Contents

KU-052-266

Guide to the book

In the Unlocking the Law books all the essential elements that make up the law are clearly defined to bring the law alive and make it memorable. In addition, the books are enhanced with learning features to reinforce learning and test your knowledge as you study. Follow this guide to make sure you get the most from reading this book.

AIMS AND OBJECTIVES

Defines what you will learn in each chapter.

definition
Find key legal terminology at a glance.

SECTION

Highlights sections from Acts.

ARTICLE

Defines Articles of the Treaty on the Functioning of the European Union (TFEU) or of the European Convention on Human Rights or other treaty.

tutor tip

Provides key ideas from lecturers on how to get ahead.

CLAUSE

Shows a bill going through Parliament or a draft bill proposed by the Law Commission.

CASE EXAMPLE

 Illustrates the law in action.

JUDGMENT

Provides extracts from judgments on cases.

QUOTATION

Encourages you to engage with secondary sources.

Indicates that you will be able to test yourself further on this topic using the Key Questions and Answers section of this book on www. unlockingthe law.co.uk

ACTIVITY

Enables you to test yourself as you progress through the chapter.

student mentor tip

Offers advice from law graduates on the best way to achieve the results you want

SAMPLE ESSAY QUESTIONS

Provide you with real-life sample essays and show you the best way to plan your answer.

SUMMARY

Concludes each chapter to reinforce learning.

Acknowledgments

Preface

The 'Unlocking' series is designed to make learning each subject area more accessible by focusing on learning needs, and by providing a range of different supporting materials and features.

All topic areas are broken up into 'bite size' sections with a logical progression and extensive use of headings and numerous sub-headings. Each book in the series also contains a variety of charts, diagrams and key fact summaries to reinforce the information in the body of the text. Diagrams and flow charts are particularly useful because they can provide a quick and easy understanding of the key points, especially when revising for examinations. Key facts charts not only provide a quick visual guide through the subject but are useful for revision purposes also.

The books have a number of common features in the layout. Important cases are separated out for easy access and have full citation in the text as well as the table of cases for ease of reference. The emphasis of the series is on depth of understanding much more than breadth. For this reason each text also includes key extracts from judgments where appropriate. Extracts from academic comment from journal articles and leading texts are also included to give some insight into the debates on complex or controversial areas. In both cases these are indented to make them clear from the body of the text.

Finally, the books also include much formative 'self-testing', with a variety of activities including subject specific comprehension and application of the law amongst others to help the student gain a good idea of his or her progress in the course.

Table of Cases

Table of Statutory Instruments

Table of Legislation

This mostly relates to British legislation, with European legislation following.

1

Introduction to company law

AIMS AND OBJECTIVES

After reading this chapter you should understand:

- The scope of 'company law'
- The relationship between core company law, insolvency law, securities regulation and corporate governance
- The sources of company law
- The importance in the study of company law of foundation course legal knowledge and skills
- The historical development of the registered company and its statutory framework
- The arguments for and against limited liability
- The influence of the European Union on UK company law
- The importance of the 1998 Company Law Review
- The rationale behind the Companies Act 2006 and its initial impact
- The key changes introduced by the Companies Act 2006

1.1 Who this book is for

This book is written primarily for undergraduate law students studying company law. It aims to guide students to an understanding of:

- the scope of company law and how it is linked to other specialist legal subjects such as securities regulation and insolvency law
- the sources of company law
- key legal principles of company law
- key moot, or unsettled, issues in company law.

It is also written to assist students to develop their ability to:

- understand and appreciate the context in which company law operates
- apply key principles of company law to solve problem questions
- interpret legislation
- use precedents to construct logical and persuasive arguments and discuss moot points of law
- think reflectively and critically about the strengths, shortcomings and implications of various aspects of company law.

Company law and company law scholarship have grown rapidly in volume in recent years making it unrealistic to cover the whole of even 'core' company law (a term explained in the next section) in what is usually little more than two terms if students are to achieve *understanding* rather than acquire a superficial level of knowledge. Three filters commonly used to limit the volume of material covered are adopted in this book, which focuses on:

- companies formed to *run businesses for profit*, not companies formed for charitable or other non profit-making purposes;
- *registered limited liability companies with a share capital* rather than other types of registered company such as unlimited companies or companies limited by guarantee;
- the *Companies Act 2006*, with limited coverage of securities regulation (also known as capital markets law or financial services law) or insolvency law.

Whilst students choose to study company law for a number of reasons, all share the aim of successfully completing their assessment(s). The activities and sample essay questions in each chapter of this book are designed to help you to test your knowledge and understanding and develop a successful approach to answering company law questions.

1.2 What we mean by 'company law'

core company law

the law governing the creation and operation of registered companies

1.2.1 Core company law

The focus of this book is what is sometimes referred to as 'core company law', which is essentially the law governing the creation and operation of registered companies. It is very easy to identify core company law today as it is almost all contained in the 1,300 sections and 16 schedules of the Companies Act 2006, regulations made pursuant to that Act, and cases clarifying the application of the statutory rules and principles.

That said, the Companies Act 2006 is not a comprehensive code of core company law in the sense of a body of rules that has replaced all common law rules and equitable principles previously found in cases. Certain aspects of core company law, such as remedies available for breach of directors' duties, remain case-stated law distinct from statute law and many cases interpreting provisions of past Companies Acts remain relevant today. The Companies Act 2006 is also not the only current statute containing core company law. Key relevant statutes and the role of case law in core company law are considered in section 1.3 below under the heading 'Sources of company law'.

Limits of core company law

A comprehensive review of law relevant to companies would include insolvency law and securities regulation (also known as capital markets law or financial services law) to the extent that they apply to companies. In the last 25 years, each of these areas of law has become a highly developed and voluminous legal subject in its own right. Realistically neither can be covered in any depth in a company law textbook of moderate length.

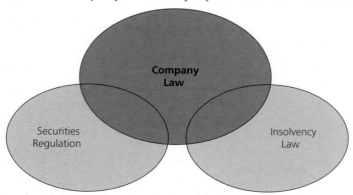

Figure 1.1 Company law includes parts of securities regulation and insolvency law

Corporate governance has attracted a great deal of attention as an important aspect of company law and it is appropriate to say a few words about it in the context of setting out what we mean by company law. Corporate governance is not a legal term, rather, it is a label, or heading under which to analyse the questions how, by whom, and to what end corporate decisions must or should be taken. Within that debate, the issue of how far the law can and should be used to achieve good corporate governance arises.

Those who support extensive use of law and regulation to improve corporate governance are said to support the 'juridification' of corporate governance, those against are said to prefer 'private ordering'. Company law and corporate governance overlap to the extent that a large part of company law is about how and by whom corporate decisions can or must be made.

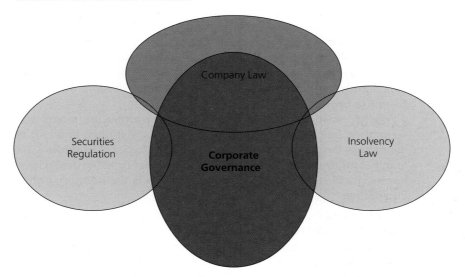

Figure 1.2 Corporate governance

Textbooks on company law differ in the extent to which they deal with insolvency law, securities regulation and corporate governance. The approach taken in this book to each is set out in the following three sections.

1.2.2 Insolvency law

Even though in theory they could, companies do not tend to continue in existence forever. They either outlive their usefulness or become financially unviable. Before a company ceases to exist, or is 'dissolved', to use the legal term, its ongoing operations are brought to an end, its assets are sold and the proceeds of sale are used to pay those to whom it owes money. This process is called 'winding up' or 'liquidating' the company.

Some companies that are wound up or liquidated are able to pay all their debts in full, that is, they are 'solvent', yet the law governing winding up of *solvent* companies is set out in the Insolvency Act 1986 (and rules made pursuant to that Act, the most important of which are the Insolvency Rules 1986). The explanation for this is that most winding ups involve *insolvent* companies and when, in the mid-1980s, the law governing insolvent company winding ups was moved out of company law legislation into specific insolvency legislation, it made sense to deal with solvent winding ups in the same statute. This avoided the need for duplication of those winding up provisions relevant to both solvent and insolvent companies in both the Companies Act 1985 (now replaced by the Companies Act 2006) and the Insolvency Act 1986.

Note that insolvency is a term relevant to both companies and individuals but in the UK the term bankruptcy is used only to refer to the insolvency of individuals, not companies. It is legally incorrect to refer to a company going bankrupt.

Insolvency law is a highly detailed and specialised area of legal practice requiring study of specialist texts for a full understanding of its scope and complexity. Of the four key formal processes: voluntary arrangements, receivership, administration and liquidation (the process by which companies are wound up), voluntary arrangements and administration are outlined in Chapter 15 (in which receivership is also mentioned), and liquidation is examined in Chapter 16.

During the liquidation process, the person appointed to conduct the winding up of a company, the 'liquidator', has the power (amongst others), to apply to court for orders that certain individuals, often directors or people closely connected with directors, contribute sums to the company to swell the assets available for distribution to creditors. It is important for anyone seeking to understand the law governing directors to understand the full range of potential liabilities and exposures of directors and for this reason the relevant provisions of the Insolvency Act 1986 are included in Chapter 16.

Liquidators also have powers to review and challenge the validity of certain transactions entered into by the company in the 'twilight zone', that is, in the period of up to two years leading up to the commencement of winding up proceedings. Clearly, it is important for anybody seeking to understand the rights of those who deal with companies, to understand the potential for twilight zone transactions to be challenged by a liquidator and for this reason the relevant provisions are also covered, in Chapter 16, of this book.

Finally, once the assets of a company have been turned into money and any contributions secured, a liquidator is required to follow a statutory order of distribution which determines the priority of payment of different types of creditors. Given the significance of this statutory ordering to the decision whether or not to deal with a company and the terms on which to do so, Chapter 16 also covers the statutory order of distribution on liquidation.

1.2.3 Securities regulation

It is difficult to decide which, if any, part of securities regulation to include in a core company law textbook. The object of securities law is essentially to provide protections to those who decide to invest their money in securities (which are basically shares and corporate bonds), and the large number of complex investment products financial service providers have built around securities.

Securities regulation is part of what is often called finance law. For our purposes, finance law can be viewed as made up of three parts: banking law; the regulation of those who conduct investment business and the markets on which investments are traded; and, increasingly, the regulation of companies whose securities (shares and bonds) are offered to the public. Regulatory shortcomings highlighted by the global financial crisis of 2008 and its aftermath have resulted in extensive, ongoing reform of finance law. Most of the changes relate to the regulation of banks and the re-alignment of regulatory responsibilities amongst the Financial Services Authority (FSA), the Bank of England and the Treasury. This realignment will be effected by the Financial Services Bill (2012 Bill) which is making its way through Parliament at the time of writing. It is expected to become law at some time in 2012 to take effect in 2013. A new 'macro-prudential authority' will be established, called the Financial Policy Committee (FPC), and the two key regulators sitting underneath this umbrella will be the Prudential Regulation Authority (PRA), which will be a subsidiary of the Bank of England, and the Financial Conduct Authority (FCA) which will be the re-focused FSA. Fortunately, apart from the relevant regulator being renamed, the framework of securities regulation will remain intact.

The key securities regulation statute in the UK is the Financial Services and Markets Act 2000 (FSMA), as amended (most recently by the Financial Services Act 2010), and to be further amended by the 2012 Bill. That Act established and empowers the main securities regulator to make detailed rules governing securities. At the time of writing, the name of the regulator remains the Financial Services Authority (FSA) and the detailed rules are found in the FSA Handbook. Once the 2012 Bill comes into effect, the functions of the FSA will be split, with some functions being performed by the Prudential Regulation

Authority (PRA). The securities regulatory functions of the FSA will be performed by the Financial Conduct Authority (FCA) which can be viewed as the FSA with a new name.

The heart of securities regulation is disclosure of accurate information. This theme has been supplemented in recent years, in no small part because securities regulation is being used to implement legal initiatives to achieve good corporate governance, which is seen as supportive of efficient capital markets and essential to achieve economic growth. As for the sources of securities regulation, statutory provisions in the FMSA are supported by detailed rules (the FSA Handbook) produced by the FSA pursuant to powers under the FSMA, which rules are underpinned and supplemented by soft law such as the UK Corporate Governance Code and the Stewardship Code.

Aspects of securities regulation touched upon in this book are the prospectus rules, which are outlined in Chapter 7, and the ongoing disclosure obligations, which are outlined in Chapter 17 and touched upon at various points in the text where the Companies Act 2006 disclosures that they supplement are discussed.

1.2.4 Corporate governance

corporate governance

the system by which companies are directed and controlled

Corporate governance means different things to different people in different contexts. Whenever the term is used, the first question to ask is, in what sense is it being used by the writer? If this is not made clear, it is usually helpful to examine the context in which the term is being used. Subject to this caveat, two definitions of corporate governance are often referenced (as, for example, in the recent European Commission Green Paper, The EU Corporate Governance Framework (COM(2011) 164 final).

The first is a definition laid down in 1992 in the Report of the Cadbury Committee, a Committee established by the Financial Reporting Council, the London Stock Exchange and the Accountancy Profession to consider the Financial Aspects of Corporate Governance. According to the Cadbury Committee (at para 2.5), 'Corporate Governance is the system by which companies are directed and controlled'.

The second definition is that first provided by the Organisation of Economic Cooperation and Development (OECD) in 1999 and repeated in the preamble to its revised Principles of Corporate Governance in 2004 in which corporate governance is identified as one key element in improving economic efficiency and growth as well as enhancing investor confidence.

QUOTATION

'Corporate governance involves a set of relationships between a company's management, its board, its shareholders and other stakeholders. Corporate governance also provides the structure through which the objectives of the company are set, and the means of attaining those objectives and monitoring performance are determined.'

OECD, Principles of Corporate Governance (2004) at p.11

Corporate governance and small companies

The vast majority of independent companies, that is, companies that are not part of a larger corporate group of companies, are managed by individuals who own or control the company or a large part of it. Additional shareholders are typically related to the majority owner or participate in managing the company alongside the majority owner, and it is not uncommon for them to be both relatives and co-managers. Most of these companies are not large and are registered as private rather than public companies. Questions about how such a company is governed usually arise out of one of two types of dispute.

The first type of dispute raises the question whether the board of directors or the majority shareholder can behave, or cause the company to behave (ie can the company be governed), in a manner objectionable to, and alleged to be inconsistent with the interests of its minority shareholders. The second type of dispute raises the question whether or not the board of directors or the shareholders can behave, or cause the company to behave (ie can the company be governed), in a manner that undermines the ability of the company to pay its creditors.

Whilst other groups, such as employees, suppliers and customers, may be affected by the manner in which a small company is governed, such impacts are typically either relatively minor or can be worked around simply because of the size of the company's operation. Also, self-interested action by managers or directors of small companies is not generally an issue because the manager/directors own the company. To the extent that the managers/directors do not own all of the shares, their pursuit of self-interest raises issues of not only, or even mainly, how to prevent abuse of management power, but rather what legal constraints exist, or should exist, on majority shareholders.

Company laws important to regulating small company governance include not only obvious topics such as directors' duties and disclosure obligations but, as the above demonstrates, constraints on majority shareholders and the remedies available to minority shareholders, particularly in the context of unfairly prejudicial conduct petitions (see Chapter 14). Principally found in the Companies Act 2006, relevant laws can also be found in insolvency law.

For the above reasons, a legalistic approach to the concept of corporate governance has often been taken and can be justified in relation to small, if not all, private companies. Corporate governance initiatives have traditionally focused on companies with shares traded on stock exchanges or listed companies. This is unlikely to remain the case for much longer. Driven by political focus on small and medium sized enterprises (SMEs, a term explained at section 2.2.2), as important drivers of economic growth and employment, there is increasing interest in improving SME corporate governance, particularly at EU level as evidenced by the recent EU Green paper on the EU Corporate Governance Framework:

QUOTATION

'Good corporate governance may also matter to shareholders in unlisted companies. While certain corporate governance issues are already addressed by company law provision on private companies, many areas are not covered. Corporate governance guidelines for unlisted companies may need to be encouraged: proper and efficient governance is valuable also for unlisted companies, especially taking into account the economic importance of certain very large unlisted companies. Moreover, putting excessive burdens on listed companies could make listing less attractive. However, principles designed for listed companies cannot be simply transposed to unlisted companies, as the challenges they face are different. Some voluntary codes have already been drafted and initiatives taken by professional bodies at European or national level. So the question is whether any EU action is needed on corporate governance in unlisted companies.'

European Commission Green Paper, The EU Corporate Governance Framework
(COM(2011) 164 final at p.4

Corporate governance and large companies

In relation to large companies, corporate governance is typically addressed as a much more complex and broad-ranging concept because of the clear impact the quality of corporate governance of large companies with extensive business operations has on the economy and society. It is the role of *law* in corporate governance, however, that is, and must be, the focus of law courses. Even if we set aside questions of the role the law could and should play in improving corporate governance, the study of how existing company law influences corporate governance is more complex in relation to large companies than it is in relation to small companies. This complexity arises in part out of the model of ownership of many large companies.

The scope of impact of business operations

The larger the business of a company, the larger the impact its operations will have on a larger number of individuals and, consequently, the economy. Consider the potential for the environment to be very significantly adversely affected by a company that owns and is actively expanding its network of oil pipelines. Similarly, a large company may run nuclear power stations producing by-products, best practice waste-management of which involves the storage into the long term future of active nuclear material. A large company may employ a significant proportion of workers in a locality. It may be the largest purchaser of a particular product or products in the country so that producers are dependent upon it continuing to buy a large share of their output (Tesco as a purchaser of milk, and Marks & Spencer as a purchaser of quality ready-meals, exemplify this). A large company may be one of only a handful of suppliers of a particular product or service, such as mobile telephony, with millions of consumer (distinct from business) customers.

The point to note is that the effect of decision-making by such companies is not confined to the shareholders of the company or even to those (typically other companies or businesses) who have *chosen* to do business with the company. Decision-making by large companies can significantly affect the environment, the local community, the livelihood of large numbers of people who work for the company, consumer choice and the viability of suppliers. The various groups affected by, or interested in, a company are sometimes referred to as 'stakeholders'.

The extent to which the interests of different stakeholders:

- as a matter of *law*, must be
- as a matter of *fact*, are
- as a matter of *policy*, should be

taken into account in company decision-making are important questions that fall within the corporate governance rubric. Closely related questions are who *must be*, who *is* and who *should* be involved in company decision-making.

The extent to which each question is explored in a company law course will depend in large part upon the interests of the lecturers and tutors delivering the course. On a course in which the traditional approach, sometimes referred to as a 'black letter law' approach, is adopted, the focus will be on current rules and regulations to answer the first question and its corollary: as a matter of law to what extent *must* the interests of different stakeholders be taken into account and who *must be* involved in company decision-making. Even where this approach is adopted, however, introduction into core company law, in s 172 of the Companies Act 2006, of the concept of 'enlightened shareholder value' (a concept examined at 11.3.2) means that some analysis of the larger issues of corporate governance are called for, if only to explain this development and provide some insight into how s 172 may be interpreted in the future by boards of directors and the courts.

On a course in which a 'law in context' approach or a 'socio-legal studies' approach is adopted, time is likely to be spent focused on the third question and its corollary: as a matter of policy, to what extent *should* the interests of different stakeholders be taken into account in company decision-making and who *should be* involved in company decision-making. A wide range of approaches can be taken to this line of enquiry. An historical approach, for example, may involve reviewing initiatives in the UK over the years to engage workers in company decision-making. A comparative law approach may involve reviewing, comparing and contrasting company decision-making in a selection of legal jurisdictions across the world. A European Union perspective may be adopted, perhaps examining the dichotomy within the European Union between Member States with worker participation (such as Germany) and those without (such as the UK), a matter that has presented insuperable difficulties in harmonising company law in the European Union.

Writings of theorists in an array of scholarly disciplines, sociology and economics to name but two, may be drawn upon to explore corporate governance (as well as other aspects of company law) and underpin policy proposals. In particular, theories and models developed by economists have been drawn upon (extensively in the USA, in the EU and to a lesser, albeit influential, extent in the UK) to explore the operation of law, predict the effects of changes to company law and, more contentiously, propose what the law should be. This law and economics scholarship is more developed in relation to corporate governance issues raised by the phenomenon of the separation of ownership from the control/management of companies, addressed in the next section.

The second of the three questions identified above: to what extent are the interests of different stakeholders taken into account as a matter of practice and who *actually* takes part in (or perhaps the question should be, who actually influences) company decision-making, are questions of fact. The focus here needs to be on empirical studies yet, as it appears that little empirical research has taken place in the UK on decision-making in companies, this question is often answered, somewhat unsatisfactorily, by making assumptions.

Corporate governance and the separation of ownership and control of companies

The second factor adding to the complexity of corporate governance of large companies is the model of ownership of large publicly traded companies. Separation of those who own a company (the shareholders) from those who manage the company (the directors and executives) has long been a feature of large companies in the UK. This separation raises the problem of ensuring that those who manage companies do not run them for their own personal benefit rather than for the benefit of those on whose behalf the law requires companies to be managed.

The management self-interest problem is exacerbated where a company's shares are owned by a large number of shareholders with no single person owning a significant shareholding. This pattern of shareholding is called 'atomistic' or 'dispersed'. The interest of shareholders in publicly traded companies is first and foremost, if not exclusively, financial in nature. Shareholders seek dividends, increased share value (that is, they want the price at which they can sell their shares to increase) and, ideally, both.

In this type of company legal protection based on a balance of power between the board of directors and shareholders has little if any meaningful effect because shareholders have little inclination to exercise the powers reserved to the shareholding body: the divorce of ownership and control is virtually complete. Yet it is precisely here that the most stringent laws promoting good practice in corporate governance are believed to be necessary. This explains why corporate governance law is more developed for companies with shares listed on stock exchanges than it is for private companies and unlisted public companies. It also explains why relevant laws are found not in core company law, but in securities law. Corporate governance law, beyond the Companies Act 2006, is made up of a combination of hard law (legislation such as the Financial Markets and Services Act 2006 and regulations and rules made pursuant to that Act) and 'soft law' such as guidance and, particularly, codes.

Two important codes designed to promote good corporate governance can be found on the Financial Reporting Council website referred to at the end of this chapter. The UK Corporate Governance Code (September 2012) (the successor to the Combined Code) sets out good practice for boards of directors of companies with shares with a premium listing on the Main Market of the London Stock Exchange. The directors of these companies must either cause the company to comply or explain in the company's annual report why, and the extent to which, they have chosen not to comply. The newer, UK Stewardship Code (also September 2012) is aimed at enhancing the quality of engagement between institutional investors and the companies they invest in. It sets out good practice on engagement with companies, to which institutional investors should aspire, to help improve efficient exercise of governance responsibilities. Currently, no legal obligation to comply with this code exists and no reporting obligations exist in relation to it. Corporate governance codes from all around the world can be accessed on the European Corporate Governance Institute website referenced at the end of this chapter.

Corporate governance and large private and unquoted companies

Large private companies and large public companies that are not quoted companies present a challenge to corporate governance law. They highlight what seems to be a structural difficulty with the current law, namely that enhancements to corporate governance laws believed to be required for *large* companies have been implemented by laws applicable only to listed companies. An example of this is the requirement introduced by s 417 of the Companies Act 2006 that companies report to the public information about the impact of their operations and decisions on the physical and social environment, company employees and the community, as well as disclosing company policies on these matters and the effectiveness of those policies. This obligation applies only if the company is a 'quoted company' as that term is defined in the Companies Act 2006. No private company or unquoted public company, regardless of how extensive its operations may be, is subject to these reporting obligations.

Overlooked in the reform resulting in the Companies Act 2006, how to regulate the governance of large *unquoted or unlisted* companies is an important challenge facing company law. In addition to being raised in the EU Corporate Governance Framework Green Paper quoted from above, the Reflection Group on the Future of EU Company Law, appointed by the European Commission, addressed this issue in its report published in April 2011.

QUOTATION

'As it is important to avoid broad and imprecise categorisations, the Reflection Group is particularly concerned about the distinction between public and private limited companies that has traditionally dominated legislation within company law for more than a century. The origin of the distinction is the still correct observation that a company with a large and dispersed crowd of shareholders may in certain respects warrant different regulation from a company with a small and closely knit circle of shareholders. However, in its traditional form the distinction relies on an inapt choice of company form, whereby a company is deemed "public" or "private" simply by its choice of company form. Thus, a "public company" does not necessarily have a large and dispersed crowd of shareholders; in fact, it may not even be listed and may have a single shareholder. Nor does a "private company" have to be a small company in any way; it can have more shareholders, more employees and a greater turnover than a "public company".'

Report of the Reflection Group on the Future of EU Company Law,
Brussels, 5 April 2011, European Commission

The approach to corporate governance taken in this book

Large parts of the Companies Act 2006 can be characterised as laws existing to support and promote good practice in corporate governance. Being so pervasive, these laws are not separated out and expressly dealt with under the rubric 'corporate governance'. The Companies Act 2006 corporate governance provisions are supplemented by securities regulation for companies with shares listed on stock exchanges. Whilst these aspects of securities laws may be characterised as part of core company law, limited space requires that a line be drawn somewhere and the only corporate governance rules outside the Companies Act 2006 covered briefly in this book are the periodic and insider information reporting requirements (see Chapter 17).

The impact of the quality of corporate governance on the political economy makes it an important topic of scholarly interest. Beyond examining the existing law, this book simply introduces readers to the enormous potential scope of this area of study and provides those interested in expanding their understanding with suggestions for further reading. An excellent starting point for those seeking to understand the European Union's current approach to corporate governance is the European Commission EU Corporate Governance Framework Green Paper already referred to.

1.3 Sources of company law

1.3.1 Legislation

Statute law takes the lead in the sources of company law. The main statute containing company law is currently the Companies Act 2006. The most important statutes containing provisions regarded as part of core company law are:

- Companies Act 2006
- Insolvency Act 1986
- Company Directors Disqualification Act 1986
- Financial Services and Markets Act 2000
- Criminal Justice Act 1993 (insider dealing)
- Companies Act 1985 (company investigations)
- Companies (Audit, Investigations and Community Enterprise) Act 2004 (company investigations and community interest companies (CICs)).

The Companies Act 2006 is the most recent statute pursuant to which a company can be registered. Each successive Act setting out the process for registration since 1862 has been called the Companies Act. It is often important to know pursuant to which Companies Act a company has been registered and to consult that Act because the content of the model articles of association scheduled to each Act is different.

The Companies Act 2006 and other relevant statutes are supplemented by detailed rules contained in statutory regulations. The 2006 Act and regulations can be found by following links on the Department for Business, Innovation and Skills (BIS) Companies Act 2006 website referenced at the end of this chapter.

The term 'Companies Acts' is defined in s 2 of the Companies Act 2006. It essentially means the company law provisions (Pts 1–39) of the Companies Act 2006 and the community interest provisions (Pt 2) of the Companies (Audit, Investigations and Community Enterprise) Act 2004. The term is sometimes used in a different sense, however, to refer to the Companies Acts over time, in aggregate.

1.3.2 Case law

The study of cases is an important part of understanding company law. Principles that remain case-stated distinct from principles set out in the relevant statutes make up only a small part of company law but even though many common law and equitable principles are now set out in the Companies Act 2006 or another current statute, the cases in which they were developed remain relevant to demonstrate how they apply in practice.

Provided that the Act is intended simply to state the existing law rather than change it, old cases help us to understand how a statutory rule will be applied in the future. A good example of this is the general duty owed by a director to the company set out in s 171(b) of the Companies Act 2006, the duty of a director to only exercise powers for the purposes for which they are conferred. The general duties owed by a director to the company have been developed by judges in case law over more than 150 years before becoming statutory duties set out in the Companies Act 2006. This case law provides a rich source of examples of application of the principles in practice, or 'declaratory precedent'.

Clearly, before old case law can be relied upon, it is essential to know in relation to any given section of the Act, whether the Act is intended to change the law or not. Change may render some but not all past cases irrelevant. It may also render a part only but not all of a case irrelevant. The key learning is that in this situation, great care needs to be taken when seeking to rely on past cases.

Many core company law cases are concerned with the meaning and application of repealed statutes, particularly sections from previous Companies Acts. Here, again, if the earlier statutory rule appears to have been re-enacted in the Companies Act 2006, care must be taken to determine whether or not there has been a change in the statutory language and, if the language has changed, whether or not the change is intended:

BIS
the Department for Business, Innovation and Skills (formerly BERR and before that the DTI) is the government department responsible for company law (amongst other things)

- To make no change to the law, that is, no substantive change. The language may have been changed to clean up the drafting, perhaps to make the section easier to understand or to reconcile the language with related sections of the Act.
- To incorporate case law-development of the meaning of a section of the Act. An example of this is s 33 which, unlike s 14 of the Companies Act 1985 (the predecessor provision), makes it clear that the contract in a company's articles of association can be enforced against the company, a point established in *Hickman v Kent or Romney Sheep Breeders' Association* [1915] 1 Ch 881.
- To change the law.

The intention of the legislature, particularly where it is to change the law, may be clear from the face of the new section. An example of this is s 188 of the Companies Act 2006. Section 188 requires shareholder approval by general resolution of a director's service contract that can run for more than *two* years whereas s 319 of the Companies Act 1985 (the predecessor section) required shareholder approval for a director's service contract that could run for more than *five* years. In places, however, the legislative intention is not clear. An example of this is s 168 of the Companies Act 2006. Section 168, which provides for a director to be removed from office by the shareholders by general resolution, omits reference to provision to the contrary in the company's articles. The predecessor section, s 303 of the Companies Act 1985, referred to the company's articles. The effect of this omission from the new section is not clear.

1.3.3 Foundation legal knowledge and company law

Company law should not be approached as a self-contained body of legal learning. Students beginning to study company law are usually familiar with most if not all foundation law subjects: English Legal System, Public Law, Criminal Law, Contract and Tort Law, Property Law, European Union Law and Equity and Trust Law and the importance of foundation legal subjects to the study of company law should not be underestimated. You will enhance your understanding of company law by drawing on your knowledge of these subjects.

At many points in your study of company law you will need to draw on your foundation law knowledge, apply foundation law concepts and utilise the general legal skills you have been developing in your legal studies to date. When reading and applying sections of the main company law statute, the Companies Act 2006, for example, you will need to draw on your statutory interpretation skills. When examining potentially irreconcilable judgments you will need to exercise your ability to distinguish cases on their facts, extend legal principles by analogy to new fact situations and develop persuasive arguments, expressed concisely, to demonstrate your understanding.

Knowledge of *contract law* is essential to understand the debate around the extent to which the articles of a company form a legally enforceable contract. As almost all company contracts are entered into by individuals acting on behalf of the company, ie by individuals acting as agents, knowledge of *agency law* also helps when considering when a company is and is not bound by a contract.

Parts of *trust law* are very relevant to the study of company law. Directors and trustees share the legal characteristic of 'fiduciaries' which renders them subject to fiduciary duties. Whilst equitable duties have now been replaced by statutory duties owed by directors, when it comes to considering remedies for breach, students will come across the same cases and the same equitable principles operating, whether it is a breach of duty by a trustee or by a director.

Familiarity with different types of *European Union (EU) law*; how it comes into being and is incorporated into English law will also help your study of company law. UK membership of the European Union has had an important effect on the development of company law and will continue to do so. European Union company law initiatives, past, present and planned for the future, are considered in section 1.5 below.

More examples could be given, including examples from *criminal, tort* and *property law*. The general point, however, has been made: drawing on your existing knowledge and skills will make it much easier to understand company law.

The discussion above demonstrates that the study of core company law involves application of general legal knowledge and understanding of how law evolves and is reformed, whether by case law or legislation. Due to the prominent role played by statute law, statutory interpretation is particularly important. It is also important to use precedents to build arguments to answer questions of company law the answers to which are 'moot', meaning open to argument or discussion.

1.4 Historical development of company law

1.4.1 The first registered companies

This book is about the law applicable to registered companies. The opportunity to create a company by an inexpensive process (registration of documents) and as a matter of right (rather than discretion or favour), has existed in England for over 160 years, since the passing of the Joint Stock Companies Act 1844. Whilst theoretically possible, it is extremely unlikely that a company would today be formed to run a business for profit by the old processes of Parliament passing a special Act or the Crown granting a Royal Charter to bring the company into existence.

The 1844 Act followed the influential report earlier that year of the first Parliamentary Committee on joint stock companies chaired by William Gladstone. Another significant feature of modern company law that can be traced back to Gladstone's report and the 1844 Act is public disclosure of information about registered companies. Information about a company, its directors and members and annual reports and accounts must be filed at Companies House with the registrar of companies where it is available for inspection by members of the public (see Chapter 17).

Companies House
an executive agency of BIS by which the registrar of companies performs the functions of the registrar including the incorporation and dissolution of registered companies, the examination and storage of information delivered under the Companies Act, and, where required, the making public of that information

When a company is registered with the registrar at Companies House, we speak about it being 'incorporated'. The term is used in s 15(1) of the Companies Act 2006: 'On the registration of a company, the registrar of companies shall give a certificate that the company is incorporated'. The term comes from the Latin verb 'corporare' which means 'to furnish with a body'. The process of registering a company brings into existence, or 'embodies' a new legal person. All legal persons, registered companies included, enjoy legal rights and are subject to enforceable legal liabilities.

Significant legal benefits arise when a company owns and conducts a business rather than that business being owned and conducted mutually by a group of individuals. Complexity is swept away regarding such questions as, who are the parties to a contract entered into in the course of the business? Who can be sued to recover money lent to the business? Who owns the property used in the business? Instead of multiple individuals (everyone who owns a part of the business or participates in management) being named as parties to a contract or litigation, a single legal person is substituted: the company. This benefits both those owning and running the business and those with whom business is conducted. In this respect companies, unlike unincorporated business structures (on which, see Chapter 2), simplify and, therefore, facilitate the efficient conduct of business.

The use of a company to conduct a business brings the efficiency benefits outlined above but also brings with it the potential for the company to have insufficient funds to pay those to whom it owes money, its 'creditors'. Owners, or 'members', of companies registered under the 1844 Act were required to contribute funds to an unlimited amount to the company to enable the company to pay its creditors. These first registered companies were what we now call 'unlimited companies', a term used in s 3(4) of the Companies Act 2006 to describe a company in which, 'there is no limit on the liability of its members'. It is still possible to register an unlimited company but as this book is about companies formed for profit and unlimited companies are rarely used for this purpose, little will be found about unlimited companies in this book.

1.4.2 Limited liability for company members

The question whether or not to allow companies to be registered with members, or shareholders, who are *not* required to contribute any sum to the company beyond the price agreed to be paid to buy shares in the company was debated throughout the first half of the nineteenth century. The main argument against allowing members limited liability was that it would encourage and facilitate even more recklessness and fraudulent activity than was increasingly rife in the growing financial and corporate services markets. Supporters argued limited liability would:

- encourage investment in companies
- facilitate transferability of shares
- provide clarity and certainty as to the assets available to creditors of the company.

All of which, it was said, were essential to access capital needed to fund the growth of capital-intensive industries such as the railways and mining. Demands for limited liability finally succeeded. This was due in no small part to the fact that shortly after incorporation was made easily available, various attempts to enforce the unlimited liability system provided for in the 1844 Act proved it to be unworkable.

The Limited Liability Act 1855 was enacted and quickly replaced, along with the 1844 Act, by the Joint Stock Companies Act 1856. The 1856 Act is regarded as the first modern Companies Act although it was the next consolidating Act, adopted in 1862, that bore the modern name, 'Companies Act'.

Limited liability was introduced to provide protection and encouragement to investors in companies and as a direct result of the difficulty of operating a system of unlimited liability of members of companies with freely transferable shares. When company shares are traded on a public stock exchange the list of members is typically long and rapidly changing which makes it difficult to track members down and enforce contributions.

1.4.3 The model company for which company law was designed

Introduction of limited liability is an example of how, in its early stages, company law developed to cater for companies with a relatively large number of shareholders and publicly traded shares. This model of ownership assumes that the owners of the company (the members or shareholders) are different individuals from the managers of the company (the directors). This separation of ownership and control gives rise to one of the key problems company law exists to regulate, namely the inclination of managers/directors to act in their own self interest rather than in the interests of the company and its owners/shareholders. It is this problem that underlies the imposition of strict 'fiduciary' duties on directors and extensive public disclosure obligations on companies.

In fact, today, the shares of only a tiny proportion (significantly less than 1 per cent) of registered companies are traded on a public stock exchange. Out of more than two million non-dormant registered companies, approximately 1,100 companies have shares traded on the Main Market of the London Stock Exchange and approximately 900 companies have shares traded on AIM, a market for smaller companies that is also run by the London Stock Exchange.

1.4.4 Single member and closely held companies

By far the most common type of company is a small company with a handful, if not (as is increasingly the case), a single shareholder. The directors of these companies are significant shareholders if not the sole shareholder. Separation of ownership and control is either not present or insignificant. These companies are sometimes referred to as 'closely-held' companies, referring to the small number of shareholders. The key problem company law wrestles with in closely held companies is not how to control management/the directors, but how to protect minority shareholders (who may or may not be involved in management) from the self-interested behaviour of majority shareholders.

Use of the registered limited company as a corporate structure by sole-trader businessmen gathered pace in the 1890s. This development was legally contentious. Whereas the Companies Act 1862 required a company to have a minimum of seven shareholders, businessmen satisfied this requirement by issuing one share each to members of their families, or to other individuals to hold the share on trust for the benefit of the businessman. They thereby created, in fact if not in law, a company owned and controlled by a sole member.

In the seminal case of *Salomon v A Salomon and Co Ltd* [1897] AC 22 (HL), creditors of just such a company challenged this practice as an abuse of the Companies Act 1862 registration process. They were successful both at first instance and in the Court of Appeal. It took an appeal to the House of Lords for the judges to clarify that the Companies Act 1862 permitted the registration of a company owned and controlled, in effect, by a single shareholder who could not be sued to recover the debts of the company and whose liability to contribute funds to the company was limited. It is interesting to reflect how different company law might be today if the strident judgments of the members of the Court of Appeal, firmly set against endorsing limited liability for sole traders 'hiding' behind registered companies, had not been appealed and overturned by the House of Lords.

Introduction in the Companies Act 1907 of the distinction between 'private' and 'public' companies (for the current distinction see Table 2.1) was evidence of acceptance by the legislature that:

- the registered company was not the sole preserve of companies with publicly traded shares; and
- not all laws developed with companies with publicly traded shares in mind were appropriate for closely held companies.

The 1907 Act requirement for public companies to disclose their annual balance sheets, for example, was not considered appropriate for private companies. Private companies were not required to disclose annual accounts until 1967.

By 1911, two out of every three of the 50,000 companies registered were private companies. The preponderance of private companies is even more emphasised today. By 2012, 99 out of every 100 registered companies were private companies (the percentage that are public companies is in fact 0.3 per cent).

A simplified company template to allow single member companies to save on transaction costs and unnecessary formalities was proposed by the Reflection Group on the Future of EU Company Law in its report in April 2011 (see 1.5.4 below) and BIS sees consideration of the need for a new corporate form for single person businesses as an area on which to focus. The BIS website states: 'At present there are hundreds of thousands of limited companies that are owned and run by a single person, and that person has to comply with extensive rules designed to balance the interests of multiple shareholders and directors'.

1.4.5 Twentieth century developments

Until the UK joined the European Union in 1973, company law was periodically reformed and consolidated following a review and report by a committee established for the purpose by the government department responsible for trade, now the Department for Business Innovation and Skills (BIS). The main committees, reports and resulting legislation are set out in Table 1.1 below.

Committee	Year of report	Amending Act	Consolidating Act
Loreburn Committee	1906 (Cmnd 3052)	Companies Act 1907	Companies (Consolidation) Act 1908
Wrenbury Committee	1918 (Cd 9138)	Companies Act 1929	
Greene Committee	1926 (Cmnd 2657)		
Cohen Committee	1945 (Cmnd 6659)	Companies Act 1948	
Jenkins Committee	1962 (Cmnd 1749)	Companies Act 1967 Companies Bill 1973 (lapsed)	

Table 1.1 Pre-European Union (1900–1973)

Following UK membership of the European Union, company law continued to be subject to in-depth national reviews (see Table 1.2 below). Significant reforms were made in the 1980s in the *specialised areas* of securities regulation (financial services law) and insolvency law. These areas of law were restructured, with relevant parts of company law being carved-out, reformed and relocated in the Financial Services Act 1986 (since replaced by the Financial Services and Markets Act 2000), the Insolvency Act 1986 and the Company Directors Disqualification Act 1986 (an Act that provides for the disqualification of directors from participating in the management of another company in a range of circumstances). In contrast, notwithstanding the consolidation and partial re-writing of disparate statutes resulting in the Companies Act 1985, reform of *core company law* was neither fundamental nor structured.

Changes to core company law in the period 1973–2006 occurred piecemeal, mainly in response to European Union initiatives (see section 1.5 below). The result was unacceptable. Company law increasingly lacked coherence and contained obvious conceptual inconsistencies, many arising from the obligatory implementation of a number of rules and principles set out in EU company law directives that did not sit comfortably with UK company law.

Company law reviews, reforms and consolidations excluding EU initiatives		
Reform initiative	**Year**	**Act**
Bullock Committee (Employee representation)	1977 (Cmnd 6706)	None
Cork Committee (Insolvency law)	1982 (Cmnd 8558)	Insolvency Act 1985 Insolvency Act 1986
Gower Review (Financial services law/securities regulation)	1982 (Cmnd 9125) 1984 (Cmnd 9125)	Financial Services Act 1986
Law Commission (Shareholder remedies)	Consultation Paper No 142 Report No 246	None
Law Commission (Directors' duties)	Consultation Paper No 153 Report No 261/173	None

Table 1.2 Post-European Union (1973–1998)

Not until 1998 was a root and branch review of company law announced with a clear commitment from the Government to enact a Companies Act fit for purpose in the twenty-first century. To the surprise of many onlookers who doubted that parliamentary time would be committed to such, relatively speaking, apolitical legislation, the Government honoured its commitment with the enactment of the Companies Act 2006. The Company Law Review, which resulted in the enactment of the Companies Act 2006, is examined in section 1.6 below.

1.5 European Union company law initiatives

Membership of the European Union (EU) continues to have a significant influence on the development of UK company law. As with developments at the UK level, EU core company law initiatives have been accompanied by EU financial services, securities or capital markets law initiatives. The latter developments overlap with core company law to the extent that they affect companies with shares traded on stock exchanges. (There have been no significant EU insolvency law initiatives relevant to core company law.)

Whilst the division of the European Commission responsible for company and capital markets law is the Internal Market and Services Directorate General, referred to as DG MARKT, another division of the European Commission, DG Enterprise and Industry, has become increasingly important in the direction taken in relation to company law at EU level. The influence of DG Enterprise and Industry has resulted in initiatives to simplify company law, particularly for micro, small and medium sized companies, as part of the focus on SMEs as the key driver for economic growth, innovation, employment and social integration in the EU. This, together with expansion in the membership of the EU, the change in approach to EU law-making required in response to this expansion (sometimes referred to as 'modernisation'), and the need to question the effectiveness of company and financial services law following both the financial and economic crisis that hit the EU and USA in 2008 and the earlier corporate scandals involving Enron and Parmalat, culminated in the European Commission, in February 2012, launching an 'in-depth consultation on the future of EU company law'. This public consultation is cast in the broadest of terms (see 1.5.4 below).

A brief overview of key EU company law developments follows. It is divided into four parts. The first EU company law development phase concentrated on harmonisation of core company law across Member States and required Member States to make significant, often technical, changes to their national company law. This phase is covered in 1.5.1 below. The phase following core company law harmonisation involved publication (in 2000 and 2003 respectively) and implementation of the Financial Services Action Plan (FSAP) and the Action Plan on Company Law and Corporate Governance (the Company Law Action Plan). These plans are considered in 1.5.2. Alongside these legislative initiatives, the European Court has passed judgment in a number of cases involving the incorporation of companies in Member States by nationals of other Member States intending to run the companies from their home Member State and the establishment of branches of companies in other Member States. In these cases the court has laid down a clear and robust view of the operation of the right to freedom of establishment in relation to companies. This development is reviewed in 1.5.3. Finally, the future of EU company law is considered in 1.5.4.

Efforts have also been made by the European Commission, with greater and lesser success, to put supra-national European company structures in place. The results to date of these efforts are the availability of EEIGs, European Companies and European Co-operative Societies. A proposal to make available a European Private Company has also attracted a great deal of attention. Each of these entities and proposals to make available other European entities in the non-profit field are covered in Chapter 2.

1.5.1 Core company law harmonisation

The enormous program of work that made up the company law harmonisation program supported the policy to achieve free movement of persons, goods, services and capital throughout all Member States. The aims of the Company Law harmonisation programme included:

- providing equivalent protection through the EU for shareholders and other parties concerned with companies
- ensuring freedom of establishment for companies throughout the EU
- fostering efficiency and competitiveness of business
- promoting cross-border cooperation between companies in different Member States.

In later years, the following was added:

- stimulating discussions between Member States on the modernisation of company law and corporate governance.

The earliest step to harmonise company law across EU Member States, the First European Company Law Directive, predated UK membership. It was implemented in the UK by the European Communities Act 1972 when the UK joined the European Economic Community, as the EU then was, on 1 January 1973. Of the 13 core company law directives proposed by the European Commission, the 11 in place as at the end of 2008 (having been implemented by further primary legislation in 1980, 1981, 1989 and 2006 as well as occasional secondary legislation), are listed in Table 1.3 below together with an indication of the topics with which they deal. EU company law directives apply across the European Economic Area (EEA).

Thirteenth Company Law Directive 2004/25/EC	21 April 2004	on takeover bids
Twelfth Company Law Directive 89/667/EEC	21 December 1989	on single-member private limited-liability companies
Eleventh Company Law Directive 89/666/EEC	21 December 1989	concerning disclosure requirements in respect of branches opened in a Member State by certain types of company governed by the law of another State
Tenth Company Law Directive 2005/56/EC	26 October 2005	on cross-border mergers of limited liability companies
Draft Ninth Company Law Council Directive	Withdrawn	on relationship of companies within corporate groups
Eighth Company Law Directive 84/253/EEC (as amended)	10 April 1984	on the approval of persons responsible for carrying out the statutory audits of accounting documents
Seventh Company Law Directive 83/349/EEC	3 June 1983	on consolidated accounts
Sixth Company Law Directive 82/891/EEC (as amended by 2007/63/EC)	17 December 1982	concerning the division of public limited liability companies
Draft Fifth Company Law Directive	Progress halted	on the structure of public companies
Fourth Company Law Directive 78/660/EEC (as amended)	25 July 1978	on the annual accounts of certain types of companies
Third Company Law Directive 78/855/EEC (as amended by 2007/63/EC)	9 October 1978	concerning mergers of public limited liability companies
Second Company Law Directive 77/91/EEC (as amended by 92/101/EEC & 2006/68/EC)	13 December 1976	on co-ordination of safeguards required by Member States of companies in respect of the formation of public limited liability companies and the maintenance and alteration of their capital, with a view to making such safeguards equivalent
First Company Law Directive 68/151/EEC (as amended by 2003/58/EC)	9 March 1968	on co-ordination of safeguards required by Member States of companies with a view to making such safeguards equivalent throughout the EU

Table 1.3 Main European Union company law harmonisation directives

Neither the fifth nor the ninth draft directives have been finalised. The draft ninth directive, on the relationship between companies within a corporate group, has been withdrawn and the view expressed in the Action Plan is that there is no need for it to be revived. The draft fifth directive concerns the structure of public companies but the inability of Member States to reach agreement on worker representation on boards of directors has halted progress. The original draft tenth directive, dealing with cross-border mergers, published in 1984, was withdrawn in 2001 because agreement could not be reached on provisions for employee participation rights but a new draft directive on cross-border mergers, proposed pursuant to the Action Plan, was finally adopted on 26 October 2005 (Directive 2005/56/EC). A fourteenth company law directive on the cross-border transfer of registered office of limited companies, published by the European Commission in October 2008, is currently on hold pending the outcome of the public consultation on the future of European company law which includes consultation on cross-border mobility for companies (see 1.5.4 below).

1.5.2 The Financial Services and Company Law Action Plans

The beginning of the twenty-first century saw the European Commission focusing on cross-border capital flows and laws to support and develop a Single Market in financial services. In May 1999, the European Commission launched its framework for action in the form of a Communication entitled Financial Services: Implementing the framework for financial markets: Action Plan (COM(1999)232) (FSAP). Agreed to by Member States in 2000, the FSAP was an EU policy priority. It consisted of a set of measures intended to fill gaps and remove barriers to provide a legal and regulatory environment to support integration of the *financial markets* in Member States. The FSAP measures covered a wide range of issues including the issue of securities and security trading, corporate accounts, corporate restructuring and corporate insolvency.

Although its focus was on financial services, the European Commission appointed a High Level Group of Company Law Experts to consider the next stage of development for core company law. The group reported in 2002.

QUOTATION

'A fundamental review of company law in Europe was certainly due. Many agree that EU company law has not kept up with developments which shape its role and application, in particular the creation of a single EU market which companies and their investors wish to use to the optimum, the development of European securities markets and their regulation, the development of modern information and communication technologies which should be facilitated and could be used to improve company law arrangements and the development of corporate governance practices and standards. Indeed, we believe company law in Europe must catch up with these developments.'

Letter from the Chairman, Report of the High Level Group of Company Law Experts on a Modern Regulatory Framework for Company Law in Europe (2002) European Commission

The European Commission responded to the report with the 2003 European Commission Communication, Modernising Company Law and Enhancing Corporate Governance in the EU – A Plan to Move Forward (COM(2003) 284). The main aims of the Company Law Action Plan were to strengthen shareholders rights, reinforce protection for employees and creditors and increase the efficiency and competitiveness of business. In particular, it proposed a series of corporate governance initiatives aimed at boosting confidence in capital markets (stock exchanges for our purposes). Proposed areas for reform, set out in Appendix 1 of the communication, were divided into three phases, the short term (2003–5), the medium term (2006–8) and 2009 onwards. At the end of phase 1 the European Commission consulted on the future of the plan. This consultation was believed necessary in the light of broader EU developments and priorities, particularly efforts to make European industry more competitive (the Lisbon agenda) and the EU better regulation policy, both of which potentially called for a different approach to EU company law. Following this consultation, even more significant events led to confidence in the financial and economic structures in place in Europe being undermined. The challenges of the twenty-first century have left the European Union unsure as to how to proceed with the development of European company law.

The legislative phase for the FSAP drew to a close in 2005 with significant progress having been made towards putting in place directives to achieve an integrated, open, and more competitive and efficient European financial market. *Implementation* of the directives by Member States was not, however, as complete as the European Commission would have wished for and when, in December 2005, the European Commission presented its financial services strategy for 2005–2010, one key challenge identified was to consolidate progress and for Member States to work together on *applying* the better regulatory disciplines provided for in the directives.

The key EU directives relevant to core company law put in place since 2001 are set out in Table 1.4 below.

Directive 2007/36/EC	11 July 2007	on shareholders rights in listed companies (Shareholder Rights Directive)
Directive 2004/109/EC	15 December 2004	on the harmonisation of transparency requirements on listed companies (Transparency Directive) (amends 2001/34/EC below)
Directive 2004/39/EC	21 April 2004	on markets in financial instruments (MiFID)
Directive 2003/71/EC	4 November 2003	on prospectuses when securities are offered to the public or admitted to trading (Prospectus Directive) (amends 2001/34/EC below)
Directive 2003/6/EC	28 January 2003	on insider dealing and market manipulation (Market Abuse Directive)
Directive 2001/34/EC	6 July 2001	on the admission of securities to listing and information to be published

Table 1.4 Key EU Directives derived from the Company Law Action Plan and the FSAP relevant to core company law

1.5.3 Freedom of establishment and cross-border mobility

Alongside the European Commission's efforts to develop European company law, the European Court (previously the European Court of Justice) has been faced with a number of issues important to European company law. The most important of these is the operation in the context of companies of the fundamental right of freedom of establishment, currently set out in Article 49 of The Treaty on the Functioning of the European Union (TFEU).

ARTICLE

'49 Within the framework of the provisions set out below, restrictions on the freedom of establishment of nationals of a Member State in the territory of another Member State shall be prohibited. Such prohibition shall also apply to restrictions on the setting-up of agencies, branches or subsidiaries by nationals of any Member State established in the territory of any Member State.

Freedom of establishment shall include the right to take up and pursue activities as self-employed persons and to set up and manage undertakings, in particular companies or firms within the meaning of the second paragraph of Article 54, under the conditions laid down for its own nationals by the law of the country where such establishment is effected, subject to the provisions of the Chapter relating to capital.'

Article 49 provides that freedom of establishment shall include the right of nationals of a Member State to incorporate and manage companies in another Member States under the same conditions as local people, that is, without being discriminated against because they are not nationals of the state of incorporation. A UK national, for example, can incorporate a company in any Member State and must be subjected to the same rules as those that apply to a national of the chosen Member State who sets up a company.

The scope of this freedom in the context of companies has been examined in four key cases. The decision in the fourth case, *Re Sevic Systems AG* (Case C-411/03 [2005] ECR I-10805), is not considered here because it has been superseded by the tenth Company Law Directive on cross-border mergers (see Table 1.3 above). Of the three cases considered in this section, two concerned the choice of Member State of incorporation and one concerned a company moving its central administration from one Member State to another whilst remaining incorporated in the original Member State.

The key issue underlying the first two cases is whether or not freedom of establishment opens up the opportunity for forum shopping within the EU, that is, the opportunity to decide to incorporate a company in the jurisdiction with the most attractive (often the least demanding) incorporation regime, regardless of where in the EU the company is and is not to carry on business. The most obvious case of forum shopping is where those incorporating the company have no intention of the company carrying on business in the Member State of incorporation. The first case, *Centros Ltd v Erhvervs-og Selskabsstyrelsen* (Case C-212/97 [1999] ECR I-1549) involving the incorporation of a company in England by a Danish couple based in Denmark, was just such a case.

The Danish couple chose England because the requirements of incorporation in England were more easily complied with than the requirements to incorporate in Denmark. In particular, at the time, a minimum share capital of 200,000 Danish krona was required, whereas in England the minimum share capital of a private company was (and still is) the nominal value of one share, which can be as little as one pence. An application to register a branch of the English company in Denmark was made which the Danish Trade and Companies Board (DTCB) turned down. As the company carried on no business in England and intended to carry on its only business in Denmark, the DTCB considered the couple to be in breach of Danish company law. Denmark's minimum capital rules, it was argued, were for the benefit of creditors. The Danish couple took the DTCB to court in Denmark, lost the case, appealed, and the Danish appeal court referred the point to the European Court for a preliminary ruling under Article 177 (now TFEU Article 267). The court ruling was in favour of the Danish couple. The force of the argument that the minimum capital rules were for the benefit of creditors was undermined by the fact that foreign companies with foreign operations could register branches in Denmark without complying with Danish minimum capital requirements.

JUDGMENT

'26 In the present case, the provisions of national law, application of which the parties concerned have sought to avoid, are rules governing the formation of companies and not rules concerning the carrying on of certain trades, professions or businesses. The provisions of the Treaty on freedom of establishment are intended specifically to enable companies formed in accordance with the law of a Member State and having their registered office, central administration or principal place of business within the Community to pursue activities in other Member States through an agency, branch or subsidiary.

27 That being so, the fact that a national of a Member State who wishes to set up a company chooses to form it in the Member State whose rules of company law seem to him the least restrictive and to set up branches in other Member States cannot, in itself, constitute an abuse of the right of establishment. The right to form a company in accordance with the law of a Member State and to set up branches in other Member States is inherent in the exercise, in a single market, of the freedom of establishment guaranteed by the Treaty.'

In *Kamer van Koophandel en Fabrieken voor Amsterdam v Inspire Art Ltd* (Case C-167/01 [2003] ECR I-10155) the Dutch authorities sought to impose both a disclosure obligation not imposed on Dutch companies, and Dutch minimum capital requirements and director liability rules, on an English company that had registered a branch in Amsterdam. On an application from the Dutch court for a preliminary ruling, the court ruled that both infringed the guarantee in the treaty of freedom of establishment.

JUDGMENT

'143 It is contrary to Article 2 of the Eleventh Directive for national legislation ... to impose on the branch of a company formed in accordance with the laws of another Member State disclosure obligations not provided for by that directive.

It is contrary to Article ... [49 TFEU] ... for national legislation ... to impose on the exercise of freedom of secondary establishment in that State by a company formed in accordance with the law of another Member State certain conditions provided for in domestic company law in respect of company formation relating to minimum capital and directors' liability. The reasons for which the company was formed in that other Member State, and the fact that it carries on its activities exclusively or almost exclusively in the Member State of establishment, do not deprive it of the right to invoke the freedom of establishment guaranteed by the ... [TFEU] ... save where the existence of an abuse is established on a case-by-case basis.'

In *Uberseering BV v Nordic Construction Co Baumanagement GmbH (NCC) (Case C-208/00 [2002] ECR I-9919)*, a company incorporated in the Netherlands came to find itself in a position where all its shareholders and business activities were in Germany. It moved its central administrative offices from the Netherlands to Germany. When it attempted to sue a supplier of defective services in the German courts, it was denied the right to do so on the basis that as it was not incorporated under German law and the German court did not recognise it as a company incorporated under Dutch law, it had no capacity to sue. This was because German law does not embrace the 'incorporation theory', whereby the internal affairs of a company, including its status, are governed by the law of the place of its incorporation. Rather, German law embraces the 'company seat' theory, whereby the internal affairs of a company, including its status, are governed by the law of the place of its actual centre of administration. The court's ruling on a preliminary reference from the German Federal Court, was again in favour of the company:

JUDGMENT

'1. Where a company formed in accordance with the law of a Member State ("A") in which it has its registered office is deemed, under the law of another Member State ("B"), to have moved its actual centre of administration to Member State B, Articles 43 EC and 48 EC preclude Member State B from denying the company legal capacity and, consequently, the capacity to bring legal proceedings before its national courts for the purpose of enforcing rights under a contract with a company established in Member State B.

2. Where a company formed in accordance with the law of a Member State ("A") in which it has its registered office exercises its freedom of establishment in another Member State ("B"), Articles 43 EC and 48 EC require Member State B to recognise the legal capacity and, consequently, the capacity to be a party to legal proceedings which the company enjoys under the law of its State of incorporation ("A").'

As these cases illustrate, the European Court has laid down a clear and robust view of the right to freedom of establishment as it operates in relation to companies incorporated in the EU. The question of cross-border mobility of companies, however, is complex and involves a number of difficult issues apart from freedom of establishment. It was one of three areas focused on and upon which extensive recommendations were made by the Reflection Group on the Future of Company Law in 2011.

1.5.4 The future of EU company law

At the time of writing the European Commission is consulting on the way forward for European company law. The consultation was announced on 20 February 2012.

QUOTATION

'What does the public consultation cover?

Input is requested both on the general orientation of European company law and on more specific initiatives that could be envisaged in the future. The following issues are covered in the consultation:

- **Objectives and scope of European company law** – What should be the main objectives of European company law? Are the current rules fit for today's challenges? In which areas is there need for further evolution? What relationship between company law and corporate governance?
- **Codification of European company law** – Should the existing company law Directives be merged in a single instrument in order to make the regulatory framework more accessible and user-friendly?
- **The future of company legal forms at European level** – What are the advantages and shortcomings of European company forms? Do existing company forms need to be reviewed? Should alternative instruments be explored?
- **Cross-border mobility for companies** – What can be done to facilitate the cross-border transfer of a company's seat? What if a company splits into different entities cross-border – should the rules on cross-border mergers be reviewed?
- **Groups of companies** – ie a set of companies under a single management or source of control – Is there need for EU policy action in this field?
- **Capital regime for European companies** – Should the existing minimum legal capital requirements and rules on capital maintenance be modified and updated?'

European Commission Press Release 20 February 2012: European Company Law – what way forward Reference: IP/12/149

The consultation is taking place principally following the Report of the Reflection Group on the Future of EU Company Law, commissioned by the European Commission and published in April 2011. The Report coincided with the publication of the European Commission Green Paper on The EU Corporate Governance Framework (COM(2011) 164 final). Whilst consultation on the Green Paper took place in 2011, the current public consultation should be seen as underpinned by both documents. Post-consultation developments can be followed on the website referenced at the end of this chapter.

1.6 The Company Law Review and the Companies Act 2006

The Companies Act 2006 is the most significant reform of company law since the Companies Act 1862. The eight and a half year reform process leading up to the Act involved a three-year Company Law Review (CLR), involving expert review and public consultation, followed by Government review and parliamentary scrutiny, the key stages of which are indicated in Table 1.5. The key documents, along with numerous consultative documents and a wealth of consultation material, can be accessed via the BIS Companies Act website referenced under further reading at the end of this chapter.

Stage of CLR	Date of completion of stage/publication	Key document
Launch	March 1998	Modern Company Law for a Competitive Economy (MCLCE)
The Strategic Stage	February 1999	MCLCE: The Strategic Framework
The Development Stage	March 2000	MCLCE: Developing the Framework
The Completion Stage	November 2000	MCLCE: Completing the Structure
The Final Stage	July 2001	MCLCE: Final Report
White Paper	July 2002	Modernising Company Law (with partial draft Act) (Cm 5553)
Second White Paper	March 2005	Company Law Reform (Cm 6456)
Introduction into House of Lords	November 2005	Company Law Reform Bill
Royal Assent	8 November 2006	Companies Act 2006

Table 1.5 Company Law Review and Companies Act 2006 key stages

The resultant 1,300 section, 16 schedule Act required over 80 statutory instruments, including eight Commencement Orders and seven Consequential Amendments Orders to implement it and provide essential detail left out of the body of the Act. Enabling powers in the Act ensure that the extensive detailed regulations may be put in place without taking up parliamentary time. The Act and all relevant regulations may be accessed on the BIS Companies Act 2006 website. The Act can also be accessed directly on the UK government legislation website. Note that the latest available online version of the Act is the Act as amended from time to time. If the most recent amendments have not been made to the online version, an indication of where to find the amendments is included.

For those familiar with the pre-Companies Act 2006 law, which is largely contained in the Companies Act 1985, the key changes introduced by the 2006 Act are set out in Appendix 1 at the end of this book.

1.7 Evaluating the Companies Act 2006

The objectives of the Companies Act 2006, as stated in the final White Paper, were:

- to enhance shareholder engagement and a long-term investment culture
- to ensure better regulation and a 'think small first' approach
- to make it easier to set up and run a company
- to provide flexibility for the future.

Whilst it remains too early to state whether or not these objectives have been achieved, two recent reports provide some insight into the initial impact of the Act. A project to evaluate the immediate impact of the major provisions of the Act, commenced by BIS in September 2009, resulted in a two volume report published in August 2010 (the BIS Report) and, in January 2012, the Secretary of State for BIS presented to parliament a Memorandum to the Business, Innovation and Skills Select Committee Post-Legislative Assessment of the Companies Act 2006 (Cm 8255) (Memorandum) containing a preliminary assessment of the Act.

QUOTATION

'Many of the changes introduced through the Act appear to have been perceived as a piece of good house-keeping, enabling somewhat archaic provisions to be removed, bringing Company Law into the twenty first century, rather than radical change. It must be borne in mind when reviewing these findings that the Companies Act 2006 is primarily an enabling Act, so it is for a company to decide whether it wishes to take advantage of the measures provided and when it wishes to do so. Thus further time must elapse to allow companies to decide how they wish to proceed. It appears that some companies have made changes in tranches rather than all in one go, and also that advisors have been hugely influential in which changes have been made. That aside, awareness levels, particularly those relating to small private companies, were higher than some stakeholders expected and so too were levels of compliance/adoption with certain measures such as auditor limited liability agreements.'

BIS Evaluation of the Companies Act Volume 1 (August 2010) at p.5

In terms of simply being aware of individual changes made by the Act, the BIS Report states that awareness of the following changes was highest:

- directors' addresses (85 per cent);
- access to company information and filing times (84 per cent); and
- the business review (81 per cent).

Companies are reportedly least aware of the changes made to capital maintenance (57 per cent), and those simplifying the law and making it more accessible (62 per cent).

Levels of adoption of measures so as to benefit from the changes were predictably much lower than awareness levels but this must be read with the understanding that the Companies Act 2006 is essentially an enabling Act. As many of the changes simply create opportunities to benefit, adoption is likely to increase over time. Interestingly, 17 per cent of companies have taken (or their auditors have taken) the opportunity, introduced by the Act, to limit their auditor's liability by entering into an auditor limited liability agreement (see Chapter 17).

Positive outcomes from the Act noted in the Memorandum were:

- a reduction in bureaucracy;
- greater privacy for directors and shareholders;
- greater clarity on directors' duties; and
- greater engagement with shareholders.

SUMMARY

Core company law

The law governing the creation and operation of registered companies. Although primarily found in the Companies Act 2006, it contains parts of insolvency law and securities regulation.

Sources of company law

The key sources of company law are case law, statutes, statutory instruments or government regulations and self-regulatory rules and codes such as the UK Corporate Governance Code and the UK Stewardship Code (July 2010). The principal statutes are:

- Companies Act 2006
- Insolvency Act 1986
- Company Directors Disqualification Act 1986
- Financial Services and Markets Act 2000
- Criminal Justice Act 1993 (insider dealing)
- Companies Act 1985 (company investigations)
- Companies (Audit, Investigations and Community Enterprise) Act 2004.

Historical development of the registered company

- Registered companies have existed in the UK since 1844.
- Limited liability was first available for registered companies in 1855.
- Private and public companies were first distinguished in 1907.

■ Since 1973 UK membership of the European Union has influenced the development of UK company law as EU harmonisation and a single market have been pursued, including through the Company Law Action Plan, the Financial Services Action Plan and freedom of establishment.

Most recent key development

■ The Companies Act 2006, which followed a major government Company Law Review initiated in 1998, aims to enhance shareholder engagement and a long-term investment culture, ensure better regulation and a Think Small First approach, make companies easier to set up and run and provide flexibility for the future.

■ The 2006 Act is viewed in practice as a piece of good house-keeping rather than a radical reforming statute.

■ The European Commission commenced a consultation on the way forward for European company law in February 2012.

ACTIVITY

Self-test questions

1. Explain how securities regulation and insolvency law are relevant to company law.
2. What does the term 'corporate governance' mean?
3. Name seven statutes relevant to company law and identify the most important of them.
4. How has the UK's membership of the European Union affected company law in the UK?
5. What are the objectives of the Companies Act 2006?

Further reading

Useful websites

BIS Companies Act 2006 website:
http://www.bis.gov.uk/policies/business-law/company-and-partnership-law/company-law
European Commission Company Law and Corporate Governance website:
http://ec.europa.eu/internal_market/company/index_en.htm
European Commission Financial Services Action Plan website:
http://ec.europa.eu/internal_market/finances/actionplan/index_en.htm
The European Corporate Governance Institute website:
www.ecgi.org/index.htm
Financial Reporting Council Corporate Governance website:
www.frc.org.uk/corporate
Companies Act 2006 as amended online version:
http://www.legislation.gov.uk/ukpga/2006/46/contents

Articles

Ireland, P, 'Capitalism Without the Capitalist: the Joint Stock Company Share and the Emergence of the Modern Doctrine of Separate Corporate Personality' (1996) 17 *Journal of Legal History* 63.
Pekmezovic, A, 'Determinants of corporate ownership: the question of legal origin: Part 1' (2007) 18 ICCLR 97.
Pekmezovic, A, 'Determinants of corporate ownership: the question of legal origin: Part 2' (2007) 18 ICCLR 147.
Ueda, J, 'Modernizing company law and regulatory competition: some economic implications' (2008) 29 Stat LR 154.

Reports

Company Law Review 1998 Steering Group and Government documents (see Table 1.5 above, available at BIS Companies Act 2006 website above).

Department for Business Innovation & Skills, Evaluation of the Companies Act Volumes 1 & 2 (August 2010) (URN 10/1360).

European Commission Communication, Implementing the framework for financial markets: action plan (COM(1999) 232 final).

European Commission Communication, Modernising Company Law and Enhancing Corporate Governance in the EU – A Plan to Move Forward (COM(2003) 284).

European Commission Green Paper, The EU corporate governance framework (COM(2011) 164).

European Commission Internal Market and Services, Report of the Reflection Group on the Future of EU Company Law, Brussels 5 April 2011.

Memorandum to the Business, Innovation and Skills Select Committee, Post-Legislative Assessment of the Companies Act 2006 (Cm 8255) (January 2012).

Books

Cheffins, B, *Corporate Ownership and Control: British Business Transformed* (Oxford University Press, 2008).

Harris, R, *Industrializing English Law Entrepreneurship and Business Organization, 1720–1844* (Cambridge University Press, 2000).

Hudson, A, *Finance Law* (Sweet & Maxwell, 2009).

de Lacey, J (ed), *The Reform of United Kingdom Company Law* (Cavendish Publishing, 2002), particularly:

Parkinson, J, 'Inclusive Company Law'

Rickford, J, 'A History of the Company Law Review'

Riley, C, 'The Juridification of Corporate Governance'

McCahery, J, and Vermeulen, E, *Corporate Governance of Non-listed Companies* (Oxford University Press, 2008).

2

Legal structures of business organisations

AIMS AND OBJECTIVES

After reading this chapter you should be able to:

- Categorise private businesses in the UK according to legal structure
- Recognise unincorporated business organisation legal structures
- Recognise incorporated business organisation legal structures
- Understand the different types of registered companies available
- Identify the key differences between private and public companies
- Understand that not all public companies have shares listed on a stock exchange
- Compare and contrast the main features of partnerships, LLPs and registered companies
- Appreciate the variety of legal structures used in the social economy
- Identify the special features that attach to community interest companies compared to ordinary registered companies
- Understand EU-level organisational legal structures introduced for use by businesses and in the social economy

2.1 Introduction

This book is about business organisation law in the UK, specifically the law applicable to companies registered under the Companies Acts formed to own and conduct one or more businesses run for profit. The aim of this chapter is to put business organisations structured as registered companies into context.

First, profit-making business organisations are categorised according to their legal structure and size. The appropriateness of using the legal structure adopted by a business organisation to determine the applicability of certain mandatory laws such as public disclosure is questioned. The different legal structures through which businesses may be conducted in the UK are then examined, looking first at unincorporated, then incorporated business forms.

Due to the increasing political, social and economic importance of not-for-profit organisations, or 'social enterprises', interest is growing at both national and European Union (EU) level in the legal structures used in this 'third sector' or 'civil society'. Although detailed consideration of these legal structures is outside the scope of this book, it is important to be aware of this development and the final section of this chapter looks at some of the more popular legal structures used in the third sector. Finally, in the last section of this chapter, we look at EU initiatives in relation to business organisations and civil society entities.

2.2 Categorising private businesses in the UK

2.2.1 Categorisation of private businesses by legal structure

According to statistics published by BIS there were approximately 4.5 million private business enterprises in the UK at the beginning of 2011, a figure that excludes government and non-profit organisations. Of these, almost two thirds are sole traders, just over 10 per cent are partnerships and just over one-quarter are registered companies.

A number of difficult issues arise in attempting to achieve accurate and comparable statistics which render the figures that follow indicative rather than definitive numbers. Subject to this proviso, if we focus on private business enterprises in which more than one person is involved, either as an owner or employee, the total number of enterprises drops from 4.5 million to around 1.5 million. This reflects two key facts. First, a fact that might not come as a surprise is that of 2.8 million sole traders, only 10 per cent employ another person or persons. What might come as a surprise, however, is that approximately 40 per cent of companies are 'one man band' companies, that is, they have only one person, the owner, working in them. The term 'working' is used here rather than 'employed' because as a matter of law the owner, who will be a shareholder and a director, may or may not also be an employee of the company.

Figure 2.1 Private business enterprises in the UK 2011

Figure 2.2 Private business enterprises with two or more persons in the UK 2011

When one man band enterprises are excluded, the proportion of the business enterprises using each of the three most popular legal structures changes considerably. Companies are the most popular legal structure, at 50 per cent of the total, followed by partnerships at 30 per cent and sole traders make up 20 per cent of the total.

The Limited Liability Partnership (LLP) does not feature in the national statistics referenced above. The LLP is a legal structure available only since 2001 and whilst as at March 2006 approximately 17,500 were registered, that figure more than doubled in the following five years to approximately 43,000 as at March 2011. Notwithstanding the limited number the LLP is an important structure to understand, not least because of its popularity amongst professionals, including lawyers. The LLP is the legal structure of choice for firms of accountants and solicitors. It is discussed below at section 2.4.2.

2.2.2 Categorisation of private businesses by size

Business enterprises are increasingly considered in terms of small and medium enterprises (SMEs) on the one hand and large enterprises on the other with increasing political focus on SMEs. Support for SMEs is one of the European Commission's priorities for economic growth, job creation and economic and social cohesion. Eligibility for EU measures such as community programmes, grants and loans very often depends upon an enterprise meeting the SME criteria. In the EU, SMEs are believed to account for more than 99 per cent of all business enterprises and 67 per cent of all employment. Figures in the UK are 99.9 per cent and 59 per cent, although, again, care must be taken in interpreting the figures as they are not directly comparable due to different underlying methodologies used to compile them. What appears to be clear is that in the twenty-first century to date, both in the UK and the EU, new jobs have been created primarily by SMEs, not be large companies.

No single consistent definition of the term SME exists. Where the term is used, the meaning should always be confirmed. The EU defines SME as 'micro, small and medium-sized enterprises' (making it an odd abbreviation since the introduction of the 'micro' category) (see Commission Recommendation of 6 May 2003 (2003/361/EC) OJ L 124 p.36).

The three criteria used by the EU to assess whether an enterprise is micro, small or medium-sized are the number of employees (or headcount), the annual turnover (the sum received for goods and services in a year) and the annual balance sheet total (the total value of the assets or property of the enterprise, less the amount it owes). An enterprise must meet the employee threshold and one of the other two criteria thresholds to come within a particular category. Any enterprise that employs 250 or more individuals is a large enterprise, not an SME, regardless of its income or assets. The thresholds current as at April 2012 are set out in Figure 2.3 below.

2.2.3 Categorisation relevant to determining applicable laws

Size, to some extent, determines the legal rules applicable to a company registered under the Companies Acts and to an LLP. The Companies Act 2006, for example, applies less rigorous public disclosure and audit requirements to small and medium-sized companies, as those terms are defined in the Companies Act 2006 (as amended and supplemented by the Companies Act 2006 (Amendment) (Accounts and Reports) Regulations 2008 (SI 2008/393)). The requirements to qualify as a small or medium sized company for these purposes are set out in Figure 2.4 below.

Rather than size, however, by far the more important factor determining the legal rules that apply to a private business is the legal form it takes, and, within the category of registered companies limited by shares, whether it is a private company (Ltd or Limited) or a public company (PLC). This key distinction is drawn at various points throughout this book and the differences are summarised in Table 2.1 below.

Increasingly, laws are being developed to regulate companies with shares traded on stock exchanges. This makes it very important to distinguish between those companies with, and those without, shares traded on a stock exchange. Great care needs to be taken here, as a number of terms are used in law to determine the scope of application of particular legal provisions. 'Quoted company' (s 385), 'traded company' (s 360C) and 'listed company' (a term with more than one legal definition) come to mind. Always check to which type of company particular laws apply.

Also, be aware that the use of a term in law may be very different from its general (non-legal) usage. For example, in general usage, the term 'quoted' refers to shares traded on *any* stock exchange. In contrast, the term 'quoted company' as defined in the Companies Act 2006, includes companies with shares traded on the Main Market of the London Stock Exchange (and certain other markets) but *does not include* companies with shares traded on AIM, which is the second most important market for shares in London. Figure 2.6 below represents the Companies Act 2006 definition of quoted company figuratively. To complicate matters further, the London Stock Exchange defines shares listed on AIM as 'quoted', in contrast to shares listed on the Main Market, which it defines as 'listed'.

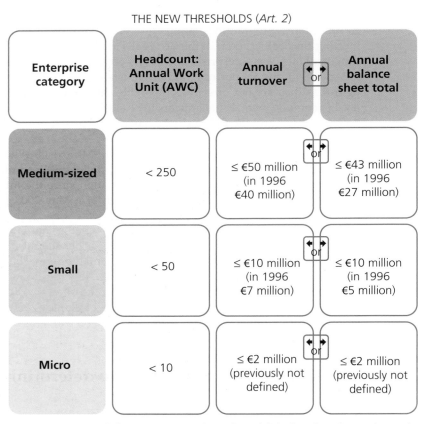

THE NEW THRESHOLDS (*Art. 2*)

Enterprise category	Headcount: Annual Work Unit (AWC)	Annual turnover	or	Annual balance sheet total
Medium-sized	< 250	≤ €50 million (in 1996 €40 million)	or	≤ €43 million (in 1996 €27 million)
Small	< 50	≤ €10 million (in 1996 €7 million)	or	≤ €10 million (in 1996 €5 million)
Micro	< 10	≤ €2 million (previously not defined)	or	≤ €2 million (previously not defined)

The new SME definition: User guide and model declaration, Enterprise and Industry publications, European Commission Publications Office

Figure 2.3 EU definition of SME from 1 January 2005

The appropriateness of legal-form based regulation is open to question. For example, why should a large partnership be subject to no public disclosure rules when a similarly sized company is required to make extensive information, including details about its owners, directors and share capital, and annual accounts and reports available to the public? It is noteworthy that the first company statute, the Joint Stock Company Act 1844, required *any* new business organisation with more than 25 members to register as a company, a threshold lowered to 20 by the Joint Stock Company Act 1856. Large business organisations (size being gauged by reference to the number of owners) were thereby subject to public disclosure requirements. The size limit of 20 on partnerships (the only effective alternative legal structure) was eroded by more and more exceptions over the years until it was finally abolished in 2002. Today, there is no limit on the number of partners a partnership can have.

> **Medium-sized company: Companies Act 2006, s 465**
>
> Must satisfy 2 out of 3 of:
>
> > ≤ £25.9m annual turnover
> > ≤ £12.9m balance sheet
> > ≤ 250 employees
>
> to take advantage of accounts & reports rules for medium sized companies, must also be a private company (s 467)
>
> **Small company: Companies Act 2006, s 382**
>
> Must satisfy 2 out of 3 of:
>
> > ≤ £6.5m annual turnover
> > ≤ £3.26m balance sheet
> > ≤ 50 employees
>
> to take advantage of accounts & reports small companies regime, must also be a private company (s 384)
>
> to be exempt from filing a directors' report with the registrar, must also be a private company (s 415A)
>
> to be exempt from audit must satisfy both turnover and balance sheet tests and be a private company (ss 477 & 488)

Figure 2.4 Small and medium sized companies for Companies Act 2006 purposes

Public disclosure to enable scrutiny is acknowledged to be an important and effective tool to drive best practice in business organisation governance in the public interest. The public interest is increasingly concerned with business organisation governance, environmental protection, the impact of business on the community, and the interests of stakeholders in businesses other than owners and creditors. As the interests served by public disclosure are expanded, it may be more appropriate for disclosure obligations to be triggered by size of business rather than by the legal structure adopted as this would ensure that large businesses are subjected to adequate scrutiny.

It is arguable that size is a more appropriate basis on which to impose a more onerous legal regime, rather than legal rules being triggered based on registration as a private or public company or based on a company being quoted, traded or listed. Quoted companies are subject to the most onerous narrative reporting under the Companies Act 2006, for more on which, see Chapter 17 below. As company law becomes more concerned with a variety of stakeholders in addition to shareholders and creditors, the public/private, quoted/unquoted, traded/untraded and listed/unlisted company distinctions may be eclipsed by categorisation by size as the trigger for the application of more onerous company laws.

A current and important relevant trend before the credit crunch was for private equity firms to acquire larger and larger companies. If the company acquired is a quoted company, its shares may be withdrawn from being traded on a stock market (usually the Main Market of the London Stock Exchange), and removed from the official list. This removes the company from both the higher level of public disclosure imposed on quoted companies by the Companies Act 2006 tiered disclosure regime and the public disclosure obligations imposed by securities regulation on companies with shares traded on a stock market, the result being less effective public scrutiny. An example of this was the acquisition in June 2007 of Alliance Boots plc, the company that owns the Boots high street chain of chemists, by A B Acquisitions Limited, a company controlled by private equity funds. Since its acquisition, its shares are no longer traded on a stock exchange, it is no longer a quoted, traded or listed company, and Alliance Boots plc has been reregistered as a private company: Alliance Boots Ltd.

2.3 Unincorporated business organisation legal structures

Unincorporated organisations are organisations that are not persons, in the eyes of the law, separate from their members. They are not corporate entities or artificial legal persons. Businesses *run for profit* that are not organised as corporate entities almost all take the form of sole traders or partnerships. Each of these business forms is considered in this section. Unincorporated organisations that are not sole traders or partnerships are often referred to as 'unincorporated associations'. As running a business to make profits is not usually the principal purpose of these organisations (most of them are clubs or cooperatives), they are considered later in this chapter along with other social enterprise private legal structures (see 2.6 below).

2.3.1 Sole traders

No 'core' business organisation law exists relevant to sole traders or 'sole practitioners' (the term preferred by professionals) because there is no organisation to regulate. A sole trader is an individual who offers goods or services to others in return for payment. In the context of distinguishing a sole trader from an employee, a sole trader is referred to as an 'independent contractor'.

The individual who is the sole trader is the party to contracts, owns all the property he or she uses in the course of trade or business, and receives all the income and profits from the business. A sole trader can contract with individuals to help in the business, whether by entering into a contract for services with an independent contractor or a contract of employment (a contract of service) with an employee. In the latter case, the individual sole trader is the employer. Approximately 10 per cent of sole traders employee others in their business.

The individual who is the sole trader is also the person sued if anything goes wrong in the course of the business. If a judgment is obtained against the individual, all of his or her assets (whether personal or used in the business) are available to settle or pay that judgment debt.

No legal person, separate from the individual, is created, therefore the sole trader carries on an unincorporated business. The individual cannot be an employee of the business because he cannot contract with himself. Both of these points mean that, in contrast to establishing a company through which to conduct a business, there is little opportunity for a sole trader to minimise his or her tax liability. A sole trader is taxed as a self-employed person and the profit from carrying on the business is subject to income tax. If the individual has taxable income from outside the business, perhaps interest on his or her savings in a Building Society, the business profits are added to that income and the rates of tax (50 per cent, 40 per cent and 20 per cent) are applied to the total income.

Setting up in business as a sole trader is easy. The sole trader simply needs to register as self-employed with Her Majesty's Revenue & Customs (HMRC). Any laws applicable to the particular type of business or practice in which the sole trader is involved also need to be complied with. A sole trader who employs others must register for PAYE purposes and if earnings of the business are expected to exceed the relevant threshold (£77,000 per annum in 2012–13) a sole trader will also need to register for value added tax (VAT) purposes. No information about a sole trader's business needs to be made available to the public: a sole trader has financial and business privacy.

Individuals who wish to own and manage a business on their own can choose to conduct that business as a sole trader or through a company. The decision of an individual to establish a company may, however, be customer-led, and, to this extent, less a choice of the individual rather than a trading necessity. Potential customers, preferring to contract with a company to provide the services of an individual rather than contracting directly with that individual, may exclude sole traders from consideration

sole trader
an individual who is in business on his own account ie, he is not in partnership nor does he trade through a corporate body

when deciding to whom to award a contract. The reasoning behind this practice, prevalent in the IT industry, is that customers do not wish to incur the consequences of an individual being found to be an employee. An employee has far more rights against the customer/employer than arise out of a contract for services with a service delivering company. Furthermore, an employer must pay employer national insurance (13.8 per cent in 2012–13) on the earnings of an employee, and incur the administrative cost and inconvenience of deducting employee national insurance contributions and income tax from an employee's earnings and paying the deducted sum to HMRC under the 'pay as you earn' (PAYE) system.

2.3.2 Partnerships

General partnerships

partnership
the relation which subsists between persons carrying on a business in common with a view of profit

Partnership is a legal relationship defined in the Partnership Act 1890 (in this section, 'the Act'). The Act has set out the basic structure of partnership law with no significant substantive change for over a century. There are no necessary formalities required to create a partnership.

SECTION

'Partnership Act 1890, section 1(1)
Partnership is the relation which subsists between persons carrying on a business in common with a view of profit.'

Whether or not a partnership exists is decided by applying the statutory test to the facts. Whether an express (written or oral) or implied agreement is entered into or not, if two or more persons carry on a business together ('in common'), with the intention of making a profit, a partnership will exist because the arrangement falls within s 1(1) of the Act. The relationship between the members of a company is *not* a partnership, a point put beyond doubt by s 1(2).

Section 2 contains rules to help to decide whether or not a partnership exists. These rules deal with sharing profits (*prima facie* evidence of partnership, s 2(3)), and sharing income and ownership of property (neither, in themselves, enough to evidence a partnership, ss 2(2) and 2(1) respectively). The Act defines partners collectively as a firm (s 4).

The Act continues, setting out internal rules governing relations between the partners themselves, and external rules governing relations between the partnership and those dealing with the partnership. Most internal rules in the Act are not mandatory rules but default or 'opt-out' rules, that is, rules that apply unless the partners agree otherwise. Agreement otherwise can be oral or evidenced by behaviour but is most commonly evidenced by a written contract between the partners setting out the main terms on which the partnership is to operate. Written partnership agreements range from very simple to massively detailed documents. Law firm partnership agreements are typically very long and involved.

Two important examples of simple default rules regularly opted out of and in many cases replaced by long and complex provisions, are (1) the capital and profit sharing rule, and (2) the management rule, both found in s 24 of the Act.

SECTION

'Partnership Act 1890, s 24
(1) All the partners are entitled to share equally in the capital and profits of the business, and must contribute equally towards the losses whether of capital or otherwise sustained by the firm …
(5) Every partner may take part in the management of the partnership business.'

In law, partnerships are *not* legal persons or entities distinct from the partners. A partnership is an unincorporated association. A partnership cannot own legal property, the property is owned by the partners (using a trust in many cases to vest the legal title in a limited number of partners to be held for all partners). Nor can a partnership enter into a contract. Contracts, even those which appear on the face of the contractual document to be with a firm, or the partnership because the firm is named as the party to the agreement, are in fact contracts with the individuals who are the partners in the firm. The Law Commission has described the unincorporated legal status of partnerships as 'a throwback to the nineteenth century' and an anomaly which it considers it long past time to end. As discussed later in this section, however, the Government has chosen not to implement the Law Commission's proposals for partnerships to be incorporated organisations.

The unincorporated status of partnerships makes the external rules that apply between partners and third parties critically important. In default of agreement to the contrary, partners have authority to bind the other partners in the firm to contracts: partners are agents of one another. Moreover, s 9 confirms that every partner in a firm is liable, jointly with the other partners, for all debts and obligations of the firm incurred whilst he is a partner. Section 10 extends this liability to cover wrongful acts or omissions of any partner acting in the ordinary course of the partnership business. A partner's liability is unlimited (although see limited partnerships below for the special case where a non-managing partner can limit his contribution to the sum invested in the partnership).

Unlike companies and LLPs, partnerships are not subject to public disclosure obligations. This is an important factor for those who choose to operate their business as a partnership. With the abolition of the restriction on the size of partnerships, it is arguable that, for large partnerships, this absence of public disclosure should be revisited.

A partnership is automatically dissolved every time there is a change of partner, a state of affairs described by the Law Commission in 2003 as, 'far removed from the ordinary perceptions of those involved'.

QUOTATION

'Any change in the membership of a firm, whether the withdrawal of a partner or the admission of a new partner, "destroys the identity of the firm". The "old" firm is dissolved. If the surviving partners continue in partnership (with or without additional partners) a 'new' firm is created. The new firm can take over the assets of the old one and assume its obligations. This involves a contractual arrangement between members of the old firm and the new firm, to continue the old firm's business. In addition, the transfer of an obligation will normally require the consent of the creditor. Continuing a partnership's business in this way does not continue the partnership itself. Even an agreement in advance that partners will continue to practise in partnership on the retirement of one of their number does not prevent the partnership which practises the day after the retirement from being a different partnership from that in business on the previous day.'

Partnership Law, The Law Commission (Law Com No 283, 2003) at para 2.6

One of the main aims of this chapter is to draw attention to distinguishing features between partnerships and registered companies. Transferability of shares is a key characteristic of registered companies. Shareholders are able to sell their shares, that is, they can, in effect, withdraw their investment in the company, without affecting the company's financial position. The shareholder exits the company by receiving his investment back from the new owner of the shares. Transferability exists for shareholders of companies with publicly traded shares but is not always a reality for the owner of private company shares for which it can be very difficult to find a buyer. This ability of the company to continue *unaffected by changes in ownership* is in stark contrast to partnerships. Or at least it is in theory. In practice, tax rules combined with appropriate provisions in partnership agreements can mean that whilst in theory a change in partners operates to terminate a partnership, in fact, the partnership business is not wound up and the business continues largely as before, with one less or one more partner.

Limited liability is often portrayed as the principal distinction between partnerships and registered companies. More recently, however, business organisation law theorists have turned their attention to 'entity shielding' or, as it is also called, 'affirmative asset partitioning'. Entity shielding describes the situation in which the assets or property of a business organisation are protected from the claims of the owner's personal creditors. Entity shielding is strong in registered companies. The assets are owned by the company and if a shareholder owes money to a personal creditor, that creditor cannot enforce the debt against the company. Nor can the shareholder force the company to wind up and pay out the value of his shares to him to enable him to pay his creditors. The company is protected as a going concern.

In contrast, the personal creditors of a partner can demand a payout of the partner's share of the assets to meet the debts that the partner, in his personal capacity, owes to them. The only entity shielding that exists in the context of a partnership is 'weak' entity shielding in that the claims of personal creditors of a partner are subordinated to the claims of the creditors of the partnership: the creditors of the partnership must all have been paid in full before partnership assets can be used to pay personal debts of any of its partners. The different degrees of entity shielding in partnerships and companies has been described as an even more important distinction than limited liability (Hansmann, Kraakman & Squire (2007)).

Following detailed review, comprehensive proposals for reform of partnership law, including a draft Bill, were put forward in 2003 by the Law Commission (see Law Com No 283). The most significant aspect of the proposals was that partnerships, whether general or limited (on which see below), should be separate persons, ie *incorporated* business organisations. Note, however, that the Law Commission did not propose limited liability for partners. Even if the proposals were to be adopted, partners would remain personally responsible, without limit, for the debts and other liabilities of the partnership.

Following DTI (now BIS) consultation on the economic impact of the proposals, in July 2006, the Government announced its decision not to implement the proposals in respect of general partnership law 'for the moment'. As at April 2012, no steps had been taken to implement the proposals in either England or Scotland in relation to general partnerships.

Limited partnerships

limited partnership

a partnership having one or more but not all limited partners ie, sleeping partners whose liability in the event of the partnership's insolvency is limited to the amount that such partner has agreed to contribute

Limited partnerships are *unincorporated* firms provided for by the Limited Partnership Act 1907. They should not be confused with limited liability partnerships (LLPs). LLPs are *incorporated* entities provided for by the Limited Liability Partnership Act 2000 and are considered below at section 2.4.2.

Limited partnerships are partnerships with at least one general partner and one or more limited partners who contribute an agreed sum to the partnership and are not liable for the debts and obligations of the firm beyond that amount. Limited partners may *not* participate in management of the partnership and have no power to bind the firm.

Limited partnerships must be registered at Companies House and the registrar of companies issues a certificate of registration. The names of all of the partners (general and limited) and the sums contributed by limited partners are available for public inspection but there is no requirement for a limited partnership to file accounts. Approximately 1,000 limited partnerships per annum have been registered in recent years and as at the end of March 2011, just under 19,000 limited partnerships were registered at Companies House. Since 1987 (when certain tax guidelines were agreed to by HMRC), limited partnerships have been popular with private equity firms for use as venture capital funds to acquire companies.

The Government's initial indication, in 2006, that it proposed to implement the Law Commission proposals that *limited partnerships* should become legal entities led to a legislative proposal, in 2008, to substantially rewrite the Limited Partnership Act 1907. As a result of the consultation, very few of the changes were found to be unequivocally supported resulting in BIS adopting what it describes as a 'modular approach' to reform. The ensuing Legislative Reform (Limited Partnerships) Order 2009 (SI 2009/1940) effected very limited changes, the two main changes being making a certificate of registration conclusive evidence that a limited partnership has been formed at the date shown on the certificate; and introduction of a requirement that all *new* limited partnerships include 'Limited Partnership' or 'LP' or equivalent at the end of their names. Further reforms are expected as part of a programme of modernising limited partnership law and progress can be followed on the Partnership and LLP law page of the BIS website.

Quasi-partnership companies

'Quasi-partnership company' is not a legally defined term. Company law sometimes acknowledges the fact that a business that is owned and conducted by a registered company has been:

- established with partnership expectations, including, in particular, the expectation that all owners are entitled to participate in management; and
- run by the owners as if it were a partnership, for example, by all owners taking a part in management.

Recognition of these characteristics has led judges to develop special rules for such 'quasi-partnership' companies. Three areas of company law where this is the case are:

- Enforcement of a company's articles of association, specifically, the willingness of the court to permit members of a quasi-partnership company to sue each other directly to enforce the articles of association (*Rayfield v Hands* [1960] Ch 1).
- Companies Act 2006, s 994 petitions, specifically the willingness of the court to grant a remedy based on a finding that even in the absence of any breaches of rights, the affairs of a quasi-partnership company have been conducted in a manner that is unfairly prejudicial to the interests of one or more members.
- Insolvency Act 1986, s 124 applications to wind up a company based on it being just and equitable to do so.

2.4 Incorporated business organisation legal structures

2.4.1 Registered companies

As seen above in section 2.2, if single member businesses are excluded (on the basis that they are not really 'organisations'), the registered company, the focus of this book, is the most popular legal structure for business organisations in the UK. The types of companies that can be registered in the UK are displayed in Figure 2.5.

This book focuses on companies limited by shares, both public and private. Companies limited by guarantee and unlimited companies are dealt with very briefly immediately below and community interest companies (CICs) are considered along with other social enterprise private legal structures (see section 2.6.3).

Companies limited by guarantee

company limited by guarantee
a company the articles of which contains an undertaking by members to contribute a specified amount on a winding up towards the payment of its debts and the expenses of winding up

Section 3(1) of the Companies Act 2006 states that a company is a limited liability company if the liability of its members is limited by its constitution. The liability of members may be limited by shares or limited by guarantee. A company is limited by guarantee if the liability of its members is limited to the amount specified in the articles that the members undertake to contribute to the assets of the company in the event of the company being wound up (s 3(3)).

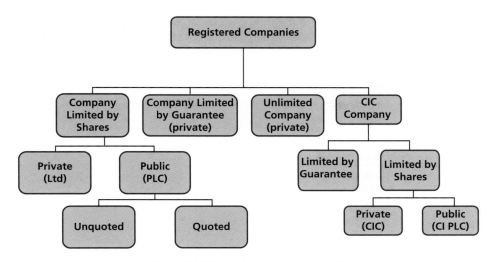

Figure 2.5 Types of registered companies

Companies limited by guarantee are not commonly used in business. They are all private companies but a separate set of Model Articles for Companies Limited by Guarantee has been enacted, alongside those for private and public companies limited by shares (see the Companies (Model Articles) Regulations 2008 (SI 2008/3229)). Traditionally, companies limited by guarantee have been the registered company of choice for charitable companies (meaning companies registered under the Companies Acts with exclusively charitable objects). A new form of company is soon to become available for charities, the Charitable Incorporated Organisation (CIO). Developed to avoid the double burden that charitable companies have long endured of having to register and file documents with both the Charity Commission and the registrar of companies, CIOs are expected to prove more popular than the company limited by guarantee (CIOs are considered below under social enterprise legal structures, at section 2.6.2).

Interestingly, Network Rail Ltd is a private company limited by guarantee. Formed in 2002 to take over Railtrack and responsibility for the UK's rail network, it is a not for profit organisation that receives significant funds from the government. Nonetheless, it asserts on its website that it 'operates as a commercial business' and that the board runs the company 'to the standards required of a publicly listed company'.

Unlimited companies

unlimited company
a company, the liability of whose members to contribute on a winding up to the company, to enable it to pay its debts, is not limited, by shares, guarantee or otherwise

Unlimited companies, which must be private companies, are similarly uncommon in business. They are companies, the liability of whose members to contribute on a winding up to the company to enable it to pay its debts is not limited. They sometimes occur in business contexts as part of a tax planning structure due to some overseas tax authorities (including the US revenue service) regarding them as tax transparent, or 'flow-through' entities, ie ignoring them for tax purposes. In the event of a winding up, the members of an unlimited company are required to contribute sums to the company sufficient for payment of its debts and liabilities (Insolvency Act 1986, s 74(1)).

Companies limited by shares

private company
a registered company that is not a public company

Companies limited by shares have shareholders who own shares in the company. The concept of 'limited' is explored at section 3.5. Essentially, the shareholders of a limited company are *not* required to contribute sums to the company sufficient for payment of its debts and liabilities but are simply required to pay to the company the amount (if any) unpaid on the shares held by them (s 3(2)).

public limited company
a company registered as a public company the name of which ends with the letters plc (or the words represented by those letters in full)

Companies limited by shares may be public companies or private companies. The principal legal difference between public (PLC) and private companies (Ltd or Limited) is that public companies may offer their shares to the public. A private company may not offer its shares to the public (Companies Act 2006, s 755). The main differences between public and private limited companies are set out in Table 2.1 below.

Difference	Companies Act 2006
The name of a public limited company must end with 'plc' or 'public limited company' and the name of a private limited company with 'Ltd' or 'Limited'	ss 58 and 59
Ltd cannot offer shares to the public	s 755
Ltd can have one director, plc needs a minimum of two	s 154
No authorised minimum nominal value of allotted share capital for Ltds, £50,000 for plcs of which a minimum of 25% must be paid up	ss 761 and 763
Plc needs a trading certificate before it can do business or exercise any borrowing powers	s 761
A different set of model articles exists for private companies limited by shares and public companies	s 19(2) and regulations made thereunder
Ltd need not hold AGMs; only needs meetings to remove directors pursuant to s 168 or remove auditors pursuant to s 510	N/A
Ltds need not have a company secretary	s 270
Ltds can pass written resolutions of shareholders	ss 288–300
Ltds can give financial assistance for the purchase of their own shares	N/A
Ltds can purchase and redeem shares out of capital	s 710
Ltds can reduce their share capital without court approval by special resolution and a solvency statement	ss 641–643
Ltds can, if they meet the criteria, qualify for the small companies regime for accounts and reports and/or for the small company exemption from audit; plcs do not qualify for either (ss 384 and 478)	s 381 (accounts) s 477 (audit)

Table 2.1 Key legal differences between private (Ltd) and public (plc) limited companies

Certain sections of the Companies Act 2006 are applicable to some public companies (plcs) and not others. Two subdivisions of public companies relevant to the application of the Act are quoted and unquoted companies (s 385) and traded and untraded companies (s 360C).

Quoted companies

Quoted company is the term used in the Companies Act 2006 to identify registered companies with (in simple terms) equity shares traded on a UK or other EEA regulated stock market or one of the two most famous US stock markets, the New York Stock Exchange and NASDAQ (see Companies Act 2006, s 385 for the precise definition of quoted company). Quoted companies are illustrated diagrammatically in Figure 2.6. Important requirements of the Act, such as the enhanced disclosure obligations in the business review in the directors' report, apply only to quoted companies (see s 417(5)).

Traded companies

The traded company concept introduced into the Companies Act 2006 with effect from August 2009 as part of implementation in the UK of the Shareholder Rights Directive (2007/36/EC) (by The Companies (Shareholders' Rights) Regulations 2009 (SI 2009/1632)) is a company with shares that carry the right to vote at a general meeting admitted to trading on a UK or other EEA regulated stock market (s 360C). It is relevant to shareholder resolutions and meetings.

Somewhat unhelpfully, the term traded company was already present in s 146 of the Act, for which purpose it simply means 'a company whose shares are admitted to trading on a regulated market'. Section 146 enables a person who owns shares on behalf

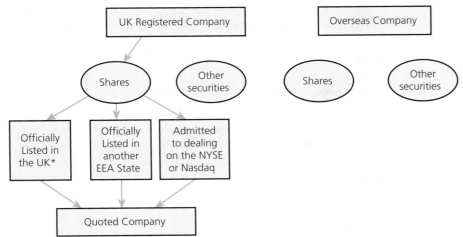

* Note that the two UK markets for officially listed shares are the London Stock Exchange Main Market and the ISDX Main Board Market.

Figure 2.6 Quoted companies (Companies Act 2006, s 385)

UK Listing Authority or UKLA

the Financial Services Authority when it acts as the competent authority under Part VI of FSMA 2000, ie the UK's securities regulator

official list

the list maintained by the Financial Services Authority as UK Listing Authority pursuant to FSMA 2000 s 74(1) being a list of securities issued by companies for the purpose of being traded on a UK regulated market (the most important of which markets for equity shares is the Main Market of the London Stock Exchange)

of another to nominate the beneficial owner as the person to receive information from the company, that is, to have 'information rights'.

Listed companies, listed shares and listed securities

The term 'listed company' is not defined in the Companies Act 2006. It has several definitions in securities regulation and, if you see it used, it is essential to check which definition applies. In securities regulation, the term 'listed' is often attached to a particular class of securities, such as a class of shares or a class of debt securities (on which see Chapter 6), issued by a company. The details of securities regulation are beyond the scope of this book. For the purposes of core company law, a listed company can be regarded as a company that has a class of its shares admitted to the official list of securities and traded on a regulated stock exchange. Listed shares, or listed securities, are shares or securities admitted to the UK official list.

The UK official list is a list of securities maintained by the Financial Services Authority (FSA), acting as the UK 'competent authority' or 'listing authority', pursuant to s 74 of the Financial Services and Markets Act 2000 (FSMA). A security is only admitted to the official list following a successful application to the FSA (s 75) and the FSA will not admit a security to the official list unless it has been accepted for trading on a regulated market for listed securities. The most important of those markets in the UK is the London Stock Exchange (LSE) Main Market *but it is not the only one*. Another is the ISDX Main Board Market.

A company seeking to have its securities admitted to the official list must:

- comply with the Listing Rules published by the FSA; *and*
- obtain the security's admission to trading on a regulated market for listed securities (usually *but not always* the LSE Main Market).

The LSE used to be the UK competent authority. In a 2008 discussion paper the FSA described two principal consequences arising from the fact that the FSA, rather than the LSE, is now the UK competent authority (also referred to as the UK Listing Authority (UKLA)).

QUOTATION

'First, there is considerable scope for confusion about what the term "Listing" means in the UK. In most jurisdictions, it is synonymous with admission to trading on an exchange, whereas in the UK, admission to the Official List and admission to trading are different (although linked) concepts. Second, although historically long-associated with the London Stock Exchange's (LSE) Main Market, the Official List is not in fact … linked to any single trading platform or venue.'

A Review of the Structure of the Listing Regime (FSA Discussion Paper 08/01: January 2008)

Accordingly, whilst most listed securities in the UK are traded on the LSE Main Market, some are not.

All companies with securities officially listed in the UK need to comply with the Listing Rules promulgated by the FSA pursuant to the FSMA *and* with the rules imposed by the regulated market on which the securities are admitted to trading. The relevant rules of the LSE Main Market are the LSE Admission and Disclosure Standards and those for PLUS are the PLUS Market's Admission and Disclosure Standards.

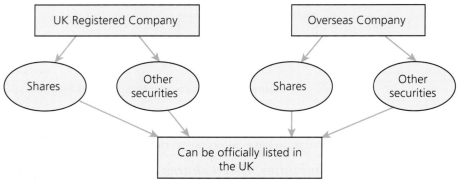

Note that registered companies with shares with a Premium Listing on the London Stock Exchange Main Market are subject to the most stringent regulations. They must comply with 'super-equivalent' listing standards.

Figure 2.7 Listed securities

Note that the Listing Rules provide for equity shares to have a Standard Listing or a Premium Listing. The regulatory requirements imposed on a company with shares with a Standard Listing are based on EU directives. A company with shares with a Premium Listing must comply with 'super-equivalent listing standards'. Super-equivalent listing standards are higher than the minimum standards required by the EU. They have been credited as partly responsible for the success of the UK securities markets because they are seen to offer additional protection and comfort to investors. Differences between UK companies and overseas companies were removed in the 2010 review and restructuring of the Listing Rules so that now both UK and overseas companies can choose to have either a Standard or Premium Listing.

All companies with a Premium Listing (whether UK or overseas companies) are required to state in their annual report and accounts whether or not they have complied with the UK Corporate Governance Code and give reasons for any non-compliance (see Listing Rule 9.8.6R and 9.8.7R).

Numbers of registered companies

As at March 2011, approximately 2.5 million companies were registered at Companies House. BIS figures, on the other hand, indicate the existence of approximately 1.3 million private business enterprises conducted by registered companies. This leaves over a million companies to be accounted for. These 'missing' companies include:

- registered companies not incorporated for business purposes (such as charitable companies);
- dormant companies (companies with no significant accounting entries in any given year which almost certainly account for more than 20 per cent of registered companies and perhaps significantly more than that);
- subsidiary companies within a corporate group.

UK Corporate Governance Code

the code on corporate governance published by the FRC, most recently updated and renamed in September 2012 previously called the Combined Code on Corporate Governance

A corporate group may count as a single entity in business statistics, yet it may be made up of an unlimited number of separate registered companies. In law, each company within a corporate group is treated as a separate legal person with its own debts and other liabilities.

Of all registered companies, only approximately 8,000 (0.3 per cent) are public companies. This means that only approximately 8,000 UK registered companies *may* offer their shares to the public. Not all of them do so. Moreover, do not assume that all public company shares are traded on a stock market. Only approximately 2,000 UK registered companies have shares traded on a stock exchange, ie 25 per cent of public registered companies, and substantially less than 1 per cent of all registered companies. These 2,000 companies are split primarily between the London Stock Exchange's Main Market (1,100) and AIM (900).

Sizes of registered companies and corporate groups

Registered company business organisations range considerably in size from sole member companies with no employees, no paid-up share capital owning no property/having no assets, to companies such as BT Group plc with over 100,000 employees, over £10 billion worth of assets, and annual income in excess of £20 billion. In fact, BT Group plc is the parent company of a large group of companies. Its operations are conducted and income is earned by legally distinct operating companies within the group. Assets are owned by holding companies and/or operating companies and employees are employed by a number of companies within the group. A list of the principal operating subsidiaries within the BT Group plc group can be seen in its 2011 Annual Report (at page 155) accessible on the webpage referenced at the end of this chapter. The actual number of companies within the group will be substantially more than those listed.

Most companies are small companies. Using share capital as an indicator of size, of all companies on the companies register as at March 2011, 74 per cent had issued share capital of £100 or less and 87 per cent had issued share capital of £5,000 or less. Of the approximately 400,000 companies first registered in 2010–11, close to 95 per cent had issued share capital of £5,000 or less. Using the definition of small company for audit exemption purposes (set out above in Figure 2.4) as an indicator of size, 71 per cent of annual accounts filed at Companies House in 2010–11 were exempt from audit.

It is important, however, not to assume that all private companies are small companies (just as not all public companies are large companies). Of the circa 200 companies registered at Companies House in 2010–11 with an issued share capital of £100 million or more, only 12 were public companies, 94 per cent were private companies.

Key legal characteristics of registered companies

The registered company is believed to have become popular because, since 1862, it has offered businessmen the following five attractive characteristics:

- Separate legal personality
- Limited liability
- Transferable shares
- A legal framework designed to pre-empt and provide remedies for problems arising out of the separation of ownership (by shareholders) and control (by the board of directors)
- Asset shielding.

Separate legal personality and limited liability

Separate legal personality and limited liability are considered in detail in Chapter 3. It is worth mentioning here, however, that in relation to *private* companies, significant limits to the enjoyment of these characteristics exist in practice. The fundamental rule that a shareholder is not liable for the debts and liabilities of a company, for example, is regularly contractually undermined by the creditors of a private company requiring the shareholders to guarantee the company's liabilities. This practice does not undermine the principles of separate personality or limited liability in legal theory but it does go a long way to removing their beneficial consequences.

Transferable shares

The transferability of shares in considered in Chapter 7. Again, it is worth mentioning here that provisions in a private company's constitution often carefully limit a shareholder's right to transfer shares. Even in the absence of such constitutional or contractual limits on the right of a member to sell his or her shares, it is often very difficult to sell shares in a private company because they cannot be offered to the public, they are difficult to value, they are usually regarded as a speculative investment carrying significant risk, and anybody buying them will face the same problems finding a buyer when they come to sell shares.

Internal dispute resolution

Laws responding to the fourth characteristic of a registered company, that company law is designed to pre-empt or provide remedies in respect of problems that arise from the separation of ownership from control, are considered at a number of places in this book, including Chapters 11, 12, 13 and 14. Certain laws are more important for small companies than for large companies, such as the right to petition the court for relief from the affairs of the company being conducted in an unfair and prejudicial manner pursuant to s 994 of the Companies Act 2006.

Essentially, company law was originally designed (and to this day in large part remains designed) to deal with companies controlled by one group of individuals, the directors and owned by a different, larger group of individuals, the shareholders. Management of a registered company is invariably vested not in the shareholders (the owners) but in the board of directors. Shareholders have limited powers to direct the board on specific points and can remove one or more of the directors, or the entire board, so it is sometimes said that shareholders retain 'residual' control. In reality, this separation of ownership and control is largely irrelevant to most small companies because the directors are the shareholders.

For large companies, the legal framework of company law, and, increasingly, securities law, facilitates exploitation of the benefits of having professional managers running a business funded by 'investor' shareholders. The main interest of a shareholder with a small shareholding in a large company is to receive a dividend each year and to benefit from an increase in value of his or her shares which value can be realised by selling the shares to a third party, ideally on a stock market.

Asset shielding

The fact that the assets of a company are shielded from the claims of the personal creditors of shareholders is a characteristic of the registered company that has received increasing attention in recent years. The benefit this characteristic brings is not enjoyed by the shareholder directly, but by the company and its creditors. If a personal creditor of a shareholder wishes to realise the value of the shareholders' interest in a company, the company cannot be made to pay-out any money to the shareholder. In this way, the finances of the company are protected from the insolvency of the owners, something which reduces the risk of doing business with a company, and therefore, it is argued, promotes efficient commerce.

Small private companies

In light of the discussion above, it may be asked what, then, are the principal benefits of incorporation to private or small companies? Ease of contracting and the protection from unlimited liability to trade creditors that separate legal personality offers should not be overlooked. Two further benefits that are often influential in a businessman choosing to establish a company rather than using another legal structure of business organisation are:

■ Customer protection from employer obligations
■ Tax planning opportunities.

The first of these is explained above, at the end of section 2.3.1. The second is illustrated by contrasting a business run by a sole trader and the same business being run by a company established by an otherwise would-be sole trader. The profits of the business run by the sole trader are income of the sole trader in the year in which they arise. They are added to other taxable income of the sole trader and the aggregate sum is subject to income tax. There is little, if any, scope for tax planning to minimise taxes.

In contrast, the profits of the company can be dealt with in a variety of ways. The value that the profits represent can be transferred to the owner of the company and/ or people close to him who have been issued with shares in the company as dividends, capital gains, above-market-rate remuneration for services and above market interest on shareholder loans to the company.

Corporate taxation is complex and detailed 'anti-avoidance' rules exist to prevent individuals using companies to avoid paying tax. The following is simply intended to introduce you to some basic principles and the scope for tax planning. Essentially, the profits of a company are subject to corporation tax in the year in which they arise. The rate of corporation tax for small companies is lower than income tax rates. Taxed profits can be retained in the company, increasing the value of the company and therefore the value of shares in the company. This value can then be accessed by the shareholder selling his or her shares. The sale of shares for more than was paid for them precipitates a capital gain. Capital gains are subject to capital gains tax, not income tax. Also, the gain can be taken in any number of years and may be spread across a number of years by a few shares being sold each year.

Alternatively, taxed profits made by a company can be paid out to the shareholder as dividends. They may be paid out not only in the year in which they arise but also, provided they have not been cancelled out by losses in the meantime, in subsequent years. This provides the opportunity to spread taxes over a number of years to achieve an overall lower rate of tax. Dividends are subject to income tax but the income tax payable is in effect reduced by a tax credit to take into account the fact that corporation tax has already been paid. It may be possible for the businessman's family to be shareholders in the company so that the profits can be divided amongst a number of individual shareholders to avoid higher rate taxes.

Finally, the profits of a company can be artificially depressed by the payment of above-market-rate remuneration to employees of the company. These employees may be the sole shareholder or members of his family employed by the company. Again, the point is not to understand the detail of tax law (the details of which change from year to year) but to appreciate that the establishment of a company introduces flexibility that can be used to the advantage of the tax-paying owner or owners of the business. The recent case of *Jones v Garnett (Inspector of Taxes)* [2007] 1 WLR 2030 HL illustrates the use of the limited company to minimise taxes.

2.4.2 Limited liability partnerships (LLP)

limited liability partnership

a body corporate, the liability of whose members is limited, formed by registration under the Limited Liability Partnerships Act 2000 which has the organisational flexibility of a partnership and is taxed as a partnership

The limited liability partnership (LLP) combines the organisational flexibility and tax status of a partnership with limited liability for its members and entity shielding for creditors. It exists due to intense lobbying by the accountancy profession. Accountants sought, and in the LLP have secured, protection from unlimited liability, particularly in relation to auditing service shortcomings. Companies that have not been audited properly may sue the company's auditors (see Chapter 17).

Limited Liability Partnerships are incorporated organisations governed by the Limited Liability Partnerships Act 2000 and extensive regulations made pursuant to both that Act and the Companies Act 2006. The Limited Liability Partnerships Regulations 2001 (SI 2001/1090) applied provisions of the Companies Act 1985 and the Insolvency Act 1986, suitably amended, to LLPs. Those regulations have been amended and in large part (but not totally) replaced by regulations applying to LLPs appropriate parts of the Companies Act 2006 (and regulations made under it). The principal regulations are the Limited Liability Partnerships (Application of Companies Act 2006) Regulations 2009 (SI 2009/1804). They apply to LLPs the Companies Act 2006 provisions governing:

- the formalities of doing business
- names and trading disclosures
- registered offices
- the register of directors and protection from disclosure of residential addresses
- debentures
- annual returns
- the registration of charges
- arrangements and reconstructions
- fraudulent trading
- protection of members against unfair prejudice
- dissolution and restoration to the register
- the registrar of companies.

Specific regulations apply the accounts and audit provisions of the 2006 Act to LLPs, with modification (see The Limited Liability Partnerships (Accounts and Audit) (Application of Companies Act 2006) Regulations 2008 (SI 2008/1911)). The special reports and accounts regimes for small companies (SI 2008/409) and medium and large companies (SI 2008/410) have also been adapted and applied to LLPs (see SI 2008/1912 for small LLP and SI 2008/1913 for medium and large LLPs).

LLPs are separate legal entities from their members yet they are 'tax transparent'. This means that HMRC looks through the LLP, ignoring its existence for tax purposes, and treats the profits of the LLP business as if they have been earned by the members of the LLP, just as in an ordinary partnership.

The limited liability of members of an LLP mirrors the liability of a shareholder in a limited company. This is achieved by the version of s 74 of the Insolvency Act 1986 applicable to LLPs (as substituted by reg 5(2)(f) and Sched 3 of the Limited Liability Partnership Regulations 2001 (SI 2001/1090)), set out below.

SECTION

'When a limited liability partnership is wound up every present and past member of the limited liability partnership who has agreed with the other members or with the limited liability partnership that he will, in circumstances which have arisen, be liable to contribute to the assets of the limited liability partnership in the event that the limited liability partnership goes into liquidation is liable, to the extent that he has so agreed, to contribute to its assets to any amount sufficient for payment of its debts and liabilities, and the expenses of the winding up, and for the adjustment of the rights of the contributories among themselves.

However, a past member shall only be liable if the obligation arising from such agreement survived his ceasing to be a member of the limited liability partnership.'

LLPs offer the benefits of asset shielding and continue in existence notwithstanding the death or resignation of a member. For a number of reasons a member is unlikely to be able to exit with the ease with which shareholders can exit a company with publicly traded shares. Even were the LLP agreement to permit transfer, a member is likely to find difficulty finding a buyer for his interest. Provisions in the LLP agreement are likely to preclude transfer and contain provisions governing the rights of an existing member to withdraw his or her investments. The principal features of LLPs, registered companies and partnerships are compared and contrasted in Table 2.2 below.

2.4.3 Chartered and statutory corporations

Formation of a business corporation by obtaining a charter of incorporation from the Crown or securing a private Act of Parliament is unlikely to happen today. It is much easier and less expensive to register a company, and a grant or Act would be unlikely to be forthcoming for a purely profit-making venture. As at March 2011, Companies House records stated that 828 corporations incorporated by Royal Charter and 45 corporations incorporated by special Acts of Parliament existed. Although once used to run private businesses, many of these corporations are not-for-profit organisations.

The Privy Council is responsible for overseeing the grant of new Royal Charters.

QUOTATION

'New grants of Royal Charters are these days reserved for eminent professional bodies or charities which have a solid record of achievement and are financially sound. In the case of professional bodies they should represent a field of activity which is unique and not covered by other professional bodies.

At least 75 per cent of the corporate members should be qualified to first degree level standard. Finally, both in the case of charities and professional bodies, incorporation by Charter should be in the public interest.'

Privy Council website, Chartered bodies, accessed 9 April 2012

A list of all Royal Charters granted since the first, which was granted in 1261 to the University of Cambridge, can be found on the website of the Privy Council. Examples of corporations formed by Royal Charter are the Law Society (1845) and the Institute of Chartered Accountants (1880). Three new Royal Charters were granted in 2011, all to professional bodies: The Chartered Institute for the Management of Sport and Physical Activity, The Chartered Institute of Legal Executives and the Institution of Engineering Designers. No new corporations were formed by special Act of Parliament in 2010/11.

2.5 Partnerships, LLPs and Registered Companies compared and contrasted

The most important aspects of the three basic legal structure options available when more than one person is involved in *ownership* of a business: partnerships, LLPs and registered companies, are summarised, compared and contrasted in Table 2.2 below. The sole trader is omitted from this comparative exercise due to the absence of any business organisation laws uniquely applicable to sole traders. Contract and employment law are the key areas of law governing the operation of a business by a sole trader.

	Partnerships	Limited Liability Partnerships (LLP)	Registered Companies Limited by Shares (Ltd/PLC)
Main legislation	Partnership Act 1890.	Limited Liability Partnerships Act 2000.	Companies Act 2006.
Formation	Exist from the point in time at which two or more persons begin to carry on a business in common with a view to making a profit.	Incorporated by statute. Formed by registering an incorporation document with the Registrar of Companies.	Incorporated by statute. Formed by registering specified documents and forms with the Registrar of Companies.
Separate personality	A partnership has no separate legal personality from its partners.	An LLP has a separate legal personality from its members.	A registered company has a separate legal personality from its owners and managers.

	Partnerships	Limited Liability Partnerships (LLP)	Registered Companies Limited by Shares (Ltd/PLC)
Maximum and minimum numbers	Minimum of two partners. No maximum number of partners.	Minimum of two members. No maximum number of members.	Minimum of one member. No maximum number of members.
Liability of members	Partners have unlimited liability for the debts and liabilities of the partnership. A 'Limited Partnership' is a special kind of partnership that can have one or more partners with limited liability but must be registered: Limited Partnership Act 1907.	Members have no liability for the debts and liabilities of the LLP. On a winding up, members are liable to contribute to the LLP the amount (if any) agreed in the LLP Agreement: Insolvency Act 1986, s 74 as substituted by LLP Regulations 2001.	Members have no liability for the debts and liabilities of the company. When called upon or on a winding up, members are required to contribute any unpaid part of the nominal value of the shares they own. Insolvency Act 1986, s 74(d). Private companies can be registered as unlimited companies.
Capacity to act	A partnership is not a person separate from the partners therefore no question of its capacity arises.	LLP has the capacity of a natural person. No doctrine of *ultra vires*.	Company has capacity of a natural person. *Ultra vires* doctrine has applied historically but Companies Act 2006 ends its application to both old and newly registered companies except charitable companies
Public disclosure	No public disclosure obligations. Partnership agreement and accounts are private.	Extensive public disclosure requirements apply similar to the registered companies' regime. LLP agreement is private.	Extensive public disclosure requirements including constitutional documents, details of capital, details of members and directors, annual returns and accounts and reports.
Audit of accounts	Accounts need not be audited.	Accounts must be audited. Exemptions similar to registered companies regime apply.	Accounts must be audited. Exemptions for small (s 477) and dormant (s 480) companies.
Management	Managed by the partners.	Managed by the members. Minimum of two designated members have administration responsibilities.	Directors are responsible for the management of the company almost always. Rules stipulating how a registered company is to be managed are agreed in the articles. Model Articles (private and public companies) provide for directors to manage.
Entry into contracts	Every partner has implied authority to act as agent and bind the firm and the other partners to a contract: partners are agents of each other.	All members are agents of the LLP. Members are not agents of each other.	The board of directors can exercise all the powers of the company and bind the company to contracts. No member has any implied authority to bind the company.

	Partnerships	Limited Liability Partnerships (LLP)	Registered Companies Limited by Shares (Ltd/PLC)
Effect of change of membership	In legal theory, the death or bankruptcy of a partner and any change in the partners, whether by a partner leaving or a partner joining, results in the old partnership coming to an end and a new partnership coming into existence. In practice, tax rules combined with appropriate provisions in partnership agreements can mean that such a termination and commencement are legal technicalities. The partnership business is not wound up and the business continues.	An LLP continues in existence regardless of change in its membership.	A company continues in existence regardless of change in its members.
Transferring ownership rights	A partner can transfer his right to receive a share of the partnership profits and his right, on winding up, to receive a share of the partnership assets, to an assignee *but the partner must continue to be a partner*. If a partner wishes to withdraw from the partnership he cannot transfer his interest in the partnership to a third party who is to step into the firm as a partner in his place, as his exit will bring the partnership to an end and the third party may or may not be accepted as a partner in the new partnership	Members cannot transfer their ownership interest without the agreement of the other members.	A member/shareholder can transfer his shares to another person and cease to be a member of the company without the consent of the company or other members unless there is provision otherwise in the articles. Restrictions on transfer are commonly found in private company articles.
Period of existence and dissolution	A partnership continues in existence as long as the partners carry on a business in common with a view to making a profit.	LLP remains in existence until it is terminated by removal from the register.	Company remains in existence until it is dissolved by the registrar of companies removing its name from the register of companies.
Ownership of property	Property of a partnership is owned by the partners in common.	Property is owned by the LLP.	Property is owned by the company.
Rights of personal creditors of members to business property	A partner's personal creditors can claim against partnership property but their claims are subordinated to the claims of partnership creditors.	Members' creditors have no claim against the assets of the LLP.	Members' creditors have no claim against the assets of the company.
Floating charges	Partnerships may not grant floating charges.	LLPs may grant floating charges over LLP property.	Companies may grant floating charges over company property.

	Partnerships	Limited Liability Partnerships (LLP)	Registered Companies Limited by Shares (Ltd/PLC)
Status of managers	Partners are not employees of the partnership.	Members are not employees of the LLP.	Directors may be employees of the company. 'Executive director' normally describes a person who is appointed to be a director and has a contract of employment with the company.
Taxation	Tax on partnership profits payable by partners (income tax). No employer NIC contributions payable in relation to partners. Employer NIC contributions payable by the partners as a business expense as employer of employees.	Tax on LLP profits payable by members as if the LLP was a partnership (income tax). No employer NIC contributions for members. Employer NIC contributions payable by the LLP as a business expense as employer of employees.	Tax on company profits payable by the company (corporation tax). Shareholders taxed on dividends (income tax) and gains on sale of shares (capital gains tax). Employer NIC contributions payable by the company as a business expense as employer of employees.

Table 2.2 Partnerships, Limited Liability Partnerships (LLPs) and Registered Companies compared and contrasted

unincorporated association

an organisation typically formed or run to advance social, environmental or cultural objectives for the benefit of its members, the local community or the public generally, including sports or other social clubs and cooperatives, often charities, not being incorporated or a sole trader or a partnership

2.6 Social enterprise private legal structures

A great deal of definitional uncertainty exists in the world of 'social enterprise', 'civil society' or the 'third sector'. The terms are generally used to describe organisations that are neither run purely for profit nor government organisations. A wide range of legal structures are used by social enterprise organisations and the aim of this section is simply to introduce you to some of the more common legal structures that are not used in the private for-profit sector.

2.6.1 Unincorporated associations

An unincorporated organisation that is neither a sole trader nor a partnership is often referred to as an unincorporated association. Lawton LJ described an unincorporated association in *Conservative & Unionist Central Office v Burrell* [1982] 1 WLR 522 CA as:

JUDGMENT

'. . . two or more persons bound together for one or more common purposes, not being business purposes, by mutual undertakings, each having mutual duties and obligations, in an organisation which has rules which identify in whom control of it and its funds rests and upon what terms and which can be joined or left at will.'

Lawton LJ

This definition is useful in that it identifies key characteristics required before a contractual arrangement between individuals will be regarded as establishing an 'association'. Contrary to the definition, many unincorporated associations do engage in business. Current guidance on corporation tax provided by HMRC makes this clear.

QUOTATION

'The characteristics of an unincorporated association have emerged primarily from case law.
An unincorporated association:
- is not a legal entity,
- is an organisation of persons or bodies (more than one) with an identifiable membership (possibly changing),
- has a membership who are bound together for a common purpose by an identifiable constitution or rules (which may be written or oral),
- is an organisation where the form of association is not one which is recognised in law as being something else (for example, an incorporated body or a partnership),
- must have an existence distinct from those persons who would be regarded as its members,
- the tie between the persons need not be a legally enforceable contract.

Whether an organisation is an unincorporated association is a question of fact and will depend upon a consideration of all the relevant circumstances. It cannot be determined by simply looking at what the organisation calls itself or the form of its rules.
There is no reason why an unincorporated body should not have trading or business objects, or carry on significant commercial activities.
There are a wide variety of unincorporated associations varying from small thrift clubs to substantial business organisations. In all cases, the facts of the particular organisation must be looked at.
Unincorporated associations can include:
- Various types of members' club
- Investment clubs
- Thrift funds and Christmas or holiday clubs
- Voluntary organisations, including those set up 'for good causes'
- Religious communities.'

HMRC Company Taxation Manual, Particular Bodies, CTM41305 as at April 2012

The point to note is that unincorporated associations rarely engage in business purely to make profits; they tend to be 'not-for-profit' organisations.

A number of legal problems stem from an unincorporated association not having a separate legal personality. First, an unincorporated association cannot own property. The legal title to property will usually vest in one, several or all of the members on trust for the benefit of the members. In relation to criminal liability, the exposure of unincorporated associations to criminal liability depends upon whether the crime is a common law or statutory offence. An unincorporated association is incapable of being liable for a common law offence because of its lack of separate personality. A number of statutes, however, treat unincorporated associations as persons that can commit statutory offences.

Turning to tort liability, where a third party has a tortious claim against an unincorporated association, they can name the unincorporated association and its office bearers as the defendants to the legal claim. In the reported English law case in which action has been brought, the funds of the unincorporated association, (including, crucially, access to insurance payments), have been sufficient to pay the claim in full. If the funds were to be inadequate, it remains unclear whether the members would be held to be jointly and severally liable. A member of an unincorporated association may be surprised to know that they may be sued for a sum that may be substantially in excess of the amount of any subscriptions they have agreed to pay. This lack of clarity renders the law unsatisfactory.

Finally, because it is not a separate person in law, an unincorporated association cannot enter into a contract. The law relating to unincorporated association contracts is unacceptably unclear. A person seeking to supply an unincorporated association with goods or services, for example, depending upon the facts, contracts with all, a number of, or one of the members. That member is, or those members are, usually a member or members of the management committee of the unincorporated association. Members will be bound personally by the contract based on having expressly or impliedly authorised the person who signs (or otherwise performs the act of agreeing to the contract) to bind them (see *Steele v Gourley* (1886) 3 TLR 118).

2.6.2 Charitable incorporated organisations (CIO)

Charities are established using different legal structures, both unincorporated and incorporated. Charities can be established as companies registered with the registrar of companies under the Companies Acts. Whilst it is possible to establish a charity as a company limited by shares, this is extremely unusual and most incorporated charities are companies limited by guarantee. Note that this does not mean that it is unusual for charities to own companies limited by shares through which to run businesses for the benefit of the parent charity. Many charities own companies limited by shares, the profits made by which are paid out to the charity as dividends.

The Charities Act 2006 provides for a new form of company specifically designed for charities, the Charitable Incorporated Organisation (CIO). Delays in finalising the governing regulations mean that as at September 2012 CIOs were still not available. A principal benefit of CIOs will be that charities wishing to have a corporate structure will be able to register a CIO with the Charity Commission, allowing them to deal with only one regulator, rather than two as is currently the case with charities having to register as a charity with the Charity Commission and, if they wish to have a corporate structure, having to also register a company with the Registrar of Companies. Less onerous accounting rules are also expected to apply to CIOs. CIO developments can be tracked on the Charity Commission website referenced at the end of this chapter.

2.6.3 Community interest companies (CIC)

The community interest company (CIC) is a relatively new corporate vehicle, introduced in October 2004 as a unique legal structure to assist social enterprise, that is, organisations that combine social purpose with commercial activities. They are governed by a combination of the Companies Act 2006 and Pt 2 of the Companies (Audit, Investigations and Community Enterprise) Act 2004. Approximately 6,397 CICs existed in April 2012, a threefold increase since October 2008. CICs are formed by registering (with the Registrar of Companies at Companies House) a public or private limited company which satisfies additional regulation, compliance with which is supervised by the Regulator of Community Interest Companies. Approximately 75 per cent of CICs are limited by guarantee and 25 per cent are limited by shares.

A CIC has three main additional characteristics:

- It must be carried on for the benefit of the community.
- It is subject to an 'asset lock', which is a general term to describe various restrictions on profits and assets designed to ensure that it is being run for the benefit of the community.
- It must file community interest annual reports which are available to the public.

The main legal differences between a CIC and a non-CIC registered company are set out in Table 2.3 below.

	Community interest company (CIC)	Non-CIC private or public company limited by shares (Ltd or PLC)
Main legislation	Companies Act 2006 which has effect subject to Pt 2 of the Companies (Audit, Investigations and Community Enterprise) Act 2004 (CAICEA)	Companies Act 2006

	Community interest company (CIC)	Non-CIC private or public company limited by shares (Ltd or PLC)
Purpose for which it is formed and run	A CIC must be set up and run for the benefit of the community. If a reasonable person might consider that its activities are being carried on for the benefit of the community, this requirement is satisfied (CAICEA, s 35(2)). A CIC cannot be a charity or politically motivated or set up by for the benefit of an unduly restrictive group.	A non-CIC registered company can be set up and run for any purpose that is not illegal.
Can it make a profit?	A CIC limited by shares may aim to make profit: however, restrictions apply to the distribution of profits to members as the profit should be made and applied for the benefit of the community. A CIC limited by guarantee is a not for profit organisation.	Non-CIC registered companies limited by shares are almost all set up with the aim of making profits.
Asset lock issue: Right to distribute profits to shareholders	The amount that can be paid to shareholders as dividends in any year is capped and the cap has three elements: ▪ The maximum dividend that can be paid on any share is 5% above the Bank of England base lending rate (BLR) (eg on a £1 share, if BLR is 5%, the dividend cannot exceed 9 pence (5% + 4% = 9%). ▪ Only 35% of distributable profit can be paid out as dividends. ▪ If distributable profits are retained for five years they cannot then be used to pay dividends. The dividend cap will not apply to shares held by an asset-locked body specified in the articles as a possible recipient of the CIC's assets or if the CIC Regulator has consented to the dividend.	A non-CIC registered company can pay all of its distributable profits to shareholders as dividends.
Asset lock issue: Right to transfer company assets out of the company	The articles of association must contain at least the statutory minimum restrictions on the transfer of assets out of the company. More stringent restrictions can be included. The minimum restrictions require a transfer to be: ▪ made for full consideration (ie at market value); or ▪ made to another asset locked body which is specified in the CIC's articles; or ▪ made to another asset locked body with the consent of the CIC Regulator; or ▪ otherwise made for the benefit of the community.	This is regulated by directors' duties owed to the company which may be breached if assets are transferred at an undervalue, etc.
Asset lock issue: Rate of interest paid on performance-related loans	Loans, the interest payable on which is linked to the performance of the borrower are rare but could provide a way for a CIC to avoid the dividend cap. For this reason, the rate of interest payable is capped.	This is a matter to be decided by the board of directors in accordance with the duties the directors owe to the company.

	Community interest company (CIC)	Non-CIC private or public company limited by shares (Ltd or PLC)
Asset lock issue: Remuneration of directors	The position is the same as for non-CIC registered companies except that if the level of remuneration is not reasonable, that factor will be considered by the CIC Regulator in deciding whether or not the company is being run for the benefit of the community. He may decide that it is being run for the benefit of the directors. Unlike a non-CIC, the articles of a CIC often state that the members may, by general resolution, specify the remuneration of directors.	The board of directors is normally empowered by the articles of association to pay fees to individual directors for services to the company. If a director is also an employee of the company, a service contract will be agreed to on behalf of the company by the board of directors, although shareholder approval is needed for service contracts of more than two years' duration.
Control issue: Power to appoint directors	No powers to appoint directors may be given to anyone who is not a member of the CIC, which immediately after their exercise could result in the majority of directors having been appointed by non-members.	Rules providing for appointment of directors are set out in the articles of association. No comparable restriction applies.
Relevant public disclosures	A CIC has to make a community interest statement for the public record describing what it will do, who it will help and how. A CIC must deliver a community interest company report to the Registrar of Companies which is placed on the public register along with its annual return and its annual reports and accounts.	Not applicable. A non-CIC registered company must deliver an annual return and annual reports and accounts to the Registrar of Companies which are placed on the public register.
Distribution of assets on a winding up	Any assets remaining after creditors have been paid in full will be distributed to an asset locked company specified in the articles or chosen by the CIC Regulator.	Any assets remaining after creditors have been paid in full are distributable amongst the shareholders.
Charitable status	A CIC cannot be a charity.	A non-CIC registered company may be a charity.

Table 2.3 Community interest companies and non-CIC registered companies limited by shares: the main differences

2.6.4 UK mutual organisations

Mutual organisation is not a specifically defined term. It is sometimes used to refer to an organisation, whether incorporated or not, run for the benefit of its members, who are its customers, rather than an organisation run to provide services for one group, its customers, from which to make profits for another group, its shareholders. Organisations run for the benefit of both members and the public, and, even, organisations run for the benefit of persons other than its members are also sometimes included under the 'mutual organisations' rubric. Another name given to mutual organisations is 'co-operatives'.

Mutual organisations, or co-operatives can be established using different legal structures, including the registered company. In the UK a number of insurers, such as the NFU Mutual and the Police Mutual Assurance, are mutual organisations. Many mutual organisations are financial organisations such as building societies, credit unions and friendly societies, each of which is considered below.

As part of its role as registrar of mutual societies, the Financial Services Authority maintains a 'mutuals register'. It is a public record of industrial and provident societies, building societies, credit unions and the various kinds of society registered under the Friendly Societies Acts. As at April 2012, the mutuals register contained just over 10,000 organisations.

The Legislative Reform (Industrial and Provident Societies and Credit Unions) Order 2011 introduces changes to the regulation of mutual organisations designed to broaden their scope of activity and allow them to grow larger and operate with fewer legal constraints.

Industrial and provident societies

A society qualifies for registration as an industrial and provident society under the Industrial and Provident Societies Act 1965 if it has at least three members, runs a business and either is a *bona fide* co-operative or that business is run for the benefit of *the community*. The society also has to demonstrate that there are special reasons why it should not be registered as a company under the Companies Acts before it will be registered under the 1965 Act. Community in this context means persons other than its own members. The principal benefits of registration are that the society obtains incorporated status and its members have limited liability.

The registering authority for organisations registered under the Industrial and Provident Societies Act 1965 is the Financial Services Authority, but note that this role is separate and distinct from the FSA's role under the Financial Services and Markets Act 2000. If an industrial and provident society has charitable objects it is an exempt charity and is not required to register with the Charity Commission. Working men's clubs, benevolent societies and specially authorised societies registered under the Friendly Societies Act 1974 are permitted to re-register as industrial and provident societies. As at April 2012 approximately 80 per cent of the organisations on the mutuals register were registered under the 1965 Act.

Friendly societies

The FSA defines a friendly society as: 'a voluntary mutual organisation whose main purpose is to assist members (usually financially) during sickness, unemployment or retirement, and to provide life assurance'.

Having grown in number prior to the establishment of the welfare state to provide financial assistance to people in ill health or old age, there are now only about 1,500 friendly societies in existence. Friendly societies were originally all unincorporated and registered under the Friendly Societies Act 1974 and this remains the case for most. Since 1993, however, as a result of the Friendly Societies Act 1992, new friendly societies may register as incorporated and existing, unincorporated friendly societies may re-register under the 1992 Act and become incorporated. Surprisingly few have made the transition.

Credit unions

In September 2011, in addition to 20 credit unions registered under the Industrial and Provident Societies Act 1965, there were 460 credit unions in Great Britain registered under the Credit Unions Act 1979. They are incorporated entities with limited liability and are subject to FSA regulation under the Financial Services and Markets Act 2000. As their name suggests, credit unions lend money to their members.

Building societies

As at April 2012, 48 building societies were listed on the mutuals register. This does not include a number of well known finance businesses such as Halifax, Alliance & Leicester and Northern Rock that used to be, but are no longer, building societies having 'demutualised' and turned into banks. The Nationwide owns around half the assets owned by all building societies.

Building societies are regulated by the FSA which took over the functions of the Building Societies Commissioner following enactment of the Financial Services and Markets Act 2000. Building Societies become incorporated on being registered and issued with a certificate of incorporation pursuant to the Building Societies Act 1986 (as extensively amended). The 1986 Act governs building societies in much the same way as the Companies Act 2006 governs registered companies. It regulates, for example, the constitution, governance, purpose and public disclosures required of building societies.

Section 5(1) of the 1986 Act states that an organisation may register as a building society if, and only if, 'Its purpose or principal purpose is that of making loans which are secured on residential property and are funded substantially by its members'. Following deregulation in 1994 and 1997 many building societies expanded into a wider range of financial products making them very similar in their product offerings to banks. Like banks, they fund loans by borrowing on the wholesale money markets, although they are limited by s 7 of the 1986 Act which requires 50 per cent of lending to be funded by member deposits.

Building societies are owned by their members, hence they are mutual organisations. Members who are indebted to the building society are called 'borrowing members' and those with savings deposited are called 'shareholding members'. The liability of building society members is limited (Building Societies Act 1986, para 6 of Sched 2 and para 7(4) of Sched 15).

2.7 European organisation legal structures

The European Commission has proposed a number of pan-European forms of organisation. Forms of business organisation have been proposed (and two adopted) as part of its programme of company law reform (which is part of the European Commission's efforts to make a single market a reality in the EU). Forms of 'social enterprise' enterprises, on the other hand, have been proposed under the European Commission's social economy programme (one of the principal concerns of which is the level of employment within the EU). Initiatives to establish pan-European forms of organisation have not been as successful as the European Commission's efforts to harmonise company law.

2.7.1 European business organisation structures

The EU has established two pan-European corporate forms and the European Commission has issued a draft Regulation for a third. This development has been referred to as the development of a 'distinct 28th company law regime' and members of the Reflection Group on the Future of EU Company Law were split on the merits of such a development (see page 29 of their report, referenced at the end of Chapter 1).

European Economic Interest Group (EEIG)

European Economic Interest Group (EEIG)

a legal entity separate from its members at least two members of which must be from different Member States and all members of which must carry on business within the European Union (EU) and have their principal administration within the EU

A European Economic Interest Group (EEIG) is a legal entity separate from its members that has been available since 1989. Members may be individuals or other business organisations, the condition for membership being that each member carries on business within the EU with its principal administration within the EU and, if it is not an individual, is an entity formed in accordance with the laws of a Member State with its registered office in the EU. At least two members must be from different Member States.

The EEIG is available to those carrying on businesses (in its widest sense) in different Member States who wish to work more closely together but do not wish to merge or have one business organisation take over the other, or, perhaps a merger is too expensive or difficult. It can be seen as a type of joint venture although it is different from the typical joint ventures in the UK which are:

- corporate vehicle joint ventures (in which two or more business organisations establish a jointly owned company to pursue a shared venture)

- contractual joint ventures (in which two or more business organisations enter into a contract governing their respective rights and obligations in relation to a joint business venture).

The EEIGs are not established to make profit themselves, but to facilitate their members' profit-making by facilitating cross-border co-operation. Like LLPs, even though they are separate legal entities and can enter into contracts and own property, they are tax-transparent. Unlike LLPs and most registered companies, however, the members of an EEIG do *not* benefit from limited liability. Members are jointly and severally liable for the debts and other liabilities of the EEIG. The EEIGs are registered with the company's registrar in the Member State in which they have their principal place of establishment, and as at 31 March 2011, 238 EEIGs had been registered at Companies House. The governing legislation is EC Regulation 2137/85 and the European Economic Interest Grouping Regulations 1989 (SI 1989/638). An example of where an EEIG might be used is if research companies in different Member States wish to co-operate in a large research project, or if producers of complementary products in different Member States wish to launch a joint marketing operation.

Societas Europaea (SE)
a corporate vehicle designed for corporate groups which operate in more than one European Union member state

European Public Limited Liability Company or Societas Europaea (SE)

European Community plans in the 1970s to create a European supra-national company registration system allowing for incorporation of supra-national European companies not registered in any particular Member State proved to be premature. The organisational entity ultimately made available as a result of this initiative is the European public limited liability company, or Societas Europaea (SE). It has been possible to register an SE with a Member State company registrar since 8 October 2004.

SEs have not proved popular to date. As at 31 March 2011, 23 SEs had been registered at Companies House. This limited use of the SE form of organisation is due in part to the limited circumstances in which an SE can be formed. SEs may be formed:

- by merging two or more public companies registered in at least two different Member States (different Member State companies (DMSCs))
- as a holding company of two or more DMSCs
- as a subsidiary of two or more DMSCs
- by transforming into an SE a public company that has had a subsidiary in a different Member State for at least two years.

The SE is a separate legal person, treated as if formed under the laws of the Member State in which it is registered. The SE allows the parent company of a corporate group operating in more than one Member State to be governed by a single applicable law. That law is found in part in EC Regulation 2157/2001 (supplemented by Directive 2001/86/EC) but the applicable law is in large part the law of the Member State in which the SE is registered. In the UK that is the European Public Limited Liability Company Regulations 2004 (SI 2004/2326).

The Reflection Group on the Future of EU Company Law has highlighted shortcomings with the current form of SE available and called for reform.

QUOTATION

'The SE Regulation ... appears inadequate in several important aspects.

The SE cannot be formed by a decision *ab initio*, but requires the previous incorporation of companies with different Home States that either merge into an SE or form the SE as a subsidiary, and it is only available to national companies of the public type (SA/AG/PLC, etc). Some Members of the Reflection Group think that all limited companies should also be able to create an SE.

The SE company form is not a truly European form due to the substantial references to national law in the SE Statute Regulation, which effectively provides many different variations depending on the national company law of the Member State where it was formed.

The subscribed capital (legal capital) must be at least €120,000. It is almost five times higher than the legal capital required of a national public limited company according to the Second Company Law Directive, and may prove too high a threshold for medium-sized entrepreneurs. The registered office must be in the Member State where the real seat is located. This reduces the flexibility of the SE, which ought to be its primary *raison d'être*. National companies incorporated under the laws of Member States that do not impose the same requirement can move their real seat freely within the Union; an option that is not open to the SE.

The separate regime on worker participation effectively imposes this particular element of the national company law of some Member States on other Member States, where it is alien to the domestic law.

If the SE is to become a viable alternative to national companies, the Commission has to prepare a reform of the SE Regulation, as is required by such regulation, and take into account inspiration from the flexibility available for national companies. The amended Regulation should be simplified which means that it should limit as much as possible the options offered to the Member States to determine the terms of application of the SE statute.'

European Commission Internal Market and Services, Report of the Reflection Group on the Future of EU Competition Law, Brussels 5 April 2011 at p.29

Societas Privata Europaea (SPE)

a form of European Private Company (SPE) proposed by the European Commission to assist both large corporate groups wishing to reduce the costs of administering their groups of subsidiaries in Europe and SMEs seeking to operate in more than one Member State

European Private Limited Liability Company or Societas Privata Europaea (SPE)

The 2003 Action Plan announced that a feasibility study should be undertaken to determine the need for a European Private Company (SPE). Such a form could assist both large corporate groups wishing to reduce the costs of administering their groups of subsidiaries in Europe and SMEs seeking to operate in more than one Member State.

The feasibility study apparently showed that stakeholders are divided as to whether there is such a need as well as on the scope and content of an SPE proposal. Nonetheless, the European Parliament adopted a resolution in 2007 requesting the European Commission to draw up an SPE Regulation which, following two consultations (part of the European Commission's impact assessment), it did in June 2008: the EC Commission Proposal for a Council Regulation on the Statute for a European private company (COM 2008 396/3). The progress of this proposal can be followed on the Europa Internal Market Company Law and Corporate Governance website referenced at the end of Chapter 1.

2.7.2 European social economy entity structures

Social economy entity structures proposed by the European Commission are outlined below. To date, the only proposal adopted is the SCE.

European Co-operative Society (SCE)

European Co-operative Societies are provided for by Council Regulation (EC) No 1435/2003 of 22 July 2003 on the Statute for a European Cooperative Society (SCE) and a supplementing Council Directive 2003/72/EC of 22 July 2003 regarding the involvement of employees.

Based on the SE model, the regulation provides for SCEs to be separate legal entities registered with the companies' registrar in one Member State with members from more than one Member State. The essential difference between an SCE and an SE is that the main object of an SCE must be the satisfaction of its members' needs (or the development of their economic and social activities), rather than pursuit of profit to pay for capital investment.

European Association and European Mutual Society

Proposals for a pan-European form for associations and mutual societies originated in the European Commission's social economy programme rather than part of the European Commission's internal market/company law programme. None the less, in its 2003 Action Plan on company law, the European Commission expressed its intention to actively support development of new European legal forms for these entities. Support was withdrawn when the European Commission reviewed the Action Plan in 2004/5 and proposed regulations were withdrawn in 2006.

European Association

The draft Regulation for a European Association was similar in its structure and aims as that for a European Co-operative Society (SCE). The key characteristic of a European Association set out in the draft Regulation was that it is a, 'permanent grouping of natural or legal persons whose members pool their knowledge or activities either for a purpose in the general interest or in order to directly or indirectly promote the trade or professional interests of its members', with its profits from any economic activity being devoted exclusively to the pursuit of its purposes and not being divided amongst its members.

European Mutual Society

Mutual societies are popular in the fields of insurance, credit and health. However, there is no agreed upon definition of a mutual association. In its review of the mutual association concept in its consultation document entitled Mutual Associations in an Enlarged Europe (2003), the European Commission identified the key characteristics of a mutual association as follows:

- Mutual societies operate on the basis of an initial capital or fund financed by the members or by borrowing. This fund is the collective and indivisible property of the mutual society.
- The main objective of mutual societies is to satisfy members' interests and, in some cases, the interests of the wider community.
- Mutual associations are not established with the aim of making profits.
- Profits made by a mutual association are reinvested to improve services to members though they can be redistributed amongst members.
- Individual members have no property rights over the assets of the mutual and if a member leaves the mutual, this has no effect on the capital, which will continue to serve the remaining members.
- Democracy, solidarity and independence from the state are principles on which mutual associations are established.

European Foundation

The 2003 Action Plan called for a feasibility study to explore the need for a pan-European form of Foundation and, following extensive studies and consultation, in February 2012, the European Commission published a Proposal for a Council Regulation on the Statute for a European Foundation (FE) (COM(2012) 35 final). European Foundations are organisations the activities of which focus on the public benefit. Examples of typical areas of activity are social and health services, fostering research and promoting culture, including by awarding grants and running projects. The European Foundation entity proposed is an incorporated entity with a public benefit purpose. Details can be found in the documents accessible from the Europa European Foundations webpage referenced at the end of this chapter.

SUMMARY

Key business structure statistics

- Almost half of all businesses in which more than one person works are structured as registered limited liability companies.
- Firms of professionals are increasingly structured as limited liability partnerships (LLPs) rather than general partnerships.

Key unincorporated business organisations legal structures

- Sole traders (no governing act; no limited liability; can employ others).
- Partnerships (governed by the Partnership Act 1890; participation of non-managing limited partners possible: Limited Partnership Act 1907).
- Unincorporated associations are used for non-profit enterprises.

Key incorporated business organisations legal structures

- Registered companies.
- Limited Liability Partnerships (governed by the Limited Liability Partnerships Act 2000; tax transparent but otherwise separate legal entities from the members).
- Chartered and statutory companies (largely long-standing organisations; new grants of charters reserved for eminent professional bodies or charities).

Different types of companies can be registered

- Limited rather than unlimited companies are used for business enterprises.
- Limited companies may be either public or private companies. Public companies can offer shares to the public (but not all of them do). Private companies cannot (s 755) and are subject to a less stringent administrative and reporting regime.
- Public companies may (but do not have to be):
  - quoted companies (s 385)
  - traded companies (s 360C)
  - listed companies (not defined in the Companies Act 2006).
- Public companies that have shares traded on the Main Market of the LSE may have a Premium Listing or Standard Listing. Super-equivalent listing standards apply to all companies with a Premium Listing only.

Key social enterprise private legal structures

- Unincorporated associations (the governing law is very under-developed).
- Charitable incorporated organisations (introduced by Charities Act 2006, implementation delayed).
- Community interest companies (CICs) (governed by Companies Act 2006 and Part 2 of the Companies (Audit, Investigations and Community Enterprise) Act 2004).
- UK mutual organisations (include industrial and provident societies, friendly societies, credit unions and building societies).

Key European business organisation structures

- Exisiting structures: European Economic Interest Group (EEIGs) and Societas Europaea (SEs) have not proved popular.
- Proposed structure: Societas Privata Europaea (SPEs).

Key European social economy entity structures

- European social economy entity structures, at different stages of development, are the European co-operative society, European Association, European Mutual Society and the European Foundation.

ACTIVITY

Cherie, Tony and Harriet are Karate experts. They have a dream to run a Karate school for children and identify premises near to three schools they believe would be a perfect location. They make enquiries and the premises are available to let on a three-year lease at £12,000 per annum with a deposit of £10,000 payable. The premises are in need of decoration and they believe this would cost £10,000. Equipment is expected to cost a further £10,000. They draw up a business plan and visit the Blair Bank which indicates a willingness to lend them £40,000 provided they set up their business with an acceptable legal structure and can offer Blair Bank 'the usual protections'. Cherie and Harriet own a house together. Tony is their tenant.

Advise Cherie, Tony and Harriet on the legal structures available to them, the benefits and shortcomings of each, and the nature of the 'usual protections' to which Blair Bank has referred.

SAMPLE ESSAY QUESTION

Compare and contrast the key legal structures available for running a business.

Unpack the question

You should ensure at the outset that you have identified each and every part of the question. This is important so that you do not overlook an important aspect and provide an incomplete answer. It also means that you do not proceed to write an overly-generic answer because you have identified the focus of the question. You should separate out:

- Identification of the key legal structures available
- Identification of those that are appropriate *for running a business*
- Identification of features of organisation structures that are important to businessmen
- The need to make a comparison of different structures.

State that you have assumed that the question is focused on businesses *run solely for profit*.

Identify the key legal structures available

- sole trader
- partnership (possibly with one or more limited partners)
- limited liability partnership
- registered company – various types: most appropriate: limited by shares; can be either private or public

You could mention (to dismiss) other structures more suited where businesses are not run solely for profit.

Decide how to structure your discussion

You could structure you answer by taking each structure in turn and addressing its key legal characteristics. This would mean that you would have to then go on to compare and contrast the identified differences in a later part of your essay in order to actually do what the question asks you to do. Because of this, it may make more sense to structure you answer by taking a number of key characteristics about business organisation structures and examine how each type of business organisation option deals with it. Using this structure, the similarities and differences will become immediately apparent and you will be answering the question.

Identify a number of key issues to form the basis of your comparison and contrasting exercise

Key issues you should consider are:

- owner risk/liability
- confidentiality/disclosure obligations
- flexibility/structural obligations
- protection of business assets from non-business creditors of the owners
- availability of assets of the owners to the business to satisfy business creditors
- minimum start-up capital requirements
- availability and cost of capital
- any minimum number of owner requirements
- ease of change of owners/the ability of participants to access their invested capital.

Tables 2.1 and 2.2 suggest a number of other issues you could add in here.

Reflect on your analysis

Explain the importance of indentifying the issues most important to the particular individuals seeking to set up and run the business, before being able to advise them as to the form of organisation that best suits their requirements. You might also mention that the decision as to which form of organisation to establish should only be made after taking tax advice as well as legal advice.

CONCLUDE

Further reading

Useful websites

Companies House website:
www.companieshouse.gov.uk/
Community Interest Companies Regulator website:
http://www.bis.gov.uk/cicregulator/
Charity Commission Charitable Incorporated Organisation website:
http://www.charity-commission.gov.uk/Start_up_a_charity/Do_I_need_to_register/CIOs/cios_general_information.aspx
Europa Social Economy Enterprises website:
http://ec.europa.eu/enterprise/entrepreneurship/coop/index.htm
Europa European Foundations webpage:
http://ec.europa.eu/internal_market/company/eufoundation/index_en.htm

Articles

Cross, S, 'New legal forms for charities in the United Kingdom' [2008] JBL 662–87.
Hansmann, Kraakman & Squire, 'The New Business Entities in Evolutionary Perspective' (2007) 8 EBOR 59 at 65.
Schmidt, J, 'SE and SCE: two new European company forms – and more to come!' (2006) 27 Comp Law 99.

Reports

Partnership Law, The Law Commission (Law Com No 283, 2003).
BIS, A Guide to Legal Forms for Business (November 2011) available at:
http://www.bis.gov.uk/assets/biscore/business-law/docs/g/11-1399-guide-legal-forms-for-business.pdf.
BT Group plc Annual Report available at:
http://www.btplc.com/sharesandperformance/annualreportandreview/pdf/btgroupan-nualreport2011.pdf.

Books

Faber, D, 'Legal Structures for Small Businesses' in de Lacey, J, (ed), *The Reform of United Kingdom Company Law* (Cavendish Publishing Ltd, 2002).
Morse, G, *Partnership Law* (7th edn, Oxford University Press, 2010).
Smith, P, *Limited Liability Partnerships Handbook* (3rd edn, Bloomsbury Professional, 2012).

3

The company as a distinct and legal person

AIMS AND OBJECTIVES

After reading this chapter you should be able to:

■ Understand the consequences of a company having a separate legal personality from its owners and managers

■ Understand the concept of the limited liability of shareholders

■ Analyse and distinguish

● separate legal personality of a company

● shareholder limited liability

■ Critically assess the operation and effect of separate legal personality in the context of a corporate group

■ Identify three basic ways of supplementing or curtailing the operation of the separate legal personality doctrine

■ Apply self-help remedies to fact situations to work around the separate legal personality doctrine

■ Understand the situations in which a court will ignore the separate legal personality of a company and the basis for doing so

■ Understand how a court will approach interpretation of a statute to determine whether or not it requires a court to ignore the separate legal personality of a company

■ Consider fact situations and determine whether or not a claimant against a company may have a remedy against any other person

3.1 The registered company as a corporation

Section 15(1) of the Companies Act 2006 makes it clear that registered companies become incorporated and separate legal persons on registration.

SECTION

'On the registration of a company, the registrar of companies shall give a certificate that the company is incorporated.'

Section 16(2) of the Companies Act 2006 makes it clear who the members of a registered company are and that the members may vary over time.

SECTION

'The subscribers to the memorandum, together with such other persons as may from time to time become members of the company, are a body corporate by the name stated in the certificate of incorporation.'

3.2 What is a corporation?

To understand the meaning of corporation, it is important to understand the concept of a legal person. A legal person is a being or entity with the capacity to both:

- enjoy (by virtue of its existence), or acquire, enforceable legal rights or property; and
- be (by virtue of its existence), or become subject to, enforceable legal obligations and liabilities.

Legal persons fall into two categories:

- natural persons (individuals, including you yourself); and
- artificial or juristic persons.

The word 'individual' is used in this book to refer to a natural person. The term 'person' is used to cover both natural and artificial persons. All artificial or juristic persons are corporations. 'Corporation' and 'to incorporate' come from the Latin verb 'corporare' which means to furnish with a body or to infuse with substance. This is what the law does when it creates or recognises an artificial or juristic corporation: it furnishes an artificial construct with substance in the eyes of the law; with the ability to have legal rights and incur legal liabilities.

Corporations fall into two categories:

- Corporations sole;
- Corporations aggregate.

Corporations sole are limited by law to one member at any given time. Corporations sole are often attached as an incident of an office. Examples are the Crown and the Archbishop of Canterbury. Mayors are also generally corporations sole. The corporation

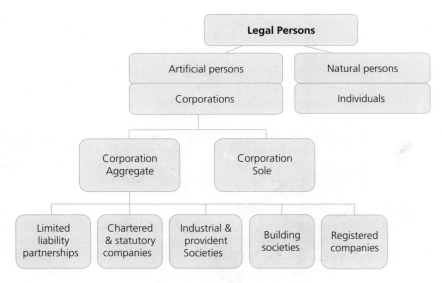

Figure 3.1 Types of legal persons

sole is distinct in law from the individual who occupies the post at any point in time. The individual office-holder changes over time, but the corporation sole continues with no need to transfer any property or rights to the new incumbent. The individual's acts in the capacity of the corporation are separate from the individual's personal acts.

In the study of business organisations, we are not concerned with corporations sole, we are concerned with corporations aggregate. Corporations aggregate may (but need not) have more than one member at any given time. Statutory corporations, chartered corporations, registered companies, building societies, industrial and provident societies and limited liability partnerships are all examples of corporations aggregate. Figure 3.1 illustrates the classification of legal persons.

incorporation
the process by which a legal entity, separate from its owners and managers, is formed

3.3 The consequences of incorporation/separate legal personality

In general terms, a company, because it is a corporation, is a person in law separate from any and all of the individuals involved in the company whether those individuals are its owners/shareholders, its managers/directors or are involved in some other way.

In general terms a company has the capacity to both:

- enjoy (by virtue of its existence), or acquire, enforceable legal rights or property; and
- be (by virtue of its existence), or become subject to, enforceable legal obligations and liabilities.

In specific terms, a company:

- can own property
- can be a party to a contract
- can act tortiously
- can be a victim of tortious behaviour
- can commit a crime
- can be the victim of a crime
- can sue and be sued
- has a nationality
- has a domicile
- has human rights.

All of the above rights and liabilities parallel the capacity of an individual but the scope and content of some of those rights and liabilities are not exactly the same as those of an individual. For example, although some human rights make sense in the context of an artificial person, others do not. Examples of human rights set out in the European Convention on Human Rights (ECHR) exercisable by companies are:

- the right to require a fair trial in the determination of its civil rights and obligations or any criminal charge against it (ECHR, Art 6) (see *R (Alconbury Developments Ltd) v Secretary of State for the Environment, Transport and Regions* [2003] 2 AC 295);
- freedom of expression (ECHR, Art 10) (see *R (Northern Cyprus Tourist Centre Limited) v Transport for London* [2005] UKHRR 1231);
- prohibition of discrimination (ECHR Article 14);
- the right to protection of company property (ECHR, Art 1 of Protocol 1).

The ECHR cases brought to protect the rights of companies are tracked on the Human Rights of Companies website referenced at the end of this chapter.

In relation to criminal liability, a number of criminal offences are specifically aimed at companies, particularly under the Companies Act 2006, and do not apply to individuals. Others have been drafted with companies as one class of accused in mind, for example, offences under the Health and Safety at Work Act 1974. In relation to crime generally, many crimes were established with individuals in mind and the courts have wrestled to establish principles governing when an artificial entity will be considered to have the requisite *mens rea* and/or acted out the requisite *actus reus*, ie for our purposes, when an offence will be imputed to a company. The leading principle, derived from *Lennard's Carrying Co Ltd v Asiatic Petroleum Co Ltd* [1915] AC 705 (HL) and developed by the courts is referred to as the 'directing mind and will test', the 'identification theory' or the 'alter ego principle'. It was applied in the leading case of *Tesco Supermarkets Ltd v Nattrass* [1972] AC 153 (HL), which involved Tesco advertising goods for sale at a price less than that at which it was actually offering them for sale, an offence under the Trade Descriptions Act 1968 at the time (since repealed and replaced by a different offence under the Consumer Protection Act 1987). The theory requires an individual to be 'identified' with the company for criminal liability to attach to the company. This arises where the individual is considered to be the 'directing mind and will' of the company. This attribution theory has resulted in difficult case law and the test has been called 'dysfunctional' (see *Sullivan* (1996)).

The narrowness of the identification theory inhibited successful prosecution of companies following such national tragedies as the capsizing of the Herald of Free Enterprise (which caused 192 deaths), the Piper Alpha North Sea oil platform explosion (which caused 167 deaths) and the Paddington rail crash (which caused 31 deaths). Public outcry at the failure of the courts to deliver 'justice' resulted in the passage of the Corporate Manslaughter and Corporate Homicide Act 2007 which took effect in April 2008 and reflects a systems-based principle of organisational behaviour rather than the individualistic principle developed by the courts. An overview of the Act can be found on the Ministry of Justice website, referenced at the end of this chapter. Under the Act, convicted companies face unlimited fines, remedial orders and publicity orders.

The first successful prosecution under the 2007 Act occurred in February 2011. Following the death of a geologist employee when a trial pit he was working in collapsed, Cotswold Geotechnical (Holdings) Ltd was convicted of corporate manslaughter. The company was found guilty of failing to ensure the safety of the employee and was fined £385,000, to be paid over ten years. The fine was upheld on appeal and the company was put into creditors' voluntary liquidation. The trial in a second prosecution under the Act is expected to take place in June 2012 when a storage product manufacturing company, Lion Steel Equipment Ltd, will be prosecuted for corporate manslaughter after an employee of the company died when he fell through a roof at one of its factories.

Difficulties implicit in imputing wrongful acts to a company are not confined to criminal law. The question of attribution arises in other areas of law, including tort and contract. In those areas, what would otherwise be attribution issues are largely dealt with by applying the principle of vicarious liability and agency law.

A company *differs* from a natural person in that it:

- has perpetual existence until dissolved
- has owners.

3.4 *Salomon v A Salomon & Co Ltd*

tutor tip

"Take a moment to check how 'Salomon' is spelt and impress your tutor by being in the minority of students who spell it correctly"

The most famous case illustrating the operation of the concept of the separate legal personality of a company is *Salomon v A Salomon & Co Ltd* [1897] AC 22 (HL). The case was hard fought, all the way to the House of Lords, by the liquidator on behalf of the unsecured creditors of a company that had become insolvent very soon after being registered under the Companies Act 1862. The case is important because it confirmed the ability of a sole trader to transfer his business into a registered company and thereby insulate himself from the liabilities of the business.

Before this case, the full significance of the ability to incorporate a limited liability company by registration was not appreciated. As the judgments at first instance and in the Court of Appeal indicate, as the nineteenth century was drawing to a close, it was not widely understood that sole trader owners of small businesses could use the Act to secure limited liability and insulate their personal property from business risks.

CASE EXAMPLE

Salomon v A Salomon & Co Ltd [1897] AC 22 (HL)

Mr Salomon owned and ran a profitable boot and shoe manufacturing business as a sole trader. He wished to run his business through a limited company which he achieved by registering a company and selling his business to that company.

The statute governing company registrations at that time required seven subscribers to the memorandum of association, ie seven original members or shareholders. Mr Salomon satisfied this requirement by himself, his wife and his five grown-up children becoming subscribers (under the Companies Act 2006 only one subscriber or member is required). The initial nominal share capital of the company was £40,000. This was divided into 40,000 shares with a nominal value of £1 each. Seven £1 shares were issued, one being issued to each shareholder/member/subscriber which made the initial issued share capital of the company £7. The first directors were appointed by the shareholders and were Mr Salomon and his two eldest sons.

The sale price of the business to the company was 'the sanguine expectations of a fond owner', rather than the market value of the business. In short, the business was sold to the company at an overvalue. In return for the business being transferred to the company, the £39,000 purchase price for the business was 'paid' by the company to Mr Salomon in the following way:

- £9,000 was paid in cash (£8,000 of which, with no legal obligation to do so, Mr Salomon used to pay off debts of the business)
- 20,000 shares of £1 each were issued to Mr Salomon, credited as fully paid-up shares (ie the shares were regarded as having been paid for by Mr Salomon, not in cash but 'in kind', by the transfer to the company of £20,000 pounds' worth of the business)
- A £10,000 secured loan note, or, 'debenture' was issued to Mr Salomon recording that the company owed Mr Salomon £10,000 pounds secured by a charge over the company's assets.

Virtually immediately after the transfer, the profitability of the business began to decline. The company found itself in debt and unable to pay its debts as they fell due. Mr Salomon cancelled his loan note, the debenture, and the company entered into loan arrangements/debentures with Mr Broderip who became a secured creditor of the company. The company failed to pay interest on the loan when it fell due and Mr Broderip exercised his right, as a secured creditor, to have a receiver appointed. Shortly thereafter the company went into liquidation. The company's assets were sold by the liquidator to realise cash to pay both the secured and the unsecured creditors of the company.

Secured creditors are entitled to be paid before the unsecured creditors of a company (see Chapter 15). The proceeds of sale of the company's assets were insufficient even to pay the secured creditor, Mr Broderip, in full. In these unhappy circumstances, the liquidator brought an action against Mr Broderip and Mr Salomon alleging the loan notes issued by the company were fraudulent and invalid. The liquidator was successful at first instance and in the Court of Appeal but was appealed to the House of Lords. Held: Mr Salomon had done nothing wrong, was not liable for the debts of the company, and the loans between him and the company and Broderip and the company were valid.

3.4.1 The first instance and Court of Appeal decisions

The first instance judge in *Salomon* decided that fraud was *not* established on the facts of the case. He did, however, use agency principles to decide that the company was Mr Salomon's agent and on that basis he ordered Mr Salomon, the principal, to indemnify the company, the agent, for the debts the company had incurred as his agent. The Court of Appeal rejected the first instance agency argument. Lindley LJ preferred to hold that the company was the trustee of Mr Salomon who was the beneficiary. Lindley LJ described the company as, 'A trustee improperly brought into existence by him to enable him to do what the statute prohibits', therefore, he held, the beneficiary (Mr Salomon) must indemnify the trustee, the company.

Lopes LJ regarded the family member/shareholders as 'dummies'. What the Act required, he stated, were, 'seven independent *bona fide* members, who had a mind and a will of their own'. According to Lopes LJ, 'The transaction is a device to apply the machinery of the [1862 Act] to a state of things never contemplated by that Act – an ingenious device to obtain the protections of the Act, and in my judgment in a way inconsistent with and opposed to its policy and provisions'. He ordered that the sale of the business to the company be set aside as a sale by Salomon to himself with none of the incidents of a sale, but being a fiction.

3.4.2 The House of Lords decision

In dismissing the claims of the liquidator, members of the House of Lords totally disagreed with the decisions at first instance and in the Court of Appeal which, they said, had misconceived the scope and effect of the 1862 Act. Lord MacNaghten's judgment was particularly lucid:

JUDGMENT

'[T]hough it may be that after incorporation the business is precisely the same as it was before, and the same persons are managers and the same hands receive the profits, the company is not in law the agent of the subscribers or trustee of them. Nor are the members liable, in any shape or form, except to the extent and in the manner provided by the Act.'

Writing in 1944, Kahn-Freund commented:

QUOTATION

'In this country as elsewhere company law has, to a large extent, changed its economic and social function. The privileges of incorporation or of limited liability were originally granted in order to enable a number of capitalists to embark upon risky adventures without shouldering the burden of personal liability. … However, owing to the ease with which companies can be formed in this country, and owing to the rigidity with which the courts applied the corporate entity concept ever since the calamitous decision in *Salomon v Salomon & Co Ltd*, a single trader or a group of traders are almost tempted by the law to conduct their business in the form of a limited company, even where no particular business risk is involved, and where no outside capital is required …

The metaphysical separation between a man in his individual capacity and his capacity as a one-man-company can be used to defraud his creditors who are exposed to grave injury owing to the timidity of the Courts and of the Companies Act.'

Kahn-Freund, 'Some Reflections on Company Law Reform' (1944) 7 MLR 54

3.4.3 Separate legal personality and insurance

One area in particular in which difficulty arose as a result of the failure of businessmen to appreciate the 'tyrannical sway' the corporate entity metaphor holds over the courts is insurance of company property. In a triad of cases (*Macaura* (see below), *General Accident v Midland Bank Ltd* [1940] 2 KB 388 and *Levinger v Licences etc Insurance Co* (1936) 54 LL L Rep 68), insurance companies have avoided paying out under insurance contracts for which they have received premiums, based on the insured property being owned not by the party insuring it (the shareholder of the company), but, rather by the company itself.

CASE EXAMPLE

Macaura v Northern Assurance Co [1925] AC 619 (HL)

After selling his property (timber) to a company in return for shares, Macaura, the sole shareholder of Irish Canadian Sawmills Ltd, insured the timber against fire in his own name.

The timber was destroyed by fire and Macaura claimed on the insurance policy. Held: The property belonged to the company, not to the shareholder. Even though the timber had been destroyed by an insured event, Macaura had no insurable interest in the timber as 'he stood in no "legal or equitable relation" to it' and so could not recover under the insurance policy.

3.5 Limited liability: a concept distinct from separate legal personality

It follows inexorably from the separate identity of the company from its owners/shareholders and managers/directors that if a company incurs debts, those debts are the debts of the company, owed by the company to the lender/creditor. Without more, the debts of the company are not the debts of any other person. This means that not even the owners/shareholders of the company are liable to pay any sum owed by the company to the lender/creditor. Any legal action to recover the debt must be brought by the creditor naming the company as the defendant in the legal action. The owners/shareholders of the company are not parties to the contract pursuant to which the sum owed (the debt) is due to the creditor therefore action against them will fail.

One important question that cannot be answered simply by referring to the separate legal personality of the company is this:

■ what, if any, liability does an owner/shareholder of a company have to contribute money *to the company* to enable the company to pay its lenders/creditors?

The answer to this question depends upon whether the company in question is a limited or unlimited company.

limited company
a company the liability of whose members to contribute to the company to enable it to pay its debts is limited by shares or guarantee

3.5.1 Limited and unlimited companies

Owners of registered companies do not necessarily or always limit their liability to contribute sums to the company so that the company can pay the sums it, the company, owes to third parties: limited liability is an *option* available to incorporators of a registered company. As Figure 2.5 shows, it is possible to register a private company under the Companies Act 2006 with unlimited liability. Section 3(4) makes this clear.

SECTION

'If there is no limit on the liability of its members, the company is an "unlimited company".'

Unlimited companies are not popular vehicles for business organisations, but it is useful to focus on them here as they throw into sharp relief the difference between the concepts of separate legal personality and limited liability, concepts which are often treated as a single concept by students, resulting in misunderstanding. The liability of a shareholder to pay money into a company needs to be considered both when the company is trading, and when the company has ceased trading and is being wound up.

3.5.2 Shareholder payments to a company that is trading

A person can become a shareholder by acquiring shares in a company either from the company itself or from an existing shareholder. Most shares obtained from existing shareholders involve a stock exchange transaction. Most stock exchanges forbid trading in shares in relation to which any sum remains payable to the company by the shareholder. For this reason, this section will concentrate on shares acquired from the company. Acquisition of shares from an existing shareholder will not be considered further.

Shares may be allotted and issued by a company and acquired by a shareholder on a fully paid-up, partly paid-up or nil-paid basis. Shares are fully paid-up when the shareholder pays to the company the whole of the share price (the amount due to the company) on allotment. As long as the company continues to trade, the company has no legal right to require a shareholder with fully paid-up shares to pay any further sum of money into the company. This is true, whether the company is a limited or unlimited company.

Where shares are obtained from a company on a partly paid, or nil-paid, basis the shareholder, at the time of allotment, does not pay to the company a part, or any part (as the case may be), of the price payable for the shares. In such a case the company is entitled to call upon the shareholder to pay to the company any part, or the whole, of the amount of the share price as yet unpaid, at any time.

The power to make such calls on shareholders, to determine when and how much, is ordinarily given to the directors of the company who must exercise the power in accordance with their duties to the company. The common law rule that all shareholders must be treated equally when calls are made (see *Preston v Grand Collier Dock Co* (1840) 11 Sim 327), can now be contracted out of by including a provision in the articles of association of a company permitting shares to be allotted on the basis that different calls can be made on different shareholders at different times (see s 581(a) of the Companies Act 2006).

Whilst a company continues to trade, the most a shareholder can be required to pay into the company is the price he has agreed to pay, but has not yet paid, for his or her shares.

winding up
the liquidation of a company

3.5.3 Shareholder payments to a company that is being wound up

The law governing the obligation of a shareholder to contribute money to a company that has ceased trading and is being wound up is found in s 74 of the Insolvency Act 1986. When a company is being wound up, it is essential to distinguish limited and unlimited companies.

The starting point for both limited and unlimited companies is s 74(1) which provided that:

SECTION

'When a company is wound up, every past and present member is liable to contribute to its assets to any amount sufficient for payment of its debts and liabilities.'

In the event of a company being wound up, a shareholder, without more, is required to contribute to the assets of a company sufficient to enable the company to pay its creditors and meet its other liabilities. Note, however, that even in relation to an unlimited company, a member is *not* liable to contribute to debts or liabilities incurred by the company *after* he or she has ceased to be a member and also is not liable to contribute anything at all if he or she has not been a member for a year or more at the time of the commencement of the winding up (see s 74(2)(a) and (b)).

Section 74 goes on to make specific provision for a company limited by shares. Section 74(2)(d) provides:

SECTION

'[I]n the case of a company limited by shares, no contribution is required from any member exceeding the amount (if any) unpaid on the shares in respect of which he is liable as a present or past member.'

In relation to a company limited by shares, whether a public or a private company, s 74(2)(d) of the Insolvency Act 1986 is the statutory basis on which the liability of shareholders to contribute to the company to enable it to pay its debts and other liabilities is limited. The limit is the amount (if any) unpaid on the shares. If that amount has been paid to the company, a shareholder is under no further obligation to contribute.

3.5.4 Justifications for limited liability

Shareholders of the first registered companies did not have limited liability. As outlined in Chapter 1, the debate as to the costs and benefits limited liability would bring were still being debated in 1844, when the first incorporation statute was enacted. Although the debate was soon won by those advocating the beneficial consequences of limiting the liability of shareholders, limited liability was initially introduced for large companies only, that is, companies with a minimum of 25 shareholders that met certain minimum share value and issued share capital requirements (see s 1 of the Limited Liability Act 1855). This restricted availability was relaxed the very next year by the Joint Stock Companies Act 1856.

The key benefits of limited liability are:

- Encouragement of investment by members of the public in companies.
- Facilitation of the transferability of shares.
- Clarity and certainty as to the assets available to creditors of the company.

3.6 Corporate groups and separate legal personality

It follows from the separate legal personality of companies and the ability of a company to own property that one company can own shares in another company. This is the basis for the existence of corporate groups that can be, and are not uncommonly, made up of over one hundred companies, all owned, ultimately, by one parent company.

QUOTATION

'The international group of companies – not the single company – has become *the* prevailing form of European large-sized enterprises, which business activity is typically organised and conducted through a network of individual subsidiaries located in several States inside and outside Europe.

The group management is the heart of this leading business organisation: the main reason for its success consists in the sophisticated and flexible management issuing from the optimal combination of central control exercised by the parent and local autonomy granted to subsidiaries. No successful regulation could ignore this central feature. *Any EU legislation and/or recommendation on groups of companies should seek to maintain and enhance the flexibility of the management of groups in its international business activities*.'

European Commission Internal Market and Services, Report of the Reflection Group on the Future of EU Competition Law, Brussels 5 April 2011 at p.59

A corporate group is a single *economic* entity. Public disclosure laws recognise this to the extent that accounts made available to the public must be compiled on a group basis (see Chapter 17). Fundamentally, however, company law sees a corporate group as a series of individual companies. Each company within the group owns its own property and is liable for its own debts and other liabilities. It is preservation of the reputation of the parent of a corporate group that in many cases will cause a parent company to 'pay' claims made against its subsidiaries, rather than any legal obligation to do so, for, as we have seen, a shareholder, and, therefore, a parent company, is not liable for the debts or other liabilities of the company. If the liability of a subsidiary is large enough, a parent company will incur the public opprobrium suffered from leaving it to 'sink', ie become insolvent, and leave creditors wholly or only partly paid. There is no law that prevents a parent company from doing this.

The right of one company to establish a wholly owned subsidiary company to perform risky operations and thereby protect the assets of other companies in the corporate group from the claims of persons damaged by the risky activity is clear in English law. It is not universally accepted as a satisfactory state of affairs and is not the case throughout Europe. Attempts to change the law to introduce parent liability for its subsidiaries have been made as part of the European Union company

parent company

a company is the parent company of another company if it holds the majority voting rights in that company, is a member and can appoint or remove all the directors, or is a member and controls a majority of the voting rights either alone or pursuant to an agreement with other members of the company

subsidiary company

a company is a subsidiary of another company, known as its holding or parent company, if that other company holds the majority of its voting rights, is a member and can appoint or remove all of its directors, or is a member and controls a majority of its voting rights either alone or pursuant to an agreement with other members law harmonisation programme, but, as we have seen in Chapter 1, the draft ninth company law directive containing proposals on this issue was withdrawn through lack of consensus and years passed with no expectation of it being revived. How to address groups forms part of the consultation on the future of European company law announced in February 2012.

Attempts have also been made in a number of cases to argue that one company in a corporate group is required as a matter of law to pay liabilities incurred by another company in the corporate group based on a 'single economic entity' theory. Notwithstanding one or two cases in which this theory seemed to have been accepted, the most famous of which was *DHN Food Distributors Ltd v Tower Hamlets LBC* [1976] 1 WLR 852 (CA), this basis for imposing liability has now been firmly rejected by the English courts. Use by corporate groups of the separate legal personality of group member companies to minimise exposure to business creditors is illustrated in *Multinational Gas and Petrochemical Company v Multinational Gas and Petrochemical Services Ltd* [1983] Ch 258. The more difficult scenario to accept is the organisation of a corporate group deliberately so as to minimise exposure of the group's wealth to tort victims. The Court of Appeal confirmed that English law endorses this behaviour in *Adams v Cape Industries plc* [1990] Ch 433. Note, however, the Court of Appeal confirmation in *Chandler v Cape plc* [2012] EWCA Civ 525 that a patent company may be liable in tort for personal injury caused by its subsidiaries based on application of *Caparo Industries Plc v Dickman* [1990] 2 AC 605 (HL) and watch out for an appeal to the Supreme Court.

CASE EXAMPLE

Adams v Cape Industries plc [1990] Ch 433 (CA)

A number of class actions were brought in Texan courts by US workers injured by exposure to asbestos mined in South Africa by subsidiary companies within the Cape corporate group. The asbestos had been marketed in the US by NAAC, a wholly owned subsidiary company within the Cape corporate group, incorporated in Illinois. NAAC ceased to trade and was put into liquidation and two new subsidiaries, CPC (incorporated in Illinois) and AMC (a Liechtenstein entity), were incorporated by the Cape corporate group to market asbestos in the US. Judgments were awarded by the Texan court, against, amongst others, Cape (the group parent company) and Capasco (another wholly owned subsidiary within the Cape corporate group, incorporated in England). The case is concerned with the circumstances in which a judgment awarded by a foreign court will be enforced by the English courts. Essentially, Jimmy Adams, the applicant in England, had to show that at the relevant time the judgment debtors (Cape and Capasco) were present in the US. Adams' counsel, Mr Morison, argued:

- NAAC was part of the same corporate group as Cape and Capasco and the presence of NAAC in the US should constitute presence of Cape and Capasco
- AMC and CPC, through which asbestos was marketed into the US after NAAC ceased to trade, were sham companies established to mask the real situation and the veil should be lifted and their presence treated as the presence of Cape and Capasco
- Cape and Capasco were present through marketing and selling asbestos through their agents, NAAC, AMC and CPC.

Held: The Texan judgments would not be enforced by the English courts. (See below at 3.7.3 for further information and extracts from this case.)

In refusing to allow enforcement of the Texan judgments and finding in favour of Cape, the court rejected each of the arguments to overcome the separate legal personality of each company member of a corporate group. In the course of rejecting them, the Court of Appeal reviewed the circumstances in which English courts are willing to avoid the consequences of the separate legal personality of a company in order to allow a creditor of a company a remedy against the company's shareholder. These circumstances and certain noteworthy comments of the court on the argument put to it that a corporate group is a single economic unit and therefore should be treated as a single legal entity are set out below at section 3.7.3.

The claimant in *Adams v Cape* (1990) represented the victims of tortious behaviour of a company and the victims were denied a remedy against the shareholder (the parent company) which had valuable assets to meet the judgments. Pettet notes that the vulnerability of tort victims was not part of the debate that took place in the nineteenth century about whether or not to extend limited liability to the shareholders of registered companies. The debate focussed on trade and financial creditors who, it is argued, providing they have access to accurate information, can look after themselves in that they can negotiate protections or reflect the risk of doing business with a particular company in their terms of business and pricing. If this is accepted, there is no reason for the law to require shareholders to contribute to a company to enable it to pay its debts. Rather, the focus of the law should be adequate public disclosure of information. This reasoning is not compelling in relation to tort victims.

KEY FACTS

Separate legal personality	
On registration a company becomes a separate legal person, s 15(1).	
A company registered under the Companies Act 2006 has the legal capacity of a natural person, s 39.	
Without more, the shareholders of a company *cannot* be sued to enforce contracts to which the company is a party	*Salomon v A Salomon & Co Ltd* (1897) *Ord v Belhaven* (1998)
Property owned by the company is not owned by its shareholders and shareholders have no insurable interest in it.	*Macaura v Northern Assurance Co* (1925)
Companies may own shares in other companies and corporate groups are very common.	
Corporate groups may be organised so as to minimise the legal liabilities of individual companies in the group.	*Adams v Cape* (1990)
Shareholder limited liability	
A shareholder of an *unlimited* company must contribute sums to the company in a winding up to enable the company to pay its creditors in full.	Insolvency Act 1986, s 74(1)
A shareholder of a *limited* company is not required to contribute more than the amount unpaid for the shares he owns.	Insolvency Act 1986, s 74(2)(d)
A company can make calls on nil-paid or partly paid shares until all shares are fully paid-up.	*Preston v Grand Collier Dock Co* (1840)

3.7 Limits on the implications of incorporation/separate legal personality

We have identified the main consequences of the separate legal personality of a company (section 3.3 above). It is important to understand the ways in which these consequences may be supplemented or curtailed so as to provide a person with a remedy different from that dictated by a strict application of the separate legal personality doctrine. There are three routes by which to supplement or curtail the doctrine to achieve such a remedy. The most common outcome is for a claimant against a company to be awarded a remedy against the company's shareholder. In some cases, however, a remedy is sought against a company owned or controlled by a person against whom a claimant has its principal remedy. The judgment of the Supreme Court in the appeal in *VTB Capital plc v Nutritek International Corp* [2012] EWCA Civ 808 is pending at the time of going to press. This will clarify the law on piercing the corporate veil, particularly, the remedies available.

Self-help action

First, a person dealing with a company can often **work around** the main consequence of the company being a person separate from its shareholders, that its shareholders are not liable for the debts and obligations of the company, by putting appropriate **contractual or agency arrangements** in place. This behaviour is often called 'self-help' action.

Piercing the corporate veil

Second, the courts sometimes **refuse to apply the doctrine of separate legal personality**. The terms 'lifting the corporate veil' and 'piercing the corporate veil' are used in this context. Such imagery, however, can hinder rather than help to explain what the court is doing and why; particularly as these terms have not always been used consistently. It is easy to overestimate the importance of this topic. There was a time when the courts were very receptive to arguments urging them to ignore the separate legal personality of a company. This approach is evidenced by Lord Denning in *DHN Ltd v Tower Hamlets LBC* (1976) (CA) (considered below) and *Littlewoods Mail Order Stores Limited v Commissioner of Inland Revenue* [1969] 1 WLR 1241. That era is believed to be over and courts have in recent years adopted a much stricter approach to suggested departures from the separate personality doctrine.

Statutory provisions

Finally, statutory provisions may, in certain circumstances, **supplement or otherwise affect rights**. If a person has a right against a company, a statutory provision may supplement that person's rights by providing a statutory right in addition to the existing rights. This right may be against the shareholders or the directors, for example. Alternatively, a statutory provision may state that the acts of one company are to be regarded as the acts of its parent company (the shareholder), perhaps for the purpose of determining whether or not compensation is payable pursuant to the statute. Statutory provisions that operate when a company is being wound up are especially important and need to be addressed separately from those applicable when a company is still trading, or, as it is said, is still 'a going concern'.

Each of these three routes is explored below. First, it is helpful to consider typical scenarios in which there is a wish to provide a claimant with a different remedy from that dictated by a strict application of the separate personality doctrine.

3.7.1 Typical scenarios

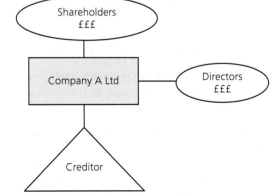

A company has insufficient assets to pay its creditors. Its directors and shareholders have assets.

Can the creditor sue either the directors or the shareholders to recover the sum owed to it by Company A Ltd?

Figure 3.2 Typical scenario 1

**A company has insufficient assets to pay its creditors.
It has a sole shareholder/director who has assets**

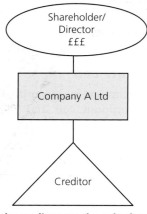

**Can the creditor sue the sole shareholder/director to
recover the sum owed to it by Company A Ltd?**

Figure 3.3 Typical scenario 2

**Company A Ltd has insufficient assets to pay its creditors.
It is a wholly owned subsidiary of Company B Ltd
which has assets.**

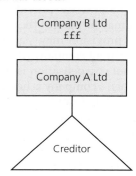

**Can the creditor sue Company B Ltd to recover the
sum owed to it by Company A Ltd?**

Figure 3.4 Typical scenario 3

E is employed by O as a salesman.

E's contract of employment contains restrictive covenants.

**One covenant prohibits E from selling products to any of the
customers of his employer for 12 months after his
employment terminates.**

E decides to resign his employment with O.

E forms Company Ex Ltd which sells products to a customer of O.

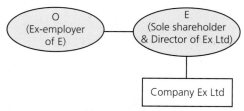

**Can O obtain an injunction restraining Company Ex Ltd
from selling to O's customers?**

Figure 3.5 Using a company to avoid existing obligations

3.7.2 Self-help action to mitigate the consequences of incorporation

Contractual arrangements

In each of Figures 3.2 to 3.4, the creditor could have insisted that the shareholder (or one or more of the shareholders) guarantee the obligations of Company A Ltd under any loan between the creditor and Company A Ltd. Such guarantees are very common in the context of corporate groups, when they are called 'parent guarantees'. They are also very common in the context of sole member or closely held companies.

In Figure 3.5, O, the ex-employer, could protect itself by appropriate language in E's contract of employment. The contractual clause containing the restrictive covenant could be drafted so that the restriction covered sales to O's customers by E or any company owned or controlled by E. It would also be sensible to define control for the purposes of the covenant.

These are two illustrations of how contracts can be used to work around the consequences of incorporation. Agency is a particular type of contractual relationship. An agency relationship may be put in place between a company and its shareholder. A claimant often seeks to establish that a company is the agent of its shareholder so that the claimant has a claim against the principal (the shareholder) rather than the (insolvent) agent/company.

Agency and the consequences of incorporation

There is *no presumption* of agency between a company and its shareholder(s). If the facts support the argument, however, it may be possible to argue in the context of Figures 3.3 and 3.4 (ignoring Figure 3.2 because this argument is less likely to succeed where there is more than one shareholder), that when it entered into the loan agreement (or whichever contract has given rise to the sum of money being owed to the creditor), Company A Ltd acted as the agent of the shareholder/parent company. If this argument succeeds, the shareholder/parent company, as the principal, is the party to the loan/contract, not Company A Ltd, and the creditor can sue the shareholder/parent company to recover the sum owed because it is owed by the shareholder/ parent company.

In such a case, agency does not override or undermine the separate personality of Company A Ltd. Company A Ltd must be a separate legal entity from its shareholder/ parent company to play the role of agent. Its separate legal personality is a pre-condition to the agency argument succeeding.

In *Adams v Cape* (1990), it was argued that certain subsidiaries of Cape that were present in the US acted as Cape's agent. Although it was clear that the subsidiaries in question acted as the agent of Cape *for certain specific purposes*, it was found as *a matter of fact* that there was no agency between the subsidiaries and Cape such as to make the presence of the subsidiaries in the US the presence of Cape. This case highlights the difficulty in establishing an agency relationship between a parent and a subsidiary company in the absence of clear written evidence that such a relationship has been agreed by both parties. In this light, agency can be seen as a contractual self-help remedy.

Agency was used in a different way as a step in an argument (which failed) to impose liability on the indirect owner of a company in *Yukong Lines Ltd of Korea v Rendsburg Investments Corporation of Liberia, The Rialto No 2* [1998] 1 WLR 294 (QBD).

CASE EXAMPLE

Yukong Lines Ltd of Korea v Rendsburg Investments Corporation of Liberia, The Rialto No 2 [1998] 1 WLR 294 (QBD)

Yukong was a Korean shipping company. It negotiated with Marcan to enter into a charterparty (a lease of a ship). Marcan was the agent of Rendsburg, a Lyberian company, and the parties to the charterparty were Yukong and Rendsburg. Before the ship was delivered by Yukong, assets were moved out of Rendsburg and Rendsburg repudiated the charterparty. Yukong found itself with a right to sue a company, Rendsburg, which had no money to pay the damages suffered by Yukong as a result of the repudiatory breach. Yukong argued that Mr Yamvrias, a director of Marcam and the indirect owner (along with his family) of both Marcan and Rendsburg, was the undisclosed principal of Rendsburg. If this could be proved, Mr Yamvrias (a wealthy man) would be the correct party to the charterparty and Yukong could sue Mr Yamvrias for damages for breach of contract. Held:

- Mr Yamvrias controlled Rendsburg and the ultimate beneficial interest in both Rendsburg and Marcam companies rested with him and other members of his family.
- Mr Yamvrias had caused assets of Rendsburg to be moved out of the company to put those assets beyond the reach of Yukong.
- Mr Yamvrias had signed the charterparty expressly as agent for Rendsburg.
- The parties to the charterparty were Rendsburg and Yukong.
- Yamvrias did *not* enter into the charterparty as undisclosed principal of Rendsburg: there was no evidence of this.
- Movement of the funds out of Rendsburg was not enough to treat Yamvrias as a party to the charterparty.
- Yukong must look to the insolvency laws to protect itself in a case such as this where it finds itself to be a contingent judgment creditor of an insolvent company (Rendsburg).

Although the claimant, Yukong, was unsuccessful in *The Rialto No 2*, the case illustrates how agency *may* provide a claimant with a remedy against a shareholder of a company.

To summarise, claimants dissatisfied with their rights against a company have often put forward agency arguments to support a remedy against the shareholder. This will succeed or fail depending upon whether or not the facts support the assertion that an agency relationship exists making the company the agent of the shareholder.

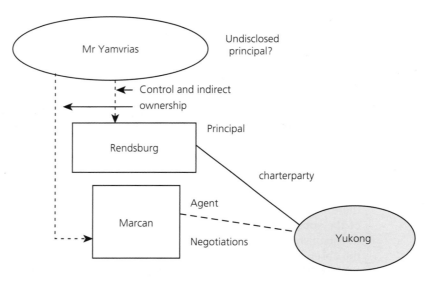

Figure 3.6 The Rialto No 2

3.7.3 Piercing the corporate veil: court-developed limits on the consequences of incorporation

Over the years, claimants have put forward three further arguments to support requests for remedies against one or more shareholders of the company. These arguments are based on the single economic entity theory, the justice theory, and the façade theory.

Each of these theories was exhaustively examined in *Adams v Cape* (1990) (above), the leading authority on this area of company law. As a result of that examination, it may be stated with confidence that of the three theories, only the façade theory provides a basis for 'piercing the corporate veil', that is, treating a company and the shareholder standing behind the company, as a single entity in law so that the rights, liabilities or activities of the company are the rights, liabilities or activities of the shareholder (see *Atlas Maritime Company SA v Avalon Maritime Limited (No 1)* [1991] 4 All ER 769) and *vice versa*.

Single economic entity theory

The proposition that a court can treat a group of companies as a single entity in law because they are/it is a single economic entity is false (see section 3.6 above). In *Adams v Cape* (1990), Slade LJ quoted with approval the following words of Goff LJ (as he then was) in *Bank of Tokyo Ltd v Karoon* (1987) (CA):

JUDGMENT

'Counsel suggested beguilingly that it would be technical for us to distinguish between parent and subsidiary company in this context; economically, he said, they were one. But we are concerned not with economics but the law. The distinction between the two is, in law, fundamental and cannot here be bridged.'

The apparent acceptance of the single economic entity theory by Lord Denning in *DHN Ltd v Tower Hamlets LBC* (1976) (CA), can no longer be regarded as good law. The correctness of the reasoning in the case has been doubted by the House of Lords in *Woolfson v Strathclyde RC* (1978) SC 90 (HL) in which, referencing the *DHN* decision, Lord Keith of Kinkel said:

JUDGMENT

'I have some doubts whether in this respect the Court of Appeal properly applied the principle that it is appropriate to pierce the corporate veil only where special circumstances exist indicating that it is a mere façade concealing the true facts.'

DHN involved compensation under the Land Compensation Act 1961. It is now regarded as an example of a case involving interpretation of a statutory provision pursuant to which a parent and two subsidiary companies were to be treated as one unit for the purposes of entitlement to statutory compensation for disturbance, a point made by Slade LJ in *Adams v Cape Industries plc* (1990).

Ord v Belhaven Pubs Ltd [1998] 2 BCC 607 (CA) provides a clear illustration of the single entity theory being rejected because it offends against the separate legal personality doctrine.

CASE EXAMPLE

Ord v Belhaven Pubs Ltd [1998] 2 BCC 607 (CA)

The plaintiff sued the defendant company in contract and tort arising out of the entry into a lease of a pub from the defendant in 1989. During proceedings the defendant company ceased trading, had no assets and the plaintiff sought to replace its parent, Ascot Holdings Ltd, or a sister company in the group, Ascot Estates Ltd, as the defendant. In an attempt to rationalise the group's operating structure, the group had been reorganised to consolidate the hotels business and assets in the defendant and the pubs in Ascot Estates Ltd. Properties had been transferred at book value. In 1992 assets were transferred from the defendant company to its parent company, Ascot Holdings Ltd, at above book value. At first instance the judge decided to treat the group as a single entity and permitted the substitution of the parent company as the defendant in the action. She spoke of the parent company being the 'controlling mind' of the subsidiaries and of the 'concept of corporate benefit' or 'concept of the economic unit'. On appeal, Held: Reversing the first instance decision, neither the parent nor the sister company were liable for the liabilities of the defendant. To disregard the distinction between the legal entities involved in order to render the holding company potentially liable was at odds with the whole concept of corporate personality, limited liability and the decision in *Salomon v Salomon*.

As we have seen above at section 3.6, the court in *Adams v Cape Industries plc* (1990) rejected the single legal entity theory in a case involving tort victims of a subsidiary company who had suffered physical injury, unlike the Ords who had suffered purely economic loss. The court in *Adams v Cape* denied the tort victims access to parent company funds to pay unpaid judgments obtained against subsidiary companies. Slade LJ's comments on the right of companies to structure corporate groups to minimise the exposure of parent companies are noteworthy.

JUDGMENT

'The "single economic unit" argument

There is no general principle that all companies in a group of companies are to be regarded as one. On the contrary, the fundamental principle is that "each company in a group of companies (a relatively modern concept) is a separate legal entity possessed of separate legal rights and liabilities": *The Albazero* [1977] AC. 774, 807, *per* Roskill LJ ...

The "corporate veil" point

It is thus indisputable that each of Cape, Capasco, N.A.A.C. and C.P.C. were in law separate legal entities ... Our law, for better or worse, recognises the creation of subsidiary companies, which though in one sense the creatures of their parent companies, will nevertheless under the general law fall to be treated as separate legal entities with all the rights and liabilities which would normally attach to separate legal entities ...

As to Cape's purpose in making the arrangements for the liquidation of N.A.A.C. and the creation of A.M.C. and C.P.C. ... The allegation of impropriety was, in our view, rightly abandoned. The inference which we draw from all the evidence was that Cape's intention was to enable sales of asbestos from the South African subsidiaries to continue to be made in the United States while (a) reducing the appearance of any involvement therein of Cape or its subsidiaries, and (b) reducing by any lawful means available to it the risk of any subsidiary or of Cape as parent company being held liable for United States taxation or subject to the jurisdiction of the United States courts, whether state or federal, and the risk of any default judgment by such a court being held to be enforceable in this country ...

Is the legal position altered by the facts that Cape's intention, in making the relevant arrangements (as we infer), was to enable sales of asbestos from the South African subsidiaries to be made while (a) reducing if not eliminating the appearance of any involvement therein of Cape or its subsidiaries, and (b) reducing by any lawful means available to it the risk of any subsidiary or of Cape as parent company being held liable for United States taxation or subject to the jurisdiction of the United States courts and the risk of any default judgment by such a court being held to be enforceable in this country?

We think not. Mr Morison submitted that the court will lift the corporate veil where a defendant by the device of a corporate structure attempts to evade (i) limitations imposed on his conduct by law; (ii) such rights of relief against him as third parties already possess; and (iii) such rights of relief as third parties may in the future acquire. Assuming that the first and second of these three conditions will suffice in law to justify such a course, neither of them apply in the present case. It is not suggested that the arrangements involved any actual or potential illegality or were intended to deprive anyone of their existing rights. Whether or not such a course deserves moral approval, there was nothing illegal as such in Cape arranging its affairs (whether by the use of subsidiaries or otherwise) so as to attract the minimum publicity to its involvement in the sale of Cape asbestos in the United States of America. As to condition (iii), we do not accept as a matter of law that the court is entitled to lift the corporate veil as against a defendant company which is the member of a corporate group merely because the corporate structure has been used so as to ensure that the legal liability (if any) in respect of particular future activities of the group (and correspondingly the risk of enforcement of that liability) will fall on another member of the group rather than the defendant company. Whether or not this is desirable, the right to use a corporate structure in this manner is inherent in our corporate law. Mr Morison urged on us that the purpose of the operation was in substance that Cape would have the practical benefit of the group's asbestos trade in the United States of America without the risks of tortious liability. This may be so. However, in our judgment, Cape was in law entitled to organise the group's affairs in that manner and … to expect that the court would apply the principle of *Salomon v A Salomon & Co Ltd* [1897] AC 22 in the ordinary way.'

Notwithstanding the formidable array of cases denying the single economic entity theory as a basis for piercing the veil, reference to that theory in two recent cases (*Becket Investment Management Group Ltd v Hall* [2007] EWCA Civ 613 and *Adelson v Associated Newspapers Ltd* [2007] EWHC 3028 has stirred commentary that it may be time for *Adams v Cape* to be revisited.

Façade theory

If the company is a 'mere façade concealing the true facts', the corporate veil will be pierced. Authority for this proposition is the House of Lords decision in *Woolfson v Strathclyde Regional Council* (above), although Lord Kinkel cited no authority for this proposition and gave no indication of the meaning of 'façade'. Ten years later, LJ Slade commented on the authorities on 'façade' in the Court of Appeal in *Adams v Cape* (1990) (at 543):

JUDGMENT

'From the authorities cited to us we are left with rather sparse guidance as to the principles which should guide the court in determining whether or not the arrangements of a corporate group involve a façade within the meaning of that word as used by the House of Lords in *Woolfson*.'

In the cases in which the courts have treated the company and the shareholder as one, the terms used to describe the company, apart from 'façade', are 'device', 'stratagem', 'mask', 'cloak' and 'sham' (all of which terms were used in *Gilford Motor Company Ltd v Horne* [1933] Ch 935). This basis for ignoring the separate legal personality of the company may be seen as an application, in the context of formation or use of a company, of a legal principle or doctrine of general application, the 'sham doctrine'. The sham doctrine was acknowledged by LJ Diplock in *Snook v London and West Riding Investments Ltd* [1967] 2 QB 786, 803 in the following terms:

JUDGMENT

'[I]t means acts done or documents executed by the parties to the "sham" which are intended by them to give to third parties or to the court the appearance of creating between the parties legal rights and obligations different from the actual legal rights and obligations (if any) which the parties intend to create.'

The consequence of the finding that acts or documents are a sham is illustrated by the words of LJ Lindley in *Yorkshire Railway Wagon Co v Maclure* (1882) 21 Ch D 309, 318. Speaking in the context of a transaction entered into by a company he stated, 'If it were a mere cloak or screen for another transaction one could see through it'. If a company is a sham, it is ignored, and this act of ignoring it is a piercing of the corporate veil.

The drawing together of the circumstances in which the courts rely on the existence of a sham and recognition of the existence of a general legal doctrine, the 'sham doctrine', is relatively new (see *Conaglen* (2008)). Exploration of the pre-requisites to a finding of a sham in the wider context is likely to aid understanding of when a court will pierce the corporate veil, supplementing the 'sparse guidance' in the company cases referred to by LJ Slade in *Adams v Cape* (1990).

We have seen how, because of the apparently unlimited range of circumstances in which it is possible to create a separate legal personality, two or more legal persons may exist where there is only one economic entity or economic interest in existence. This is the case where an individual forms a sole member company (or a company in which a number of shareholders hold their shares on trust for one individual), or where a company forms and owns all the shares in another company (a 'wholly owned subsidiary company'). The sham-based cases are situations in which in fact, or in substance (if not in legal form), there is no difference between one person's economic interest and the company's economic interest.

Where a company is formed with the intention of using it to avoid an existing legal liability, the court will pierce the veil based on a finding of sham.

CASE EXAMPLE

Gilford Motor Company Ltd v Horne [1933] Ch 935

An ex-employee was unable to escape a restrictive covenant in favour of his ex-employer by carrying out the restricted activity through a company he had formed for that purpose (see Figure 3.5 above).

CASE EXAMPLE

Jones v Lipman [1962] 1 WLR 832 (Ch Div)

A person who had contracted to sell a piece of land was not permitted to avoid an order for specific performance by transferring the land to a company created solely for the purpose of avoiding the transfer to the buyer. The company was subject to the specific decree order.

It is not necessary to establish that the company was formed with the intention to avoid an existing legal obligation. *Trustor v Smallbone (No 2)* [2001] WLR 1177 (Ch Div) demonstrates that a company may have been formed for a perfectly proper purpose but if it is later used as a vehicle to facilitate a breach of duty, its separate legal personality will not be allowed to inhibit a court ordering a remedy reflecting the reality of the situation.

CASE EXAMPLE

Trustor v Smallbone (No 2) [2001] WLR 1177 (Ch Div)

Dishonestly, without authority and in breach of duty to Trustor AB, its managing director, Smallbone, transferred c. £20 million to a Gibraltarian company, Introcom Ltd. Introcom Ltd was owned indirectly, via a Lichtenstein trust, by Smallbone who also controlled the company. Introcom Ltd had been set up earlier, in connection with another matter, as a vehicle for remuneration for Smallbone. The court ordered Introcom Ltd to repay the sum received to Trustor AB on the ground that it had knowingly received the money, ie had received the money with knowledge of Smallbone's breach of fiduciary duty. Trustor AB then sought to make Smallbone liable to repay the money received by Introcom Ltd. Held: The court was entitled to pierce the corporate veil and recognise the receipt of the company (Introcom Ltd) as that of the individual in control of the company (Smallbone). The company was used as a device or façade in that it was used as the vehicle for the receipt of the money and its use was improper as it was the means by which Smallbone committed inexcusable breaches of his duty as a director of Trustor AB.

Justice theory

It has been argued that if justice requires it, a remedy should be available against the shareholder for a wrong done by the company. Presented in these general terms, the argument offends against the doctrine of legal certainty and may be rejected for this reason alone. Delivering the judgment of the Court of Appeal in *Adams v Cape* (1990) (see above at section 3.6), Slade LJ rejected the argument as unfounded.

JUDGMENT

'Mr Morison ... submitted that the court will, in appropriate circumstances, ignore the distinction in law between members of a group of companies treating them as one, and that broadly speaking, it will do so whenever it considers that justice so demands. In support of this submission, he referred us to a number of authorities ... Mr Morison described the theme of all these cases as being that where legal technicalities would produce injustice in cases involving members of a group of companies, such technicalities should not be allowed to prevail. We do not think that the cases relied on go nearly so far as this. As Sir Godfray submitted, save in cases which turn on the wording of particular statutes or contracts, the court is not free to disregard the principle of *Salomon v A Salomon & Co Ltd* [1897] AC 22 merely because it considers that justice so requires.'

There are, however, many situations when courts will look through a company and ignore its existence. The façade theory, above, provides examples of this. Other examples exist that do not fit together neatly into a theory. Rather than attempting to create a general theory for when courts will pierce the corporate veil, the approach suggested by Davies and others to explain these cases is to examine the purpose of the legal rule or principle in issue in each case.

Approached in this way, the existence of a company becomes simply a fact in the context of the application of the rule or principle. In each case, the court is refining the rule or principle in issue by explaining how that rule operates in the context involving a company, rather than the court developing a general rule or principle of company law that must be applied regardless of the rule or principle in issue.

Such an approach is analogous to the interpretation and application by the courts of a statutory provision, such as happened in *DHN* as explained in *Woolfson* and *Adams v Cape* (1990). The treatment of the grocery group in *DHN* as a single business for the purposes of awarding compensation pursuant to the statute was driven by the compensation rules in the statute, not by a general principle of company law that the separate legal personality of a company should be ignored when it is a member of a corporate group.

An example is provided by *Ratiu v Conway* [2006] 1 All ER 571 in which the issue arose as to whom does a solicitor retained by a company owe professional duties. Do those duties stop at the company, or do they extend to a sole shareholder who controls the company?

CASE EXAMPLE

Ratiu v Conway [2006] 1 All ER 571

Mr Conway, a solicitor, was retained in relation to the purchase and sale of a number of properties in London by two companies, both ultimately owned and controlled by Mr Ratiu, RHP Ltd and Pristbrook Ltd. Mr Conway sued Mr Ratiu for damages for libel and won. On Mr Ratiu's appeal the issue arose of to whom a solicitor owes professional duties. Mr Conway argued that he was never under any professional duty to Mr Ratiu because he had been retained by the companies, RHP Ltd and Pristbrook Ltd. Held: On the facts, the reality was that Mr Conway knew that his client was Mr Ratiu and not RHP Ltd or Pristbrook, which were simply vehicles controlled by Mr Ratiu. In this case, Mr Conway owed professional duties, fiduciary duties, to the shareholder.

JUDGMENT

LJ Auld, at paragraph 78 stated, 'There is, it seems to me, a powerful argument of principle, in this intensely personal context of trust, confidence and loyalty, for lifting the corporate veil where the facts require it to include those in or behind the company who are in reality the persons whose trust in and reliance upon the fiduciary may be confounded.'

JUDGMENT

LJ Sedley, at paragraph 188 stated, 'I recognise that there is an asymmetry between the law's longstanding insistence on the discreet legal personality of limited liability companies and its willingness to lift the veil, as the expression is, in a case like the present. But it is the latter, not the former, which accords with common sense and justice when the issue is who a solicitor owes his professional duties to.'

3.7.4 Statutory provisions supplementing available remedies

Statutory provisions regularly supplement or otherwise affect the rights of individuals and companies. A statute may, for example, create a statutory cause of action, or it may provide a defence to a claim. Ordinarily, these provisions do not impinge on the separate legal personalities of companies. Occasionally, however, the operation of a statute may result in the separate legal personality of a company being ignored, or, put another way, the corporate veil being pierced. This was the case in *DHN* (above at section 3.7.3).

The approach to statutory interpretation to be adopted when the interpretation of a statute will result in the piercing of the corporate veil is found in *Dimbleby & Sons Ltd v National Union of Journalists* [1984] 1 WLR 427 (HL).

In *Dimbleby*, the House of Lords has expressed the view that whilst, if it is the intention of Parliament that the separate personality of one or more companies be ignored, one would expect this to be expressly stated in the statute, even in the absence of clear words, such an intention may be the inexorable result of a purposive construction of the statute. Such result was not inexorable in the *Dimbleby* case in which the National Union of Journalists (NUJ) argued, unsuccessfully, that a sister company of the employer company with which the NUJ was in dispute, was itself 'an employer who is party to the dispute'.

JUDGMENT

'The "corporate veil" in the case of companies incorporated under the Companies Act is drawn by statute and it can be pierced by some other statute if such other statute so provides; but in view of its *raison d'être* and its consistent recognition by the courts since *Salomon v Salomon and Co Ltd* [1897] AC 22, one would expect that any parliamentary intention to pierce the corporate veil would be expressed in clear and unequivocal language. I do not wholly exclude the possibility that even in the absence of express words stating that in specified circumstances one company, although separately incorporated, is to be treated as sharing the same legal personality of another, a purposive construction of the statute may nevertheless lead inexorably to the conclusion that such must have been the intention of Parliament.'

trading certificate

the certificate issued by the registrar of companies a public company is required to obtain before it can lawfully trade or borrow

Examples of statutory provisions that supplement or otherwise affect the rights of a claimant in relation to a company are set out below. The examples are taken from company law and insolvency law. They are not an exhaustive list. A number of tax statute provisions are designed to preclude the use of the corporate form to avoid liabilities and to achieve this, the statutory provisions sometimes require the separate legal personality of companies to be ignored.

Companies Act 2006, s 767(3)

The Companies Act 2006 imposes a minimum share capital requirement on public companies which must be complied with before the Registrar of Companies will issue a trading certificate under s 761. Where a public company does business or exercises any borrowing powers without having a trading certificate it contravenes s 761. If the company defaults on any obligation under a transaction entered into whilst in contravention of s 761, s 767(3) operates to make the directors of the company jointly and severally liable to indemnify any other party to the transaction in respect of any loss or damage suffered by him by reason of the company's failure to comply with its obligations. This is an example of a statutory provision supplementing the rights of a person with rights against a company by rendering the directors of the company liable for the obligations of the company.

Company Directors Disqualification Act 1986, s 15

Section 15 of the Company Directors Disqualification Act 1986 (CDDA) operates to make a person who is involved in the management of a company whilst disqualified pursuant to the Act jointly and severally liable with the company for debts incurred by the company during the time he was so involved. This is another example of a statutory provision supplementing the rights of a person who has rights against the company. The operation of s 15 (CDDA) and s 767(3) of the Companies Act 2006 are illustrated in Figure 3.7.

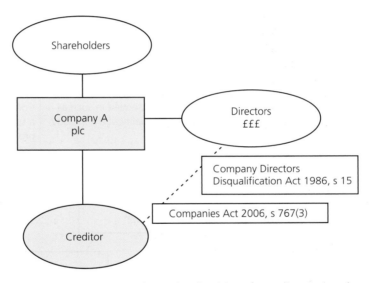

Figure 3.7 Statutory provisions supplementing the rights of a creditor against the company

Fraudulent or wrongful trading, Insolvency Act 1986, ss 213 and 214

When a company has ceased trading and is being wound-up, statutory provisions enable the liquidator to apply to the court for orders against any persons who were knowingly a party to fraudulent trading by the company (s 213) or any director who allowed the company to continue to trade when he knew or should have known there was no reasonable prospect of avoiding insolvent liquidation (s 214). The orders require those persons to contribute to the assets of the company.

These statutory provisions do not give rights directly to creditors of a company but they are important examples of how the strict consequence of the separate legal personality of the company, that creditors have access only to the assets of the company, is ameliorated by entitling the liquidator to bring actions that will benefit creditors against directors and (in some cases) shareholders. These and similar statutory provisions are examined towards the end of this book, see Chapter 16.

KEY FACTS

Limits on the implications of incorporation/separate legal personality	
Persons dealing with a company can take self-help action to mitigate the consequences of each company having a separate legal personality.	
Personal guarantees and parent company guarantees are very common.	
Statutes sometimes provide a person dealing with a company with an alternative remedy to the remedy they have against the company.	
A disqualified director who takes part in management will be liable for the debts and other liabilities of the company.	Company Directors Disqualification Act 1986, s 15
It is a matter of statutory interpretation whether or not a statute permits or requires the separate legal personality of a company to be ignored.	*Dimbleby v National Union of Journalists* (1984)
The liquidator of a company has a range of statutory powers to bring actions against directors and others to swell the assets available for distribution to creditors.	Insolvency Act 1986, ss 212–214
The court will pierce the corporate veil and disregard the separate legal personality of a company in some, very limited, circumstances.	
If the company is a sham its separate legal personality will be ignored.	*Jones v Lipman* (1962) *Gilford v Horne* (1933) *Trustor v Smallbone (No 2)* (2001)
Occasionally, a rule of law will be extended in such a way as to make the separate personality of a company unimportant.	*Conway v Ratiu* (2006) involved a solicitor being found to owe professional duties to the sole shareholder of client companies.

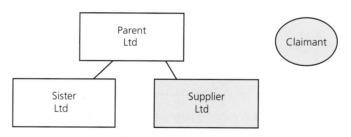

Figure 3.8 Who can the claimant sue?

ACTIVITY

Applying the law

Consider Figure 3.8 and the following facts:

Claimant contracted with Supplier Ltd for the supply of widgets. Supplier Ltd failed to supply the widgets and Claimant suffered loss of profits on the resale of the widgets. Claimant has discovered that Supplier Ltd is a subsidiary company of Parent Ltd which is also the parent company of Sister Ltd. Each of Parent Ltd and Sister Ltd have substantial assets but Supplier Ltd has no assets.

Against whom does Claimant have a cause of action? Would your answer be different if the assets of Supplier Ltd had been transferred from Supplier Ltd to Parent Ltd or Sister Ltd after Supplier Ltd had breached the contract of supply with Claimant? What enquiries would you make about the circumstances of the asset transfer in order to advise Parent Ltd and Sister Ltd as to their potential liabilities?

SAMPLE ESSAY QUESTION

Critically analyse the concepts of limited liability and separate corporate personality explaining how they complement one another.

Unpack the question

This is the first essential step which you must take time to do properly. You should separate out:

- The concept of limited liability
- The concept of separate corporate personality
- The need to consider how these two concepts relate to/complement one another
- The need for analysis
- The need for evaluation, i.e., critique of the concepts/relationship.

Explain the meaning of limited liability

- Show that you understand the concept
- Explain that it is the liability of the shareholders/members to contribute to the assets of the company to enable it to pay its debts that is limited
- The starting point is that on a winding up the members of a company are liable to contribute to the company to any amount sufficient for payment of its debts and liabilities, i.e., liability is not limited: Insolvency Act 1986 s 74
- For shareholders of a limited company, this liability is restricted to the amount, if any, unpaid on his shares: s 74(2)(d).

Explain the meaning and consequences of separate corporate personality

- Show that you understand the concept
- The debts of the company are not the debts of one or more of the owners of the company, therefore the owner is *not* liable to pay any sum owed *by the company* to the lender/creditor
- Illustrate with cases any/all of the following consequences: a company can own property, can be a party to a contract, can act tortiously, can be a victim of tortious behaviour, has human rights, can commit a crime, can be the victim of a crime, can sue and be sued, has perpetual existence until dissolved

- Emphasize that a company's liability is unlimited, as in the case of individuals, unless limited under a contract/by effective notice, but its ability to meet its liabilities when it is trading is limited to the value of its own assets/resources.

Explore the relationship between the two concepts

- Note that it is possible to establish a separate corporate personality able to incur debts and liabilities, without limiting the liability of its members (an unlimited company)
- Consider whether the reverse is true. It would be extremely difficult to implement limited liability without a separate corporate personality, and legal regulation of exclusion and limitation of liability (clauses/notices etc) would almost certainly preclude an effective outcome.

Reflect on the concepts

- Move beyond a technical explanation of the concepts to consider the implications and attractiveness of the concepts
- You should refer to the basic debate between those who see limited liability as encouraging undercapitalised and irresponsible business initiatives and those who so it as essential to facilitate investment in business
- You could also discuss the plight of the tort victim who did not choose to do business with the company.

CONCLUDE

SUMMARY

Registered companies are artificial persons called corporations

- On registration a company becomes a separate legal person, s 15(1).
- A company registered under the Companies Act 2006 has the legal capacity of a natural person, s 39.

The consequences of incorporation/separate legal personality

- Without more, the shareholders of a company cannot be sued to enforce contracts to which the company is a party (*Salomon v A Salomon & Co Ltd* (1897); *Ord v Belhaven* (1998)).
- Property owned by the company is not owned by its shareholders and shareholders have no insurable interest in it (*Macaura v Northern Assurance Co* (1925)).

- Companies may own shares in other companies and corporate groups are very common.
- Corporate groups may be organised so as to minimise the legal liabilities of individual companies in the group (*Adams v Cape* (1990)).

Limited liability: a concept distinct from separate legal personality

- A shareholder of an unlimited company must contribute sums to the company in a winding up to enable the company to pay its creditors in full (Insolvency Act 1986, s 74(1)).
- A shareholder of a limited company is not required to contribute more than the amount unpaid for the shares he owns (Insolvency Act 1986, s 74(2)(d)).
- A company can make calls on nil-paid or partly paid shares until all shares are fully paid-up (*Preston v Grand Collier Dock Co* (1840)).

Limits on the implication of incorporation/separate legal personality

- Persons dealing with a company can take self-help action to mitigate the consequences of each company having a separate legal personality.
- Personal guarantees and parent company guarantees are very common.
- Statutes sometimes provide a person dealing with a company with an alternative remedy to the remedy they have against the company.
- A disqualified director who takes part in management will be liable for the debts and other liabilities of the company (Company Directors Disqualification Act 1986, s 15).
- It is a matter of statutory interpretation whether or not a statute permits or requires the separate legal personality of a company to be ignored (*Dimbleby v National Union of Journalists* (1984)).
- The liquidator of a company has a range of statutory powers to bring actions against directors and others to swell the assets available for distribution to creditors (Insolvency Act 1986, ss 212–214).
- The court will pierce the corporate veil and disregard the separate legal personality of a company in some, very limited, circumstances.
- If the company is a sham its separate legal personality will be ignored (*Jones v Lipman* (1962); *Gilford v Horne* (1933); *Trustor v Smallbone (No 2)* (2001)).

Further reading

Useful websites

The Human Rights of Companies website:
http://www.thehumanrightsofcompanies.com
Understanding the Corporate Manslaughter and Corporate Homicide Act 2007 (Ministry of Justice, 2007), accessible at: www.justice.gov.uk/docs/manslaughterhomicideact07.pdf

Articles

Cheng, T K, 'The Corporate Veil Doctrine Revisited: A Comparative Study of the English and the U.S. Corporate Veil Doctrines' (2011) 34 BC Int'l & Comp. L. Rev. 329.

Conaglen, M, 'Sham Trusts' (2008) 67 CLJ 176.

Ferran, E, 'Corporate Attribution and the Directing Will' (2011) 127 LQR 239.

Hargovan, A, and Harris, J, 'Piercing the Corporate Veil in Canada: A Comparative Analysis' (2007) 28 Comp Law 58.

Kahn-Freund, O, 'Some Reflections on Company Law Reform' (1944) 7 MLR 54.

Linklater, L, 'Piercing The Corporate Veil – The Never Ending Story' (2006) 27 Comp Law 65.

Moore, M, 'A Temple Built on Faulty Foundations: Piercing the Corporate Veil and the Legacy of *Salomon v Salomon*' [2006] JBL 180.

Rixon, J, 'Lifting the Veil between Holding and Subsidiary Companies' [1986] 102 LQR 415 (on *Woolfson*).

Sullivan, G R, 'The Attribution of Culpability to Limited Companies' [1996] CLJ 515.

Books

Pinto, A and Evans, M, *Corporate Criminal Liability* (2nd edn, Sweet & Maxwell, 2008).

Wells, C, *Corporations and Criminal Responsibility* (2nd edn, Oxford University Press, 2002).

4

Company formation and linked issues

AIMS AND OBJECTIVES

After reading this chapter you should be able to:

- Register a company
- Understand the importance and usefulness of company registration numbers
- Decide whether a proposed name for a company will be accepted by the registrar of companies
- Understand when a company name may be challenged based on another's goodwill
- Advise on trading disclosures required by a company
- Recognise a promoter and explain the legal obligations he owes in relation to the proposed company
- Distinguish between a business and the company operating it
- Recognise a pre-incorporation contract
- Advise whether or not a person who signs a pre-incorporation contract on behalf of a company is liable under it or can enforce it
- Work out whether or not a company is bound by a pre-incorporation contract
- Re-register a private company as a public company and *vice versa*

4.1 Registering a UK company

registrar of companies

the registrar of companies for England and Wales, Scotland or Northern Ireland, as the case may require, to whom documents are sent to form a company and to whom the necessary returns are made during the lifetime of a company

This chapter describes how to register a UK company pursuant to the Companies Act 2006.

4.1.1 Where to register

A 'UK company' is a company registered under the Companies Act 2006 (s 1183). Although reference is made throughout the Act, and in this book, to the registrar of companies, there are in fact three registrars (s 1060):

- the registrar for England and Wales
- the registrar for Scotland
- the registrar for Northern Ireland.

registered office

the address of the office of a company to which formal notices and legal documents should be addressed and sent

memorandum of association

the document which under predecessor companies acts set out the basic details of a company: name, place of incorporation, objects, liability of the members and authorised share capital but under the Companies Act 2006 is a shorter document containing the names of the initial subscribers for shares and their agreement to form a company

certificate of incorporation

the document issued by the registrar of companies on the registration of a company under the Companies Act 2006 or a predecessor statute

The intended location of the registered office of a UK company determines to which registrar the registration documents must be delivered (s 9(6)). England and Wales, Scotland and Northern Ireland are three different legal systems with separate court systems. The law of the jurisdiction in which the company is registered will govern the internal affairs of the company.

4.1.2 Registration requirements: general

A UK company is formed by one or more persons (which may be companies) subscribing their names to a memorandum of association and complying with the registration requirements contained in ss 9–13 of the Companies Act 2006. If the registrar of companies is satisfied the registration requirements of the Act have been complied with he *must* register the documents delivered to him and *must* issue a certificate that the company is incorporated (ss 14 and 15). A refusal by the registrar to register a company is subject to judicial review.

A company may not be formed for an unlawful purpose (s 7(2)), but as there is no longer a requirement to state the purpose or purposes for which a company is being incorporated (known as the company's 'objects', s 31(1)), in any of the documents delivered to the registrar when applying to register a company, it is unlikely that the registrar will have information to be in a position to enforce this provision by refusing to register a company.

A notorious case involving a company registered to run a brothel (*R v Registrar of Companies ex parte Attorney General Ltd* [1991] BCLC 476) established that even though s 15(4) states that a certificate of incorporation is conclusive evidence 'that the requirements of this Act as to registration have been complied with', a certificate of incorporation is *not* conclusive evidence that a company has been formed for a lawful purpose.

4.1.3 Registration requirements: submitting an application to register

The registration procedure is very simple and inexpensive. An application can be made electronically with the requisite forms and documents being 'delivered' to the registrar (Companies House) online and a certificate received within hours. An application to register a company must include the following (s 9):

1 **memorandum of association** in prescribed form (ss 7 and 8):
   - only one subscriber is required and there is no maximum
   - subscriber(s) agree to take at least one share (each)
   - subscribers express the wish to form a company and agree to become members
2 **articles of association**
   - articles are the internal rules of the company
   - if none are submitted, relevant Model Articles will apply
   - may (not must) contain a statement of objects (s 31)
   - if the articles contain an entrenched provision, notice of this must be given by the company to the registrar (s 23(1))
3 **application to register a company form (INO1)**, which states and includes:
   - the proposed company name
   - whether the proposed registered office is to be in England and Wales, Scotland or Northern Ireland
   - whether or not the liability of the members is to be limited and if so by shares or guarantee
   - whether the company is to be private (Limited/Ltd) or public (plc)
4 **statement of capital and initial shareholdings** (s 10) (unless the company is to be limited by guarantee, in which case a statement of guarantee is required, see s 11), which states:
   - number of shares to be taken on registration
   - total nominal value of those shares

- for each class:
  - prescribed particulars of rights attached to those shares
  - number of shares of that class
  - total nominal value of shares of that class
- amount to be paid up and amount unpaid on each share
- prescribed particulars to identify subscribers
- in relation to each subscriber:
  - number, nominal value and class of shares he is to take
  - amount to be paid up and amount unpaid on each share
- the statement of capital must be updated each time the capital is altered, for example, if additional shares are allotted

5 **statement of proposed registered address**
6 **statement of proposed officers** (s 12)
  - proposed **directors**' particulars including residential address
  - proposed **secretary**'s particulars (if company is to have one)
7 **statement of compliance** that the registration requirements have been complied with (s 13)
8 **fee** (£13–£100 depending upon the mode of registration and whether or not same-day registration is required).

4.2 Specialist company formation companies

Rather than dealing with Companies House directly, specialist company registration businesses can be found online offering to register companies on behalf of those seeking to set up a registered company (the incorporators). The key benefits of obtaining a company from a company registration business are simplicity and the saving of the time that would otherwise be taken familiarising oneself with the process and gathering together and completing the relevant information and forms.

The main shortcoming of companies obtained from a company registration business, and of self-registered companies, is that the constitution of the company, the articles of association will not be *fully* made to order or 'bespoked' to the needs of the incorporators. In many cases no attempt to reflect the wishes of the incorporators in the articles of association is made at all. Nonetheless, the Company Law Review Steering Committee Group estimated in 2000 that approximately 60 per cent of companies being registered were registered by specialist company formation companies and there is every likelihood that this percentage has increased in the last decade and will continue to increase in the future.

4.3 Company numbers and names

tutor tip

'A company's name may change but its number cannot which is why it is good practice to include a company's number as well as its name in legal documents'

When a company is registered it is given a registered number, often called the company number (s 1066). This number appears on the certificate of incorporation and the register of companies. During its continued existence a company may change its name. A company's company number, however, never changes. When a company is registered, or a change of name is sought, the proposed name must comply with the Companies Act 2006. The company's name appears on the certificate of incorporation.

4.3.1 Company numbers

It can be very difficult to know which company entered into an agreement if, after entering into the agreement, the company changes its name. It is particularly confusing where a company's name is changed and its old name is given to a new company. An old agreement may appear to have been entered into by the new company when in fact it was entered into by the company that previously had that name. This is not an academic issue; it occurs frequently in practice and causes problems.

Identification difficulty can be avoided by including the company number as part of the identification of a company, rather than relying on referring to a company by its name. In the example given, if the old agreement stated the company number of the company that had entered into it, it would be clear that the new company, albeit having the same company name, is a different company because it has a different company number. Unfortunately, not all jurisdictions have this benefit. Companies registered in Delaware, the most popular state in which to incorporate in the USA, for example, do not have unique company numbers.

4.3.2 Company names

The law governing company names is contained in Pt 5 of the Companies Act 2006. A company sometimes trades using a business name different from its company name. A company with the company name Gas Appliances Limited, for example, may trade under the name 'Flames For You' which is its business name. Rules governing business names are contained in Pt 41 of the Companies Act 2006. The rules, which replace the Business Names Act 1985, apply not only to companies but to any person carrying on business in the UK.

The legal issues in relation to company names and company business names fall into four categories:

- limits on company names
- procedure for changing a company name
- trading disclosures
- regulation of business names (Pt 41).

Choosing a company name: limits on company names

The Companies Act 2006 provisions allow:

- the registrar of companies to refuse to register certain company names;
- the Secretary of State to direct that a company name be changed in certain circumstances;
- a company names adjudicator to order that a company name be changed, on the successful application by a person with goodwill.

These provisions need to be taken into account when choosing a company name when both registering a company and changing the name of an existing company. The detailed rights of the registrar and the Secretary of State are contained in The Company and Business Names (Miscellaneous Provisions) Regulations 2009 (SI 2009/1085), referred to as the CBN(MP) Regulations 2009. The main points are summarised in Tables 4.1 and 4.2 below. The rights of a person with goodwill are considered in the paragraphs following the tables.

Registrar of companies' rights to refuse to register a name

Prohibited names (s 53)

A company must not be registered by a name if, in the opinion of the Secretary of State, its use would constitute an offence or it is offensive.

Approval of names by the Secretary of State (SS) (ss 54 and 55)

A company will not be registered with a name that:

(i) would be likely to give the impression that the company is connected with Her Majesty's Government, a local authority or any public authority specified in the The Company, Limited Liability Partnership and Business names (Sensitive Words and Expressions) Regulations 2009 (SI 2009/2615) (these regulation replace the Company and Business Names Regulations 1981 (as amended)); or

(ii) includes a sensitive word or expression listed in those regulations unless evidence is produced that the name has been approved by the SS.

Example:

'NHS Pottery Services Limited' will not be registered without the approval of the SS who will not consider the request for approval unless provided with the reply from the Department of Health to a request in writing seeking its views.

Registrar of companies' rights to refuse to register a name
Prohibited characters (s 57) A company may not be registered by a name that includes any characters, signs, symbol or punctuation, or the placing or number thereof, that is not permitted by the CBN(MP) Regulations 2009 (see reg 2 and Sched 1). **Example:** '*Burst Limited' will not be registered because '*' cannot be used as one of the first three characters.
Indications of company type or legal form by limited companies (ss 58–64) A company name must indicate the type of company it is, in a manner provided for in the Act. **Examples:** The name of a private limited company that is not a cic, Welsh or exempt must end with 'limited' or 'ltd'. The name of a public limited company that is not a cic or Welsh must end with 'public limited company' or 'plc'.
Inappropriate use of indications of company type or form (s 65) A company must not be registered by a name that includes specified words, expressions or other indications associated with a particular type of company or form of organisation or words similar thereto prohibited by the SS in the CBN(MP) Regulations 2009 (see regs 4-6). **Example:** An unlimited company must not have a name that ends with the word 'limited'. **Names the same as the name of an existing company (s 66)** The registrar of companies will not register a company with a name that is the same as a name on the company register. The Companies Act 2006 and CBN(MP) Regulations 2009 contain guidance as to how the registrar will approach deciding whether or not one name is the same as another for these purposes and provisions to ensure that trivial difference between names will be ignored by the registrar of companies when deciding whether or not a name is 'the same as' a name on the company register (see reg 7 and Sched 3). **Example:** The proposed name 'Sands Co Public Limited Company' will not be registered if there is an existing company named 'S and S plc'. This is because gaps are ignored for the purposes of comparison, so 'S and S' is regarded as the same as 'sands', 'Co' is ignored, and 'plc' is equivalent to 'Public Limited Company'. Note that reg 8 of the CBN(MP) Regulations 2009 allows for a company to be registered with a name that would otherwise be prohibited by s 66 if the existing company consents *and* is part of the same corporate group as the company whose name is being registered or changed.

Table 4.1 Registrar of companies' rights to refuse to register a name

Secretary of State's rights to direct that a name be changed
Company ceasing to be entitled to an exemption from the requirement to end its name with 'limited' (s 64) If it appears to the Secretary of State that a company whose name does not include 'limited' or any of the permitted alternatives has ceased to be entitled to an exemption, he may direct the company to change its name so that it ends with 'limited' or one of the permitted alternatives.
Names the same as or similar to the name of an existing company (ss 67 and 68) The Secretary of State may direct a company to change its name if it has been registered in a name that is the same as or, in the opinion of the Secretary of State, too like an existing company name. Such direction must be given within 12 months of registration by the name in question.

Secretary of State's rights to direct that a name be changed
Misleading information given for the purposes of a company's registration with a particular name (s 75)
If it appears to the Secretary of State that misleading information has been given for the purposes of a company's registration by a particular name, or that an undertaking or assurance has been given for that purpose and has not been fulfilled, the Secretary of State may direct the company to change its name. Such a direction must be given within five years of the company's registration by the name in question.
Misleading indication of activities (s 76)
If in the opinion of the Secretary of State the name by which a company is registered gives so misleading an indication of the nature of its activities as to be likely to cause harm to the public, the Secretary of State may direct the company to change its name.

Table 4.2 Secretary of State's rights to direct that a name be changed

In addition to company law considerations, it is important to choose a company name that will not leave the company open to challenge based on the argument that the conduct of business under that name infringes the intellectual property rights of another person. These rights include, though they may not be limited to, the right to bring an action for infringement of a registered trade mark and the right of a trader to bring a tort action for passing-off.

Passing off

passing off

a common law tort actionable by a claimant who is the owner of goodwill (sometimes referred to as an unregistered trade mark or reputation attached to a good or service) when another person has made a misrepresentation which leads or is likely to lead to its product or service being associated with the claimant thereby deceiving the public and resulting in damage to the goodwill of the claimant

A passing off action may be brought against any person who misrepresents to the public that the goods or services it, the misrepresenting person, is providing, are associated with the claimant trader, thereby causing damage to the claimant trader. The claimant trader must demonstrate that it has goodwill that has been damaged by the misrepresentation (see *Erwen Warnick B V v J Townend & Sons (Hull) Ltd* [1979] AC 731, *per* Lord Fraser at 742 (HL)). Goodwill refers to all those attributes of a business that attract and retain customers that are not accounted for elsewhere. Goodwill is an intangible asset of a business that can be bought and sold (see section 4.5 below, transferring a business to a company). Merely calling a company a name can never amount to passing off.

Objection to a name, based on goodwill

The legal protection given to the owner of goodwill has been enhanced, on the recommendation of the Company Law Review, by the introduction of ss 69–74 of the Companies Act 2006. The Companies Act provisions are in addition to, and complement, the tort of passing off. They provide for a person with goodwill (s 69) to apply to a company names adjudicator for an order that a company name be changed (s 73). The details are contained in the Company Names Adjudicator Rules 2008 (SI 2008/1738).

The applicant must establish that the respondent company's name is the same as a name associated with the applicant in which it has goodwill, or is so sufficiently similar to such a name that its use would be likely to mislead by suggesting a connection between the respondent company and the applicant. The concept of 'goodwill' is extended for the purposes of such an application, being defined in s 69(7) to include 'reputation of any description'. There is no time limit on the making of an application which could but, as the following comments suggest, is unlikely to be made years after a company has been registered with a particular name.

The provisions are intended to catch only those cases in which the company name has been chosen to exploit another's reputation or goodwill, in other words, to provide a remedy where there has been opportunistic registration. Consequently, the provisions have been drawn very narrowly and an objection cannot be upheld, and no order that a company name be changed can be made, if the respondent company establishes any one of the following five defences:

1 that the name was registered before the commencement of the activities on which the applicant relies to show goodwill;

2 that the respondent company:
- is operating under the name; or
- is proposing to do so and has incurred substantial start-up costs in preparation; or
- was formerly operating under the name and is now dormant;

3 that the name was registered in the ordinary course of a company formation business and the company is available for sale to the applicant on the standard terms of that business;

4 that the name was adopted in good faith;

5 that the interests of the applicant are not adversely affected to any significant extent.

Any decision of a company names adjudicator may be appealed to the court (s 74).

Procedure to change a company name

A company may change its name by the following process (ss 77–81):

1 The company:
- passes a special resolution;
- forwards a copy of the resolution to the registrar of companies;
- gives notice of change of name to the registrar of companies.

2 The registrar:
- satisfies himself that:
  - the new name complies with the requirements of the Act; and
  - the other requirements of the Act have been complied with;
- enters the new name on the register of companies in place of the old name;
- issues a new certificate of incorporation.

The change of name has effect from the date on which the new certificate is issued (s 81). If the articles provide another means by which the company's name can be changed, that means is substituted for the special resolution in the process above. There are special provisions to accommodate a change of name directed or ordered by the Secretary of State, a company names adjudicator or the court (s 77).

Trading disclosures

The trading disclosures required by regulations made pursuant to ss 82 and 84 of the Companies Act 2006 extend beyond the obligation to disclose the company name in specified locations. All information mandated by The Companies (Trading Disclosures) Regulations 2008 (SI 2008/495) (as amended) must be readable by the naked eye (reg 2).

Basically, a company is required to:

1 display its company name, so that the name may be easily seen by any visitor (regs 3–5), at:
- its registered office;
- any place where it keeps company records;
- any place at which it carries on business.

2 disclose its company name on (reg 6):
- its websites;
- its business letters, notices and other official publications;
- its bills of exchange, promissory notes, endorsements and order forms;
- cheques purporting to be signed by or on behalf of the company:
  - orders for money, goods or services purporting to be signed by or on behalf of the company;
  - its bills of parcels, invoices and other demands for payment, receipts and letters of credit;
  - its applications for licences to carry on a trade or activity;
  - all other forms of its business correspondence and documentation.

3 disclose the part of the UK in which the company is registered, the company's registered number and the address of the company's registered office and ensure that any share capital referred to (which is optional) is paid-up share capital (reg 7) on:

- its websites;
- its business letters;
- its order forms.

Additionally, where a company's business letter includes the name of any director of that company, other than in the text or as a signatory, the letter must disclose the name of every director of that company (reg 8). Finally, a company must reply within five working days of a request from any person it deals with in the course of business, disclosing the address of its registered office and the place at which its records can be inspected (reg 9).

If a company fails, without reasonable excuse, to comply with any of the above requirements, an offence is committed by both the company and every officer of the company in default. Any person guilty of an offence is liable on summary conviction to a fine and, for continued contravention, a daily default fine (reg 10).

Business names used by companies

A business name is a name used in the course of carrying on a business. Just as a sole trader may carry on business under his own name or a name different from his personal name and a partnership may trade under the names of the partners or a name different from the names of the partners, so a company may trade under its company name or a different name. Although business names are not registered with any government department, business name laws must be adhered to.

The Companies Act 2006 (Pt 41 (ss 1192–1208)) governs business names used by both registered companies and in relation to businesses not carried on by registered companies. The relevant provisions replace the Business Names Act 1985 and regulations made thereunder. For non-company businesses (only) these rules extend beyond regulating the choice of name to requiring certain trading disclosures (see ss 1200–1206).

Chapter 1 of Pt 41 of the 2006 Act (ss 1192–1199) applies to registered companies. Basically, a company may not, without the approval of the Secretary of State, use a business name:

- suggesting connection with the government or a public authority (s 1193);
- that includes a sensitive word as listed from time to time in regulations (s 1194);
- inappropriately suggesting that the company is a particular type of company or has a particular legal form (s 1197); or
- giving a misleading indication of the nature of the activities conducted so as to be likely to cause harm to the public (s 1198).

The first two bullet points mirror the requirement to obtain approval before a company could be registered with the name in question (see ss 54 and 55) and the third and fourth bullet points complement ss 58, 59 and 76 regulating registrable names. Sections 54, 55, 58, 59 and 76 are covered in Tables 4.1 and 4.2 above.

4.3.3 Names and the phoenix syndrome

The phoenix syndrome describes the setting up of a company with a similar name to, and running essentially the same business that had been run by, a company that has gone into insolvent liquidation having run up significant debts, and its assets having been transferred to the second company. The imagery is of a new company arising out of the flames of its financially burnt-out predecessor. Businessmen who engage in this behaviour have little respect for the creditors (including consumers) of the companies they sequentially set up and abandon and are said to exploit the privileges of limited liability.

The law has responded to this phenomenon in a number of ways. Part of the response has been s 216 of the Insolvency Act 1986 which prohibits a person who was a director of

phoenix company

a new company formed with a name the same as or similar to that of a company that has gone into insolvent liquidation having the same director(s) as the failed company and running essentially the same business that had been run by the failed company the assets of which have been transferred to the second company a company that has gone into insolvent liquidation from being a director of or otherwise being involved in the following five years in the management of a company or a business with a prohibited name, which is a name so similar to the name by which the insolvent company was known as to suggest an association with the insolvent company. The name by which a company is or was known for these purposes may be either its company name or its business name. Mummery LJ in *Ad Valorem Factors Ltd v Ricketts* [2004] 1 All ER 894 (CA) gave guidance as to how a court will go about deciding whether or not a name is a prohibited name for s 216 purposes.

JUDGMENT

'It is necessary, of course, to make a comparison of the names of the two companies in the context of all the circumstances in which they were actually used or likely to be used: the types of product dealt in, the locations of the business, the types of customers dealing with the companies and those involved in the operations of the two companies.'

A person who contravenes s 216 is criminally liable and may be imprisoned or fined or both. Section 217 renders the director personally liable, jointly and severally with the company, for all the debts and liabilities of the new company or business incurred whilst he was involved with it in contravention of s 216.

CASE EXAMPLE

Ad Valorem Factors Ltd v Ricketts [2004] 1 All ER 894 (CA)

The defendant had been a director of Air Component Co Ltd, which had gone into insolvent liquidation. He was then a director of Air Equipment Co Ltd and it also went into insolvent liquidation. An assignee of a debt owed to Air Equipment Co Ltd sought to recover the debt from the defendant on the basis that the name of the second company was a prohibited name within s 216 of the Insolvency Act 1986 and that therefore the defendant was personally liable for the debts of the second company pursuant to s 217. Held: The second company name was so similar to the name by which the insolvent company was known as to suggest an association with the first company and was therefore a prohibited name. That being the conclusion, the court had no discretion to exercise and the director was personally liable for the debts of the second company. This was so even if the second company was not a 'phoenix syndrome' case.

Sections 216 and 217 are drafted to apply broadly. They impose personal liability notwithstanding the circumstances in question do not amount to a morally culpable 'phoenix syndrome' scenario. Customers do not have to have been deceived or misled nor is it necessary to show that assets have been transferred between the relevant companies. Arguments that the sections should be given a purposive interpretation to narrow their range of application were rejected by the Court of Appeal in *Ad Valorem Factors Ltd v Ricketts* [2004] 1 All ER 894 (CA), a case that has been applied in a number of subsequent cases not involving phoenix syndrome companies. Lewison J, for example, relied on *Ad Valorem Factors Ltd v Ricketts* in *First Independent Factors and Finance Ltd v Mountford* [2008] 2 BCLC 297.

JUDGMENT

'In my judgment it is not a permissible method of interpreting the rule to allow the ill-defined metaphorical idea of a "phoenix" to distort the meaning of the rule. As the Court of Appeal pointed out in *Ricketts v Ad Valorem Factors Ltd*, the statute … should not be given a distorted interpretation in order to confine it to "phoenix cases".'

4.4 Promoters

The term 'promoter' is used to describe a person involved in setting up a company who is not purely providing professional or administrative services (such as a solicitor or an accountant) to those who are setting up the company (the incorporators). As Bowen LJ stated in *Whaley Bridge Calico Printing v Green* (1879) 5 QBD 109, 'promoter' is not a term of law but one of business. Continuing, he stated that a promoter is a term 'usefully summing up in a single word a number of business operations familiar to the commercial world by which a company is generally brought into existence'.

A promoter is not necessarily involved in all stages of, or in all the tasks performed in, setting up a company and a promoter's role will vary with each individual project. Typical acts of a promoter are:

- raising the idea of forming a company for the purpose in question
- soliciting the interest of others
- finding directors, shareholders and other investors
- acquiring business assets for use by the new company
- negotiating business contracts on behalf of the new company.

The words of Cockburn CJ, in *Twycross v Grant* (1877), are often quoted to describe a promoter:

JUDGMENT

'[O]ne who undertakes to form a company with reference to a given project and to set it going and who takes the necessary steps to accomplish that purpose … and so long as the work of formation continues, those who carry on that work must, I think, retain the character of promoters.'

In law, it is important to know whether or not a person is a promoter, and the points in time at which he first became and ceased to be a promoter, because the law regards a promoter as a fiduciary who owes duties of loyalty and good faith to the promoted company. That said, there are no modern cases about the duties of promoters and this may be because detailed securities regulations, including the Prospectus Rules, have resulted in the fiduciary duties of promoters no longer playing an important role in protecting prospective investors in companies.

Older cases often involved one or more promoters personally acquiring property with a view to, and subsequently, selling that property, at a substantial profit, to the company they had promoted. Any profit made by promoters in this way is made as a result of their position as fiduciaries and, paralleling the position of trustees, is a breach of fiduciary duty unless the arrangements have been fully disclosed to, and consent has been obtained from, the 'beneficiary'. The difficulties the courts faced applying this basic fiduciary principle to promoters were in deciding what constituted full disclosure and whose consent was needed in the context of a newly formed company with a board of directors, initial shareholders (the subscribers to the memorandum who were often the promoters themselves) and additional shareholders who had joined the company as the result of shares being offered to the public by the issuing of a prospectus.

The courts found that if there was a board of directors independent from the promoters, the promoters could disclose their interest to the board and the board could decide on behalf of the company whether or not to purchase the promoters' property. Provided this happened, there was no breach of fiduciary duty by the promoters.

CASE EXAMPLE

Erlanger v New Sombrero Phosphate Company (1878) 3 App Cas 1218 (HL)

The lease of a West Indies island was acquired for £55,000 by a syndicate of bankers headed by Erlanger. The lease was sold for £110,000, through a nominee company, to a company promoted by Erlanger. The purchase of the lease was 'ratified' without enquiry at a board meeting of the newly formed company at which not all directors were present and only one director was independent of Erlanger. The public subscribed for shares without the real circumstances of the sale being disclosed to them. The sale of the lease was approved (without proper disclosure) at the first shareholders' meeting. The company's business went badly, the true facts were discovered, the original directors were removed and the new directors brought legal proceedings to have the sale of the lease to the company rescinded. Held: The contract should be set aside with an order for members of the syndicate to repay the purchase monies.

JUDGMENT

Lord Cairns stated '[I]t is … incumbent upon the promoters to take care that in forming the company they provide it with an executive, that is, to say, with a board of directors, who shall both be aware that the property which they are asked to buy is the property of the promoters, and who shall be competent and impartial judges as to whether the purchase ought or ought not to be made. I do not say that the owner of the property may not promote and form a … company, and then sell his property to it, but I do say that if he does he is bound that he sells it to the company through the medium of a board of directors who can and do exercise an independent judgment on the transaction and who are not left under the belief that the property belongs not to the promoter but to some other person.'

Where, as was often the case, there was no board of directors independent of the promoters, the promoters needed to make disclosure to the shareholders and secure their consent but this worked only if the shareholders were independent of the promoters. Full disclosure of the arrangements in a prospectus, so that any shareholder who decided to invest in the company did so with knowledge of the arrangements, was found to be enough to prevent a breach of fiduciary duty.

CASE EXAMPLE

Lagunas Nitrate Co v Lagunas Syndicate [1899] 2 Ch 392

Two promoters were the only directors of a company and the first two shareholders (subscribers to the memorandum). The company therefore did not have an independent board. A prospectus was published inviting members of the public to take shares in the company in which the interest of the promoters in the property they had sold to the company was made clear. The Court of Appeal held that there was no breach of fiduciary duty because there had been adequate disclosure.

The point in time at which a promoter acquires property that he subsequently sells to the company is relevant. If he acquires property *before* becoming a promoter and subsequently sells the property to a company he has promoted, the rights of the company are not wholly clear from the cases. If the promoter has not disclosed his interest, the company can rescind the contract. Where rescission is not possible, however (perhaps because the property cannot be returned to the promoter), the promoter is apparently *not* liable to account to the company for any profit he has made on the sale (*Re Lady Forrest (Murchison) Gold Mine Ltd* [1901] 1 Ch 582). Whether or not the company can claim equitable compensation to recoup its losses from the promoter is not clear. Conaglen (2003) argues that the promoter will be liable to pay equitable compensation.

4.5 Transferring a business to a company

It is very common for a company to be registered for the specific purpose of acquiring an already existing business that is being run by a sole trader or a partnership. In *Salomon*, for example, Mr Salomon sold the boot and shoe manufacturing business he had been carrying on as a sole trader to a company formed to acquire it. It is essential to understand that 'the business' is something separate from the entity running the business. In legal terms, the business is a bundle of assets, contract rights and liabilities.

A business sale contract, describing the business, will be entered into between the company (the buyer) and the seller (the sole trader, etc). Pursuant to that contract, legal title to the business property will be transferred to the company by complying with the formalities necessary to transfer each particular type of property (land, assets (choses in possession) different types of choses in action (rights under contracts, debts, different types of intellectual property etc). Legal transfer of liabilities is more difficult and liabilities are often left with the seller, or assigned in equity to the company with the company agreeing to indemnify the seller against any costs it incurs should it, rather than the company, be pursued and have to satisfy a business liability.

The difference between the net asset value of the business (that is, the sum of the business assets less the liabilities of the business to be assumed by the buyer) and the purchase price paid for the business, is called 'goodwill'. The value of the goodwill associated with a business that is sold as a 'going concern' (that is, when there is no break in trading) is often very significant.

The seller is often the principal, if not the sole, shareholder of the new company/buyer. The purchase price for the business is rarely paid to the seller in cash by the new company as the new company will usually have no, or very little, money, only its initial paid-up share capital. The seller will typically receive a mixture of shares and loan notes equivalent in value to the purchase price for the business. This will make the seller both a major shareholder and a financial creditor of the company. The loan notes are liabilities of the company; they are debts owed by the company to the seller. The value of the shares held by the seller will be, basically, the difference between the purchase price and the debts. If, as is usual, this value exceeds the nominal value of the shares, the shares will be treated as if they have been issued at a premium. If this paragraph is confusing, do not worry. Once you have read Chapter 7 on shareholders, shares and share capital, you will be better placed to understand the difference between the nominal value of a share, the paid-up value of a share and the market value of a share.

4.6 Pre-incorporation contracts

4.6.1 What is a pre-incorporation contract?

A pre-incorporation contract is a contract to which a company appears to be a party that has been entered into before the company has been registered. It is a contract made before the company exists.

Agency law, a combination of common law and equity, governed the rights of those involved in a pre-incorporation contract situation before EU law required the UK to legislate to change the law. Agency law stated that:

1 An agent cannot bind a non-existent principal.
2 If the company did not exist at the time a contract is entered into, the contract is not binding on the subsequently formed company.
3 A person who purports to contract on behalf of a non-existent company may or may not:
   - be personally liable pursuant to the contract;
   - have rights to sue the other party to the contract.
4 Whether or not a person is liable or has rights depends upon the real intent as revealed by the contract, that is, the correct construction of the contract. In the words of Oliver

LJ, 'what we have to look at is whether the agent intended himself to be a party to the contract?' (*Phonogram Ltd v Lane* [1982] QB 938 (CA) at 945, approved in *Cotronic (UK) Ltd v Dezonie* [1991] BCC 200).

5   The real intent was often ascertained based on the way in which the contract had been signed so that if the contract was signed 'on behalf of' a company, the person signing would usually be personally liable (see *Kelner v Baxter* (1866–67) LR 2 CP 174). If, however, the contract was signed as if the signatory was the company, such as a signature appearing above the printed company name, the signatory would not usually be liable (see *Newborne v Sensolid* [1954] 1 QB 45).

6   If the person is not personally liable under the contract, the third party may be able to sue him or her for breach of warranty of authority.

These rules involved fine distinctions being drawn and did not provide much protection to a third party who believed that he was contracting with the company. The law has been amended by what is now s 51 of the Companies Act 2006, the predecessor provision of which was introduced to implement Art 7 of the First Company Law Directive (68/151/EEC). The Directive and s 51 focus on protection of the third party.

SECTION

's 51(1)
A contract that purports to be made by or on behalf of a company at a time when the company has not been formed has effect, *subject to any agreement to the contrary,* as one made with the person purporting to act for the company or as agent for it, and *he is personally liable on the contract* accordingly.' (emphasis added)

4.6.2 What is meant by 'subject to any agreement to the contrary'?

Section 51 states that the person purporting to act for, or as agent of, the company is personally liable on the contract unless there is any agreement to the contrary. The meaning of these words was considered in a case involving the pop group Cheap, Mean and Nasty.

CASE EXAMPLE

Phonogram Ltd v Lane [1982] QB 938 (CA)

Lane negotiated with a record company, Phonogram Limited, to obtain a recording deal for the pop group Cheap Mean and Nasty. He signed a contract with Phonogram Limited which provided for an advance of £6,000. He signed the contract 'for and on behalf of Fragile Management Limited'. The sum advanced became repayable and Phonogram Limited discovered that Fragile Management Limited had never existed. It sued Lane to recover the money, relying on the predecessor section to what is now s 51 of the Companies Act 2006. Held: Lane was ordered to repay the money.

In the course of his judgment Lord Denning MR gave the words 'subject to any agreement to the contrary' a very narrow meaning.

JUDGMENT

'If there was an express agreement that the man who was signing was not to be liable, the section would not apply. But unless there is a clear exclusion of personal liability [s 51(1)] should be given its full effect. It means that … where a person purports to contract on behalf of a company not yet formed, then however he expresses his signature he himself is personally liable on the contract.'

4.6.3 Can the person made liable by s 51 enforce the contract?

Section 51(1) states that the person who purports to enter into the contract *'is personally liable on the contract'* which, it has been argued, implies that the person cannot enforce the agreement. This interpretation of the statutory provision was rejected by Arden LJ in *Braymist Ltd v Wise Finance Co Ltd* [2002] Ch 273 (CA) in a judgment that examined the correct approach to the interpretation of 'domestic directive-based legislation'.

CASE EXAMPLE

Braymist Ltd v Wise Finance Co Ltd [2002] Ch 273 (CA)

A firm of solicitors, Sturges, signed a contract as agents on behalf of an as yet unregistered company, Braymist Ltd. The contract was an agreement for Braymist to sell land to Wise, a property developer. Wise changed its mind and did not want to perform the contract. Sturges sued to enforce the contract. Held: Sturges was entitled to enforce the contract against Wise. Parliament did not intend to determine the rules and it is the common law rules that apply to determine whether a person who is *made liable* on a contract by (what is now) s 51 is entitled to *enforce* the contract.

JUDGMENT

'[A]s I see it, the purpose of [s 51] was limited to: (i) complying with the UK treaty obligations to implement art 7 of the Directive, (ii) removing the possibility that the agent would be held not liable on the ground that he merely confirmed the company's signature, and (iii) putting such persons or agents in the same position as regards the enforcement of the contract as they would be at common law and in particular (in the case of agents) this is the same position as agents who contracted as agents.'

4.6.4 Can a company ratify or adopt a pre-incorporation contract?

A company cannot unilaterally, by adoption or ratification, obtain the benefit of a contract purporting to have been made on its behalf before the company came into existence.

CASE EXAMPLE

Re Northumberland Avenue Hotel Co (1866) 33 Ch D 16 (CA)

Doyle, acting as agent for a hotel company, entered into an agreement with Wallis to lease certain property and build on it. The company was not incorporated until after the contract had been entered into. The articles of the company purported to adopt the contract, the company took possession of the land, and the company assumed that the contract was an existing and binding contract. The building was not completed, the company went into liquidation and Wallis claimed in the liquidation. Held: The contract did not bind the company.

JUDGMENT

Lopes LJ stated, 'It is ... clear that the company, after it came into existence, could not ratify that contract, because the company was not in existence at the time the contract was made. No doubt the company, after it came into existence, might have entered into a new contract upon the same terms as the agreement ... and we are asked to infer such a contract from the conduct and transactions of the company after it came into existence.'

This inability to ratify a pre-incorporation contract has been reversed in a number of common-law jurisdictions but remains law in England, notwithstanding recommendations by the Jenkins Committee (Cmnd 1749, 1962) that it be reversed.

Note that if an off the shelf company is in existence at the time a contract was entered into, that company can ratify the contract and the signatory will not be liable pursuant to s 51, *provided*, however, there is evidence that the off the shelf company was the company that was intended to be a party to the contract (see *Oshkosh B'Gosh Inc v Dan Marbel Inc Ltd* [1989] BCLC 507).

4.6.5 How can a company become a party to a pre-incorporation contract?

The answer to how a company can become a party to a pre-incorporation contract is found in *Braymist*:

JUDGMENT

'The United Kingdom's implementation of article 7 makes no reference to the possibility of the company enforcing the contract when it has been formed. Since so far as it was concerned the contract was a nullity it could only do this by entering into a contract of novation with the agent.'

Novation is a tripartite transaction in which the parties to the original agreement, together with the company, enter into a *new* agreement. Novation is usually achieved by all three parties signing a formal document. It is possible, however, for a new agreement to be found to exist based on evidence of conduct such as changes to the contract having been agreed to by the company and the third party, such that the court is able to say that a new contract has come into existence, as was found in *Howard v Patent Ivory Manufacturing Co* (1888) 38 Ch D 156. Such instances are rare, however, and the difficulty of establishing novation of a pre-incorporation contract by conduct can be seen from the decision of the Privy Council in *Natal Land Co & Colonization Ltd v Pauline Colliery and Development Syndicate Ltd* [1964] AC 120 (PC).

4.7 Re-registration of a company

The status of a registered company as a public or private company and as a limited or unlimited company can be altered by re-registration under Pt 7 (ss 89–111) of the Companies Act 2006. Alteration from private to public and *vice versa* are commented on in this section. The relevant provisions differ very little from the predecessor provisions under the Companies Act 1985.

4.7.1 From private to public

Few companies are registered as public companies from the start. Most public companies begin life as a private company and are re-registered as a public company at a later date, usually to enable the company to offer shares to the public, something a private company is prohibited from doing by s 755. The first time a company offers shares to the public by floating on a stock exchange is called an IPO, an 'initial public offering'.

Re-registration as a public company is a relatively straightforward process (ss 90–96) but does require the company to involve its auditors. The involvement of the auditors is to ensure that the balance sheet gives a true and fair view of the company's financial position. Where, as is very common, a private company has received non-cash assets (such as a business – see section 4.5 above) in return for issuing shares, the auditor's report will confirm that the assets have been accounted for in accordance with the requirements of the Companies Act 2006.

A re-registration application is made by delivering to the registrar:

- A statement of the company's proposed name on re-registration.
- A statement of the proposed secretary (if the company does not already have one).
- A copy of the special resolution that has been passed that the company should be re-registered.
- A copy of the articles as proposed to be amended.
- A copy of the company's balance sheet together with an unqualified report by the company's auditors on the balance sheet, and a statement by the auditor that in his opinion at the balance sheet date the amount of the company's net assets was not less than the sum of its called-up share capital and undistributable reserves.
- A statement of compliance that the requirements as to re-registration have been complied with.

The requirements as to re-registration not reflected in the documents above compliance with which are confirmed by the statement of compliance are that:

1 At the time the special resolution is passed:
- the nominal value of the allotted share capital must not be less than the authorised minimum (£50,000); and
- each allotted share must be paid up at least as to one-quarter of the nominal value of the share and the whole of any premium.
2 Between the balance sheet date and the date on which the application for re-registration is delivered there must have been no change in the company's financial position that results in the amount of the company's net assets being less than the aggregate of its called-up share capital and undistributable reserves.

If the registrar is satisfied that the company is entitled to be re-registered, he must issue a certificate of incorporation reflecting the alteration (s 96(2)). Unlike companies registered in the first instance as public companies, the re-registered company does *not* need a trading certificate (s 761(1)). This is because the conditions for issuance of a trading certificate (that the nominal value of the allotted share capital is not less than the authorised minimum (£50,000) and each allotted share is paid up at least as to one-quarter of the nominal value of the share and the whole of any premium) are covered by the re-registration process (s 91).

4.7.2 From public to private

It is also common for a public company to be re-registered as a private company. One situation in which this may occur is in a reconstruction following a take-over in which a public company has been acquired and the new owner re-registers it as a private company. Re-registration may also be required because the share capital of a public company falls below the mandatory authorised minimum.

A less common but not unknown scenario for such a re-registration is where an entrepreneur has grown his company, taken it public, offered shares to the public, listed those shares on the stock exchange but retained a substantial shareholding himself. He may then decide that he/the company (for he may not distinguish between the two in his mind quite to the extent required by law) is too constrained by the rigours of securities regulations and market forces and take the company private again.

Richard Branson is an example. Virgin Group Limited is now a private company. The company was registered as a plc and floated on the stock market in 1986. Its shares were removed from listing two years later and it was changed from a plc to a private company. The term 'take private' is not always used technically and does not necessarily mean that a public company has been re-registered as a private company; it is sometimes used to mean that the company no longer has shares listed on a stock exchange.

Re-registration of a public company as a private company is governed by ss 97–101. The process is straightforward unless one or more minority shareholders object. As for re-registration from private to public, a special resolution that the company should be re-registered is needed. Most companies with their registered office and place of central management and control in the UK are subject to the protections of the City Code on Takeovers and Mergers. When such a company is being taken private, shareholders need to be informed, before voting on the resolution, of the protections they will be giving up by agreeing to the company's re-registration and the Code Executive should be consulted on this. The articles need to be amended and copies of the proposed articles and the special resolution, together with a statement of compliance as to the requirements of re-registration, need to be sent to the registrar who, provided he is satisfied that the company is entitled to be re-registered, must re-register the company and issue an altered certificate of incorporation (s 96).

Shares of a private company are usually far more difficult to sell than shares in a public company, and this is certainly the case if the public company is a quoted company. For this reason, shareholders may object to a company being taken private. Shareholders who together hold at least 5 per cent of the nominal value of the company's shares or 50 or more shareholders, provided they have not voted in favour of the re-registration, may, within 28 days of it being passed, apply to court to cancel a re-registration resolution. The court may confirm or cancel the resolution and may do so 'on such terms as it thinks fit'. Section 98 provides no indication of the factors a court is to take into consideration when exercising its discretionary powers. Section 98(5) does, however, expressly provide that the court may provide that the company purchase the shares of the opposing minority shareholders, and this will resolve the problem going private presents for most minority shareholders.

KEY FACTS

Promoters and pre-incorporation contracts	
Promoters	
Defined: a business term used to describe a person involved in setting up a business who is not purely providing professional or administrative services.	
A promoter owes fiduciary duties to the company.	*Erlanger v New Sombrero* (1878)
Must disclose his interest in a company contract to the company.	*Lagunas Nitrate v Lagunas Syndicate* (1899)
Failure to disclose renders the agreement voidable. Whether or not the promoter must account for profits if contract cannot be rescinded is moot.	*Re Lady Forrest (Murchison) Gold Mine Ltd* (1901) suggests not
Common law and equitable duties have largely been superseded by securities regulation.	Financial Services and Markets Act 2000 Prospectus Rules
Pre-incorporation contracts	
Defined: a contract entered into before the company is registered/in existence.	
The company cannot be bound.	
The signatory purporting to act for the company is bound by the contract.	s 51
Unless there is a clear exclusion of personal liability.	*Phonogram Ltd v Lane* (1982)
The person made liable by s 51 may also *enforce* the contract.	*Braymist Ltd v Wise Finance Co Ltd* (2002)
A company may NOT become a party to a pre-incorporation contract by ratification.	*Re Northumberland Avenue Hotel Co Ltd* (1866)
A company may become a party to a pre-incorporation contract by novation.	*Howard v Patent Ivory* (1888)

SAMPLE ESSAY QUESTION

Explain the impact of section 51 of the Companies Act 2006 indicating how, if at all, the law might be improved.

Unpack the question

This is the first essential step which you must take time to do properly. You should separate out:

- Explaining the law before s 51/its predecessor was put in place: agency principles applied to promoters
- Explaining s 51
- Identifying the changes brought about by s 51
- Identifying any shortcomings in the operation of s 51
- Suggesting improvements to the law.

Agency principles applied to promoters

- An agent cannot act for a non-existent principal
- The company is not bound by a pre-incorporation contract: *Kelner v Baxter*
- The agent may or may not be bound: *Newborne v Sensolid; Kelner v Baxter*
- The test to determine is the agent bound is stated in *Phonogram Ltd v Lane*
- Pre-incorporation contract cannot be ratified: *Kelner v Baxter*
- Novation is required: *Howard v Patent Ivory Manufacturing Co.*

Section 51 and how it changed the common law position

- As the implementation of Article 7 of the First Company Law Directive (68/151/EEC) it is focused on protection of the third party
- The company is not bound but the agent is bound
- The agent can enforce the contract: *Braymist Ltd v Wise Finance Co Ltd*
- The language "subject to any agreement to the contrary" is interpreted narrowly: *Phonogram Ltd v Lane.*

Shortcomings of s 51 and improvements to the law

- The agent is not the intended party to the contract, the company is
- Permit ratification of pre-incorporation contracts (Recommended by Jenkins Committee 1962)
- Align the law more fully with Article 7 of the First EU Company Law Directive by making the company liable.

CONCLUDE

ACTIVITY

Applying the law

Darren, Erin and Chandra are partners in a successful beauty treatment practice. As they are planning to move to new, larger premises and employ two new people, they decide to set up a company to be called 'Beauty 4 U Limited'. Chandra signs a three-year lease for the new premises 'for and on behalf of Beauty 4 U Limited'. The lease states at clause 8: 'In no event whatsoever shall any person other than Beauty 4 U Limited be legally bound in any way or liable pursuant to this lease'. Beauty 4 U Limited is registered the day after the lease has been signed.

Advise Beauty 4 U Ltd and Chandra on their rights and liabilities under the lease. What, if any, steps would you advise them to take?

SUMMARY

Registering a UK company

- Companies are registered with the registrar of companies in Cardiff, Edinburgh or Belfast by submitting Form INO1, a Memorandum of Association and the relevant fee.
- On registration and issue of a certificate of incorporation by the Registrar of Companies an artificial person comes into existence.
- A company number is issued on registration and never changes.
- Company names are subject to detailed regulation.

Promoters

- Promoter: a business term used to describe a person involved in setting up a business who is not purely providing professional or administrative services.
- Promoter owes fiduciary duties to the company (*Erlanger v New Sombrero* (1878)); must disclose his interest in a company contract to the company (*Lagunas Nitrate v Lagunas Syndicate* (1899)).
- Failure to disclose renders the agreement voidable. Whether or not the promoter must account for profits if the contract cannot be rescinded is moot (*Re Lady Forrest (Murchison) Gold Mine Ltd* (1901) suggests not).
- Common law and equitable duties have largely been superseded by securities regulation (see Financial Services and Markets Act 2000 and the Prospectus Rules).

Pre-incorporation contracts

▪ Defined: a contract entered into before the company is registered/in existence.

▪ The company cannot be bound and the signatory purporting to act for the company is bound by the contract (s 51) unless there is a clear exclusion of personal liability (*Phonogram Ltd v Lane* (1982)).

▪ The person made liable by s 51 may also enforce the contract (*Braymist Ltd v Wise Finance Co Ltd* (2002)). A company may not become a party to a pre-incorporation contract by ratification (*Re Northumberland Avenue Hotel Co Ltd* (1866)).

▪ A company may become a party to a pre-incorporation contract by novation (*Howard v Patent Ivory* (1888)).

Re-registration of a company

Companies may re-register from private to public (and must do so before issuing shares to the public) and from public to private.

Further reading

Articles

Bourne, N, 'Pre-incorporation contracts' (2002) 28 Bus LR 110.

Cain, B, 'Company Names Adjudicator Rules' (2008) 32 CSR 25.

Conaglen, M, 'Equitable compensation for breach of fiduciary dealing rules' (2003) 119 LQR 246.

Francies, M, McLaughlin, C & Hardy, A, 'From public to private: changing direction' (2003) 14 PLC 21.

Mayer, T, 'Personal liability for trading in a prohibited name: sections 216–217 Insolvency Act 1986' (2006) 27 Comp Law 14.

Pennington, R, 'The Validation of Pre-Incorporation Contracts' (2002) 23(9) Comp Law 284.

Savirimuthu, J, 'Pre-incorporation contracts and the problem of corporate fundamentalism: are promoters proverbially profuse?' (2003) 24 Comp Law 196.

5

The constitution of the company

AIMS AND OBJECTIVES

After reading this chapter you should be able to:

- Identify the key documents making up the constitution of pre-2006 Act and post-2006 Act registered companies
- Explain the key respects in which a pre-2006 Act company's constitution differs from that of a post-2006 Act company
- Understand the historical importance of the *ultra vires* doctrine and objects clauses
- Appreciate the effect, enforceability and importance of shareholders' agreements
- Understand the role and importance of a company's articles of association
- Understand the role and relevance of the model articles
- Identify matters typically dealt with in a company's articles
- Understand the legal limitations on what may be included in articles
- Appreciate that the articles are a statutory contract and identify the unique characteristics of that contract
- Understand the legal problems and limits associated with enforcement of provisions of a company's articles
- Identify the statutory provisions governing amendment of a company's articles
- Discuss the court-developed restrictions on amendment of a company's articles
- Explain when articles will be implied as terms in contracts and the reasons why this may be necessary

5.1 What is the constitution of a company?

No comprehensive legal definition of the constitution of a company exists and the partial definition in s 17 of the Companies Act 2006 is not particularly helpful. The constitution is the company's governance system; the rules and principles prescribing how it is to function. This governance system is a combination of:

1 legal rules and principles found in statutes and case law (general company law); and
2 rules and principles adopted by members of the company contained in
   - the articles of association;
   - special resolutions;

- 'any resolution or agreement agreed to by all the members ... that, if not so agreed, would not have been effective for its purpose unless passed by a special resolution' (s 29).

Unfortunately, exactly which shareholder decisions and agreements fall into the final sub-bullet point is not clear. This is an important issue because all constitutional documents, decisions and agreements must be registered with the registrar of companies, are available for public scrutiny (s 30), and must be sent to a member on request (s 32) with criminal liability for the company and every officer in default arising in the event of non-compliance. Some shareholders' agreements fall within s 29 and therefore must be registered and some do not. Shareholders' agreements are discussed at section 5.7 below.

For the purposes of supplying members with copies, the meaning of constitutional documents is extended to include a current statement of capital (or, in the case of a company limited by guarantee, the statement of guarantee), and the current (as well as any past) certificate of incorporation (s 32).

Today, the most important constitutional document of a company is its articles of association. Before focusing on the articles, it is helpful to consider the background to the regime in the Companies Act 2006 and place the constitution of a company in context. In this chapter, first we look at pre-Companies Act 2006 constitutions and the effect the 2006 Act has had on the constitutions of companies in existence when the relevant provisions of the Act came into effect (1 October 2009). We then examine the articles in detail, followed by a look at the role played by shareholders' agreements that exist alongside the formal constitutional documents required by the Companies Acts.

5.2 Pre-Companies Act 2006 constitutions

There are a number of reasons why it is important to understand some of the key principles of company law relevant to company constitutions prior to the 2006 Act. Those reasons include:

- many company law cases, of continued relevance under the 2006 Act, are difficult to understand without a basic understanding of the concepts of the objects and capacity of a company and the doctrine of *ultra vires*; and
- most pre-2006 Act companies continue to have 'old-style memoranda of associations' and so it is important to know about these, their original role, and the effect the 2006 Act has had on the role they play.

5.3 The objects and capacity of a company

5.3.1 Pre-Companies Act 2006 companies

Old-style memoranda of association

The objects and capacity of a pre-Companies Act 2006 company are rooted in its memorandum of association which makes it important to consider the role and content of an 'old-style' memorandum of association. Until 1 October 2009, each company had an old-style memorandum which contained the fundamental information listed below. Provisions of a memorandum could only be amended in limited circumstances following specified procedures.

An old-style memorandum could be used to entrench one or more provisions of a company's constitution. Members could remove one or more provisions completely from the statutory power to amend, or render one or more provisions subject to a more restrictive amendment procedure than the statutory requirements. This was achieved by placing the relevant provision in the memorandum and stating either that it could not be amended, or, that it could be amended only if the specified procedure was gone through.

memorandum of association

the document which under predecessor companies acts set out the basic details of a company: name, place of incorporation, objects, liability of the members and authorised share capital but under the Companies Act 2006 is a shorter document containing the names of the initial subscribers for shares and their agreement to form a company

objects clause

the clause in an old style memorandum of association which sets out the business(es) the company proposes to carry on. Under the Companies Act 2006, the objects clause of pre-2006 Act companies has become a provision of the articles of association. A company incorporated under the 2006 Act may but need not have an objects clause in its articles

ultra vires

the expression used to refer to a transaction entered into by a company that is beyond its legal capacity (historically, outside the scope of its objects clause). In this strict sense, *ultra vires* has been abolished in relation to non-charitable registered Companies. Sometimes used to refer to a transaction beyond the powers of the directors, which use is best avoided

The mandatory provisions of an old-style memorandum of a company limited by shares (Companies Act 1985, s 2) were:

- The company name.
- If the company was to be registered as a public company, this fact had to be stated.
- Whether the registered office was to be in England, Wales or Scotland.
- The company's objects.
- That the liability of the members was limited.
- The share capital and how it was divided into shares of fixed amount.
- The names and addresses of each of the subscribers (the first members of the company) and the number of shares each agreed to acquire on registration.

Objects, capacity and the *ultra vires* doctrine

Companies registered under a pre-2006 Act companies act (ie, registered prior to 1 October 2009), had to be registered to pursue one or more 'objects' or types of business. A pre-2006 Act company's object or objects were set out in the objects clause of the company's old-style memorandum of association. Traditionally, the object of a company would be specific, such as 'to operate a railway'.

The rationale for requiring a registered company to state its object or objects was to ensure that members and creditors of the company were clearly informed of the line of business the company had been formed to pursue. Before the landmark decision of the House of Lords in *Ashbury Carriage and Iron Company Ltd v Riche* (1875) LR 7 HL 653, the *legal* effect of stating objects in the memorandum of a registered company was not clear. It was unclear whether a registered company had the legal capacity of a natural person (essentially unlimited capacity), or a more limited legal capacity, namely the legal capacity to pursue its objects as stated in its memorandum of association and nothing more.

If the capacity of a registered company was limited, registered companies would be subject to the doctrine of *ultra vires*. *Ultra vires* is a doctrine of general application, not of relevance only to registered companies. It applies to all legal persons whose legal capacity to act is subject to limits, rendering acts outside the legal capacity of the person null and void.

In *Ashbury Carriage* the House of Lords decided that the doctrine of *ultra vires* did apply to registered companies, the legal capacity of which was limited to pursuit of the objects for which they were formed, as specified in the memorandum of association. This, the House of Lords, stated, was the Legislature's intention and the correct statutory interpretation of the Joint Stock Companies Act 1862.

CASE EXAMPLE

Ashbury Carriage and Iron Company Ltd v Riche (1875) LR 7 HL 653

Ashbury Carriage and Iron Company Ltd was registered under the Joint Stock Companies Act 1862 with the objects, specified in its memorandum of association, of dealing in railway carriages and other railway plant and related lines of business which did not include the funding or construction of railway lines. The company entered into a contract to provide finance for the construction of a railway line in Belgium. When the company was sued to enforce the contract it argued that entry into the contract was *ultra vires* the company, the contract was void, and that this remained the legal position even if the shareholders had authorised the contract or subsequently approved entry into it. Held: In favour of the company, *per* Lord Cairns: 'In my opinion, beyond all doubt, on the true construction of the statute of 1862, creating this corporation, it appears that it was the intention of the Legislature, not implied, but actually expressed, that the corporation should not enter, having regard to its memorandum of association, into a contract of this description ... every Court ... is bound to treat that contract, entered into contrary to the enactment, I will not say as illegal, but as *extra vires*, and wholly null and void ... I am clearly of opinion that this contract was entirely, as I have said, beyond the objects in the memorandum of association. If so, it was thereby placed beyond the powers of the company to make the contract. If so, my Lords, it is not a question whether the contract ever was ratified or was not ratified. It was a contract void from its beginning, it was void because the company could not make the contract.'

tutor tip

"In company law the term *ultra vires* should be confined to acts beyond the *legal capacity* of a *company*, which is now only going to arise in relation to charitable companies. Avoid using the term in relation to acts *outside the authority* of the *directors*"

Unfortunately, the term *ultra vires* is not always used in this strict sense and a great deal of confusion has arisen, particularly as a result of the term being used to describe a situation where, although the company has the legal capacity to act in a certain way, the particular individual within the company who performs the act (often, although not necessarily, a director), does not have the authority to do so. This is not a case of *ultra vires*, but rather a case of 'excess of powers' in that an agent of the company acts outside the scope of his authority, not outside the capacity of the company.

Very early in the history of the registered company, objects clauses began to be drafted to provide for a company to pursue more than one object or a range of objects. It became increasingly popular for specific objects in objects clauses to be followed by generic wording such as the right 'to carry on any other trade or business whatsoever which can, in the opinion of the board of directors, be advantageously carried on by the company in connection with or as ancillary to any of the above business or the general businesses of the company' (language accepted as a valid object by the Court of Appeal in *Bell Houses Ltd v City Wall Properties Ltd* [1966] 2 QB 656).

The practice of drafting the objects of a company very broadly rendered the strict *ultra vires* doctrine of little practical relevance to most companies as almost any conceivable act would fall within the broadly stated objects. Even where *ultra vires* remained relevant to a given company, the effect of a company acting outside its capacity was altered by statute when the First European Company Law Directive was implemented in the UK (by s 9(1) of the European Communities Act 1972). Rather than protecting company members, this Directive focused on protecting those who traded with companies. At common law, if a third party contracted with a company and entry into the contract turned out to be outside the capacity of the company and therefore *ultra vires*, the legal right of the company to walk away (because the contract was null and void) protected the shareholders from the board of directors using company assets to pursue goals outside the line of business shareholders understood to be the object of the company when they invested in the company. This preserved the expectations of shareholders but left the third party's expectations defeated as he was unable to enforce the contract.

In contrast, the Directive focused on protecting the third party dealing with the company. UK implementation of the Directive was, however, half-hearted. It provided that in favour of a person dealing in good faith with a company, any transaction decided upon by the directors was deemed to be within the capacity of the company. This left the *ultra vires* doctrine to operate in a number of situations, such as where the third party did not act in good faith. It also allowed a third party seeking to avoid a contract to invoke the *ultra vires* doctrine as the statute deemed the contract to be within the capacity of the company only *in favour of a person dealing with the company* and not in favour of the company. The company could not rely on the statutory provision.

The next stage in the reform of the *ultra vires* doctrine came with the Companies Act 1989 amendments to the Companies Act 1985. First, the practice of drafting objects clauses so as to allow a company to pursue virtually any line of business was endorsed and encouraged by the introduction of s 3A into the Companies Act 1985. Section 3A provided that where there is a statement in the memorandum that the company's object is to carry on business as a 'general commercial company', this means that its object is to carry on any trade or business whatsoever and the company has power to do all such things as are incidental or conducive to the carrying on of any trade or business. Second, the *ultra vires* doctrine was dealt a severe blow by the putting in place of s 35 (now s 39(1) of the Companies Act 2006).

SECTION

'The validity of an act done by a company shall not be called into question on the ground of lack of capacity by reason of anything in the company's [memorandum]* [constitution].**'
* Companies Act 1985; ** Companies Act 2006

Section 35 did not abolish the *ultra vires* doctrine completely. Traces of it remained and it is often said that it was abolished only in relation to outsiders. Companies still had to have objects clauses in their memoranda and the *ultra vires* doctrine was preserved insofar as it had implications for the rights of members in relation to the company and company insiders, the directors in particular. What remained was referred to as the 'insider dimension' of the *ultra vires* doctrine.

The remnants (or 'insider dimension') of the *ultra vires* doctrine were watered down even further by the Companies Act 2006. Nowadays, not only does a company have unlimited legal capacity as a result of what is now s 39 (above), but, due to the operation of s 28 (below), the legal effect of an objects clause has changed. All that now appears to remain of the *ultra vires* doctrine is the ability of an *individual* shareholder to obtain an injunction to restrain the doing of any act outside the objects of the company, the existence of which rule of law is referred to in s 40(4). Even this right is confined to the period *before* any legal obligations have been incurred by the company (s 40(4)).

The right of the company to sue any director who causes the company to engage in activity outside its objects is sometimes cited as a remaining aspect of the *ultra vires* doctrine but it is more helpfully portrayed as the right of the company to sue for breach of the directors' duty, now set out in s 171(a), to act in accordance with the company's constitution. The legal effects of restrictions on a company's objects are considered more fully in the following section.

Note that special rules relating to *ultra vires* exist for charitable companies. The *ultra vires* doctrine has not been abolished in relation to charitable companies (s 42).

Impact of the 2006 Act on the constitution of pre-2006 Act companies

Every pre-2006 Act company once had, and most will continue to have an old-style memorandum registered with the registrar of companies as there is no obligation to take any action to change this situation. However, s 28 of the Companies Act 2006 fundamentally changes the effect of that document and the provisions contained in it.

's 28(1)
Provisions that immediately before the commencement of this Part were contained in a company's memorandum but are not provisions of the kind mentioned in section 8 (provisions of new-style memorandum) are to be treated after the commencement of this Part as provisions of the company's articles.'

An objects clause in a company's memorandum of association is now treated as a provision of the company's articles. Objects clauses in the articles of a company *will not limit the capacity of the company* (s 39) and, with the exception of charities (as to which see s 42), and (possibly) the right referred to in s 40(4) (see above), the *ultra vires* doctrine will not be relevant to registered companies.

Objects clauses will, however, remain relevant but for different legal reasons. Being deemed to be provisions of the articles:

1 they will operate as a limitation on the authority of the board of directors to bind the company (although the common law position on this is significantly altered by ss 40 and 41 in order to protect third parties, see Chapter 10);

2 they will operate as a provision of the company's constitution: and
  - a director owes the company a duty to act in accordance with the company's constitution (s 171);
  - a shareholder can apply for an injunction to prevent a company from acting outside its constitution, that is, beyond its restricted objects (*Stevens v Mysore Reefs (Kangundi) Mining Co Ltd* [1902] 1 Ch 745);

3 should the object no longer be pursuable or capable of achievement, the 'substratum' of the company may be regarded as gone which has been held to be a good ground for the court to order that the company be wound up under the Insolvency Act 1986, s 122(1)(g), on the basis that 'the court is of the opinion that it is just and equitable that the company should be wound up'.

5.3.2 Companies registered under the Companies Act 2006

The registration provisions of the Companies Act 2006 came into effect on 1 October 2009. Any company registered since that day is a UK company and this section, rather than section 5.3.1 above, is relevant.

New-style memoranda of association

A company registered under the Companies Act 2006 will have a new-style memorandum of association which is simply a prescribed-form document to be completed and filed with the registrar of companies at the time the company is registered. Unlike an old-style memorandum, a new-style memorandum will not be updated. It simply states (s 8), as a matter of record, that the subscribers:

- wish to form a company under the Act;
- agree to become members and, if the company is to have a share capital, to take at least one share each.

articles of association

the regulations governing a company's internal management including the rights of shareholders, the conduct of meetings and the appointment, removal and powers of directors. Separate Model Articles for public and private limited companies operate as the articles of a company to the extent that they have not been excluded or modified

Only one member is required for a Company registered under the 2006 Act, whether it is a public or private company (s 7(1)). Single member *private* companies were permitted under the 1985 Act, but public companies were required to have a minimum of two members. This technical requirement was regularly satisfied by simply allotting one share to a person to hold the legal title as bare trustee for the other, main shareholder as beneficiary.

Objects, capacity and the ultra vires doctrine

As a result of s 39(1) (previously s 35, set out above), together with the change in the role of the memorandum of association, the *ultra vires* doctrine is no longer relevant to registered companies that are not charities. All non-charitable companies have the capacity of a natural person.

A company registered under the 2006 Act need not state the objects it is registered to pursue and, unless the articles specifically restrict them, the objects of the company are unrestricted (s 31(1)). Companies are not expected to choose to state objects in their articles. Some companies will, and the legal implications of an objects statement in the articles will be the same as the legal implications of an objects clause of a pre-2006 Act company that has been deemed to be a provision of its articles. (See section 5.3.1 above where the impact of the 2006 Act on pre-2006 Act companies is addressed.)

The Company's Constitution	
Constitutional documents of a company formed under the Companies Act 2006 are (ss 29 and 32):	
Articles	
Special resolutions	
Resolutions/agreements of all members that would otherwise have to have been made by special resolution	
Current statement of capital	
Certificate of incorporation	
Pre-Companies Act 2006 companies objects and capacity	
Historically, had to have an object clause in its memorandum of association.	From 1 October 2009, all clauses in the memorandum are treated as article provisions (s 28).
The impact on persons dealing with the company had been removed although traces of the *ultra vires* doctrine remained in the Companies Act 1985.	The *ultra vires* doctrine is wholly abolished and the company has the capacity of a natural person (s 39).
Companies registered under the Companies Act 2006 objects and capacity	
May choose to but need not restrict its objects in its articles (s 31).	The company has the capacity of a natural person (s 39).
Potential impact of restricted objects on third parties is as a limitation on the powers of the board/authority of a company agent which is relevant only to persons dealing with the company in bad faith (s 40).	
Shareholders' agreements	
Shareholders' agreements may undermine the rule preventing articles overriding mandatory statutory rights of the company such as the right to alter the articles by special resolution.	*Russell v Northern Bank Development Corporation* (1992)

5.4 The Articles of Association

5.4.1 What are the articles of association?

The articles of association contain the internal rules of the company. They state the organisational structure of the company, allocate powers to and between the organs of the company (the board of directors and the shareholders), and prescribe procedures for decision-making. They make up the most important constitutional document of a company registered under the Companies Act 2006 (due to the fundamental nature of the content of an old-style memorandum of association, before the Companies Act 2006 came into effect, it was regarded as the most important constitutional document of a pre-2006 Act company).

5.4.2 Drafting articles and model articles

Although articles could be drafted from scratch, they rarely are. Company legislation has always contained model or default sets of articles and different sets of model articles exist for different types of companies. The model articles for companies limited by share capital registered under the Companies Act 1985 is known as 'Table A', and is relevant to both public and private companies. Under the 2006 Act, the name of the default articles

model articles
the default articles which, by operation of the Companies Act 2006, s 20, form part or all of the articles of a registered company on its formation to the extent that the incorporators do not register bespoke articles

has been changed to 'model articles' and the Model Articles for Private Companies Limited by Shares are different, containing a shorter and less formal set of rules (53 articles), from the Model Articles for Public Companies (86 articles) (see The Companies (Model Articles) Regulations 2008 (SI 2008/3229)).

Model articles apply in the absence of alternative articles being filed on registration of the company (s 20(1)(a)). Past normal practice has been for part only of the relevant default articles to be adopted, supplemented by particular articles appropriate to the circumstances in which the company is being formed and the wishes of the prospective members. This is achieved by drafting a document that:

- states 'The annexed version of the model articles shall be the articles of the company except as provided otherwise herein';
- contains a list of individual articles from the model articles that do *not* apply;
- contains replacement and supplementary individual articles as required.

There is no reason to believe that this practice will not continue in the future. Note, however, the importance of stating clearly in the proposed articles those articles within the model articles that do *not* apply, as s 20(1)(b) provides that the relevant model articles will apply in so far as the proposed articles 'do not exclude or modify the relevant model articles'.

5.4.3 Ascertaining the articles of association

On registration of the company, the initial articles are registered with the registrar of companies and are a document of public record. Articles can be amended, usually by special resolution, so it is always important to check that you have the most up to date version of the articles of a company. If you are reviewing a company search (documents about a company supplied from the public register), always check whether, since inception, there have been any amendments and whether a new set of articles has been adopted.

For older companies, always check which 'Table A' forms the basis of the articles as there have been different versions over time. Where a copy has not been attached, but simply referred to, it is sometimes necessary to dig out Table A from the companies act current at the time the company was incorporated.

5.4.4 Content of the articles of association

Range of issues typically covered by the articles

The following list is not comprehensive but gives a general indication of the principal matters covered by the articles of a company limited by share capital:

1 Directors:
- Directors' powers and responsibilities;
- Decision-making by directors;
- Appointment of directors;
- Directors' indemnity and insurance.
2 Decision-making by members:
- Organisation of general meetings;
- Voting at general meetings;
- Restrictions on members' rights;
- Application of rules to class meetings.
3 Shares and distributions:
- Issue of shares;
- Interests in shares;
- Share certificates and uncertificated shares;
- Liability of members;
- Partly paid shares;
- Transfer of shares;
- Distributions (dividends);
- Capitalisation of profits.

This list is based on the Model Articles for Public Companies but most of the matters covered are also relevant to private companies limited by share capital.

Limits on the content of the articles

The content of the articles is a matter to be agreed upon by the original members of the company and may be changed from time to time as the company develops (see amendment of articles below). Basically, any matter may be included in the articles subject to the general principle that articles inconsistent with the law are void and unenforceable. Articles that purport to override certain statutory rights or powers have been held to be void and unenforceable. Two clear examples of this are *Re Peveril Gold Mines Ltd* [1898] 1 Ch 122 (CA) concerning an attempt to override the statutory right of shareholders to petition to wind-up the company, and *Allen v Gold Reefs of West Africa Ltd* [1900] 1 Ch 656 (CA) concerning an attempt to exclude the statutory right to amend the articles.

CASE EXAMPLE

Re Peveril Gold Mines Ltd [1898] 1 Ch 122 (CA)

A provision in the articles of the company purported to limit the statutory right of a shareholder to petition the court to wind up the company under s 82 of the Companies Act 1862 (now s 124(1) of the Insolvency Act 1986). Held: The article was void. *Per* Chitty, LJ: 'In my opinion, this condition is annexed to the incorporation of a company with limited liability – that the company may be wound up under the circumstances, and at the instance of the persons, prescribed by the Act, and the articles of association cannot validly provide that the shareholders, who are entitled under s 82 to petition for a winding up, shall not do so except on certain conditions.'

The power of a company to amend its articles by special resolution, currently found in s 21 of the Companies Act 2006 and considered below, has appeared in previous companies acts. The long established principle that a company cannot deprive itself of this statutory power by putting a provision to that effect in its articles, was confirmed by Lindley MR in the Court of Appeal in the leading case on amendment of the articles, *Allen v Gold Reefs of West Africa Ltd* [1900] 1 Ch 656 (CA):

JUDGMENT

'[T]he company is empowered by the statute to alter the regulations contained in its articles from time to time by special resolution … and any regulation or article purporting to deprive the company of this power is invalid on the ground that it is contrary to the statute … The power thus conferred on companies to alter the regulations contained in their articles is limited only by the provisions contained in the statute …'

The principle that a company cannot use its articles to exclude or limit the s 21 power to amend is subject to the statutory power, in s 22, to protect certain articles from amendment, ie to entrench certain articles. It is only those attempts to entrench articles that do not comply with s 22 that will be null and void.

The principle that articles inconsistent with the law are void is simple to state but can be difficult to apply. It presupposes clarity as to which laws are mandatory and which may be opted-out of, something not always clear in company law. Even if a particular statutory provision is asserted to be mandatory, on a number of occasions the courts have endorsed arrangements that in effect, if not in form, permit the statutory provision to be opted-out of. Three cases exemplify this. *Bushell v Faith* [1969] 2 Ch 438 (HL) and *Amalgamated Pest Control v McCarron* [1995] 1QdR 583 (Queensland Supreme Court, Australia) involve weighted voting rights in the context of the statutory right to remove directors by ordinary resolution and the passing of special resolutions. The third, *Russell v Northern Bank Development Corporation* [1992] 1 WLR 588 (HL), involved the impact of a voting agreement in a shareholders' agreement and for this reason is discussed under shareholders' agreements in section 5.7 below.

CASE EXAMPLE

Bushell v Faith [1969] 2 Ch 438 (HL)

A company had a share capital of 300 × £1 shares with 100 shares owned by each of Mr Faith, Mrs Bushell & Dr Bayne. An Article provided: 'In the event of a resolution being proposed at any general meeting of the company for the removal from office of any director, any shares held by that director shall on a pole in respect of such resolution carry the right to three votes per share'. An attempt was made to remove Mr Faith by ordinary resolution of the shareholders, relying on what is now s 168 Companies Act 2006. Held: Mr Faith could insist on three votes per share in any resolution to remove him from office, the result being that he could always outvote the other two shareholders, even though they owned two thirds of the shares and could carry any other ordinary resolution.

JUDGMENT

Per Lord Donavon: 'Any case where the articles prescribed that a director should be removable during his period of office only by a special resolution or an extraordinary resolution ... is overridden by [the Companies Act s 168]. A simple majority of the votes will now suffice ... It is now contended, however, that [s 168] does something more; namely that it provides in effect that when the ordinary resolution proposing the removal of the director is put to the meeting each member present shall have one vote per share ... Why should this be? The section does not say so as it easily could ... Parliament followed its practice of leaving to companies and their shareholders liberty to allocate voting rights as they please.'

Is s 168 a mandatory rule or not? It can be circumvented by the use of weighted voting rights which suggests that it is not. Note, however, that the Listing Rules forbid the circumventing of s 168 by provisions such as this in the articles. The rule for companies with listed shares is therefore different than the rule for other companies (whether private or public). For companies with listed shares, s 168 is a mandatory rule.

The reasoning in *Bushell v Faith* was followed in the case of *Amalgamated Pest Control* [1995] 1QdR 583 (Queensland Supreme Court, Australia). There, the articles of association gave one member 26 per cent of the votes on any special resolution with the result that he could defeat any special resolution. The Queensland Supreme Court upheld this allocation of voting rights.

Although articles are a type of agreement between all of the shareholders of a company, they are a document of public record and subject to unique rules, including rules as to amendment and enforcement, which makes them a '*sui generis*' arrangement. Because of this, shareholders often prefer to capture the agreement between them in a separate agreement, a 'shareholders' agreement'. Shareholders' agreements often contain important arrangements that impact on the way a company is managed and may render the articles misleading if not read in conjunction with the shareholders' agreement. Shareholders' agreements are considered in 5.7 below.

5.4.5 Effect of the articles of association

5.4.5.1 The articles as a statutory contract

Section 33(1) of the Companies Act 2006 makes it clear that a contract is created by the articles of association.

> 'The provisions of a company's constitution bind the company and its members to the same extent as if there were covenants on the part of the company and of each member to observe those provisions.'

Although not made clear by the language used in the predecessor section (immediately before the 2006 Act, s 14 of the Companies Act 1985), s 33 has been redrafted to make it clear that the company is a party to the statutory contract. Each member is a party to the statutory contract which is not just a contract between each member and the company, but also between each member and each other member (*Salmon v Quin & Axtens Ltd* [1909] AC 442 (HL) and *Rayfield v Hands* [1960] Ch 1, each considered below).

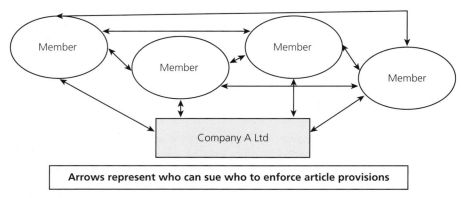

Figure 5.1 Contractual relationships created by the s 33 statutory contract

The statutory contract has noteworthy characteristics that distinguish it from a typical contract as follows:

- Amendment of a contract usually requires the agreement of all parties, yet the articles can be amended (subject to entrenchment) by a special resolution, which requires the support of only 75 per cent of the members (s 21(1)).
- A contract usually binds only those parties who agree to it, yet all members *at any time* are bound by the articles, so that a new member who has played no part in the drafting of the articles, upon being registered as a member, is bound by the articles.
- The articles cannot be challenged based on the doctrines of misrepresentation, mistake (common law or equitable) or undue influence (*Bratton Seymour Service Co Ltd v Oxborough* [1992] BCLC 693 (CA)).
- The court may not rectify the articles even if they do not represent the intentions of the members on incorporation (*Evans v Chapman* (1902) 86 LT 381; *Scott v Frank F. Scott (London) Ltd* [1940] Ch 749 (CA)).
- The articles are exempt from the Contract (Rights of Third Parties) Act 1999 (see s 6(2) of that Act), so that a third party cannot enforce a provision in the articles.
- The articles are not subject to ss 2–4 of the Unfair Contract Terms Act 1977 (see Sched 1, para 1(d) to that Act).

The impact is yet to be seen on the interpretation of articles of association of the judgment of Lord Hoffmann in *Attorney General of Belize v Belize Telecom Ltd* [2009] UKPC 10 (PC). Hoffmann applied the general principle of construction regarding the implication of terms in commercial contracts to the articles of a company when earlier decisions had suggested that more restrictive rules applied. Distinguishing *Bratton*, Hoffmann stated that the principle governing the implication of a term is, 'Is that what the instrument, read as a whole against the relevant background, would reasonably be understood to mean? From this perspective, an implied term is not an addition to the articles but simply spells out what the articles mean'.

CASE EXAMPLE

Attorney General of Belize v Belize Telecom Ltd [2009] UKPC 10 (PC)

The articles of the company incorporated to take over the business of the Belize Telecommunications Authority provided that any person who held a special or golden share and class C ordinary shares amounting to 37.5 per cent or more of the issued ordinary shares in the company could appoint or remove two directors. A shareholder that had originally met both criteria ceased to hold the required percentage of ordinary shares. The question arose as to whether or not the directors appointed by that shareholder could be removed or required to vacate office. The only person who had the power to remove them under the articles was the person with power to appoint them but no such person existed and the articles were silent on vacation of office. The Privy Council, reversing the decision of the Belize Court of Appeal, held that a term should be implied that a director who had been appointed by a person holding the requisite percentage of ordinary shares vacated his office if the person appointing him ceased to hold such a shareholding. The implication was required to avoid defeating what appeared to have been the overriding purpose of the machinery of appointment and removal of directors which was to have a board of directors that reflected the interests of the various participants in the company.

In the recent case of *McKillen v Misland (Cyprus) Investments Ltd* [2012] EWCA Civ 179 (CA), the hearing of a preliminary issue in a s 994 petition, the Court of Appeal applied the test from *Belize* when interpreting the pre-emption provisions in the articles and a shareholders' agreement of a company incorporated to invest in hotels.

5.4.5.2 Enforcement of the provisions of the articles

If the articles were an ordinary contract, enforcement of its provisions would be straightforward; parties to the contract could both enforce the contract and have the contract enforced against them. Unfortunately, in relation to the statutory contract, the answer is not that straightforward.

Enforcement by the company

The company can enforce the articles against individual members, as illustrated by *Hickman v Kent or Romney Sheep Breeders Association* [1915] 1 Ch 881.

CASE EXAMPLE

Hickman v Kent or Romney Sheep Breeders Association [1915] 1 Ch 881

Articles provided for disputes between a member and the company to be referred to arbitration. A member sued *in court* to enforce his rights as a member, including his right to have his sheep registered by the company in its published flock book.

Held: The court stayed the court proceedings brought by the member as the member was bound by the articles to arbitrate the dispute and the company was entitled to enforce the arbitration clause in the articles against the member.

tutor tip

"Link claims by shareholders to enforce the articles based on s 33 with the availability of the broader-based right to petition the court for a remedy based on unfairly prejudicial conduct under s 994"

In *Hickman*, the rights the member was seeking to enforce were rights common to all members: they were 'membership rights'. The company was permitted to enforce the arbitration clause in the articles because the dispute between the member and the company related to membership rights. The company cannot enforce provisions in the articles against a member if the provision relates to rights of the member in a different capacity, such as in his capacity as a director or solicitor (see *Bisgood v Henderson's Transvaal Estates Ltd* [1908] 1 Ch 743).

Enforcement by members

Some of the provisions in the articles can be enforced by a member, whether against the company (as in *Wood v Odessa Waterworks Co* (1889) 42 Ch D 636, below) or against other members (as in *Rayfield v Hands* [1960] Ch 1, below).

CASE EXAMPLE

Wood v Odessa Waterworks Co (1889) 42 Ch D 636

Provisions in the articles of association governed the rights of the members in respect of the division of the profits of the company. A member, on behalf of himself and all other members, brought an action for an injunction to restrain the company from acting on an ordinary resolution supporting a board proposal that profits be used to give debenture bonds to members instead of dividends, on the ground that to do so contravened the articles of association of the company. Held: *Per* Stirling J: 'What I have to determine is, whether that which is proposed to be done is in accordance with the articles of association as they stand, and, in my judgment, it is not, and therefore the Plaintiff is entitled to an injunction so far as relates to the payment of dividends.'

CASE EXAMPLE

Rayfield v Hands [1960] Ch 1

Articles provided that a shareholder wishing to sell his shares must offer them to those members who were directors and those member/directors were required to buy the shares at a fair price. The member/directors refused to buy the shares and Mr Rayfield sued them to enforce the provision in the articles. Held: Mr Rayfield could enforce the article against the member/directors who were ordered to take the shares. Note that Vaisey J sounded a note of caution as to the range of application of this principle of direct enforcement by one member against another: 'The conclusion to which I have come may not be of so general application as to extend to articles of association of every company, for it is, I think, material to remember that this private company is one of that class of companies which bears a close analogy to a partnership.'

It appears that some types of provisions in the articles may not be enforceable by members. The cases in which the courts have imposed restrictions on enforcement fall into two categories, cases concerning enforcement of outsider rights and cases concerning internal irregularities.

Can a member sue to enforce outsider rights in the articles?

It is unclear, even today, whether or not a member can sue to enforce an article that confers on him an 'outsider right'. An outsider right is a right that attaches to a person in a capacity other than as a member (such as the right to be a director or the company solicitor) rather than in his capacity as member (such as the right to attend and vote at meetings). The case law is inconsistent, rendering this a moot issue.

The more widely held view appears to be that a member cannot sue to enforce outsider rights. The cases of *Eley v Positive Government Security Life Assurance Co* (1876) 1 ExD 88 (CA), *Browne v La Trinidad* (1887) 37 Ch D 1, *Hickman v Kent or Romney Sheep Breeders Association* [1915] 1 Ch 881 and *Beattie v E & F Beattie Ltd* [1938] Ch 708 (CA), are commonly cited in support of this restriction on enforcement.

CASE EXAMPLE

Eley v Positive Government Security Life Assurance Co (1876) 1 ExD 88 (CA)

Articles required the company to employ Eley as its solicitor unless he had been guilty of misconduct. The company used a different solicitor and Eley sued the company for breach of contract arguing that the articles formed a contract between himself and the company. Eley was treated as suing in his capacity as an 'outsider', not as a member. Held: Eley could *not* rely on or enforce the articles which were 'a matter between the directors and shareholders, and not between them and the plaintiff.' The court also rejected the argument that the relevant article was evidence of an agreement between the company and Eley separate from the articles.

Eley clearly supports the proposition that the articles can only confer rights on a member, not on a third party or 'outsider'. However this is merely an illustration of the doctrine of privity: the outsider is not a party to the contract and therefore cannot enforce the contract. In fact, although he was not a member at the time the articles were adopted (on incorporation of the company), Eley was a member of the company at the time of the court case but this fact does not seem to have been brought to the attention of the court as it was not addressed in the judgment. It is not clear that this case would have been decided the same way if Eley had sued as a member ('*qua member*'), rather than as an outsider. On its face, the case is *not* authority for the proposition that a member cannot enforce outsider rights, but for the more limited and obvious common law proposition that a non-party to a contract cannot sue to enforce the contract.

CASE EXAMPLE

Browne v La Trinidad (1887) 37 Ch D 1 (CA)

Articles entitled Mr Browne to be a director for a fixed period. Browne was a member of the company but could not enforce the right to be a director, even in his capacity as a member, as it was a matter 'not connected with the holding of shares'.

The third case cited in support of the unenforceability of outsider rights by a member is *Hickman* (above), yet, on its facts, *Hickman* involved membership rights, not outsider rights. The right in the articles enforced by the court was the right of members and the association to have disputes between members and the association arbitrated rather than litigated. Also, the underlying dispute between the member and the association related to membership rights (including the right of all members to have their flocks listed in the flock book published by the association). Consequently, anything said in that case about enforcement of outsider rights is strictly *obiter dictum*, not being necessary to support the decision in the case. It is unfortunate, therefore, that the Court of Appeal in *Beattie* placed such importance on two oft-quoted passages from the judgment of Astbury J in *Hickman*:

JUDGMENT

'An outsider to whom rights purport to be given by the articles in his capacity as such outsider, whether he is or subsequently becomes a member, cannot sue on those articles treating them as contracts between himself and the company to enforce those rights. Those rights are not part of the general regulations of the company applicable alike to all shareholders and can only exist by virtue of some contact between such person and the company.

... no right merely purporting to be given by an article to a person, whether as a member or not, in a capacity other than that of member, as, for instance, as solicitor, promoter, director, can be enforced against the company.'

The most important case supporting the unenforceability of outsider rights is *Beattie v E & F Beattie Ltd* [1938] Ch 708 (CA).

CASE EXAMPLE

Beattie v E & F Beattie Ltd [1938] Ch 708 (CA)

A derivative action was brought on behalf of the company by a member seeking an injunction stopping a director, Ernest Beattie (EB), from denying the member access to the books and accounts of the company. In effect, the company was suing a director for breach of duty in his capacity as director. EB was both a director and a member of the company. He applied to have the action stayed on the ground that the articles contained a provision requiring all disputes between members of the company or between members and the company to be referred to arbitration. (If a valid arbitration clause exists the courts will normally 'stay' or pause court proceedings to enable the dispute to be resolved by arbitration.)

Held: EB could not invoke the article and insist on arbitration as this was not a dispute between the company and himself *as a member*. It was an action against him in his capacity as a director (an outsider) and the articles were not relevant. Per Wilfred Greene MR: '[T]he contractual force given to the articles of association by [s 33] is limited to such provisions of the articles as apply to the relationship of the members in their capacity as members.'

Note that Ernest Beattie was not seeking to enforce the articles *'qua member'*. Rather, in proceedings already underway in which he was being sued in his capacity as a director, he sought to assert his contractual rights as a member of the company. Focusing on this aspect of the case, it could be said that this case, like *Eley*, is simply an illustration of privity: Ernest Beattie, the director, was not, in that capacity, a party to the contract in the articles. Nor was the dispute between him and the company a dispute between the company and a member as member. As Greene MR commented, by seeking to have the dispute referred to arbitration, 'he is not, in my judgment, seeking to enforce a right which is common to himself and all other members'. The question was left open in this case whether the court would have stayed the derivative action if an action had been brought by a member (even Mr Beattie himself), as member, to enforce the arbitration clause in the articles, thereby requiring what was a dispute between members and the company (about access to company records) to be arbitrated.

Turning to the authorities for the proposition that outsider rights in the articles *are* enforceable, in the leading case, *Salmon v Quinn & Axtens Ltd* [1909] 1 Ch 311 (HL), the House of Lords permitted a shareholder to enforce a veto given to him in the articles in his capacity of managing director.

CASE EXAMPLE

Salmon v Quinn & Axtens Ltd [1909] 1 Ch 311 (HL)

Messrs Axtens and Salmon held a large majority of shares in the company. By the articles:

- General management of the company was given to the board of directors subject to the right of members, by ordinary resolution 'being not inconsistent with the articles', to decide matters.
- Each of two managing directors (Messrs Axtens and Salmon) was given power to veto decisions of the board relating to acquiring and letting premises.

In accordance with the articles, as managing director, Mr Salmon (S) vetoed a decision but his veto was ignored and the other directors secured an ordinary resolution of the members to support their decision. S, in his capacity as a member of the company enforcing the articles, sought an injunction to restrain the decision being carried out. Held: The House of Lords granted the injunction reasoning that this was an attempt to by-pass rules on decision-making contained within the articles. It was an attempt to amend the articles by an ordinary resolution rather than by a special resolution (see the next section on amendment of articles). The court would prevent the company acting on a decision taken unconstitutionally.

Mr Salmon, a director and member of the company, in effect enforced the rights in the articles given to a managing director. The managing director's veto right was not common to all shareholders, thus Mr Salmon enforced an 'outsider' right. He enforced this 'outsider' right by bringing an action *as a member* to enforce the articles. Lord Wedderburn has argued that this case establishes that members can indirectly enforce outsider rights in the articles by suing as members to require the company not to depart from the contract in the articles (Wedderburn (1957)).

Can a member sue to enforce the articles where there has been an internal irregularity?

Courts will not provide a remedy to an individual shareholder seeking to enforce a limitation or procedure set out in the articles if a majority of the members could, consistently with the statute and the articles, bring about the outcome being complained of. This is based on the principle of majority rule: an individual member of a company cannot usurp the power of the majority of the members. The concept of internal irregularity limits the personal rights of an individual member, that he can enforce. Internal irregularities are breaches of obligations on the company that can be enforced only by a majority of the members. If a majority of the members condones or 'ratifies' the irregularity, an individual shareholder is powerless to enforce the stipulated limit or procedure.

In the case of *Grant v UK Switchback Railways Company* (1888) 40 Ch D 135 (CA), directors acted in breach of restrictions imposed by the articles but an individual shareholder could not bring an action because the matter in issue was a mere internal irregularity that could be and had been ratified by an ordinary resolution (ie by a simple majority vote) of shareholders.

CASE EXAMPLE

Grant v UK Switchback Railways Company (1888) 40 Ch D 135 (CA)

The articles disqualified a director from voting to approve entry into any contract in which he was personally interested. The board of directors entered into a contract to sell the business of the company. All but one of the directors were personally interested in the sale contract. A member applied for an injunction restraining the company from carrying out the contract as it was entered into in breach of the articles. Before the application was heard a general meeting of the company was held at which an ordinary resolution was passed approving and adopting the contract and authorising the directors to carry it into effect. Held: The Court of Appeal refused to grant an injunction. The directors had no authority to enter into the contract but the shareholders could ratify the unauthorised act by ordinary resolution and had done so.

In the earlier case of *MacDougall v Gardiner* (1875) 1 Ch D 13 (CA), the Court of Appeal had strongly asserted the importance of not engaging the courts in matters internal to a company at the suit of an individual shareholder. Mellish LJ stressed the importance of respecting majority rule. He did not require the majority to have expressed its will to defeat the action of an individual shareholder, it was enough that a meeting could be called at which the majority could correct the irregularity.

CASE EXAMPLE

MacDougall v Gardiner (1875) 1 Ch D 13 (CA)

The articles gave the chairman at a general meeting power, with the consent of the members, to adjourn the meeting, and also provided for taking a poll if demanded by five shareholders. At a general meeting the adjournment of the meeting was proposed and declared by the chairman to be carried on a show of hands. A poll was duly demanded, but the chairman ruled that there could not be a poll on the question of adjournment. A shareholder brought an action on behalf of himself and all other shareholders except the directors seeking (i) a declaration that the conduct of the chairman was illegal and improper, and (ii) an injunction to restrain the directors from carrying out certain arrangements he alleged the directors were seeking to carry out without consulting the shareholders, without submitting them to the shareholders for their approval. Held: No remedy was granted. The matters complained of were internal irregularities. *Per* Mellish LJ, '[T]here can be no use in having a litigation … the ultimate end of which is only that a meeting has to be called, and then ultimately the majority gets its wishes … [I]f what is complained of is simply that something which the majority are entitled to do has been done or undone irregularly, then I think it is quite right that nobody should have a right to set that aside, or to institute a suit in Chancery about it, except the company itself.'

MacDougall, which clearly asserts the unwillingness of the courts to interfere in the internal management of companies, contrasts with cases such as *Pender v Lushington* (1877) 6 Ch D 70 that focus on the rights of shareholders.

Pender v Lushington (1877) 6 Ch D 70

The articles provided for one vote for every 10 shares with no member entitled to more than 100 votes in total. Pender transferred some of his shares to nominees to hold on trust and those nominees sought to vote along with Pender on a resolution.

The chairman of the company refused to count the nominee's votes and the resolution was defeated. Pender and the nominee shareholders brought an action seeking an injunction. Held: They were entitled to an injunction preventing the company from acting contrary to the resolution. *Per* Jessel MR, 'This is an action by Mr Pender for himself. He is a member of the company, and … he is entitled to have his vote recorded – an individual right in respect of which he has a right to sue. That has nothing to do with the question like that raised in *Foss v Harbottle* and that line of cases. He has a right to say, 'you shall record my vote, as that is a right of property belonging to my interest in this company, and if you refuse to record my vote I will institute legal proceedings against you to compel you'.

It is very difficult to reconcile these very different approaches taken by the courts. A great deal of uncertainty remains as to which rights stated in the articles can be enforced by members and, consequently, it is impossible to provide a comprehensive definition of the personal rights of a shareholder.

KEY FACTS

Articles of association	
Source and content	
If articles are not registered relevant model articles will apply.	s 20(1)(a)
Model articles apply insofar as registered articles do not exclude or modify them.	s 20(1)(b)
Typical content includes internal company rules about: directors (powers and responsibilities; decision-making; appointment) decision-making by shareholders (organisation and voting at general meetings; restrictions on shareholders' rights) shares and distributions (issue and interests in shares; liability of members; transfer of shares; distributions/dividends; capitalisation of profits).	
See: Model Articles for Private Companies Limited by Shares and Model Articles for Public Companies	
Articles may not override mandatory laws such as the right of a shareholder to petition the court to wind up the company.	*Re Peveril Gold Mines* (1898)
Weighted voting rights may operate to undermine the mandatory nature of statutory provisions.	*Bushell v Faith* (1969)
	But note: Listing rules prohibit weighted voting rights undermining the right of shareholders to remove directors by ordinary resolution
Effect of the articles of association	
The articles form a statutory contract	s 33
Enforcement of the provisions of the articles raises a number of moot issues including:	
Can a shareholder enforce non-membership rights?	*Beattie v Beattie* (1938) says no (*obiter*) *Salmon v Quinn & Axtens* (1909) suggests yes
Can a shareholder require the company to act in accordance with the articles if an ordinary resolution could authorise or ratify the challenged behaviour?	*Grant v UK Switchback Railways* (1888) says no (but it is unclear what amounts to an internal management matter and what amounts to a personal right)
Can one shareholder enforce the articles against another shareholder?	*Rayfield v Hands* (1960) says yes but cautions that the decision may be confined to quasi-partnership cases

5.5 Amending the articles of association

5.5.1 Statutory provisions governing amendment

Section 21 states that a company may amend its articles by special resolution. The relevant special resolution (s 30) and a copy of the new articles (s 26) must be sent to the registrar of companies. A shareholder is not bound by an amendment that requires him to take more shares or increases his liability to pay money to the company (s 25).

By way of exceptions to the need for a special resolution to amend the articles, s 551(8) states that a resolution to give, vary, revoke or renew authorisation of the directors to exercise the power of the company to allot shares in the company may be an ordinary resolution 'even though it amends the company's articles'. Section 551(9) brings any such resolution within the s 30 obligation to forward a copy to the registrar of companies. Section 685(2) also acknowledges that changes to the articles can be brought about by ordinary resolutions in cases in which the directors are authorised by ordinary resolution, pursuant to s 685(1), to determine the terms and conditions of redemption of shares.

5.5.2 Contractual provisions affecting amendment

Provisions in the articles

The common law principle that a company cannot, by putting a provision to that effect in its articles, deprive itself of the statutory power to amend its articles by special resolution is subject to the s 22 right to entrench provisions in the articles. This new statutory right to restrict the power of the company to amend its articles replaces the previous right of a company to place those provisions of its constitution it wished to entrench into its memorandum of association and state either that they could not be amended, or, that they could be amended only if the procedure specified in the memorandum was gone through.

SECTION

's 22(1) A company's articles may contain provision ('provision for entrenchment') to the effect that specified provisions of the articles may be amended or repealed only if conditions are met, or procedures are complied with, that are more restrictive than those applicable in the case of a special resolution.

(2) Provision for entrenchment may only be made –
    (a) in the company's articles on formation, or
    (b) by an amendment of the company's articles agreed to by all the members of the company.
(3) Provision for entrenchment does not prevent amendment of the company's articles –
    (a) by agreement of all the members of the company,
    (b) by order of a court.'

Article provisions can only be entrenched on incorporation or, if at a later date, only by unanimous consent of the shareholders and the existence of a provision for entrenchment must be drawn to the attention of the registrar of companies (s 23).

Company contracts

A company cannot enter into a specifically enforceable agreement not to exercise its statutory power to amend its articles (see *Russell v Northern Bank Development Corporation* [1992] 1 WLR 588 (HL), considered at section 5.7.3). A company may amend its articles and act on the amended articles even if this means that the company is in breach of a contract previously entered into. The remedy for the other party to the contract is damages, not an injunction, if the effect of an injunction would be to stop the company relying on its amended articles, thereby, in effect, restricting its power to amend its articles.

CASE EXAMPLE

Southern Foundries (1926) Ltd v Shirlaw [1940] AC 701 (HL)

The company contracted with Shirlaw that he was to be managing director of the company for 10 years. The articles provided that if a managing director ceased to be a director his appointment as managing director would also end. The company was taken over and the new owners amended the articles to provide that they could remove any director by written instrument. Shirlaw was removed as a director and the company treated his managing directorship as also at an end, relying on the relevant article, even though this contradicted the agreement between Shirlaw and the company as Shirlaw had only been the managing director for just over two years. Shirlaw sued the company and the new owner for damages. Held: Shirlaw was entitled to damages. The company was entitled to rely on the amended articles. No injunction could be granted to prevent the adoption of new articles. *Per* L Porter 'A company cannot be precluded from altering its articles thereby giving itself power to act upon the provisions of the altered articles – but so to act may nevertheless be a breach of the contract if it is contrary to a stipulation in a contract validly made before variation'.

Shareholders' agreements

Unlike a company agreement, a shareholders' agreement can have a significant effect on the statutory power of a company to amend its articles. This is considered below at section 5.7.3.

5.5.3 Court-developed restrictions on amendment

In addition to statutory provisions expressly addressing amendment of the articles and contractual provisions affecting the statutory power of a company to amend its articles, the courts have developed restrictions governing exercise of the statutory power to amend the articles.

No amendment to remove accrued rights

An amendment that deprives a shareholder of rights retrospectively, that is, rights that have already accrued, will not be effective unless the shareholder agrees to it (*James v Buena Ventura Nitrate Grounds Syndicate Limited* [1896] 1 Ch 456).

No amendment to introduce an article that could not have been included on incorporation

Articles inconsistent with mandatory company law rules are void and unenforceable (see above at section 5.4.4). It follows that any amended article purporting to override such a company law rule, equally, is void and unenforceable. Note, however, that even if it is permissible to include a particular provision in the articles at the outset, when a company is originally incorporated, it does not necessarily follow that such a provision may be added to the articles by amendment by special resolution.

There seems to be at least one type of provision courts permit on incorporation but will not allow to be introduced into the articles by amendment, at least not without the consent of the affected shareholder(s). This is a bare squeeze-out provision (also known as a bare compulsory transfer provision) which allows a shareholder to be bought out and excluded from continued participation in a company without that right to exclude being conditional upon behaviour of the shareholder that would in some way justify exclusion, such as competing with the company. Bare squeeze-out clauses may be included in articles on incorporation (*Phillips v Manufacturers' Securities Limited* (1917) 116 LT 290 (CA)). The cases on whether or not such a clause may be introduced by amendment of the articles by special resolution are not clear cut. Hannigan (2007) concludes that such a clause cannot be introduced. She reaches this conclusion notwithstanding the uncertainty expressed in *Constable v Executive Connections Ltd* [2005] 2 BCLC 638 and the fact that in cases in which the validity of introduction of such a clause have been considered, judges have approached the issue purely as a question of whether or not the amendment is *bona fide* for the benefit of the company as a whole (see section below), an approach that is problematic and artificial.

However the courts articulate the principle they are applying, the cases on bare squeeze-outs are consistent with a rule that a shareholders' right to continue to own shares in a company cannot be taken away by amendment of the articles by special resolution except where:

- the amendment provides for the shareholder to receive fair value for his shares; *and*
- the shareholders' continued membership in the company is detrimental to the conduct of the company's affairs so that the exclusion is for a proper purpose.

This approach, taken by the Australian courts in *Gambotto v WCP Ltd* (1995) 182 CLR 432 (Australian High Court), is a more compelling approach to regulating squeeze-out clauses in articles than the *bona fide* test. Nonetheless, Lord Hoffmann has stated categorically (albeit in the Privy Council, making his statement persuasive rather than binding on English courts) that the proper purpose doctrine expounded in *Gambotto* is not part of English law (*Citco Banking Corporation NV v Pusser's Limited* [2007] UKPC 13 (PC)) and that the correct test to apply is whether or not the amendment is *bona fide* in the interests of the company as a whole. For this reason, the key trio of cases on squeeze-out rights, *Sidebottom v Kershaw, Leese & Co Ltd* [1920] 1 Ch 154, *Brown v British Abrasive Wheel Co Ltd* [1919] 1 Ch 290 and *Dafen Tinplate Co Ltd v Llanelly Steel Company* (1907) Ltd [1920] 2 Ch 124, are discussed in the following section.

Amendment must be *bona fide* for the benefit of the company as a whole

We now turn to the most important judicial restriction on the power of amendment of the articles. In *Allen v Gold Reefs of West Africa Ltd* [1900] 1 Ch 656 (CA), referring to what is now s 22 of the 2006 Act, Lindley MR stated what has come to be regarded as the definitive, if not always helpful, statement of the common law restriction on the exercise of the power to amend the articles, that the statutory power to amend must be exercised '*bona fide* for the benefit of the company as a whole'. The burden of proof is on the person who challenges the validity of the amendment (see *Peters' American Delicacy Co Ltd v Heath* (1939) 61 CLR 457).

Lindley MR's statement raises more questions about the application of the principle than it answers, or, as Meagher JA commented in *Gambotto v WCP Ltd* (1995) 182 CLR 432 (Australian High Court) 'these words have beguiled and confused the Courts ever since'. Less respectfully, in *Peters' American Delicacy Company Ltd v Heath* (1939) 61 CLR 457, Dixon, J described the words as 'almost meaningless'.

CASE EXAMPLE

Allen v Gold Reefs of West Africa Ltd [1900] 1 Ch 656 (CA)

Emilio Zuccani owned partly paid shares and was the only owner of fully paid shares in the company. He died owing the company over £6,000, the aggregate sums called-up but still unpaid on his partly paid shares. Articles provided for a lien in favour of the company 'upon all shares (not being fully paid) held by such member in respect of debts owed by a shareholder to the company'. After Mr Zuccani's death the company amended the articles to omit the language in brackets thereby extending the company's lien to cover fully paid-up shares. Mr Zuccani's executors sought a declaration that the company had no lien upon the fully paid-up shares. They argued, amongst other points, that the resolution creating a lien upon Mr Zuccani's fully paid-up shares was an oppressive act as against him, he being the only holder of fully paid-up shares in the company. Held: The amendment was valid. Any suspicions excited by the fact that the amendment only affected Zucanni's executor were dispelled once it was realised that this was because Zuccani was the only holder of paid-up shares who at the time was in arrear of calls. The altered articles applied to all holders of fully paid shares, made no distinction between them, and therefore the directors could not be charged with bad faith. Lindley, MR stated the following now famous words: 'The power … conferred on companies to alter … their articles … must, like all other powers, be exercised subject to those general principles of law and equity which are applicable to all powers conferred on majorities and enabling them to bind minorities. *It must be exercised not only in the manner required by law, but also, bona fide for the benefit of the company as a whole and it must not be exceeded.* These conditions are always implied, and are seldom, if ever, expressed. But if they are complied with, I can discover no ground for judicially putting any other restrictions on the power conferred by the section than those contained in it.' (emphasis added)

Application of the *Allen* principle where the company's interests are not affected by the amendment

In *Allen* the amendment directly affected the interests of the company. As Romer LJ stated:

JUDGMENT

'It appears to me the shareholders were acting in the truest and best interests of the company in exercising the legal right to alter the articles so that the company might as one result obtain payment of the debt due from Mr Zuccani. The shareholders were only bound to look to the interests of the company. They were not bound to consult or consider Mr Zuccani's separate or private interests.'

The *Allen* principle is more difficult to apply where the amendment in question does not particularly affect the interests of the company as a separate entity, but rather solely impacts on shareholders and has different effects on the minority and majority shareholders. Examples are amendments affecting the distribution of dividends or capital and amendments affecting the power of shareholders to retain and dispose of their shares. The Court of Appeal in *Greenhalgh v Arderne Cinemas Ltd* [1951] Ch 286 (CA) tried to deal with this by developing what has subsequently come to be known as the 'discrimination test'.

CASE EXAMPLE

Greenhalgh v Arderne Cinemas Ltd [1951] Ch 286 (CA)

Pre-emption rights in the articles gave existing shareholders the right to buy shares of any shareholder who wished to sell. The articles were amended to add a provision that any member could transfer shares to anyone if the transfer was approved by ordinary resolution. The effect of this amendment was to take away from the minority the right to acquire other members' shares (provided an ordinary resolution could be secured). Held: The amendment was valid. The court applied the principle in *Allen v Gold Reefs of West Africa* but Evershed MR sought to explain the application of the principle. He stated, 'a special resolution … would be liable to be impeached if the effect of it were to discriminate between the majority shareholders and the minority shareholders, so as to give the former an advantage of which the latter were deprived'.

The fact that the amendment in *Greenhalgh* was held not to bring about the type of discrimination that fell within the scope of the principle immediately created uncertainty as to exactly which type of discrimination was such as to cause a court to restrain the majority. In *Citco Banking Corporation v Pusser's Ltd* (2007) Bus LR 960 (PC) Lord Hoffmann reviewed the cases, including *Greenhalgh*, and expressed the view that the *Allen* test was not helpful in cases in which the interests of the company are not affected. Although he stated that another test of validity is required for such cases, it was not necessary to decide the case to expound an alternative, which he declined to do.

JUDGMENT

'It must however be acknowledged that the test of "*bona fide* for the benefit of the company as a whole" will not enable one to decide all cases in which amendments of the articles operate to the disadvantage of some shareholder or group of shareholders. Such amendments are sometimes only for the purpose of regulating the rights of shareholders in matters in which the company as a corporate entity has no interest, such as the distribution of dividends or capital or the power to dispose of shares … Some other test of validity is required.'

Application of the *Allen* principle in squeeze-out cases

As discussed above, the *Allen* principle has been applied to amendments introducing squeeze-out provisions in three leading cases.

CASE EXAMPLE

Sidebottom v Kershaw, Leese & Co Ltd [1920] 1 Ch 154 (CA)

The articles were amended to provide that any shareholder *who competed with the company* could be compelled to sell his shares to nominees of the directors at full value, ie a compulsory transfer/expulsion provision but conditioned on the shareholder behaving contrary to the interests of the company. Held: An expulsion clause can be included in articles on the registration of a company. Articles can be amended to include such a provision provided the exercise of the power of alteration is *bona fide* for the benefit of the company as a whole. An alteration applicable to all shareholders is not open to challenge *solely* on the basis of its impact on a particular shareholder. Here, the amendment was passed *bona fide* for the benefit of the company as a whole therefore was allowed to stand.

CASE EXAMPLE

Brown v British Abrasive Wheel Co Ltd [1919] 1 Ch 290

Holders of 98 per cent of the shares in the company were willing to provide capital to fund development of the company only if they could acquire the other 2 per cent. They sought to amend the articles to permit them to acquire the shares at fair value. Held: The minority shareholder was entitled to an injunction preventing the shareholders from altering the articles. The court found as a matter of fact that the majority had acted for their own benefit, not the benefit of the company.

CASE EXAMPLE

Dafen Tinplate v Llanelly Steel Company (1907) Ltd [1920] 2 Ch 124

The company had been founded on the expectation that shareholders would purchase their supplies from the company. A shareholder began sourcing supplies from a competing company in which he had an interest. The articles were amended to provide a right of the majority shareholders to decide that the shares of any member (other than one principal shareholder) be offered for sale by the directors to anyone the directors chose, at fair value as decided by the directors. Held: The court *did not allow the amendment to stand* on the basis that to say that such an unrestricted power of expropriation was for the benefit of the company was to confuse the interests of the majority with the benefit of the company as a whole.

The Australian case of *Gambotto v WCP Ltd* (1995) 182 CLR 432 (Australian High Court), concerned an amendment to introduce squeeze-out rights that was clearly in the interests of the company and in relation to which there was no evidence of bad faith on the part of the majority shareholders. Nonetheless, the amendment was disallowed. The court rejected the *Allen* principle in favour of a new 'proper purpose test, which involves asking whether or not the amendment is 'beyond any purpose contemplated by the articles or oppressive as that expression is understood in the law relating to corporations'. This test has excited a great deal of academic comment. The Company Law Review Steering Group considered the case and rejected calls to amend English law along similar lines on the basis that the case introduced more complexity with no more certainty than currently exists in English law.

Reform of the *Allen* principle

In relation to the right of majorities to bind minorities, calls for the governing legal principles to be clarified or changed and, in either case, placed on a statutory footing in the 2006 Act, have not been acted upon. Justifications advanced for leaving the law as it is included reference to the difficulty of coming up with more appropriate legal principles to govern than those found in the case law (see, for example, comments on the Australian case of *Gambotto* above), and the belief that this is not a particularly important area of law to clarify because a shareholder who is not satisfied with an amendment can obtain an appropriate remedy by bringing an unfair prejudice petition under s 994 of the 2006 Act, a point made by Rixon (1986).

Unfair prejudice petitions are considered in Chapter 13, from which review it can be seen that it is not clear that amendment of the articles in accordance with the statutory power (s 21) would found a successful unfair prejudice petition in other than quasi-partnership companies, the petition being based on unfair prejudice to the *interests* of the shareholder rather than a breach of his strict legal rights.

5.6 Contracts with terms derived from the articles

Individual articles (often, confusingly referred to in cases as 'regulations') are often found to have been embodied in, and form part of, a separate contract between a company and a third person. This approach has regularly been taken in cases involving directors suing for remuneration stated in the articles. These cases are examples of the courts applying principles of contract law to identify the express terms of an agreement, implying terms into that agreement (where appropriate), and construing (give meaning to) those terms. It is important not to confuse this use of one or more individual articles (as evidence of the terms of a separate agreement between the company and the relevant third party), with enforcement of the statutory contract. The argument was rejected in *Eley* (above section 5.4.5) but was accepted in *Re New British Iron Co, ex parte Beckwith* [1898] 1 Ch 324.

CASE EXAMPLE

Re New British Iron Co, ex parte Beckwith [1898] 1 Ch 324

Article 62 fixed the sum of £1,000 as payable as remuneration to the board of directors, to be divided amongst them as they saw fit. When the company went into liquidation, without having paid any remuneration, it became important to determine whether or not the remuneration was due to the directors as members (the directors were also shareholders in the company) or otherwise. Held: *Per* Wright, J: 'That article is not in itself a contract between the company and the directors … But where on the footing of that article the directors are employed by the company and accept office the terms of art 62 are embodied in and form part of the contract between the company and the directors'. The remuneration was due to the directors, 'under a distinct contract with the company'.

Guinness plc v Saunders [1990] 2 AC 663 is a relatively recent case in which the court treated the relevant articles as terms embodied in a separate contract between a director and the company. This is not an express part of the decision in the case but must be a step in the reasoning.

CASE EXAMPLE

Guinness plc v Saunders [1990] 2 AC 663

Articles provided that remuneration for work outside the scope of the ordinary duties of a director had to be fixed by the board of directors as a whole. Mr Ward was a director of Guinness plc who performed work outside the normal scope and was given special remuneration of £5.2 million by a committee of the board. The sum should have been fixed by the board of directors as the committee had no authority to make the payment. Mr Ward was ordered to repay the money to the company. Mr Ward argued that a *quantum meruit* sum was owed to him. Held: Where parties to a contract have agreed how remuneration is to be determined, the court will not award a *quantum meruit* even if the agreement has not been implemented.

KEY FACTS

Amending articles and contracts with terms derived from the articles	
Amending the articles of association	
Articles may be amended by special resolution	s 21
Unless they are entrenched	s 22
A contract clause not to amend its articles will not be specifically enforced against a company but the company may be liable in damages if it alters its articles in breach of the contract.	*Russell v Northern Bank Development Corporation* (1992) *Southern Foundries (1926) Ltd v Shirlaw* (1940)
Accrued rights may not be removed by amendment of the articles.	*James v Buena Ventura Nitrate Grounds Syndicate Limited* (1896)
Amendments must be *bona fide* for the benefit of the company as a whole.	*Allen v Gold Reefs of West Africa Ltd* (1900)
Where the company as an entity is not impacted by the amendment, such as squeeze out cases, the test is difficult to apply.	*Greenhalgh v Arderne Cinemas Ltd* (1951) *Sidebottom v Kershaw* (1920) *Brown v British Abrasive Wheel* (1919) *Dafen Tinplate v Llanelly Steel Company* (1907)
Contracts with terms derived from the articles	
Article provisions may be found to be embodied in a separate contract between a company and a third person, typically a director's service contract.	*Re New British Iron Co, ex parte Beckwith* (1898) *Guinness plc v Saunders* (1990)

ACTIVITY

'The more one looks at the decided cases the more hard it is to know precisely where the line is to be drawn between those cases where the introduction of a compulsory transfer provision will be upheld and those where it will not.' *Constable v Executive Connections Ltd* [2005] BCLC 638 at 652.

Do you agree with this statement? State the current law on the right of a majority to exclude a minority shareholder from a company.

5.7 Shareholders' agreements

Shareholders' agreements are often entered into when the company is first registered but may be entered into at any time. They may or may not be part of the 'official' constitution of the company subject to the relevant registration requirements. Whether or not they are registrable, they can fundamentally affect the way a company is managed and controlled. Shareholders' agreements are often entered into, rather than putting the relevant provisions in the articles, to provide clarity in relation to enforceability compared to the lack of clarity surrounding enforceability of the articles of association, as discussed in section 5.4.5 above. Another reason why shareholders agreements are used is to preserve confidentiality, yet it is incorrect to assume that all shareholders' agreements can lawfully be kept confidential. Great care must be taken when drafting a shareholders' agreement to ensure that, if confidentiality is required, it does not fall within s 29 of the Companies Act 2006 and therefore become registrable with the registrar of companies pursuant to s 30 and available for public scrutiny. Failure to register a registrable shareholders' agreement is a criminal offence committed by the company and every officer in default.

Shareholders' agreements are used by the shareholders of closely held companies, meaning companies with a small number of shareholders. They are impractical for companies with a large number of shareholders and are rarely of interest to those who buy company shares purely as a financial investment. Shareholders' agreements are used as a matter of course in a number of common business transactions, such as joint ventures. The document usually referred to as the 'joint venture agreement' is a particular type of shareholders' agreement.

5.7.1 Matters addressed in shareholders' agreements

Many provisions in shareholders' agreements could appear in the articles but are deliberately put into a shareholders' agreement, usually in pursuit of confidentiality and enforceability. The matters dealt with in shareholders' agreements vary depending upon the context in which the agreement is put in place. Examples of matters commonly provided for are:

1 Appointment of directors for fixed terms.
2 Protection from removal of particular individuals from the board of directors using weighted voting rights.
3 Shareholder approval to be needed for major company decisions.
4 No issue of shares without unanimous shareholder approval.
5 Rights regarding withdrawal from the company:
   - Pre-emption rights providing that if one shareholder wishes to sell his shares he must first offer them to the others.
   - Obligations on shareholders to buy shares of a shareholder who wishes to exit the company at a fair/market price or price to be ascertained in a stipulated way.
6 Payment of dividends:
   - Shareholder agreements may contain clauses dealing with the proportion of distributable profits to be distributed annually. A joint venture agreement between two company shareholders, for example, may provide for all legally distributable profits to be distributed each year.
7 Restrictive covenants:
   - Where a shareholder has brought particular expertise to a company he may contract with other shareholders not to use that expertise in any other business (note, however, that public policy rules operate to preclude enforcement of restrictive covenants that are unreasonable restraints on trade).

5.7.2 Who is party to a shareholders' agreement?

Shareholders' agreements are contracts entered into by two or more shareholders. Ordinary rules of contract apply which means that shareholders' agreements bind only those shareholders who enter into the agreement and can only be amended with the agreement of all parties to the agreement.

The company can be, and often is, made a party to a shareholders' agreement. The contractual undertakings of the company are subject to special considerations, examined below at section 5.7.4, which often make the contractual obligations of the company unenforceable. Unenforceability of one or more of the company's obligations may or may not affect the operation of the agreement *between the shareholders*; whether or not it does will depend upon the correct construction of the agreement. It is important to draft the agreement so that, as far as possible, the obligations of the shareholders are stated separately from the obligations of the company. This provides the best likelihood that the problematic obligations can be deleted, or 'blue-lined' out of the agreement, leaving the obligations of the shareholders intact.

5.7.3 Enforcing shareholders' agreements

If a shareholder who is a party to a shareholders' agreement breaches the agreement, any other shareholder who is a party to the agreement who has suffered loss caused by the breach that is not too remote may sue for damages for breach of contract. The availability of other remedies, such as mandatory injunctions, depends upon the application of contract law principles. The leading case on enforcement of shareholders agreements is *Russell v Northern Bank Development Corporation* [1992] 1 WLR 588 (HL).

CASE EXAMPLE

Russell v Northern Bank Development Corporation [1992] 1 WLR 588 (HL)

A shareholders' agreement was entered into between the five shareholders of Tyrone Brick Limited. The company was also a party to the agreement. Clause 3 provided, amongst other things, that no further share capital was to be created without the written consent of all parties to the agreement. The board of directors proposed a resolution to increase the share capital. One shareholder, Russell, sought an injunction restraining the other shareholders who were party to the agreement from voting in support of the resolution and a declaration that clause 3 was valid and binding on both the shareholders and the company. Held: In relation to the shareholders, the agreement was not a restriction on the statutory powers of the company to alter its share capital, its memorandum or articles of association. Clause 3 was valid and enforceable between the shareholders and Russell was entitled to a declaration that the shareholders were bound by clause 3 as to how to exercise their votes and in an appropriate case would be entitled to an injunction. The agreement was held to be unenforceable against the company.

5.7.4 The effect of the enforceability of shareholders' agreements

In *Russell* the House of Lords confirmed that shareholders' agreements can be enforced *against shareholders*. Enforcing a shareholders' agreement can and often does have the effect of circumventing a statutory provision that appears to be mandatory and which the courts will not permit the company to contract out of directly.

By way of illustration, s 21 of the Companies Act 2006 states that a company may amend its articles by special resolution, a power that has appeared in previous Companies Acts. It is a long established principle that a company cannot deprive itself of this statutory power by putting a provision to that effect in its articles (see *Allen v Gold Reefs of West Africa Ltd* [1900] 1 Ch 656, discussed in Chapter 6). *Russell v Northern Bank Development Corporation* (1992) decided that a company also cannot contract out of this statutory power by entering into an agreement the performance of which has the effect of denying the company the power to exercise its statutory power to amend its articles.

Such an undertaking by the company was described as, 'as obnoxious as if it had been contained in the articles of association and therefore ... unenforceable as being contrary to the [Act]'. In reality, however, the *company* does not need to contract out of this statutory power. The same result, that the power to amend its articles cannot be exercised, can be achieved by the *shareholders* entering into a voting arrangement in a shareholders' agreement. Farrar describes this state of the law as a 'triumph of form over substance', for although we can state categorically that a company cannot contract out of the mandatory power in the Companies Act 2006 (the form), that mandatory power can effectively be excluded (the substance). This is a further example of the courts upholding arrangements that circumvent supposedly mandatory statutory provisions (see *Bushell v Faith* [1969] 2 Ch 438 (HL) and *Amalgamated Pest Control v McCarron* [1995] 1 QdR 583 (Queensland Supreme Court, Australia), both considered in section 5.4.4).

SUMMARY

The constitution of a company

The key constitutional documents of a company formed under the Companies Act 2006 are its articles of association and any special resolutions, its current statement of capital and its certificate of incorporation.

Pre-2006 Act constitutions

- Historically, a registered company had to have an objects clause in its memorandum of association. The Companies Act 2006 treats all provisions in a memoranda of association as article provisions (s 28).
- The *ultra vires* doctrine has been wholly abolished for non-charitable companies and a company has the capacity of a natural person (s 39).

2006 Act registered companies

- May but need not restrict its objects in its articles (s 31). The company has the capacity of a natural person (s 39).
- Potential impact of restricted objects on third parties is as a limitation on the powers of the board/authority of a company agent which is ignored in favour of a person dealing with the company in good faith (s 40).

The articles of association including the model articles

- If articles are not registered relevant model articles will apply (s 20(1)(a)).
- Model articles apply insofar as registered articles do not exclude or modify them (s 20(1)(b)). See: Model Articles for Private Companies Limited by Shares and Model Articles for Public Companies.
- Articles may not override mandatory laws such as the right of a shareholder to petition the court to wind up the company (*Re Peveril Gold Mines* (1898)).
- Weighted voting rights may operate to undermine the mandatory nature of statutory provisions (*Bushell v Faith* (1969)), but Listing Rules prohibit weighted voting rights undermining the right of shareholders to remove directors.

The articles are a statutory contract and enforcement is restricted

- The articles form a statutory contract (s 33) enforcement of the provisions of which raises a number of moot issues including:
  - Can a shareholder enforce non-membership rights? (*Beattie v Beattie* (1938) says no (*obiter*); *Salmon v Quinn & Axtens* (1909) suggests yes.)
  - Can a shareholder require the company to act in accordance with the articles if an ordinary resolution could authorise or ratify the challenged behaviour? (*Grant v UK Switchback Railways* (1888) says no (but it is unclear what amounts to an internal management matter and what amounts to a personal right.)
  - Can one shareholder enforce the articles against another shareholder? (*Rayfield v Hands* (1960) says yes but cautions that the decision may be confined to quasi-partnership cases.)

Contracts with terms derived from the articles

Article provisions may be found to be embodied in a separate contract between a company and a third person, typically a director's service contract (*Re New British Iron Co, ex parte Beckwith* (1898); *Guinness plc v Saunders* (1990)).

Alteration of the constitution

- Articles may be amended by special resolution (s 21), unless they are entrenched (s 22).
- A contract clause not to amend its articles will not be specifically enforced against a company but the company may be liable in damages if it alters its articles in breach of the contract (*Russell v Northern Bank Development Corporation* (1992); *Southern Foundries (1926) Ltd v Shirlaw* (1940)).
- Accrued rights may not be removed by amendment of the articles (*James v Buena Ventura Nitrate Grounds Syndicate Limited* (1896)).
- Amendments must be *bona fide* for the benefit of the company as a whole (*Allen v Gold Reefs of West Africa Ltd* (1900)).
- Where the company as an entity is not impacted by the amendment, such as squeeze out cases, the test is difficult to apply (*Greenhalgh v Arderne Cinemas Ltd* (1951); *Sidebottom v Kershaw* (1920); *Brown v British Abrasive Wheel* (1919) and *Dafen Tinplate v Llanelly Steel Company* (1907)).

Shareholder agreements

Shareholders' agreements may undermine the rule preventing articles overriding mandatory statutory rights of the company such as the right to alter the articles by special resolution (*Russell v Northern Bank Development Corporation* (1992)).

ACTIVITY

Discuss the key developments in the relevance of the doctrine of *ultra vires* to registered companies in the UK including the effect of the Companies Act 2006 on companies registered pursuant to the 2006 Act and companies already in existence when the 2006 Act came into effect.

SAMPLE ESSAY QUESTION

> Critically analyse case law on the rights of shareholders to enforce the articles of association to demonstrate why you agree or disagree with the proposition that the contractual effect of the articles is limited to provisions of the articles concerned with the membership and constitution of the company.

Unpack the question

This is the first essential step which you must take time to do properly. You should separate out:

- Explaining what the articles of association are
- Identification of the articles as a contract
- Identifying the types of rights protected under s 33 and the case law
- The concept of a membership right/outsider right and the case law
- Provisions concerned with the constitution of the company and the internal management and majority rule principle and the case law
- Your reasoned views on the accuracy of the proposition.

The articles: what they are and contractual character

- The internal rules of the company registered on incorporation or appropriate Model Articles apply: s 20
- A contract between the company and members and between the members *inter se*: s 33
- Explain ways in which the articles are a unique type of contract.

The types of rights protected under s 33 and the cases

Discuss the cases on membership rights and outsider rights:

- *Eley v Positive Govenment Security Life Assurance Co*
- *Browne v La Trinidad*
- *Beattie v Beattie*
- *Hickman v Kent or Romney Sheep Breeders Association* (note classic words of Astbury, J).

Discuss constitutional rights and the internal management and majority rule principle

- Discuss *Salmon v Quinn & Axtens*
- Discuss the internal management and majority rule cases: *Grant v UK Switchback Railways Company; MacDougall v Gardiner*
- Discuss Wedderburn's (1957) interpretation.

CONCLUDE

Express your reasoned opinion as to the accuracy or otherwise of the statement.

Further reading

Articles

Bourne, N, 'Drafting objects clauses and *ultra vires*' (2004) 25 Bus LR 258 (Note that this article is on the pre-2006 Act law).

Cheung, R, 'The use of statutory unanimous shareholder agreements and entrenched articles in reserving minority shareholders' rights: a comparative analysis' (2008) 29 Comp Law 234.

Davenport, B, 'What did *Russell v Northern Bank Development Corporation Ltd* Decide?' [1993] LQR 553.

Drury, R, 'The relative nature of a shareholder's right to enforce the company contract' [1986] CLJ 219.

Griffin, S, 'The rise and fall of the *ultra vires* rule in corporate law' (1998) 2 MJLS 5.

Griffin, S, 'The Limited Contractual Nature of s. 14 of The Companies Act 1985' (1993) 14 Comp Law 217.

Hannigan, B, 'Altering the Articles to Provide for Compulsory Transfer – Dragging the Minority to a Reluctant Exit' [2007] JBL 471.

Martin, S, 'Statutory procedures' (2008) 32 CSR 16.

Prentice, D, 'Alteration of articles of association – expropriation of shares' (1996) 112 LQR 194.

Rixon, 'Competing Interests and Conflicting Principles: an Examination of the Power of Alteration of Articles of Association' (1986) 49 MLR 446.

Wedderburn, K, 'Shareholders' Rights and the Rule in *Foss v Harbottle*' [1957] CLJ 194.

Books

Cheffins, B, *Company Law, Theory, Structure and Operation* (Clarendon Press, 1997).

Reece Thomas, K, and Ryan, C, *The Law and Practice of Shareholders' Agreements* (3rd edn, LexisNexis, 2009).

6

Financing a company

AIMS AND OBJECTIVES

After reading this chapter you should be able to:

- Identify the basic methods of funding a company's operations
- Recognise a financing lease distinct from an operating lease
- Identify six types of debt financing
- State the benefits to a lender of a secured loan compared to an unsecured loan
- Discuss the main legal restrictions on share finance that do not apply to debt finance
- Understand the composition of share capital
- Understand the key distinguishing features of debt and equity financing

6.1 Introduction

The aim of this chapter is to introduce you to:

- how a registered company limited by shares funds or obtains the money and assets it requires in order to conduct its business operations;
- the basic legal principles governing different types of funding or financing arrangements.

The financing structure of a company is not static. It changes over time in response to the business needs of the company and the relative costs of different types of financing. The financing structure of a closely held company may also often change in response to the needs of its shareholders.

The *amount* of funding a company needs will be determined by the business needs of the company from time to time. If a company seeks to expand its business for which it requires new manufacturing equipment but does not have the money to pay for the required machinery, for example, it will need to fund the acquisition of the machinery.

The *type* of financing arrangement used to obtain the required funding will largely be determined by the relative costs of different types of financing. It is assumed that a company run for profit will seek to minimise the cost of funding its business operations as part of its endeavour to maximise profits. If this is correct, all other things being equal, the structure of a company's fina ncing will change over time in response to one type of finance becoming less expensive than another. All other things being equal, when interest rates are high, we would expect to see a company that has borrowed a lot of money at an interest rate that varies with market rates seeking to refinance its debt, possibly by raising money from the issue of shares and using that money (equity financing) to reduce its borrowings (debt financing).

The cost of funding is a combination of the sums payable to the provider of the funding, such as interest payable to a bank pursuant to a bank loan, and the administration costs of setting up and managing the relationship with the funding provider (referred to as 'transaction costs'), such as lawyer's fees for advice and drafting contracts, and other expenses incurred to ensure compliance with applicable laws and regulations. What appears to be a cheap source of funds may turn out to be an expensive funding option if the transaction costs to access it are high. The interest rate payable on money borrowed from a bank or banking syndicate may be higher than the rate payable on money borrowed from members of the public, yet the costs of entering into debt arrangements with the public, typically by the issue of debenture stock, are high. Once transaction costs are taken into account, the bank loan may be the less expensive funding option.

A third factor, critical in assessing the relative cost of funding options, is the impact of the proposed financial arrangements on the tax position of the company. The growth of lease financing in the period up to the mid-1980s was driven by tax incentives which made lease financing a relatively inexpensive type of financing arrangement. Corporate tax is a complex subject on which companies seek advice from highly specialised accountants and lawyers. Extremely complicated financing arrangements are often put in place because they are 'tax efficient'. Even for small, family owned companies, tax efficiency is a significant factor affecting the company's financing arrangements. The aim in such cases will not necessarily be to minimise the taxes payable by the company, but to arrive at the most tax efficient position for the sole or major shareholders. This involves consideration of the taxes payable by both the company and the shareholder.

The financing arrangements of a large listed company are likely to be far more complex than those of a small, closely held company, yet the basic legal framework of corporate financing explained here is the same for all companies limited by shares.

6.2 Types of corporate financing

The basic methods of funding a company's operations are:

- Issue shares: equity financing.
- Borrow money: debt financing.

Equipment needed by a company can also be acquired by lease financing.

Most companies are financed by a combination of debt and equity financing. A company with a high proportion of its financing in the form of debt is knows as a highly geared company. It is also described as highly leveraged. A highly geared, or highly leveraged company is more vulnerable to insolvency than a company with low gearing. This is because it must service its debts, that is, make the payments due under its loan agreements, regardless of its turnover or profits. In contrast, the level of dividend paid to equity shareholders will reflect the profitability of the company and will fall following an extensive period of poor trading. Moreover, it is unlawful for a company to pay a dividend to its shareholders unless it has distributable profits out of which to pay it.

The law governing debt financing is principally contract law. Other sources of governing law are banking law and, if the company is borrowing directly from the public by the issuing of debt securities (also called debenture stock), securities regulation.

Core company law focuses on equity financing: the relationship between the company and its shareholders. The introduction to equity financing in the final section of this chapter leads into the more detailed consideration of shares, shareholders and share capital in the next chapter.

6.3 Lease financing

Lease financing is separated out from equity and debt as a type of financing because it is legally distinct from both. From a financial and accounting perspective, however, finance leases are essentially the same as term loans. If a company requires a particularly costly asset for use in its operation, instead of borrowing or issuing shares in return for the money to buy the asset, it may decide to hire the asset under a contract. The contract is called a lease.

Certain types of leases are regarded as part of corporate finance because *from a non-legal perspective* they function in the same way as borrowing a sum of money and spending the borrowed money on the relevant asset. These 'finance leases' are distinguished from operating leases by key characteristics:

- they are typically long term (10 years is not unusual) and cannot be terminated earlier by the company except in very limited circumstances involving cause (for example, the asset is defective) or payment of a significant sum;
- the sum of the lease payments is at least 90 per cent of, and is almost always more than, the price at which the company could buy the leased asset;
- the asset is not intended to be hired out to any other person: the term (length) of the lease is at least as long as the useful lifespan, or economic life, of the leased asset;
- the lessee is responsible for the servicing and maintenance of the leased asset so assumes substantially all the risks of ownership (as well as the rewards, ie the right to possession and use).

The true nature of finance leases is indicated by the fact that the lessor is usually a finance company, a bank or a banking subsidiary. Special rules govern how finance leases, distinct from operating leases, have to be accounted for. Essentially, these special accounting rules result in the same accounting entries in the balance sheet of a company in relation to a finance lease as for a loan and subsequent purchase of an asset with the borrowed sum. Even if *in law* the company is neither the owner of the asset nor a borrower of money it must regard itself as such for finance and accounting purposes.

6.4 Debt financing: creditors

creditor
a person to whom a debt is owed

Debt financing occurs when a company enters into *a contract to borrow money* from another person, typically a bank, which lends money to the company. The cost of borrowing is usually expressed as interest on the sum borrowed (the capital sum) and interest payments are a tax-deductible business expense payable by the company.

Lenders are a type of creditor and are often called 'financial creditors' to distinguish them from other creditors to whom the company owes sums of money. Unlike other creditors, even if lending money is not the principal business of a financial creditor, it is the principal purpose of the financial creditor's transaction with the company.

judgment creditor
a creditor who has sued the company owing him money and obtained judgment from the court in his favour against the company

Other types of creditors are trade creditors and judgment creditors. An example of a trade creditor is a supplier to the company who agrees that the company may pay for the goods or services supplied to the company some time after delivery or performance. A judgment debtor is a person who has secured a judgment for a sum of money against the company which the company has not paid. The judgment may have arisen out of a range of legal wrongs, including, for example, negligence on the part of the company. If a company fails to pay its taxes by the due date, HM Revenue & Customs (HMRC) will also be a creditor of the company.

Critical legal characteristics of debt financing

Subject to generic legal limits to contract enforcement such as illegality and public policy considerations, essentially, the law will give contractual effect to whatever bargain a lender and company reach. The legal essence of debt financing is that if the company defaults on any payment due under the loan agreement, whether interest payments, repayment of the sum borrowed or both, the lender can sue the company to recover the unpaid sums.

Critical tax characteristics of debt financing

The different tax treatment of the cost of debt finance (interest payments) and the cost of equity finance (dividends) has made debt financing very popular in the UK.

The cost of debt financing is deducted, along with other costs of doing business, from the receipts of the company from its business operations, in the calculation of a company's profits. The cost of debt finance is paid out of pre-tax profit. In contrast, the cost of equity finance is paid out of the profits of a company after tax has been paid on those profits. The cost of equity finance is paid out of post-tax profits. This difference in taxation gives debt finance a tax benefit over equity financing. All other things being equal, UK tax treatment makes debt financing less expensive than equity financing.

The key characteristics of common types of debt financing are examined below.

6.4.1 Overdraft facilities

The most common type of debt or loan financing is an overdraft facility. An overdraft is called a 'facility' because it is an arrangement available to the borrower should the borrower wish to use it or 'draw-down' on it. It is a revolving facility because the borrower can repay sums borrowed and draw-down further sums at will, so that the sum borrowed increases and decreases over the life of the facility.

The relationship between a bank and a company (or any person) that has an account with an overdraft facility is contractual. When the company deposits money in the bank account, the bank becomes the debtor and the company is the creditor: the bank owes money to the company. When the account becomes overdrawn, the character of the parties to the contract is reversed and the bank becomes the creditor and the company is now the debtor: the company owes money to the bank.

The terms of the overdraft contract will state, amongst other things, the limit of the overdraft facility, ie the maximum sum the company may owe the bank at any point in time, the interest rate payable by the company on any sum borrowed/overdrawn and the circumstances in which the bank can require the company to repay the sum borrowed/overdrawn.

Understanding how an overdraft works is a precondition to understanding the application in certain circumstances of laws governing transaction avoidance procedures available to a liquidator (see Chapter 16 below).

6.4.2 Simple loan contracts

The simplest type of debt or loan financing is a term loan. Consider the following simple example:

- a bank (the creditor) (the lender);
- contracts to lend (a loan);
- to a company (the debtor) (the borrower);
- £100,000 (the capital sum);
- at a fixed rate of interest of 6 per cent per annum (or at a variable rate of interest);
- interest is payable annually on the outstanding capital;
- capital is repayable in 10 annual instalments of £10,000 ;
- if the company fails to make any capital or interest payment on the due date, the total outstanding sum and accrued interest becomes repayable immediately.

6.4.3 Syndicated loans

The term syndicated loan simply refers to a loan entered into between the company and more than one lender, the 'syndicate' of lenders or 'banking syndicate'. The loan is usually large and the contractual arrangements between the various lenders and the company can be very complicated. There is usually a lead lender or 'underwriter' of the loan which is usually the bank providing the largest part of the loan. The main reason for syndicated loans is to share amongst a number of lenders the risk of the company not being able to repay the large sum of money borrowed.

6.4.4 Subordinated loans

A subordinated loan is a loan that provides for the company to repay to the lender the sum borrowed only after the lender has first repaid in full sums owed to other specified lenders under specified loans. The subordinated loan is said to rank *after* those other specified loans. The subordination makes the loan riskier for the lender than it otherwise would be as, should the borrowing company run into financial difficulties, the lender has less chance of being repaid the sum lent than it would have if the loan was not subordinated.

6.4.5 Debt securities

Rather than borrowing money from a bank or other financial institution, a company may choose to borrow money from the public directly. The money banks and other financial institutions lend to companies is ultimately accessed from the public, who deposit money in current or savings accounts. Accessing the public directly can save a company costs by cutting out the bank's and/or other middle man's costs and profits.

Company borrowing from the public most commonly takes the form of a company issuing corporate bonds (such as eurobonds and medium term notes) or 'loan notes' (also referred to as 'loan stock' or 'debenture stock') all of which are forms of 'debt security'. Debt security is a broad term encompassing securities issued by a range of issuers which includes companies but also includes, for example, the Government. Treasury bonds, for example, are debt securities.

Securities regulation imposes strict legal rules on companies offering debt securities to the public. Compliance involves significant legal and administrative costs. Consequently, the issue of debt securities is only practical for raising large sums. Also, the issue of debt securities can only realistically be contemplated by companies that have established good commercial track records and are therefore attractive to investors.

Corporate debt securities are instruments of indebtedness of the company. They are usually freely transferable by the lender and are typically listed on a stock exchange where they are bought and sold just like shares: they are traded in the capital market. The term 'debenture stock' is usually reserved for corporate debt securities that are secured, typically by a floating charge. 'Secured' basically means that the contractual right to be paid is reinforced by a property right (see the next section). This is not always the case, however, and some debenture stock, notwithstanding its name, is not secured.

6.4.6 Secured lending

Banks are unwilling to lend large sums to companies on an unsecured basis. Revisit the example of a simple, unsecured, loan contract set out at section 6.4.2 above and consider what the bank can do if the company fails to make a payment to the bank under the agreement, ie 'defaults' on payment of interest, repayment of the sum lent (the capital or principal) or an instalment thereof, or both. Apart from writing letters demanding payment or renegotiating the terms of the loan, the bank may:

- sue the company to recover the sum payable under the terms of the loan agreement, seek to enforce the judgment and, if execution of the judgment debt fails, petition the court to have the company wound up;
- issue a statutory demand for payment (if £750 or more is owed) following which, if the company fails to pay, petition the court to have the company wound up.

Provided a company has the money to pay the sum owed, receipt of a statutory demand normally results in swift payment without the need for further legal action. If, however, a company cannot repay the sum due because it does not have the money, it is likely that the company will owe money to more than one creditor. Even if there are no judgment creditors, it is likely to have a mixture of financial and trade creditors and HM Revenue & Customs is likely to be a creditor due to unpaid taxes.

If a company cannot pay its debts as they fall due, it is insolvent, and, unless the company has a realistic opportunity to borrow more money to enable it to pay its debts as they fall due and trade its way out of insolvency, the company is likely to enter insolvent liquidation. This means that the company will be wound up (liquidated) and its assets distributed amongst its creditors. Once a company has entered into insolvent liquidation, creditors cannot bring legal actions to enforce debts owed to them but must rely on the liquidator to distribute to them their fair share of the company's assets as determined by the application of the legally dictated order of distribution in Chapter VIII of the Insolvency Act 1986 and the *pari passu* principle.

If a loan is unsecured the lender's rights against the company are purely contractual and the right to enforce the contract is lost should the company enter into insolvent liquidation. An unsecured lender has not negotiated and secured any property rights, such as the right, in the event that the company defaults on repayment of the sum borrowed, to take possession of specified valuable property owned by the company, sell that property, and recover from the proceeds of sale the debt owed to it by the company. In the absence of property rights, in the event of the company entering into insolvent liquidation, the unsecured lender will rank alongside all other unsecured and non-preferential creditors (trade and judgment creditors and HM Revenue and Customs) when the liquidator distributes the assets of the company.

In addition to the right to enforce the loan contract, which is a personal right the lender can assert only against the borrower, a secured lender has property rights (also referred to as real rights).

Consider the following example of a simple secured loan:

- the bank (lender/creditor/chargee);
- contracts to lend the agreed amount *and* secure the loan amount and any interest outstanding from time to time (the sum charged);
- against specified property (the charged property);
- owned by the company (borrower/debtor/chargor);
- by contractually requiring the company to grant a fixed charge against the specified property in favour of the bank (contractual right);
- the company, in performance of the contractual obligation, takes any and all steps (including the execution of any necessary documents) required to grant the fixed charge to the bank (the formalities);
- the bank has a property right, or real right, in the specified property.

Two key qualities of property rights, or real rights, are:

- The lender can assert its property rights against an indefinite number of people, not only the person that granted the property rights to the lender.
- The lender can take the property in which it has property rights out of an insolvency process (including the insolvent liquidation of a company).

This means that the secured creditor is entitled to retain the proceeds of sale of the property against which its loan is secured (the property in which the property rights exist), up to the value of the sum secured against the property. It is the rights of the holder of a *fixed* charge against one or more items of property (assets) of the company that is described here. The property rights arising out of *fixed* charge secured lending are illustrated diagrammatically in Figures 6.1 and 6.2.

insolvent

a company is insolvent and an application to wind it up can be made if it is unable to pay its debts

secured creditor

a creditor who has a property interest in all or part of the property of the company to secure the debt

fixed charge

a property interest in specified property preventing the owner of the property from selling or otherwise dealing with it without first either paying back the sum secured against it or obtaining the consent of the chargeholder. Also called a specific charge

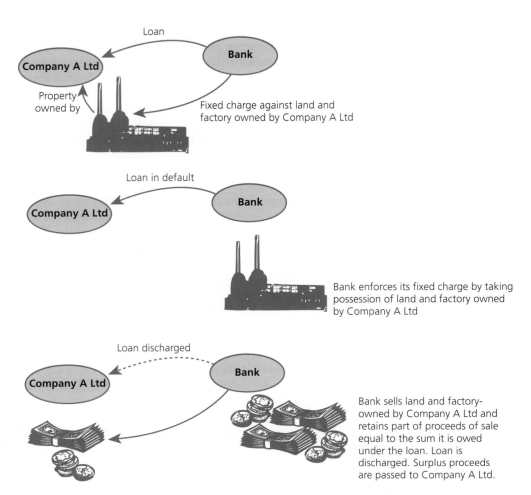

Figure 6.1 Fixed charge against real property: stages of enforcement

floating charge

a security by way of charge over one or more specified classes of assets, present and future, prior to enforcement of which charge, the company is free to carry on business in the ordinary way in relation to those assets, including removing any assets from the security

The distinction between secured and unsecured lending is critical because of the enhanced rights of a secured lender relative to an unsecured lender. This is the key point to appreciate here.

Within secured lending, a key distinction exists between fixed charge security and floating charge security. The property rights, or real rights, of a lender that has secured its loan to a company by taking a *floating* charge against company property are subordinated by statute to certain other debts (preferential debts), expenses of the liquidator and statutory charges. The rights of a floating charge holder are not as clear cut or strong as the property rights of a fixed charge holder. The most important time to analyse the rights of different types of secured lenders (basically, fixed and floating charge holders) is when a company is in insolvent liquidation. If the liquidator is to distribute the assets of the company amongst the various creditors in accordance with the statutory order of distribution provided for in Chapter VIII of the Insolvency Act 1986, he must first establish the rights of the different types of creditors, including the rights of the different types of secured creditors. For this reason, secured lending, including the distinction between fixed and floating charges, is considered in further detail towards the end of this book, in Chapter 16.

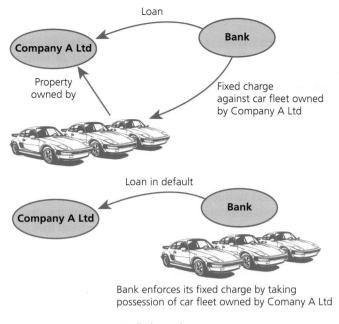

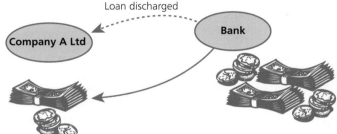

Bank enforces its fixed charge by taking
possession of car fleet owned by Comany A Ltd

Bank sells car fleet owned by
Company A Ltd and retains part
of proceeds of sale equal to sum
owed under the loan. Loan is
discharged. Surplus proceeds are
passed to Company A Ltd

Figure 6.2 Fixed charge against personal property: stages of enforcement

debenture

a document
which either
creates a debt or
acknowledges it.
Usually, though
by no means al-
ways, a debenture
is secured

6.4.7 Debentures

The term 'debenture' is used widely to describe a range of debts, documents evidencing
debts and the security attached to debts. It is important not to ascribe too narrow a
meaning to the term or to make assumptions about a debt or 'instrument' described as
a debenture.

A partial definition of the term debenture is included in s 738 of the Companies Act
2006. The provision simply clarifies that where the term debenture is used in the Act, it
includes collective debentures, ie debenture stock.

SECTION

. . . .

'738 Meaning of "debenture"
In the Companies Acts 'debenture' includes debenture stock, bonds and any other securities of
a company, whether or not constituting a charge on the assets of the company.'

Perhaps the best explanation of the term debenture can be found in *Levy v Abercorris Slate
and Slab Co* (1887) 37 Ch D 260.

JUDGMENT

'[Debenture] ... means a document which either creates a debt or acknowledges it ... [there is
no] precise legal definition of the term, it is not either in law or commerce a strictly technical
term, or what is called a term of art.'

6.5 Equity financing: shareholders

Equity financing occurs where a company issues shares to one or more investors who become members of the company, or 'shareholders'. In return for the shares, the shareholder pays the issue price of the shares to the company. The company receives its funding and the shareholder receives and owns a valuable asset, shares in the company. The shareholder has contributed 'equity capital' to the company (the finance term), which is also called 'share capital' (the legal term).

Only public companies, not private companies, may offer shares to the public (s 755). Any company making a public offer must comply with strict legal rules contained in securities regulation. Although the most obvious case of a public offer is an offer of shares that are to be listed on a stock exchange (when a prospectus will be required), securities regulation is not confined to this type of public offer by the company. The regulations governing different types of public offers and applications for shares to be admitted to listing on a stock exchange are detailed and highly technical (see the Financial Services and Markets Act 2000, the Prospectus Rules made by the Financial Services Authority (FSA) pursuant to that Act and Chapter 7, at section 7.5, below).

The shareholder usually has the option to:

- hold onto his shares and receive his share of such of the profits of the company as the company decides to distribute in any year in the form of dividend payments; or
- sell his shares to a third party, ideally for a higher price than he paid for them, thereby receiving back, or 'realising' the sum invested and making a profit in the form of a capital gain.

The cost to the company of equity financing in a given year is the sum of the dividend amounts paid to shareholders in that year. This corresponds to the annual interest paid on a loan, which is the cost of debt financing. Due to the law governing equity financing, it is far more flexible to 'service' or pay for equity financing than it is to service debt financing, a point that is particularly important in difficult trading times.

6.5.1 No shareholder right to receive payment for equity capital

The cost of debt financing is solely a matter of contract to be agreed between the company and the lender. Once agreed, a lender may enforce the contractual obligation of the company to pay interest in accordance with the terms of the loan by legal action. In contrast, any agreement between the company and a shareholder relating to payments by the company to the shareholder must comply with mandatory company laws which together are referred to as capital maintenance rules. The most important of these legal rules is that a company may only pay dividends out of profits available for the purpose (s 830) (and a public company must also comply with s 831). If a company and shareholder purport to agree that a shareholder is *entitled* to receive an annual dividend equal to 10 per cent of the nominal price of the share, for example, this contractual obligation will *not* be enforceable in a year in which the company does not have sufficient profits to make the dividend payment.

Furthermore, the default or presumptive legal rules governing payment of dividends, ie the rules contained in the model articles that apply if the company and the shareholders do not agree otherwise, provide that no dividend is payable unless both the board of directors recommends a dividend, and that level of dividend, or a lesser amount, is declared payable by an ordinary resolution of the shareholders (see Art 70 of the Model Articles for Public Companies and Article 30 of the Model Articles for Private Companies Limited by Shares). This default legal position places the decision as to if and when to pay dividends in the hands of the company which makes the payment terms for equity finance legally very flexible.

This flexibility may be restricted by the company agreeing with a shareholder to issue shares with rights to receive dividends at specified rates (such as in the example in the first paragraph of this section). Even in such a case, the shareholder is unable to insist on receiving a dividend, or any other payment for the supply of equity capital, if the company has no profits out of which to make the payment.

The inability of a shareholder legally to insist on receipt of a return on equity capital invested in a company is a critical distinction between debt and equity. This flexibility in the hands of the company as to whether and when to pay dividends is part of the reason why:

- investment in shares is more risky than lending money to a company, by investing in debenture stock, for example;
- the degree of leveraging of a company's financing is an extremely important factor in how likely a company will be able to remain solvent and therefore survive harsh trading conditions, when profits are low or non-existent.

The degree of leveraging is the ratio of a company's debt financing to equity financing. A company is more highly leveraged the larger the proportion of its funding that is debt financing rather than equity financing. Because the cost of debt financing is contractually fixed and does not change in difficult trading times, it can become very difficult for a company to keep up payments under its loan agreements. In contrast, the cost of servicing equity finance may be zero in difficult trading times and must be zero if the company has no distributable profits out of which to pay dividends. In difficult trading, it is far better to be funded largely by equity than debt.

If the company defaults on debt interest or capital repayments, the lender may bring legal action to recover any overdue sum and may have the company wound up. The Bank of England is concerned about the enhanced instability of the UK economy resulting from the high degree of leveraging of companies owned by private equity firms. Private equity-owned companies are highly leveraged because in good trading times this makes a lot of money for their owners. In bad times, these companies are more at risk of becoming insolvent and ceasing to trade than less highly leveraged companies.

6.5.2 No shareholder right to receive share capital back from the company

The essence of debt financing is that the company is contractually obliged to repay the sum borrowed in accordance with the terms of repayment set out in the loan agreement. In contrast, an ordinary shareholder is not entitled to insist on the return of his share capital. This is known as the share capital maintenance principle, the rules supporting which are found in the Companies Act 2006.

The company is entitled to keep any sum provided as share capital until the company is wound up (liquidated) and the assets of the company are distributed. In that distribution, the shareholder ranks last in line and will not share in the distribution unless all creditors and costs of the winding up have been paid in full.

Any agreement entitling a shareholder to insist on the return of share capital (such as where the shareholder has been issued with redeemable shares) and any action by the company to return share capital to the shareholder (such as by a reduction of share capital) must be in accordance with the Companies Act 2006, s 617 of which states that a limited company having a share capital may *not* alter its share capital except in the ways listed in that section. The two key relevant ways to return share capital to shareholders included in the s 617 list are:

- reduction of share capital in accordance with ss 641–657;
- the power of a private company to purchase its own shares out of capital, including redeeming redeemable shares, in accordance with ss 658–737 (especially ss 709–723).

6.5.3 The composition of share capital

In this chapter we have referred to equity capital and share capital as if it is of uniform composition and those terms have been used interchangeably. The rights attached to each share in a class of shares are uniform in all respects (*Birch v Cropper* (1899) 14 App Cas 525, see now s 629) therefore if a company has only one class of shares its equity capital is of uniform composition. Also, if a company has only one class of shares those shares must be equity shares, the whole of its share capital is equity capital and those terms may be used interchangeably.

As matter of law, however, the equity share capital (the term used in the Companies Act 2006) of a company may not be the same as the company's share capital, but rather a part only of the share capital. Where a company has a class of shares that 'neither as respects dividends nor as respects capital, carries any right to participate beyond a specified amount in a distribution', those shares are part of the share capital of the company but they are *not* equity shares and do *not* form part of the equity share capital of the company (s 548).

As discussed in section 6.6 below, a company may have as many classes of shares as it likes and it is in the development of various types of shares that financing flexibility has been delivered to companies. Although certain types of shares with certain key characteristics are given names such as 'preference shares', these are not legal terms but are merely descriptive of one characteristic of the shares (preference shares typically have preference rights versus ordinary shareholders in relation to either or both dividends and return of capital), or those to whom the shares are typically issued. Outside capital maintenance rules, there is a great deal of contractual flexibility as to the terms that can be agreed between the company and the owner of a particular class of shares. The key point to note is that each class of shares is governed by its own particular terms of issue. That said, certain typical classes of shares are considered in the next chapter on shares, shareholders and share capital. Note that *all* shares, not just equity shares, are subject to company law restrictions on payment of dividends and return of capital.

6.5.4 Nature of the relationship between a shareholder and the company

The relationship between a company and a shareholder is partly, but not solely, contractual in nature. The extent to which the law will give contractual effect to the bargain the company and the shareholders reach is subject not only to generic legal limits to contract enforcement such as illegality and public policy considerations, but also to mandatory rules of company law.

In a widely held company, a shareholder is one of many shareholders. This emphasises the importance of the relationship being governed by a 'standard form contract', the same for each shareholder (or at least for each shareholder holding a given class of shares). This 'standard form' is provided by the constitution of the company. The principal constitutional document of a company is the articles of association and, as we have seen in Chapter 5, the articles establish a statutory contract between each shareholder and the company (they also establish a contractual relationship between one shareholder and another but this is not important here).

The articles may not be the only contractual terms of the relationship between the company and a shareholder. The company and a shareholder may establish additional contractual arrangements governing their relationship. These additional arrangements are typical where a different class of shares is created and issued, such as preference shares or redeemable shares. The terms of issue of these shares, typically contained in the issue document, supplement the provisions in the articles. Again, the terms of issue establishing the rights of the company and the shareholders will be subject to mandatory company law rules.

The terms of the relationship between the company and a shareholder are affected and supplemented by rules of law to a far greater extent than is true of other financing relationships such as that between the company and a lender. Some of those rules regulate the financial terms of the company/shareholder relationship but many of the laws apply because, and are relevant to, the additional character of a shareholder as a part-owner of the company. As such, a shareholder does not simply have rights *against* the company but also has rights to participate in the company. Many rules of law regulate this management role of the shareholder. As it is built around the right to vote at general meetings, a large part of company law concerning the company/shareholder relationship is not relevant to non-voting shares or shares with voting rights restricted to specific matters, such as matters relevant to the financial rights of the shareholder.

The right to participate in the company carries with it responsibilities, one aspect of which we have seen above when, in chapter 5, we considered the obligation of shareholders voting to amend the articles to act '*bona fide* for the benefit of the company as a whole' (*per* Lindley MR in *Allen v Gold Reefs of West Africa Ltd* [1900] 1 Ch 656 (CA)). The role of a shareholder as part of the decision-making of the company, manifest in the voting rights attached to his shares, is considered later, in Chapter 9, dealing with the governance of the company.

6.6 Hybrid financing

The distinction between equity finance and debt finance is important in the practice of financing, for tax purposes and in law. Although far more rules of law affect the company/shareholder relationship than affect the company/lender relationship, both relationships are essentially contractual. Significant scope exists for the company and a supplier of finance, be it a lender or putative shareholder, to agree the terms on which they will deal with one another.

This is particularly so where a company has more than one class of shares. Although some rules of company law apply to all shares (such as the prohibition on dividends unless the company has distributable profits out of which to pay them (s 830) and the prioritising of creditors over shareholders in a winding up (Chapter VIII of the Insolvency Act 1986)), other legal requirements can be satisfied by one class of shares. This allows for second and subsequent classes of shares to be set up with fewer legal constraints. Consider the following examples:

- Provided a company has a class of shares entitled to vote at general meetings, it may create classes of non-voting shares.
- Provided a company has a class of shares entitled to share the surplus assets on a winding up, it may limit the rights to return of capital of the holders of one, several or all other classes of shares.
- Provided a company has a class of non-redeemable shares, it can establish second and further classes of redeemable shares.

The number of classes of shares a company may have is unlimited.

Demand for flexibility from both sides has resulted in enormous variety in the types of financial arrangements in place between companies and suppliers of funds. Arrangements do not always fit obviously into the legal categories of 'equity' and 'debt': the delivery of commercial flexibility in financing often results in legally complex arrangements with characteristics of both equity and debt, sometimes called 'hybrid' financing. It is possible to have shares that look very much like debt and debt that looks very much like equity.

Preference shares are an example of equity financing with one or more characteristics that make them resemble debt. Convertible loan stock is a debt arrangement which, at the option of the holder, can be replaced by ordinary shares, becoming equity financing, usually at a specified conversion price and on a specified date or on the occurrence of a specified event.

Corporate financing
Basic types of corporate financing:
Equity financing Debt financing Lease financing
Basic types of debt financing:
Overdraft facilities Simple loan contracts Syndicated loans Subordinated loans Debt securities: corporate bonds and loan notes/loan stock/debenture stock Secured lending
Debenture
Not a term of art. Refers to all debts and the documents evidencing them.
Equity financing:
Equity shares: bear the greatest risk of any form of corporate financing. No right to dividends, last to participate on a winding up Non-equity shares: 'neither as respects dividends nor as respects capital, carr[y] any right to participate beyond a specified amount in a distribution' s 548

Key distinguishing features of debt and equity financing		
	Debt	**Equity**
Is the provider of the finance *entitled* receive payment for the sum of money provided to the company?	This is purely a matter of contract for the company and the lender to agree. Typically, a company is contractually obliged to pay interest at the contractually specified annual rate on the sum borrowed.	This matter is regulated by the articles, the terms of issue of the shares and company law, particularly capital maintenance laws. Typically, an ordinary shareholder is entitled to receive such dividends as the directors recommend and the shareholders declare by ordinary resolution. If the company has no distributable profits, the company may not pay a dividend (s 830). (See also s 831 for public companies.)
Is the provider of the finance entitled to receive the sum of money provided to the company back from the company?	This is purely a matter of contract for the company and the lender to agree. The essence of a loan is that the company is contractually obliged to repay the sum borrowed in accordance with the terms of repayment set out in the loan agreement.	This matter is regulated by the articles, the terms of issue of the shares and company law, particularly capital maintenance laws. An ordinary shareholder is not entitled to insist in the return of his share capital. The company is entitled to keep any sum provided as 'equity' until the company is wound up and the assets of the company are distributed. Any agreement otherwise and any action by the company to return capital to the shareholder must be in accordance with the Companies Act 2006.

Key distinguishing features of debt and equity financing		
	Debt	**Equity**
	If the lender needs the money earlier than in accordance with the repayment schedule he may be able to assign the benefit of the debt in return for a lump sum, ie sell the debt.	Provided a company has a class of non-redeemable shares it can issue redeemable shares. A holder of redeemable shares can insist on the shares being redeemed, ie can receive the sum of money paid to the company back in accordance with their terms of issues provided the relevant sections of the Companies Act 2006 are complied with. A shareholder can sell his shares to a third party unless the articles prohibit this or the shareholder has entered into an agreement not to do so.
Is the cost of funding paid out of pre- or post-tax income?	The cost of debt finance is paid out of pre-tax profit: the cost is deducted as a business expense in the calculation of company profits.	The cost of equity finance is paid out of post-tax profits: dividend payments are not a tax-deductible business expense but must be paid out of the profits of a company after tax has been paid on those profits.

ACTIVITY

Self-testing questions

1. What are the basic methods of funding a company's operations?
2. What are the key characteristics of a finance lease?
3. Why is it important to recognise a lease as a finance lease rather than an operating lease?
4. Identify six types of debt financing.
5. What is the legal relationship between a bank and a company that has a current account with the bank?
6. May all registered companies offer loan securities to the public?
7. What is a secured loan?
8. Name two types of loan security.
9. What benefit does security confer on a lender?
10. What are the two key legal restrictions on share finance that do not apply to debt finance?
11. State three distinguishing features of equity compared to debt financing.
12. Distinguish equity share capital from non-equity share capital.

SUMMARY

Funding a company's operations

The basic methods of funding a company's operations are debt and equity financing. Lease financing is also available.

Debt financing

- Typical debt arrangements are overdraft facilities, simple loan contracts, syndicated loans, subordinated loans, debt securities and secured lending.
- The rights of creditors are basically contractual though these rights may be supplemented by property rights by way of charges over property of the company put in place to secure debts so that the creditor becomes a secured creditor.
- Security is usually by way of a charge which may be a fixed charge or a floating charge.

Debentures

- A debenture is a document which either creates a debt or acknowledges it. Not all debentures evidence secured debt, though most do.

Equity financing

- The relationship between a company and a shareholder is partly contractual in nature but in addition to generic legal limits to contract enforcement, mandatory rules of company law regulate the relationship. A company can have any number of classes of shares but the rights attached to each share in a class of shares are uniform (*Birch v Cropper* (1899) 14 App Cas 525; s 629).

Hybrid financing

- The myriad financial arrangements between companies and suppliers of funds do not always fit obviously into the legal categories of 'equity' and 'debt'.
- Preference shares are equity financing resembling debt.
- Convertible loan stock is a debt arrangement which can be converted into ordinary shares, becoming equity financing.

Further reading

Books

Ferran, E, *Principles of Corporate Finance Law* (Oxford University Press, 2008).

Ferran, E, *Company Law and Corporate Finance* (Oxford University Press, 1999) (do not rely on this book for current legal detail because it is written based on the Companies Act 1985).

7

Shareholders, shares and share capital

AIMS AND OBJECTIVES

After reading this chapter you should be able to:

- Understand the nature of a share and the rights and liabilities of a shareholder
- Explain the concept of a class of shares
- Distinguish equity and non-equity shares
- Discuss what is and what is not a variation of rights
- Explain the difference between the old regime of authorised share capital and the new regime of share capital statements
- Use the language of share capital accurately
- Discuss why and how a company may increase its share capital
- Discuss the role of pre-emption rights and when they are applicable
- Identify which companies may offer shares to the public and when a prospectus is required

7.1 Introduction

This chapter is divided into five parts. The first part examines the fundamental financial entitlements of ordinary shareholders and the corresponding risk of losing the value of their investment in a company. The second part examines the legal nature of a share, the rights attached to different classes of shares and variation of class rights. Part three examines the language and structure of the share capital of a company and part four examines how to increase a company's share capital. Reducing a company's share capital is a far more problematic step than increasing it and is dealt with in the next chapter, as part of our study of capital maintenance. The final part outlines offering shares to the public.

7.2 Shareholders

7.2.1 Who is entitled to the residual wealth of a company?

A company operating a business for profit owns the business assets. In *Salomon v A Salomon and Co Ltd* [1897] AC 22 (HL), the company owned the shoe manufacturing business. A company that operates a successful business makes profits and those profits belong to the company. Profits may be retained and re-invested to expand the business. This increases the value of the company's business assets and allows the company to generate bigger profits. If this happens, the company becomes wealthier. Yet the company is an artificial person. As an artificial entity it cannot enjoy that wealth and the question arises, what happens to the wealth generated by the company? To whom does the benefit of the generated wealth accrue?

The term 'residual wealth of the company' is used here to mean the value that would remain were all sums legally owed by the company paid in full. It is sometimes referred to as the 'net worth' or the 'net assets' of the company. It is held by the company for the benefit of its shareholders and is also referred to as 'shareholders' equity'.

7.2.2 How may shareholders realise the residual wealth of the company?

Capital maintenance

A shareholder cannot demand that the company pay him the value of his shares out of the assets of the company.

QUOTATION

'[T]the essence of the association [the company] is that the investment made by each shareholder is permanent.'

Hannigan, Altering the Articles to Allow for Compulsory Transfer – Dragging Minority Shareholders to a Reluctant Exit (2007) JBL 471 at 490

Even in the context of a 'quasi-partnership' company, without more, a shareholder is unable to unilaterally withdraw from the company by requiring either the company or the other shareholders to buy him out (*O'Neill v Phillips* [1999] 2 BCLC 1). The permanency of the capital contribution made by a shareholder, or, put another way, the retention of share capital by the company *vis-à-vis* the shareholder, is a fundamental principle of company law.

Not only can an individual shareholder not demand his share of the company's wealth from the company (which can be seen as protecting the majority of shareholders from individual shareholders who could otherwise jeopardise the finances of the company) but, under the rationale of creditor-protection, the courts established the principle that the company is prohibited from returning share capital to shareholders: a prohibition that operates regardless of the wishes of the majority of shareholders.

In support of this 'capital maintenance' principle, elaborate statutory procedures have been enacted in an effort to ensure that various mechanisms used by companies for legitimate purposes cannot be misused to remove share capital from the company when it is not in the creditors' interest for this to be done. Sealy described the pre-2006 Act statutory provisions as 'byzantine obfuscation'. Moreover, evidence exists that creditors do not place great reliance on the share capital of a company when deciding the creditworthiness of a company. Although the 2006 Act has taken steps to deregulate this area in relation to private companies, the second European Company Law Directive prevents significant deregulation in relation to public companies. Consequently, the capital maintenance laws, which are considered in the next chapter, remain complex.

Distribution of profits

As its name implies, the capital maintenance principle, and the rules enacted to support it, apply to the sums of money paid by shareholders to the company: the share capital. The share capital of a company is discussed further below at section 7.4. The capital maintenance principle is not intended to prevent the distribution to shareholders of that part of the wealth of the company that has been achieved by the company generating profits.

Profits may be paid out, or distributed, to shareholders and this typically occurs by the payment of annual or bi-annual dividends. An individual shareholder may not insist on receiving his share of retained profits. The power to pay out profits is for the company to exercise and rules governing exercise of the power are set out in the company's articles. As under the model articles for both public and private companies and Table A before them, the board of directors is typically empowered to recommend dividends which are then approved, or declared, by resolution of the shareholders. The shareholders may declare a smaller dividend than the board recommends but cannot by ordinary resolution declare a dividend higher than that recommended by the board. As a part of managing the business of the company, and before recommending a dividend, the board of directors must ask: which use of the profits is most likely to promote the success of the company?

Transferability of shares

Whilst a shareholder cannot withdraw his capital from the company, he may realise the value of his shares by selling them to a third party who becomes a shareholder and member of the company in his place. Without more, a share is freely transferable. This key characteristic of a share is now stated in s 544(1). Buckley LJ explained the core company law position in *Re Discoverers Finance Corporation Ltd, Lindlar's Case* [1910] 1 Ch 312 at 316:

JUDGMENT

'The regulations [articles] of the company may impose fetters upon the right of transfer. In the absence of restrictions in the articles the shareholder has by virtue of the statute the right to transfer his shares without the consent of anybody to any transferee.'

The ability to restrict transferability by inserting provisions in the articles is regularly exercised by private companies. Although the model articles for private companies limited by shares do not contain any such restrictions, this is because there are a number of ways in which transfer may be restricted and it was not considered appropriate to select one particular restriction formula for inclusion in the model articles as a default rule.

In contrast, and with rare exception, securities regulation provides that no restrictions may be placed on the transferability of listed shares (Listing Rule 2.2.4(1)). Restrictions on transfer are inconsistent with the operation of stock markets where shares are bought and sold without reference to the articles.

Special rules govern the sale, or legal transfer/assignment of shares. The process depends upon whether the shares are certificated or uncertificated shares.

Dematerialised or uncertificated shares

Shares traded on stock exchanges, listed shares, are uncertificated, also known as 'dematerialised' shares. The legal title to a dematerialised share is recorded in, and transfers are made by, CREST, the national computerised securities depository and electronic transfer system first established in 1996. Buyers and sellers of uncertificated shares must have access to the CREST system. They may be a member of CREST or access CREST through a broker. Many share transfers take place in the name of nominee brokers who hold legal title to the shares on trust for the beneficiary seller/buyer.

If all shares of a company are uncertificated, the company's register of members will be maintained by CREST. If some shares are uncertificated and some certificated, the company's register of members will be kept in two parts; the uncertificated share part will be maintained by CREST and the certificated share part will be maintained by the company. A buyer (or his nominee) normally becomes the legal owner of shares when those shares are credited to his (or his nominee's) CREST account and his name is entered in the register of members maintained by CREST. The Companies Act 2006 contains provisions enabling the Treasury and the Secretary of State to make regulations governing the transfer of title to uncertificated shares (see ss 783 to 790). The current governing regulations are The Uncertificated Securities Regulations 2001 (SI 2001/3755)

CREST

an electronic holding and settlement system in which legal title to a dematerialised share is recorded and by which share transfers are made. Shares held and transferred in this way are called 'dematerialised' as amended by The Companies Act 2006 (Commencement No 2, Consequential Amendments, Transitional Provisions and Savings) Order 2007 (SI 2007/1093).

Certificated shares

certificated

a paper-based system of holding shares, represented by share certificates

share certificate

the documentary evidence issued by a company and held by a shareholder to indicate the ownership of shares

stock transfer form

the form completed by the transferor of certificated shares to transfer the shares to the transferee

Certificated shares are transferred by the seller, or transferor, executing a stock transfer form prescribed by the Stock Transfer Act 1963. In relation to fully paid shares, a stock transfer form may be used even if the articles provide for a different form or procedure but the provisions in the articles will take precedence in relation to partly paid shares as the 1963 Act does not apply to them. The stock transfer form is sent, together with any share certificates that may have been issued, to the registered office of the company. Legal title normally vests in the buyer, or transferee, when his name is entered in the company's register of members. A stock transfer form is not a 'proper instrument of transfer' for the purposes of s 770(1)(a) of the Companies Act 2006 unless it has been stamped, indicating that stamp duty has been paid on it. Consequently, as a company may not register a transfer of shares unless a proper instrument of transfer is presented, transfer of the legal title to shares is conditional upon the payment of stamp duty on the value of the transfer. Some transfers are exempt from stamp duty, such as transfers the consideration for which is no more than £1,000. In such a case, the transferor signs an exemption certificate, which appears on the back of a standard form stock transfer form, and the form is sent directly to the company without the need for it to be sent to the Stamp Office.

Equitable title to certificated shares can arise at an earlier stage in the transfer procedure, when the transferor has done everything equity requires of him to transfer the shares. This principle, applied and developed in *Re Rose* [1952] Ch 499 and *Pennington v Waine* [2002] All ER (D) 24 (Mar) (CA), is one that you are likely to come across in property or trusts law.

Winding up the company

Shareholders can obtain the company's residual wealth by having the company wound up. Note that the power to wind up the company does not lie with an individual shareholder. Shareholders with 75 per cent or more of the votes must pass a special resolution to voluntarily wind up a company (Insolvency Act 1986, s 84(1)(b)).

Winding up the company is a terminal step. The company ceases to trade, all the assets of the company are sold and the proceeds distributed to creditors and shareholders, the company is removed from the register of companies and, at that point, the company ceases to exist (the dissolution). If a company is profitable it is rare for shareholders to wish to wind it up as this would be to kill the goose that lays the golden eggs.

7.2.3 Who is required to contribute to a company with unpaid debts?

The reverse side of the coin to the question of entitlement to share in the wealth generated by a company is: who is responsible (directly and indirectly) for the debts of a company? If, rather than generating wealth, a company not only dissipates, or loses, the money paid to it by shareholders in return for shares (the share capital), but also borrows money and loses that money in poor trading so that it cannot pay it back, the company has no residual wealth, but rather has unpaid debts. Just as the wealth, above, is owned *by the company*, the debts are owed *by the company*.

Creditors of the company cannot sue the shareholders to obtain payment, as the creditors' legal rights of action are against the company. The obligations of shareholders to contribute to the assets of the company in such circumstances to enable the company to pay its debts have been examined above, when we considered the limitation of liability principle in Chapter 3. In essence, the liability of a shareholder to pay money to the company is limited to payment for his shares. If his shares are fully paid, he cannot be required to contribute any further. Shares and share capital play an important role in limiting shareholder liability.

7.3 Legal nature of a share

7.3.1 Share as a bundle of rights and liabilities

A share in a company is a legally complex concept. The limited statutory definition of share in s 540 is far from illuminating.

SECTION

'540. In the Companies Acts "share", in relation to a company, means share in the company's, share capital'

The Act confirms that a share is a piece of personal property (s 541), and the House of Lords in *Colonial Bank v Whinney* (1886) 11 App Cas 426 confirmed that a share is a chose in action. Classification as a chose in action is usually relevant to determine the rules governing legal transfer: assignment of a chose in action is governed by s 136 of the Law of Property Act 1925. As special rules govern the transfer of legal title to most shares (see section 7.2.2 above), the status of a share as a chose in action is of limited practical relevance.

Both the entitlement ('interest') and liability aspects of a share mentioned in section 7.2 of this chapter and the contractual nature of the relationship between a shareholder and the company explored in Chapter 5 are identified in Farwell J's classic judicial statement of the nature of a share in *Borland's Trustee v Steel* [1901] 1 Ch 279:

JUDGMENT

'A share is the interest of a shareholder in the company measured by a sum of money for the purposes of liability in the first place, and of interest in the second, but also consisting of a series of mutual covenants entered into by all the shareholders *inter se* in accordance with section [33] of the Companies Act [2006]. The contract contained in the articles of association is one of the original incidents of the share. A share … is an interest measured by a sum of money and made up of various rights contained in the contract.'

This statement does not stress the rights of a shareholder to vote and thereby participate in decision-making, or the exercise of powers, by the company. This decision-making, or voting participation, aspect of share ownership is focused on in Chapter 9.

7.3.2 Presumption of equality of shares and classes of shares

There is a legal presumption that each share in a company provides the owner with the same rights and liabilities as every other share. This is called the 'presumption of equality' (see *Birch v Cropper* (1899) 14 App Cas 525 HL).

The presumption can be displaced by the company issuing shares with different rights attaching to them. Shares with the same rights and liabilities are called a class of shares. A new class of shares is created by a company issuing shares with rights or liabilities that differ in some respect from all existing shares in the company. There is no legal limit to the number of classes of shares a company may have.

Residual ordinary shares

Most companies have only one class of shares, called here 'residual ordinary shares'. The rights of a residual ordinary shareholder are found in company law (common law principles and statutory provisions) and in the constitution of the company (principally the articles). As has been noted above, shareholders are entitled to share the wealth generated by a company. Residual ordinary shares carry the same right to share in the *profits* of the company as every other residual ordinary share. Should the company be wound up, each residual ordinary share will carry the right to share in the *residual wealth* of the company as every other residual ordinary share. The third right attached to a residual ordinary share is the right to *vote* on shareholder resolutions. Without more, every residual ordinary shareholder has one vote in respect of each share on a resolution on a poll (s 284 and see Chapter 9 for the meaning of poll).

Other classes of shares

A company is only able to issue shares with restrictions or rights different from the shares already in issue if it is permitted to do so by its articles of association. The model articles for both private and public companies contain such an article (articles 22 and 43 respectively). Different classes of shares usually arise from the creation of shares differing from residual ordinary shares (and any other already existing classes) in one or more of the following key respects:

- nominal value (*Greenhalgh v Arderne Cinema's Ltd* [1946] 1 All ER 512 (CA));
- rights to participate in declared dividends;
- rights to participate in residual wealth on a winding up;
- voting rights.

That said, a new class of shares *may* be created when a share is issued with rights differing *in any way* from the residual ordinary shares and any other classes of shares the company already has. The precise range of rights that are in law 'class rights' becomes important when a company seeks to vary the rights of one class of shareholders. Unless provision is made otherwise in the articles, class rights may be varied only with the consent of holders of 75 per cent of the class. To understand when consent of the class is needed, it is necessary to know what is and what is not a class right. This issue is explored further under class rights and variation.

Ascertaining the rights attached to shares

The specific rights of second and subsequent classes of shares are found in the articles or the shareholders' resolution authorising their issue. Those rights may override or be supplemented by common law principles and statutory provisions. Following the issue of new shares, the rights and liabilities attaching to them must be stated in the amended statement of capital that must be sent, along with the return of allotment, to the registrar of companies (s 555).

The specific rights of new classes of shares should be stated clearly in the articles or authorising resolution. This avoids the need to depend upon presumptions or implied terms in determining those rights. Current practice is for the rights to be set out very clearly in the articles but this has not always been the case. The courts have regularly been called upon to determine the rights and liabilities attached to a class of shares that have been issued without the precise rights intended to attach having been captured in the articles or authorising resolution.

In the course of deciding these cases the courts have developed a number of rules or 'canons' of construction for the purposes of working out the rights of shares issues with inadequately stated rights and liabilities. The main canons of construction are:

- All shares have the same rights and liabilities unless the company and the shareholder have agreed otherwise (*Birch v Cropper* (1899), above).
- If new shares are issued those shares will carry the same rights and liabilities as the residual ordinary shares except to the extent provided otherwise.
- If voting rights have been specified, those rights are presumed to be exhaustive: the shares carry no right to vote on a resolution on any matter beyond those matters (*Re Bradford Investment Ltd* [1991] BCLC 224).
- If dividend rights have been specified, those rights are presumed to be exhaustive: the shares carry no rights to participate in dividends beyond the expressly stated rights (*Will v United Lankat Plantations Co* [1914] AC 11 (HL)).
- If capital participation rights have been specified, those rights are presumed to be exhaustive: the shares carry no rights to participate in capital beyond the expressly stated rights (*Scottish Insurance Corporation Ltd v Wilsons & Clyde Coal Co Ltd* [1949] AC 462 (HL)).

- If shares carry a right to receive a dividend of a specified amount before other shares (known as a 'preferential dividend'), such as 10 per cent of the nominal price per year, the dividend rights are presumed to be cumulative: if 10 per cent is not paid in one year, 20 per cent will be payable in the second year and, if not paid, 30 per cent will be payable in the third year, etc) (*Webb v Earle* (1875) LR 20 Eq 566).
- A preferential dividend is presumed to be not payable unless it has been declared by the company. Whilst this presumption will be rebutted by language suggesting otherwise, such as provision in the articles or authorising resolution that, subject to distributable profits being available, dividends are automatically payable on 1 May of each year, it would be courting negligence on the part of a solicitor to allow the terms of issue not to deal clearly with this matter as the legal presumption does *not* reflect commercial reality (*Re Roberts & Cooper Ltd* [1929] 2 Ch 383 and *Re Bradford Investments Plc (No 1)* [1991] BCLC 224).

The presumption that stated class rights are deemed to be exhaustive was set out in *Re National Telephone Company* [1914] 1 Ch 755.

JUDGMENT

'[E]ither with regard to dividends or with regard to the rights in a winding up, the express gift or attachment of preferential rights to preference shares, on their creation, is *prima facie*, a definition of the whole of their rights in that respect and negatives any further or other right to which, but for the specified rights, they would have been entitled.'

Class names

The names given to certain types of shares with certain key characteristics are not always legally significant. They may be merely descriptive, whether of one or more characteristic of the shares, such as 'preference shares' or of those to whom the shares are typically issued, such as 'employees' shares' or 'founders' shares'. The name 'preference shares' is simply a name indicating that the shares have some degree of preference versus other shareholders in relation to either, or both, dividends and capital participation.

'Redeemable shares', on the other hand, is not only a name but also a legal description (s 684(1)) of shares that are liable to be redeemed at the option of the company or the shareholder and must be so redeemed in accordance with the Companies Act 2006 (ss 684–689). Difficulties can arise when shares that are not redeemable shares for the purposes of the 2006 Act are none the less given the name 'redeemable shares'.

Equity and non-equity shares

Where a company has a class of shares that 'neither as respects dividends nor as respects capital, carries any right to participate beyond a specified amount in a distribution', those shares are part of the share capital of the company but they are *not* equity shares and do *not* form part of the equity share capital of the company (s 548). The distinction between equity and non-equity shares reflects the fact some shares are in many ways fulfilling the role of debt. One typical type of preference shareholder, in return for the first bite of the company's wealth after the creditors in the form of preferential rights to a fixed rate dividend *and* receipt of the sum they paid to the company back in priority to other (equity) shareholders receiving any capital back, foregoes the right to participate to any greater extent in the wealth generated by the company and is a non-equity shareholder.

Equity share capital connotes:

- an *unlimited* opportunity to share in the financial success of the company, which opportunity becomes a right in the event of a solvent winding up;
- the first layer of capital at risk and to be lost in the event of insolvency.

Class rights and variation

A company may seek to vary the rights attaching to a class of shares. Shares entitled to a 10 per cent preferential dividend, for example, may be considered a very expensive way

---

cumulative dividend

if any dividend due is not paid, it accrues to the shareholder and is payable with the next dividend due at the next payment date. Usually associated with preference shares

preference shares

shares giving the holder preferential rights, usually in respect of dividends and/or return of capital on a winding up

redeemable shares

fully paid-up shares that either will be redeemed (bought back by the company), or may be redeemed at the option of the company or the shareholder, on such date or dates and subject to such terms as are stated in the articles or company resolution

equity share capital

the issued share capital of a

company excluding any part which, neither as respects dividends nor as respects capital, carries any right to participate beyond a specified amount in a distribution

to access capital. The company may wish to either reduce the rate of preferred dividend or reduce the share capital and get rid of the preference shares altogether.

The statutory procedure to be complied with before class rights may be varied is set out in the Companies Act 2006 (ss 630–640). The articles may provide less protection than is provided by the statute (s 630(2)(a)). Alternatively, more onerous restrictions on the variation of rights than those in the statute may be imposed and these may be in the articles or in the authorising resolution of the class of shares.

Essentially, under the statute, holders of 75 per cent by nominal value of the shares in the affected class must approve a variation in advance (s 630(4)). Even if 75 per cent of the holders approve the variation, the holders of 15 per cent may, within 21 days of approval, apply to the court to have the variation cancelled (s 633(1)). The court may disallow the variation if it is satisfied that, having regard to all the circumstances of the case, the variation would unfairly prejudice the shareholders of the class represented by the applicant (s 633(5)). The minority shareholders believing themselves to be unfairly prejudiced by a variation supported by a majority of the class may, as an alternative course of action, petition the court under s 994 (considered below). In view of the broad-ranging remedies available to a court under s 994, it is likely to be a preferable route for disaffected minority shareholders, which may explain why there appears to be only one reported case on what is now s 633 (*Re Sound City (Films) Ltd* [1947] Ch 169).

The strength or weakness of the protection given to holders of classes of shares by the statutory provision and provisions in the articles depends upon the breadth or narrowness of interpretation of the terms 'variation' and 'class right'.

Variation

No comprehensive definition of variation exists for the purposes of s 630. A variation of rights can be a variation to improve or enhance the rights of the class as well as a variation adversely affecting those rights. Also, the Act makes it clear that an abrogation of rights is a variation for the purposes of the Act (s 630(6)). Consequently, a reduction of capital by way of repayment of capital and cancellation of shares of a particular class may be a variation.

The courts have confined the concept of variation by drawing a distinction between class rights and the enjoyment of class rights. This has resulted in it being possible to adversely affect the financial position of holders of a class of shares in a number of ways without the company having to go through the variation procedure because the change is merely a change in the *enjoyment* of class rights.

Example

The dilution of voting control by the issue of more shares of the same class (in the case in hand, preference shares) to ordinary shareholders has been held not to be a variation of rights necessarily.

CASE EXAMPLE

White v Bristol Aeroplane Co [1953] Ch 65 (CA)

The company proposed to issue further preference shares to ordinary shareholders, to be paid for out of company reserves. This would dilute the voting control of existing preference shareholders. The articles contained a provision governing when the consent of a class was required. The articles stated that all or any *rights and privileges attached to any class of shares* forming part of the capital from time to time of the company might be affected, modified, varied, dealt with or abrogated in any manner with the sanction of an extraordinary resolution passed at a separate meeting of the members of that class. The preference shareholders objected to the proposed issue, arguing that the issue of the new preference shares would 'affect' the rights attached to their shares. Held: The issue of further preference shares would not be a variation of, or affect the rights attached to the shares and therefore preference shareholder consent was not needed. The proposed issue would affect the *enjoyment of existing rights* not the rights themselves.

Example

Reduction of the absolute amount of preferred dividend payable by the company brought about by reducing the nominal value of the preference shares has been held not to be a variation of rights because the express right to a preferential dividend of 4 per cent remained the same.

CASE EXAMPLE

Re Mackenzie & Co Ltd [1916] 2 Ch 450

Preference shareholders were entitled to a dividend of 4 per cent of the amount paid-up on their £20 shares and no priority as to capital on a winding up. The ordinary shareholders in general meeting agreed a reduction in the company's share capital, reducing the nominal value of all shares, both ordinary and preference shares, rateably, that is, by the same proportion. Each preference share was reduced in nominal value to £12. Even though the preferential dividend expressed in percentage terms was not changed but remained at 4 per cent, the change in nominal value reduced the dividend provided for on a fully paid-up preference share from 80 pence (4 per cent of £20) to 48 pence (4 per cent of £12). Held: The reduction in share capital was *not* a variation of the preference shareholders' rights. The right to a 4 per cent dividend remained the same even if the enjoyment of the right was changed.

The following three cases decide that a company may reduce its share capital by returning nominal capital to preference shareholders with priority rights to return of capital on a winding up *and no further capital participation* without approval of the holders of the class and the preference shareholders can not complain about the loss of the right to share in the future wealth of the company by continuing to receive their preferential dividends.

CASE EXAMPLE

Scottish Assurance v Wilsons & Clyde Coal Co [1949] AC 462 (HL)

The company sought court approval for a reduction in its share capital by paying nominal share capital back to its 7 per cent preference shareholders and extinguishing their shares. Preference shareholders argued that the reduction should not be approved as it was unfair to them. Held: As a matter of interpretation of the rights attached to the preference shares, they entitled the holder to priority return of capital but no further participation in capital on a winding up. The capital reduction was fair.

CASE EXAMPLE

House of Fraser v AGCE Investments Ltd [1987] AC 387 (HL)

Preference shareholders were entitled to prior repayment of nominal capital 'on a winding up or otherwise' but no further participation in the capital. Preference share capital was not needed by the company which reduced its share capital by a special resolution of ordinary shareholders in general meeting, returning the preference share capital to the class of preference shareholders and extinguishing the shares. The articles provided for class approval if the special rights attaching to a class were 'modified, commuted, affected or dealt with'. No class meeting was held to approve the reduction. When the company sought court approval for the reduction in capital, as required by the Act, the preference shareholders argued the court could not approve the reduction of capital in the absence of consent of the holders of the class. Held: The reduction was not a modification, etc of the preference shareholders' rights but an extinction of the shares in strict accordance with the contract in the articles. Applying *Re Saltdean Estate Co Ltd* [1968] 1 WLR 1844, the right to prior return of nominal capital on a winding up meant that the preference shares could be cancelled on a reduction of share capital.

CASE EXAMPLE

Re Hunting Plc [2005] 2 BCLC 211

On an application by the company for confirmation by the court of a resolution to reduce its issued share capital by the cancellation of convertible preference shares, preference shareholders argued that the scheme of reduction was unfair to them. Held: The reduction was approved. A company is entitled to reduce its capital by cancelling preference shares to replace the preference share capital with cheaper capital. The reduction was not unfair to the preference shareholders because they knew when they acquired their shares they were assuming the risk of being paid off in full.

In *Re Saltdean Estate Co Ltd* [1968] 1 WLR 1844, Buckley J confirmed that prior payment of preference shares on a reduction of capital is part of the bargain a preference shareholder enters into:.

JUDGMENT

'The liability to prior repayment on a reduction of capital, corresponding to their right to prior return of capital in a winding up ... is part of the bargain between the shareholders and forms an integral part of the definition or delimitation of the bundle of rights which make up a preference share. Giving effect to it does not involve the variation or abrogation of any right attached to such a share.'

The rights of the preference shareholders may be enhanced by provisions in the articles which specify that particular action by the company does amount to a variation of rights for which approval of the class is required.

CASE EXAMPLE

Re Northern Engineering Industries plc [1994] 2 BCLC 704 (CA)

The company proposed to reduce its capital by way of paying off its preference shares and cancelling them. The articles provided that the rights attached to any class of shares shall be deemed to be varied by 'the reduction of the capital paid up on those shares' (7(b)) and for the consent of 75 per cent of the holders of a class of shares to be obtained before the rights could be varied or abrogated (6). The judge refused to confirm the reduction of capital on the grounds that it was a variation of the rights of the preference shares to which the consent of the holders had not been obtained. The company appealed. Held: Dismissing the appeal, the reduction proposed by the company was caught by article 7(b) which was inserted to protect the rights of preference shareholders and the protection required the class holders to give their consent by an appropriate class vote not only where the reduction was piecemeal but also where it involved a complete repayment of their investment.

In view of the narrow protection afforded by the statutory provisions and the often narrow interpretation of provisions in articles, those intending to become holders of class rights will need to ensure that there are sufficiently protective provisions in the authorising resolution or in the articles, requiring their consent to changes that affect the enjoyment of the rights as well as to changes to the rights themselves, or for adequate compensation to be paid when the enjoyment of rights are taken away.

A specific example of the latter has become the norm as a result of the decisions that demonstrated that it is not, without more, unfair and is consistent with the statutory protection, for a company, without securing approval of the class, to repay and remove from the company *at any time* the holders of shares with limited capital participation rights simply by paying them the nominal value of their shares (*Scottish Assurance v Wilsons & Clyde Coal Co* [1949] AC 462 (HL), *House of Fraser v AGCE Investments Ltd* [1987] AC 387 (HL)). These decisions confirmed that limited capital participation shares are, in effect, shares redeemable at the will of the company. This led to the introduction of the 'Spens formula', language inserted into the rights of listed shares with limited capital participation rights but *full dividend participation rights*, providing for payment to shareholders of the market price rather than the nominal price of their shares should the shares be cancelled before the company is wound up.

To the extent that, at the point of cancellation, a company has retained profits (rather than having paid them out as dividends), those profits are reflected in the market price of the shares. The Spens formula protects the class shareholders against losing those valuable dividend rights. The Spens formula does not offer protection from loss of the expected future profits.

Class rights

There is no comprehensive definition of 'class rights' for the purposes of s 630. The concept was explored in *Cumbrian Newspapers Group Ltd v Cumberland and Westmoreland Newspaper and Printing Co Ltd* [1987] Ch 1 which recognised as class rights for the purposes of s 630, rights not attaching to any particular shares, but exercisable only for so long as the shareholder was owner of shares in the company. The decision in the case has attracted criticism and may no longer be good law as a result of s 629(1) which states:

SECTION

'For the purposes of the Companies Acts shares are of one class if the rights attached to them are in all respects uniform.'

By expressly referring to rights *attached to shares*, this section *may* have excluded from class rights the type of rights in *Cumberland*, but the effect of s 629 remains to be determined.

CASE EXAMPLE

Cumbrian Newspapers Group Ltd v Cumberland and Westmoreland Newspaper and Printing Co Ltd [1987] Ch 1

Pursuant to an agreement by which Cumberland acquired one of Cumbrian's newspapers, Cumbrian acquired just over 10 per cent of the shares in Cumberland and the articles of Cumberland were amended to allow Cumbrian to prevent a take-over of Cumberland by giving Cumbrian (only) the following rights: (i) rights of pre-emption over other ordinary shares, (ii) rights in respect of unissued shares, and (iii) so long as Cumbrian held no less than 10 per cent of the shares in Cumberland, the right to appoint a director. Cumberland sought to remove these rights by special resolution of the ordinary shareholders. Cumbrian argued removal of the rights was a variation of class rights for the purposes of the statute (now s 630) therefore its (the class holder's) approval was needed. Removal of the rights would be a variation, being an 'abrogation', but the question was, were they 'class rights'? Held: Even though they were not attached to particular shares, the rights were conferred on Cumbrian in the capacity of shareholder of the company and therefore were class rights and could not be varied without the approval of holders of 75 per cent of the class.

Notwithstanding this case, a dearth of judicial consideration means that the concept of class rights remains unclear in English law. Three ways of interpreting the concept are discussed by Ferran (1999):

- Class rights are those rights which are exclusive to the class and distinct from right attaching to any other class (the narrow concept).
- Class rights are all the rights which, under the constitution, attach to shares in the company, irrespective of whether those rights are exclusive to a particular class or also enjoyed by other classes (the broad concept).
- Class rights are rights which are exclusive to the class and dividend and capital rights, rights to vote and rights relating to protection of class rights (the middle concept).

Greenhalgh v Arderne Cinema's Ltd [1946] 1 All ER 512 (CA) is cited as supporting the middle concept by implication but in the absence of more compelling authority, the issue of what are and are not class rights remains moot. This continuing uncertainty surrounding the concept of class rights is a further reason why it is important to spell out clearly, in the articles or authorising resolution, the situations in which the holders of particular shares are protected from the company's actions, whether by requiring approval of the holders of 75 per cent or by some other protective mechanism.

KEY FACTS

Shares	
The classic judicial statement of the nature of a share is found in:	*Borland's Trustee v Steel* (1901) *per* Farwell J
A share is a chose in action.	*Colonial Bank v Whinney* (1886)
A share is transferable subject to provisions in the articles.	s 544 and *Re Discoverers Finance Corporation Ltd, Lindlar's Case* (1910)
Certificated shares are transferred by completion of a stock transfer form, stamp duty adjudication and entry of the transferee's name in the register of members.	s 770 and Stock Transfer Act 1963
Uncertificated shares are transferred using the CREST system.	The Uncertificated Securities Regulations 2001 (as amended)
Each share is rebuttably presumed to have the same rights as every other share.	*Birch v Cropper* (1899)
A company may have any number of classes of shares and the main rights that differ from class to class are:	Voting rights Dividend rights Capital participation rights Nominal share value
The concept of a class right is unclear. The Companies Act 2006 may have narrowed it.	*Cumbrian Newspapers v Cumberland and Westmoreland* (1987) s 629
Shares with restricted rights in respect of dividends and capital are not equity shares and pre-emption rights do not arise on their issue or in favour of their holders.	ss 548 and 560
Class rights may be varied with the consent of 75% class holders or as otherwise provided in the articles.	ss 630–640
Courts interpret variation of class rights narrowly. A mere change in the enjoyment of rights is not a variation.	*White v Bristol Aeroplane Co* (1953)

7.4 Share capital

The share capital rules for companies registered under the Companies Act 2006 focus on *issued* shares. The old concept of *authorised* share capital has been abandoned but it remains necessary to be familiar with authorised share capital to understand the old cases and the documentation of companies incorporated before the relevant sections of the 2006 Act came into effect.

7.4.1 The old regime: authorised share capital

The pre-2006 Act law requires a company to state its authorised share capital, also known as its 'registered capital' or 'nominal capital', in its (old-style) memorandum of association. The authorised share capital is a statement of:

1 the maximum share capital the company can have;
2 the classes of shares of which the share capital amount may be made up;
3 for each class of shares:
   - the nominal value of the shares;
   - the maximum number of shares the company can have.

Example: Company A Ltd

1 The (old-style) memorandum of association of Company A Ltd states:
   'The share capital of the company is £1 million (one million pounds sterling) divided into 1 million ordinary shares of £1 (one pound sterling) each'.
2 B and C both subscribe to the memorandum of association in which they agree to take 1 × £1 share each.
3 The company issues 1 × £1 share to B and 1 × £1 to C.
4 Neither B nor C pay for their shares which are issued on a nil-paid basis.
5 No further shares are issued.

Company A Ltd has:
   - Authorised share capital: £1 million
   - Issued share capital: £2
   - Called-up share capital: 0

The reasoning behind companies not being required to have authorised share capitals in future is that the concept is of little use and potentially misleading, as the example above demonstrates. The constitution of the company refers to £1 million yet all that figure operates as is a *maximum* share capital and the figure commonly chosen is often totally unrelated to any realistic expectation as to what the issued share capital is likely to be. The figures used in the example are not exaggerated to make the point. In terms of operating as a meaningful limit on the share capital of the company, not only are very large figures adopted, but s 121 of the Companies Act 1985 permitted a company to increase its authorised share capital by the shareholders passing an ordinary resolution.

7.4.2 The new law: share capital statements

The first shareholders of a company are those who sign the memorandum of association at the time of registration and thereby agree to become a member of the company and take at least one share (s 8). The shares taken by, or issued to, those who sign the memorandum of association make up the initial share capital of the company.

A statement of initial share capital must be included in the application to register a company (s 9(4)), and an updated statement of capital must be sent or 'returned' to the registrar of companies each time the company's share capital is altered. The statement of share capital of a company therefore contains details of the *issued* share capital. A statement of share capital must state:

1 the total number of issued shares of the company;
2 the total nominal value of those issued shares;
3 for each class:
   - the prescribed particulars of rights attached to those shares;
   - the number of issued shares of that class;
   - the total nominal value of shares of that class;
4 the amount paid up and the amount unpaid on each issued share (whether on account of the nominal value or by way of premium).

Example: Company B Ltd

1   C and D both subscribe to the (new-style) memorandum of association of Company B Ltd in which they each agree to take 1 × £1 share.
2   The company issues 1 × £1 share to C and 1 × £1 to D.
3   Neither C nor D pay for their shares which are issued on a nil-paid basis.
4   The statement of initial share capital states:

- Total number of shares issued: 2
- Total nominal value of those shares: £2
- The amount paid-up on each share: Nil
- The amount payable   £1 per share
- All shares are ordinary shares.

share capital
the shares of a company that have been issued, including those taken on the formation of the company by those who subscribed to the memorandum of association

nominal value
the value attached to a share when it is issued. The nominal value of a share need not bear any correlation to the market value of that share

premium
the amount paid for a share over and above the nominal value when it is allotted by the company

7.4.3 The new law: the language of share capital

The share capital of Company B Ltd in the example above is £2. This is the 'issued share capital'. Issued share capital is the total nominal value of the issued shares. 'Nominal value' is the fixed monetary value attached to the share, also referred to as the 'par' value. It is also the minimum amount for which the share can be issued, that is, a holder must be required to contribute at least the nominal value. A share issued at less than nominal value is issued at a discount, which is prohibited (s 580(1)). The nominal value of all shares in Company A Ltd and Company B Ltd in the examples above is £1.

Nominal value and premium

All shares must have a fixed nominal value (s 542). Like authorised share capital, the nominal value of a share can be misleading and is regarded by some to be unnecessary. The nominal value bears no necessary relationship to the issue price of the share or the market or underlying value of the share. Shares are often issued at a price higher than nominal value. The difference between the issue price and the nominal value of a share is called the share premium. If a share with a nominal value of £1 is issued at £1.20, the share premium is 20 pence. Share premiums do *not* technically form part of the company's share capital. That said, the limits on what a company can do with share premium amounts are very similar to the limits on the share capital.

Nominal value is important to work out the proportion, or rateable share, of the residual wealth of the company to which each shareholder is entitled. If a company has share capital of £100 made up of 100 × £1 ordinary shares, each share entitles its owner to one hundredth of the residual wealth of the company.

If a company issues 100 × £1 shares and 100 × £2 shares, it has 200 issued shares and £300 share capital. Even if the only difference in the shares is their nominal value, the shares are different classes of shares (*Greenhalgh* (1946), above). They will not be treated as having equal entitlement to share in the residual assets of the company and this difference in rights is brought about by the nominal value. Without more being stated in the articles or other authorising resolution, each will be entitled to receive back the nominal share value before any remaining surplus is distributed. How the surplus is to be distributed is a question of interpretation of the rights attaching to the shares and great care should be taken to ensure that this issue is dealt with clearly. The nominal value, fixed at the time of issue and, unlike the issue price, the same for all shares in the class, is therefore important. If nominal values are abolished, a fixed value that does not vary over time will still need to be attached to each share for the purpose of ascertaining the capital to be returned to each shareholder. At the moment we call that fixed value the nominal value.

The issue price of a share does not have to be paid when the share is issued. All or part of the price can be deferred: the issued share capital of a company is not necessarily the same as the 'paid-up share capital'. The paid-up share capital is the sum of those parts of the nominal value of issued shares already contributed to the company. Company B Ltd's issued share capital is £2 but its paid-up share capital is 0. The fact that the unpaid part of the purchase price can be called up distinguishes a partly paid share (which is permitted) from a share issued at a discount (which is prohibited).

called-up capital

the sum of the amounts paid for shares when issued, sums subsequently called-up (even if the called amounts have not been paid), and sums due on a specified date without further call

Called-up share capital (s 547)

The issued share capital figure (s 546(2)) is important because it reflects the minimum sum shareholders are required to pay to the company. The company can issue calls on shareholders to pay the amount outstanding on their shares. Company B Ltd can call on C and D to pay £1 each. If C and D had paid 40 pence on each share when the shares were issued, the paid-up share capital of the company would be 80 pence (2 × 40 pence). Company B Ltd could call on C and D to pay up to 60 pence each, either in one call or in a series of calls of parts of the outstanding 60 pence. The 'called-up share capital' is the sum of the amounts paid for shares when issued, sums subsequently called-up (even if the called amounts have not been paid), and sums due on a specified date without further call (s 547). If C and D had each paid 40 pence on their shares on issue and Company B Ltd subsequently called-up 20 pence per share, Company B Ltd's called-up share capital would be £1.20 calculated as follows:

paid-up share capital (80 pence) + called-up amount (2 × 20 pence = 40 pence) = £1.20

If a part of the share capital has not been called-up or paid-up and the company enters into insolvent liquidation, or is wound-up, the liquidator can require the shareholders to pay the un-paid amount if this is needed to pay the creditors of the company. Where shares are fully paid, as virtually all listed shares are, a shareholder is under no obligation to contribute further to the company. Where shares are issued at nominal value, the nominal share value (£1) and the issued share capital (£2) establishes the limit on the liability of a shareholder.

7.5 Alteration of share capital

The initial share capital of a company is determined by the shares taken by those who sign the memorandum of association. A company may not alter its share capital except in a way provided for in s 617 of the Companies Act 2006. The 2006 Act contained extensive rules regulating alterations of capital most of which are focused on share capital reduction. Share capital reduction, briefly touched upon in the final paragraphs of this section, is considered in detail in the following chapter as part of our consideration of capital maintenance. In the remaining part of this section we focus on how to increase the share capital of a company.

7.5.1 Increasing the share capital

After registration the company may decide to increase its share capital. By s 617(2)(a), a company may increase its share capital but must do so in accordance with Pt 17 of the Act. Unlike a reduction, an increase in share capital is not considered by the courts and legislature to be a particularly problematic issue. As value is being added to the company, the issue of new shares is not regarded as threatening the position of the company's creditors. Core company law rules regulating the issue of new shares are designed to protect the rights of existing shareholders.

If the capital of a company is to be increased by the offering of shares to the public, detailed securities regulation must be complied with. A private company may not offer shares to the public, but if it wishes to raise money from the public it may re-register as a public company and then make an 'initial public offering' (see section 7.6 below). This section is concerned with the core company law rules on share issues.

Reasons for increasing the share capital

There are many reasons why a company may wish to increase its share capital. Some of the more common, acceptable, reasons are:

- To raise money for the running of the company (*Punt v Symons & Co Ltd* [1903] 2 Ch 506).
- To issue shares in return for assets transferred to the business (such as in return for the boot business in *Salomon*).

A couple of unacceptable reasons for increasing share capital are:

- To forestall a takeover bid (*Hogg v Cramphorn Ltd* [1967] Ch 254).
- To change the seat of control of a company (*Howard Smith v Ampol Petroleum Ltd* [1974] AC 821 (PC)).

allotment
shares in a company are taken to be allotted when a person acquires the unconditional right to be included in the company's register of members in respect of the shares

Procedure for the allotment and issue of shares

Note on terminology
The terms 'allotment' and 'issue' are often used interchangeably and in most contexts this is unobjectionable. The distinction between the terms is important when focussing on the process for becoming a shareholder. First there is an allotment of shares, which occurs when a contract for the issue of shares is put in place.

SECTION

> **'s 558 When shares are allotted**
> For the purposes of the Companies Acts shares in a company are taken to be allotted when a person acquires the unconditional right to be included in the company's register of members in respect of the shares.'

member
a person becomes a member of a company when his name is entered in the register of members. For companies with a share capital the term is synonymous with shareholder

Allotment is followed by the actual *issue* of the shares, which occurs when the name of the owner is registered in the company's register of members (*National Westminster Bank v IRC* [1995] 1 AC 111 (HL)). A person obtains legal title to the shares and becomes a member of the company when his name is registered.

The terms 'member' and 'shareholder' are also often used interchangeably and, again, this is unobjectionable in most contexts. Member is a generic term covering shareholders, guarantors (of companies limited by guarantee) and members of unlimited companies. All shareholders are members of a company, but not all members are shareholders.

Does the board of directors have authority to allot new shares?

Whether or not the board of directors has authority to allot shares is determined by ss 550 and 551 of the Act, the company's articles and relevant shareholder resolutions authorising the board of directors to allot shares. The rules are summarised in Table 7.1.

Type of company	Source of authority of directors to issue shares	Provisions in the articles
Private company with one class of shares only	The Act authorises the directors to issue shares of the same class (s 550)	None are needed but articles *may* restrict the power of the directors to issue shares (s 550)
Private company with more than one class of shares	Either the articles can authorise the directors to issue shares, or an ordinary resolution is needed to authorise the directors to issue shares (s 551(1))	Art 22 of the Model Articles for Private Company Limited by Shares and Art 43 of the Model Articles for Public companies provide that the company may issues shares with such rights or restrictions as are determined by ordinary resolution and that the company may issue redeemable shares and the directors may determine the terms, condition and manner of redemption of such redeemable shares
Public company	The grant of authority to issue must state the maximum amount of shares that may be allotted under it (ss 551(3)) The authority must be for no longer than 5 years (s 551(3)) The authority can be varied or revoked at any time by ordinary resolution (s 551(4))	

Table 7.1 Authority to allot and issue shares

Exercise of the authority to allot and issue shares

If the board is authorised to allot and issue shares, the power will be exercised by the board deciding to exercise that authority, or power, usually by passing a board resolution. A director who knowingly makes an unauthorised allotment or permits or authorises an unauthorised allotment of shares is guilty of an offence (s 549(4)) and liable to a fine. If shares are allotted without authority the allotment will not, however, be invalid for that reason (s 549(6)).

Directors who participate in the board decision to allot must act in accordance with their duties to the company. One of those duties is set out in s 171.

SECTION

's 171 Duty to act within powers
A director of a company must –
(a) act in accordance with the company's constitution, and
(b) only exercise powers for the purposes for which they are conferred.'

An allotment for the purpose of manipulating voting power of one group of shareholder at the expense of another is an allotment for an improper purpose and will be set aside (subject to protection of third party rights) (*Howard Smith v Ampol Petroleum Limited* [1974] AC 821). Also, an allotment with the dominant purpose of preserving the directors' control of the management of the company is an allotment for an improper purpose and will be set aside (subject to protection of third party rights) (*Hogg v Cramphorn Ltd* [1967] Ch 254). Section 171 is considered further in Chapter 11.

Statutory pre-emption rights of existing shareholders

pre-emption rights

the rights of existing equity shareholders to be offered new equity shares first in proportion to their existing equity shareholdings

The purpose of pre-emption rights is to protect existing equity shareholders from their rights in the equity or residual wealth of the company, and their share of the voting rights, from being diluted by the issue of new shares. Statutory pre-emption rights, in ss 560–577 of the Act, give equity shareholders the right of first refusal to take up any new equity shares. Each equity shareholder is entitled to be offered that proportion of the new shares as would preserve his proportionate interest in the equitable share capital of the company. This is his *pro rata* share of the new issue. The operation of pre-emption rights is best illustrated by an example.

pro rata

rateably or in proportion

Example

Company C Ltd (a private company) has a share capital of 100 × £1 ordinary shares. E, F, G & H each own 25 of those shares. The directors of Company C Ltd decide the company needs to raise £100. They decide to exercise their authority to issue new shares to issue £100 × £1 ordinary shares. An investor (I) approaches the directors and offers to pay £1.20 per share for the shares.

Are the directors permitted to issue the shares to I?

Before the directors can issue the shares to the investor they must determine whether or not any of E, F, G or H, the existing equity shareholders, is entitled to exercise statutory pre-emption rights in relation to the new shares.

If no pre-emption rights exist, the directors can issue the shares to I and the interests in the share capital of the company would be as set out in Table 7.2.

Shareholder	Number of shares owned	Share of equity share capital owned and share of voting rights	
		Before	After
E	25	25%	12.5%
F	25	25%	12.5%
G	25	25%	12.5%
H	25	25%	12.5%
I	100	0%	50%
Total	200	100%	100%

Table 7.2 Interests in the share capital of Company C Ltd

There has been significant dilution of the proportionate interests of the original shareholders in the equity share capital.

If the statutory rights apply to all the existing shareholders, E, F, G & H, the new shares must be offered to them in proportion to their existing shares of the equity share capital. The equity share capital is £100 of which each of E, F, G & H own £25, 25 per cent or one quarter. They must each be offered 25 per cent or one quarter of the new shares, which is 25 shares each and the offer must be open for acceptance for at least 21 days (s 562(5)). If they all accept the offer, after the new shares are issued, they will each own 50 shares equal to £50 or 25 per cent or one quarter of the £200 equity share capital of the company. The interests in the share capital of the company would be as set out in Table 7.3.

Shareholder	Number of shares owned	Share of equity share capital owned and share of voting rights	
		Before	After
E	50	25%	25%
F	50	25%	25%
G	50	25%	25%
H	50	25%	25%
Total	200	100%	100%

Table 7.3 Interests in the share capital of Company C Ltd (2)

There has been no dilution of their proportionate interests in the equity share capital. Note that it is the nominal share value of the shares (£1) that determines the share capital, not the issue price of the shares (£1.20). The shares must be offered to the existing shareholders at the same price (£1.20) or a more favourable price than they would be offered to I. It is common practice for listed companies to offer new shares to existing ordinary shareholders at below market value (see rights issues below).

Each of the shareholders is free to refuse the offer, in which event, if the shares they are offered are subsequently taken-up by somebody else, perhaps I, the shareholder will have a reduced proportion of the equity share capital. Let's assume that E & F take up their share of the new shares but G & H decline to take up the shares offered to them. The 50 shares offered to G & H are taken up by I. The interests in the share capital of the company would be as set out in Table 7.4.

Shareholder	Number of shares owned	Share of equity share capital owned and share of voting rights	
		Before	After
E	50	25%	25%
F	50	25%	25%
G	25	25%	12.5%
H	25	25%	12.5%
I	50	0	25%
Total	200	100%	100%

Table 7.4 Interests in the shares of Company C Ltd (3)

This demonstrates how the share interests of G & H have been diluted, by them not exercising their pre-emption rights, from 25 per cent to 12.5 per cent. Pre-emption offers can be made on an open or renounceable basis. Each can only be accepted by the shareholder to whom it is made but a renounceable offer, once accepted, may be assigned to another person (see rights issues below).

Limits on the application of statutory pre-emption rights

Statutory pre-emption rights apply only to the issue of equity securities (s 560) and only in favour of the holders of equity shares which are referred to in s 560 as ordinary shares. A share is not an ordinary share or an equity security which 'neither as respects dividends nor as respects capital, carries any right to participate beyond a specified amount in a distribution'.

Example

A £1, 6 per cent dividend preference share with priority as to return of nominal capital is not an ordinary share or equity security for the purposes of pre-emption rights because:

- the right to participate in dividends is limited to 6 per cent of the nominal share value per annum, which is a specified amount: 6 pence per annum
- the right to participate in capital is limited to return of nominal capital, which is a specified amount: £1 per share.

Statutory pre-emption rights also do *not* apply to the issue of:

- bonus shares (s 564)
- shares for non-cash consideration (whether wholly or only in-part (s 565))
- shares to be held under an employee share scheme (s 566).

The removal of shares issued for partly or wholly non-cash consideration from their scope makes it relatively easy for a company to avoid statutory pre-emption rights.

Statutory pre-emption rights may not apply in a variety of circumstances as follows:

- A private company may exclude the statutory pre-emption rights by provision in its articles (s 567).
- If a company's articles contain intra-class pre-emption rights, that is, provision for new shares *of a particular class* of ordinary shares to be offered *pro rata* to existing *members of that class* of ordinary shares, the statutory pre-emption rights will not apply if the pre-emption rights in the articles have been complied with (s 568).
- A private company with only one class of shares may authorise its directors, by provision in the articles or by special resolution, to allot shares of that class without pre-emption rights or with modified pre-emption rights (s 569).
- A company in which the directors have been authorised pursuant to s 551 to allot shares may authorise its directors, by provision in the articles or by special resolution, to allot shares without pre-emption rights or with modified pre-emption rights (s 570).
- A company may disapply or modify the statutory pre-emption rights in relation to a specified allotment by passing a special resolution (s 571) recommended by the directors and supported by a written statement of the directors setting out the reasons for the dis-application, the price and justification for the price of the shares to be allotted.

Consequences of contravention of statutory pre-emption rights

If shares are allotted in contravention of the statutory pre-emption rights of existing shareholders, the allotment is not, for that reason, invalid. Section 563 provides a statutory right to compensation to any person to whom an offer should have been made for any loss, damage, costs or expenses sustained or incurred by reason of the contravention. The company and every officer who knowingly authorised or permitted the contravention are jointly and severally liable to compensate the shareholders. A two year limitation period runs from delivery of the return of allotment to the registrar of companies.

No criminal penalties apply to contravention of the statutory pre-emption rights but there is criminal liability for false statements in directors' written statements supporting a recommendation for a special resolution to disapply pre-emption rights (s 572).

Companies with listed shares: rights issues and open offers

In addition to the statutory pre-emption right provisions described above, companies with listed shares must comply with the Listing Rules issued by the FSA. The relevant rules are found in Listing Rules 9.3.11 and 9.3.12.

An existing shareholder who has pre-emption rights may not be in a financial position to exercise them and therefore faces dilution of his voting and interest in the company. Where shares are traded on a stock exchange, shareholders face the additional prospect of an immediate reduction in the market price of their existing shares when, as is often the case, shares are offered to existing shareholders at a discount to the market price. To avoid this immediate adverse financial impact, most new issues of equity shares by listed companies take the form of a 'rights issue'. This is in contrast to an 'open offer'. The details of how rights issues are structured are beyond the scope of this book. They can be found in books on securities regulation or corporate finance.

rights issue

the offer by a listed company of new shares to existing equity shareholders on a *pro rata* basis on a renounceable basis which entails issuing renounceable letters of allotment. The new shares are offered at a discount to the market price and the rights can be assigned for consideration

Basically, rights issues involve the provisional allotment of a *pro rata* proportion of new equity shares to existing equity shareholders, by way of a provisional allotment letter (PAL). The provisionally allotted shares are nil-paid, that is, the price of the shares remains wholly unpaid. A shareholder may take up the offer, by subscribing and paying the company for the provisionally allotted shares, or he can renounce the offer. If the shareholder renounces the offer, that is not the end of the story. The shareholder can trade, or sell, the right to subscribe for the pre-emption shares by signing the PAL and passing it to a purchaser of the rights. The shareholder receives consideration for the transfer of the rights to the third party and the third party subscribes and pays for the shares. The benefit of an open offer cannot be transferred in this way. For this reason, listing rules restrict the discount from market price that can be applied to shares offered on an open offer pre-emptive basis. The normal maximum discount for an open offer is 10 per cent of market value (though this is subject to exceptions (Listing Rule 9.5.10)).

Public disclosure of an increase of share capital

A return of allotment and (updated) statement of capital must be sent to the registrar of companies within one month of making an allotment (s 555). In the case of a public company, the registrar must publish receipt of the return and statement of capital, which is satisfied by a notice of receipt appearing in a supplement to the London Gazette (ss 1077 and 1078).

Issue price and payment for shares

All shares must have a fixed nominal value (s 542). Shares may not be issued at a discount (s 580) which means that the issue price may not be less than the nominal share value. If shares are issued at a discount the owner is liable to pay the company the discount amount and interest on the discount amount (s 580(2)). One way around the prohibition on discounts would be for the company to agree to pay a commission to a person who agrees to buy shares. Consider a £1 ordinary share issued for £1. It is not issued at a discount. If, however, the company has agreed with the shareholder to pay a commission of 20 per cent for agreeing to purchase the share, the net effect is that the company ends up with 80 pence, which is less than the nominal value. The Act regulates this loophole by prohibiting such commission payments both to the shareholder and to any person in return for them finding a purchaser (s 552) unless the articles authorise the payment of such commissions and the commission is no more than 10 per cent of the issue price (s 553).

The prohibition on issuing shares at below nominal value is intended to protect creditors and existing shareholders. Creditors are assured that the company has had (or has rights to call-up) the full amount of the stated share capital and share capital has traditionally been regarded as considered important by creditors as a financial cushion (see capital maintenance in Chapter 8). Shareholders are protected from new shareholders obtaining, at a reduced price, equivalent rights to participate in the voting and wealth of the company as they, the existing shareholders, have (remember, the company's wealth is shared between shareholders based on the number of shares owned and their nominal value).

These protections are lost if shares can be paid for with non-cash consideration which is over-valued. Shares may be paid for in money or money's worth (s 582) and the form that payment, or the consideration for the shares, is to take will be agreed as part of the terms of issue.

Example

Company D Ltd wishes to issue 1 million × £1 ordinary shares. The shares cannot be issued for less than £1 each, a total £1 million consideration. The company agrees to issue the shares to J in return for J transferring a plot of land to the company. The company and the new shareholder agree that the land is worth £1 million so the shares are issued fully paid. If the land is in fact worth less than £1 million, the shares have been issued in return for less real value than their nominal value.

What, if any, law governs the valuation of asset or services provided as payment (in whole or in part) of the issue price? The answer is that a private company and a new shareholder are essentially free to agree the value to be assigned. The 2006 Act provisions addressing the form that non-cash consideration may take and the potential for over-valuation apply only to public companies.

A public company may not accept as payment for shares:

- an undertaking by any person that he or another will do work or perform services for the company or any other person (s 585)
- an undertaking to be performed more than five years after the date of allotment (s 587)
- non-cash consideration, unless the consideration has been independently valued in accordance with the Act (s 593) (but note that cash consideration is given a broad definition in the Act (s 583)).

Shares may be issued nil-paid, partly paid or fully paid. The company may call up, or require the shareholder to pay, the whole or any unpaid part of the issue price (not just the nominal value) from time to time. All shareholders within the relevant class must be treated equally unless the articles authorise the company to agree otherwise, in which case, shares can be issued with different paid-up amounts and different times for payment of calls for different shareholders (s 581). Although a company has the right to call-up any outstanding part of the issue price, which must be at least the nominal value, a bird in the hand is worth two in the bush and the value of the right to call is only as good as the ability of the shareholder to pay. The amount of a call is owed by the shareholder to the company as a debt and the debtor/shareholder may be unable to pay the debt. Public companies are therefore required to issue shares on which at least 25 per cent of the nominal value and the full amount of any premium is paid-up at the time of issue (s 586).

share premium account

an account into which all payments made for shares over and above their nominal value are credited

The issue price may be more than the nominal value and the extent to which the issue price exceeds the nominal value is called the premium. The premium amount is credited to a share premium account (s 610). If existing shareholders are to be protected, the issue price of a new share of the same class should be the 'real value' of an existing share. There are a number of different ways of arriving at the real value of a share. For listed shares, the real value is often taken to be the price at which the shares are trading in the market: the quoted share price. The market price of a share can be volatile, and may be very different from the value of the share based on the net assets of the company (very crudely, the residual wealth of the company divided by the number of shares) or the earnings potential of the company. Consequently, there is enormous scope for judgement in arriving at the appropriate issue price of a share.

Directors who exercise the power or authority to allot shares must exercise that power in accordance with the duties that as directors they owe to the company. In particular, when involved in deciding the issue price, a director will need to act in accordance with s 172 of the Act and, 'act in the way he considers, in good faith, would be most likely to promote the success of the company for the benefit of its members as a whole'. This duty is examined in Chapter 11.

Completing the issue of shares

A shareholder does not have legal title to shares and those shares have not been issued unless and until his name appears in relation to those shares in the register of members. An allotment of shares must be registered, that is, the register of members must reflect the new shareholdings, as soon as possible and in any event within two months of the date of the allotment (s 554).

If a company fails to register shares it fails to carry out the contract of allotment and the person to whom the shares should be issued may sue the company for breach of contract and recover damages, or, if damages are not adequate, the court may order specific performance of the contract of allotment. Damages are likely to be adequate if the shares are available on the secondary market, that is, if the person can obtain shares from another shareholder (*Re BTR plc* (1987) 4 BCC 45).

A company must complete share certificates in relation to allotted shares within two months of the allotment (s 769), although this obligation can be expressly overridden and does not apply to uncertificated, that is, dematerialised shares.

Capitalisation: issue of bonus shares

bonus issue

fully paid shares of the same class issued free of charge to existing shareholders in proportion to their existing shareholding also referred to as a capitalisation issue

A company may issue shares to its existing members credited as fully paid. This is called a bonus share issue. Bonus shares are paid for, and may only be paid for, by the company out of the sums previously received as premium, or undistributed profits. The effect is that sums reflected in the accounts of the company as premium or undistributed profits of the company are turned into share capital. This is called 'capitalisation'. If the shares are paid for out of undistributed profits, the company will reduce its ability to pay dividends to the extent of the capitalisation.

Example

Company E Ltd has a share capital of £1,000 made up of $1,000 \times £1$ shares. 500 of those shares were issued at nominal value (£1) on registration of the company to K and 500 were issued two years later at an issue price of £1.10 to L. The company has been trading for 5 years and has not distributed any of the £500 profits it has made. It has an undistributed profit reserve of £500. The relevant accounts of the company will show:

	£
Share capital	1,000
Premium Account	50
Distributable reserves	500

The company decides to issue $550 \times £1$ bonus shares. K and L each receive 275 fully paid-up £1 shares. The relevant accounts now show:

	£
Share capital	1,550
Premium Account	0
Distributable reserves	0

Company E Ltd has a larger share capital than before. It has no distributable profits and will be unable to declare any dividends until it has generated more profits.

7.5.2 Reduction of share capital

There are many reasons why a company may wish to reduce its share capital. Some of the more common, acceptable reasons are:

- the capital is no longer needed by the company, perhaps because the trading operations of the company have been slimmed-down;
- to refinance the company, replacing expensive share capital with debt funding;
- to buy-out a founding shareholder who is retiring.

The importance of directors acting on the second of these reasons was emphasised by Lord Greene MR in the Court of Appeal decision in *Prudential Assurance Co v Chatterley*

Whitfield Collieries [1949] AC 512 (HL) *sub nom Re Chatterley-Whitfield Collieries Ltd* [1948] 2 All ER 593 CA:

JUDGMENT

'A company which has issued preference shares carrying a high rate of dividend and finds its business so curtailed that it has capital surplus to its requirements and sees the likelihood, or at any rate the possibility, that its preference capital will not, if I may use the expression, "earn its keep", would be guilty of financial ineptitude if it did not take steps to reduce its capital by paying off preference capital so far as the law allowed it to do so. That is mere common-place in company finance.'

Some unacceptable reasons for reducing share capital are:

- to exclude one or more shareholders from the company;
- to reduce the voting control of one or more shareholders.

A company cannot reduce its share capital except in one of the ways listed in s 617 of the Act. Here, core company law is concerned to protect the company's creditors. The House of Lords has characterised return of legal share capital to shareholders as likely to reduce the ability of the company to pay its debts, see *Trevor v Whitworth* (1887) 12 App Cas 409, discussed when reduction of share capital is examined in detail in the next chapter.

KEY FACTS

Share capital and alteration of share capital	
Share capital	
A company is no longer required to have an *authorised* share capital	
Share capital statements are statements of *issued* share capital (s 9(4))	
Each share must have a fixed *nominal value* (s 542)	
The difference between the nominal value and the issue price is the *share premium*	
The part of the nominal share capital that has been paid to the company is the *paid up share capital*	
The paid-up share capital + any sum called up or due without call is the *called-up share capital*	
Alteration of share capital	
Reduction of share capital must be in accordance with strict procedures in the Companies Act 2006 (see chapter 8)	
Share capital is increased by allotting and issuing new shares: see Table 7.1	
Directors must not allot shares for an improper purpose	*Howard Smith v Ampol Petroleum* (1974)
	Hogg v Cramphorn Ltd (1967)
Existing *equity* shareholders are entitled to statutory pre-emption rights when *equity* shares are allotted	s 561
Pre-emption rights do not apply to the issue of bonus shares, shares for non-cash consideration or shares issued to certain employees' share schemes	ss 564–566
Pre-emption rights can be excluded and dis-applied in a variety of ways including by special resolution	ss 567–571

7.6 Offering shares to the public

A private company is prohibited from offering its shares to the public (s 755). The meaning of 'offer to the public' for these purposes is found in s 756 and is very broad. Accordingly, rules governing the offer of shares to the public are relevant only to *public* companies.

The detailed rules requiring extensive accurate information to be available when shares in a company are offered to the public or admitted to trading on a regulated market, the principal aim of which is investor protection, are found not in core company law but in the Financial Services and Markets Act 2000 (FSMA) and the Prospectus Rules issued by the Financial Securities Authority (FSA) pursuant to that Act (FSMA s 84). The relevant rules implement in the UK the European Prospectus Directive (2003/71/EC), although the UK law goes beyond implementation of that directive. The Prospectus Directive has been amended by Directive 2010/73/EU which has been implemented in part in the UK at the time of writing by the Prospectus Regulations 2011 SI 2011/1668 with further regulations to follow. The FSMA and Prospectus Rules should not be seen as applying exclusively to companies with shares listed, or to be listed, on a regulated market. Public offers of shares by public companies that do not have listed shares are also subject to regulation. An example is a public offer by a company with shares quoted on AIM. Again, the detailed rules are beyond the scope of this book and can be found in books on securities regulation or corporate finance. The following paragraphs contain a brief outline of the law on prospectuses.

Basically, FSMA s 85 provides that subject to exemptions (FSMA s 86), a company must publish a prospectus before it:

prospectus

a document containing information about the company and its shares which enables prospective investors to decide whether or not to invest and/or is supplied to the financial regulator to obtain admission of shares to the Official List

- makes an offer of shares to the public; or
- applies for the admission of shares to trading on a regulated market.

The principal regulated market in the UK is the Main Market of the London Stock Exchange. AIM is not a regulated market for the purposes of a prospectus being required.

Some of the main exemptions from the requirement to publish a prospectus are:

- offers to qualified investors only;
- offers to fewer than 150 investors other than qualified investors;
- offers where the total consideration is less than €5 million (c. £4 million);
- offers where the minimum investment by one investor is €100,000 (c. £80,000) or more.

The prospectus must have been submitted to, and approved in advance by, the FSA (FSMA s 85). Advertisements published by the company in the context of offering shares to the public are also regulated (see PR 3.3). A person who fails to comply with the prospectus requirements is guilty of an offence for which the penalty is imprisonment for up to 2 years or an unlimited fine, or both (s 85(3)). Non-issue of a prospectus in contravention of s 85 is also actionable at the suit of a person who suffers loss as a result of the contravention (s 85(4)).

Section 87A of the FSMA sets out the principles governing the content of prospectuses and the Prospectus Rules specify the detailed content. Essentially, a prospectus must contain all information necessary to enable investors to make an informed assessment of the assets, liabilities, financial position, profits and losses and prospects of the company and the rights attaching to the shares (s 87A(2)). The information must be presented in an easily analysable and comprehensible form and must be summarised in non-technical language (s 87A(3)–(6)). Civil liability for untrue and misleading statements in a prospectus or omission of required information is governed by s 90 and such information or omission may give rise to liability pursuant to a number of other causes of action such as action pursuant to the Misrepresentation Act 1967, deceit, common law negligence, or for breach of contract.

KEY FACTS

Offering shares to the public	
A private company is prohibited from offering its shares to the public	s 755
Securities regulations mandate when a *prospectus* must be published in connection with: an offer of shares to the public admission of shares to trading on a regulated market	Financial Services and Markets Act 2000 (FMSA) s 85 and Prospectus Rules (PR) promulgated pursuant thereto.
Advertisements published in the context of offering shares to the public are also regulated	PR 3.3
A prospectus must contain all information necessary to enable investors to make an *informed assessment* of the assets, liabilities, financial position, profits and losses and prospects of the company and the rights attaching to the shares	FSMA s 87A PRs contain detailed rules as to content.
Failure to publish a prospectus when required is a criminal offence punishable by imprisonment or an unlimited fine	s 85(3)
Civil actions can be brought for non-issue or for omissions or untrue or misleading statements in prospectuses	ss 85(4), 90, various torts and breach of contract

ACTIVITY

Self-test questions

A. What is the meaning of each of the following terms? Identify the source of your definition.
1. Member of a company
2. Shareholder
3. Share
4. Class of shares
5. Preference share
6. Equity share
7. Nominal value
8. Authorised share capital
9. Nominal share capital
10. Share capital
11. Market value of a share
12. Allot or allotment
13. Nil paid share
14. Partly paid share
15. Fully paid share
16. Share premium
17. Called-up share capital
18. Pre-emption rights
19. Rights issue
20. Offer to the public

Applying the law

B. Andy and Betty recently registered a company called Myco Ltd. Each subscribed for 5,000 fully paid £1 shares and each of them is a director. They could not secure a bank loan but have found an investor, Ian, who is prepared to invest £20,000 in their company. Ian has asked for preference shares with a 10 per cent return. Andy and Betty are anxious to ensure

Ian will not be able to interfere in management or otherwise control 'their' company. They also wish to be able to pay Ian back when they can afford to and thereby remove him from the company, even if he does not want to leave. Advise Andy and Betty.

SUMMARY

The legal nature of a share

- A share is a chose in action (*Colonial Bank v Whinney* (1886)), is transferable subject to provisions in the articles (s 544 and *Re Discoverers Finance Corporation Ltd*, *Lindlar's Case* (1910)), and is classically defined in *Borland's Trustee v Steel* (1901).

Different types of shares and class rights

- Subject to the articles permitting different classes of shares, a company may have any number of classes of shares.
- The main rights that differ from class to class are voting rights, dividend rights and capital participation rights.
- What are and what are not class *rights* is a moot issue in English law.
- Shares with rights restricted to a specified amount in respect of dividends and capital are not equity shares for the purposes of the Companies Act 2006 (ss 548).

Variation of class rights

- Class rights may be varied with the consent of 75 per cent class holders or as otherwise provided in the articles (ss 630–640).
- Holders of 15 per cent may apply to the court to have a variation cancelled (s 633(1)) or may wish to petition the court under s 994.
- Courts interpret variation of class rights narrowly. A mere change in the enjoyment of rights is not a variation (*White v Bristol Aeroplane Co* (1953)).

Share capital

- The share capital of a company is the number of shares issues multiplied by the nominal value.
- All shares must have a fixed nominal value (s 542) which determines both the capital repayable before the surplus is distributed and the share of the surplus to which a shareholder is entitled in the event of a solvent winding up.

Alteration of share capital

- Share capital can be increased by the issue of shares or decreased by following a number of processes, in either case, the process followed must be strictly in accordance with the Companies Act 2006.

The allotment and issue of shares

- Rules governing the authority to issue shares are set out in Table 8.1 above.
- Directors must issues shares in the accordance with the constitution of the company and for the purpose for which the power is issue shares is conferred on them, ie not for an improper purpose such as to thwart a takeover bid (*Howard Smith v Ampol Petroleum Ltd* (1974)).

Payment for shares, discounts and premiums

- Shares may not be issued at a discount to the nominal value (s 580).
- Shares may be paid for in money or money's worth (s 582).
- Rules regulating payment for shares of public companies are stricter than for private companies (for public companies see ss 584-609).

- If shares are issued at a price higher than the nominal value the sum in excess is called the premium and must be transferred to a share premium account (s 610).
- Directors must exercise the power to decide the issue price of shares in accordance with their directors' duties.

Pre-emption rights

- To preserve their share of the company, existing equity shareholders are entitled to statutory pre-emption rights when equity shares are allotted (s 561).
- Pre-emption rights do not apply in certain situations (ss 564–566) and can be excluded and dis-applied in a variety of ways including by special resolution (ss 567–571).

Offering shares to the public

- A private company is prohibited from offering its shares to the public (s 755).
- A company is required to publish a prospectus before it makes an offer of securities to the public or applies for the admission of securities to trading on a regulated market.
- Key exemptions are: offers to qualified investors only; offers to fewer than 150 investors other than qualified investors; offers where the total consideration is less than €5 million, and offers where the minimum nominal value of a share or payable by one investor is €100,000 or more.
- Prospectuses are not required solely for admission of securities to AIM.
- A prospectus must contain all information necessary to enable investors to make an informed assessment of the assets and liabilities, financial position, profits and losses, and prospects of the company and any guarantor and the rights attaching to the shares (FSMA s 87A) and specific content requirements are found in the Prospectus Rules.
- Failure to publish an approved prospectus where one is required is a criminal offence (s 85(3)).
- Statutory compensation may be payable 'the persons responsible' for a prospectus for non-issue of a prospectus (s 85(4)) or publication of untrue or misleading statements in a prospectus (s 90).
- Common law remedies may also be available.

Further reading

Useful websites

The Financial Services Authority Handbook which contains, amongst other things, the Prospectus Rules is available at:
http://fsahandbook.info/FSA/html/handbook/

Articles

Armour, J, 'Share Capital and Creditor Protection: Efficient Rules for a Modern Company Law' (2000) 63 MLR 355.
Steele, A, 'Rights issue reform' (2009) 32 CSR 158.
Worthington, S, 'Shares and shareholders: property, power and entitlement (Part 1)' (2001) 22 Comp Law 258.
Worthington, S, 'Shares and shareholders: property, power and entitlement (Part 2)' (2001) 22 Comp Law 307.

Books

Davies, P, *Gower & Davies' Principles of Modern Company Law* (8th edn, Sweet & Maxwell, 2008).
Ferran, E, *Company Law and Corporate Finance* (Oxford University Press, 1999).

8

Capital maintenance and distributions

AIMS AND OBJECTIVES

After reading this chapter you should be able to:

- Understand how share capital can protect a creditor and why its relevance declines over the life of a company
- Explain the scope of 'capital maintenance' laws
- State the minimum share capital requirements
- Appreciate the exceptions to the statutory prohibition on reduction of share capital
- Advise on the availability of the solvency statement process for reducing share capital and the steps required to complete the process
- Advise on the procedure a public company must follow to reduce its share capital
- Advise on the availability of and steps required to acquire shares out of capital
- Appreciate statutory and common law restrictions on distributions
- Recognise potentially disguised distributions
- Understand how the legal restrictions are relaxed for distributions in kind
- Discuss the remedies available for payment of unlawful distributions
- State the shareholder last principle
- Discuss whether a principle of no truly gratuitous payments is needed or not
- Know the rules governing company political donations
- Recognise financial assistance and know when it is prohibited

8.1 Introduction

In the previous chapter we learned about a company's share capital. We know that the share capital of a company is the number of issued shares × nominal value of those shares (100 × £1 = £100, for example). On registration, a company begins life with its initial share capital, which it can increase from time to time by issuing more shares. The company uses its share capital to fund its trading operations with the aim of making profits. The company may supplement its share capital by incurring debt, that is, borrowing money from creditors to fund its trading operations.

In this chapter we review the laws governing minimum share capital and the reduction of share capital. We examine the importance of share capital to creditors and we also examine the laws regulating other actions by which companies return money to shareholders, principally by distributions. Together with the shareholder last principle, these laws are often referred to as 'capital maintenance'. We then look at the broader issue of how the law regulates gratuitous payments by a company to non-shareholders, including political donations. The final section of this chapter deals with the prohibition on a company giving financial assistance for the purchase of its own shares which is an extension to the prohibition on a company buying its own shares but is aimed at a different mischief from capital maintenance laws.

8.1.1 Can share capital protect a creditor against company trading losses?

At the start of a company's life, a financial creditor will be very interested to know how much share capital the company has before the creditor will be prepared to lend money to the company. The creditor wishes to be paid interest on any sum it lends to the company and to be paid back that sum at the point, or various points, in the future at which it becomes due and repayable.

If a company has a negligible share capital, virtually the entire risk of the company making trading losses lies with the creditor. Every £1 the company loses in trading is £1 it cannot pay back to the lender. The creditor may have a legal right to sue the company to recover the sum contractually due and payable to it but that right is only valuable if the company has the money to pay the sum due (see Example 1 below).

If, however, a company has substantial share capital, the risk of the company making trading losses lies with the shareholders up to the amount of the share capital. Every £1 the company loses, up to the amount of the share capital, is a loss borne by the shareholders. This is because the shareholders cannot insist on taking their capital back from the company whilst it is a going concern and, if the company is wound-up, its shareholders are only entitled to receive money back from the company after all the creditors have been paid in full (the shareholder last principle) (see Example 2 and section 8.6 below).

The company may not reduce its share capital and return money to its shareholders (except as authorised by, and subject to compliance with procedures in, the 2006 Act) *and* the company cannot pay money to shareholders, whether in the form of dividends or otherwise, unless the company has profits out of which to make the payment.

The following examples illustrate the importance of share capital in the early stages of a company's operation. They also introduce you to the concepts of assets, liabilities and capital in the balance sheet of a company. Understanding the basics of how share capital and profits and losses affect a company's balance sheet is essential to understanding capital maintenance. The following examples are simplified to demonstrate the basic principles.

Example 1 A company with virtually no share capital

Company A Ltd is registered with a share capital of £1 made up of 1 × £1 ordinary share, fully paid-up. Company A Ltd borrows £1,000 from B, repayable in 12 months. Company A Ltd has assets of £1,001. This is stated in its balance sheet as follows:

Balance Sheet of Company A Ltd as at 1 January 2008

		£
Assets		
	Cash at bank	1,001
Liabilities		
	Sum owed to B	1,000
Net assets		1
Capital		
	Share capital	1 (Number of issued shares × nominal value)

The basic balance sheet equation, or accounting equation, is:

$$\text{Assets} = \text{Liabilities} + \text{Capital}$$

'Capital' is made up of a number of components, the main ones are:

Capital = share capital + share premium + reserves (accumulated profits and losses)
The only component of capital in the above balance sheet is share capital.
'Net assets' is also an important concept:

$$\text{Assets} - \text{Liabilities} = \text{net assets}$$
$$£1,001 - £1,000 = £1$$

Net assets is also equal to Capital. In this balance sheet, net assets is equal to the share capital because share capital is equal to the Capital but net assets will not always equal the share capital. Indeed, the moment the company has profits or losses its net assets will diverge from its share capital, as the following 1 January 2009 balance sheet of Company A Ltd shows.

Company A Ltd trades for 12 months and incurs trading losses of £500. It then has £501. B demands repayment of the £1,000 owed and due to it from Company A Ltd. Even if B sues Company A Ltd, the most it can receive is £501 because that is all the money Company A Ltd has. The balance sheet now looks as follows:

Balance Sheet of Company A Ltd as at 1 January 2009

		£	
Assets			
	Cash at bank	501	
Liabilities			
	Sum owed to B	1,000	
Net assets		(499)	
Capital			
	Share capital	1	(Number of issued shares × nominal value)
	Profit & loss	(500)	(Accumulated profits and losses)

Brackets around a number indicate that it is a negative number. Note that the share capital amount remains the same. It reflects the number of shares in issue and their nominal value. It does not change unless more shares are issued (a share capital increase) or issued shares are cancelled (a share capital reduction). In this balance sheet, net assets is:

$$\text{Assets} - \text{Liabilities}$$
$$£501 - £1,000 = (£499)$$

This is *not* equal to the share capital of £1 because there are two components to Capital: share capital and accumulated profits and losses. The accumulated profits and loss here is a loss of £500, so Capital is:

$$\text{share capital} + \text{profit and loss (accumulated profits and losses)}$$
$$£1 + (500) = (£499)$$

The shareholders cannot receive their share capital back from Company A Ltd whilst the company is a going concern. The company cannot pay a dividend to shareholders because it has no profits available for the purpose (it has made a loss). B is entitled to all the assets of the company. Even if he receives them he remains only partly repaid. He has borne all but £1 of the trading risk of the company; he has absorbed all but £1 of the trading losses.

Example 2 A company with substantial share capital

Company C Ltd is registered with a share capital of £1,000 made up of 1,000 £1 ordinary shares, fully paid-up. Company C Ltd borrows £1,000 from B, repayable in 12 months. Company C Ltd has assets of £2,000. This is stated in its balance sheet as follows:

Balance Sheet of Company C Ltd as at 1 January 2008

£

Assets

Cash at bank	2,000	

Liabilities

Sum owed to B	1,000	
Net assets	1,000	

Capital

Share capital	1,000 (Number of issued shares × nominal value)	

Company C Ltd trades for 12 months and incurs trading losses of £500. It then has £1,500. B demands repayment of the £1,000 owed and due from Company C Ltd. Even though Company C Ltd has lost £500, it is still able to repay B.

Balance Sheet of Company C Ltd as at 1 January 2009

£

Assets

Cash at bank	1,500	

Liabilities

Sum owed to B	1,000	
Net assets	500	

Capital

Share capital	1,000 (Number of issued shares × nominal value)	
Profit & loss	(500) (Accumulated profits and losses)	

The shareholders cannot receive their share capital back whilst Company C Ltd is a going concern. The company cannot pay a dividend to shareholders because it has no profits available for the purpose (it has made a loss). The trading loss is borne by the shareholders as, after B has been paid £1,000, only £500 remains of their £1,000 share capital. Their shares are worth only £500, or 50 pence each. Unlike in Example 1, the creditor has been protected from the trading losses of the company by the share capital and will be protected until the net assets of the company are zero.

Example 3 Shares issued at a premium

If a company issues shares at an issue price above the nominal value of the shares, the amount by which the issue price exceeds the nominal value is the premium. The issue of £1 ordinary shares at an issue price of £2 is an example. The amount of the premium is not reflected in the share capital but in the share premium account, and the premium account balance appears in the balance sheet. With two exceptions, the premium account amount is subject to the same maintenance rules as the share capital. It is an 'undistributable reserve'. It cannot be returned to shareholders (except as authorised by, and subject to compliance with procedures in, the 2006 Act) and it does not count as profits for the purposes of distribution.

If the £1 ordinary shares of Company C Ltd in Example 2 above had been issued at the issue price of £2, the balance sheet of Company C Ltd would have looked like this:

Balance Sheet of Company C Ltd as at 1 January 2008

£

Assets

Cash at bank	3,000	

Liabilities

Sum owed to B	1,000	
Net assets	2,000	

Capital

Share capital	1,000 (Number of issued shares × nominal value)	
Share premium	1,000 (premium paid on issue of shares)	

Neither the share capital nor the share premium account balance may be distributed to shareholders: the creditors will be protected by the amount of the share premium as well as the share capital.

In *Trevor v Whitworth* (1887) 12 App Cas 409 (HL), Lord Watson explained the creditor-protection rationale for the existence of capital maintenance rules:

JUDGMENT

'[P]ersons who deal with, and give credit to a limited company, naturally rely upon the fact that the company is trading with a certain amount of capital already paid, as well as upon the responsibility of its members for the capital remaining at call; and they are entitled to assume that no part of the capital which has been paid into the coffers of the company has been subsequently paid out, except in the legitimate course of its business.'

8.1.2 The relevance of share capital over the life of a company

The examples in section 8.1.1 above demonstrate how share capital can protect a creditor from losing money due to a company experiencing trading losses. They are based on a single, financial creditor lending money to a company at the outset of its operations and cover only the first year of the company's life. In such a simple, somewhat unrealistic, scenario share capital is observed to represent a cushion for creditors against the risk of default of the company. In reality, a financial creditor will seek to *secure* any sum lent to the company. Taking security offers far greater protection to a creditor than the initial share capital contributed to a company (secured debt is explained at section 6.5.6 and Chapter 16).

In reality, the ability of the share capital to protect creditors and the importance of share capital to creditors reduces over the life of a company. First, the initial share capital becomes an increasingly historic figure, eroded in real terms by inflation. Second, creditors who extend credit to a company with a trading record will have more information about the company available to them than the limited information available on formation. The relevance of share capital to creditors is picked up again below, at 8.4, after we have reviewed the rules designed to prevent it being returned to shareholders.

8.1.3 The meaning of 'capital maintenance'

Capital maintenance is referred to as a 'principle', 'doctrine', or 'core concept' of company law. It is not a straightforward concept and its precise scope is unclear. It is necessary to break the concept down into its components.

Lord Russell identified the two key components of capital maintenance (when a company is not being wound-up) in *Hill v Permanent Trustee Company of New South Wales* [1930] AC 720 (PC):

JUDGMENT

'A limited company not in liquidation can make no payment by way of return of capital to its shareholders except as a step in an authorised reduction of capital. Any other payment made by it by means of which it parts with moneys to its shareholders must and can only be made by way of dividing profits. Whether the payment is called "dividend" or "bonus", or any other name, it still must remain a payment on division of profits.'

The two fundamental legal principles identified in Lord Russell's judgment can now be found in the Companies Act 2006:

- a limited company having a share capital may not reduce its share capital except as authorised by statute (s 617);
- distributions of a company's assets to its members, whether in cash or otherwise, may only be made out of profits available for the purpose (s 830 and see also s 831 in relation to public companies).

To appreciate the operation and role played by capital maintenance in company law, it is important also to be aware of legal rules supporting and refining these key principles. Accordingly, the capital maintenance concept can be regarded as shorthand for:

- minimum share capital rules (ss 763–767);
- the basic prohibition on a company reducing its share capital (s 617);
- detailed exceptions to the prohibition on a company reducing its share capital (Pts 17 and 18 of the 2006 Act);
- the requirement that distributions to shareholders may only be paid out of profits available for the purpose (ss 829–853);
- the shareholder last principle on winding up (Insolvency Act 1986 ss 107 and 143(1); *Ayerst (Inspector of Taxes) v C & K (Construction) Ltd* [1976] AC 167).

Each of these components of capital maintenance is considered in turn in the following sections of this chapter.

8.2 Minimum share capital requirement

8.2.1 Requirement to have a share capital

Public companies and private companies limited by shares must have a share capital. Incorporators are required to register a statement of capital and initial shareholdings on registration indicating the number of shares to be taken on formation by the subscribers and their nominal value (s 10).

8.2.2 Private companies

The share capital of a private company can be as small as the incorporators choose, for example, 1 share of 1 penny.

8.2.3 Public companies

Public companies must have allotted shares of no less than the authorised minimum as a condition of the registrar of companies issuing a trading certificate and a public company must not do business without having a trading certificate (s 761). The authorised minimum nominal value of the issued shares of a public company is £50,000 or the prescribed euro equivalent (ss 761(2) and 763).

Public companies may not issue shares unless they are paid up as to at least one quarter nominal value (s 586) and shares issued at the time of incorporation must be paid for in cash (s 584). The result is that a company registered as a public company must have at least £12,500 in cash when it commences business and the right to call for at least a further £37,500 from shareholders. Laws governing payment for shares, considered in section 7.5.1 above, are important to ensure that the company is entitled to receive from a shareholder at least the nominal value of his shares: shares may not be issued at a discount (s 580).

The importance to creditors of the requirement that a company has a share capital and the minimum required for public companies are considered in section 8.4 below.

8.3 Statutory prohibition on reduction of share capital except in accordance with the Act and company articles

Once a company has been registered with its initial share capital, the company may not *alter* its share capital except in the ways set out in s 617. Section 617 permits *reduction* of share capital in accordance with ss 641–657. There is no need for specific authorisation in a company's articles to reduce its share capital in accordance with the Act. If, however, articles contain any restriction or prohibition on reduction of share capital, the provisions in the articles must be complied with (s 641(6)).

8.3.1 Private company reduction of share capital

A private company may reduce its share capital by either of two procedures. It may use the old procedure (the only procedure available to a public company to reduce its share capital), which requires confirmation by court order and is considered in the next subsection. Alternatively, it can use the new procedure, first introduced by the Companies Act 2006 and contained in ss 641–644. This procedure is part of the deregulation of company law for private companies as the old rules were regarded as unnecessarily complicated. No court confirmation of the reduction is required and the fact that the procedure has been introduced essentially acknowledges that maintaining share capital is not important to the creditors of private companies. The critical basis for a reduction is the opinion of the directors that the company is solvent and will remain solvent for the following year.

The solvency statement process

A private company may reduce its share capital by the following process (ss 641(1)(a) and 642–644):

1 Directors conduct a review of the company's solvency.
2 Every director signs a solvency statement.
3 Directors send a proposed special resolution to members (with a copy of the solvency statement if the resolution is to be a written resolution).
4 Shareholders pass a special resolution (which can be passed at a meeting or a written resolution) within 15 days of the date of the solvency statement.
5 The following must be registered with the registrar (s 644):
   - copy of solvency statement
   - special resolution
   - statement of capital as reduced
   - confirmatory statement regarding compliance with the reduction of capital process.

The reduction does not take effect until the required documents and statements have been registered.

The solvency statement (s 643)

The solvency statement needed to support a share capital reduction is a prescribed-form statement, s 643(3). It must be signed by *all* directors. Each director must confirm that he has formed the opinion that:

- on the date of the statement there is no ground on which the company could be found to be unable to pay (or otherwise discharge) its debts; and
- the company will be able to pay (or otherwise discharge) its debts as they fall due during the year immediately following the date of the statement.

If the directors make a solvency statement without having reasonable grounds for the opinion expressed in it, which is then delivered to the registrar, every director who is in default commits a criminal offence and is liable for imprisonment of up to 12 months or a fine or both (s 643(4) and (5)).

Right of shareholders and creditors to object

In contrast with a reduction of capital by confirmation of the court (ss 645 and 646), neither creditors nor those shareholders who do not support the reduction of share capital have an opportunity during the process to object to a reduction of capital effected by the solvency statement route. Note, however, the need to ensure that if there is a variation of class rights, the variation of class rights procedure is gone through (see Chapter 7). Minority shareholders who object may be able to bring a derivative claim if the directors have breached their duties in the course of the reduction, or the circumstances may found a successful unfair prejudice petition. Both of these procedures are examined in Chapter 14 below.

8.3.2 Public company reduction of share capital

A public company (and a private company, although it seems unlikely that a private company will use this more cumbersome procedure in future) may reduce its share capital by special resolution but must secure a confirmation order from the court (ss 641(1)(b) and 645–651).

The process

1 A special resolution must be passed.
2 The company must settle a list of creditors for the court and either:
    - obtain the consent of all creditors or
    - pay off, or set aside a sum to pay off, any creditor who does not consent.
3 The company must present a petition to the court to confirm the reduction.
4 The court may make an order confirming the reduction 'on such terms and conditions as it thinks fit' (s 648(1)).
5 The following must be registered with the registrar (s 649):
    - special resolution
    - copy of the court order
    - statement of capital as reduced, approved by the court.

The reduction does not take effect until the required documents and statements have been registered.

Court confirmation

When the court is considering a petition to reduce share capital it must consider the interests of the creditors, the shareholders and members of the public who may invest or become creditors of the company (*Ex parte Westburn Sugar Refineries Ltd* [1951] AC 625). In relation to creditors, the court must not confirm the reduction unless it is satisfied in relation to every creditor who has not consented to the reduction that either his debt has been paid off or a sum has been set aside by the company to pay him off (s 648(2)). An offence is committed, punishable by fine, by every officer of the company who intentionally or recklessly conceals the name of a creditor or misrepresents the nature or amount of a creditor's debt or claim (s 647). Section 646 of the Act, which entitles a creditor to object to the reduction, has been amended to require that to succeed, the creditor must demonstrate that its claim is at risk and that the company has not provided adequate safeguards, (a mandatory requirement arising from European Directive 2006/68, implemented by the Companies (Share Capital and Acquisition by Company of Its Own Shares) Regulations 2009 (SI 2009/2022)).

In relation to shareholders, the court must consider whether or not the reduction is fair and equitable as between shareholders, whether of the same or different classes (see *Scottish Insurance Corporation Ltd v Wilsons & Clyde Coal Co Ltd* [1949] AC 462 (HL)). Note that where the reduction involves a particular class of shareholders, the variation of rights procedure may have to be gone through (see section 7.3.2 and the cases considered there).

8.3.3 Acquisition of own shares

Section 617 expressly states that the statutory prohibition on a company reducing its share capital does *not* affect the power of a company to acquire its own shares in accordance with Pt 18 of the Act. This is supported in Pt 18 by s 658 which prohibits the acquisition by a company of its own shares, 'except in accordance with the provisions of this Part'. The company may acquire its shares either by purchasing shares or redeeming redeemable shares.

Public companies

The statutory power of a public company to acquire its own shares is basically restricted to acquisition using distributable profits or the proceeds of a new issue of shares made for the purpose (ss 687(2) and 692(2)).

Acquisition of own shares out of the proceeds of a new issue of shares

Where shares are bought by a company out of the proceeds of a new issue of shares, the acquired shares are cancelled and the share capital is reduced (ss 688 and 706), but new shares have been issued which increase the share capital by at least the amount of the reduction. The overall effect is that there is no reduction in share capital. For this reason, such an acquisition is not considered further in this chapter.

Acquisition of own shares using distributable profits

No effective reduction of share capital is also the result achieved by the operation of s 733 in relation to the acquisition by a company of its own shares using distributable profits. Where shares are bought by a company using distributable profits, the acquired shares are cancelled and the share capital is reduced (ss 688 and 706), but s 733 requires a sum equal to the nominal value of the shares acquired (the reduction in capital), to be transferred to an account called the 'capital redemption reserve'. Section 733(6) provides that, with one exception, the provisions of the Act relating to the reduction of share capital apply to the capital redemption reserve. Consequently, *the capital redemption reserve is treated like share capital and is undistributable*. If the share capital account and the capital redemption reserve account are added together they equal the share capital amount before the acquisition of the shares. This means that the company's share capital is technically reduced but in practical terms the company must be operated as if its share capital remained the same as before the reduction.

The exception to treating the capital redemption reserve in the same way as share capital is that the capital redemption reserve can be used to pay up new shares issued to existing shareholders as fully paid bonus shares. The result of such an issue is to turn the amount used from the capital redemption reserve to fund the bonus share issue back into share capital. That being the case, the exception is consistent with the acquisition of shares using distributable profits being *in practical effect* not a reduction of share capital at all. For this reason, such an acquisition is not considered further in this chapter.

A public company seeking to acquire shares *out of capital* must use the reduction of capital procedure considered at section 8.3.2 above for which court confirmation is required.

Private companies

In addition to being able to acquire its own shares using distributable profits or the proceeds of a new issue of shares made for the purpose, just as a public company can, a private company is permitted to acquire its own shares out of capital (ss 687(1) and 692(1)) provided it does so in accordance with Chapter 5 of Pt 18 of the Act (ss 709–723). When a company acquires its own shares out of capital, the shares are cancelled and there is a real reduction in share capital.

Are the acquisition of shares out of capital provisions redundant?

The procedure in Chapter 5 of Pt 18 of the Act (ss 709–723) by which a private company may use capital to acquire its own shares existed, albeit in a slightly different form, before the 2006 Act. It is much more onerous than the new solvency statement procedure by which a private company may reduce its share capital introduced by the Companies Act 2006. It is expected that most future share acquisitions will be effected by way of a reduction of share capital in accordance with the solvency statement procedure (ss 642–644) and it may be questioned why ss 709–723 remain in the Act.

The reason for a company to go through the more onerous ss 709–723 procedure is not apparent: indeed, the Company Law Review concluded that introduction of the solvency statement process for capital reduction would make the rules on purchase of shares out of capital redundant. Respondents to the White Paper consultation, however, convinced the Government otherwise. In the Companies Act 2006 Regulatory Impact Assessment (January 2007), the Government expressed the view that what are now ss 709–723 should be retained in order to allow private companies to continue to use the uncontroversial mechanism of paying a premium out of capital on a purchase of its own shares. Since the 2006 Act came into effect, London Gazette notices of use of this procedure (s 719 notices) have appeared in the London Gazette at the rate of around one per week.

Acquisition of shares out of capital

If a private company intends to redeem (s 687) or purchase (s 690) its own shares out of capital, the shares must be fully paid up and paid for on acquisition (although on a redemption of shares, payment may be deferred if the terms of redemption so provide) (ss 686 and 691). In addition to ss 709–723 (the provisions specifically relevant to the *use of capital* to pay for a share acquisition), redeemable shares will be redeemed in accordance with their terms of redemption, and the 'off-market' purchase procedure set out in the Act will need to be complied with for other purchases of shares (ss 693–700 and 702–708).

Briefly:

1 The purchase contract must be available for inspection (s 702).
2 The terms of the purchase contract must be made available to shareholders (s 696).
3 A special resolution must be passed authorising the terms of the purchase contract (s 694).
4 All profits available for distribution and the proceeds of any fresh issue of shares must be applied to pay for acquisition *before* any capital may be used (s 710).
5 Directors must enquire into the affairs and prospects of the company (s 714).
6 A directors' statement is required including:
   - the amount of the capital payment permissible;
   - a solvency statement as in s 643 (see above at section 8.3.1) (s 714).
7 An auditor's report is required (s 714(6)) stating that:
   - the amount of the permissible capital payment is in his view properly determined;
   - he is not aware of anything to indicate that the opinion expressed by the directors in their statement is unreasonable in the circumstances.
8 The directors' statement and auditor's report must be available for inspection (s 720).
9 The directors' and auditors' report must be made available to shareholders (s 718).
10 A special resolution must be passed authorising payment out of capital (s 716).
11 Public notice (in the Gazette) of any proposed payment out of capital is required (s 719).
12 The shares must be cancelled (ss 688 and 706).
13 The following must be sent to the registrar:
   - Notice of redemption (s 689) or purchase of shares (s 707) as the case may be;
   - Statement of capital (ss 689 and 708);
   - Both special resolutions.

The directors' statement must be in prescribed form containing the prescribed information and paragraph 5 of the Companies (Shares And Share Capital) Order 2009 (SI No 2009/388) states that it must be signed by *all* directors.

Creditors and any shareholder who has not consented have five weeks from the date of the special resolution authorising the payment of capital within which to object to the use of the capital to redeem or acquire the company's shares. The objection is made by application to the court to cancel the special resolution (s 721).

Minimum share capital requirement	
Public limited companies (only):	
required to have minimum £50,000 or euro equivalent	ss 761 and 763
paid up as to at least 25% nominal value in cash	s 586 and s 584
Reduction of share capital	
Prohibited at common law except as permitted by statute	*Trevor v Whitworth (1887)*
Private company:	
may reduce share capital by solvency statement route or	ss 641–644
court approval route	ss 641 and 645–651
may acquire its own shares out of capital	ss 687, 690 and 709–723
Public company:	ss 641 and 645–651
May reduce share capital by court approval route	*Ex parte Westburn Sugar Refineries Ltd* (1951)
May acquire its own shares but not out of capital	ss 687(2) and 692(2)

8.4 Is capital maintenance important to creditors?

Focusing on share capital, private companies must have a share capital but it may be wholly minimal, such as, in theory, one share of one penny. Although public companies are required to have a minimum share capital of £50,000, this is not a substantial sum of money for a company in business in today's world.

In practice, of the companies formed and registered in 2010–11 that had a share capital, 90 per cent were incorporated with initial share capital of £100 or less and 97.5 per cent with a share capital of £5,000 or less. Of all companies on the register as at March 2011, 77 per cent had issued capital of £100 or less and 82 per cent had issued capital of £5,000 or less.

The rules and facts above indicate that in relation to most companies share capital offers little comfort to creditors that the company will be able to pay its debts. Evidence received by the Company Law Review Steering Group suggests creditors do not regard a company's share capital as particularly important.

QUOTATION

'The view of the substantial majority of consultees … was that a company's share capital is nowadays relatively unimportant as a measure of its ability to repay credit, and that other measures, including net assets, cash flow and interest cover are considerably more important.'

Company Law Reform, Modern Company Law for a Competitive Economy, Company Formation and Capital Maintenance, consultation document (October 1999 at para 3.5)

This raises the question of why the Companies Act 2006 contains such detailed rules relating to reductions in share capital, redemption of shares and a company acquiring its own shares?

In relation to private companies, the law has been simplified in relation to reduction of share capital, but the procedure for a private company to redeem or acquire its own shares out of capital remain unnecessarily complex. In relation to public companies, notwithstanding the stated aims of the reform of company law culminating in the 2006 Act, the law has not been simplified. This is in part explained by UK law having to reflect EU law, specifically, the Second Company Law Directive (77/91/EEC) which mandates capital maintenance rules for public companies. Sealy's comment that the pre-2006 Act statutory provisions were of 'byzantine obfuscation', unfortunately, remains applicable to the 2006 Act provisions.

8.5 Regulation of distributions

Restrictions on the ability of a company to reduce its share capital or acquire its own shares using capital do not prevent a company from paying sums of money to shareholders that do not cause a reduction in the company's formal share capital. The payment of value to shareholders is further controlled by restrictions on distributions to shareholders. These restrictions are found in both case law (*Re Exchange Banking Co, Flitcroft's Case* (1882) 21 Ch D 519 (CA)), and the Companies Act 2006 (ss 829–853).

The common law and statutory restrictions are cumulative (s 851) and, as a result of s 831, the statutory restrictions are stricter for public companies than they are for private companies.

8.5.1 Distributions

Definition of distribution

Distribution for the purposes of the statutory restrictions is very widely defined in s 829 as 'every distribution of a company's assets to shareholders, whether in cash or otherwise'. The following four activities are expressly excluded from the statutory definition either because they are subject to control by other provisions of the Act or do not give rise to any problem:

- a reduction of share capital (considered at sections 8.3.1 and 8.3.2 above)
- acquisition of shares in accordance with the Act (considered at section 8.3.3 above)
- the issue of bonus shares (this increases the share capital of the company)
- a distribution of assets to shareholders on its winding up (this will only occur after all creditors have been paid in full; see the shareholder last principle considered at section 8.6 below).

Dividends

dividend

a payment made to members out of a company's distributable profits, in proportion to their shareholding

The most common type of distribution is a dividend. Dividends are the amounts companies pay shareholders in return for share capital. Although an individual shareholder may not insist on receiving a dividend, large companies generally need to meet shareholder expectations by paying dividends or face a fall in their share price.

Authority to declare and pay dividends is not dealt with in the Act but in a company's articles. Companies typically pay an annual dividend, also referred to as a 'final dividend', and may pay interim dividends. The Model Articles for Private Companies Limited by Shares and those for public companies provide for annual or final dividends to be recommended by directors and declared by general resolution of the shareholders. Shareholders cannot declare a dividend of an amount greater than that recommended by the directors, although they may substitute a smaller amount. Directors are usually authorised by the articles to pay interim dividends without recourse to the shareholders in which event they may do so from time to time during the course of the financial year of the company. Quoted companies often pay dividends twice per year. Directors are also usually authorised to pay at intervals any dividend payable at a fixed rate if it appears to them that the profits available for distribution justify the payment. This allows dividends to be paid on preference shares without recourse to shareholders. Model articles 30 (private companies) and 70 (public companies) provide for all of the above.

At common law a dividend is paid based on the nominal value of shares held by shareholders. Although the Model Articles for Private Companies Limited by Shares are silent on this point, it is common for articles to provide that dividends should be paid based on the amounts paid up on the shares (see Model Articles for Public Companies, Art 71). This means that if a dividend of 8 pence is declared on £1 ordinary shares, the holder of a fully paid up £1 ordinary share will receive 8 pence whereas the holder of a £1 ordinary share on which only 50 pence is paid up will receive only 4 pence.

Dividends must be paid in cash unless the articles permit payment otherwise (*Wood v Odessa Waterworks Co* (1889) 42 Ch D 636). Once a dividend has been declared, it becomes a debt payable by the company to the shareholder and a shareholder may sue to enforce that debt (*Re Severn and Wye and Severn Bridge Railway Co* [1896] 1 Ch 559).

Disguised distributions

Transactions with shareholders in a different capacity than that of shareholder may need to be assessed to determine whether or not they are 'disguised' distributions or payments out of capital. Typical transactions that need to be considered are:

1 Sale of company property at an undervalue to a buyer who is a shareholder
    ● *Aveling Barford Ltd v Perion Ltd* [1989] BCLC 626
2 Purchase of property at an over-value by the company from a seller who is a shareholder
3 Payment of excessive director's fees to directors who are shareholders
    ● *Re Halt Garage (1964) Ltd* [1982] 3 All ER 1016
4 Payment of excessive employees' wages to employees who are shareholders
5 Excessive group service payments: excessive sums paid by subsidiaries to parent companies in return for a bundle of corporate services
6 Corporate gifts to shareholders.

These will not be permitted to the extent that the net gain by the shareholder is a payment out of capital or the company does not have distributable profits equal to or greater than that net gain. Net gain means the amount by which the value obtained by the shareholder exceeds the value obtained by the company from the transaction. In other words, the company is not permitted to make disguised gifts to shareholders.

Example

Shareholder A has property valued at £100,000. He sells the property to the company for £150,000. This is a disguised distribution of £50,000. The company has, in effect, given the shareholder £50,000 of company money.

The test applied is not a wholly subjective test based on the honesty of the directors approving the payment. Nor is it for the court to substitute its own commercial judgement. Patent excess or unreasonableness will cast doubt on the genuineness of the transaction (*Re Halt Garage (1964) Ltd* [1982] 3 All ER 1016). The Supreme Court in *Progress Property Co Ltd v Moore and another* [2010] UKSC 55 stated the court's real task to be 'to inquire into the true purpose and substance of the impugned transaction'.

8.5.2 Restrictions applicable to both private and public companies

Common law restriction

At common law, a company may not pay a dividend out of capital. This principle was stated and demonstrated clearly in *Re Exchange Banking Co, Flitcroft's Case* (1882) 21 Ch D 519 (CA).

CASE EXAMPLE

distributable profits

profits available for the purpose of paying a dividend as defined in s 830 of the Companies Act 2006

Re Exchange Banking Co, Flitcroft's Case (1882) 21 Ch D 519 (CA)

Between 1873 and 1875 the directors of a banking company had presented reports and balance sheets to shareholders in which debts known by the directors to be bad were entered as assets. As a result, apparent profits were shown when the directors knew the company had no distributable profits. In reliance on those accounts, the shareholders passed resolutions declaring dividends and those dividends were paid. The liquidator of the insolvent company sought an order that five of its former directors were jointly and severally liable to repay the amount of dividends paid to shareholders out of capital. Held: *Per* Cotton LJ, 'The assets of a company are to be dealt with only for purposes of its business. The application of the capital in paying dividends was therefore a misapplication'. As regards each dividend the court held that persons who were directors when it was paid were jointly and severally liable for the whole amount paid. The shareholders could not ratify such payments even if they knew the facts because a payment of dividends out of capital is incapable of ratification.

Statutory restriction: s 830

Section 830 of the Companies Act 2006 states that 'a company may only make a distribution out of profits available for the purpose'.

Profits available for the purpose

Profits available for the purpose are defined in s 830(2):

SECTION

'A company's profits available for distribution are its accumulated, realised profits, so far as not previously utilised by distribution or capitalisation, less its accumulated, realised losses, so far as not previously written off in a reduction or reorganisation of capital duly made.'

Setting aside for a moment the difficult question of whether or not a profit or loss has been 'realised', if a company is to be sure that it complies with s 830 it must keep a running total of its realised profits, less its realised losses and distributions already made, from the day it commences business. Only if the figure is positive at the time the company wishes to make a distribution does the company have profits available to distribute.

Example

Company A Ltd is registered on 1 January 2000. It has the following realised profits and realised losses, makes no distributions and has the following profits available for the purpose of distribution at the end of each of its first five years of operation:

	2000	2001	2002	2003	2004
Realised Profits (RP)	10	15	10	5	0
Realised Losses (RL)	5	10	5	10	5
RP–RL	5	5	5	(5)	(5)
PROFITS AVAILABLE FOR THE PURPOSE: Cumulative RP–RL	5	10	15	10	5

Notes: All figures are in 000s; figures in brackets are negative.

Company A Ltd could have paid a dividend of £15,000 at the end of 2002. It did not and because it made a loss in 2003 it could only have paid a dividend of £10,000 at the end of 2003. Due to a further loss in 2004, it could only pay a dividend of £5,000 at the end of 2004.

If Company A Ltd pays the dividends indicated in the following table in the year indicated, the 'profits available for the purpose' figure is adjusted accordingly:

	2000	2001	2002	2003	2004
Cumulative RP-RL	5	10	15	10	5
Dividend paid (Ds)	0	5	0	5	0
Cumulative Ds (CD)	0	5	5	10	10
PROFITS AVAILABLE FOR THE PURPOSE: Cumulative (RP–RL) – CD (or zero)	5	5	10	0	0

Relevant accounts

Whether or not a distribution may be made without contravening the Act is determined by reference to a company's accounts and the Act uses the concept of 'relevant accounts' (s 836). These will usually be the last annual individual accounts of the company compiled in accordance with the Act accompanied (unless the company is exempt) by an auditor's report (s 837(3)). If the auditor's report is qualified, s 837(4) requires a written statement to be made by the auditor as to whether or not the matters in respect of which his report is qualified are material to determining whether a distribution complies with the statutory distribution provisions and either a copy of that statement must be sent to each member of a private company or it must be laid before a meeting of a public company.

As a result of the European Regulation on the Application of International Accounting Standards (EC No 1606/2002) (the IAS Regulation (s 474)), publicly traded companies must prepare their *group* accounts in accordance with EU International Financial Reporting Standards (EU-IFRS), referred to in the Act as International Accounting Standards (IAS). Dividends are *not*, however, justified by reference to group accounts but individual company accounts. In relation to *individual* company accounts, all companies have the choice of preparing their individual accounts in accordance with EU IFRS (IAS individual accounts) or UK Generally Accepted Accounting Practice (UK GAAP) (Companies Act individual accounts) (s 395).

If a company wishes to make a distribution before the end of its first year, *initial accounts* need to be compiled that satisfy s 839. These will be the relevant accounts for the purposes of the distribution. If a company wishes to make an interim dividend based on trading after the date of the last annual accounts, it will need to justify that distribution by reference to *interim accounts* that satisfy s 838.

'Realised profits' and 'realised losses'

Notwithstanding the fundamental importance of the concept of 'realised' to the ability of a company to make a distribution, there is no requirement to identify those profits and losses that are realised and those that are unrealised in the relevant accounts. The only time the directors need to form a view on whether profits are realised or not is when they wish to use them to make a distribution. The directors often use a Statement of Total Recognised Gains and Losses to help them to determine distributable profits.

Apart from clarifying a couple of specific points in relation to revaluation of fixed assets (s 841) and dividends in kind (ss 845 and 846, see below), the Act delegates to the accounting industry the task of establishing standards and practices for determining when a profit or loss is and when it is not realised by s 853(4):

SECTION

'References to "realised profits" and "realised losses", in relation to a company's accounts, are to such profits or losses of the company as fall to be treated as realised in accordance with principles generally accepted at the time when the accounts are prepared, with respect to the determination for accounting purposes of realised profits or losses.'

Profits received by the company in cash or as some other asset (provided the cash value of that asset can be realised with reasonable certainty) are treated as 'realised' for accounting purposes. Whilst this is the essence of 'realised', realised is a far more complex concept than this (see Financial Reporting Standard (FRS) 18 (FRSs are part of UK GAAP)).

The ascertainment of distributable profits can be a very complex process. It involves far more than simply checking the company's profit and loss account. It is even sometimes the case that amounts reported outside the profit and loss account are available for distribution. Detailed consideration can be found in the most recent technical release issued by the Institute of Chartered Accountants (ICA) which, at the time of writing, was Tech 02/10 on determination of realised profits and losses in the context of distributions under the Companies Act 2006.

8.5.3 Additional limit on distributions by public company: net asset test

In addition to distributions having to come out of profits available for the purpose in accordance with s 830, s 831 states that a *public* company may only make a distribution up to the amount by which its net assets exceed the aggregate of its called-up share capital and undistributable reserves.

Undistributable reserves are listed in s 831(4) as:

- The share premium account (see Example 3 in section 8.1.1 above).
- The capital redemption reserve (see section 8.3.3 above).
- The amount by which its accumulated, unrealised profits (so far as not previously utilised by capitalisation) exceed its accumulated, unrealised losses (so far as not previously written off in a reduction or reorganisation of capital duly made) (note that if the losses exceed profits this will be a net *unrealised loss which is not reflected in this figure which is never less than zero*).
- Any other reserve the company is prohibited from distributing by any enactment or by its articles.

The effect of s 831 is that a public company's net *unrealised* losses must be deducted from its net *realised* profits (the company's 'profits available for the purpose of distribution' pursuant to s 830) to determine whether or not the company may make a distribution in accordance with the Act. Again, exactly what is and what is not an 'unrealised loss' for these purposes is determined by generally accepted accounting practice (see s 853(4) above).

8.5.4 Distributions in kind

If authorised by the articles, dividends may be made 'in kind'. Distributions to shareholders often take a non-cash form such as the transfer of an asset from a subsidiary to its parent. Even a distribution by a company to a sister company (a company with which it shares a parent company) will be treated as a distribution to its shareholder for the purposes of s 829 and could potentially also be a transfer of capital to a shareholder (*Aveling Barford Ltd v Perion Ltd* [1989] BCLC 626).

Sections 845, 846 and 851(2) of the 2006 Act clarify the previously uncertain legal position relating to the transfer of an asset to a shareholder (or any company controlled by its shareholder) where the market value of the asset is higher than the value of the asset in the company's balance sheet, the asset's 'book value'.

Transfer of an asset at book value

It is not uncommon for a company to transfer assets to its parent company in return for consideration equal to the book value of the transferred asset. If the market value of the asset is the same as its book value, there is no distribution and no unlawful return of capital: the company has received full value for the asset. If, however, the market value of the asset is more than the book value, in the absence of specific statutory provisions otherwise, transfer at book value would be a distribution of the amount by which the market value of the asset exceeded the book value, the company having, in effect, made a gift of the difference to its shareholder.

Example

Company A Ltd bought a piece of property in 2000 for £100,000. The value of the property in the accounts (or 'books') of Company A Ltd is £100,000 (book value). In 2008 the market value of the property has risen to £150,000. Company A Ltd transfers the property to its parent company for £100,000. In the absence of specific statutory provisions otherwise, this would be a disguised distribution of £50,000, the company having, in effect, given the shareholder £50,000 of company money. If such a transaction were to take place when the company did not have distributable profits at least equal to the difference between the book price and the market price the company would, without more, have made an unlawful distribution.

Sections 845, 846 and 851 provide relief in specific circumstances thereby ensuring that such a transaction is not an unlawful distribution and will not be regarded as a transfer of capital contrary to the common law principle in *Flitcroft's Case*, by reason of the market value and the book value being different.

If, as in the example above, the property is transferred at book value, provided the company has distributable profits, the amount of the distribution will be taken to be zero (s 845(2)(a) and s 845(2)). There will be no distribution for the purposes of s 829, or the common law. It is s 851(2) that takes away the danger of the transfer being regarded as a transfer of capital to a shareholder contrary to the common law prohibition.

Transfer of an asset at above book value

If property is transferred at *above* book value, again, subject to the company having distributable profits, the amount of the distribution will be taken to be zero. Also, s 845(3) provides that, solely for the purpose of meeting the pre-condition for the application of s 845(2) that a company has distributable profits, the distributable profits of the company may be treated as increased by the amount by which the price paid for the asset exceeds its book value.

Transfer of an asset at below book value

If the asset is transferred for a consideration *less than* its book value, s 845 operates to render the amount of the distribution equal only to the shortfall versus book value (rather than the difference between the actual consideration and market value). For the distribution to be in accordance with the Act, this shortfall will need to be covered by distributable profits.

Finally, s 846 allows a company with a revalued asset in its balance sheet, so that it is showing an *un*realised profit in its accounts, to treat that profit as a *realised* profit. The concession applies only for the purposes of a distribution by way of transfer of that particular revalued asset.

8.5.5 Remedies for payment of unlawful distributions

The unlawful payment of a distribution is not a criminal offence. Section 847(2) provides a civil remedy against a shareholder and s 847(3) preserves the common law and equitable remedies available against a shareholder who receives a distribution made unlawfully to him. Common law and equity also potentially provide remedies against the directors involved in the making of such payments. Additionally, unless a company is entitled to rely on the small or dormant company exemption from audit, the relevant accounts by which a distribution has been justified will have been reviewed by the company's auditor and an audit report signed. If it can be established that the unlawfulness of the distribution has resulted from negligence or breach of contract by the auditor, a company may be able to claim damages from its auditor (auditor liability is considered in Chapter 17). The sections below explore the potential liability of directors and shareholders in more detail.

Remedies available against the directors

Although the 2006 Act is silent in relation to the liability of directors who pay company capital to shareholders or make unlawful distributions, it is clear from *Flitcroft's Case* (above at section 8.5.2) that the directors at the time of the payment are jointly and severally liable to compensate the company for the whole amount paid.

This was applied in *Bairstow v Queen's Moat Houses* [2001] 2 BCLC 531 even though the directors did not actually know that the distributions were unlawful. *Bairstow* also made it clear that the liability of the directors is not limited to cases where distributions are demonstrably made out of capital, and applies whether or not the company is insolvent. The precise circumstances in which a director will be liable to the company in respect of unlawfully paid dividends and the test for liability, however, remain unclear.

The liability of a potentially *de facto* director for breach of trust in paying out dividends in the absence of profits available for the purpose was in issue in *Holland v Commissioners for Her Majesty's Revenue and Customs* [2008] EWHC 2200 (Ch), the first instance decision of a case ultimately appealed to the Supreme Court (which appeal is considered in the next chapter under *de facto* directors). The defendant had based the ability to pay dividends on accounts in which no provision had been made for payment of higher rate tax, provision for which would have reduced the profits. A provision is 'any amount retained as reasonably necessary for the purpose of providing for any liability the nature of which is clearly defined and which is either likely to be incurred, or certain to be incurred but uncertain as to amount or as to the date on which it will arise'. It was decided at first instance that the defendant was a *de facto* director (the issue appealed and reversed by the Supreme Court), but that before receiving categorical advice that the company was liability to pay higher rate tax, and in relation to dividends paid before that advice, he had made a judgement call as to whether or not it was reasonably necessary to retain an amount as a provision in relation to higher rate tax and, although with hindsight, that judgement call had been wrong, no breach of trust had occurred and therefore he would not be required to compensate the company in respect of the dividends. The decision was not appealed on this issue.

Remedies available against a shareholder

Remedies against a shareholder arise both under s 847 and pursuant to the common law principle that payment of an unlawful distribution is a misapplication of corporate funds.

The s 847 statutory remedy

Section 847(1) makes a shareholder liable to repay any sum received in contravention of the statutory distribution rules if at the time the distribution was made he knew or had reasonable grounds for believing the distribution was made in contravention of the statutory distribution rules. Accordingly, liability arises where the shareholder *actually* knows or has *reasonable grounds for believing*. But what precisely is it that the shareholder has to know or have reasonable grounds for believing?

In *It's a Wrap (UK) Ltd v Gula and another* [2006] 2 BCLC 634, the Court of Appeal considered the question whether the knowledge (actual or otherwise) required by the section is of:

- the relevant facts constituting the contravention; or
- those facts and, in addition, the fact that the Act was contravened.

The court applied the general presumption that ignorance of the law is no defence to decide that it is the former: there is no requirement that the shareholder knew, actually or otherwise, that the Act was contravened.

Section 847 implements Art 16 of the Second Company Law Directive and *It's a Wrap* is an excellent illustration of the court applying, in the context of company law, the *Marleasing* principle of conforming interpretation (*Marleasing SA v La Comercial Internacional de Alimentacion* Case C-106/89 [1990] ECR I-4135), that the courts must interpret a statute in a manner that is so far as possible in conformity with the provisions and objectives of the directive it was enacted to implement and general principles of

Community law. The court considered that there was nothing in the wording or purpose of Art 16 to oust the general principle that a person is deemed to know the law.

ARTICLE

'Article 16
Any distribution made contrary to art 15 must be returned by shareholders who have received it if the company proves that these shareholders knew of the irregularity of the distribution made to them, or could not in view of the circumstances have been unaware of it.'

The test for determining whether or not a shareholder has 'reasonable grounds for believing' that the distribution was made in contravention of the statutory distribution rules is not clear. It was not in issue in *It's a Wrap* because in that case the shareholders knew the distributions were not made out of profits, ie had actual knowledge of the facts constituting the contravention. Nonetheless, Arden LJ made some interesting *obiter* statements as to the meaning of 'reasonable grounds for believing'.

JUDGMENT

'[I]t is by no means self-evident that they are to be equated with "constructive knowledge" if by that expression is meant knowledge which a person would have but for his negligence. I do not think that the composite phrase "knows or has reasonable grounds for believing" has the same meaning as "knows or ought to know".'

Interpretation of the phrase will be influenced by application of the *Marleasing* principle and Art 16 uses very different wording: 'could not in view of the circumstances have been unaware of'. The Art 16 language supports Arden LJ's suggested interpretation, that the phrase is narrower than constructive knowledge and that more must be established by the company than negligence on the part of the shareholder, such as the deliberate turning of a blind eye to relevant facts. Arden LJ's comments are, however, only *obiter*, and the meaning of 'knows or has reasonable grounds for believing' remains moot.

Common law and equitable remedies

A shareholder who receives a distribution that contravenes the common law prohibition on distributions out of capital or (due to s 847(3)) the statutory rules may be required to repay the sum received to the company based on the imposition of a constructive trust (*Precision Dippings Ltd v Precision Dippings Marketing Ltd* [1986] Ch 447 (CA)). This will be a more effective remedy than recovery pursuant to s 847 because it is a proprietary remedy. If the shareholder becomes bankrupt or insolvent after the imposition of the constructive trust, the constructive trust funds will not be available to the other creditors of the shareholder. The circumstances in which a constructive trust will be imposed on a shareholder may not be exactly the same as those in which a repayment would be ordered under s 847. A constructive trust may be imposed where the shareholder is still in possession of the dividend or its traceable proceeds and is not a *bona fide* purchaser for value without notice of the wrongful payment.

The company may also be able to obtain a personal remedy against a shareholder in an action for money had and received at common law, or if an equitable proprietary claim can be successfully argued (knowing receipt or dishonest assistance). These topics are usually covered in courses on Trusts and Equity.

8.6 Shareholder last principle on a winding up

Shareholders have no claim to return of their contribution in a winding up until all creditor claims have been satisfied (Insolvency Act 1986, ss 107 and 143(1)). This supports the principle that the share capital sum is there to provide a buffer for creditors against poor trading and is not to be returned to shareholders ahead of creditors being paid.

8.7 A broader concept of capital maintenance?

8.7.1 Gratuitous payments to non-shareholders

Capital maintenance rules regulate the transfer of value *to shareholders*. It is interesting to consider the extent to which the law regulates gratuitous transfers of value by a company to persons *other than shareholders*. The most obvious example of a gratuitous transfer of value is a gift but any activity that takes value out of the company for no apparently good commercial reason could be characterised as a 'disguised gift'.

Examples of un-commercial arrangements are:

- Sale of company property at an undervalue (below market value)
- Purchase of property by the company at an overvalue (above market value)
- Payment of excessive directors' fees
- Payment of excessive employees' wages
- Excessive payment for goods or services
- Corporate gifts delivering no benefit to the company commensurate with cost.

8.7.2 Gratuitous payments as *ultra vires*

Historically, gifts made by companies were challenged as beyond the legal capacity of the company, or *'ultra vires'*, based on them falling outside the objects of the company. The practice of adopting broad objects clauses resulted in this argument rarely succeeding. In *Re Horsley & Weight Ltd* [1982] Ch 422, the Court of Appeal even confirmed that the giving of gifts is capable of being a distinct object of a company. In any event, the *ultra vires* argument is no longer available (see Chapter 5).

8.7.3 The 'Cakes and Ale Case Law'

Cases as recently as *Barclays Bank v British and Commonwealth Holdings plc* [1996] BCLC 1, appear to support the existence of a principle that 'no company may make truly gratuitous dispositions of its assets'. This line of cases has been dubbed the 'Cakes and Ale Case Law' (see McGuinness (2007)), as it can be traced back to Bowen LJ's often quoted words from *Hutton v West Cork Railway Co* (1883) Ch D 654 (CA):

JUDGMENT

'The law does not say that there are to be no cakes and ale, but there are to be no cakes and ale except such as are required for the benefit of the company.'

The principle has been criticised by Ferran who argues that 'the principle that a company cannot give away its capital is not part of English company law' (Ferran (1999)). It appears to remain good law in Canada (McGuinness (2007)) and the issue is best regarded as moot in English law. What seems to be clear is that a principle that truly gratuitous dispositions are unlawful is not needed as other legal principles adequately regulate the mischief it addresses, whether the decision to make the gratuitous payment is made by the directors or the shareholders.

Decisions by directors

In most cases the decision to make the gift will be made by the directors. Directors must act in accordance with their duties to the company and the principle can be seen as an application of those duties. The two most relevant duties where payments are made to parties unrelated to the directors are the duty to exercise powers only for the purposes for which they are conferred (s 171) and the duty to act in the way that the director considers in good faith would be most likely to promote the success of the company (s 172). If a director does not consider in good faith that the payment would be most likely to promote the success of the company (see s 172), the court may find the director to be in breach of duty. The ability of the company to recover from third parties any sums actually paid will be determined by rules governing remedies available against third parties when there has been a breach of fiduciary duty. You may examine these remedies in your study of equity in the context of trusts. Where the decision to make a gift is made by directors, there appears to be no need for an additional principle of law. The mischief is dealt with by enforcement of directors' duties (see Chapters 11 and 12).

Decisions by shareholders

In *Hutton* it was the shareholders of the company who voted for payments to be made to employees, for loss of their employment. The company had no obligation to make such payments and a dissenting minority successfully challenged the payments. The importance of the principle, that a company cannot make gifts unless for the benefit of its business, could be said to be that it operates to constrain the action of the majority of shareholders: it precludes a majority from forcing the gratuitous disposition of corporate assets on a minority. Yet is such a specific principle needed?

In *Re Halt Garage (1964) Ltd* [1982] 3 All ER 1016, Oliver, J explained *Hutton* as an application of a more general abuse of powers principle. We considered the 'general principles of law and equity which are applicable to all powers conferred on majorities and enabling them to bind minorities', when we examined the constraints on shareholders voting to amend the articles (see Chapter 5 at section 5.5.3). *Hutton* may be seen as a particular application of those principles which require the shareholders to exercise the power of the company to make gifts 'not only in the manner required by law, but also, *bona fide* for the benefit of the company as a whole and it must not be exceeded' (*per* Lindley MR in *Allen v Gold Reefs of West Africa Ltd* [1900] 1 Ch 656 (CA)). Yet this principle appears only to have been applied to amendment of the articles of a company. Moreover, it seems to contradict the principle that a shareholder is entitled to exercise his voting rights in his own interest, a principle based on the theory of the right to vote being a property right (*Northern Counties Securities Ltd v Jackson & Steeple Ltd* [1974] 1 WLR 1133). Consequently, the law remains unclear.

The business judgment rule

A no truly gratuitous dispositions principle would require courts to be called upon to analyse and pass judgment on whether or not a decision was or was not 'truly gratuitous'. To determine such involves deciding whether or not the company could benefit in any way from the payment. This potentially requires judges to second-guess business decisions which they have generally shown great reluctance to do as they are not businessmen and such decisions are best left to the board of directors. As most payments are made when a company is a going concern, it will almost always be possible to articulate some benefit to the company that flows from the payment and it is interesting to note that in both *Hutton* and *Parke v Daily News Ltd* [1962] Ch 927 (a case in which the principle from *Hutton* was applied), the companies had ceased to carry on business before the challenged payments were agreed to. The companies remained in existence solely for the purpose of being wound up, in which circumstances it was difficult to argue that the making of payments to employees could benefit the companies in any way.

Note that today, s 247 of the Companies Act 2006 empowers companies to make provision for employees on cessation or transfer of the business of the company. Consequently, the payments in both *Hutton* and *Parke* would not be problematic today.

Gratuitous payments out of capital or profits

In *Re George Newman & Co* [1895] 1 Ch 674, Lindley LJ appears to have restricted the principle against gratuitous payments to payments made *out of capital*.

JUDGMENT

'The shareholders, at a meeting duly convened ... can, if they think proper, remunerate directors for their trouble or make presents to them for their services out of assets properly divisible amongst the shareholders themselves ... But to make presents out of profits is one thing and to make them out of capital or out of money borrowed by the company is a very different matter. Such money cannot lawfully be divided amongst the shareholders themselves nor can it be given away by them for nothing to their directors so as to bind the company in its corporate capacity.'

Many cases in which the principle has been asserted have involved indirect returns of capital (*Barclays v British & Commonwealth Holdings*) and unlawful distributions (*Aveling Barford Ltd v Perion Ltd* [1989] BCLC 626) *to shareholders*. These cases could have been adequately dealt with applying capital maintenance rules. In other cases in which the principle has been asserted the payment has also been challenged based on the *ultra vires* argument (*Ridge Securities Ltd v IRC* [1964] 1 All ER 275 at 288). This has often resulted in confused judgments the status of which are unclear following the demise of the *ultra vires* doctrine.

Whether or not there is a general principle prohibiting gratuitous payments, a number of legal principles and specific legal rules are available to regulate gifts and 'disguised gift' transactions:

1. If the payments are authorised by directors, the company can challenge the directors based on **breaches of their directors' duties.**
2. Breaches by the company and directors of **specific provisions of the 2006 Act** such as long service agreements (s 188); asset/loan transactions with directors (ss 190 & 197).
3. If the transaction has been authorised by shareholders, a minority can seek relief by:
   - **Derivative action on behalf of the company based on breach of duty by a director** that the shareholders are prepared to condone (especially if those directors are shareholders purporting to condone the transaction) (s 260).
   - **Unfair prejudice petition** (s 994).
   - Assertion of the **improper purpose principle** (*Re Halt Garage (1964) Ltd* [1982] 3 All ER 1016).
4. If the transaction takes place in the twilight zone, the liquidator can challenge it based on it being:
   - a **voidable preference** pursuant to s 239 Insolvency Act 1986;
   - an **invalid floating charge** pursuant to s 245 Insolvency Act 1986;
   - a **transfer at an undervalue** (TUV) pursuant to s 238 Insolvency Act 1986;
   - a liquidator can enforce breaches of directors' duties using s 212 Insolvency Act 1986.
5. A liquidator can apply for contribution orders based on **wrongful or fraudulent trading** (ss 213 and 214 of the Insolvency Act 1986).

Each of these legal principles and rules is considered at the appropriate place in this book.

8.8 Political donations

The making of political donations and incurring of political expenditure by a company is specifically regulated by the Companies Act 2006 (ss 366–379), although companies may make political donations of up to £5,000 in any 12 month period without complying with the statutory provisions (s 378). Also, donations and subscriptions to trade unions other than to the union's political fund are not political contributions and all-party parliamentary groups are not political organisations for the purposes of the statutory provisions (ss 374–376).

Subject to the foregoing, no political donations or expenses are permitted unless authorised by both the shareholders of the company and, if the company is part of a group, by the shareholders of the ultimate holding company (s 366). A wholly owned subsidiary company is not required to pass such a resolution (but the parent company must) (s 366). Shareholder approval has been required since 2000.

A resolution generally authorising such has effect for four years or such shorter period as the articles require or the directors determine (s 368). All directors are jointly and severally liable to repay any payments or expenses incurred without authorisation and compensate the company for any consequent loss or damage (s 369), and there are special provisions governing the rights of shareholders to enforce the directors' liabilities (ss 370–373).

KEY FACTS

Distributions, s 829	
Distributions may be disguised	*Aveling Barford Ltd v Perion Ltd* (1989)
	Re Halt Garage (1964) Ltd (1982)
Companies may only pay distributions out of profits available for the purpose	*Re Exchange Banking Co, Flitcroft's Case* (1882)
	s 830
Public companies must also take unrealised losses into account	s 831
Transfer of assets to sister companies may be a distribution	*Aveling Barford Ltd v Perion Ltd* (1989)
	ss 845, 846 and 851
Remedies for payment of unlawful distributions may be available against:	
Directors (jointly and severally liable)	*Re Exchange Banking Co, Flitcroft's Case* (1882) *Bairstow v Queen's Moat Houses* (2001)
Shareholders (pursuant to both statute and case law)	s 847 *It's a Wrap (UK) Ltd v Gula* (2006) *Precision Dippings Ltd v Precision Dippings Marketing Ltd* (1986)
Shareholder last principle on a winding up	
Shareholders have no claim until creditors have been paid in full	ss 107 and 143(1) Insolvency Act 1986
Gratuitous payments to non-shareholders	
The existence of a principle banning truly gratuitous payments is moot	*Hutton v West Cork Railway Co* (1883) *Barclays Bank v British & Commonwealth Holdings* (1996) *Re George Newman & Co* (1895)
Political donations	
Up to £5,000 in any 12 month period is not regulated by statute	s 378
Beyond that amount, shareholder approval is required	s 366

8.9 Financial assistance for the purchase of its own shares

8.9.1 Background to the current rules

The provision of financial assistance by a company for the acquisition of its own shares by another person was first prohibited in 1928. It was made, and for public companies remains, a criminal offence (s 680). The rule is usually considered in conjunction with capital maintenance rules because it was proposed by Lord Greene (as Chair of the Company Law Amendment Committee), and introduced, in part, as an extension of the rule against a company purchasing and trading, or 'trafficking', in its own shares. The mischief sought to be addressed, however, was not a diminution in the resources of the company brought about by the assistance. The purpose of the rule is not to preserve assets of the company for the benefit of creditors. Consequently, it does not fit well under the capital maintenance rubric.

8.9.2 Reasons for the statutory prohibition

The ban was introduced to deal with two perceived mischiefs:

- manipulation of a company's share price brought about by the company providing assistance for the purchase of its shares;
- use of an acquired company's assets to pay off the debt incurred to buy the company.

The second mischief explains why the prohibition applies to assistance provided *after* (s 678(3)), as well as before or at the same time as (s 678(1)), the acquisition of shares takes place. According to Lord Greene MR, the practice, following the end of the First World War, of a financier taking out a short-term loan (sometimes called a bridging loan) to finance the acquisition of shares in a company and then using the assets of that company to repay the loan 'gave rise to great dissatisfaction and, in some cases, great scandals' (*Re VGM Holdings Ltd* [1942] Ch 235 at 239).

In fact, the practice Lord Greene describes is not uncommon today and is not regarded as contentious. It is quite acceptable, and within the law, for one company to borrow significantly to finance the acquisition of another company and, following acquisition, to cause the acquired company to pay out as much as it can *by way of lawful dividend* to its new parent to enable the parent to pay back as much of its acquisition borrowings as possible. The legality of this is assured by s 681(2) taking 'a distribution of a company's assets by way of dividend lawfully made' outside the statutory prohibition.

Also, if the acquired company has a lot of cash or readily realisable assets, loans from the subsidiary to the parent can be put in place enabling the parent company to pay back acquisition borrowings. This may, however, be caught by the prohibition. The fact that such a loan is innocuous, yet it is not clear whether or not it would be caught by the statutory prohibition, is but one way in which the provisions prohibiting financial assistance are unsatisfactory. Gower captures the unsatisfactory nature of the rule in the following words:

JUDGMENT

'The history of the rule does not constitute one of the most glorious episodes in British company law. The rationale for its introduction was under-articulated; it has proved capable of rendering unlawful what seem from any perspective to be perfectly innocuous transactions; and it has proved resistant to a reformulation which would avoid these problems.'

Gower (2008), para 13–26

Although the 2006 Act removed the prohibition in relation to private companies (that are not subsidiaries of public companies), the prohibition remains for public companies as part of the UK's implementation of the European Second Company Law Directive

(Directive 77/91/EEC) (though note that the UK has not implemented relaxations made to that directive by Directive 2006/68/EC).

8.9.3 Typical examples of financial assistance

Typical examples of a company providing financial assistance for the purchase of its shares are:

- Company A plc lends money to X and X uses that money to buy shares in Company A plc.
- Company B plc guarantees a loan made by Bank E to Y and Y uses the borrowed money to buy shares in Company B plc.
- Z borrows money from Bank F and uses it to buy Company C Ltd. Z then uses the resources of Company C Ltd to repay the loan monies to Bank F.

8.9.4 What is prohibited?

By ss 678 and 679 it is not lawful for:

- a public company
- to give financial assistance
- directly or indirectly
- for the purpose of acquisition of its shares or shares in its private holding company
- either before or at the same time as the acquisition
- or for the purpose of reducing or discharging a liability incurred for the purpose of the acquisition.

Financial assistance is defined very widely in s 677. The section lists specific examples of ways in which financial assistance can be given and also contains generic language, as follows:

- gift, guarantee, security, indemnity, release, waiver and loan;
- any other financial assistance given by the company where the net assets of the company are reduced to a material extent by the giving of the assistance or the company has no net assets (s 677(d)).

The prohibition now applies only to public companies, not to private companies (see reform, below at section 8.9.8). This means that if a public company is acquired and the parent company wishes to use its assets to reduce or discharge a liability incurred for the purpose of the acquisition, even if the acquired company is not able to pay money to the parent as dividends, the acquired company can be re-registered as a private company following which there is no prohibition on it providing financial assistance.

8.9.5 Limits and exceptions to the prohibition

The main limits to the prohibition are the 'principal purpose' and 'incidental part' carve-outs.

The 'principal purpose' carve-out

If the company's principal purpose in giving assistance is not to give it for the purpose of acquisition of shares, or to reduce or discharge any liability incurred for the purpose of the acquisition of shares, *and* the assistance is given in good faith in the interests of the company, it is not prohibited (ss 678(2)(a),(4)(a) and 679(2)(a),(4)(a)).

The 'incidental part' carve-out

If the giving of the assistance for the acquisition of shares, or to reduce or discharge any liability incurred for the purpose of the acquisition of shares, is only an incidental part of some larger purpose of the company *and* the assistance is given in good faith in the interests of the company, it is not prohibited (ss 678(2)(b),(4)(b) and 679(2)(b),(4)(b)).

The scope of these carve-outs was considered in *Brady v Brady* [1989] AC 755 (HL). The narrow approach taken has been fiercely criticised and seems at odds with the more liberal approach generally taken to exceptions operating in the context of criminal offences (although the case was in fact a civil case in which one party sought specific performance of an agreement which included the provision of financial assistance). Nonetheless, notwithstanding the proposal to replace the words 'principal purpose' with 'predominant reason', the 2006 Act retains the old language.

CASE EXAMPLE

Brady v Brady [1989] AC 755 (HL)

Two brothers were unable to run the family company together. To save the company from being run down they made arrangements to split the businesses of the company with one brother, Robert, to run the soft drinks side and the other brother, Jack, to run the road haulier business. Arrangements were put in place which included the original company providing financial assistance to a new company to allow the new company to purchase shares in the old company. Jack sued Robert for specific performance of the agreement but Robert argued that the agreement provided for the giving of unlawful financial assistance and was therefore void and unenforceable. Jack argued that the 'incidental part of some larger purpose' exception applied. Held: The financial assistance did not fall within the incidental part exception (though specific performance was granted based on other grounds). The purpose of the assistance was to acquire shares even if that was not the reason for assistance 'reason is not the same as purpose'; and 'larger is not the same thing as "more important"'. *Per* Lord Oliver: 'The purpose and the only purpose of the financial assistance is and remains that of enabling the shares to be acquired and the financial or commercial advantages flowing from the acquisition, whilst they may form the reason for forming the purpose of providing assistance, are a by-product of it rather than an independent purpose of which the assistance can properly be considered to be an incident'.

Exceptions to the prohibition, contained in ss 681 and 682, are detailed. In addition to the particularly important exception noted above of a dividend lawfully made, s 681 removes from the prohibition allotment of bonus shares and reductions of capital and redemption or purchase of shares in accordance with the Act. The s 682 exceptions are conditional upon either the company's net assets not being reduced or any such reduction being provided out of distributable profits. The main arrangements excluded by s 682 are arrangements by which employees acquire shares.

8.9.6 Criminal sanctions for contravention

Section 680 states that if the company contravenes the prohibition on the giving of financial assistance, the company and every officer of the company in default commits an offence. The company is liable to a fine and officers are liable to up to 12 months' imprisonment, a fine, or both.

8.9.7 Civil remedies for breach

The Act does not specify the civil consequences of the company contravening the prohibition and providing unlawful financial assistance. The consequences must be found in the cases and the approach of the judges has changed over time. It is necessary to consider the position of the following:

- the company giving the unlawful financial assistance
- the person purchasing the shares
- any third party involved such as a bank lending money to the purchaser of the shares the guarantee of which by the company amounts to unlawful financial assistance
- the directors of the company.

The current position can be summarised as:

- An agreement between the purchaser and the company for the provision of unlawful financial assistance is void and unenforceable by either party (*Brady v Brady* [1989] AC 755 (HL)).
- If the agreement to provide unlawful financial assistance and the agreement to purchase shares form a single composite transaction and the financial assistance provisions cannot be severed from the agreement so as to leave an enforceable agreement, the entire agreement will be unlawful and unenforceable by the company or the purchaser (*South Western Mineral Water Co Ltd v Ashmore* [1967] 1 WLR 1110).
- Connected transactions are not tainted by the unlawfulness of the unlawful financial assistance so that, for example, a purchaser cannot avoid an obligation to buy shares relying on the argument that the company has agreed to provide unlawful financial assistance in relation to the purchase (unless the two are one composite agreement).
- Any agreement by which the unlawful financial assistance is to be given is void and unenforceable (*Heald v O'Connor* [1971] WLR 497).
- The directors are liable to the company for breach of duty.
- If company assets have been transferred by way of financial assistance the company *may* be able to recover those assets based on the recipient holding the assets on constructive trust arising as a result of the breaches of fiduciary duty by the directors.

8.9.8 Reform

As mentioned above, implementing Company Law Review proposals, the Companies Act 2006 does not apply the prohibition on financial assistance to private companies. Commentators have questioned the impact on the common law position of simply excluding private companies from the scope of the statutory prohibition on financial assistance. Essentially, common law capital maintenance principles expounded in the nineteenth century in the context of undeveloped accounting principles and practices have not been developed because statutory developments have, in large part, removed the need for recourse to the common law.

There is no specific common law prohibition on financial assistance but any financial assistance by a private company will need to comply with the general principles of capital maintenance outlined in this chapter. For example, if an existing shareholder were to be given company funds to buy shares in the company at a time when the company had no distributable profits, it would be an unlawful distribution. If the sum was a return of capital, that would be an unlawful return of capital. Where the decision to provide the funds is taken by directors, the duties they owe to the company will also regulate behaviour.

Financial assistance remains in place for public companies because of the European Second Company Law Directive (see above at 8.9.2).

KEY FACTS

Financial assistance for the purchase of its own shares	
Public companies may not provide financial assistance for purchase of its own shares subject to:	ss 678 and 679
criminal sanctions	s 680
civil remedies for breach	*Brady v Brady* (1989) *South Western Mineral Water Co Ltd v Ashmore* (1967) *Heald v O'Connor* (1971)
Statutory prohibition abolished for private companies by the Companies Act 2006	Behaviour principally regulated by directors' duties

SAMPLE ESSAY QUESTION

Discuss the extent to which current laws applicable to private companies support the doctrine of capital maintenance.

Unpack the question

This is the first essential step which you must take time to do properly. You should separate out:

- Explaining the doctrine of capital maintenance and the reason for it
- Identifying deregulation for private companies as an aim of the 2006 Act
- The irrelevance of minimum share capital to private companies
- Outlining the statutory procedures for reduction of capital/redemption and purchase of shares by private companies
- Control of dividends/other distributions
- Explanation of the shareholder last rule on winding-up
- Assessment of the extent to which the law supports the doctrine in relation to private companies.

The doctrine of capital maintenance

Identify the "capital maintenance" doctrine as shorthand for:

- minimum share capital rules: ss 763–767
- the basic prohibition on a company reducing its share capital: s 617
- detailed exceptions to the prohibition on a company reducing its share capital: Pts 17 and 18 of the 2006 Act
- the requirement that distributions to shareholders may only be paid out of profits available for the purpose: ss 829–853
- the shareholder last principle on winding-up: Insolvency Act 1986 ss 107.

Possibly characterise financial assistance as related but separate from the doctrine. Explain the rationale, creditor protection: *Trevor v Whitworth*.

> **Review the extent to which the law supports the doctrine in relation to private companies**
>
> - Recognise the irrelevance of minimum share capital to private companies
> - Identify the inroads into the prohibition on share capital reduction by outlining the new and old statutory procedure for reduction of capital
> - Outline the provisions enabling private companies to redemption and purchase shares out of capital
> - Explain s 830 control of dividends/other distributions and identify this as the critical protection
> - Explain how the shareholder last rule on winding-up preserves the assets for creditors.

> **CONCLUDE**
>
> Express your reasoned conclusion as to whether the law supports capital maintenance for private companies.

ACTIVITY

Applying the law

A. Revisit Andy, Betty and Myco Ltd from the activity at the end of Chapter 7. Explain the process they would need to go through to repay and remove Ian from Myco Ltd if they had issued (i) non-voting preference shares with limited dividend and capital rights; and (ii) preference shares which only differed from ordinary shares in relation to the dividend right, which is fixed at 10 per cent.

B. Company A Ltd bought an asset, V, for £100,000 in 1990. The asset appreciated in value and was revalued in 2000. V is now entered in the accounts of Company A Ltd as worth £150,000. The market value of V is estimated to be £400k. Company A Ltd has distributable profits of £100k. A wishes to transfer S, lawfully, to its sister company, I, for the lowest price possible. Advise A.

SUMMARY

The doctrine of capital maintenance

Capital maintenance is essentially two principles now found in the Companies Act 2006:

- A limited company having a share capital may not reduce its share capital except as authorised by statute (s 617).
- Distributions of a company's assets to its members, whether in cash or otherwise, may only be made out of profits available for the purpose (s 830 and see also s 831 in relation to public companies).

Minimum share capital requirements

Public limited companies (only) are required to have minimum £50,000 or euro equivalent paid up as to at least 25 per cent nominal value in cash (ss 761, 763, 584 & 586).

Capital reductions

Reduction of share capital is prohibited both at common law and by statute except as permitted by statute, (*Trevor v Whitworth* (1887); s 617).

Private company:

▨ May reduce share capital by solvency statement route, (ss 641–644) or court approval route, (ss 641 and 645–651).
▨ May acquire or redeem its own shares out of capital, (ss 687, 690 and 709–723).

Public company:

▨ May reduce share capital only by court approval route, (ss 641 and 645–651; *Ex parte Westburn Sugar Refineries Ltd* (1951)).
▨ May acquire or redeem its own shares only out of profits or the proceeds of a new issue.

Dividends and distributions

▨ Companies may only pay distributions out of profits available for the purpose (*Re Exchange Banking Co, Flitcroft's Case* (1882); s 830).
▨ Public companies must also take unrealised losses into account when calculating profits (s 831).
▨ Remedies for payment of unlawful distributions may be available against:
  ● Directors (jointly and severally liable) (*Re Exchange Banking Co, Flitcroft's Case* (1882); *Bairstow v Queen's Moat Houses* (2001)); and
  ● Shareholders (pursuant to both statute and case law) (s 847; *It's a Wrap (UK) Ltd v Gula* (2006); *Precision Dippings Ltd v Precision Dippings Marketing Ltd* (1986)).

Shareholder last principle

▨ Shareholders have no claim until creditors have been paid in full (Insolvency Act 1986 ss 107 and 143(1)).

Financial assistance

▨ Public companies may not provide financial assistance for purchase of its own shares, (ss 678 and 679) subject to criminal sanctions (s 680) and civil remedies for breach (*Brady v Brady* (1989); *South Western Mineral Water Co Ltd v Ashmore* (1967); *Heald v O'Connor* (1971)).
▨ Statutory prohibition abolished for private companies by the Companies Act 2006 (behaviour principally regulated by directors' duties).

Further reading

Useful websites
ICA guidance on determination of realised profits and losses in the context of determining profits available for distribution can be accessed at:
www.icaew.com/index.cfm/route/154655/icaew_ga/en/pdf

Articles
Daehnert, A, 'The minimum capital requirement – an anachronism under conservation: Part 1' (2009) 30 Comp Law 3.
Daehnert, A, 'The minimum capital requirement – an anachronism under conservation: Part 2' (2009) 30 Comp Law 34.

Ferran, E, 'Corporate transactions and financial assistance: shifting policy perspectives but static law' (2004) 63 CLJ 225.

Ferran, E,' Directors' liability for unlawful dividends' (2011) 70 CLJ 321.

Niranjan, V, and Naravane, S, 'A reassessment of fundamental dividend principles' (2009) 20 ICCLR 88.

Proctor, C, 'Financial assistance: new proposals and new perspectives?' (2007) 28 Comp Law 3.

See 'European Business Law Review', part 5 of the 15th volume for articles on capital maintenance and its reform.

Reports

Company Law Amendment Committee Report (1926) Cmnd 2657 (The Greene Report).

'Reforming Capital: Report of the Interdisciplinary Group on Capital Maintenance' edited by Jonathan Rickford (2004) 15 EBL Rev 919.

Books

Davies, P, (2008) *Gower & Davies' Principles of Modern Company Law* (8th edn, Sweet & Maxwell).

McGuinness, K, (2007) *Corporate Law* (2nd edn, LexisNexis Canada).

9

Governance of the company

AIMS AND OBJECTIVES

After reading this chapter you should be able to:

- Identify the key organs of governance of a company
- Discuss the division of power between the board of directors and shareholders
- Discuss four methods by which shareholders make valid decisions
- Call a company meeting
- Discuss how boards of directors make valid decisions
- Identify different types of directors and the roles each plays
- Appoint and remove directors
- Discuss how the law governs director remuneration
- State the role of a company secretary
- Identify the officers of a company

9.1 Introduction and key organs of governance of a company

This chapter is about the constitutional system by which the affairs of a company are governed or controlled. This system is established by a combination of law and the constitutional documents of the company. The central questions are *who* is empowered to make decisions about the company's affairs and *how* are those decisions taken.

The key organs of governance of a company are the board of directors and the shareholders. As a governing organ or body of the company, the shareholders are often referred to as 'the shareholders in general meeting'. This description is accurate for public companies because decision-making by public company shareholders must take place by resolutions being passed at a shareholders' meeting (s 281(2)). The terminology is not particularly appropriate for private companies, however, because there is no requirement for a private company to hold shareholders' meetings and private company shareholders may make decisions without meetings, by written resolution (s 281(1)).

In this chapter, the shareholders as a body and the board of directors are considered in turn followed by examination of the appointment and removal of individual directors. We then take a very brief look at the role of the company secretary and a company's officers.

9.2 Shareholder governance

9.2.1 Introduction

The role of shareholders in the governance of any given company is established by a combination of:

- constitutional rules of the company (the articles of association)
- statute law (the Companies Act 2006 and the Insolvency Act 1986)
- cases recognising the power of the shareholders in certain circumstances.

Shareholders are sometimes referred to as 'residual controllers' of the company. Four main points support this:

- the law requires certain fundamental decisions to be made by the shareholders
- whilst the articles normally entrust management to the board of directors they also usually reserve a right for shareholders to direct the board by special resolution on any specified matter
- if the board is unable to act, power will revert to the shareholders
- shareholders have the right to remove directors from office.

It is important to distinguish clearly between a shareholder acting as part of the decision-making governance body of the company and a shareholder acting in an individual capacity to enforce his or her personal rights. The rights and obligations of a shareholder acting in his personal capacity were dealt with in part in Chapter 5 when we considered the rights of a shareholder to enforce provisions in the articles and are also considered in Chapter 14. They are not considered further in this chapter.

Shareholders in closely held companies

The role played by shareholders in a closely held company is typically very different from the role played by shareholders of a company with dispersed ownership. Closely held companies are usually 'owner-managed' companies. The practical difficulty here is that decision-making can be very informal. Very often, the major shareholders are the directors who are also the executives/managers of the company. The shareholder/director/manager individual is usually focused on running the business of the company, not figuring out in which capacity the law requires him to take a particular decision. He has no practical concern to 'get the legal paperwork right'. Compared to the procedures in place for public companies, the law provides simpler, less formal procedures for decisions to be made by both shareholders (essentially no need for annual general meetings and the option to make written resolutions) and boards of directors of private companies.

Shareholders in listed companies

The scenario outlined above is in stark contrast to a large public company with many shareholders in which the main, indeed virtually sole, interest of shareholders is to see the price of their shares increase and receive adequate dividends on their shares. Consider, for example, individuals who own shares in Vodaphone Group plc, BT Group plc or in the parent company of a banking group, such as Lloyds Banking Group plc.

Invitations to shareholder meetings, received through the post, are often regarded by shareholders of dispersed ownership companies as not unlike junk mail. Little or no interest is shown in filling out the proxy form enclosed with the invitation empowering another to exercise their vote at the meeting on the proposed resolutions also included with the invitation to the meeting. Consequently, attendance at shareholder meetings is very poor. In all, the governance of the company is wholly entrusted by such shareholders to the board of directors.

The proportion of shares of companies listed on the London Stock Exchange, by value, owned directly by individuals at the beginning of 2011 was 11.5 per cent. The figure has risen slightly in recent years, reversing a long trend downwards to a low of 10.2 per cent at the beginning of 2009. Beyond this, it is difficult to know for whom shares are held as registers of members (shareholders) record nominee names, not the beneficiaries of shares. Forty-five per cent by value of all shares recorded in Crest shareholder registers are in multiple ownership pooled nominee accounts. The Office of National Statistics has estimated that the proportion of listed shares by value owned by insurance companies at the beginning of 2011 was between 8 and 13 per cent and that pension funds owned approximately 5.1 per cent. These figures are much smaller than fifty years ago but the significance of this drop is not clear as a growing proportion of shares are owned as part of non-insurance company and non-pension fund pooled investment funds of different types. Indirect ownership of shares by individuals is significantly higher than direct ownership. The proportion of shares of companies listed on the London Stock Exchange, by value, owned by those outside the UK at the beginning of 2011 was more than 41 per cent (a one third increase in overseas ownership since 1998).

Institutional investors have faced severe criticism over the years for their failure to take their role as shareholders seriously and for failing to exert adequate influence over boards of directors of the companies in which they invest. Introduced in 2010 as a response to apathy, and revised in September 2012 the aim of the non-statutory Stewardship Code ('the Code') is to encourage institutional shareholders to play a more active role in corporate governance than has been the case to date.

The Kay Review of UK Equity Markets, published in July 2012, and the Government response published in November 2012 call for company directors, asset managers and asset holders to embrace Good Practice Statements aimed at encouraging long-term value creation. This evolving regulatory policy can be tracked on the BIS website.

QUOTATION

'The Code sets out good practice on engagement with investee companies to which the FRC believes institutional investors should aspire. It provides an opportunity to build a critical mass of UK and overseas investors committed to the high quality dialogue with companies needed to underpin good governance. By creating a sound basis of engagement it should create a much needed stronger link between governance and the investment process, and lend greater substance to the concept of "comply or explain" as applied by listed companies. The FRC therefore sees it as complementary to the UK Corporate Governance Code for listed companies, as revised in June 2010.'

FRC, The Stewardship Code, July 2010, p.1

In addition to the non-statutory code, changes have been made to the Companies Act 2006 by the Companies (Shareholders' Rights) Regulations 2009 (SI 2009/1632) (the Shareholder Rights Regulations), implementing the Shareholder Rights Directive (2007/36/EC), in an attempt to improve shareholder engagement in the governance of traded companies.

9.2.2 Division of powers in the articles

Article 3 of both the Model Articles for Private Companies Limited by Shares and those for public companies establishes the board of directors as the principal organ of management of the company:

MODEL ARTICLE

'Subject to the articles, the directors are responsible for the management of the company's business, for which purpose they may exercise all the powers of the company.'

In addition to being expressly subject to the company's other articles, this power is also subject to the provisions of the Companies Act 2006.

Article 4 of both the Model Articles for Private Companies Limited by Shares and for Public Companies establishes a reserve power for the shareholders:

MODEL ARTICLE

'The shareholders may, by special resolution, direct the directors to take, or refrain from taking, specified action.'

Attempts by shareholders to usurp board powers by passing ordinary resolutions or acting in any other way inconsistently with the articles will not succeed.

CASE EXAMPLE

Automatic Self Cleansing v Cuninghame [1906] 2 Ch 34

Powers of general management were vested in the board subject to directions from the shareholders by extraordinary resolution. The shareholders passed an ordinary resolution directing the board to sell the company's business. The directors objected to the sale. Held: The board of directors could lawfully refuse to comply as direction by ordinary resolution was insufficient. On a true construction of the articles the shareholders were only competent to intervene by extraordinary general meeting. [Note that extraordinary resolutions are no longer provided for in the Companies Act 2006. They required 75 per cent support and had to be passed at an extraordinary general meeting.]

CASE EXAMPLE

John Shaw & Sons (Salford) Ltd v Shaw [1935] 2 KB 113 (CA)

Articles vested general powers of management in 'permanent directors'. The permanent directors resolved to institute legal proceedings against three 'ordinary directors' who were shareholders. The shareholders passed a resolution to discontinue the company's legal proceedings. Held: The shareholders had no power to overrule the decision of the permanent directors. The options available to the shareholder were (i) to change the articles, or (ii) to remove the board of directors.

The decision whether or not a company should commence legal action in given circumstances is part of the general management of the company so will ordinarily be vested in the board of directors pursuant to Art 3. The applicability of the basic rule against usurpation by shareholders to the decision to litigate or not was confirmed in *Breckland Group Holdings Ltd v London & Suffolk Properties Ltd* [1989] BCLC 100. Harman J restrained the majority shareholder from taking any further action in litigation commenced by the shareholder without authority of the board until a board meeting could be held at which it could be resolved whether to continue or discontinue the legal action.

9.2.3 Statutory powers of shareholders

The statutory powers given to shareholders are mainly in the Companies Act 2006 but also arise from the Insolvency Act 1986.

Powers given to shareholders by the Companies Act 2006

The main powers given to shareholders by the Companies Act 2006 are:

- To amend the company's constitution (s 21(1) and see Chapter 5).
- To resolve to reregister the company eg from private to public or vice versa (ss 90 and 97 and see Chapter 4).
- To remove directors by ordinary resolution (s 168 and see section 9.3.3 below).
- To approve director service contracts if employment is guaranteed for more than 2 years (s 188(2) and see section 9.3.4) below).
- To approve substantial property transactions (s 190(1)) and loans (s 197) between the company and a director (see Chapter 12).
- To approve compensation to a director for loss of office (s 217 and see section 9.3.4 below).
- To ratify directors' breaches of duty (s 239 and see Chapter 13).
- To authorise political donations in excess of £5,000 (s 366 and see Chapter 8).
- To approve appointment of the company auditor (s 489(4) and see Chapter 17).
- To authorise the board to allot shares (s 551) (Though board power to allot is automatic for a private company with only one class of shares, s 550) (see Chapter 7).
- To disapply pre-emption rights (ss 569–571 and see Chapter 7).
- To reduce share capital (s 641(1) and see Chapter 8).
- To authorise the company to purchase its own shares (ss 694, 701 and see Chapter 8).
- To approve a payment out of capital for redemption or other acquisition of a company's own shares (s 716 and see Chapter 8).

Note that whilst the shareholders have a statutory power to remove directors (s 168), shareholders have no *statutory* power to appoint directors. Appointment of directors is provided for in the company's articles.

Power given to shareholders by the Insolvency Act 2006

The main power given to shareholders by the Insolvency Act 1986 is to decide, by special resolution, to wind-up the company voluntarily (Insolvency Act 1986 s 84(1)).

9.2.4 Default powers of shareholders

Management power will revert to the shareholders in circumstances where the board is unable to act.

CASE EXAMPLE

Barron v Potter [1914] 1 Ch 895

A company had two directors and the articles gave directors power to appoint additional directors. One director would not attend any board meeting at which the other was present. Held: A general resolution appointing an additional director was valid. *Per* Warrington J, 'If directors having certain powers are unable or unwilling to exercise them … there must be some power in the company to do itself that which under other circumstances would be otherwise done … in my opinion the company in general meeting has power to make the appointment'.

9.2.5 How shareholders exercise their powers

Shareholders exercise their powers by taking decisions and the rules governing how decisions are to be taken are determined by a combination of the articles, statute and common law. The 2006 Act requires shareholder resolutions in a number of situations and shareholder decisions are usually taken by resolutions in accordance with the provisions of the Act (ss 281–299). The common law is, however, preserved which leaves open the potential for shareholder decisions to be effective even if they are made otherwise than by passing a resolution (s 281(4)(a)). The common law may also override the statutory

resolution

the formal way in which a decision of the shareholders or the directors is proposed and passed rules as to the circumstances in which a resolution is or is not treated as having been passed and undermine the statutory rules insofar as the common law may preclude a person from alleging that a resolution has not been duly passed (s 281(4)(b) and (c)). The common law rules are considered after the statutory rules.

Statutory provisions on resolutions

The 2006 Act states that resolutions of the shareholders of a *public* company must be passed at shareholders' meetings held and conducted in accordance with the 2006 Act for which notice has been given in accordance with the Act (ss 281(2) and 301). *Private* company shareholders must pass resolutions either at similarly conforming shareholders' meetings or by written resolution (s 288(1)).

It is only possible to determine whether or not a resolution has been validly passed if we know:

- which shareholders have the right to vote
- the proportion of votes needed to pass the resolution; and
- how votes are to be counted.

Voting rights

A company must have at least one class of shares that carry the right to vote. Unless the articles provide otherwise, every share carries one vote on every resolution put to shareholders (s 284), except in a vote by show of hands, when, regardless of the number of shares he owns, a shareholder has only one vote (see voting methods below). Articles may provide for weighted voting rights which can give rise to surprising outcomes. The decision in *Bushell v Faith* [1970] AC 1099 (HL) has rendered s 168, by which shareholders may remove a director by ordinary resolution, a presumptive rather than mandatory rule of law (see the discussion in Chapter 5), and the decision in *Amalgamated Pest Control v McCarron* [1995] 1 QdR 583 permitted incorporators to use weighted voting rights to give a less than 25 per cent minority shareholder a veto on any special resolution.

Even where a company has different classes of shares, the starting point is that all shares carry the right to one vote. The articles or resolution authorising allotment may state that a certain class of shares carries the right to vote on resolutions on matters affecting the rights of the class. Even if it is not stated expressly that these are the *only* voting rights attaching to the shares, the court may use the principle of exhaustion of rights to construe such a provision in the articles as excluding any other voting rights (see *Re Bradford Investment Ltd* [1991] BCLC 224 and section 7.3.2).

Proportion of votes needed to pass resolutions

The two basic types of resolution passed by shareholders are ordinary resolutions and special resolutions. Ordinary resolutions must be passed by not less than a simple majority (50 per cent +1) (s 282) and special resolutions must be passed by not less than 75 per cent (s 283). Provisions of the Companies Act 2006 mandating shareholder approval of certain acts or empowering shareholders usually require a special resolution or a general resolution.

Curiously, s 282 appears to have inadvertently changed the law in relation to the right of the chairman of a shareholders' meeting to have a casting vote. The chairman is usually a director of the company who may or may not be a shareholder. Nonetheless, traditionally, it was common for articles to provide for the chairman to have a casting vote in the event of an equality of votes for and against an ordinary resolution and reg 50 of Table A contained just such a provision. Without more, s 282 overrides an article giving the chairman a casting vote.

This outcome has been partly reversed by a provision in The Companies Act 2006 (Commencement No 5, Transitional Provisions and Savings) Order 2007) (SI 2007/3495) which provides that companies whose articles contained a provision giving the chairman a casting vote immediately before 1 October 2007 may continue to rely on that article

written resolution

a resolution of the members of a private company proposed and passed in accordance with the Companies Act 2006

ordinary resolution

a resolution of the members of a company passed by a simple majority of 50% plus one vote of those eligible to vote

special resolution

a resolution of the members of a company used for significant decisions requiring a 75% majority of the votes of those eligible to vote which must be described as a special resolution and the text of which must be set out in any notice notwithstanding s 282. Companies incorporated after 1 October 2007 may not rely on such a provision in their articles, nor can such a provision be introduced by a company that did not have such a provision before 1 October 2007. This saving has no application to traded companies (as that term is defined in the Companies Act s 360C), and traded companies cannot allow the chairman of a shareholders' meeting to have a casting vote (see regulation 22 of the Shareholders Rights Regulations (implementing the Shareholder Rights Directive)).

Voting methods
Three different voting methods are used to pass resolutions. Two are used at shareholders' meetings and the third, available to private companies only, is used for written resolutions.

Vote on a show of hands
A vote on a show of hands is very simple, being based on shareholders in attendance at a meeting raising their hands to indicate support for, or opposition to, a resolution put to the meeting. A resolution passed on a show of hands is a general resolution if it is passed by not less than a simple majority of the shareholders (including duly appointed proxies) who vote on the resolution (being eligible to do so). It is a special resolution if passed by not less than 75 per cent of shareholders (including duly appointed proxies) who vote on the resolution (being eligible to do so).

Example 1
Ten shareholders attend a meeting and are eligible to vote on a resolution. Six shareholders raise their hands in support of the resolution. The resolution has been passed as a general resolution.

If only three shareholders had raised their hands in support, the chairman of the meeting would have been required to ask those who wished to vote against the resolution to raise their hands. If only two shareholders voted against the resolution, the resolution would have been passed as a general resolution because a simple majority (three) of those who voted (five) supported it. If three or more shareholders had voted against the resolution, it would not have been passed.

poll
a vote in writing at a general meeting where shareholders or their proxies vote in proportion to their voting shareholdings

Poll vote
A poll vote is not based on the number of shareholders who vote, but on the voting rights of the shareholders who vote. A resolution passed on a poll is a general resolution if passed by shareholders representing not less than a simple majority of the total voting rights of shareholders who vote (in person or by proxy) on the resolution. It is a special resolution if passed by shareholders representing not less than 75 per cent of the total voting rights of shareholders who vote (in person or by proxy) on the resolution. A person with more than one vote is under no obligation to cast all his votes or to cast those he uses in the same way (s 322).

Additional provisions apply to quoted and traded companies in relation to poll votes, including the obligation to make the results and associated information about poll votes available on the company's website (s 341).

Example 2
The same ten shareholders as appeared in Example 1 attend the same meeting and are eligible to vote on the resolution. There is a call for a poll vote on the resolution. Nine of the shareholders own ten ordinary shares each. The tenth shareholder owns 910 ordinary shares in the company. The number of votes that can potentially be cast at the meeting is 1,000. The six shareholders who passed the general resolution in Example 1 each have ten shares. They vote in favour of the resolution. They represent only 6 per cent of the voting rights of shareholders who could vote. The holder of 910 shares votes against the resolution. The resolution is not passed. If the holder of 910 votes attended the meeting but decided to abstain from voting in the poll vote, the six shareholders could pass the resolution as a general resolution.

Written resolution vote

A written resolution is based not on the number of shareholders who actually vote, and not on the voting rights of the shareholders who actually vote, but on the voting rights of all shareholders eligible to vote. The relevant date for determining eligibility to vote on a written resolution is the date on which the written resolution is sent to shareholders (ss 289 and 290). Essentially, copies of a proposed written resolution are sent to shareholders who sign the copy of the resolution and send it back to the company, although any signed or otherwise authenticated document referencing the resolution and indicating the shareholder's agreement to it, sent or emailed to the company, suffices (s 296).

In one respect, voting on a written resolution is calculated in the same way as on a poll vote: it is the proportion of *votes* held by those shareholders who support and oppose the resolution that counts. Calculation of votes differs from a poll vote, however, in that a written resolution must be passed by shareholders representing no less than a simple majority (for a general resolution) or no less than 75 per cent (for a special resolution) of the *total voting rights of eligible shareholders*. In contrast, a poll vote is based on the voting rights of only those shareholders who are in attendance at the meeting (in person or by proxy) and who actually vote on the particular resolution.

As indicated above, written resolutions can only be used by private companies (s 288) and even private companies may *not* use the written resolution procedure to remove a director pursuant to s 168 or to remove an auditor before expiry of his term of office (s 288(2)).

Proxies and corporate representatives

A shareholder is entitled to appoint another person as his proxy to exercise all or any of his rights to attend, speak and vote at a meeting of the company (s 324). Proxies are entitled to vote on votes by a show of hands as well as on poll vote. The availability of proxy voting has been expanded and the rules improved by the 2009 regulations. A clear statement of the obligation of a proxy has been introduced as a new s 324A to the Act.

proxy

a person appointed by a member entitled to vote at a general meeting to attend the meeting and vote in his place. The proxy can speak at the meeting and vote on a show of hands and on a poll. The proxy need not be a member of the company

SECTION

'**Section 324   Obligation of Proxy to Vote in Accordance with Instructions**
A proxy must vote in accordance with any instructions given by the member by whom the proxy is appointed.'

The changes to the proxy rules applicable to all companies essentially allow proxies for more than one shareholder to cast votes both for and against a resolution where their instructions from different shareholders requires such. Some of the changes apply only to traded companies which must provide an electronic address for the return of proxies and, although the appointment and termination of a proxy's authority must be in writing, for these purposes, writing includes by electronic communication (ss 327 and 333A).

Companies, being artificial entities, cannot attend meetings of the companies in which they own shares. For this reason the Companies Act provides for companies to appoint corporate representatives. A corporate representative is an individual who has been authorised by resolution of the directors of a company (Company A) to represent Company A at any meeting of a company of which Company A is a shareholder (s 323). The individual is then empowered to exercise the same powers on behalf of the company as if it were an individual member of the company, ie from the company's perspective, the corporate representative is, for all intents and purposes, the member/shareholder and has the full rights of the corporate shareholder he or she represents.

Note that, following confusion, s 323 has been amended by the Shareholders' Rights Regulations 2009 and it is now clear that where a shareholder company appoints more than one corporate representative, the corporate representatives are permitted to vote in different ways from one another in respect of different blocks of shares.

Statutory provisions on shareholder meetings (ss 301–361)

quorum

the minimum number of people necessary for the transaction of business at general meeting or board meeting

Rules governing shareholder meetings, also called company meetings, are an important part of shareholder decision-making. A company with only one shareholder may hold a properly constituted meeting (s 318). Apart from that circumstance, and unless the articles require a higher number, two shareholders (or corporate representatives of proxies) present at a meeting are a quorum (s 318). This means that even if one individual present represents two or more shareholders, the meeting is not a properly constituted meeting and no business can be conducted.

Annual general meetings (AGM)

annual general meeting (AGM)

a general meeting of the members of a company which public companies must hold each calendar year within six months of the financial year end

Every *public* company must hold an annual general meeting (AGM) within six months of the end of its financial year and if the company fails to do so a criminal offence is committed by every director and the company secretary (s 336). At least 21 days' notice of an AGM, stating that it is an AGM, must be given (s 307(2)) to all shareholders and directors (s 310) unless *all* shareholders entitled to attend and vote agree to shorter notice (s 337(2)). Except for the longer minimum notice of meeting period (21 days rather than 14), the need for unanimous consent to short notice (rather than 90 per cent (for private companies) or 95 per cent (for public companies)) and the rules requiring the company to circulate notice of shareholders' resolutions to be moved at the AGM (s 338), the rules for general meetings set out below apply to AGMs.

General meetings

general meeting

a meeting of the members of a company

The directors may call a general meeting (s 302) and are required to call a general meeting if holders of at least 5 per cent of the voting rights of shareholders having a right to vote at general meetings request (in writing or electronic form) that the directors do so (ss 303 and 304). If the directors fail to call a general meeting within 21 days of such a request, or to hold the meeting within 28 days of the request, the shareholders who made the request may call a meeting and hold it within three months of the request, in which event their reasonable expenses are reimbursable by the company (s 305).

If it is impracticable for a meeting to be called or conducted in accordance with the articles of the company or the 2006 Act, the court may, on application by a director or any shareholder who would be entitled to vote at the meeting, or of its own volition, order a meeting to be called, held and conducted in any manner the court thinks fit (s 306).

All shareholders and directors are entitled to receive notice of every general meeting unless the articles provide otherwise (s 310). At least 14 days' notice of a meeting must be given unless shareholders holding not less than 90 per cent (for a private company) or 95 per cent (for a public company) of the nominal value of the shares held by those entitled to attend and vote at the meeting agree to shorter notice. A notice must state the general nature of the business to be dealt with as well as the time, date and place of the meeting (s 311). If notice is given of a meeting any accidental failure to give notice to one or more shareholders will not render the notice invalid (s 313).

Shareholders with at least 5 per cent of the voting rights of shareholders eligible to vote on the proposed matter may require the company to circulate a statement of up to 1,000 words relating to a proposed resolution or any other business to be dealt with at the meeting (s 314). A similar right exists in relation to written resolutions (s 293).

special notice

the notice required from the proposing shareholders to the company, of ordinary resolutions to remove a director or remove, appoint or re-appoint an auditor

Special notice is required of four resolutions:

- to remove a director pursuant to s 168;
- to appoint someone in his place at the removal meeting;
- to remove an auditor (s 511); and
- to appoint a new auditor (s 515).

Special notice is given *by* the shareholder *to* the company of his intention to move the resolution and must be not less than 28 days before the date of the meeting at which the resolution is to be voted on (s 312). Be sure to distinguish special notice of a resolution given by a shareholder to the company from notice of a meeting given by a company to shareholders.

The rules governing general meetings were altered for trading companies by the Shareholders' Rights Regulations 2009. Amongst other rights, the shareholders of a traded company have the right to ask questions at a general meeting (s 319A). The obligation of the company to answer shareholders' questions is circumscribed, in addition to not being required to answer if to do so would involve the disclosure of confidential information, no answer is required if, 'it is undesirable in the interests of the company or the food order of the meeting that the question by answered'.

Class meetings

Meetings of holders of a particular class of shares are called class meetings. The rules governing class meetings are essentially the same as for general meetings, being applicable 'with necessary modifications' (s 334).

Court-ordered meetings

If it is impracticable for a meeting to be called or conducted in accordance with the articles of the company or the 2006 Act, the court may, on application by a director or any shareholder who would be entitled to vote at the meeting, or of its own volition, order a meeting to be called, held and conducted in any manner the court thinks fit (s 306).

Shareholder decisions recognised at common law

The principle that the shareholders of a company may unanimously reach a decision without the need for compliance with formal procedures is known as the 'Duomatic principle'. The principle was in fact established long before it was applied in *Re Duomatic Ltd* [1969] 2 Ch 365. Lord Davey referred to the principle in *Salomon* to confirm that the company was bound by the purchase of the boot manufacturing business because the unanimous agreement of the shareholders of the company was an inevitable inference from the circumstances. The principle was applied in the very simple circumstances of *Re Express Engineering Works Ltd* [1920] 1 Ch 466 (CA).

CASE EXAMPLE

Re Express Engineering Works Ltd [1920] 1 Ch 466 (CA)

The purchase of property paid for by the issues of debentures had been approved by resolution of the five directors of the company at a directors' meeting. All directors in attendance at the meeting were disqualified from acting because they were all interested in the seller of the property, so the directors' resolution was ineffective. The directors were also the shareholders of the company. The liquidator of the company argued that the issue of the debentures was invalid. Held: The court refused to set the debentures aside. The meeting was a directors' meeting but it might be considered a general meeting. If the five persons present had said, 'We will now constitute this a general meeting' it would have been within their powers to do so and it appeared to Lord Sterndale MR that that was in fact what they did and the company was bound by the unanimous agreement of the shareholders.

The principle has been applied in a wide range of circumstances, including when different types of resolutions would otherwise have been required, such as a special resolution (*Cane v Jones* [1980] 1 WLR 1451). Mummery LJ described the principle in the following terms in *Euro Brokers Holdings Ltd v Monecor (London) Ltd* [2003] BCLC 506 (CA).

JUDGMENT

'[The Duomatic principle] is a sound and sensible principle of company law allowing the members of the company to reach an agreement without the need for strict compliance with formal procedures, where they exist only for the benefit of those who are agreed not to comply with them. What matters is the unanimous assent of those who ultimately exercise power over the affairs of the company through their right to attend and vote at a general meeting. It does not matter whether the formal procedures in question are stipulated for in the articles of association, in the Companies Acts or in a separate contract between the members of the company concerned. What matters is that all the members have reached an agreement. If they have they cannot be heard to say that they are not bound by it because the formal procedures were not followed. The position is treated in the same way as if the agreed formal procedure had been followed.'

Judicial constraint on the exercise of voting rights by a shareholder

Tension exists between two lines of cases relevant to the exercise of shareholder voting rights. There is no principle that the position of shareholder gives rise to fiduciary obligations to the company but the range of decisions in relation to which a shareholder is required to think beyond his own self interest is unclear.

The *Allen v Gold Reefs of West Africa Ltd* [1900] 1 Ch 656 (CA) line of cases focuses on when voting shareholders are exercising a power conferred on majorities enabling them to bind minorities. They apply the general principles of law and equity applicable to such powers and require a shareholder to exercise his votes *bona fide* for the benefit of the company. With the exception of Oliver J (as he then was) in *Re Halt Garage (1964) Ltd* [1982] 3 All ER 1016 explaining the decision in *Hutton v West Cork Railway Co* (1883) Ch D 654 (CA) as an application of these general principles, cases asserting the requirement that a shareholder must exercise his votes *bona fide* for the benefit of the company appear to be confined to cases amending the articles.

In contrast, a number of cases, reaching back to *Pender v Lushington* (1877) 6 Ch D 70, have emphasised the unrestrained right of a shareholder to vote in his own individual interest. In the words of Sir George Jessel MR in *Pender*:

JUDGMENT

'There is, if I may say so, no obligation on a shareholder of a company to give his vote merely with a view to what other persons may consider the interests of the company at large. He has a right, if he thinks fit, to give his vote from motives or promptings of what he considers his own individual interest.'

Subsequent cases have stressed the individual *property* nature of the voting rights attaching to shares. In *Re Astec (BSR) plc* [1998] 2 BCLC 556, Johnathon Parker J stated:

JUDGMENT

'The starting point is the proposition that in general the right of a shareholder to vote his shares is a right of property which the shareholder is free to exercise in what he regards as his own best interests. He is not obliged to cast his vote in what others may regard as the best interests of the general body of shareholders, or in the best interests of the company as an entity in its own right.'

Northern Counties Securities Ltd v Jackson & Steeple Ltd [1974] 2 All ER 625 seems to be the high water mark of this approach. The question in issue was whether or not shareholders would be in contempt of court if they voted against a resolution that had to be passed if the company was to comply with an undertaking it had given to the court. Walton LJ (sitting in the Chancery Division) held that not even a shareholder who was also a director was required to vote in anything other than his own interest.

JUDGMENT

'When a shareholder is voting for or against a particular resolution he is voting as a person owing no fiduciary duty to the company and who is exercising his own right of property, to vote as he thinks fit. ... a shareholder who casts his vote in general meeting is not casting it as an agent of the company in any shape or form. His act therefore, in voting as he pleases, cannot in any way be regarded as an act of the company.'

In *Re Unisoft Group Ltd (No 3)* [1994] 1 BCLC 609, Harman J attempted to reconcile the *Allen* and *Pender* lines of cases by asserting the freedom of the shareholder in strong terms but emphasising the distinction between the act of a shareholder in voting for or against a resolution and the resolution itself.

JUDGMENT

'It is important to remember that shareholders' rights to deal with or vote their shares are separate from the rights of the company as a corporate entity and shareholders' relationships with it. Shareholders are entitled to sell their shares, to vote their shares, to take any course they like in general meeting without regard to any other person's rights or position. In my judgment the law is that a shareholder may act with malice in voting his shares against a particular resolution and there can be no objection to that.'

Where self-interested voting behaviour results in a special resolution to amend the articles, it is the special resolution which is an act of the corporate entity, Harman J appears to be saying, that may be challenged as not *bona fide* for the benefit of the company. Harman J's analysis implicitly emphasises the substantive rights of minority shareholders. Although it is a valiant attempt to reconcile apparently irreconcilable case law, his approach is difficult to reconcile with the *language* of the *Allen* cases.

KEY FACTS

Division of powers and shareholder decision-making	
Division of powers	
Company powers allocated in articles:	
Management and all powers of the company vested in board of directors	Model Art 3 (public and private)
Shareholders may direct board to take specified action by special resolution	Model Art 4 (public and private)
Shareholders may not usurp power by ordinary resolution or otherwise contrary to the articles	*Automatic Self Cleansing v Cuninghame* (1906)
Shareholders also have:	
statutory powers	Companies Act 2006 and Insolvency Act 1986 (listed at section 9.2.3)
common law default powers if board is unable to act	*Barron v Potter* (1914)
How shareholders exercise their powers	
Presumption that shares have equal voting rights unless articles provide otherwise	*Birch v Cropper* (1889) and s 284
Shareholder resolutions:	s 284
Vote on show of hands	One vote per shareholder at meeting
Poll vote	One vote per share of those present or represented at meeting
Written resolution (private company)	One vote per share
Ordinary resolutions: simple majority	s 282
Special resolutions: 75%	s 283
Unanimous informal decisions are effective	*Re Duomatic Ltd* (1969)
	Re Express Engineering Works Ltd (1920)
Shareholders are entitled to vote in their own self-interest, subject to:	*Northern Counties Securities v Jackson & Steeple* (1974)
requirement to exercise votes *bona fide* for the benefit of the company applies when amending the articles	*Allen v Gold Reefs of West Africa Ltd* (1900)
unclear whether of wider application	*Re Halt Garages (1964) Ltd* (1982)

9.3 Board of directors

We turn away from the shareholders of a company now to look at the board of directors. In the first part of this section we focus on the board of directors as a decision-making organ of the company; on the powers vested in the board and how the board exercises those powers by taking decisions. In the second part of this section we consider the composition of the board of directors; how directors are appointed and removed. Finally, we focus on directors' terms of service and remuneration, a subject that has attracted a great deal of attention as it is in relation to this that boards of directors may be most keenly tempted to behave not in the best interests of the company, but rather in their own best interests.

9.3.1 Board powers and decision-making

Powers of the board

As stated above, Art 3 of both the Model Articles for Private Companies Limited by Shares and those for public companies establishes the board of directors as the principal organ of management of the company:

MODEL ARTICLE

'Subject to the articles, the directors are responsible for the management of the company's business, for which purpose they may exercise all the powers of the company.'

When considering these powers and the exercise of them, it is essential to view the board of directors as a body distinct from the individual directors making it up. It is the board collectively that is entrusted by the articles with the responsibility to manage the company and it is the board collectively, as an organ of government of the company, that is empowered to exercise all the powers of the company for this purpose. Sir George Mellish LJ made this point clearly in *Re Marseilles Extension Railway Company, ex parte Credit Foncier and Mobilier of England* (1871) LR 7 Ch App 161 (CA) (cited in *Mayson, French & Ryan on Company Law* (2008)).

JUDGMENT

'It appears to me, that a director is simply a person appointed to act as one of a board, with power to bind the company when acting as a board, but having otherwise no power to bind them.'

The collective nature of the responsibility of the board is also emphasised in the first principle of the UK Corporate Governance Code (2010).

QUOTATION

'Every company should be headed by an effective board, which is *collectively* responsible for the success of the company.' (emphasis added)

FRC UK Corporate Governance Code (June 2010) at p.6

Although the Model Articles do not contain any particular limitation, it is not uncommon for the articles of a company to limit the general allocation of management and powers to the board of directors by, typically, requiring shareholder approval before certain powers of the company may be exercised. An example would be an article providing that shareholder approval in advance is required before £1 million or more can be borrowed by the company.

When advising a company or a director, it is always essential to check a company's articles to be aware of any such limitation. If the power is exercised without first obtaining shareholder approval, the board and every director involved in the decision is acting outside his authority. Section 40 of the Companies Act 2006 operates in such a case in favour of a person dealing with the company in good faith. The powers of the board of directors are deemed, in that person's favour, to be free of any such limitation. The consequences of the board and individual directors acting outside their authority and the operation and effect of s 40 are considered in Chapter 10 when we look at binding the company.

Delegation and authorisation

In the course of management of a company, company powers are not only exercised by the board of directors. Delegation of power is essential if a company is to be run efficiently. Article 5 of both the Model Articles for Private Companies Limited by Shares and those for public companies empowers the board of directors to delegate any power conferred on it by the articles.

MODEL ARTICLE

'Directors may delegate

5(1) Subject to the articles, the directors may delegate any of the powers which are conferred on them under the articles—
(a) to such person or committee;
(b) by such means (including by power of attorney);
(c) to such an extent;
(d) in relation to such matters or territories; and
(e) on such terms and conditions;
   as they think fit.
(2) If the directors so specify, any such delegation may authorise further delegation of the directors' powers by any person to whom they are delegated.
(3) The directors may revoke any delegation in whole or part, or alter its terms and conditions.'

The board's power to delegate is broad. From the perspective of knowing who is authorised to exercise which power, it would be ideal if the board of directors passed resolutions approving lists of powers delegated to named individuals. Ideals, however, are all too often unrealistic and in most companies the practice of documenting delegation is very poor. Notice that subsection (2) of model Art 5 allows a cascade of delegation by enabling any person to whom the board has delegated powers to further delegate those powers.

All too often it is unclear whether or not an individual director, executive or employee has the authority to exercise a particular power. The governing area of law here is agency law. A person to whom the board delegates power is an agent of the company. Evidence of express actual agency is often missing so it is necessary to examine the fact situation to determine whether or not the individual in question has implied actual authority or even ostensible (also known as apparent), authority to exercise the power in question. The operation of agency principles in the company context is examined in the next chapter. In this chapter, we are not concerned with a situation in which delegation is in issue, but with how *the board of directors* exercises the powers conferred on it.

Board decision-making

Sole director companies

The remainder of this section on board decision-making is not relevant to a private company that has only one director and no provision in its articles requiring it to have more than one. Article 7(2) of the Model Articles for Private Companies Limited by

Shares allows such a director to take decisions without regard to any of the provisions of the articles relating to directors' quorums and decision-making.

Board decisions

Statute does not regulate board decision-making. Establishing the rules for how the board of directors is to take decisions is an important part of the articles of both private and public companies. Part 2 of both the Model Articles for Private Companies Limited by Shares and those for public companies contain extensive rules with which you should familiarise yourself. Rules relating to participation of an individual director who is interested in a matter on which the board is taking a decision are not considered here but are addressed in Chapter 12 in the context of directors' duties.

Public companies

The Model Articles for Public Companies provisions governing the taking of decisions by the board are relatively straightforward. Article 7(1) provides that, subject to the articles, decisions of the directors must be taken:

- at a directors' meeting (at which resolutions are passed by a majority of those participating with every director having one vote unless the articles provide otherwise (Art 13)); or
- in the form of a directors' written resolution (which require the unanimous support of all directors (Art 18)).

Be careful not to confuse shareholder written resolutions, a form of resolution permitted only by private companies (s 288), with written *board* resolutions of public companies.

Private companies

The private company Model Articles governing the taking of decisions by the board are not drafted as clearly as those for public companies. This is the legacy of the consultative process which saw the draft Model Articles amended on more than one occasion. The end result provides less informality than originally proposed, the original proposal having been in line with the deregulatory theme for private companies of the Companies Act 2006. Article 7 sets out the basic rule and Art 8 then provides for unanimous decision-making outside board meetings. Unanimous informal decisions may be arrived at in a number of ways.

MODEL ARTICLE

'Directors to take decisions collectively
7.   (1) The general rule about decision-making by directors is that any decision of the directors must be either a majority decision at a meeting or a decision taken in accordance with Article 8.
      ...
8.   (1) A decision of the directors is taken in accordance with this article when all eligible directors indicate to each other by any means that they share a common view on a matter.
      (2) Such a decision may take the form of a resolution in writing, copies of which have been signed by each eligible director or to which each eligible director has otherwise indicated agreement in writing.'

It is clear that *majority* decisions of directors outside board meetings will *not* be effective in any circumstances except where a specific provision permitting majority decisions to be taken outside directors' meetings appears in the articles of association of the company.

Board meetings

Board meetings of a public or private company may be called by any director by giving notice to the other directors (Model Articles, Art 9 (private company), Art 8 (public company)). The notice provisions of Table A (the predecessor default articles to the Model Articles) were often amended to meet the specific requirements of companies, a practice that may continue.

The Model Articles establish the quorum, that is, the number of directors who must be present before decisions may be taken or any other business conducted at a meeting of directors. The provisions are straightforward: the quorum may be fixed from time to time by a decision of the directors, must never be less than two, and, unless otherwise fixed, is two (Art 11 (private company), Art 10 (public company)). Both sets of Model Articles allow directors at meetings without a quorum to appoint further directors and call a general meeting to enable shareholders to appoint further directors (Art 11).

In the event of an equal number of votes on a particular resolution, the chairman or other director chairing the meeting will have a casting vote (Art 13 (private company), Art 14 (public company)). Again, this is a default/Model Article that has historically been amended.

9.3.2 Definition and classification of directors

director
any person occupying the position of a director by whatever name he is called

Most directors are appointed in accordance with the articles of the company, their details are recorded by the company in the register of directors (s 162) and their appointment is notified to the registrar of companies (s 167). There is no doubt as to the status of such individuals; they are directors for all legal purposes.

Occasionally, however, individuals behave, openly, like directors without the formalities of appointment having taken place (*de facto* directors). A different but related situation is where an individual does not patently behave as a director but gives directions and instructions that the other directors of the company follow (a shadow director). In both situations the question often arises of the extent of application of the law applicable to formally appointed directors (*de jure* directors). In particular, are *de facto* and/or shadow directors for the purposes of owing directors' duties to the company?

In its 1998 Consultation Paper on company directors (No 153), the Law Commission explained the approach to be taken to determining whether or not a particular statutory provision extends beyond *de jure* directors.

QUOTATION

'The meaning of "director" varies according to the context in which it is to be found, and it is a matter of construction whether a particular section covers a person who is a *de facto* director.'
Law Commission, Company Directors: Regulating Conflicts of Interest and Formulating a Statement of Duties No 153 (1998) at p.309

The courts must examine the statute and determine, as a matter of statutory interpretation, the intention of the legislature and the meaning and effect of the particular provision of the Act in question.

In the following paragraphs we examine different types of directors. The legal starting point is s 250(1) of the Companies Act 2006.

SECTION

de jure director
a person who has not only been properly appointed but who has satisfied the legal formalities that have to be observed by directors

'In the Companies Acts, "director" includes any person occupying the position of director, by whatever name called.'

De jure directors

Directors appointed in accordance with the articles of association and the appointment of whom is registered and filed in accordance with the requirements of the Companies Act 2006 are *de jure* directors.

de facto director

a person who has not been properly appointed but who has assumed the role of a director

De facto directors

Directors who have not been legally appointed, including where a purported appointment is irregular, but nevertheless openly assume the position of director, despite a lack of authority and right to act, are *de facto* directors. The key issue is not what the individual does but whether there is an assumption of responsibility by him or her to act as director. *De facto* directors are clearly capable of coming within the definition of director in s 250.

The concept of *de facto* director was has been recently considered by the Supreme Court in *Revenue and Customs Commissioners v Holland* [2010] UKSC 51 (SC). The case, the first instance decision in which is discussed in section 8.5.5 of Chapter 8, involved an alleged breach of trust by an allegedly *de facto* director. In that context, the majority of the court confirmed that a person is only a *de facto* director if he or she has assumed responsibility, that is, has 'opted in' to the role of director of a company. Lord Collins stated, 'For almost 150 years *de facto* directors in English law were persons who had been appointed as directors, but whose appointment was defective, or had come to an end, but who acted or continued to act as directors'. The decision of the first instance court was reversed on the grounds that the Mr Holland had not been a *de facto* director. It is not clear that this is the test that was applied in the subsequent Court of Appeal decision in *Re Mumtaz Properties* [2011] EWCA Civ 610 in which the court appears to have focussed on whether or not the individual was part of the corporate governance structure of the company.

shadow director

any person in accordance with whose directions or instructions the directors are accustomed to act, except where that person gives advice in a professional capacity (eg a solicitor or accountant)

Shadow directors

Shadow director is defined in s 251.

SECTION

'"Shadow director", in relation to a company, means a person in accordance with whose directions or instructions the directors of the company are accustomed to act.'

Note, however, the saving for professional advisers in s 251(2). If the directors of a company act on the advice of another individual given in a professional capacity, this will not be enough to render that individual a shadow director.

Shadow directors are not prohibited by law and no penalty attaches to occupying the status of shadow director. They are expressly referred to in a number of provisions of the Companies Act 2006, such as in s 170(5) which provides that the general duties of directors apply to shadow directors, 'where, and to the extent that, the corresponding common law rules or equitable principles so apply'. Where the Act does not expressly refer to shadow directors, the courts will need to ascertain the meaning and effect of the statutory provision to determine whether or not it extends to shadow directors.

Executive and non-executive directors

'Executive director' is not defined in core company law. It is a term used to refer to a director who usually has extensive powers delegated to him by reason of the role he performs in the company and who almost certainly has a service contract with the company. His service contract will be separate from his appointment as a director.

non-executive director (NED)

a director who is not an employee of the company and who has no executive responsibilities

Non-executive directors are essentially directors without service contracts who do not work day to day in the company. Most large companies have both types of directors on their boards. Both types have overall and equal responsibility for the leadership of the company. In the words of, speaking in the context of core company law:

QUOTATION

'Non-executive directors are subject to the same legal framework as their executive counterparts. Accordingly, their position can be somewhat invidious in many cases where they are expected to act without the executives' day to day decision-making power and detailed knowledge of the business. The duty of care owed by non-executive directors would also appear to be the same as that expected of executive directors. However the non-executive is likely to have to do less than an executive director to discharge his duty.'

Law Commission, Company Directors: Regulating Conflicts of Interest and Formulating a Statement of Duties, Consultation Paper No 153 (1998) at paragraph 17.23

The UK Corporate Governance Code (2010) (with which companies with shares with premium listings on the London Stock Exchange Main Market must comply or explain why they do not) ('the Code'), draws a distinction between executive directors and non-executive directors, or 'NEDs', and places important reliance on NEDs. The role of NEDs is set out in the supporting principles to the first main principle that all companies should be headed by an effective board.

QUOTATION

'A.4   Non-executive Directors
Main Principle
As part of their role as members of a unitary board, non-executive directors should constructively challenge and help develop proposals on strategy.
Supporting Principle
Non-executive directors should scrutinise the performance of management in meeting agreed goals and objectives and monitor the reporting of performance. They should satisfy themselves on the integrity of financial information and that financial controls and systems of risk management are robust and defensible. They are responsible for determining appropriate levels of remuneration of executive directors and have a prime role in appointing and, where necessary, removing executive directors, and in succession planning.
Code Provisions
A.4.1 The board should appoint one of the independent non-executive directors to be the senior independent director to provide a sounding board for the chairman and to serve as an intermediary for the other directors when necessary. The senior independent director should be available to shareholders if they have concerns which contact through the normal channels of chairman, chief executive or other executive directors has failed to resolve or for which such contact is inappropriate.
A.4.2 The chairman should hold meetings with the non-executive directors without the executives present. Led by the senior independent director, the non-executive directors should meet without the chairman present at least annually to appraise the chairman's performance and on such other occasions as are deemed appropriate.
A.4.3 Where directors have concerns which cannot be resolved about the running of the company or a proposed action, they should ensure that their concerns are recorded in the board minutes. On resignation, a nonexecutive director should provide a written statement to the chairman, for circulation to the board, if they have any such concerns.'

Financial Reporting Council, UK Code of Corporate Governance (June 2010)

The Code further distinguishes between NEDs and *independent* NEDs. The supporting principles of the effectiveness section of the Code provides that the board should include an appropriate combination of executive and non-executive directors (and, in particular, independent non-executive directors) such that no individual or small group of individuals can dominate the board's decision-taking.

QUOTATION

'**Code Provisions**
B.1.1 The board should identify in the annual report each non-executive director it considers to be independent. The board should determine whether the director is independent in character and judgement and whether there are relationships or circumstances which are likely to affect, or could appear to affect, the director's judgement. The board should state its reasons if it determines that a director is independent notwithstanding the existence of

relationships or circumstances which may appear relevant to its determination, including if the director:

- ▪ has been an employee of the company or group within the last five years;
- ▪ has, or has had within the last three years, a material business relationship with the company either directly, or as a partner, shareholder, director or senior employee of a body that has such a relationship with the company;
- ▪ has received or receives additional remuneration from the company apart from a director's fee, participates in the company's share option or a performance-related pay scheme, or is a member of the company's pension scheme;
- ▪ has close family ties with any of the company's advisers, directors or senior employees;
- ▪ holds cross-directorships or has significant links with other directors through involvement in other companies or bodies;
- ▪ represents a significant shareholder; or
- ▪ has served on the board for more than nine years from the date of their first election.'

Financial Reporting Council, UK Code of Corporate Governance (June 2010)

The Code also provides that at least 50 per cent of the boards of companies in the FTSE 350 or larger should be independent NEDs. Independence is a question of whether the director is independent in character and judgement based on whether there are relationships or circumstances which are likely to affect, or could appear to affect, the director's judgement.

Nominee directors

'Nominee director' is not a legal term but a term usually used to describe a director who, in practice, is expected to act in accordance with some understanding or arrangement which creates an obligation or mutual expectation of loyalty to someone other than the company as a whole. A nominee director must *not*, however, put the interests of this principal above those of the company (*Scottish Co-operative Wholesale Society v Meyer* [1959] AC 324).

Managing director

Table A made specific reference to appointing a member of the board to be a managing director. The Model Articles do not mention managing director. The term used to be legally important because of cases indicating the breadth of authority an individual given the title would be regarded by the courts as having. Today, a person historically called the managing director is more likely to be called the Chief Executive Officer, or CEO.

9.3.3 Appointing and removing directors

Appointing directors

The Companies Act 2006 is silent on how directors are to be appointed (except for providing that special notice must be given of any intention to appoint, *at the removal meeting*, a director in place of a director to be removed pursuant to s 168). The Act requires the names and details of each new director, with his signed consent to act as a director, to be notified to the registrar (s 167), who must keep a register, and the company must also maintain a register of directors (s 162).

Both registers are open to public inspection but changes introduced by the 2006 Act mean that even though a director's residential address must be disclosed to both the registrar and the company, it is protected from public inspection (ss 240–242). This is achieved by a director providing both his residential address and a service address (which may be his residential address but will often be the company's registered address) to the company and the registrar. The registers that the public can inspect contain only the service address. Before the 2006 Act a director could only protect his residential address if he could demonstrate that he was at serious risk of violence or intimidation.

Rules regarding appointment of directors are normally set out in the articles and both the Model Articles for Private Companies Limited by Shares (Art 17) and those for public companies (Art 20) provide for directors to be appointed either by ordinary resolution or by a decision of the directors. Where the number of appointed directors is less than a quorum to hold a directors' meeting, the Model Articles provide that the appointed director or directors may appoint sufficient number of directors to make up a quorum (Art 11 for both private and public companies). The Model Articles for Public Companies provide for a director appointed by the directors to retire at the next AGM, the practice being for him to be re-appointed by the shareholders, and for all directors to retire every three years, although they may be, and regularly are, re-appointed (Art 21).

If the articles do not expressly deal with appointment, the default articles will apply unless excluded (the relevant Table A for companies registered under pre-2006 statutes, the Model Articles for Private Companies Limited by Shares or Public Companies, as the case may be, for companies registered under the 2006 Act). Furthermore, the shareholders have inherent power to appoint directors by general resolution (*Link Agricultural Property Ltd v Shanahan* (1998) 28 ACSR 498). This would be important in the unusual circumstance of articles not dealing with appointment *and* exclusion of the default articles. Where articles deal with appointment but do not mention the rights of shareholders it is a question of construction of the particular language of the articles to determine whether or not this inherent power has been excluded.

Number of directors

A private company must have at least one director and a public company must have a minimum of two directors (s 154) but no statutory maximum number of directors is set for either private or public companies. There are no provisions governing the numbers of directors in the Model Articles for Private Companies Limited by Shares or those for public companies.

Who can be a director?

A director need not be an individual. A company, for example, may be a director of another company. The Act does, however, require every company to have at least one director who is a natural person (s 155). Consequently, if a company is a sole director company, that director must be an individual. The main categories of persons *not* permitted to act as a director are:

- A person who has not attained the age of 16 (s 157). Directors who were not yet 16 when this provision came into effect on 1 October 2008, ceased to be directors from that date.
- A bankrupt person (unless he secures permission of the court) (Company Directors Disqualification Act 1986 (CDDA) s 11).
- Persons subject to a disqualified order, or an undertaking in lieu thereof, under the Company Directors Disqualification Act 1986 (as amended) (CDDA).

The CDDA is considered in further detail in Chapter 13.

In addition to statutory disqualifications, the articles may extend the list of persons disqualified from being a director or may impose conditions on those who are directors. Historically, directors were typically required to own a specified number of shares in the company, but this is no longer a common requirement. In practice, directors of private companies are often major shareholders, if not the sole shareholder, and in large companies directors often own shares (and/or share options) acquired as part of their remuneration or incentive packages.

Removal of directors

Statutory provisions

Unlike appointment of directors, in relation to which it confines itself largely to disclosure obligations, the Companies Act 2006 contains a very important provision entitling shareholders to remove one, several or all directors (s 168(1)).

SECTION

'A company may by ordinary resolution at a meeting remove a director before the expiration of his period of office, notwithstanding anything in any agreement between it and him.'

A meeting is required for the statutory power of removal to be exercised and this is the case even for private companies: the written resolution procedure cannot be used to remove a director pursuant to s 168. Section 168(2) states that special notice must be given of a resolution to remove a director. This means that the company must receive notice that the removal resolution is to be moved, from the shareholder proposing the resolution, at least 28 days before the meeting to consider it is held.

On receipt of notice of an intended resolution to remove a director, the company must send a copy to the director concerned. The director may require the company to circulate written representations to the shareholders and is also entitled to address the meeting at which the resolution is to be considered, s 169.

The shares held by a director may carry additional voting rights when his removal is being sought. It may therefore be possible for the director to use such additional voting rights to defeat the wishes of controlling shareholders (*Bushell v Faith* [1970] AC 1099). There is no provision for weighted voting rights in the Model Articles and they are prohibited for listed companies by the Listing Rules made pursuant to the Financial Services and Markets Act 2000.

The final point to note is that s 168(5) states that removal under s 168(1) does not prejudice any right the director may have to compensation for early termination of a service contract.

Articles

The articles of a company usually state grounds for automatic retirement of directors and Art 18 of the Model Articles for Private Companies Limited by Shares and Art 22 of those for public companies do just that, essentially providing for a director to cease to hold office if he:

- ceases to be a director by virtue of any provision of the Companies Act 2006 or is prohibited from being a director by law
- is bankrupted or makes a composition with his creditors
- is physically or mentally incapable of acting as a director
- has notified the company that he is resigning or retiring from office.

As already mentioned, Art 21 of the Model Articles for Public Companies further provides for:

- a director appointed by the directors to retire at the next AGM, the practice being for him to be re-appointed by the shareholders at that AGM, and
- all directors to retire every three years, known as 'retirement by rotation', although directors may be, and regularly are, re-appointed.

A stricter regime governing the periods of office of directors of companies with Premium Listings is set out in the UK Corporate Governance Code.

QUOTATION

'B.7   Re-election
Main Principle
All directors should be submitted for re-election at regular intervals, subject to continued satisfactory performance.
Code Provisions
B.7.1 All directors of FTSE 350 companies should be subject to annual election by shareholders. All other directors should be subject to election by shareholders at the first annual general meeting after their appointment, and to re-election thereafter at intervals of no more than

three years. Nonexecutive directors who have served longer than nine years should be subject to annual re-election. The names of directors submitted for election or re-election should be accompanied by sufficient biographical details and any other relevant information to enable shareholders to take an informed decision on their election.'

Financial Reporting Council, UK Corporate Governance Code (June 2010)

9.3.4 Remuneration of directors

Directors as directors, employees and independent contractors

It is important to realise that a director who works for a company *beyond* attending and preparing for meetings of the board of directors and committees of the board will have two relationships with the company. He will be:

1 a director, which is an 'office', governed by trust principles as developed in the corporate environment; and

2 either:

- an employee, which is a contractual relationship supplemented by employment law as developed in the corporate environment; or
- an independent contractor (if the non-board related services are part-time or occasional and do not render him an employee), which is also a contractual relationship.

Directors are *not* employees of the company simply because they have been appointed as a director. Family owned companies often appoint the spouse and/or grown-up children, or other relatives of the person who runs the business, to be directors and those individuals do not play any role in the company apart from being a director (a role to which they often-times pay little attention). Clearly, they are not employees of the company. Non-executive directors of large companies are also not employees of the company. They are paid directors' fees and are reimbursed their expenses incurred in the performance of the role of director.

On the other hand, a person who works full-time running the family owned company, or an executive director of a large company, is an employee of the company. A large company will negotiate and enter into a service contract with each of its executives, executive directors included. Due to the potential for self-interested action by board members, director service contracts and remuneration are subject to laws and regulations designed to inhibit excess. Small companies often do not formalise employee relationships with its directors by the company and the director/employees signing written service contracts.

A legal grey area exists where directors perform occasional or part-time services for a company beyond those strictly required of a director. The terms on which the services are rendered should be agreed and clearly documented and this is likely to establish the director as an independent contractor with the company, rather than an employee. If the services are such as to bring the director within the definition of employee, however, he will be an employee. If terms have not been clearly agreed, to be entitled to payment for services the director will need to establish that the services performed were not merely performance of the role of director.

Payment for performing the role of director

Directors are not entitled to be paid for their services to the company as directors because the office of director was historically aligned in law with that of a trustee who is not entitled to payment. If either the articles permit payment *or* the shareholders approve payment, the company can pay its directors and the sums paid are sometime called directors' fees but are also called remuneration. It is standard practice for articles to authorise the payment of directors' fees, and the Model Articles for Private Companies Limited by Shares (Art 19(2)) and those for public companies (Art 23) provide that directors are entitled to such remuneration as the directors determine for their services to the company as directors.

Payment on termination of office

Payments for loss of office as a director (as defined in ss 215 and 216) must not be made unless the payment does not exceed £200 (s 221), or it has been approved by ordinary resolution of the shareholders (s 217). Note that this requirement does *not* apply to payments made pursuant to a legal obligation or by way of damages for breach of a legal obligation or settlement of any claim related to a legal obligation (s 220). Payment in lieu of notice under a service contract and other payments provided for under a service contract are outside the s 217 prohibition.

Payment for non-director services provided as an independent contractor

The trustee-like nature of the role of director also precludes the company from paying remuneration for services beyond services as a director unless payment is authorised by the articles or the shareholders. Again, the Model Articles for Private Companies Limited by Shares (Art 19) and those for public companies (Art 23) provide that in addition to payment for services as a director, directors are entitled to such remuneration as the directors determine for 'any other service which they undertake for the company'.

Where a director has performed additional services but the procedure by which the articles require payment to be determined has not been gone through (under the Model Articles that is determination by the directors), the House of Lords decision in *Guinness plc v Saunders* [1990] 2 AC 663 (HL), appears to preclude a successful *quantum meruit* claim by a director.

CASE EXAMPLE

Guinness plc v Saunders [1990] 2 AC 663 (HL)

The articles of Guinness plc provided that remuneration for work outside the scope of the ordinary duties of a director had to be fixed by the board of directors as a whole.

Mr Ward was a director who performed work outside the normal scope and was given special remuneration of £5.2 million by a committee of the board. The committee had no authority to make the payment which Mr Ward was ordered to repay to the company. Mr Ward argued that a *quantum meruit* sum was owed to him. Held: Where parties to a contract have agreed how remuneration is to be determined the court will not award a *quantum meruit* even if the agreement has not been implemented. The court considered the relevant articles as terms embodied in a contract between Mr Ward and the company (a contract separate from the s 33 contract).

The general principle that a person who has performed services requested and freely accepted by another is entitled to a *quantum meruit* payment has no application where the amount of the payment has been contractually agreed, nor where a mechanism for the determination of the payment amount has been specified in a contract. As a director is not entitled to payment unless the articles authorise payment, the only time a director is able to contemplate a *quantum meruit* claim is if the articles authorise payment. Whilst a provision in the articles simply stating that a director is entitled to be paid for additional service would leave open a *quantum meruit* claim, the moment the power to determine the remuneration is allocated to the directors (as in the Model Articles), or any other procedure for determination of the amount is stipulated in the articles, no *quantum meruit* claim would succeed if the mechanism for determination of payment had not been adhered to.

Where the Model Articles apply, the director whose remuneration is being determined must not participate as a director in the board of directors' decision nor will he count towards quorum because he has a conflict of interest (Art 14 (private companies) and Art 16 (public companies)).

Service contracts

Model Articles 19 (for private companies) and 23 (for public companies) also apply to permit the directors to determine remuneration payable pursuant to directors' service contracts (also known as contracts of employment). Again, individual directors are normally precluded by the articles from voting to approve their own service contracts because they have a conflict of interest (see Model Arts 14 (for private companies) and 16 (for public companies)).

Companies Act protections in relation to service contracts and remuneration

Due to the potential for mutual self-interested action by directors, who could otherwise award each other long-term service contracts and excessively generous compensation packages and other remuneration, statutory protections have been enacted in relation to directors' service contracts and remuneration generally to protect shareholders and creditors.

Shareholder approval of long-term director service contracts

Section 188 requires shareholder approval in advance of directors' service contracts (as defined in s 227, see below) of longer than two years. A copy of the entire proposed contract must be available for inspection by shareholders or, in the case of a written resolution, sent to shareholders before the shareholders' resolution is passed (s 188(5)). Technically, it is only the provision of the contract relating to its length that must be approved (s 188(2)), and the consequences of failure to secure shareholder approval are that:

- the provision is void to the extent of the contravention so that the contract can run for a maximum of two years; and
- the contract is deemed to contain a term entitling the company to terminate the contract at any time by giving reasonable notice.

Shareholder inspection of director service contracts

Companies are required to keep copies of directors' service contracts, make them available for inspection by shareholders without charge, and provide copies to shareholders on request. Failure to do so is a criminal offence by every director, officer or manager in default (ss 228–229). As an anti-avoidance provision, service contract is defined to include the terms of appointment of a person as a director and a contract for the performance of the ordinary duties of a director (s 227(2)).

Public disclosure of director remuneration

The law requiring public disclosure of directors' remuneration becomes more demanding as one moves along the spectrum from small companies, through other unquoted companies and quoted companies, to companies with listed securities.

Small companies

The small companies regime effectively removes small companies from any requirement to disclose director remuneration to the public. Information in the notes to the accounts can be deleted from the accounts filed with the registrar of companies (see the Small Companies and Groups (Accounts and Directors' Report) Regulations 2008 (SI 2008/409)).

Unquoted companies

The notes to the annual accounts of unquoted companies must state the total remuneration paid to all directors as a single figure, the amount paid to the highest paid director and the total sum paid as compensation for loss of office (s 412 and the Large and Medium-sized Companies and Groups (Accounts and Reports) Regulations 2008 (SI 2008/410), reg 8 and Sched 5). This information is filed with the registrar of companies as part of the accounts.

Quoted companies

As with unquoted companies, the notes to the annual accounts of quoted companies must state the total remuneration paid to all directors as a single figure. Further detailed disclosure relevant to directors' remuneration is mandated in an annual directors' remuneration report the directors of a quoted company are required to prepare (ss 420–422 and the Large and Medium-sized Companies and Groups (Accounts and Reports) Regulations 2008 (SI 2008/410), reg 11 and Sched 8). The company's auditors must audit the auditable part of the remuneration report and state in their audit report whether or not that part has been properly prepared in accordance with the 2006 Act (s 497).

Section 439 requires quoted companies to put a resolution approving the remuneration report to the meeting of shareholders at which its annual accounts are presented. Currently, the resolution is advisory only in that s 439(5) states that no entitlement to remuneration is made conditional upon the resolution being passed, but see reforms below.

Securities regulation additional protections

Quoted companies with equity shares listed in the UK (essentially, companies with shares traded on the London Stock Exchange Main Market, *not* companies with shares traded on AIM), are generally subject to additional corporate governance and disclosure rules and these rules include disclosure relating to directors and their remuneration. The Disclosure and Transparency Rules (DTRs), which apply to companies traded on the Main Market, whether they have premium or standard listings, requires companies to make a corporate governance statement in its directors' report (DTR 7.2). This report will includes information about how director remuneration is managed.

In contrast, the continuing disclosure obligations in the Listing Rules apply only to companies with Premium Listings (see Listing Rule 9.1). These are the most detailed and stringent rules (see Listing Rules 9.8.6–9.8 9, the information required by which must be audited (Listing Rules 9.8.10–12)). It is here that we find the obligation for a company to comply or explain why, and the extent to which it has not complied, with the UK Corporate Governance Code, section D of which is focused on remuneration. The Code provides that companies should have a remuneration committee of independent non-executive directors to which the board should delegate responsibility for setting executive director remuneration and the remuneration of the chairman of the board. The committee should also monitor and recommend the level and structure of remuneration for senior management. It is worth taking a look at the Code in this regard, which can be found on the FRC website.

Reform

Reform of the law relating to director remuneration is imminent. The Enterprise and Regulatory Reform Bill 2012, (in its committee stage in the House of Lords at the time of going to press), contains amendments to the Companies Act 2006 relevant to quoted companies (as defined in s. 385). The reforms will add two new sections to the 2006 Act: s. 439A, containing detailed rules providing for the members of quoted companies to approve the company's directors' remuneration policy, and ss. 226A–226F, stating that a quoted company may not make a remuneration payment or a payment for loss of office to a director (past, present or future) unless the payment is consistent with the approved directors' remuneration policy, or is approved by resolution of the members. Any payment in contravention will have "no effect", will be held by the recipient on trust, and any director who authorised the payment will be jointly and severally liable to indemnify the company. Related amendments to the contents of directors' remuneration reports and information to appear on the company's website are also included in the Bill. Regulations will contain detailed requirements as to the information about remuneration to be disclosed.

9.4 Company secretary and officers

9.4.1 Company secretary

A private company is not required to have a company secretary (s 270). A public company, however, must have a company secretary (s 271). The directors of a public company are required to take reasonable steps to ensure that the secretary is a person who appears to them to have (s 273):

company secretary
the chief administrative officer of the company which all public companies must have and of whose qualifications, knowledge and experience to discharge the role, the directors of a public company must take reasonable steps to satisfy themselves

- the requisite knowledge and experience to discharge the functions of company secretary; and
- one or more of the qualifications listed in the Act.

Barristers, solicitors, accountants and members of the Institute of Chartered Secretaries and Administrators (ICSA) meet the second qualification requirement (but the directors must also take reasonable steps to ensure that they have the requisite knowledge and skill to meet the first requirement).

The functions of the company secretary are not defined in the Act. They are administrative rather than of a business nature (*Re Maidstone Buildings Provisions Ltd* [1971] 1 WLR 1085).

JUDGMENT

'[A] secretary … is not concerned in the management [of] the company. Equally, I think he is not concerned in carrying on the business of the company … a person who holds the office of secretary may in some other capacity be concerned in the management of the company's business.'

9.4.2 Officers

The term officer is frequently used in the Companies Act 2006. Where it is used in a provision imposing criminal liability, officer is defined, by s 1121(2), to mean any director, manager or secretary of the company as well as any person treated as an officer for the purposes of the particular offence.

KEY FACTS

Board of directors	
Board powers and decision-making	
Management and all powers of the company vested in board of directors	Model Art 3
Board may delegate any of its powers	Model Art 5
Board is empowered to act collectively	*Re Marseilles Extension Railway Company, ex parte Credit Foncier and Mobilier of England* (1871)
Decision-making and board meetings are governed by articles	Model Arts 7 and 10 (private company) Model Arts 7 and 9 (public company)
Definition and classification of directors, s 250(1)	
*De jure/de facto/*shadow/executive/non-executive/nominee/managing directors	
Appointing and removing directors	
Appointment is governed by the articles	Model Art 17 (private company) Model Art 20 (public company)
Notification of appointment to registrar	s 167
Register of directors	s 162
Statutory right to remove by ordinary resolution at a meeting supplements article provisions	s 168
Public company articles provide for retirement by rotation	Model Art 21 (public companies)

Board of directors	
Remuneration of directors	
Payment must be permitted by articles or approved by shareholders: for holding office of a director as an independent contractor as an employee	Model Art 19(2) (private company) Model Art 23 (public company)
Quantum meruit unlikely to be payable	*Guinness v Saunders* (1990)
Tiered public disclosure of remuneration for all but small companies	
Shareholder approval required for more than 2-year service term	s 188
Shareholders may inspect service contracts	ss 228–229
Disclosure obligations are becoming more detailed over time for listed companies	DTR 7.2; LR 9.8; UK Corporate Governance Code, Section D

SAMPLE ESSAY QUESTION

Discuss the extent to which you agree or disagree with the statement that the shareholders are the 'residual controllers' of the company.

Unpack the question

This is the first essential step which you must take time to do properly. You should separate out:

- Consideration of the meaning of "shareholders" and the need to distinguish shareholders in their individual capacity
- Identification of alternative/day to day controllers of the company – the board of directors
- Review of the decisions and powers vested in shareholders
- Reflection on the implications of this for the balance of powers
- Assessment of the extent the control vested in shareholders constitutes "residual control".

Define "shareholders" and identify the board as the second decision making organ

- Identify the shareholders and the board of directors as the two decision-making organs of a company
- Consider the phrase "shareholders in general meeting", identify majority rule and the need for a super-majority for some decisions
- Explain that the powers of the company are vested in the board of directors, collectively: Model Article 3
- Explain that the general power to manage is subject to the articles and the law requiring specific decisions to be taken by the shareholders.

Review of the control vested in shareholders

- Emphasize the importance of the right to remove directors from office: s 168
- Identify a range of other fundamental decisions to be made by the shareholders: see list at 10.2.3
- Identify the right of the shareholders to direct the board by special resolution on any specified matter: Model Article 4
- Explain that power will revert to the shareholders if the board is unable to act: *Barron v Potter*.

Reflect on the implications of the balance of power

Consider to what extent shareholders *must be involved* in decision making, otherwise the company cannot act, and how far the behaviour of the board takes place in the shadow of shareholder power to remove members of the board.

CONCLUDE

Express your reasoned opinion as to whether or not you believe it correct to regard shareholders as the *residual* controllers of companies.

SUMMARY

Division of power between the board of directors and the general meeting

- Shareholders are the residual controllers of the company as the result of the articles of association; statute law (the Companies Act 2006 and the Insolvency Act 1986) and cases recognising their power in certain circumstances.
- The board of directors is responsible for the management of the company's business, for which purpose they may exercise all the powers of the company (Model Article 3).
- Shareholders may direct the board on particular issues by special resolution (Model Article 4).
- Management power will revert to the shareholders in circumstances where the board is unable to act.

Shareholders

- Shareholders make decisions by resolutions at general meetings (s 284), private companies can make decisions by written resolution (s 288) and informal unanimous decision-making is sometimes possible *Re Duomatic Ltd* (1969).
- Ordinary resolutions require a simple majority of votes (50 per cent plus one), special resolutions require 75 per cent.

Directors

- Directors take decisions by majority at board meetings or unanimously outside board meetings.
- A private company must have at least one director and a public company two directors.
- Types of directors include *de jure* directors, *de facto* directors, shadow director, executive and non-executive directors (NED)(some of whom are independent and some are not) and nominee directors.
- Rules regarding appointment and the quorum of directors are normally set out in the articles.
- A director may be removed by ordinary resolution at a meeting (s 168(1)).
- The Company Directors Disqualification Act 1986 empowers the Secretary of State to apply to the court for an order disqualifying a director from being concerned or taking part in the promotion, formation or management of a company.
- A director who performs additional work will be either an employee or an independent contractor and remuneration for each must be considered separately from fees for being a director.
- The Act regulates payments on termination of office (s 217) and the length of service contracts (s 188) so that the right to remove directors is not priced out of existence.
- The rules on disclosure of board remuneration have been tightened over the years and are increasingly onerous depending upon whether the company is a small, unquoted, quoted or has a Premium Listing on the London Stock Exchange Main Market.

Company secretary

- Public companies must have a company secretary, private companies need not.
- Directors of a public company are required to take reasonable steps to ensure that the secretary is a person who appears to them to have the requisite knowledge and experience to discharge the functions of company secretary, and one or more of the qualifications listed in the Companies Act 2006.
- The precise role and responsibilities of a secretary will vary from company to company but is administrative.

Officers

Officers of the company are defined in s 1121(2) for the purposes of the Act imposing criminal liability, typically on 'any officer in default'.

ACTIVITY

Self-test questions

1. Name the two key organs of governance of a company.
2. Is it appropriate to call the shareholders of a private company the 'shareholders in general meeting'?
3. Identify 15 key powers of a company reserved to the shareholders.
4. When will management revert to the shareholders?
5. Describe the voting rights on a resolution taken by a show of hands, poll and written resolution.
6. What proportion of votes is required to pass a written resolution?
7. May the board of directors take majority decisions outside a board meeting?
8. Who can appoint directors?
9. Who can remove directors and how?
10. What is a nominee director?
11. How does an executive director differ from a non-executive director?
12. When is a director entitled to a *quantum meruit* payment for services performed for the company?

Further reading

Useful websites

The Financial Services Authority webpage for access to the FSA Handbook:
http://www.fsa.gov.uk/handbook
The Financial Reporting Council website for access to the UK Corporate Governance Code
and the Stewardship Code:
http://www.frc.org.uk/

Articles

De Lacey, J, 'The Concept of a Company Director: Time for a New Expanded and Unified
Statutory Concept' [2006] JBL 267.
Noonan, C and Watson, S, 'Examining company directors through the lens of *de facto* direc-
torship' (2008) 7 JBL 587.

Reports

Law Commission, Company Directors: Regulating Conflicts of Interest and Formulating a
Statement of Duties No 153, 1998.

Books

Mayson, French & Ryan on Company Law 2012–2013 (29th edn, Oxford University Press, 2012).
Walters, A and Davis-White, M, *Directors' Disqualification and Bankruptcy Restrictions* (3rd
edn, Sweet & Maxwell, 2009).

10

Legally binding the company

AIMS AND OBJECTIVES

After reading this chapter you should understand:

- How companies execute and become bound by deeds
- When a company will be bound by an apparently properly executed deed or other formal document which in fact has been improperly executed
- The role and use of company seals
- The authority of the board of directors to bind the company
- The effect of s 40 of the Companies Act 2006
- The broad and narrow interpretations of the scope of s 40
- How to ascertain whether an individual has authority to bind the company
- When actual authority (express and implied) will be found to exist in the corporate context
- When ostensible or apparent authority will be found to exist in the corporate context
- The differences between implied actual authority and ostensible authority

10.1 Introduction

The legal position of a company can be changed by deed or as a result of less formal documents and/or behaviour. The most frequently changed rights and liabilities are its contractual rights and liabilities and the main focus of this chapter is how a company acquires or becomes subject to contractual rights and liabilities (section 10.4). Contractual rights and liabilities can arise from contracts by way of deed but most arise as a result of simple contracts.

The key issue in relation to simple contracts and covered in detail in this chapter, is whether or not an individual purporting to act on behalf of the company has authority to change the legal position of the company in the way in which he has purported to change it. The requirement of 'authority' of the individual is not, however, confined to simple contracts. The recent case of *Lovett v Carson Country Homes Ltd* [2009] EWHC 1143 (Ch), considered at 10.2.3 below, is a reminder of the relevance of authority in relation to deeds.

This chapter begins with an examination of how a company becomes bound by a deed (section 10.2). Historically, seals were required to bind a company to a deed. Although this is no longer the case, seals are still in use today by some companies and it is appropriate, therefore, to examine the relevance and role of company seals today (section 10.3) before turning to focus on contracts (section 10.4) and the authority of the board of directors and individuals (whether directors or not), to bind the company to a contract.

10.2 Deeds that bind the company

10.2.1 Use of deeds

deed

a formal document conforming with the requirements of a deed set out in the Law of Property (Miscellaneous Provisions) Act 1989 and, in the case of a registered company, executed as a deed in accordance with the Companies Act 2006, s 44

Deeds are used in a wider range of situations than entry into contracts. You will recall from your property and contract studies that deeds are formal documents, sometimes called instruments, affecting the legal rights and obligations of one or more legal persons. A deed may convey (effect the legal transfer of) property from one person to another. This type of deed is usually executed, or 'made', as a deed by the transferor (the person transferring the property) only. A deed may also contain the terms of an agreement entered into between two or more legal persons, in which case it is called a formal contract and is executed as a deed by all parties to the contract.

10.2.2 Requirements for a company to be bound by a deed

A company can be a party to a deed. The requirements for a company to be bound by a deed, as a deed, are set out in a combination of the Law of Property (Miscellaneous Provisions) Act 1989 (c. 34) (referenced as the LP(MP)A 1989) and the Companies Act 2006. It is important to start with the LP(MP)A 1989, s 1(2) of which states:

SECTION

'(2) An instrument shall not be a deed unless—
   (a) it makes it clear on its face that it is intended to be a deed by the person making it or, as the case may be, by the parties to it (whether by describing itself as a deed or expressing itself to be executed or signed as a deed or otherwise); and
   (b) it is validly executed as a deed by that person or, as the case may be, one or more of those parties.'

Section 1 of the LP(MP)A 1989 goes on to set out how an individual complies with s 1(2)(b), that is, how a natural person validly executes a document as a deed. The rules for how a company validly executes a deed to comply with s 1(2)(b) are found in ss 44 and 46 of the Companies Act 2006. Even if ss 44 and 46 are complied with, the document must also comply with LP(MP)A 1989, s 1(2)(a): it must be clear on its face that it is intended to be a deed.

Section 44 deals with execution of *any document* by a company and s 46 focuses on execution of a document *as a deed*. Section 44 provides that a document is executed by a company if either:

1 the company's common seal is affixed to it; or
2 it is expressed to be executed by the company and is signed by:
   ● two authorised signatories (two directors or one director and the company secretary); or
   ● a director in the presence of a witness who attests to his signature.

Section 46 then adds that for a document to be validly executed as a deed for the purposes of LP(MP)A 1989, s 1(2)(b), the validly executed document must be 'delivered as a deed'.

To deliver a deed is to evince an intention to be bound (*Xenos v Wickham* (1867) LR 2 HL 296). The act of executing a document indicates just such an intention unless the facts indicate otherwise. This is now captured in s 46(2) which states that a document is presumed to be delivered upon its being executed, unless a contrary intention is proved.

Accordingly, although it is common in practice to state on the document the words 'delivered as a deed', these words are not strictly necessary. No reference to delivery needs to be made.

The presumption is that the deed is delivered *upon it being executed*. This is very often not the intention, the intention being for the deed to take effect on an agreed date that is not to be dictated by the availability of those required to execute it. It is common therefore to expressly address delivery on the face of the deed in order to pinpoint the date upon which the deed is to become effective. Typical language used in a contract by way of deed would be, 'This deed is delivered on the date written at the start of this agreement'.

10.2.3 Looking behind a deed

A deed which appears on its face to have been validly executed by a company may not have been validly executed. To protect third parties dealing with companies in good faith, the Companies Act 1989 introduced a provision that if a document *purports* to be signed in accordance with s 44(2) (see above), it is deemed to have been duly executed (s 44(5)). The subsection operates only in favour of a purchaser in good faith for valuable consideration. Consequently, a volunteer cannot use s 44(5) to argue that a document has been properly executed. Although the company also cannot rely on s 44(5), in a case in which a company seeks to rely on a defectively executed deed, ratification will often be possible.

The relationship of s 44(5) with the law on forged documents was considered by the Law Commission in its Consultation Paper entitled 'The Execution of Deeds and Documents by or on behalf of Bodies Corporate' (1996 No 143) and its subsequent Report of the same title (1998 No 253). Even though a majority of the consultees who commented were in favour of clarification, the Law Commission concluded, 'We do not consider that there should be any legislative amendments to clarify the relationship between the presumptions of due execution and the rules governing forged documents'. This recommendation has been described by the court in *Lovett v Carson Country Homes Ltd* [2009] EWHC 1143 (Ch) as, in hindsight, unfortunate.

In *Lovett*, the court considered the argument, based on *Ruben v Great Fingall Consolidated* [1906] AC 439 (HL), that a document with a forged signature is not even a 'document' and therefore a third party seeking to rely on a forged deed cannot rely on s 44(5) to validate it, for the simple reason that there is no document to validate. Justice Davis rejected the general proposition that a forgery can never be validated:

JUDGMENT

'89 ... [I]t seems to be the case that by and large *Ruben* has, nevertheless, been represented as setting out the general position that a forgery is a nullity which cannot be validated, albeit there may be circumstances in which a party may be estopped from disputing the validity of a forged document; see *Halsbury's Laws of England*, 4th edn (London: LexisNexis), Vol.13, para.72. ...

90 No doubt a forged corporate document is a nullity in the sense that no one has actual authority on the part of a company to issue a forged document. But as the exception of estoppel shows, that does not mean that the forged document can in no circumstances have any effect whatsoever: just because circumstances can arise whereby the company may be estopped from disputing its validity. But once one accepts that, then, in my opinion, that immediately opens up the prospect that such a document cannot be sidelined as a nullity for all purposes in the case of apparent authority. Indeed, the principles of apparent authority are a broad reflection of the general principles of estoppel. That that may be so is borne out by *Ruben* itself in my view: for, admittedly in somewhat grudging terms, *Shaw v Port Philip & Colonial Gold Mining Co Ltd* (1883–84) LR 13 QBD 103 (QBD) was not formally disapproved as a decision but instead was distinguished as being capable on its facts as connoting that the secretary was held out as having authority to warrant the genuineness of a certificate.'

The court in *Lovett* did not decide that any forged document that appears on its face to have been validly executed is capable of validation by s 44(5). Where there is no estoppel by subsequent acquiescence of the company (on which form of estoppel, see *Morris v CW Martin & Sons Ltd* [1966] 1 QB 716), and no ostensible authority (ie the person who presents the document to the third party has no ostensible authority either to warrant the genuineness of the document or to communicate the company's representation of the genuineness of the document), it remains unclear whether, and if so, in which circumstances, s 44(5) may be successfully argued to validate a forgery.

10.3 Company seals

common seal

a device used for making an impressed mark (the seal of the company) on a document to authenticate it

Company seals, or 'common seals', are anachronisms. They are literally metal presses that emboss the name and (in most cases) also the number of a registered company into the document to which they are affixed, usually where a red circle or 'wafer' has been stuck onto the document. No company is required to have a seal (s 45) and even if a company has a seal it is not necessary to use it unless the articles of the company require its use in particular circumstances. Deeds and other documents can be validly executed without a seal and share certificates can be issued without being sealed (to mention the prime examples of documents that have historically been sealed).

The Model Articles (Arts 49 (for private companies) and 81 (for public companies)) do not assume a company has a seal. They simply provide that any seal that a company has may only be used by authority of the directors. Once the seal has been affixed to a document, the model articles state that, unless the directors direct otherwise, a document must be signed by at least one authorised person in the presence of a witness who attests the signature. An authorised person for this purpose is a director, the company secretary or any person authorised by the directors for the purpose of signing documents to which the common seal is applied.

10.4 Contracts that bind the company

Reflecting back on your contract law studies you will recall that contracts can be classified into:

- formal agreements (deeds); and
- simple contracts (parol agreements).

A company can be a party to either type of agreement. The difficulty a company has, like other artificial legal persons, is *how* it can enter into such contracts.

10.4.1 Formal agreements (deeds)

If the terms of a contract are set out in a document that makes it clear on its face that it is intended to be a deed and which is executed and delivered as a deed by the company in accordance with the rules set out earlier in this chapter, the company will be legally bound by that formal contract. The benefits of entering into a contract by way of deed are that, unlike in relation to simple contracts, it can be enforced without evidence of consideration and the limitation period for actions brought under it is 12 years, not six as it is for simple contracts (Limitation Act 1980, s 5).

10.4.2 Simple contracts

Simple contracts range from oral agreements not committed to paper to detailed agreements between the parties captured in lengthy documents. Even if it is evidenced by a very formal-looking document, a contract remains a simple contract for legal purposes unless the document satisfies the rules regarding deeds.

The statutory provisions governing companies entering into simple contracts discussed in this chapter apply in addition to, and must be read subject to, any legal formalities required in the case of a similar contract made by an individual (s 43(2)). A contract for the sale of land, for example, must be in writing signed by or on behalf of each of the parties to the contract (Law of Property (Miscellaneous Provisions) Act 1989, s 2). Whether the parties are individuals, companies or a mixture of the two, an agreement for the sale of land will not be valid unless it complies with this formality. The Companies Act 2006 deals with the issues arising as a result of the company being an artificial rather than a natural person.

Contracts made by a company and contracts made on behalf of a company

A distinction is drawn in the Act between contracts that are made *by* a company by writing (s 43(1)(a)) and contracts that are made *on behalf of* the company by a person acting under the company's authority, express or implied (s 43(1)(b)). To the extent that this section suggests that the contracts made *by* the company, as described in s 43(1)(a), do not involve individuals acting on behalf of the company in applying the seal or signing the document, it is misleading. Also, the omission of any reference to ostensible authority in s 43(1)(b) makes the section incomplete in terms of describing how a company may become bound by a contract.

Contracts made *by* a company

Sections 43(1)(a) and 44(4) together provide that a contract may be 'made by a company' by:

1 writing under its common seal, or
2 writing expressed to be executed by the company and signed by
   - two authorised persons or
   - a director in the presence of a witness who attests his signature.

Basically, if a contract is set out in writing and that document is either sealed or executed in accordance with s 44, the company will be bound by the contract. Contracts 'made by a company' for the purposes of s 43 may be deeds but if the document does not make it clear on its face that it is intended to be a deed, it can still be a contract 'made by the company'.

Good reason to separate out subsections s 43(1)(a) from (b) would exist if s 43(1)(a) were to establish an absolute rule such that, provided the conditions for a contract being 'made by the company' appeared on the face of the document to have been complied with, there would be no room to argue an absence of authority on the part of the individual attaching the seal, the individual signing adjacent to the seal as required by the articles (of most companies), or the authorised signatories signing the document. It is not at all clear that the section achieves this level of clarity. How far it is permitted to look behind the face of a document is not wholly clear. As we have seen when we examined looking behind a deed, above, in the circumstances most likely to arise, s 44(5), which applies not only to deeds but also to executed documents that are not deeds, bans such examination.

Example

The seal of Company A Limited is affixed to a written contract between Company A Limited and B which is also signed by a director of Company A Limited whose signature is attested by a witness, as required by Company A Limited's articles for use of the company seal. Is Company A Limited bound by the terms of the agreement?

The basic rule is that the agreement can be enforced against the company by a third party, B in this example (s 43(1)(a)).

Example

A written contract is expressed to be between Company A Limited and Company B Limited. At the end of the document it states, 'signed on behalf of Company A Limited by'. A director and the company secretary have signed the agreement in the space that follows. Is Company A Limited bound by the terms of the agreement?

The basic rule is that the agreement can be enforced against the company by a third party (ss 43(1)(a) and 44(4)).

Contracts made *on behalf of* companies

Companies can only perform acts through individuals and those individuals act *on behalf of the* company. Whether or not a contract has been made *on behalf of* a company usually involves consideration of agency law, as applied by the courts in the context of companies, and the Companies Act 2006.

The principal legal question arising in relation to whether or not a contract has been 'made on behalf of a company' is: did the individual or the organ of governance of the company (usually the board of directors) that purported to agree the terms on behalf of the company have legal authority to do so? A company will only be bound by a contract if, at the time the contract was allegedly entered into, the board of directors or the individual, on whose acts the third party is relying to allege that a contract has been entered into, was acting within the scope of its or his authority as an agent of the company.

The individual, or agent, may be a director of the company but this is not necessary. A non-director employee may be an agent of the company and an independent contractor may be appointed by the company to act as its agent for one or more particular purposes. The starting point for analysis of the existence of authority to bind the company is the authority of the board of directors.

KEY FACTS

Legally binding the company	
Deeds that bind the company	
Requirements for a company to be bound by a deed: 1) clear on face intended to be a deed, and 2) validly executed as a deed.	Law of Property (Miscellaneous Provisions) Act 1989, s 1(2)

Valid execution as a deed:
 1) a) common seal affixed; or
   b) expressed to be executed by the company and signed by
     i) two authorised signatories; or
     ii) a director in the presence of a witness who attests signature; and
	Companies Act 2006, s 44

2) delivered as a deed	Companies Act 2006, s 46
Looking behind a deed: If deed purports to be validly executed, it is deemed validly executed in relation to a purchaser in good faith for valuable consideration.	s 44(5)
If not forged but signatories lacked authority, may or may not be bound.	
Company seals	
No obligation to have a company seal	s 45
No obligation to use a company seal unless use is mandated by the articles.	No mandated use in the model articles
Contracts that bind the company	
Formal agreements (deeds) and simple contracts Purpose served by separating out of contracts made 'by a company' and 'on behalf of a company' in s 43 is unclear.	

10.5 Authority of the board of directors to bind the company

When we looked at the board of directors in Chapter 9 we saw that the articles of a company invariably state that the board is responsible for the management of the company and is empowered to exercise all the powers of the company for this purpose (Model Articles, Art 3). It is by the exercise of powers of the company that the legal rights and liabilities of the company are changed. If there are no other provisions in the articles relevant to the exercise of powers of the company, the board of directors has authority to bind the company to any contracts. Remember, the board of directors must act collectively in exercising the powers vested in it. The power to bind the company to a contract is exercised by the board of directors making a valid decision of the board, usually by board resolution (see Chapter 9 for how boards take valid decisions).

What if there are provisions in the articles, in addition to Art 3, relevant to the exercise of powers by the company? As noted in Chapter 9, notwithstanding the Art 3 default position in the model articles, it is not uncommon for the general authority of the board to exercise all powers of the company to be limited by articles that reserve certain powers to the shareholders. A typical example is an article requiring loans by the company for over a specified amount to be approved in advance by the shareholders.

What, then, are the consequences of the board of directors purporting to exercise a power of the company outside the board's actual authority? For example, what are the consequences of the board purporting to commit the company to borrow a sum beyond the level the board is authorised by the articles to commit the company to borrow?

- First, if they discover the board's plans in advance, the shareholders may be able to obtain an injunction to prevent the board acting outside its powers. This common law right is expressly preserved by s 40(4).
- Second, each director who participates in the board decision to exercise the company power outside the powers of the board, may be liable for breach of duty (see Chapter 11, directors' duties, particularly s 171). Again, this potential liability is expressly preserved by s 40(5).
- Finally, the loan contract may or may not be enforceable.

It is the enforceability of the loan contract that is examined here. Two sub-questions arise:

- Can the third party enforce the contract against the company?
- Can the company enforce the contract against the third party?

10.5.1 The Companies Act 2006, s 40 and board authority

The answer to whether or not a third party can enforce against a company a contract purportedly entered into *by the board of directors* when the board does not have the power to enter into the contract is now almost always determined by the application of s 40 of the Companies Act 2006.

SECTION

'(1) In favour of a person dealing with a company in good faith, the power of the directors to bind the company, or authorise others to do so, is deemed to be free of any limitation under the company's constitution.

(2) For this purpose–

　(a) a person 'deals with' a company if he is a party to any transaction or other act to which the company is a party.

　(b) a person dealing with a company–

　　(i) is not bound to enquire as to any limitation on the powers of the directors to bind the company or authorise others to do so,

　　(ii) is presumed to have acted in good faith unless the contrary is proved, and

　　(iii) is not to be regarded as acting in bad faith by reason only of his knowing that an act is beyond the powers of the directors under the company's constitution.'

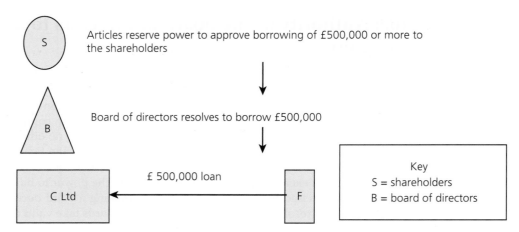

Figure 10.1 Board of directors purporting to act outside its powers

Consider the hypothetical scenario in Figure 10.1. Is C Ltd bound by the loan from F? To work out the answer, apply the following analysis:

- Is the power to approve borrowings of £500,000 or more reserved to shareholders a 'limitation under the constitution' on the power of the board of directors for the purposes of s 40? (see s 40(1))
- Is F a 'person' entitled to rely on s 40? (see s 40(2)(a))
- Was F 'dealing with [the] company'? (see s 40(2)(a))
- Was F dealing 'in good faith'? (see s 40(2)(b))

If the answer to each of the above is yes the power of the board to bind the company is deemed free of the requirement to obtain the approval in advance of the shareholders and C Ltd is bound by the loan agreement.

Person dealing with the company

In the words of the subsection, a person deals with a company for the purposes of s 40(2) (a), 'if he is a party to any transaction or other act to which the company is a party'. As the sub-section lays down a pre-condition to a decision whether the person in question is or is not a party to a transaction with the company, the language of the subsection is not at all helpful: it requires the existence of that which it is there to help to determine. Consequently, to avoid s 40 having no application at all, a purposive rather than a literal interpretation of s 40(2)(a) is required. Also, because the section is an implementation of the First European Company Law Directive, the *Marleasing* principle is once again relevant.

For the subsection to make any sense, in every case in which s 40 is relevant to a contract, 'dealing with the company' must mean being a party to a transaction *to which the company merely purports to be a party* (but to which, without s 40, it is not a party). This calls for the courts to decide whether there are any circumstances in which a person, dealing with another who purports to be acting on behalf of the company, should *not* be entitled to argue that he has the protection afforded to third parties by Art 9(2) of the First Company Law Directive, as implemented (very poorly) by s 40. Put another way, the subsection requires the courts to determine whether or not there are any circumstances in which the contracting process in issue was so defective that regardless of the good faith of the third party a court will not ignore the want of authority or other legal defect in the formation of the contract. In *Smith v Henniker-Major & Co (A firm)* [2002] 1 WLR 616 (CA), the leading case on the interpretation to be given to what is now s 40(2)(a), Carnwath LJ commented that a purposive approach to the section 'suggests a low threshold'. On the underlying approach of the courts, however, he went on to comment:

JUDGMENT

'[W]here, as here, the language of a statute, even one based on a Directive, has to be stretched in a purposive way to achieve its object, I see no reason why, in setting the limits, we should not be guided by what the common law would deem appropriate in a similar context.'

The case is not particularly helpful in relation to the question when will a third party seeking to rely on s 40 not be able to because he is not dealing with the company. Rather, it raised the question whether or not a company insider is a 'person' for the purposes of the subsection.

CASE EXAMPLE

Smith v Henniker-Major & Co (A firm) [2002] 1 WLR 616 (CA)

Smith, a director who was also the chairman and 30 per cent shareholder of a company held a meeting at which he alone was present and purported to pass a board resolution by which the company decided to assign to him the right to sue a firm of solicitors. The firm of solicitors argued that the assignment was invalid as the resolution was taken at a meeting without a quorum of two directors as required by the articles of the company. The director argued that he was a person dealing with the company in good faith and as such could rely on what is now s 40 to ignore the procedural shortcoming in the decision of the company which made the subsequent assignment unenforceable. At first instance the judge found that the director had been dealing with the company, could rely on the statutory provision, and therefore the assignment was valid. On appeal, Held: Smith could *not* rely on the section and the assignment was invalid. The words of the section were wide enough to include a director, but it was up to the courts to interpret the section and as there was no possible policy reason for interpreting it so as to enable a director in Smith's position to 'rely on his own mistake', the court would look to the common law. The case of *Morris v Kanssen* [1946] AC 459 (HL) clearly applied which decided that the law would not permit directors to rely on a presumption, 'that that is rightly done which they have themselves wrongly done' for to do so, 'is to encourage ignorance and condone dereliction from duty'.

The case does not decide that a director will never be able to rely on s 40: indeed Carnwath LJ emphasised this and considered the facts in the case to be 'quite exceptional'. It is possible for a director to seek to rely on s 40. The potential for s 40 to operate to bind the company to a contract with a director is confirmed by s 41. Section 41 provides that where, *because of s 40*, a company is bound by a contract with a director or a person connected to a director, the agreement will be voidable by the company (subject to protecting independent third party rights (s 41(6)), and the director and any other director who authorised the transaction will be liable to account to, or indemnify, the company (s 41(3)).

Dealing in good faith

As a reading of s 40(2)(b), set out above, indicates, a person dealing with the company is almost always going to be found to be acting in good faith for the purposes of s 40. The burden of proving that he was not in good faith is on the party asserting the lack of good faith, ie the company. In a sufficiently clear case, however, an absence of good faith may be found, and was so found in summary proceedings, without the benefit of a trial, in *Wrexham Association Football Club Ltd (in admin) v Crucialmove Ltd* [2008] BCLC 508 (CA), a case principally about breach of directors' duties. In summary proceedings in *Ford v Polymer Vision Ltd* [2009] EWHC 945 (Ch), Blackburne, J dismissed any question of the third party being in bad faith in relation to the validity of a debenture but referred to trial the issue of the validity of an option.

CASE EXAMPLE

Wrexham Association Football Club Ltd (in admin) v Crucialmove Ltd [2008] BCLC 508 (CA)

Two entrepreneurs, Mr Guterman and Mr Hamilton, who were interested in the exploitation of the assets of a football club established as a private company (Wrexham Association Football Club Ltd, 'the Club'), misused the fiduciary position of Mr Guterman as a director and the chairman of the Club to benefit their property development interests. In an action by the Club seeking to avoid a deed, amongst other defences, it was argued by Mr Hamilton that a third party dealing with the Club/company could rely on the predecessor section to s 40 (s 35A) to assert the validity of a deed of declaration of trust executed by the Club/company. The deed had been executed by the Club/company by Mr Guterman and the company secretary. No disclosure of his personal interest in the transaction had been made to the Club/company by Mr Guterman and he and the company secretary had no authority to execute the declaration of trust. Mr Hamilton had made no enquiries as to whether the deed had been authorised by the Club/company and argued that he was under no requirement to do so, as the predecessor provisions to s 40(2) made clear. Held: The predecessor statutory provision to s 40 did not absolve a person dealing with the Club/company from any duty to inquire whether the persons acting for the Club/company has been authorised by the board to enter into the transaction *when the circumstances were such as to put that person on inquiry*. In the unusual circumstances of the case, Mr Hamilton had been put on inquiry. Accordingly, the corporate vehicle he used, Crucialmove, which was the beneficiary of the declaration of trust, could not satisfy the requirement of good faith. The deed of declaration of trust was not binding on the Club/company and s 40 (as it now is) could not help because of the absence of good faith.

In the course of delivering the judgment of the Court of Appeal, Sir Peter Gibson quoted at length findings of fact from the first instance judgment setting out the basis for Judge Norris QC's finding of an absence of good faith.

JUDGMENT

'In my judgment it is fanciful to suggest that Mr Hamilton acted in good faith in relation to the declaration of trust when it is demonstrable from uncontroversial material or from his own case that he knew:

(a) that the whole object of Mr Guterman's and his own involvement with the Club in the first place was to promote a redevelopment of its stadium to their personal advantage ('the Wrexham project');

(b) that Mr Guterman was chairman and director of the Club;

(c) that Mr Guterman had a personal interest in the acquisition of the freehold ...;

(d) that Mr Guterman had promised Mr Hamilton that he would exercise his powers of control and management within the Club with the sole or main objective of realising the maximum potential gain from its property assets for the benefit of himself and Mr Hamilton;

(e) that the declaration of trust and transfer by the Club were the final steps to secure a benefit for Crucialmove which Mr Guterman had thought (and had explained to Mr Hamilton) could most advantageously be pursued in the name of the Club;

(f) that the Club had no independent solicitor acting for it in the transactions;

(g) that all relevant documents had only been signed by Mr Guterman and Mr Rhodes and that no board resolution authorising any step in the transaction had at any stage been produced.

If those circumstances do not demonstrate to a person acting in good faith that the transaction is improper (or put him on enquiry as to its propriety) it is difficult to know what would.'

Judge Norris QC

'In these circumstances any person acting in good faith, and particularly an experienced solicitor like Mr Hamilton, would be bound to enquire whether the transaction had been authorised or approved by the Club or its board and, if so, whether full disclosure had been made by Mr Guterman. The statement of belief by [Crucialmove] … that there was a board resolution confirming authority, rings hollow in the absence of any evidence to substantiate the reality of that belief.'

Sir Peter Gibson

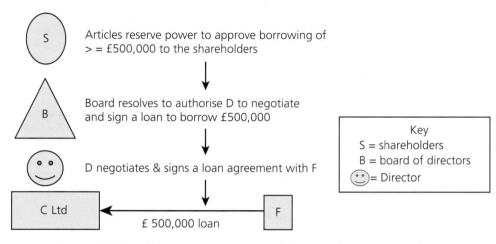

Figure 10.2 Board of directors purporting to delegate a power it does not have

Consider the hypothetical scenario in Figure 10.2. Is C Ltd bound by the loan from F? The analysis to work out the answer is almost exactly the same as it was for the hypothetical scenario in Figure 10.1. The only difference in the legal analysis is that the language of s 40(1) relied on to override the limitation in the articles is the *second* power of the directors mentioned in that subsection, 'the power of the directors to bind the company, or *authorise others to do so*' (emphasis added). The power of the board of directors of C Ltd *to authorise* D to negotiate and sign a loan agreement with F is deemed to be free of the £500,000 loan limitation on the power of the board set out in the articles. D therefore has actual authority to bind the company to the loan with F.

A narrow or broad interpretation of the scope of s 40?

An important unresolved issue regarding the scope of application of s 40 arises out of the language in s 40(1) which deems the power of *the directors* to bind the company or authorise other to do so, free of any limitation under the constitution. Section 40(1) does not state that the power of *any individual* is deemed free of any limitation under the constitution (the authority of an individual is discussed below at section 10.6 and you may understand the following discussion better after you have read that section).

Consider a third party dealing with an individual they believe to have authority to bind the company and who would have authority but for a limitation in the company's constitution. Does s 40 deem the power of the individual to be free of the limitation under the constitution? A purposive interpretation of the section would suggest s 40 should be construed broadly, giving a positive answer. The explanation would be that s 40 overrides the limit on the powers of the directors and, as every subsequent grant of authority down the chain of management in the company can be traced back to the board of directors, the benefit of the overriding operates at every level of grant of authority even where there is no express grant of authority by the board, indeed, even where the authority of the individual is ostensible authority. A narrow interpretation of s 40, on the other hand, would limit the overriding of any limit in the constitution strictly to circumstances in which the *directors* exercised the power to enter into contracts or the directors directly, and possible also expressly, authorised another person, and would result in a negative answer.

This moot issue is illustrated diagramatically in Figure 10.3. C Ltd in Figure 10.3 would be bound by the purchase agreement with F if a broad interpretation of s 40 were adopted but would not be bound if a narrow interpretation were adopted.

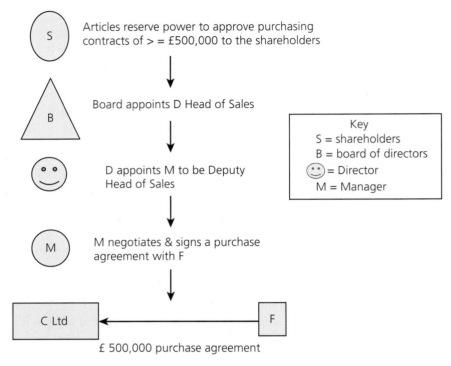

Figure 10.3 Manager is appointed to an office which carries the usual authority to enter into a contract entry into which, in the articles of the company in question, is reserved to the shareholders

Situations outside s 40

Section 40 will not be relevant in a number of situations including the following:

- If the company is seeking to rely on a contract and the third party is arguing an absence of authority, s 40 cannot be used by the company because it only operates in favour of the contractor (but note the potential for the company to ratify the contract).
- If there is no validly appointed board of directors, s 40 will not be relevant.
- If the third party is dealing with the shareholders, s 40 will not be relevant.
- If the third party is not acting in good faith, s 40 will not assist him.
- If the third party is not a 'person' dealing with the company for the purposes of the section, s 40 will not assist him.
- Potentially, if the individual purporting to act as agent of the company has not been directly granted express authority by the directors (a moot issue).

In all these situations (though only potentially in the last mentioned circumstance) the enforceability of the contract will be determined by the common law.

10.5.2 The common law position and board authority

Where s 40 does not apply, the starting point at common law is that if the board enters into a contract on behalf of the company without authority to do so, the contract cannot be enforced by the third party contractor against the company. Nor may the company enforce the contract against the third party contractor (*Re Quintex Ltd (No 2) (1990) 2 ACSR 479*). The inability of the company to enforce the contract can usually be overcome quite easily by the company adopting or ratifying the contract.

Ratification will be brought about in most cases by the shareholders passing an ordinary resolution (*Grant v UK Switchback Railway Co (1888) 40 Ch D 135 (CA)*), although it is possible for a company to ratify a contract by conduct. Ratification validates the acts of the board (or any other purported agent previously lacking authority) from the point in time when the acts took place and is, therefore, 'equivalent to an antecedent authority' (*Koenigsblatt v Sweet* [1923] 2 Ch 314). Remember from our consideration of pre-incorporation contracts that the company must have been in existence at the time the agent purported to act on its behalf. It is not possible to ratify an act performed when the principal (the company) did not exist (see Chapter 4).

Where a restriction on the power of the board exists, the board has no *actual* authority to bind the company (the principal), but what of ostensible authority? Historically, arguments that the board had *ostensible* authority were met and defeated by the constructive notice rule which deemed a person dealing with a company to have notice of the contents of the company's public documents. The most important public documents of a company are its memorandum and articles of association (although, as we saw in Chapter 5, the memorandum is much less important today than it used to be). Consequently, a third party would be deemed to have notice of any limitation on the power of the board contained in the articles. For a third party to argue he had relied on a representation that the board had authority would contradict this imputed knowledge, fail, and the contract would be unenforceable for lack of authority.

The harshness of the constructive notice rule on third parties is mitigated by the rule in *Royal British Bank v Turquand* (1856) 6 E&B 327. *Turquand's Case* established what is sometimes referred to as the 'indoor management rule', namely that a third party may assume that internal procedures specified in a company's public documents as having to be gone through to provide the board with authority have been gone through, even though they may not have been gone through. A third party who has been put on notice that those procedures have not been gone through (by something more than constructive or actual notice of the public documents) may not rely on the internal management rule. *Wrexham Association Football Club Ltd (in admin) v Crucialmove Ltd* [2007] BCC 139 (CA) (considered above at section 10.5.1) is an example of circumstances in which a third party will be considered to have been put on notice that internal procedures have not been complied with and denied the right to rely on the rule in *Turquand's Case*.

A third party who can rely on *Turquand's Case* to mitigate the constructive notice rule, may argue that the board has authority based on the statement in the articles that the board has authority to enter into the type of contract in question, the limitation on the power (such as its exercise in relation to contracts above a certain value being subject to shareholders' approval by resolution), simply calling for an internal procedure that he can assume has been gone through. Be sure to distinguish this situation from a situation in which the board is *not* authorised to enter into the type of contract in issue, for example, where the articles contain an absolute prohibition on directors entering into a certain type of contract, in which case no basis on which to argue the existence of ostensible authority will exist. As was the case in *Turquand's Case* itself, the ostensible authority argument applies where the third party finds 'not a prohibition … but a permission to do so on certain conditions' (*per* Jervis CJ).

10.6 Authority of individuals to bind the company

The articles of a company typically empower the board of directors to delegate any of its powers (Model Articles, Art 5), and authorise further delegation of its powers by any person to whom it has delegated powers. A board of directors typically delegates powers not by expressly using the terms 'delegation' and 'powers' but by allocating management responsibilities to individuals and approving the appointment of individuals to named roles within the company. In the absence of limitations on the powers of the board, *if* the allocated management responsibilities or the performance of the role involves the individual acting so as to legally bind the company, the individual will be an agent of the company with actual authority to bind the company.

If, and to what extent, the board's allocation or appointment of an individual actually delegates powers to that individual is a matter of construction of the terms of the allocation or appointment in the factual context in which it takes place. The authority of the agent is a question of fact. Exactly the same analysis applies to further delegations of power by those to whom the board has delegated powers. And so the powers of the company cascade down, to be exercised at different levels within the company, yet the authority of every agent of a company can be traced back to the board of directors.

The authority described in the previous paragraphs is *actual* authority. Concern to protect third parties dealing with companies resulted in the development of the concept of *ostensible* authority and the authority of an agent nowadays may be either actual authority (express or implied) or ostensible authority. Ostensible authority is also called apparent authority: the terms are interchangeable. Although based on very different legal reasoning, both actual and ostensible authority can be traced back to the board of directors and, ultimately, to the articles of the company. The company is, in agency terminology, the principal.

10.6.1 Actual authority

Actual authority is based on a consensual agreement between the principal (the company) and the agent. The principal consents to the agent exercising the legal power of the company to enter into contracts. The basis of actual authority was described by Diplock LJ in *Freeman & Lockyer v Buckhurst Park Properties (Mangal) Ltd* [1964] 2 QB 480.

JUDGMENT

'An "actual" authority is a legal relationship between principal and agent created by a consensual agreement to which they alone are parties. Its scope is to be ascertained by applying ordinary principles of construction of contracts, including any proper implications from the express words used, the usages of the trade, or the course of business between the parties. To this agreement the contractor is a stranger'.

In contrast, as Lord Pearson emphasised in *Hely-Hutchinson v Brayhead Ltd* [1968] 1 QB 549 (CA), ostensible authority does *not* operate between the company and the agent. It operates between the company and the third party contractor.

JUDGMENT

'If the question arises between the principal and the agent – either of them claiming against the other – actual authority must be proved. There is no question of ostensible authority as between those two parties.'

Actual authority may be express actual authority or implied actual authority.

Example 1 Express actual authority
The board of directors of Company A Limited passed a board resolution authorising the finance director, on behalf of the company, to negotiate and enter into a 10 year lease of a pasteurising machine from Extra PLC, Full PLC or Glow PLC. The finance director has express authority to bind the company to a lease falling within the description in the board resolution. He may contract with any of Extra PLC, Full PLC or Glow PLC.

Example 2 Express actual authority
Consider the hypothetical scenario in Figure 10.4. Is C Ltd bound by the loan agreement with F?

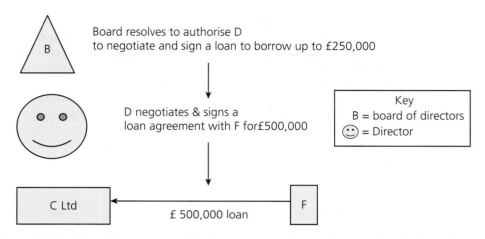

Figure 10.4 Individual director acts outside the express actual authority granted to him by the board of directors

Turning now to focus on implied actual authority, the leading case on implied actual authority in the context of a company as the principal is *Hely-Hutchinson v Brayhead Ltd* [1968] 1 QB 549 (CA). It confirms that a person appointed by the board to a position within a company will have usual authority, that is, implied actual authority, to do all such things as fall within the usual scope of that office. The case actually demonstrates another point, that is, the importance of taking into account the conduct of the company and the individual and *all the circumstances of the case*.

CASE EXAMPLE

Hely-Hutchinson v Brayhead Ltd [1968] 1 QB 549 (CA)

Richards was chairman of the board of an industrial holding company (Brayhead) and its chief executive or *'de facto* managing director'. Richards regularly entered into contracts on behalf of Brayhead which he disclosed to the board afterwards, sometimes seeking formal ratification after he had committed the company. The board acquiesced in Richards' entry into contracts. Brayhead was planning to merge with another company, Perdio. In these circumstances, Richards signed contracts purportedly binding Brayhead to guarantee Perdio's borrowings from a third party and indemnifying the third party against certain losses. The question arose, did Richards have authority to bind Brayhead to such contracts? At first instance, Roskill J found that Richards had ostensible authority. On appeal, the Court of Appeal Held: Richards had actual implied authority. Lord Denning MR found that Mr Richards had no express authority to enter into the contracts in issue on behalf of the company, nor was such authority implied from the nature of his office. Although Richards had been duly appointed chairman of the company, in itself, that office did not carry with it authority to enter into the contracts in issue without the sanction of the board. 'But *I think he had authority implied from the conduct of the parties and the circumstances of the case* … such authority being implied from the circumstance that the board by their conduct over many months had acquiesced in his acting as their chief executive and committing Brayhead Ltd to contracts without the necessity of sanction from the board'. (emphasis added)

Example 3 Implied actual authority

The board of directors of Company B Ltd resolved to approve the appointment of Paul Bailey to the position of Head of Marketing with responsibility for running the marketing department. Past Heads of Marketing have signed a range of contracts on behalf of the company such as contracts for the purchase of marketing services including television advertising time and billboard space. Paul Bailey has implied actual authority to enter into agreements on behalf of Company B Ltd but the exact scope of his implied actual authority to enter into contracts is not clear. The scope of authority is ascertained from the conduct of the board and the circumstances of the case of which the appointment to the role is an important part but it is not the only fact relevant to the existence and scope of Paul Bailey's authority.

In *Smith v Butler* [2012] EWCA Civ 314, Arden LJ examined the law relevant to ascertaining the implied authority of a managing director in the course of concluding that on the facts the MD in question had no implied authority to suspend the executive chairman.

JUDGMENT

'28 ... [the] proposition ... that, in principle, the implied powers of a managing director are those that would ordinarily be exercisable by a managing director in his position [i]n my judgment ... is correct. In *Hely-Hutchinson v Brayhead* [1968] 1 QB 549 at 583, Lord Denning MR held that the board of directors, on appointing a managing director, "thereby impliedly authorise him to do all such things as fall within the usual scope of that office." Mr Dougherty's proposition is also supported by the passage that Mr Berragan cited from *Gore-Browne on Companies*. Another way of putting that point is that the managing director's powers extend to carrying out those functions on which he did not need to obtain the specific directions of the board. This is simply the default position. It is, therefore, subject to the company's articles and anything that the parties have expressly agreed. In essence, the issue is one of interpreting the contract of appointment or employment in the light of all the relevant background, and asking what that contract would reasonably be understood to have meant (*Attorney General of Belize v Belize Telecom Ltd* [2009] 1 WLR 1485, PC, and see my judgment in *Stena Line v Merchant Navy Ratings Pension Fund Trustees Ltd* [2010] EWCA Civ 543 at 36–41).

29 On this basis, as might be expected, the test of what is within the implied actual authority of a managing director coincides with the test of what is within the ostensible authority of a managing director: see *Freeman & Lockyer v Buckhurst Park Properties (Mangal) Ltd* [1964] 2 QB 176.

30 The holder of the office of managing director might today more usually be called a chief executive officer in (at least) a public company. He or she has generally to work on the basis that his appointment does not supplant that of the role of the board and that he will have to refer back to the board for authority on matters on which the board has not clearly laid out the company's strategy. He or she would thus be expected to work within the strategy the board had actually set.

Now consider Example 3 with slightly amended facts. Consider that the resolution appointing Paul Bailey expressly stated that the Head of Marketing had authority to commit the company to marketing contracts to a value of no more than £500,000 and Paul Bailey signs a contract purporting to commit the company to purchase £600,000 of marketing services. An agent who is subject to an express limit on his authority cannot have implied actual authority that exceeds that limit. It is in just such a case that a third party must turn to ostensible authority.

10.6.2 Ostensible authority

ostensible authority
the authority that one can assume a person purporting to be an agent has based on a representation made by a person authorised by the company. Also known as apparent authority

As the words of Lord Pearson in *Hely-Hutchinson v Brayhead Ltd* quoted above make clear, unlike actual authority, ostensible authority does not operate between the company and the agent. It operates between the company and a third party. It is based on estoppel arising out of reliance by the party dealing with the company on a representation made by the company or an agent of the company.

Diplock LJ set out the conditions that need to be satisfied to establish apparent authority in *Freeman Lockyer v Buckhurst Park Properties (Mangal) Ltd* [1964] 2 QB 480 (CA):

JUDGMENT

'[T]o entitle a contractor to enforce against a company a contract entered into on behalf of the company by an agent who had no actual authority to do so … [i]t must be shown:

(1) that a representation that an agent had authority to enter on behalf of the company into a contract of the kind sought to be enforced was made to the contractor;

(2) that such representation was made by a person or persons who had "actual" authority to manage the business of the company either generally or in respect of those matters to which the contract relates;

(3) that he (the contractor) was induced by such representation to enter into the contract, ie that he in fact relied upon it; and …' (the fourth requirement is no longer relevant).

The most difficult condition for a third party contractor to satisfy is often the second condition, to show that the representation on which they relied was made by a person who had actual authority to bind the company to the contract in issue. The dealings of the third party are often confined to dealing with the individual who lacks actual authority and therefore it is representations made by that individual that the third party is often forced to assert to attempt to satisfy the condition.

In *Armagas Ltd v Mundogas SA* [1986] AC 717 (HL), the court emphasised that where the third party knows, or should know, of a general limit on the agent's actual authority, an agent cannot usually pull himself up by his own bootstraps, so to speak, and confer ostensible authority on himself by his own representations that he has more extensive authority than he actually has. Even in *Armagas*, however, Lord Keith acknowledged that there may be circumstances in which an agent who is known to have no general authority to enter into transactions of the type in issue, can be reasonably believed to have specific authority to enter into the particular transaction in issue 'by reason of circumstances created by the principal'.

The 'circumstances created by the principal' (the company) may amount to giving the agent authority to communicate to the third party notice of approval of a transaction by the person within the company authorised to approve it. In other words, it is possible for the second condition of *Freeman Lockyer* to be satisfied by a communication to the third party by, or via, the agent whose authority is in issue. This was demonstrated by *First Energy (UK) Ltd v Hungarian International Bank Ltd* [1993] 2 Lloyd's Rep 194 (CA).

CASE EXAMPLE

First Energy (UK) Ltd v Hungarian International Bank Ltd [1993] 2 Lloyd's Rep 194 (CA)

Jamison, the senior manager in charge of the Manchester office of HIB, negotiated with Croft the terms of a credit facility for First Energy. Jamison expressly told Croft that he, Jamison, had no authority to sanction a facility. Subsequently, Jamison wrote to Croft offering to finance three projects and this offer was accepted by Croft. Held: *Per* Steyn LJ, 'In context the letter was calculated to convey to First Energy that Mr. Jamison had obtained the approval of the transaction at the appropriate level at head office'. Jamison, whilst not having authority to enter into a credit facility on behalf of the bank, did have ostensible authority to communicate head office approval to Croft which is what he had done. The fact that Croft knew that Jamison's actual authority to enter into transactions on behalf of HIB was limited did not necessarily mean that his authority to communicate decisions on their behalf was limited also.

A sufficiently senior manager may have authority to communicate to a third party that another member of staff of the company has authority to commit the company to a particular matter. In *British Bank of the Middle East v Sun Life Assurance Company of Canada (UK) Ltd* [1983] 2 Lloyd's Rep 9 (HL), the leading case in which this was argued, the principle was accepted but was held not to apply on the facts as the senior manager himself did not have either authority to commit the company to the transaction in question or the authority to communicate the authority of another to do so.

CASE EXAMPLE

British Bank of the Middle East v Sun Life Assurance Company of Canada (UK) Ltd [1983] 2 Lloyd's Rep 9 (HL)

Sun Life Canada carried on the business of life insurance and granting loans on mortgages of real property in the UK. It had unit offices, branch offices and, in London, an administrative HQ. The plaintiff received an undertaking committing Sun Life to provide it with funds, signed by a unit manager, Mr Dehnel. The plaintiff did not believe that the unit manager had authority to commit Sun Life to the arrangement so wrote to the general manager of Sun Life, at Sun Life's HQ, seeking confirmation of the authority of the unit manager. A branch manager, Mr Clarke, with no actual authority to commit Sun Life to the arrangement in question, replied to the letter, confirming to the plaintiff the authority of the unit manager to sign the undertaking binding Sun Life. Held: Neither the unit manager nor the branch manager had actual authority to bind Sun Life to the undertaking and, 'It follows necessarily from that conclusion that [the branch manager] never could have had, and never did have, the actual authority, express or implied, of Sun Life UK to represent, to the bank or anyone else, that [the unit manager] had the actual authority of that company to execute singly such undertakings on its behalf'. Further, in response to the argument that Mr Clarke had ostensible authority to respond to the letter confirming Mr Dehnel's authority, it was held that he did not have ostensible authority as the [plaintiff] had no reason to suppose that Mr Clarke, by reason of his title as branch manager, had any authority to do what he did, evidence before the court indicating that it was the practice of Sun Life, and in the industry, for such undertakings to be executed at the head office.

10.6.3 Implied actual authority and ostensible authority contrasted

Although implied actual authority and ostensible authority often exist at the same time, there are a number of important differences between them. The parties between whom implied actual authority and ostensible authority operate are different. Implied actual authority operates between the principal (the company) and the individual and ostensible authority operates between the principal (the company) and the third party contractor.

The legal theory on which each type of authority is based are very different. Implied actual authority is based on consensual agreement whereas ostensible authority is based on reliance and estoppel.

Whilst both implied actual authority and ostensible authority may be present at the same time, Lord Denning MR, in his judgment in *Hely-Hutchinson v Brayhead Ltd* [1968] 1 QB 549 (CA), offered the following example of how the scope of implied actual and ostensible authority may not be coterminous.

JUDGMENT

'[S]ometimes ostensible authority exceeds actual authority. For instance, when the board appoint the managing director, they may expressly limit his authority by saying he is not to order goods worth more than £500 without the sanction of the board. In that case his actual authority is subject to the £500 limitation, but his *ostensible* authority includes all the usual authority of a managing director. The company is bound by his ostensible authority in his dealings with those who do not know of the limitation.'

Finally, implied actual authority allows a company to insist on enforcing the contract against a third party whereas a company cannot rely on the ostensible authority of its agent to enforce a contract against a third party (*Re Quintex Ltd (No 2)* (1990) 2 ACSR 479). The company can usually overcome this issue by ratifying the entry into the contract in question, although this course was not open to the company in *Re Quintex Ltd (No 2)*.

For further illustration of the interplay between different types of authority see *Waugh v HB Clifford & Sons Ltd* [1982] Ch 374 (CA) (the relationship between implied actual and apparent authority), and *SMC Electronics Ltd v Akhter Computers Ltd* [2001] 1 BCLC 433 (CA) in which the court indicated that had it not been able to find that express authority existed, it could have found the existence of both implied actual and ostensible authority.

KEY FACTS

Legally binding the company	
Authority of the board of directors to bind the company	
Statute overrides limitations in the constitution on the powers of the board in favour of a person dealing in good faith with the company.	s 40
Dealing with the company is given a purposive interpretation.	*Smith v Henniker-Major* (2002)
The person who deals in good faith with the company may be a director.	s 41
Good faith is rebuttably presumed, knowledge of lack of authority is not automatically bad faith and a person is not bound to enquire about authority.	s 40(2)(b)
But s 40(2)(b) does not absolve a person from any duty to enquire as to authority when the circumstances put him on inquiry.	*Wrexham AFC v Crucialmove Ltd* (2008)
Scope of s 40 is moot: unclear whether s 40(1) should be interpreted to deem the power of *any individual* to be free of any limitation under the constitution or only the power of *the directors* and individuals directly authorised by the board of directors and individuals directly authorised by the board of directors..	
Common law position: If board has no authority, contract does not bind the company or the third party.	*Re Quintex Ltd (No 2)* (1990)
Contract can be ratified.	*Grant v UK Switchback Railway* (1888)
Board authority may be actual or ostensible.	*Royal British Bank v Turquand* (1856)
Constructive notice of public documents doctrine mitigated by indoor management rule subject to actual notice or being put on inquiry.	*Wrexham AFC v Crucialmove Ltd* (2008)
Authority of individuals to bind the company	
Actual authority may be express or implied. Implied authority is common in company employees/agents	*Hely-Hutchinson v Brayhead* (1968)
Ostensible authority is also common in company employees/agents	*Freeman Lockyer v Buckhurst Park* (1964)
Agent may be able to communicate that a transaction has been approved by the company or may be able to communicate the authority of another person in the company but may not represent his own authority so as to create ostensible authority.	*British Bank of the Middle East v Sun Life* (1983) *First Energy v Hungarian International* (1993)

SUMMARY

Company deeds

▣ A company will only be bound by a deed if the document is clear on its face that it is intended to be a deed and is validly executed as a deed (Law of Property (Miscellaneous Provisions) Act 1989, s 1(2)).

▣ A document is validly executed as a deed by a company if:
  (i) the common seal is affixed; or
  (ii) the document is expressed to be executed by the company and is signed by two authorised signatories or a director in the presence of a witness who attests signature (Companies Act 2006, s 44); and it is delivered as a deed (Companies Act 2006, s 46).

▣ If a deed purports to be validly executed, it is deemed validly executed in relation to a purchaser in good faith for valuable consideration (s 44(5)).

Company seals

No obligation exists for a registered company to have a company seal (s 45) and no obligation to use a company seal exists unless use is mandated by the articles. Model Articles do not mandate use.

Executing company contracts

If a contract is set out in writing and that document is either sealed or executed in accordance with s 44, the company will be bound by the contract.

Contracts can also be entered into by agents acting on behalf of the company.

Companies Act 2006, s 40: statutory protection

In favour of a person dealing in good faith with the company, s 40 overrides limitations set out in the constitution on the powers of the board to bind the company.

▣ Dealing with the company is given a purposive interpretation (*Smith v Henniker-Major* (2002)).

▣ Good faith is rebuttably presumed, knowledge of lack of authority is not automatically bad faith and a person is not bound to enquire about authority (s 40(2)(b)).

▣ Section 40(2)(b) does not absolve a person from any duty to enquire as to authority when the circumstances put him on inquiry (*Wrexham AFC v Crucialmove Ltd* (2008)).

▣ The scope of s 40 is moot: it is unclear whether s 40(1) should be interpreted to deem the power of any individual to be free of any limitation under the constitution or only the power of the directors.

The common law position and the rule in *Turquand's Case*

▣ If the board has no authority to act, a contract does not bind the company or the third party (*Re Quintex Ltd (No 2)* (1990)).

▣ Board authority may be actual or ostensible and the constructive notice of public documents doctrine is mitigated by the indoor management rule (*Royal British Bank v Turquand* (1856)).

▣ If a third party has *actual* notice that the required procedure has not been gone through or has been put on inquiry, they cannot rely on the indoor management rule (*Wrexham AFC v Crucialmove Ltd* (2008)).

The authority of agents to bind the company

▣ Actual authority may be express or implied and is based on a consensual agreement between the company and the agent (*Hely-Hutchinson v Brayhead* (1968)).

▣ Ostensible authority operates between the company and the third party relying on the authority of the purported agent and is based on estoppel (*Freeman Lockyer v Buckhurst Park* (1964)).

▣ Both implied and ostensible authority is common in company employees.

ACTIVITY

Problem–question exercise

A Introduction

The question in this exercise could appear as a question in a company law examination. Remember as you work through it that the object of the exercise is to practise how to approach answering a problem-type question in an examination, not simply to learn legal rules.

The approach worked through here is only one suggested approach to answering problem-type questions. There are other approaches and you should only think of adopting this one if it makes sense to you and helps you to answer the question. Remember there is unlikely to be a 'correct' answer to a problem question. It is rare for a problem question to appear in an examination that does not raise one or more moot legal issues. If even one moot, or unresolved, legal issue arises on the facts of the question, there will be no single correct answer. Although marks are achieved for demonstrating *knowledge* of relevant legal rules and principles, even more marks can be achieved by demonstrating *skills* as you answer the question. This exercise is designed to help you to understand what those skills are and how to use them to answer a problem question.

B Question

Aspirata Ltd owns a chain of shops. The articles of Aspirata Ltd are in the form of the model articles with a small number of amendments, including a supplementary article that the board must secure a resolution of the shareholders approving any contract to borrow or to commit the company to spend £1 million or more. Annually, the board of directors passes a resolution approving a list of authority levels for personnel at different levels in the company. Members of the board are Level 1 personnel, employees who report directly to a member of the board are Level 2 personnel, employees who report directly to a Level 2 person are Level 3 personnel, and so on down the company. The board resolutions state that Level 1 personnel are authorised to commit the company to contracts with a maximum spend of £1,000,000. The corresponding figure for Level 2 is £500,000.

The board passes a board resolution appointing Barry to be a director of the company and approving his employment as Head of Purchasing. Barry takes office and meets his team including two deputy Heads of Sale who report to him, Charlie and Dirk. He is particularly impressed with Charlie. One of the first projects Barry becomes involved in is enlarging Aspirata's offering of soft drinks. He has dinner with Charlie and Ms Selit, a very successful wholesaler of soft drinks, to discuss a £1 million supply agreement. In the course of dinner he says to Ms Selit, nodding at Charlie, 'you can deal with Charlie on this one, he knows what he's doing and will get your bottles on our shelves if anyone can'. Charlie subsequently negotiates and signs a contract commiting Aspirata Ltd to purchase £1,000,000 of Nirvana Spirit from Ms Selit. The board discover the existence of the contract when Barry presents it to the board for ratification. The price is too high and it is clear that Aspirata will lose money on the contract. The board instructs Barry to call Ms Selit and explain that as Charlie had no authority, the company is not bound by the agreement.

Advise Ms Selit and Aspirata Ltd of their rights and liabilities arising out of the facts.

C Working through the question

1   Read the question through.
2   Re-read the part of the question that states *what precisely it is you are asked to do* and keep this in the front of your mind.
3   Read the question through again.
4   If you are asked to advise specific characters, try to work out and write down what those characters would want and/or the liabilities they are potentially facing in the circumstances.
5   Extract the relevant facts from the information provided:
    ● key persons and decision-making bodies
    ● different legal statuses of those persons

- relevant information about the companies in the question
- the events that have occurred.

6 Identify the legal topics, concepts, principles and rules that are relevant to the question.

7 Note the key sources of the relevant concepts, principles and rules you are going to use to answer the question (mainly cases and statutory provisions, possibly government reports, journal literature).

8 Focus on any moot points of law raised by the question and think about the different lines of argument you can make to support different conclusions in relation to each issue.

9 Decide how you are going to structure your answer:
- deal with each character in turn, or
- deal with each event in turn or
- deal with legal principles in turn
- a structured mixture of the above.

10 Construct and capture in bullet points logical arguments to apply the legal rules and principles to the facts to reach a conclusion as to the rights and/or liabilities of the characters in the fact scenario presented.

11 Write your answer:
- keep introductions to a minimum
- use connectors such as 'because', 'the reason for this is', 'it follows from this that', 'therefore', 'consequently', 'it is arguable that', 'applying this principle to the facts in the question', to build logical arguments
- keep conclusions to a minimum unless you are asked a precise question and you have not answered it in the body of your answer, in which case make sure that you answer it in the conclusion.

D Applying the approach to the question

Stage	Outcome
Read the question through	√
Re-read the part of the question that states *what precisely it is you are asked to do* and keep this in the front of your mind	**Advise Ms Selit** Rights against Aspirata Ltd, rights against Barry? Charlie? Liabilities – not in issue **Advise Aspirata Ltd** Liabilities – to Ms Selit Rights – against Barry? Against Charlie?
Read question again	√
What do the characters want and what liabilities are they potentially facing?	**Ms Selit** Wants to enforce the supply agreement against Aspirata Ltd. If not, wants damages from Aspirata Ltd, Barry or Charlie. **Aspirata Ltd** Does not want to be bound by the supply agreement with Ms Selit. If it is bound by the contract it may wish to sue Barry to recover its losses +/ remove Barry from office as a director +/ terminate Barry's employment. May wish to terminate Charlie's employment.

Stage	Outcome
Relevant facts provided **Key characters/decision-makers and statuses**	**Aspirata Ltd:** a private company with amended model articles **Shareholders:** reserve right to exercise power of company to enter into loans and purchase contracts of £1m of more. **Board of directors:** power to bind company (Art 3) limited by specific article reserving power to shareholders **Barry:** director; employee; Level 1 person; agent **Charlie:** employee; Level 2 employee; agent; signs contract **Ms Selit:** sole trader; third party contractor; hears a statement by Barry, negotiates with Charlie.
Legal topics, concepts, principles and rules relevant to the question	**Binding the company to a contract** Authority of the board: common law/articles/s 40 Authority of individual directors/employees: actual (express and implied)/ostensible authority *Freeman & Lockyer v Buckhurst Park* (1964) *Armagas Ltd v Mundogas SA* (1986) *First Energy v Hungarian International Bank* (1993) *British Bank of the Middle East v Sun Life Assurance* (1983) **Directors' duties** Acting within powers (s 171) **Removal of directors** Model articles; s 168 **Termination of service contract?** ss 168(5) and 188
Key sources	(Added into row immediately above)
Identify moot points of law	Broad or narrow interpretation of s 40 Ability of a person without actual authority to communicate to a person dealing with the company a statement sufficient to satisfy condition 2 of the *Freeman* conditions for ostensible authority

Stage	Outcome
Structure answer	See row 4 above: Work through Ms Selit's ability to enforce the agreement. Consider Aspirata Ltd – is there anything to add to the discussion about the enforceability of the contract? Consider Aspirata Ltd's rights against Barry: breach of duty, remedies, right to remove. Mention (briefly) rights of Aspirata Ltd against Charlie (probably none – all turns on the facts, may be able to discipline him – not company law).
Bullet point logical arguments applying law	Over to you!
Write answer	

SAMPLE ESSAY QUESTION

Consider the following essay question (which combines learning from this chapter and Chapter 5):

Critically analyse the proposition that objects clauses are now legally unimportant because the *ultra vires* doctrine no longer applies to registered companies.

Unpack the question

This is the first essential step which you must take time to do properly. You should separate out:

- Explanation of the meaning of "the *ultra vires* doctrine"
- Explanation of what an objects clauses is
- Explanation of the incremental reform of the doctrine vis a vis companies
- The remaining issue of the effect of an objects clause on the authority of the board to exercise the powers of the company
- Explanation of the operation of the constructive notice doctrine and *Turquand's Case*
- Explanation of the effect of s 40
- Assessment of whether or not it is correct to say that objects clauses are unimportant.

The doctrine of ultra vires and objects clauses explained

- Explain what an objects clause is and its common law effect: *Ashbury Carriage and Iron Company Ltd v Riche*.
- Explain what an objects clauses is, the evolution to extensive objects clauses encompassing comprehensive purposes and powers and endorsement of this trend in s 3A Companies Act 1985.
- Explain that ultra vires is about acts beyond the *legal capacity* of a *company*, which is now only going to arise in relation to charitable companies and note that it is important to distinguish discussion of acts *outside the authority* of the *directors*, which remains an important issue.

Explain the incremental reform of the doctrine vis a vis companies

In particular:

- Explain the effect of s 39
- Explain the effect of the 2006 Act on existing companies with objects clauses: s 28
- Note that there is no requirement for objects clauses for companies registered pursuant to the Companies Act 2006 s 31.

Discuss the effect of an objects clause

- Note the right to seek winding-up by the court because just and equitable to do so if object no longer possible: *Re Baku Consolidated Oil Fields Ltd*
- Note the right of an individual shareholder to seek an injunction: *Stevens v Mysore Reefs*
- Identify a failure to respect an objects clause as resulting in a breach of directors' duty to act otherwise than in accordance with the constitution: s 171
- Explain that the clause operates as a limit on the powers of the directors which, without more, stops a contract inconsistent with it from being binding on the company.

The position at common law and the effect of s 40 on an objects clause

- Note that at common law, the board of directors have no actual authority to act in breach of an objects clause and the doctrine of constructive notice of public documents (which included the constitutional documents of a registered company because these are on the public register) precludes the third party from establishing ostensible authority
- *Turquand's* case does not help because the prohibition on acting beyond the objects clause is absolute: it is not possible to pass an ordinary resolution empowering the board to act, or to go through some other internal procedure
- Explain the effect of s 40 on limits on powers of the directors in the articles, and that an objects clause is such a limitation which can therefore be over-ridden by s 40.

CONCLUDE

Express your reasoned opinion as to the continuing importance of objects clauses to registered companies.

Further reading

Articles

Payne, J, 'Company contracts and directors' authority' [2010] LMCLQ 187.

Payne, J and Prentice, D, 'Company contracts and vitiating factors: developments in the law on directors' authority' [2005] LMCLQ 447.

Twigg-Flesner, C, 'Full circle: Purported agent's right of enforcement under s 36C of the Companies Act 1985' (2001) 22 Comp Law 274.

Twigg-Flesner, C, 'Sections 35a and 322 revisited: Who is a "person dealing with a company"?' (2005) 26 Comp Law 195.

Walters, A, 'Section 35A and the quorum requirements: Confusion reigns' (2002) 23 Comp Law 325.

Reports

Law Commission, Consultation Paper: The Execution of Deeds and Documents by or on behalf of Bodies Corporate (1996 No 143).

Law Commission, Report: The Execution of Deeds and Documents by or on behalf of Bodies Corporate (1998 No 253).

Books

Munday, R, *Agency Law and Principles* (Oxford University Press, 2010).

Sealy, L and Hooley, R, *Commercial Law, Text, Cases and Materials* (4th edn, Oxford University Press, 2008).

11

Directors' duties: General considerations and management duties

AIMS AND OBJECTIVES

After reading this chapter you should be able to:

- Discuss the rationale behind reform of directors' duties
- Discuss the extent to which the statutory statement of directors' duties is a codification
- Understand to whom directors' duties are owed
- Understand the concept of enlightened shareholder value and how it has been introduced into directors' duties
- Appreciate when directors must focus on the interests of creditors
- Distinguish management duties and self-interest duties
- Identify general management duties and specific management duties
- Understand how the four general management duties operate:
  - to act within powers (s 171)
  - to promote the success of the company (s 172)
  - to exercise independent judgement (s 173)
  - to exercise reasonable care, skill and diligence (s 174)

11.1 Introduction

11.1.1 Approach to the study of directors' duties

The legal duties of directors are such an essential part of the legal corporate governance framework that three chapters are needed to do them justice. Following introductory remarks, the following structure is adopted for the study of directors' duties and the key statutory provisions governing directors' contracts with the company:

- Legislative reform (Chapter 11)
- To whom the duties are owed (Chapter 11)
- Management duties (Chapter 11)
- Self-interest duties (Chapter 12)
- Statutory provisions governing directors' contracts with the company (Chapter 12)
- Remedies and relief for breaches and contraventions (Chapter 13).

Classification of directors' duties into management duties and self-interest duties is depicted diagrammatically in Figure 11.1. Students regularly fail to appreciate the very different roles management and self-interest duties play. To avoid falling into this trap, you should take a few minutes to familiarise yourself with the classification in Figure 11.1 and the remainder of this introduction addresses the distinction.

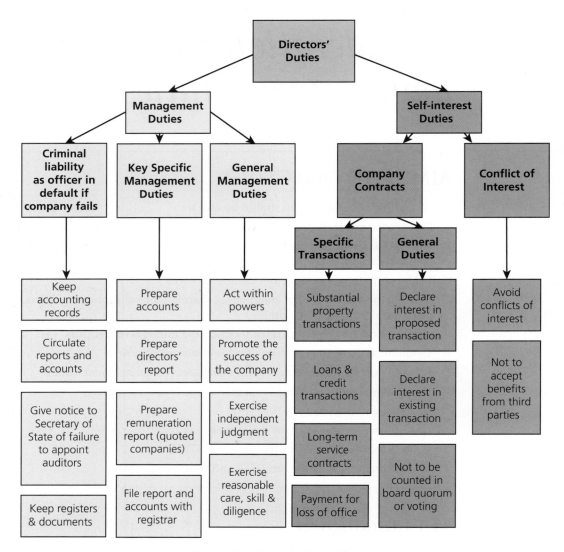

Figure 11.1 Categorisation of directors' duties

11.1.2 Control of director self-interest

The primary role of directors' duties is to discourage individuals empowered to manage companies from acting in their own self interest or in the interest of persons other than the company. It is because the directors of a company are empowered to alter the legal position of the company and in doing so are entrusted to act in the best interests of the company that they are subject to fiduciary obligations. You will come across fiduciary responsibility in agency and trust law. As a fundamental legal concept underpinning English law, it is not confined to trustees and agents.

CASE EXAMPLE

York Building Co v MacKenzie (1795) 3 Pat 378

He that is entrusted with the interest of others cannot be allowed to make the business an object of interest to himself; because from the frailty of nature, one who has the power will be too readily seized with the inclination to use the opportunity for serving his own interest at the expense of those for whom he is entrusted.

Protecting rights, particularly property rights, and establishing standards for human conscience when individuals are entrusted to protect the rights of third parties are regarded as proper matters for the civil law courts. Conflict of interest has long been discouraged by the English courts and stringent remedies awarded against transgressors.

11.1.3 Control of management behaviour

In contrast to controlling self-interest, judges have exhibited less interest in managerial competence. Courts have not considered it their role to create incentives for good management. To do so would inevitably draw judges into making judgments about the reasonableness of business decisions, a role they acknowledge they have no particular competence to play. Only relatively recently has the law given any meaningful content to what are termed here 'management duties' of directors, a development shaped by legislative intervention. The approach of the law is to require directors to arrive at decisions by satisfactory processes rather than to review the substance of management decisions.

The legislature enacts law in response to Government proposals to use law as a tool to drive behaviours considered desirable to achieve Government policy. Better corporate governance is regarded as desirable to achieve greater economic productivity with higher levels of employment, making the UK economy stronger and, ultimately, benefiting society. Although socio-economic policy, and debate as to what that policy should be and consideration of the role company law (1) does, (2) could, and (3) should play, are beyond the scope of this book, it is essential to be aware that these issues form the backdrop to the framework of legal corporate governance of which directors' duties form an important part.

The Rt Hon Margaret Hodge MP, Secretary of State for Trade and Industry, as she then was, made this clear in her Ministerial Statement on the reforms to the duties of company directors introduced by the Companies Act 2006 in which she stated:

QUOTATION

'There are two ways of looking at the statutory statement of directors' duties: on the one hand it simply codifies the existing common law obligations of company directors; on the other – especially in section 172: the duty to act in the interests of the company – it marks a radical departure in articulating the connection between what is good for a company and what is good for society at large.'

She was referring to the introduction into company law of the concept of 'enlightened shareholder value', examined later in this chapter at section 11.2.3. Although articulation of the connection between what is good for a company and what is good for society at large may be a radical step, enlightened shareholder value is far from radical. It preserves the central role of the interests of shareholders in the structure of corporate governance. Shareholders have traditionally held residual control rights in companies and it is extremely difficult to construct an alternative control mechanism. Enlightened shareholder value preserves the rights *status quo* and neither the Law Commission's review of directors' duties nor (as it became clear) the 1998 Company Law Review was established to revisit shareholder primacy or to question the fundamental role of companies or company law.

Before turning to examine management duties, it is helpful to consider directors' duties generally, including legislative reform and to whom the duties are owed.

11.2 Legislative reform of directors' duties

Directors' general duties were developed over time by the courts and remained case-based until the Companies Act 2006.

11.2.1 Statutory regulation of particular transactions

In contrast to the general duties, statutory provisions regulating *specific* transactions between a director and the company were first introduced in 1928. Prompted by financial scandals, the statutory provisions were significantly enhanced in 1980 which marked the high tide of statutory regulation of director self-interest. Company loans above a minimal amount to directors, for example, were prohibited and criminalised (a prohibition the 2006 Act removed in favour of shareholder approval).

11.2.2 General duty codification initiatives

The general duties have not been ignored by Governments through the twentieth century. A long line of committees considered consolidating or codifying general directors' duties. In 1895, the Davey Committee recommended that the duties and liabilities of promoters and directors in respect of the promotion of companies and the issue of prospectuses should be set out in statute because:

QUOTATION

'The incorporation of those principles in an Act of Parliament is more likely to bring home to promoters and directors the obligations they undertake and to shareholder and others the standard of commercial morality which they have a right to expect in those whom they are invited to trust'.

This rationale, echoed in the Government's Companies Act 2006 rationale, was not enough to cause the recommendations to be acted upon. In 1926, the Greene Committee commented that, 'To attempt by statute to define the duties of directors would be a hopeless task'. Fear of the difficulty of reducing complex duties to statutory provisions consistently stalked codification efforts.

Adopting a less defeatist stance, the Jenkins Committee, reporting in 1962, recommended a statement of the basic principles underlying the fiduciary duties owed by a director to the company. Far from codification, the statement was intended to be *non-exhaustive*. The Companies Bill 1973 contained statutory provisions stated to be 'in addition to and not in derogation of any other enactments or rules of law relating to the duties or liabilities of directors of a company'. Unfortunately, the bill fell with the Government in the first 1974 general election. A much more ambitious Companies Bill appeared in 1978. It contained duties stated to have effect 'instead of any rule of law stating the fiduciary duties of directors of companies'. Subject to severe criticism, events overtook it and in 1979 it too fell with the Government.

A Department of Trade and Industry (DTI, now the Department for Business, Innovation and Skills, or BIS) working party on directors' duties from 1993–95 failed to publish proposals, and directors' duties were next considered by the Law Commission in the late 1990s, resulting in a lengthy consultation paper entitled Company Directors: Regulating Conflicts of Interest and Formulating a Statement of Duties (No 153 (1998)). Published after the DTI (now BIS) announcement of the 1998 Company Law Review, the consultation paper significantly influenced adoption of a statutory statement of directors' duties in the Companies Act 2006.

11.2.3 Rationale for the 2006 reform

After the passing of the 2006 Act, Margaret Hodge articulated two aims of the reform of directors' duties. A third aim is found in the Law Commission's consultation paper on directors' duties:

- Providing clarity and accessibility.
- Aligning what is good for the company with what is good for society at large.
- Keeping legal regulation to the minimum necessary to safeguard stakeholders' legitimate interests.

Each is worth further consideration.

Providing clarity and accessibility

It remains too early to tell whether the post-2006 Act law on directors' duties is clearer, easier to understand and more accessible than the old law. Certainly, the headline duties are drawn together in one place in the Act. As comments in the codification section below indicate, however, the statutory provisions far from comprehensively cover all issues relevant to a directors' liability for breach of duty. It is likely that in many situations directors will continue to need to seek legal advice to understand their legal duties and the procedures available to avoid incurring liability. If this turns out to be the case, the Act will not have achieved its principal stated aim in relation to directors' duties. In the recent evaluation of the Act commissioned by BIS it is suggested that added clarity of s 172 is needed, having somewhat worryingly found evidence of directors entering into limited liability agreements with auditors 'whilst openly acknowledging they do not know of any benefits to their company'.

stakeholders
groups with an interest in the company, such as shareholders, creditors, employees, customers, suppliers and the local communities in which the company operates

Aligning what is good for the company with what is good for society at large

As indicated in the introduction to this chapter, little room was provided in the reform process for debate of the fundamental values company law ought to achieve. Debate between pluralists advocating the running of corporations in the interests of the plurality of stakeholders and those endorsing the shareholder model of the corporation was circumscribed. Although the concept of 'enlightened shareholder value' enshrined in the s 172 duty requires directors to 'have regard to' the interests of the plurality of stakeholders when taking business decisions, this duty is performed in a boardroom of individuals appointed and removable by shareholders who owe their duties to the company, the interests of which are the interests of the shareholders as a whole (s 172(1)).

Pluralist arguments faltered on the difficulty inherent in the task of establishing a mechanism of control of directors different from shareholder control. Again, it is premature to comment on the extent to which the new directors' duties will bring about a change for the good of society in the way directors make decisions. The extent to which greater emphasis will be placed on the interests of non-shareholder stakeholders, including 'the community and the environment' (s 172(1)(d)), and 'the likely consequences of any decisions in the long term' (s 172(1)(a)), remains to be observed.

Keeping legal regulation to the minimum necessary to safeguard stakeholders' legitimate interests

Economic theory has provided the principal perspective and methodology for assessing the effect of company law on commercial behaviour and predicting the effects of proposed changes to company law. The Law Commission embraced this perspective in the late 1990s. It analysed directors' duties from the starting point of the need to justify laws that interfere in and restrict business behaviour. It identified the need to strike a balance between 'necessary regulation and freedom for directors to make business decisions' as a key principle to be applied by policy makers in considering how to reform company law and it identified 'graduated regulation of conflicts of interest' and 'efficient disclosure' as two further headline principles to guide reform of the law of directors duties.

11.2.4 Have the general duties been codified?

Deliberate changes to case-based general duties

Although the general duties of directors set out in the 2006 Act are *in large part* a statutory statement of the duties as developed by the courts, those duties have been deliberately amended in a number of ways. It is not just a case of the common law and equitable duties having been stated in the statute.

Relationship between the Act and the articles

The Act has changed the respective roles of the statutory provisions and the articles of a company in the regulation of directors' self-interest, particularly in relation to the declaration of interest of a director in a company contract (see Chapter 12 below). Note that a company's articles remain an important component in determining the procedures required to protect directors from liability for breach of duty. Section 180(4) expressly provides that the general duties are not infringed by anything done (or omitted) by the directors in accordance with provision for dealing with conflicts of interest in the company's articles.

Implementation of the self-interest duties (ss 175–177) was delayed for a year beyond implementation of the other general duties, to 1 October 2008, to allow companies time to make changes to their articles to reflect and supplement the new duties. Directors' duties cannot simply be determined by reading the statutory provisions – the articles of the company must also be considered.

Do the statutory duties replace the case-based duties?

Section 170(3) appears to state that the general duties in the Act *replace* case-based directors' duties.

SECTION

'The general duties are based on certain common law rules and equitable principles as they apply in relation to directors and have effect in place of those rules and principles as regards the duties owed to a company by a director'.

The precise legal position is much more complicated than this and, rather than clarifying and making the law more accessible, it may turn out that the statutory statement has added a further layer to the legal analysis of a given situation to determine whether or not a director is in breach of duty and, if so, the remedies available.

First, a close reading of s 170(3) shows that the statutory duties have replaced 'certain common law rules and equitable principles'. It does not state that 'all' common law rules and equitable principles have been replaced. This indicates an understandable reluctance on the part of the reformers to inadvertently overlook a case-based duty. Unfortunately, it leaves the door open for obscure common law rules and equitable principles to be resurrected based on the argument that they are not the rules or principles on which the statutory duties were based.

Second, the meaning of the general duties is still to be found in case law (s 170(4)).

SECTION

'The general duties shall be interpreted and applied in the same way as common law rules or equitable principles, and regard shall be had to the corresponding common law rules and equitable principles in interpreting and applying the general duties.'

Third, the remedies for breach of duty have not been stated in the statute, rather, s 178(1) provides that the remedies are the same as for the corresponding common law rule or equitable principle.

'The consequences of breach (or threatened breach) of sections 171–177 are the same as would apply if the corresponding common law rule or equitable principle applied.'

Authorisation and ratification

Even if we assume that the general duties are a clear statement of the main duties of directors, the 2006 Act has not sought to comprehensively state the law relating to the giving of authority or ratification by the company of behaviour that would otherwise be a breach of duty. The general duties are stated in s 180(4) to have effect 'subject to any rule of law enabling the company to give authority, specifically or generally, for anything to be done (or omitted) by the directors, or any of them, that would otherwise be a breach of duty'.

This apparently reasonable subsection introduces uncertainty because the rules governing when a company may give authority for what would otherwise be a breach of duty are unclear. The manner in which a company may *ratify* a breach of duty by a director is clearly set out in s 239. Unfortunately, s 239 ends on a note of uncertainty, as it subordinates the operation of ratification provided for in the section to 'any other enactment or rule of law imposing additional requirements for valid ratification or any rule of law as to acts that are incapable of being ratified by the company'.

Consequently, the Act does not make it clear, nor is the law accessible to determine, whether or not a director may be sued for breach of duty in circumstances in which the director seeks to establish that he has been authorised to behave as he did, or subsequently excused.

11.3 To whom do directors owe their duties?

11.3.1 Directors' duties are owed to the company

The statutory general duties of directors are owed by each individual director to the company (s 170(1)). Consequently, any action for breach of duty vests in the company (*Foss v Harbottle* (1843) 2 Hare 461, considered in Chapter 14). Without more, a director does not owe duties to individual shareholders or to other stakeholders in the company (*Percival v Wright* [1902] 2 Ch 421).

When considering the *self-interest duties* of directors it is sufficient to require the director to act in the interests of 'the company' as the company's interests can be contrasted with the directors' own self-interest or the interest of a person external to the company. When considering the *management duties* of directors, however, it becomes necessary to penetrate further and ask what is meant by the interests of the company.

11.3.2 Enlightened shareholder value

The interests of the shareholders as a whole are the paramount consideration of the directors. This is captured in s 172 which requires directors to act in the way they consider to be most likely to promote the success of the company 'for the benefit of its members as a whole' (members meaning shareholders for our purposes). In performing this duty, however, the directors must have regard to the interests of other stakeholders, particularly those listed in s 172(1).

enlightened shareholder value

the doctrine enshrined in the Companies Act 2006, s 172, whereby although directors must act in the way they consider, in good faith, would be most likely to promote the success of the company for the benefit of its members as a whole, in performing this duty they must have regard to the interests of other stakeholders and the long term consequences of any decision

'A director of a company must act in the way he considers, in good faith, would be most likely to promote the success of the company for the benefit of its members as a whole, and in doing so have regard (amongst other matters) to –

(a) the likely consequences of any decision in the long term,

(b) the interests of the company's employees,

(c) the need to foster the company's business relationships with suppliers, customers and others,

(d) the impact of the company's operations on the community and the environment,

(e) the desirability of the company maintaining a reputation for high standards of business conduct, and

(f) the need to act fairly as between members of the company.'

The requirement to take various interests into account as part of acting for the benefit of the shareholders as a whole enshrines the concept of 'enlightened shareholder value'. This is illustrated in Figure 11.2.

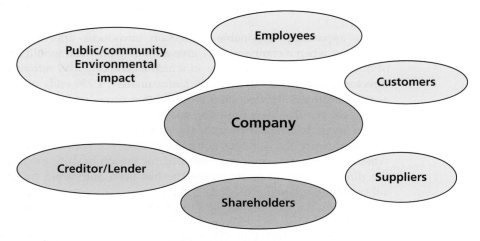

Figure 11.2 Enlightened shareholder value and s 172

11.3.3 The interests of creditors

The extent to which directors are required to take the interests of creditors into account when they are managing the company is a very important issue. Creditors are not listed alongside other obvious stakeholders in s 172(1). Instead, s 172(3) makes the duty to promote the success of the company 'for the benefit of its members as a whole' subject to 'any enactment or rule of law requiring directors, in certain circumstances, to consider or act in the interests of creditors of the company'.

The interests of creditors predominate when there is no residual wealth left in the company, that is, when shareholder equity has been dissipated, usually by poor trading (see Chapters 7 and 8). At that point, the economic owners of the company are the creditors: all the company has it owes to them. As the financial health of a company deteriorates, the directors need to increasingly focus on the interests of the creditors when they take decisions because the interests of the company become increasingly aligned with the interests of its creditors (*Facia Footwear Ltd v Hinchcliffe* [1998] 1 BCLC 218).

At the relevant point when the duty becomes 'creditor regarding', be it on insolvency (*West Mercia Safetywear v Dodd* (1988) 4 BCC 30), or at some point before insolvency, such as when the company is 'doubtfully solvent' (*Brady v Brady* [1988] BCLC 20 (CA)) (the courts have not been able to agree on the point at which the need to prioritise the interests of creditors is triggered), it is not a question of the directors owing a duty to its creditors, the duty remains owed to the company. The duty simply needs to be performed with different priorities in mind. The duty remains enforceable against the directors only by the company but note that the shareholders cannot ratify what would otherwise be a breach of duty (*Sycotex Pty Ltd v Balser* (1993) 13 ACSR 766).

The common law and equitable principles requiring directors, in certain circumstances, to consider or act in the interests of creditors, preserved by s 172(3), have not had to be developed in case law in recent years due to the enactment of s 214 of the Insolvency Act 1986. Section 214 applies when a company is being wound-up. It exposes directors to court orders to contribute to the assets of the company if knowing, or in circumstances in which they ought to have known, that the company had no reasonable prospect of not going into insolvent liquidation, they continued to trade or otherwise took steps not in the interests of creditors. Section 214 and other protections for creditors on a winding-up are considered in Chapter 16.

QUOTATION

'[T]he implementation of the allegedly ineffective wrongful trading liability that has not yet matched up to its expectations highlights the need to reassess common law duties concerning creditors in the United Kingdom. The commonly used term "duty to creditors" is a misnomer as fiduciary duties do not provide either directors with clear guidelines with regard to economical decisions, or creditors with directly enforceable claims. The UK duty to creditors provides only mitigated creditor protection by sanctioning the misappropriation of company funds and other serious opportunistic behaviour, although British company and insolvency law seems to be well equipped to deal with this type of conduct: for instance, the rules on undervalue transactions and preferential payments (s.238, 239 IA 86) efficiently redeem commercially inadequate transfers or endowments of company funds.

Though it is arguable whether directors should, when a company remains solvent yet financially instable, prioritise creditor interests when two courses of action are available, courts and legislators in both Germany and the United Kingdom have chosen not to pursue such an approach in order not to unduly restrict managerial discretion. Academic attention in both jurisdictions has thus shifted towards the duty of care and skill as a means of creditor protection … In particular the consultation of professional advisers and the initiation of directors' and shareholders' meetings to review the company's situation at an early stage in the company's decline may, *de lege lata* and *ferenda*, offer an effective back door to escape responsibility in both jurisdictions. This approach is both feasible and superior to redirecting fiduciary duties to creditors as directors are provided with hands-on recommendations and courts with straightforward criteria to evaluate liability.'

Lotz, S, 'Directors' duties with regard to creditors in German and UK (core) company law' (2011) 22 ICCLR 264 at 269 (footnotes omitted).

KEY FACTS

Directors' duties: general principles	
Legislative reform of directors' duties	
Statutory regulation of particular transactions has existed since 1928	
Common law and fiduciary duties were first stated as statutory General Duties of Directors in the Companies Act 2006	
Directors' duties are owed to the company, s 170	
Directors must promote the success of the company 'for the benefit of its members as a whole'.	s 172
When making decisions directors are required to have regard to its long-term consequences, the interests of employees, suppliers, customers and others, the impact on the community and the environment, the desirability of maintaining high standards of business conduct and the need to act fairly between members of the company.	s 172(1) 'enlightened shareholder value'
When the company is approaching insolvency directors must prioritise the interests of creditors because their interests are the interests of the company.	*Facia Footwear v Hinchcliffe* (1998) *Brady v Brady* (1988)

11.4 Management duties of directors

The duties directors are required to discharge when managing their companies may be divided into general and specific duties. The main focus of this section is the general duties. Specific duties are addressed, briefly, in the final part.

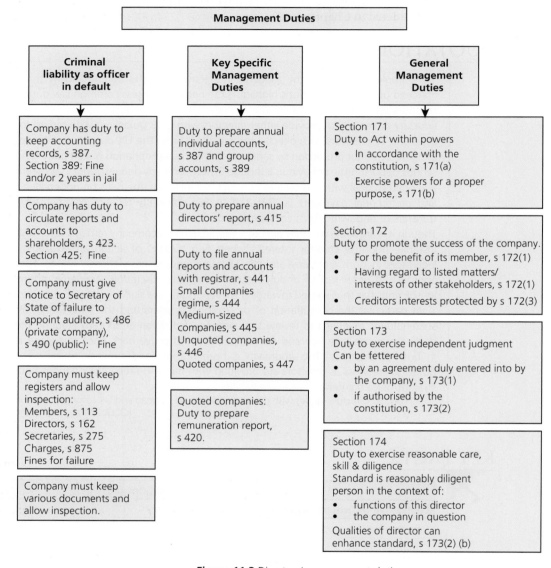

Figure 11.3 Directors' management duties

11.4.1 General management duties

Duty to Act within powers (s 171)

SECTION

'171 Duty to act within powers
A director of a company must—
(a) act in accordance with the company's constitution, and
(b) only exercise powers for the purposes for which they are conferred.'

The first general duty set out in the 2006 Act contains two limbs. The first limb, the duty to act in accordance with the company's constitution, places any director who acts outside his *actual* powers in breach of duty. A third party may be entitled to rely on ostensible authority of a director to enforce a contract against a company. This does not preclude an action for breach of duty being brought by the company against the director. Also, s 40 may operate to make an agreement binding on the company when the directors have acted outside their powers. Section 40 does *not* however, affect any liability incurred by a director by reason of exceeding his powers, a point confirmed in s 40(5) (see section 10.5.1).

Example

A company's articles require loans in excess of £200,000 to be approved in advance by the shareholders. Without shareholder approval the board unanimously resolves to enter into a loan with a third party for £500,000 and the loan is entered into. Each member of the board is in breach of s 171.

The second limb of s 171 is based on *Re Smith & Fawcett* [1942] Ch 304, *per* Greene MR:

JUDGMENT

'[Directors] must exercise their discretion *bona fide* in what they consider – not what a court may consider – is in the interests of the company, and not for any collateral purpose.'

The duty to exercise powers for a proper purpose has been particularly relevant in relation to directors issuing shares (*Hogg v Cramphorn Ltd* [1967] Ch 254 and *Howard Smith v Ampol Petroleum Ltd* [1974] AC 821 (PC)), but is not confined to such decisions. It has been applied, for example, to the power to refuse to register a transfer of shares (*Re Smith & Fawcett Ltd* [1942] Ch 304 (CA), and to the power to enter into a management agreement (*Lee Panavision v Lee Lighting Ltd* [1992] BCLC 22 (CA)).

CASE EXAMPLE

Hogg v Cramphorn Ltd [1967] Ch 254

In an effort to forestall a takeover bid it considered not to be in the interests of the company, the board of directors of Cramphorn Ltd issued shares with special voting rights to trustees of a scheme set up for the benefit of employees. Held: Even though it was accepted that the board had acted in good faith and the directors believed it was in the best interests of the company not to be taken over by Mr Baxter, the power to issue shares had been exercised for an improper purpose, the primary purpose having been to prevent Mr Baxter's bid from succeeding. (Note that the court adjourned proceedings to give the shareholders opportunity to ratify the breach by ordinary resolution, which it did. The new shares were not, and could not have been voted.)

The irrelevance of the finding in *Hogg v Cramphorn* (1967) that the directors were acting *bona fide* in what they believed to be the best interests of the company demonstrated that the duty to exercise powers for a proper purpose was different from the duty (as it then was) to act *bona fide* in what they consider to be the interests of the company. There is an objective element to the court's assessment of what is a proper purpose and what is not. How the courts approach the task of determining what is proper and what is not was addressed by Lord Wilberforce in *Howard Smith v Ampol* [1974] AC 821 (PC).

CASE EXAMPLE

Howard Smith v Ampol Petroleum Ltd [1974] AC 821 (PC)

Rival takeover offers were received for Miller Ltd. Miller's board of directors favoured the bid of Howard Smith but it was unlikely to succeed as the other bidder, Ampol, already owned

55 per cent of the shares in Miller Ltd. The board issued shares to Howard Smith with two purposes in mind: (1) to provide Miller with capital, which it needed, and (2) to convert Ampol's stake to a minority interest. The directors were not motivated by self-interest or the desire to retain control. Held: On the evidence, the *substantial purpose* for which the power was exercised was to convert Ampol's interest in the company from a majority to a minority shareholding. The power to allot share had therefore been improperly exercised and the allotment of shares was set aside.

In the course of his judgment Lord Wilberforce set out the following steps a court should take when determining whether or not there has been a breach of what is now s 171(b):

- Ascertain, on a fair view, the nature of the power.
- Define the limits within which it may be exercised.
- Examine the substantial purpose for which it was exercised.
- Reach a conclusion whether the exercise was proper or not.

JUDGMENT

'[T]o reach a conclusion whether th[e] purpose was proper or not ... [the court] will necessarily give credit to the *bona fide* opinion of the directors, if such is found to exist, and will respect their judgement as to matters of management; having done this, the ultimate conclusion has to be as to the side of a fairly broad line on which the case falls.'

Duty to promote the success of the company (s 172)

The s 172 statutory duty to promote the success of the company is set out above at section 11.3. Like the s 171 duty to act within powers, it is based on *Re Smith & Fawcett* [1942] Ch 304. In that case the court spoke in terms of directors acting *bona fide* in what they consider to be, not what a court may consider to be, in the interests of the company. Section 172, however, is couched in different language, stating that directors must act in the way they consider, in good faith, would be most likely to promote the success of the company. The section also includes guidance as to how directors should go about performing the duty (see section 11.3 above).

Focusing on the basis on which courts will find a breach of this duty, pre-2006 case law established that the court will *not* ask whether or not the decision is objectively in the interests of the company: the duty is subjective (*Regentcrest plc v Cohen* [2001] BCC 494 (Ch), a point reflected in the language of s 172 and endorsed in recent cases (see *Re Southern Counties Fresh Foods Ltd* [2011] EWHC 1370, *Cobden Investments Ltd v RWM Langport Ltd* [2008] EWHC 2810 and *Re West Coast Capital (Lios) Ltd* [2008] CSOH 72 *per* Lord Glennie).

In some circumstances, however, the courts have introduced an objective dimension into consideration of whether or not the duty has been breached. For example, where there is evidence that a director did not stop to consider the interests of the company, there is an objective 'floor' to the duty. If no intelligent and honest person in the position of the director of the company concerned could in the circumstances have reasonably believed he was acting in the interests of the company, the courts will find that the duty has been breached. Pennycuick J stated this test clearly in *Charterbridge Corporation Ltd v Lloyds Bank Ltd* [1970] Ch 62:

JUDGMENT

'The proper test, I think ... must be whether an intelligent and honest man in the position of a director of the company concerned, could, in the whole of the existing circumstances have reasonably believed that... [his actions] ... were for the benefit of the company.'

Whether or not this test survives the enactment of s 172 is unclear. Section 170(4) which states that the duties are to be interpreted and applied in the same way as common law rules or equitable principles and that regard should be had to the corresponding common law rules and equitable principles in interpreting and applying the duties suggests that it will.

Similarly unclear is the impact of the introduction of the non-exhaustive list into the section. If directors have not taken into account the various interests listed in s 172, will a court hold the directors to be in breach of s 172 on the basis of a procedural failing notwithstanding them being in good faith and considering that they have acted in the way most likely to promote the success of the company? There is evidence boards are being advised that a safe practice to avoid the potential for procedural-based liability pursuant to this section is to minute that the matters listed in s 172, and other relevant factors, have been considered before a major decision is entered into, bringing about the 'tick box' defensive board room practices it was hoped to avoid. The requirement for directors to take into account the matters listed in s 172, looked at from a different perspective, can be seen as providing boards with a defence to actions against directors for breach of s 172 instituted by shareholders convinced board decisions have not served their interests.

Judicial consideration of s 172 arose in an interesting context in *R (People & Planet) v HM Treasury* [2009] EWHC 3020, an application for permission to bring judicial review proceedings against HM Treasury relating to policy of HM Treasury in relation to the management of the government's interest in the Royal Bank of Scotland. In refusing permission, the court adopted a non-interventionist approach to management policy and decision-making by directors.

Finally, a controversial aspect of the duty to act *bona fide* in the interests of the company that now attaches to s 172 is the extent to which the duty imposes on directors a duty to disclose breaches of fiduciary duty. It is settled that if he considers it to be in the interests of the company to know, a director is under a duty to disclose to the company a breach of fiduciary duty by another director. In *Item Software (UK) Ltd v Fassihi* [2005] 2 BCLC 91 (CA), the court went further and held that a director was in breach of his duty to the company by failing to disclose *his own* earlier breach of fiduciary duty.

On the facts, the company was seeking to recover damages arising out of the company losing a contract as the result (it argued) of a director having sought to redirect the contract to himself. The damages were held not to have flowed from the initial breach of duty by the director, but would be payable if the director had been under a duty to disclose his earlier breach to the company. The Court of Appeal upheld the first instance judge's finding that the directors' failure to disclose his earlier wrong-doing was a breach for which damages were payable.

The need to plead this additional breach of duty will arise only in unusual cases as the first breach will ordinarily be sufficient to secure the required remedy. Should it be necessary, it seems correct that if a director is aware of facts that he knows it is in the interests of the company to know, he is under a duty to disclose them as part of his duty to promote the success of the company, including facts relating to his own conduct.

Duty to exercise independent judgment (s 173)

SECTION

'173 **Duty to exercise independent judgment**
(1) A director of a company must exercise independent judgment.
(2) This duty is not infringed by his acting—
  (a) in accordance with an agreement duly entered into by the company that restricts the future exercise of discretion by its directors, or
  (b) in a way authorised by the company's constitution.'

Case law establishes that directors are prohibited from fettering their discretion in the exercise of their powers, meaning that they must not enter into agreements with third parties as to how they will exercise their discretion. Whilst s 173 is based on this duty, it is not clear how far the restatement of the duty in positive terms, 'must exercise independent judgment', might have changed the common law position. The important exception to the prohibition at common law, which is captured in s 173(2)(a), which must be read in conjunction with s 172.

The result is that if a director acts in accordance with a contract binding on the company and thereby does not exercise independent discretion, no breach of s 173 occurs. Rather, a breach of s 172 may have occurred. If the directors who caused the company to enter into the contract did not consider, in good faith, entry into the contract, and the implicit fettering of future directors' discretion the contract entails, would be most likely to promote the success of the company.

As the Court of Appeal pointed out in *Fulham Football Club Ltd v Cabra Estates plc* [1994] 1 BCLC 363, to preclude directors from making contracts by which they bind themselves to the future exercise of their powers in a particular manner, when the contract taken as a whole is manifestly for the benefit of the company, would prevent companies from entering into contracts which are commercially beneficial to them. The position is summed up in the headnote to *Thorby v Goldberg* (1964) 112 CLR 597, a High Court of Australia case:

JUDGMENT

'If, when a contract is negotiated on behalf of a company, the directors *bona fide* think it in the interests of the company as a whole that the transaction should be entered into and carried into effect they may bind themselves by the contract to do whatever is necessary to effectuate it.'

The issue of exercising independent judgment can be particularly difficult for a nominee director who, without more, must not simply follow the instructions of the shareholder who has appointed him. Provided the interests of the appointing shareholder and the company coincide, no practical difficulty arises. When the interests of the shareholder who has appointed them and the company do not coincide, many nominee directors fail to appreciate that, as a member of the board, they are required to exercise independent judgment.

In *Scottish Co-op Wholesale Society Ltd v Meyer* [1959] AC 324 (HL), the Scottish Co-op Wholesale Society Ltd (SCWS) formed a private company with Meyer & Lucas (the defendants). Meyer and Lucas were the managing directors and SCWS appointed three of its own directors to the new company's board. SCWS commenced a business in competition with the company, and in the context of an action based on the affairs of the company having been conducted in a manner oppressive to some part of the members (the predecessor section to a s 994 unfair prejudice petition), Lord Denning commenting on the nominee directors, stated, 'They probably thought that "as nominees" of the co-operative society their first duty was to the co-operative society. In this they were wrong'.

Lord Denning again addressed the duty of a nominee director in *Boulting v ACTT* [1963] 2 QB 606:

JUDGMENT

'[T]ake a nominee director, that is, a director of a company who is nominated by a large shareholder to represent his interests. There is nothing wrong in it. It is done every day. Nothing wrong, that is, so long as the director is left free to exercise his best judgment in the interests of the company which he serves. But if he is put upon terms that he is bound to act in the affairs of the company in accordance with the directions of his patron, it is beyond doubt unlawful.'

Section 173(2)(b) appears to be particularly pertinent to nominee directors as it contemplates a director being able to avoid breach of s 173 if the company's constitution permits him not to exercise independent judgement. This seems to permit language in the articles, or an appropriate special resolution, providing for a nominee director to represent his nominating shareholder and authorising him to represent the interests of that shareholder. As much as this could lift from a nominee director the threat of being found in breach of s 173, the general duties are cumulative, and there is no similar way around the duty in s 172, to act in good faith to promote the success of the company for the benefit of its shareholders as a whole. Consequently, notwithstanding s 173(2)(b), where the interests of a nominating shareholder diverge from the interests of the company, the nominee director remains in a commercially unrealistic and consequently legally precarious position.

A further point arising out of the positive formulation of this duty is its effect on the ability of directors to delegate the exercise of their powers so that another person exercises the discretion or judgement which, in the absence of delegation of the power, would need to be exercised by the director. The common law principle is that a person to whom a power has been granted cannot delegate that power unless the grant empowers him to do so (*Cartmell's Case* (1874) LR 9). The articles grant the directors their powers (see Model Article 3) and invariably grant them the power to delegate any of their powers (see Model Article 5). Delegation is essential for the operation of large companies and s 173(2)(b) indicates that if authorised by the company's constitution, delegation will not, in itself, be an infringement of s 173. When deciding to delegate, selecting the delegate and supervising and reviewing the performance of the delegate, it is important for directors to act in accordance with all of their duties, including the need to comply with s 172 (above) and to act with the care and skill required by s 174 (below). In large companies, with multiple levels of delegation, this will require the board to satisfy itself that there are adequate supervision and review systems in place at all levels in the company.

Finally, the positive formulation of the duty also raises the question of the right of directors to rely on the judgement of others in taking decisions. Directors can and in many cases must take advice from experts before taking decisions. This will not be a breach of s 173 provided the director considers the advice and then, having taken the advice into account, makes his own decision. Again, other duties come into play when the director is deciding whether or not advice is required and when selecting advisors.

Duty to exercise reasonable care, skill and diligence (s 174)

SECTION

'174   Duty to exercise reasonable care, skill and diligence
(1) A director of a company must exercise reasonable care, skill and diligence.
(2) This means the care, skill and diligence that would be exercised by a reasonably diligent person with—
   (a) the general knowledge, skill and experience that may reasonably be expected of a person carrying out the functions carried out by the director in relation to the company, and
   (b) the general knowledge, skill and experience that the director has.'

The common law standard of care, skill and diligence owed by directors to their companies was developed before the modern law of negligence evolved. The degree of attendance to the affairs of the company required was negligible. In *Re Cardiff Saving Bank, Marquis of Bute* [1892] 2 Ch 100, for example, a director of a bank attended only one board meeting in the 39 years for which he was president yet was held not to be in breach of duty. The standard of care and skill required was largely subjective. In his first instance judgment in *Re City Equitable Fire Insurance Co Ltd* [1925] Ch 407, Romer J reviewed the authorities and stated that a director is not required to exhibit a greater degree of skill than may reasonably be expected from a person of his knowledge and experience. Although this case was not overruled in the years leading up to the enactment of the 2006 Act, courts had begun to work around it, preferring the statement of duty set out in s 214 of the Insolvency Act 1986.

CASE EXAMPLE

Re D'Jan (of London) Ltd [1994] 1 BCLC 561

Mr D'Jan, a director of a small company, failed, before signing it, to read an insurance proposal form that had been filled out by the company's insurance broker. Held (by Hoffmann LJ sitting in the Chancery Division at first instance): The duty of a director at common law is accurately stated in s 214 of the Insolvency Act 1986. The document was a very simple document asking a few questions that Mr D'Jan was the best person to answer and in failing to read the form he did not show reasonable diligence and was therefore in breach of his duty to the company. The court has a discretionary power [now s 1157 of the Companies Act 2006] to relieve a director wholly or in part from liability for breach of duty if the court considers he acted honestly and reasonably and ought fairly to be excused and that section contemplates that conduct may be reasonable for the purposes of the section despite amounting to lack of care at common law. His breach was not gross, it could have happened to any busy man, although this is not enough to excuse it. At the relevant time the company was solvent and prosperous and the company is and was owned by Mr D'Jan and his wife. Mr D'Jan was excused for some but not all of the liability.

This was not the first case in which Hoffmann LJ had chosen not to apply the *Re City Equitable* subjective standard of care. His approach is now reflected in s 174. The standard described in s 174(2)(a) is essentially an objective standard of care. Although it has been described as a 'universal standard', the standard is applied to the facts of each particular case (*Re Barings plc (No 5)* [1999] 1 BCLC 433, see below). In particular:

- the functions/role in the management of the company to be carried out by the particular director must be taken into account;
- the nature of its business and size of the particular company in question must be taken into account;
- the actual knowledge, skill and experience of the director can only enhance the level of care, skill and diligence required to satisfy the duty (s 174(2)(b)).

This final point is important and follows from the fact that subsections 174(2)(a) and (b) are linked by 'and' so that they are cumulative. The actual knowledge, skill and experience of a director cannot be relied on to undermine the objective standard established for a reasonably diligent person by s 174(2)(a). An experienced business accountant, for example, will be expected to show a higher level of skill in relation to financial matters than a person who does not hold himself out as having financial skills. A financial director will be expected to have the special skills expected of a person in that role (*Re Brian D Pierson (Contractors) Ltd* [2001] 1 BCLC 275).

Note that Section 174 is modelled on s 214(4) of the Insolvency Act 1986 which deals with wrongful trading by directors. In addition to wrongful trading cases providing guidance on the application of this duty, petitions under what is now s 994 (see Chapter 14) and cases involving disqualification of directors pursuant to the Company Directors Disqualification Act 1986 (see Chapter 13) often involve assessment of whether or not a director has discharged this duty. In particular, the duty of care skill and diligence was developed and clarified in the director disqualification case of *Re Barings plc (No 5)* [1999] 1 BCLC 433 (confirmed on appeal [2000] 1 BCLC 523 (CA)). The case is one of a number of cases resulting from the unauthorised trading of Nick Leeson, an employee of a subsidiary of Barings plc, which drove one of the bank's principal operating subsidiaries into insolvency. (Note, that although relevant to the question of disqualification, a finding of breach of duty of care, skill and diligence is not sufficient to establish a case for disqualification.)

CASE EXAMPLE

Re Barings plc (No 5), Secretary of State for Trade and Industry v Baker [1999] 1 BCLC 433

Disqualification orders were sought by the Secretary of State for Trade and Industry against former directors of a principal operating subsidiary of Barings plc based on their failure to institute and monitor appropriate internal management controls which resulted in Nick Leeson, a trader in its Singapore office, having sole control of both the settlement or 'back' office and the dealing or 'front' offices of the bank in Singapore. This situation continued notwithstanding an internal audit proposal that the bank should separate the roles. The issue before the court was whether the conduct of the directors was such as to make them 'unfit to be concerned in the management of a company' for the purposes of s 6 of the Company Directors Disqualification Act 1986. Held: The directors had failed properly to monitor and control Leeson's activities even though they had management responsibility for those activities. They had failed to (1) investigate a fictitious transaction discovered by internal auditors, (2) perform any proper examination of the subsidiary's profitability, (3) remove responsibility for both the front and back offices from Leeson and (4) ensure that the trading positions in Singapore were properly managed. Parker J held that the directors were incompetent to such a degree as to make them unfit to be directors and disqualified them for six years.

In the course of his judgment, Parker J stated 'each director owes duties to the company to inform himself about its affairs and to join with his co-directors in supervising and controlling them'. He summarised the relevant duties of directors:

JUDGMENT

'In summary, the following general propositions can, in my judgment, be derived from the authorities to which I was referred in relation to the duties of directors:
(i) Directors have, both collectively and individually, a continuing duty to acquire and maintain a sufficient knowledge and understanding of the company's business to enable them properly to discharge their duties as directors.
(ii) Whilst directors are entitled (subject to the articles of association of the company) to delegate particular functions to those below them in the management chain, and to trust their competence and integrity to a reasonable extent, the exercise of the power of delegation does not absolve a director from the duty to supervise the discharge of the delegated functions.
(iii) No rule of universal application can be formulated as to the duty referred to in (ii) above. The extent of the duty, and the question whether it has been discharged, must depend on the facts of each particular case, including the director's role in the management of the company'.

11.4.2 Key specific management duties

The 2006 Act sometimes imposes specific duties directly on directors and sometimes imposes specific obligations on the company. Where obligations imposed on the company are backed by criminal liability of both the company and its officers (a term that includes directors, s 1121(2)), they incentivise officers of the company to ensure that the obligations are fulfilled. These obligations therefore serve a similar function to duties. Criminal liability for default is not absolute: directors will only be liable for default if they are personally in default.

Key specific management duties and company obligations are referenced in Figures 11.1 and 11.3 above and can be looked up in the Companies Act 2006. They are touched upon in Chapter 17 in which the corporate governance role of transparency is considered.

Directors' management duties	
General management duties	
Duty to act within powers: Must act in accordance with the company's constitution Must exercise powers for a proper purpose	s 171 See Chapter 10 to determine whether or not a company is bound (s 40) *Hogg v Cramphorn* (1967) *Howard Smith v Ampol* (1974)
Duty to promote the success of the company: Incorporates enlightened shareholder value and is subjective.	s 172 *Regentcrest plc v Cohen (2001)* *Charterbridge Corporation v Lloyds Bank Ltd* (1970)
Duty to exercise independent judgment: Directors must not enter into agreements as to how to exercise their powers unless entry into the agreement is for the benefit of the company Nominee directors are in a difficult position but must not simply follow the instructions of his nominator	s 173 *Fulham Football Club Ltd v Cabra Estates Ltd* (1994) *Boulting v ACTT* (1963)
Duty to act with reasonable care, skill and diligence: Statutory duty is stricter than older common law cases indicated Duty is based on s 214 of the Insolvency Act 1986	s 174 Compare: *Re Cardiff Savings Bank, Marquis de Bute* (1892) and *Re D'jan (of London) Ltd* (1994)
Specific management duties and obligations	
In addition to specific duties imposed on directors, specific obligations are imposed on the company with criminal sanctions for officers (which term includes directors) in default	See Figure 11.3

SUMMARY

Legislative reform and codification of directors' duties

▦ Directors' general duties were developed by the courts until the Companies Act 2006 reduced them to statutory general duties.

▦ The general duties are supplemented by provisions of the Act regulating particular types of arrangement between a director and the company: substantial non-cash asset transactions (ss 190–196), loans and similar arrangements (ss 197–214); long-term service contracts (s 188) and payments for loss of office (s 215).

To whom do directors owe their duties?

▦ Directors' duties are owed to *the company* and to no other person.

Enlightened shareholder value (ESV)

▦ ESV is designed to encourage directors to take a long-term view of the success of the company, taking into account the interests of stakeholders other than shareholders, but, ultimately, promoting the success of the company *for the benefit of the shareholders as a whole* (s 172).

▦ Four general duties are particularly relevant when directors take management decisions:

  ● Duty to act within powers and to exercise powers for a proper purpose (s 171). For example, the power to issue shares should be exercised to raise capital, not to defeat a takeover.

- Duty to promote the success of the company (s 172). Stakeholder interests should be taken into account but ultimately a director must act in the way he considers in good faith would be most likely to promote the success of the company for the benefit the shareholders. Courts consider the belief of the director, not the quality of his business judgement.
- Duty to exercise independent judgment (s 173). Appropriate delegation is permitted and essential in large companies. The emphasis is then on directors ensuring management systems are in place to supervise and control delegates.
- Duty to exercise reasonable skill, care and diligence (s 174). This duty now imposes an objectively assessed standard below which no director should fall and more is expected of those with particular skills and experience.

Specific management duties and obligations

- Directors must ensure that the company keeps registers and accounting records, that accounts and reports are prepared in accordance with the Act, filed and circulated as required by the Act, and comply with numerous other specific provisions of the Companies Act 2006.

ACTIVITY

Problem–question exercise

A Question

Join Ltd was registered in 2000. Its shareholders are Arc plc and Erin, each of whom own five × £1 fully paid shares. The articles of Join Ltd provide that Arc plc and Erin are each entitled to appoint two directors and the directors shall then appoint a fifth director. Arc plc appoints John and Gary and Erin appoints herself and Helen to be directors. Paul is appointed to be the fifth director. Join Ltd's articles also provide that any new shares may only be issued if the issue has been approved in advance by special resolution.

Join Ltd is phenomenally successful. In 2008 it is valued at £10 million. It wishes to expand and needs £10 million cash. At a board meeting attended by all directors a board resolution is proposed to issue £10 million × £1 shares to Parc plc, the parent company of Arc plc, at an issue price of £1. John and Gary have been told by Arc plc to support the resolution. Arc Plc has also paid Helen £10,000 in return for Helen agreeing to support the resolution, which she does. The resolution is passed by John, Gary and Helen and the shares are issued. Join Ltd has its £10 million but Paul and Erin are outraged. What, if any, breaches of directors' duties have occurred? (You may wish to take an advance look at section 13.2.2 to enable you to produce a more complete answer.)

B Working through the question

Look again at the problem question exercise at the end of Chapter 11 to remind yourself how to approach problem-type questions. Using the table set out in section D of that exercise, work through the suggested steps and questions in the left hand column of that table to develop an answer to the question above.

Further reading

Articles

Ahern, D, 'Directors' duties, dry ink and the accessibility agenda' (2012) 128 LQR 114.
Boros, E, 'The duties of nominee and multiple directors', Part 1 (1989) 10 Comp Law 211; Part 2 (1990) 11 Comp Law 6.
Crutchfield, P, 'Nominee directors: the law and commercial reality' (1991) 12 Comp Law 136.
Davies, P, 'Directors' Creditor-Regarding Duties in Respect of Trading Decisions Taken in the Vicinity of Insolvency' [2006] EBOR 301.

Fisher, D, 'The Enlightened Shareholder – Leaving Stakeholders in the Dark: will section 172(1) of the Companies Act 2006 make directors consider the impact of their decisions on third parties?' (2009) 20 International Company and Commercial Law Review 10.

Keay, A, 'Formulating a Framework for Directors' Duties to Creditors: An Entity Maximisation Approach' [2005] CLJ 614.

Keay, A, 'The duty of directors to exercise independent judgment' (2008) 29 Comp Law 290.

Keay, A, 'Section 172(1) of the Companies Act 2006: An Interpretation and Assessment' (2007) 28 Company Lawyer 106.

Keay, A, 'Ascertaining the Corporate Objective: An Entity Maximisation and Sustainability Model' (2008) 71 Modern Law Review 663.

Keay, A, 'Enlightened Shareholder Value, the Reform of the Duties of Company Directors and the Corporate Objective' [2006] Lloyd's Maritime and Commercial Law Quarterly 335.

Kiarie, S, 'At Crossroads: Shareholder Value, Stakeholder Value and Enlightened Shareholder Value: which Road should the United Kingdom Take?' (2006) 17 International Company and Commercial Law Review 329.

Lotz, S, 'Directors' duties with regard to creditors in German and UK (core) company law' (2011) 22 ICCLR 264.

Nakajima, C, 'Whither "enlightened shareholder value"' (2007) 28 Company Lawyer 353.

Sealy, L, '"*Bona fides*" and "proper purposes" in corporate decisions' (1989) 15 Mon UL Rev 265.

Reports

Law Commission, 'Consultation Paper: Company Directors: Regulation Conflicts of Interests and Formulating a Statement of Duties' (1998 No 153).

Law Commission, 'Report: Company Directors: Regulation Conflicts of Interests and Formulating a Statement of Duties' (1999 No 261).

See also further reading at the end of Chapters 12 and 13.

12

Directors' duties: Self-interest duties

AIMS AND OBJECTIVES

After reading this chapter you should be able to:

- Distinguish:
  - a director contracting (or having an interest in a contract with) his company
  - other conflict of interest situations
- Understand the scope and operation of the two general conflict of interest duties:
  - Duty to avoid conflicts of interest (s 175)
  - Duty not to accept benefits from third parties (s 176)
- Identify director/company transactions for which shareholder approval is required
- Identify when a director is required to declare his interest in a transaction to the board of directors
- Recognise that the acts of a director may constitute breach of more than one duty
- Analyse a fact situation and identify:
  - the behaviour of each director involved
  - the directors' duties that may have been breached by each director
  - any statutory provisions governing directors' contracts with the company that may have been contravened

12.1 Introduction

As indicated in the introduction to Chapter 11, this chapter covers two essential parts of our study of directors' duties and the key statutory provisions governing directors contracting with the company, the overall scheme of our study of which is as follows:

- Legislative reform (Chapter 11).
- To whom the duties are owed (Chapter 11).
- Management duties (Chapter 11).
- Self-interest duties (Chapter 12).
- Statutory provisions governing directors' contracts with the company (Chapter 12).
- Remedies and relief for breaches and contraventions (Chapter 13).

'Self-interest duties', as that term is used in this chapter, are the duties imposed on directors primarily to discourage them from acting not only in their own self-interest but also in the interest of any person other than the company, including a person to whom they may also owe a duty. Arguably the duty in s 173 to exercise independent judgment, considered in Chapter 11, would be better placed in this chapter, as a self-interest duty, based on its role in regulating a director faced with duties both to the company and a third party (often the director's nominating shareholder). Its inclusion in the previous chapter, as a management duty, emphasises its role in requiring a director to actually exercise his judgment in the course of management, rather than abdicating responsibility.

The dual function of the duty simply highlights the fact that management duties and self-interest duties are not mutually exclusive categories. Where a director acts in his own self-interest or in the interest of another person to whom he owes a duty, he will very often also be in breach of a management duty. The same is not true in reverse, however; there is not the same likelihood that a breach of management duty will also entail a breach of a self-interest duty.

The essential learning point is that directors' duties are cumulative. A single act can be evidence of breach of a number of different duties. Section 179 states clearly, 'more than one of the general duties may apply in any given case'.

Duties regulating self-interested actions by directors fall into two categories: duties in relation to conflicts of interests and duties in relation to contracting with the company. Each category contains general duties. Additional statutory provisions govern specific types of contracts directors enter into with their companies. An overview of self-interest duties and key statutory provisions governing directors contracting with the company can be seen in Figure 12.1. In this chapter we deal with directors' conflicts of interest before turning to directors contracting with their companies.

12.2 Directors' conflicts of interest

Directors' conflicts of interests are governed by two general duties, the duty to avoid conflicts of interest (s 175) and the duty not to accept benefits from third parties (s 176).

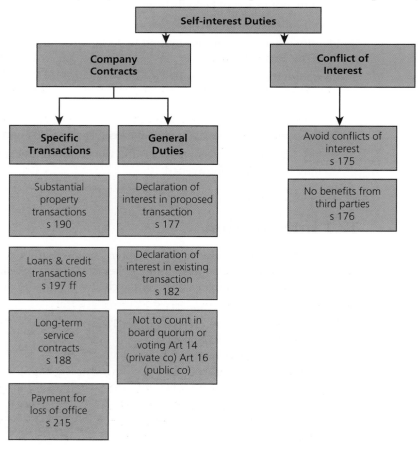

Figure 12.1 Directors' self-interest duties

12.2.1 Duty to avoid conflicts of interest

SECTION

> **'175 Duty to avoid conflicts of interest**
>
> (1) A director of a company must avoid a situation in which he has, or can have, a direct or indirect interest that conflicts, or possibly may conflict, with the interests of the company.
> (2) This applies in particular to the exploitation of any property, information or opportunity (and it is immaterial whether the company could take advantage of the property, information or opportunity).
> (3) This duty does not apply to a conflict of interest arising in relation to a transaction or arrangement with the company.
> (4) This duty is not infringed—
>   (a) if the situation cannot reasonably be regarded as likely to give rise to a conflict of interest; or
>   (b) if the matter has been authorised by the directors.
> (5) Authorisation may be given by the directors—
>   (a) where the company is a private company and nothing in the company's constitution invalidates such authorisation, by the matter being proposed to and authorised by the directors; or
>   (b) where the company is a public company and its constitution includes provision enabling the directors to authorise the matter, by the matter being proposed to and authorised by them in accordance with the constitution.
> (6) The authorisation is effective only if—
>   (a) any requirement as to the quorum at the meeting at which the matter is considered is met without counting the director in question or any other interested director, and
>   (b) the matter was agreed to without their voting or would have been agreed to if their votes had not been counted.
> (7) Any reference in this section to a conflict of interest includes a conflict of interest and duty and a conflict of duties.'

A director of a company is quite likely, at some point in his directorship, to find himself in a situation in which his duty to advance the interests of the company comes into conflict with his personal interest or a duty he owes to another person. An example of a situation with the potential to give rise to a conflict is where a director wishes to take up an opportunity that has been offered to but declined by the company. Other examples are where a director is on two or more boards of directors and one company is a major customer, supplier or competitor of the other.

Multiple directorships are common in the UK, especially amongst non-executive directors of large quoted companies. Consequently, the power to authorise conflict situations and thereby remove them from the statutory duty of a director to avoid a situation in which he has, or can have, a direct or indirect interest that conflicts, or possibly may conflict, with the interests of the company is of great practical importance.

Director authorisation

Section 175 permits the board of directors to authorise conflicts of interest. This is in contrast to the pre-2006 Act law which reserved the power to authorise conflicts of interest to the shareholders unless the articles provided otherwise (which they regularly did). The conditions for availability of s 175(5) authorisation are different for private and public companies.

Private company director authorisation of conflicts

The s 175(5) power of directors to authorise conflicts is automatic for private companies registered on or after 1 October 2008, provided nothing in its articles (constitution) invalidates such authorisation (s 175(5)(a)). Important transitional provisions state that director authorisation will only apply to private companies incorporated before that date where the shareholders have resolved (before, on or after 1 October 2008) that authorisation may be given in accordance with s 175(5) (see para 47(3) of Sched 4 to the Companies Act 2006 Fifth Commencement Order (SI 2007/3495)).

Public company director authorisation of conflicts

The board of a public company is only permitted to authorise conflicts pursuant to s 175(5) if the articles (constitution) include a provision enabling the directors to do so.

Entry into force of s 175 was delayed until 1 October 2008 to enable private companies to consider the matter and, if they so required, amend their articles to provide that director authorisation pursuant to s 175(5) was *not* permitted. Public companies, on the other hand, were to consider providing in their articles that directors may authorise conflicts pursuant to s 175(5).

Conditions for effective director authorisation

Section 175(6) governs the conditions of effective director authorisation. Any requirement as to the quorum at the meeting at which the matter is considered must be met *without* counting the director in question or any other interested director, and the matter must be agreed to *without* their voting or it must be the case that it would have been agreed to if their votes had not been counted. Note also that authorisation must be obtained in advance of acting in what would otherwise be a conflict of interest matter. When deciding whether or not to authorise a conflict, a director must, of course, act in accordance with all of the duties he owes to the company. He will be in breach of s 172, for example, if he votes to authorise a conflict if he does not consider, in good faith, that the authorisation would be most likely to promote the success of the company.

What is a conflict of interest?

Guidance in the 2006 Act

The 2006 Act contains no definition of conflict of interest. When, then, will a conflict of interest exist for the purposes of the s 175 duty?

- Section 175(7) spells out that a conflict of interest includes a conflict of interest and duty and a conflict of duties.
- Section 175(3) provides that a conflict *arising* in relation to a transaction or arrangement with the company is not a conflict covered by s 175 (regulation of these transactions and the scope of s 175(3) are considered in section 12.3 below, see in particular the example at the end of 12.3.2).
- Section 175(1) refers to the duty to avoid a situation in which the director has, or can have, a direct or indirect interest that conflicts, *or possibly may conflict*, with the interests of the company, yet s 175(4) states that the duty does not apply if the situation *cannot reasonably be regarded as likely to give rise to a conflict* of interest.
- Section 175(2) reinforces that the duty applies in particular to the exploitation of any property, information or opportunity.
- Section 175(2) goes on to state that it is immaterial whether the company could take advantage of the property, information or opportunity, yet again, it is difficult to reconcile this with the duty not applying if the situation *cannot reasonably be regarded as likely to give rise to a conflict* of interest (s 175(4)).

Beyond the clues in s 175 as to when a conflict of interest will exist, it is instructive to examine pre-2006 Act conflict of interest cases to have a sense of when a director will be found to have a conflict of interest for the purposes of s 175. Many cases have concerned directors exploiting corporate opportunities themselves after they have left the company, which raises the question when do directors' who leave a company cease to be subject to the duty. In other cases, the company has not been in a position to exploit the opportunity itself, or has decided not to. Each of these situations is considered in turn in the following paragraphs.

Corporate opportunities and directors who leave or are in the process of leaving the company

Section 170(2) specifically provides that a person who ceases to be a director continues to be subject to the duty in s 175, 'as regards the exploitation of any property, information or opportunity of which he became aware at a time when he was a director'. What is not always clear is whether such exploitation is, as a matter of fact, a conflict of interest. Two types of cases dealing with directors who leave companies and take up opportunities the companies consider they should not have exploited for their own benefit are where a director leaves deliberately in order to acquire an opportunity previously sought by and for the company, and where a director is forced out of a company. In relation to the first of these scenarios, the law is strictly applied.

CASE EXAMPLE

Canadian Aero Service Ltd v O'Mally (1973) 40 DLR (3d) 371

Two directors, the president and vice president of the company, tried to obtain a contract on behalf of the company and were active participants in the negotiations. They then resigned, formed a new company and acquired the contract for the new company. Held: The directors were liable to account to their former company for the profits made. This was a diversion of a maturing business opportunity that the company was actively pursuing. Laskin J stated that even after his resignation a director is precluded from exploiting the opportunity 'where the resignation may fairly be said to have been prompted or influenced by a wish to acquire for himself the opportunity sought by the company, or where it was his position with the company rather than a fresh initiative that led him to the opportunity which he later acquired'.

In contrast, there may be no conflict where a director performs services for a customer of the company in competition with the company, even whilst he is a director, if he is in the process of being forced out of the company. Starting from the principle illustrated in *London and Mashonaland Exploration Co Ltd v New Mashonaland Exploration Co Ltd* [1891] WN 165, that there is no completely rigid rule that a director may not be involved in the business of a company which is in competition with another company of which he is a director, the Court of Appeal in *Plus Group Ltd v Pyke* [2002] 2 BCLC 201 (CA) considered it possible for a director's duty to be 'reduced to vanishing point' on the facts because he had been squeezed out of any management role in the company. In those circumstances, a director who set up a new company to compete with the company and performed services for a major client of the company, was held *not* to be in breach of duty.

In *Foster Bryant Surveying Ltd v Bryant & Savernake Property Consultants Ltd* [2007] 2 BCLC 239 (CA), the Court of Appeal explored the duty of a director between resigning (he was effectively forced out of a company) and his resignation taking effect in the context of a customer of the company wishing to continue to secure the services of the director. Rix LJ's judgment is worth reading for its clear review of the 'corporate opportunity' authorities. He focused on the need for a link between the resignation and the obtaining of the business by the director, ie the resignation must be part of a dishonest plan. He stated that the standards of loyalty, good faith and the no-conflict rule should be tested in each case by many factors, ie a fact-intensive investigation was required to determine liability for breach. Amongst the factors to be considered in that enquiry are:

- position or office held
- nature of the corporate opportunity
- its ripeness
- its specificness
- the director's or managerial officer's relation to it
- the amount of knowledge possessed
- the circumstances in which it was obtained
- whether it was special or, indeed, even private

- the factor of time in the continuation of fiduciary duty where the alleged breach occurs after termination of the relationship with the company
- the circumstances under which the relationship was terminated, that is whether by retirement or resignation or discharge.

Note the willingness of the court in this case to engage in in-depth factual analysis when applying the conflict of interest rules to determine whether or not a conflict actually existed. This approach is in stark contrast with the approach in old cases asserting the necessity for fiduciary obligations to be applied strictly, regardless of whether or not the principal suffered a loss, to protect the principal, 'as no court is equal to the examination and ascertainment of the truth in much the greater number of cases' (*per* Lord Eldon LC in *Ex parte James* 8 Ves 337).

Companies that cannot or do not wish to pursue a corporate opportunity

The strict principle that a fiduciary may not benefit from a corporate opportunity even where the company could not have benefited from the opportunity itself, infamously applied to a solicitor and trustee in *Boardman v Phipps* [1967] 2 AC 46, has been applied to company directors in what was the leading case on conflict of interest before the 2006 Act, *Regal (Hastings) Ltd v Gulliver* [1967] 2 AC 134.

CASE EXAMPLE

Regal (Hastings) Ltd v Gulliver [1967] 2 AC 134

The board of directors of Regal (Hastings) Ltd, acting together and honestly, bought shares in a subsidiary of the company set up to facilitate the sale of the company's business. Regal (Hastings) Ltd had been given the option to acquire the shares but lacked the finances to do so. On the subsequent sale of the company and the partly owned subsidiary, the directors made profits on their shares in the subsidiary company. The new owners of the company brought proceedings against the directors to recover those profits. Held: The directors had not disclosed their intention to acquire the shares to the shareholders and obtained the approval of the shareholders to their action. Accordingly, the directors were in breach of the duty not to make a secret profit.

The reference in s 175 to it being immaterial whether the company could take advantage of the property, information or opportunity alleged to have been exploited by the director can be traced back to this case. Yet later cases, such as *Foster Bryant*, showed the willingness of the courts to take a 'common sense and merits based approach ... which reflects the equitable principles at the root of these issues' (*per* Rix LJ). As we have seen, this more flexible approach is also reflected in s 175 insofar as s 175(4)(a) states that the duty is not infringed if the situation 'cannot reasonably be regarded as likely to give rise to a conflict of interest'. It is clear that *Regal (Hastings) Ltd v Gulliver* would be decided in the same way were it to come to court today and s 175 applied to determine whether or not the directors were liable to account for the profits they made based on a breach of the duty not to put themselves in a position in which their personal interest and the interests of the company conflicted.

Further strict applications of the rule occurred in *Philip Towers v Premier Waste Management Ltd* [2011] EWCA Civ 923 (CA) and *Bhullar v Bhullar* [2003] 2 BCLC 241 (CA). In *Bhullar* two directors of a small company, which was not currently developing any further land, bought land in which the company would otherwise have been interested, for development by themselves personally. Although he approved the quotation below from the dissenting judgment of Lord Upjohn in the leading case of *Boardman v Phipps* [1967] 2 AC 46 (HL), Jonathan Parker LJ went on to find the directors liable for breach of duty, as 'reasonable men looking at the facts would think there was a real sensible possibility of conflict'.

JUDGMENT

'The phrase "possibly may conflict" requires consideration. In my view it means that the reasonable man looking at the relevant facts and circumstances of the particular case would think that there was a real sensible possibility of conflict, not that you could imagine some situation arising which might, in some conceivable possibility in events not contemplated as real sensible possibilities by any reasonable person, result in a conflict.'

12.2.2 Duty not to accept benefits from third parties

SECTION

'**176   Duty not to accept benefits from third parties**

(1) A director of a company must not accept a benefit from a third party conferred by reason of—

(a)   his being a director, or

(b)   his doing (or not doing) anything as director.

(2) A 'third party' means a person other than the company, an associated body corporate or a person acting on behalf of the company or an associated body corporate.'

The second general directors' duty aimed at protecting the company from a director acting in his own self-interest or in the interest of any person other than the company is the duty not to accept benefits from third parties. Section 176 is based on and operates in relation to directors in place of the equitable principle that fiduciaries must not accept bribes or secret commissions (see *AG of Hong Kong v Reid* [1994] 1 AC 324 (PC) but note that the Court of Appeal in *Sinclair Investments (UK) Ltd v Versailles Trade Finance* [2012] Ch. 453 (CA) declined to follow the Privy Council decision in relation to the remedy, which is an equitable account (unless the money or benefit received had been company property or arose from the director taking advantage of an opportunity or right which was properly that of the company). The section is broader than bribes and secret commissions, extending to any kind of benefit, whether financial or non-financial. Every breach of this section will fall within the duty to avoid conflicts of interest in s 175 but note that acceptance of benefits from third parties has clearly been singled out as behaviour that other directors cannot be entrusted to monitor and approve as, unlike s 175, s 176 contains no provision for board authorisation. The problem is that as the scope of s 176 is unclear, it is consequently unclear when director authorisation will work.

Unless provisions in the articles permit such (s 180(4)(b)), third party benefits must be approved by the shareholders if a director is to avoid liability. This power of the shareholders to approve receipt of third party benefits is preserved by s 180(4)(a). The exception of any benefit that cannot reasonably be regarded as likely to give rise to a conflict of interests is an important one as it takes reasonable corporate hospitality out of the realm of breach. A final point to note is that s 170(2)(b) specifically provides that a person who ceases to be a director continues to be subject to this duty 'as regards things done or omitted by him before he ceased to be a director'.

12.3 Directors contracting with their companies

We turn now to the legal rules governing directors who enter into contracts with their companies or have an interest in a contract entered into by their companies. The 2006 Act has changed the laws regulating such company contracts. Essentially, the position most companies created by including provisions in their articles has been adopted as the default legal position.

The 2006 Act imposes on directors a duty to declare interests in proposed and existing company contracts (ss 177 and 182). It also requires shareholder approval of four specific types of transactions directors may enter into with their companies.

12.3.1 Statutory declaration of interest to the board of directors

SECTION

'177 Duty to declare interest in proposed transaction or arrangement

(1) If a director of a company is in any way, directly or indirectly, interested in a proposed transaction or arrangement with the company, he must declare the nature and extent of that interest to the other directors.

(2) The declaration may (but need not) be made—
   (a) at a meeting of the directors, or
   (b) by notice to the directors in accordance with—
      (i) section 184 (notice in writing), or
      (ii) section 185 (general notice).

(3) If a declaration of interest under this section proves to be, or becomes, inaccurate or incomplete, a further declaration must be made.

(4) Any declaration required by this section must be made before the company enters into the transaction or arrangement.

(5) This section does not require a declaration of an interest of which the director is not aware or where the director is not aware of the transaction or arrangement in question.

For this purpose a director is treated as being aware of matters of which he ought reasonably to be aware.

(6) A director need not declare an interest—
   (a) if it cannot reasonably be regarded as likely to give rise to a conflict of interest;
   (b) if, or to the extent that, the other directors are already aware of it (and for this purpose the other directors are treated as aware of anything of which they ought reasonably to be aware); or
   (c) if, or to the extent that, it concerns terms of his service contract that have been or are to be considered—
      (i) by a meeting of the directors, or
      (ii) by a committee of the directors appointed for the purpose under the company's constitution.

...

182 Declaration of interest in existing transaction or arrangement

(1) Where a director of a company is in any way, directly or indirectly, interested in a transaction or arrangement that has been entered into by the company, he must declare the nature and extent of the interest to the other directors in accordance with this section. This section does not apply if or to the extent that the interest has been declared under section 177 (duty to declare interest in proposed transaction or arrangement).'

As under the 1985 Act, the 2006 Act requires a director to declare his interest in any transaction or arrangement the company proposes to enter into (s 177) or has already entered into (s 182), to the other directors. The details of how and when such declarations must be made have changed (see s 177 set out above and similar subsections in s 182).

Example

Dan is a director of E Company Ltd. Dan also owns all of the shares of Company S Ltd. Company E Ltd proposes to enter into a purchase agreement with Company S Ltd. Dan must declare his interest in Company S Ltd to the directors of Company E Ltd before the companies enter into the contract unless he can establish that his interest cannot reasonably be regarded as likely to give rise to a conflict of interest (unlikely in this case) or that the other directors are already aware of it or ought reasonably to be aware of it.

If the company actually enters into the transaction or arrangement, a director who fails to declare his interest commits a criminal offence (s 183). Of greater interest are the civil consequences of failure to comply. Sections 177 and 182 are silent as to the civil consequences of failure to comply with them. The 2006 Act does contain the general statement that the consequences of breach of the directors' general duties are the same as would apply if the corresponding common law or equitable principle applied (s 178(1)).

The problem is that there was no common law or equitable principle requiring a director to declare his interest *to the board*: ss 177 and 182 could be seen as amended re-enactments of a prior statutory provision which had no civil consequences. Section 170(3) of the Act, however, states that 'The general duties are bases on certain common law rules and equitable principles as they apply in relation to directors and have effect in place of those rules and principles as regards the duties owed to a company by a director'. Accordingly, the statutory duty of a director to declare his interest in a company contract *to the other directors* appears to operate in place of the duty of a director to make disclosure of his interest *to the company (which was the shareholders)*. On this basis, failure to declare an interest in accordance with ss 177 or 182 has the same consequences as failure to disclose to the shareholders had, and the contract is voidable by the company. Depending upon the facts, a director may also be liable to account to the company for any profits made.

If s 177 is complied with, the contract will not be voidable by the company as a result of not having been approved by the shareholders (s 180(1). Again, however, the Act is silent as to whether or not a director who makes a declaration to the other directors is protected against the company seeking an account of profits made by the director from the contract. The implication is that he is protected but the situation may be a little more involved than simply a director making a profit from a contract with his company. Consider the following example.

Example

Erin became a director of F Company Ltd in 2000. At the first board meeting she attended she learned that F Company Ltd was planning to expand into selling MP3 players in the medium term and was looking for a major supplier to open discussions with. In 2001 she was called by MiCo Ltd, an MP3 player manufacturer that was in trouble financially, was looking for new customers and wanted to discuss establishing a contract to supply F Company Ltd. Erin told MiCo Ltd that F Company Ltd was not ready to enter the MP3 player market. She expressed interest in purchasing an interest in MiCo Ltd. Erin bought shares in MiCo Ltd giving her 25 per cent of the issued shares. In 2006, F Company Ltd proposed to enter into a contract with MiCo Ltd for the supply of MP3 players. Erin declared to the other directors that she had a 25 per cent interest in MiCo Ltd. A supply contract was entered into between F Company Ltd and MiCo Ltd. MiCo Ltd made healthy profits from the contract and Erin has received dividends of £100,000 from MiCo Ltd for the last two years (compared to £100 in each of 2001–2005). Another director of F Company Ltd discovers that Erin was approached by MiCo Ltd in 2001 and is angry that Erin did not inform the board of the approach as the company may have been able to get into the MP3 player market sooner. Can F Company Ltd sue Erin for breach of s 175? Does s 175(3) prevent such an action?

In this example Erin is only able to make the profit from the contract with the company because of a conflict of interest (MiCo Ltd approaching her in 2001) that she resolved in favour of herself (by not informing F Company Ltd of the approach and purchasing an interest in MiCo Ltd herself). Surely, s 175(3) does not protect Erin from being pursued for an account of profits the potential for which arose because of the 2001 breach of s 175. Section 175(3) does not apply to 'a conflict of interest *arising* in relation to a transaction or arrangement with the company' (emphasis added). It should not protect a director where the benefit of a prior conflict of interest is crystallised by a transaction or arrangement with the company. The scope of s 175(3) is, however, far from clear.

A company's articles will invariably include provisions expressly addressing the permitted participation of a director who has an interest in a company contract in the board meeting at which the contract is considered. The Model Articles provide that when a board decision is concerned with an actual or proposed transaction or arrangement with the company in which a director is interested, a director is not to be counted as participating in the decision-making process for quorum, voting or agreement purposes (Model Articles, article 14(1) (private companies) and 16(1) (public companies)). The model articles do not, however, contain language removing the exposure of a director to being made to account for profits made out of a contract with the company provided he has declared his interest to the directors in accordance with s 177. This contrasts with Table A which invariably contained such language.

12.3.2 Shareholder approval of specified transactions

Broadly speaking, the four types of transactions between a director and the company specifically regulated under the Companies Act 1985 remain specifically regulated under the 2006 Act. *Prohibition* on loans to directors has been dropped in favour of shareholder approval, bringing the approach to loans into line with the approach to other transactions. Shareholder approval is now required for:

- Substantial property transactions (ss 190–196)
- Loans, quasi loans and other credit transactions (ss 197–214)
- Long-term service agreements (s 188)
- Payments for loss of office (s 215).

The relationship between the provisions on specific types of transactions and the general duties of directors is expressly addressed in s 180 of the Companies Act 2006. Compliance with the general duties does *not* remove the need for shareholder approval required by the specific provisions (s 180(3)). Compliance with the relevant specific provision, however, removes the requirement to comply with the general duties to avoid conflicts of interest (s 175) and not to accept benefits from third parties (s 176, s 180(2)).

Non-contractual payments to a director for loss of office (s 215) and directors' long term service contracts (s 188) have already been considered in Chapter 9 and are not further considered here. Remedies available to the company in the event that the provisions are not complied with are considered in Chapter 13.

Substantial property transactions

If a director of a company or its holding company (a parent company and any parent of its parent company are holding companies), or a person connected with him, acquires or disposes of a substantial non-cash asset from or to the company the arrangement must be approved in advance by shareholders or the acquisition or disposal must be conditional on such approval being obtained (s 190).

Examples

A director sells a flat he owns to the company for £200,000. This is a sale of a substantial non-cash asset by a director to the company. Shareholder approval is required in advance or the contract must be conditional upon such approval being obtained. Shareholder approval would also be required if the flat had been owned and sold to the company by the director's husband.

A director buys a second-hand executive car from the company for £25,000. This is an acquisition of a non-cash asset by a director from the company. If the executive car is a *substantial* non-cash asset (see below), shareholder approval is required in advance or the contract must be conditional upon such approval being obtained.

A director of Company A Ltd sells a yacht for £140,000 to Company S Ltd which is a subsidiary of Company A Ltd. This is a sale of a substantial non-cash asset to a company by a director of its holding company. Approval is required in advance by the shareholders of Company A Ltd or the contract must be conditional upon such approval being obtained.

The key points to note about the governing provisions in ss 190–196 of the Companies Act 2006 are:

1 Approval is required in advance (s 190(1)) (although if not secured, affirmation within a reasonable time after the transaction has been entered into precludes avoidance of the transaction (s 196)).
2 Approval must be by shareholder general resolution (s 190(1)).
3 An asset is not a substantial non-cash asset if its value is £5,000 or less (s 191).
4 An non-cash asset is substantial if its value exceeds £100,000 (s 191).
5 A non-cash asset valued over £5,000 but below or equal to £100,000 will also be substantial if its value exceeds10 per cent of the company's net asset value (based on annual accounts) (s 191).
6 A person can be connected with a director based on a number of relationships including (but not limited to) the following (s 252):
   - a family member (s 253), which includes a spouse, children and parents, but not sibling, aunts and uncles, nephews, nieces or grandparents;
   - a business partner;
   - a company, at least 20 per cent of the shares of which are owned by, or at least 20 per cent of the votes of which are controlled by, the director and persons connected with him.
7 Transactions between a company and its parent or wholly owned subsidiary or between two wholly owned subsidiaries of one parent company are excluded from the requirement (s 192).
8 Transactions between a company and a director in his character as a shareholder of the company are excluded from the requirement (s 192).

An example of a transaction with a director in his character as a shareholder would be a distribution made to a shareholder, who was also a director, in the form of an asset rather than cash (a distribution 'in specie').

Loans, quasi loans and other credit transactions

A company may not make a *loan* to a director of the company or its holding company, unless the transaction has been approved in advance by shareholders (s 197(1)(a)). The same applies to a *company guarantee* of a loan provided to the director by a third party, and the provision by the company of *security* in relation to such a loan (s 197(1)(b)).

For public companies (and private companies associated with public companies, such as subsidiaries), the circumstances in which shareholder approval is required are expanded to include:

- Loans and guarantees to a person connected with the director (s 200).
- A broader range of financial transactions with directors and persons connected with them: quasi loans, credit transactions and guarantees or security provided in relation to credit transaction (s 198).

The governing provisions (ss 197–214) are detailed and what follows is simply intended to capture some of the key points:

- Approval is required in advance (s 197 *et al*) (although affirmation within a reasonable time after the transaction has been entered into precludes avoidance of the transaction (s 214)).
- Approval must be by shareholder general resolution.
- No approval is required if the aggregate value of the transaction and any other relevant transactions does not exceed £10,000 (s 207).
- Advances up to £50,000 provided to a director to fund expenditure on company business are excepted (s 204).

Directors' self-interest duties	
Directors' conflict of interest duties	
Duty to avoid conflicts of interest:	s 175
Directors may approve conflicts:	s 175(4)(b)
Ltds: unless articles provide otherwise	s 175(5)
Plcs: if articles permit such	s 175(5)
Typical conflicts are diverted corporate opportunities.	*Canadian Aero Service Ltd v O'Mally* (1973) *Bhullar v Bhullar* (2003) *Regal (Hastings) Ltd v Gulliver* (1967)
New willingness of courts to engage in in-depth factual analysis to determine whether or not there has been a breach	*Foster Bryant Surveying Ltd v Bryant & Savernake* (2007)
Conflicts arising in relation to a transaction with the company fall outside this duty	s 175(3)
Situations not likely to give rise to a conflict of interest do not infringe the duty	s 175(4)(a)
Duty not to accept benefits from third parties Encompasses the fiduciary obligation not to accept bribes or secret commissions Extends to *any* kind of benefit, financial or non-financial	s 176 *AG of Hong Kong v Reid* (1994)
Duties in relation to contracting with the company	
Duty to declare interest in proposed and existing company transactions:	ss 177 and 182
Declaration is to the other directors	ss 177(1) and 182(1)
Articles typically exclude interested director from counting for quorum or voting/agreement purposes	Model Art 14 (Ltds) Model Art 16 (Plcs)
Shareholder approval of specified transactions is required:	
Substantial property transactions	ss 190–196
Loans, quasi loans and other credit transactions	ss 197–214
Long-term service agreements	s 188
Payments for loss of office	s 215

ACTIVITY

Problem–question exercise

A Introduction

When tackling problem questions on directors' duties, students all too often do not distinguish between:

▪ steps and decisions taken by a director in the performance of his role as a director and member of the board: management behaviour; and

▪ steps taken by a director as an individual, not purporting to perform his role as a director or member of the board, such as negotiating his own service contract on his own behalf or selling a piece of his personal property to the company at a profit: potentially self-interested behaviour.

Once these two types of behaviour are clearly differentiated in your mind, it becomes much easier to analyse potential breach situations. A common fact situation is a director presenting himself to a third party seeking to contract with the company as a negotiator for his company (management behaviour), obtaining information in that role (management behaviour), then contracting with the third party on his own behalf (potentially self-interested behaviour).

B Question

A Company Ltd has three directors, Alan, Barry and Carol. Alan and Barry find out informally that planning permission will be granted for a piece of land owned by A Company Ltd. They keep this information to themselves and contract with A Company Ltd to buy the land at a price that represents its value without planning permission and is far lower than its value with planning permission. The contract is approved at a board meeting attended by all directors. No shareholder approval is secured.

Discuss the potential breaches of duty by any of the directors and any contravention of the Companies Act 2006 provisions governing specific types of contract between a director and the company.

C Working through the question

Once again, look at the problem question exercise at the end of Chapter 10 to remind yourself how to approach problem-type questions. Using the table set out in section D of that exercise, work through the suggested steps and questions in the left hand column of that table to develop an answer to the question above.

SUMMARY

Directors are in a fiduciary relationship with their companies

The principal fiduciary duties of a director are:

- To avoid conflicts of interest (s 175). Conflict arising in relation to a transaction with the company is excluded from this duty (s 175(3)) and directors can authorise a conflict (s 175(5)).
- Not to accept benefits from third parties (s 176). The scope of 'benefits' is unclear. In contrast to s 175, directors cannot authorise acceptance of a benefit.

These duties continue to apply after a director has left the company as regards things done or omitted before he ceased to be a director (s 170(2)).

Directors contracts with their companies

Directors who contract with their companies or have an interest in such contracts are regulated by:

- The duty to declare any interest in proposed and existing transactions or arrangements (ss 177 and 182).
- Provisions in the company's articles.
- Provisions of the Act requiring shareholder approval in advance of:
    - substantial property transaction (ss 190–196);
    - loans and similar arrangements to directors (ss 197–214);
    - long term service contracts (s 188);
    - payment for loss of office (s 215).

Further reading

Articles

Conaglen, M, 'The nature and function of fiduciary loyalty' [2005] LQR 469.

Griffiths, B, 'Dealing with directors' conflicts of interest under the Companies Act 2006' (2008) 23 BJIB & FL 292.

Lowry, J, 'Judicial pragmatism: directors' duties and post-resignation conflicts of duty' [2008] JBL 83.

Lowry, J, & Sloszar, L, 'Judicial pragmatism: directors' duties and post-resignation conflicts of duty' [2008] Journal of Business Law 83.

Reports

Law Commission, 'Consultation Paper: Company Directors: Regulation Conflicts of Interests and Formulating a Statement of Duties; (1998 No 153).

Law Commission, 'Report: Company Directors: Regulation Conflicts of Interests and Formulating a Statement of Duties' (1999 No 261).

Books

Walters, A, and Davis-White, M, *Directors' Disqualification and Bankruptcy Restrictions* (3rd edn, Sweet & Maxwell, 2009).

See also further reading at the end of Chapters 11 and 13.

13

Directors' duties: Remedies and reliefs and director disqualification

AIMS AND OBJECTIVES

After reading this chapter you should be able to:

- Understand common law and equitable remedies for breach of directors' duties
- Understand the civil consequences of failure to comply with statutory provisions governing directors contracting with their companies
- Recognise the defences and reliefs potentially available to directors in breach of their directors' duties
- Understand the concept of ratification and the limits on directors ratifying their own wrongdoings
- Analyse a fact situation and identify:
  - the remedies potentially available for each breach of duty or contravention of the Act
  - any defence a director may be able to argue
  - any relief a director may be able to claim
  - whether or not the breach or contravention can be ratified
- Understand when a director may be disqualified from being a director or taking part in management of a company
- Understand the effects of a disqualification order or undertaking, both civil and criminal

13.1 Introduction

As indicated in the introduction to Chapter 11, this chapter covers the final part of our study of directors' duties, statutory provisions governing directors' contracts with the company and the liabilities that may flow from breaches and contraventions of those duties and statutory provision. We look in turn at the common law remedies, equitable remedies and statutory remedies before turning to reliefs from liability. In the final section of this chapter, we look briefly at the closely related issue of director disqualification pursuant to the Company Directors Disqualification Act 1986, as amended.

13.2 Remedies

Codification of the remedies for breach of directors' duties was a step too far for the reform process and the remedies potentially available for breach of s 174, a common law based duty, and ss 171–173 and 175–177, the equity-based duties, are the same as would apply if the corresponding common law rule or equitable principle applied (s 178(1)). Given that the remedies for failure to obtain shareholder approval for substantial transactions, loans and other credit arrangements between a director and the company are set out in the statute (s 195 (substantial transactions) and s 213 (loans etc): see below at section 13.2.3), it would not have been too difficult to set out the remedies for breach of the general duties in the 2006 Act. The approach taken, however, leaves the remedies flexible and able to evolve. Unfortunately this flexibility is secured at the price of not achieving the clarity and accessibility the statutory statement of directors' duties was intended to deliver.

13.2.1 Remedies for breach of duty to exercise reasonable care, skill and diligence (s 174)

The duty to exercise reasonable care, skill and diligence is a common law duty rather than an equitable duty. Consequently, the usual remedy available to the company against a director who is found to be in breach will be damages for breach of duty. Damages will be based on tort principles. Accordingly, the company must be able to show:

- loss to the company that is not too remote;
- a causal link between the breach and the company's loss (*Cohen v Selby* [2001] 1 BCLC 176).

13.2.2 Remedies for breach of the equity-based duties (ss 171–173 and 175–177)

tutor tip

"To enhance your understanding of the remedies available for breach of directors' duties cross refer to your study of remedies available for breach of fiduciary duty in trusts and equity law"

With the exception of the duty to exercise reasonable care, skill and diligence, the general duties of directors are equity-based duties for which equitable remedies may be available. Equitable remedies are never available as of right. The company must satisfy the conditions for the court to grant relief sought. Your equity or trusts studies will assist you to understand equitable remedies for breach of duty. Essentially, depending upon the circumstances, four potential remedies are available to the company, as follows:

- Return of property a director has received in breach of duty.
- Confiscation/account of profits a director has made as a result of breach of duty.
- Rescission of contracts made in breach of duty.
- Equitable compensation.

Return of property received in breach of duty

A director may be ordered to restore to the company property transferred to him in breach of fiduciary duty. This remedy is based on ordinary trust principles – the director holds such property as constructive trustee for the company (*Harrison (JJ) (Properties) Ltd v Harrison* [2001] 1 BCLC 162). See now *Sinclair Investments (UK) Ltd v Versailles Trade Finance Ltd* [2012] Ch. 453 (CA) confining the circumstances in which a constructive trust will be imposed.

Account of profits made as a result of breach of duty

A director may be ordered to account to the company for any profits he has made as a result of the breach of duty. The principal object of an account of profits is to deter directors from breaching their duties and not to compensate the company for loss (*United Pan-Europe Communications NV v Deutsche Bank AG* [2000] 2 BCLC 461). Accordingly, the director may be made to account even if the company has suffered no loss, and even if the company could not have made the profit itself, as was the case in *Regal (Hastings) Ltd v Gulliver* [1967] 2 AC 134.

JUDGMENT

'The rule of equity which insists on those, who by use of a fiduciary position make a profit, being liable to account for that profit, in no way depends on fraud, or absence of *bona fides*; or upon such questions and considerations as whether the profit would or should otherwise have gone to the plaintiff, or whether the profiteer was under a duty to obtain the source of the profit for the plaintiff, or whether he took a risk or acted as he did for the benefit of the plaintiff, or whether the plaintiff had in fact been damaged or benefited by his action. The liability arises from the mere fact of the profit having, in the stated circumstances, been made. The profiteer, however honest or well-intentioned, cannot escape the risk of being called upon to account.'

Rescission of contracts made in breach of duty

A contract made in breach of fiduciary duty may be voidable at the option of the company. Each party must return any property transferred by the other pursuant to the contract. This may be relatively straightforward where the contract is between the director and the company but where the contract is between the company and a third party, rescission may not be possible due to the effect it would have on the third party. Rescission may be awarded if the third party has requisite knowledge of the breach of duty (*Logicrose Ltd v Southend UFC Ltd* [1988] 1 WLR 1256).

Equitable compensation

A director may be ordered to pay equitable compensation to the company for loss the company has suffered as a result of the breach of duty. Equitable compensation is different from damages for breach of contract or compensation for a tort. It is closer to an indemnification, although in the commercial context a causal connection is required between the breach and the loss. The importance of causation in determining equitable compensation was made clear by Lord Brown-Wilkinson's judgment in *Target Holdings Limited v Redferns* [1996] 1 AC 421 (HL), a case in which the House of Lords quashed the Court of Appeal's order that a solicitor in breach of fiduciary duty must compensate his client for losses that had *not* been caused by the breach. The losses would have been suffered even had there been no breach of duty and therefore were not recoverable as equitable compensation for the breach of duty.

JUDGMENT

'At common law there are two principles fundamental to the award of damages. First that the defendant's wrongful act must cause the damage complained of. Second that the plaintiff is to be put "in the same position as he would have been in if he had not sustained the wrong for which he is now getting his compensation or reparation". Although … in many ways equity approaches liability for making good a breach of trust from a different starting point, in my judgment those two principles are applicable as much in equity as at common law. Under both systems liability is fault based: the defendant is only liable for the consequences of the legal wrong he has done to the plaintiff and to make good the damage caused by such wrong.'

13.2.3 Remedies for failure to obtain shareholder approval for specific transactions

In contrast to the remedies for breach of the general duties of directors, when a contract is entered into without securing statutorily required shareholder approval the remedies available against directors are set out in the 2006 Act. Section 195 (relating to substantial property transactions with directors) and s 213 (relating to loans, quasi-loans and credit transactions) provide that:

- the transaction is voidable at the instance of the company;
- a director may be required to:
  - account to the company for any benefit or profit made from the transaction; and
  - indemnify the company for any loss or damages resulting from the transaction.

Note that liability extends beyond the director who enters into the transaction. Any director of the company who has authorised the transaction is also liable to account for any profit he has made and is jointly and severally liable to indemnify the company for any loss or damage resulting from the transaction (ss 195(4)(d) and 213(4)(d)). A director could be liable even if, rather than taking any active part in authorising it, a director has merely acquiesced in the transaction (*Queensway Systems v Walker* [2006] EWHC 2496).

13.2.4 Removal from office

Where a director is in breach of duty, the shareholders may decide to remove him as a director either pursuant to any power to do so in the articles or pursuant to s 168 (see Chapter 9). The company may also seek to terminate any service contract he has with the company. The rights of the director in relation to his service contract are principally governed by employment law. In particular it will be a matter of construction of the service contract whether or not the behaviour of the director is sufficient to allow termination for cause. Company law simply provides for service contracts of longer than two years' duration entered into without securing shareholder approval, as required by s 188, to be terminable by reasonable notice.

13.3 Relief from liability, indemnification, exclusion of liability and insurance

13.3.1 Relief from liability

We have seen above that directors may be able to obtain authorisation in advance for what would otherwise be a breach of duty. This authorisation may be obtained from:

- directors in relation to conflicts of interest (s 175(5));
- shareholders, as allowed by any rule of law (s 180(4));
- a provision in the articles of the company (s 180(4)).

We have also seen that disclosure to the board in accordance with s 177 will protect a director's contract with the company, or one in which he has an interest, from being set aside (s 180(1)(b)).

In this section we focus on post-breach relief. After a breach, a director may be able to obtain relief from the consequences of his breach by:

- ratification by the shareholders pursuant to s 239;
- court-granted relief pursuant to s 1157.

Shareholder ratification (s 239)

The starting point at common law and in equity, based on majority rule and the proper plaintiff principle, is that a breach of duty by a director can be ratified after the event by the shareholders by general resolution. Section 239 is a new provision which applies to ratification of a director's conduct amounting to negligence, default, breach of duty or breach of trust in relation to the company. In effect, it provides for ratification by:

- general resolution of disinterested shareholders; or
- unanimous consent of shareholders.

Subsection 239(7) states that s 239 does not affect any other enactment or rule of law imposing additional requirements for valid ratification or any rule of law as to acts that are incapable of being ratified by the company. In doing so it preserves the uncertainty that exists regarding limits on the ratification power of shareholders. Because of s 239(7), even if a breach is apparently ratified by a disinterested majority as required by and in accordance with s 239, it may be possible to argue that the apparent ratification is ineffective. This issue could very well arise in the context of a shareholder seeking permission to continue a derivative claim (considered at section 14.3.2) as the court is precluded from giving such permission if the act complained of has been ratified (s 263(2)(c)(ii)).

Court-granted relief (s 1157)

A court that finds a director liable in respect of negligence, default, breach of duty or breach of trust may relieve the director from liability either wholly or in part if the court finds that the director acted honestly and reasonably having regard to the circumstances of the case (s 1157). The test to be applied was stated in *Re Duomatic Ltd* [1969] 2 Ch 365 at 377:

JUDGMENT

'[Was the director] … acting in the way in which a man of affairs dealing with his own affairs with reasonable care and circumspection could reasonably be expected to act in such a case.'

An example of when the court will exercise this power is *Re D'Jan (of London) Ltd* [1994] 1 BCLC 561, considered at section 11.4. In *Re D'Jan*, the court held that the predecessor to s 1157 contemplated that conduct may be reasonable for the purposes of that section despite amounting to lack of care at common law.

13.3.2 Indemnification, exclusion of liability and insurance

Subject to three important exceptions, s 232 renders void any provision which, in connection with negligence, default, breach of duty or breach of trust in relation to the company, purports to:

- exempt a director to any extent from any liability that would otherwise attach to him; or
- directly or indirectly provide a director with an indemnity to any extent against any liability.

Section 232 does not, however, prevent a company from:

- purchasing and maintaining liability insurance for its directors (s 233);
- indemnifying a director against liability he incurs to third parties (subject to limits in relation to criminal liability and proceedings) (s 234);
- indemnifying a director of a company that is a corporate occupational pension scheme trustee against liability he incurs in connection with the company's activities as trustee of the scheme (subject to limits in relation to criminal liability and proceedings) (s 235).

Also, to avoid arguments that they are exclusions of liability, otherwise lawful provisions in a company's articles dealing with conflict of interest are expressly excluded from the s 232 prohibition (s 232(4)). The model articles for both private companies (Articles 52 and 53) and public companies (Articles 85 and 86) contain identical provisions permitting the company to indemnify directors in respect of liability incurred in connection with being a director, as far as such indemnification is not prohibited or unlawful, and to purchase and maintain directors' liability insurance for the benefit of directors.

Directors' duties: remedies and relief and indemnification for breach	
Remedies for breach of directors' duties	
No statutory statement of remedies for breach of general duties, therefore need to look at common law and equitable remedies	
Common law damages for breach of s 174 duty to exercise care, skill and diligence	*Cohen v Selby* (2001) Note omission of s 174 from s 178(2)
Equitable damages for breaches of ss 171–173 and 175–177: Return of property a director has received in breach of duty Confiscation/account of profits a director has made as a result of breach of duty Rescission of contracts made in breach of duty (but note difficulty where third party involved). Equitable compensation	s 178(2) *Harrison v Harrison (2001)* *Regal (Hastings) Ltd v Gulliver* (1967) *Logicrose v Southend UFC* (1988) *Target Holdings v Redferns* (1996)
Statutory statement of remedies for failure to secure shareholder approval of specific transactions: Transaction voidable Interested director and any director authorizing the transaction is liable to account for profits and to indemnify the company for any losses resulting from the transaction	ss 195 and 213
Relief from liability and indemnification	
Shareholder ratification	s 239
Court granted relief Test is whether acting as a man of affairs dealing with his own affairs could reasonably be expected to act	s 1157 *Re Duomatic Ltd* (1969)
Exemption from liability and indemnities are void except company may: purchase liability insurance for directors indemnify directors against liability to third parties	s 232 s 233 s 234

13.4 Director disqualification

13.4.1 The basis for disqualification orders and undertakings

Director disqualification cases are now a key part of the modern law of directors' duties. Under the Company Directors Disqualification Act 1986 (CDDA), as amended (in particular by the Insolvency Act 2000), subject to the power to accept undertakings in lieu (see below), the court may (and in proceedings under s 6 and 9A must) make an order in the terms of s 1 disqualifying the defendant from promoting, forming or taking part in the management of a company or LLP, including being a director, in the following defined circumstances:

- Where a person is convicted of an indictable offence in connection with the promotion, formation, management, liquidation or striking off of a company, or with the receivership or management of a company's property (s 2).
- Where a person has been persistently in default in relation to provisions of companies legislation requiring returns or accounts to be filed with the registrar of companies (ss 3 and 5).

- Where it appears that a person has been guilty of an offence of fraudulent trading (Companies Act s 993) or any other fraud in relation to the company (s 4).
- Where a person is or has been a director of a company which has become insolvent and his conduct as a director of that company (either taken alone or taken together with his conduct as a director of any other company or companies) makes him unfit to be concerned in the management of a company (s 6).
- Where a person is or has been a director of a company and his conduct (as revealed in the course of an investigation under the Companies Act 1985 (see Chapter 17)) makes him unfit to be concerned in the management of a company (s 8).
- Where he is a director of a company that has committed a breach of competition law and his conduct as a director of that company makes him unfit to be concerned in the management of a company (s 9A).
- Where a declaration of liability is made against a person or director under the fraudulent (s 213) or wrongful (s 214) trading provisions of the Insolvency Act 1986 (s 10).

The majority of disqualification orders are made on the application of the Secretary of State under ss 6 and 8. Under both provisions, the court is required to have regard to the matters listed in Schedule 1 to the Act in determining the question of unfitness.

disqualification undertaking

an out of court procedure whereby a director accepts a binding undertaking not to act as a director for a defined disqualification period without the consent of the court, in lieu of being disqualified under the Company Directors Disqualification Act 1986 (as amended)

The option to accept a disqualification undertaking in lieu of a disqualification order was introduced in 2000 (see CDDA s 1A, 7(2A), 8(2A), 8A and 9B). Essentially, the Secretary of State can accept an undertaking if it appears to him that it is expedient in the public interest that he should do so instead of applying or proceeding with an application to court for a disqualification order. The option to accept undertakings is limited, however, to where disqualification is being considered under s 6 (insolvency and unfit director), 8 (following a company investigation) and 9A (breach of competition law).

13.4.2 The effect of disqualification orders and undertakings

A disqualification order is an order that for the period specified in the order the person shall not be a director of a company, act as a receiver of a company's property or in any way, whether directly or indirectly, be concerned or take part in the promotion, formation or management of a company unless (in each case) he has the leave of the court (s 1(1) CDDA 1986). A disqualified person could not, for example, be a company secretary.

The period of disqualification can be anything up to fifteen years depending upon the seriousness of the misconduct. In the case of s 6, if the director's conduct is found to make him unfit, the court must disqualify him for at least two years.

It is a criminal offence punishable with up to two years imprisonment and an unlimited fine for a person to act in contravention of a disqualification order or undertaking (s 13). Also, as considered in Chapter 3, a person acting in contravention of a disqualification order or undertaking may be held personally liable for the debts and liabilities of a company incurred whilst he is involved in its management (s 15).

SUMMARY
....

Remedies for breach of duty

- The remedies for breach of directors' duties are still found in case law (s 178).
- Remedies for breach of the duty of care, skill and diligence are common law remedies, the principal remedy being damages subject to causation and remoteness principles.
- Remedies for breach of the other, fiduciary duties are:
  - return of property based on a constructive trust;
  - account of profits;
  - rescission of contracts (subject to third party protection);
  - equitable compensation.

Remedies for failure to obtain shareholder approval for specific transactions

▦ Remedies are set out in the Act. In relation to substantial property transactions, loans and guarantees, ss 195 and 213 render the transaction voidable, and the interested director and any director authorizing the transaction is liable to account for profits and/or to indemnify the company for any losses resulting from the transaction.

Authorisation, ratification and court relief from liability

▦ The directors or shareholders may in some circumstances authorise or ratify acts or breaches by individual directors. Ratification is now governed by s 239 which disregards the votes of the interested director or any member connected with him.

▦ The court may grant relief from liability for breach if it considers a director to have acted honestly and reasonably having regard to the circumstances of the case (s 1157).

▦ Company granted exemptions from liability are void except that the company may purchase directors' liability insurance and may indemnify directors against liability to third parties (ss 232–234).

Director disqualification

▦ The Company Directors Disqualification Act 1986 empowers the Secretary of State in defined circumstances to apply to the court for an order disqualifying the defendant from be concerned or taking part in the promotion, formation or management of a company, or to take disqualification undertakings in lieu of an order.

SAMPLE ESSAY QUESTION

Consider the following essay question (which combines learning from Chapters 11–13):

Critically consider the extent to which the general duties of a director have not been codified.

Unpack the question

This is the first essential step which you must take time to do properly. You should separate out:

- Explanation of what is meant be "general duties of a director"
- The replacement of the case-based duties by the provisions of the 2006 Act
- Meaning of the term "codified"
- Identification and review of the relevant statutory duties: ss 171–177 & 182
- Explanation of the extent to which each was intended to be changed
- The continued relevance of the cases
- Continued relevance of the articles
- Consideration of remedies for breach
- Consideration of authorisation and ratification
- Assessment of the extent of codification/non codification.

Decide how to structure your answer

You could take each of the statutory duties in turn and discuss the issues in relation to each, or each of the issues in turn and consider the duties in turn. A combination of these two approaches is appropriate, the key point being: make a plan that covers all the aspects of the question. The boxes below are indicative of coverage, not structure.

The case-based duties and the Act

Explain:

- the case-based duties and historic efforts to state them in legislation
- the aims of the 2006 Act, particularly clarification and accessibility of the duties
- the general duties contained in the Act
- replacement but reservation of the relevance of the cases: ss 170(3) & (4)
- no attempt to codify remedies: s 178(1)
- the importance of the relationship between the duties and the articles: s 180(1) & (4)(b)
- the extent of preservation of case law governing authorisation and ratification (subject to s 239): s 180(4) & 239(7).

Deliberate changes

Identify and discuss:

- The duty to promote the success of the company: the non-exhaustive list of factors to which directors must have regard: s 172
- The objective standard for the duty to exercise care, skill and diligence: s 174
- The exceptions to the duty to avoid conflicts of interest in s 175(3) and (4)
- The change in the obligation to declare an interest from a criminal to a civil provision: s 177.

CONCLUDE

Express your reasoned opinion as to whether or not you believe the duties have been codified/the extent to which they have not.

Further reading

Articles
Conaglen, M, 'Remedial ramifications of conflicts between a fiduciary's duties' (2010) 126 LQR 72.

Worthington, S, 'Corporate Governance: Remedying and Ratifying Directors' Breaches' (2000) 116 LQR 638.

Reports
Law Commission, 'Consultation Paper: Company Directors: Regulation Conflicts of Interests and Formulating a Statement of Duties' (1998 No 153).

Law Commission, 'Report: Company Directors: Regulation Conflicts of Interests and Formulating a Statement of Duties' (1999 No 261).

Books
Walters, A, and Davis-White, M, *Directors' Disqualification and Bankruptcy Restrictions* (3rd edn, Sweet & Maxwell, 2009).

See also further reading at the end of Chapters 11 and 12.

14

Minority shareholder protection

AIMS AND OBJECTIVES

After reading this chapter you should be able to:

- Understand the proper claimant principle, its origins and shortcomings
- Advise on the circumstances in which a shareholder may commence and will be permitted to continue a statutory derivative claim (s 260)
- Recognise when a shareholder has a *personal* right he may sue to enforce in a personal capacity
- Explain why a shareholder is not able to recover reflective losses except in one circumstance and why that exception exists
- Advise whether or not a shareholder is likely to succeed in a petition based on a company's affairs having been conducted in a manner unfairly prejudicial to the interests of the shareholder (s 994)
- Advise on the basis of the just and equitable winding-up jurisdiction of the court
- Understand the relationship between s 994 and just and equitable winding-up petitions

14.1 Introduction

The introduction to this chapter highlights how the rights and claims considered in this chapter relate to one another and places those rights and claims in context.

In the following sections of the chapter, first, we examine the rule that the company is the proper claimant in proceedings in which a wrong is alleged to have been done to a company (the 'proper claimant rule'), and limits of that rule. Second, we look at the circumstances in which shareholders may commence, and will be permitted to continue, a derivative claim. Third, we consider the personal rights of a shareholder to sue in his own name for legal wrongs done to him in a personal capacity, to make good losses he has suffered, including, potentially, reflective losses. We then examine petitions based on a company's affairs having been conducted in a manner that is unfairly prejudicial to the interests of the shareholders (s 994 petitions) and their relationship to just and equitable winding-up petitions, the final type of petition covered in this chapter.

The law uses a number of legal mechanisms to protect companies from poor management and self-interested action by those in control, including imposition of the general and specific directors' duties examined in Chapters 11 and 12. If the inadequate behaviour of directors causes losses to the company, the company can sue to recover losses caused by breaches of duty (see Chapter 13). The company and the company alone has the right to sue for breach of directors' duties because, as we have learned, directors' duties are owed to the company.

Where the wrongdoers are directors, the potential exists for wrongs to be overlooked and no remedies pursued by the company because it is the wrongdoers who are managing the company. This difficulty may be overcome by the shareholders becoming the decision-making organ of the company for the purposes of ensuring legal action is brought against the directors. The problem is more difficult to overcome, however, when wrongdoer directors also own a majority of a company's shares.

We know from Chapter 9 that shareholder decisions are largely based on majority rule. Without more, then, the potential would exist for the holders of a minority of the shares in a company to have no procedure by which to assert the rights of the company when directors who were also majority shareholders acted in breach of duty to the detriment of the company. The derivative claim procedure has been developed to assist minority shareholders who find themselves in such a position to *protect the company*.

Rather than being concerned to protect the company, a minority shareholder in such a position is usually more concerned to protect himself *personally* from the adverse consequences of being a shareholder in a company with a majority shareholder managing the company in his (the majority shareholder's) own best interests rather than for the benefit of *all* shareholders. The main procedure available to a shareholder to protect himself personally is to petition the court for a remedy pursuant to the Companies Act 2006, s 994 based on the company's affairs having been conducted in a manner that is unfairly prejudicial to the interests of the minority shareholder.

If a company suffers loss caused by a breach of duty owed to the company its shareholders also usually suffer loss because the value of their shares is not as great as it would otherwise be. The shareholders' loss of share value merely reflects the loss suffered by the company, and, for this reason, is called 'reflective loss'. We know that shareholders are unable to sue wrongdoers who breach duties owed to the company, because those duties are not also owed to the shareholders.

Even where a wrongdoer owes a separate and additional duty to the shareholder, the shareholder may be unable to sue for breach of that duty and recover losses they have suffered. This is because insofar as the shareholders' losses are reflective losses, to allow recovery could result in the wrongdoer being ordered to compensate more than one person for the same loss: the company (for the loss to the company) and individual shareholders (for the reduction in share value they suffer which is a reflection of the loss to the company). As a matter of public policy, the law has set its face against allowing shareholders to recover reflective losses except in one very limited circumstance.

Traditionally, analysis of shareholder remedies has been concerned with the extent to which the law can be used by minority shareholders to secure a remedy for losses arising out of self-interested action by directors who are also majority shareholders. The remedy could be either *for the company*, by way of a derivative claim, or *for the shareholder personally*, either by asserting personal rights (subject to the limits on recovery of reflective loss), or by bringing a claim based on a company's affairs having been conducted in a manner that is unfairly prejudicial to the interests of the shareholders. This focus is, however, changing.

Increased emphasis on good corporate governance in the interests of all stakeholders in companies, the enshrinement of 'enlightened shareholder value' in s 172 of the 2006 Act, and the placing of the derivative claim on a statutory footing, have come together to raise the question of to what extent shareholder remedies may be used to enforce better management of companies in the interests of all stakeholders. Minority shareholders may challenge, or threaten to challenge, management decisions as having been taken in breach of duty by commencing a derivative claim. This has raised the spectre in some commentators' minds of minority shareholders who support public interest groups using the law to influence board decision-making in favour of public interest groups. Detailed consideration of the role of derivative claims in influencing board decision-making is outside the scope of this book but may be pursued by reading relevant literature listed under further reading at the end of this chapter.

14.2 The proper claimant principle

We know already that the company is a separate legal entity from its shareholders and consequently has legal rights and liabilities. If its rights are infringed, by a person failing to perform a contract they have entered into with the company, for example, the company may sue to enforce its rights under the contract. We also know that the decision to litigate rests with the board of directors as part of the general powers of management of the company (see Chapter 9). From this perspective, it makes perfect sense to have a basic rule, known as the rule in *Foss v Harbottle*, that in any legal proceedings in which a wrong is alleged to have been done to a company, the proper claimant is the company.

CASE EXAMPLE

Foss v Harbottle (1843) 2 Hare 461

The claimants, Foss and Turton, were *shareholders* in a company formed to buy land for use as a pleasure park. The defendants were directors and shareholders of the company. The claimant shareholders alleged that the defendants had defrauded *the company* in a number of ways including some of the defendants selling land belonging to them to the company at an exorbitant price. The claimants sought an order that the defendants make good the losses to the company. Held, dismissing the action: in any action in which a wrong is alleged to have been done to a company, the proper claimant is the company and as the company was still in existence, it was possible to call a general meeting and therefore there was nothing to prevent *the company* from dealing with the matter.

Although logical on its face, the rule has presented enormous difficulty to courts over the years.

QUOTATION

'The rules governing shareholder remedies in English company law are notoriously convoluted. Towering over this area, like Frankenstein's monster, stands the legacy of *Foss v Harbottle*. While not a Gothic novel, it has none the less generated its own horror stories of unfulfilled rights and ruinous litigation.'

Sugarman, D, 'Reconceptualising company law: reflections on the Law Commission's Consultation Paper on shareholder remedies' (1997) 18 Comp Law 226

14.2.1 Majority rule and the business judgment rule

Quite apart from reflecting the separate personality doctrine, the proper claimant principle also reflects a couple of sentiments nineteenth-century courts felt towards companies. It is perhaps an over-zealous commitment to these sentiments that resulted over the years in the unfulfilled rights and ruinous litigation to which Sugarman refers. First, is the reluctance of the courts to become involved in business decisions. Second, is the fear felt by the courts of multiplicity of legal actions arising from differences between shareholders:

JUDGMENT

'The court is not to be required on every occasion to take the management of every playhouse and brewhouse in the Kingdom.'

Carlen v Drury (1812) 1 Ves & B 149 *per* Lord Eldon

Courts have held strong to the principle that disputes amongst members of a company should be resolved by the members themselves according to the internal decision-making process provided by the company constitution and the Companies Acts (*MacDougall v Gardiner* (1875–76) LR 1 (CA)). Internal rules usually provided for majority rule, and the rule in *Foss v Harbottle* (1843) deliberately subjected minority shareholders to the rule of the majority shareholder.

14.2.2 Limits to the proper claimant principle

The courts were compelled to recognise limits to the rule in *Foss v Harbottle* (1843). The rule was not applied, for example, if a minority shareholder complained to the court about action by the company for which more than a simple majority was needed, as in *Edwards v Halliwell* [1950] 2 All ER 1064, which is a trade union case, but the principle is applicable to companies.

CASE EXAMPLE

Edwards v Halliwell [1950] 2 All ER 1064

The constitution of a trade union provided that contributions were not to be altered until a ballot vote of members had been taken and a two-thirds majority in favour obtained. Contributions were increased following a resolution supported by a simple majority. Two members sued seeking a declaration that the resolution was invalid. Held: Where a matter cannot be sanctioned by a simple majority of the members of the company but only by some special majority, an individual member is not prevented from suing by the rule in *Foss v Harbottle*.

The principal area where the rule presented difficulties was where those who control the company and, in particular, the decision to sue or not sue a person who has legally wronged the company, are themselves the wrongdoers. The most important limit to the rule, which is the only true *exception* to the rule, came to be referred to as 'fraud on the minority'. Where directors who were also majority shareholders had perpetrated a fraud on the company, a minority shareholder was permitted to commence an action based on a wrong done to the company to secure a remedy for the company. The action was called a 'derivative action'.

CASE EXAMPLE

Cook v Deeks [1916] 1 AC 554 (PC)

Three directors obtained a contract in their own name to the exclusion of the company in breach of fiduciary duty (now s 175). As holders of 75 per cent of the shares, they secured a resolution declaring the company had no interest in the contract. Held: The contract belonged in equity to the company and the directors could not use their shares to vest it in themselves. In these circumstances, where the board and majority shareholders were not willing to commence an action, minority shareholders could bring an action on behalf of the company.

The Companies Act 2006 has *replaced* the common law derivative action with a statutory derivative claim in ss 260–264 (considered below in section 14.3). All circumstances in which permission to continue a derivative action is granted may now be seen as exceptions to the proper claimant principle.

14.2.3 Example: proper claimant principle

It is helpful to illustrate how the proper claimant principle, and the exception to it, works by analysing a hypothetical scenario.

Directors as wrongdoers

Consider a company with two directors. They find out informally that planning permission will be granted for a piece of land owned by the company. They keep this information to themselves and buy the land from the company at a price representing its value without planning permission which is far lower than its value with planning permission.

In these circumstances, the directors cannot act as a decision-making organ of the company and decide to sell the land to themselves because they are conflicted-out. Articles normally provide that they cannot vote on the decision of the company to sell the land to them, and, even if the articles did not say this, and the directors cause the company to sell the land to them, they are in breach of ss 172, 175 and 190, as they have not acted to promote the success of the company (s 172), have used information obtained as directors to personal advantage (s 175), and they have failed to obtain the approval of the shareholders (s 190). Consequently, the transaction will be voidable by the company, the directors will be liable to account for any profits they have made and must indemnify the company against any losses caused by the breach of duty.

Although the directors, as the board, ordinarily have the power to decide whether or not to commence any legal action, in these circumstances control of the decision to litigate transfers to the shareholders and the shareholders, as a decision-making organ of the company, decide whether or not the company will sue the directors. The legal proceedings are still brought by the company, in the name of the company, seeking a remedy for the company.

Majority shareholders as wrongdoers

Staying with the hypothetical situation, the company has three shareholders each owning one third of the shares. Two of the shareholders are the directors. Because the wrongdoers are directors, who are not going to decide to sue themselves, the decision to litigate or not has reverted to the shareholders. Does this help the company if the wrongdoers are also shareholders?

Shareholders take most decisions by ordinary resolution, which encompasses majority rule (see Chapter 9). In our hypothetical, the wrongdoers own a majority of the shares and, as majority shareholders, they are able to pass or defeat ordinary resolutions. Are they, therefore, permitted to:

- pass an ordinary resolution approving the sale of the land pursuant to s 190?
- pass an ordinary resolution ratifying the breach pursuant to s 239?
- defeat a proposed resolution to sue the directors to recover the land?
- have any legal action commenced by the minority shareholder stopped because he is not the proper claimant?

The answer to the second question is no. On a resolution to ratify his breach of directors' duty, the votes of both the director/shareholder and any person connected with him are disregarded (s 239(4)). Curiously, there is no similar provision in s 190 requiring the votes of the director to be discounted on a resolution to approve a substantial asset transaction which leaves the matter moot and the answer to question 1 dependent upon the approach the court takes to statutory interpretation. A literal approach would suggest that all shareholders can vote, as the section does not state otherwise, whereas s 239 does state otherwise. A purposive approach may suggest otherwise. Turning to the third question, a resolution to sue the directors, if defeated, could be characterised as an indirect decision of the company to ratify a breach of duty, thereby bringing it within s 239 which requires the directors' votes to be disregarded. It is surprising that the answers to these questions are not clear-cut.

The answer to the fourth question is that, provided the minority shareholder brings the legal action as a claim under s 260, a statutory derivative claim, the action will not be stopped based on him not being the proper claimant. He will, however, need to secure the permission of the court to continue the claim. We turn now to consider the statutory derivative claim.

14.3 Statutory derivative claims

The statutory derivative claim is the only proceeding by which a minority shareholder, notwithstanding his lack of control over company decision-making, can commence legal action in respect of a cause of action vested in the company, seeking relief on behalf

derivative claim

a claim brought by a member under the Companies Act 2006, ss 260–269 against a director for an actual or proposed act or omission involving negligence, breach of duty or breach of trust by a director of a company. The claim is brought by the member for and on behalf of the company itself of the company, to remedy a wrong done to the company. The 2006 Act has expanded the grounds on which a derivative claim may be brought but requires court permission for the continuation of claims. The consequences of introduction of the new statutory procedure were not easy to predict. Although a number of claims have been commenced, the number for which permission to continue has been granted by the court to date has been very small.

QUOTATION

'The statutory derivative action is designed to make the law more flexible, efficient and cost-effective. But there were concerns that reform would open the floodgate and lead to vexatious claims with the effect of discouraging individuals to accept appointments as directors. In response, the Law Commission cautioned that members "should be able to maintain proceedings about wrongs done to the company only in exceptional circumstances" and that without good cause shareholders should not be encouraged to involve the company in litigation. As a result, the 2006 Act introduced a strict leave procedure and gave the courts new case management powers with the objective of protecting companies from disruptive litigations which are inimical to their interests. On the one hand, the law is concerned to uphold the majority rule principle in *Foss*. On the other hand, it recognises the need to protect the minority shareholders from abuse by the majority. The law aims to strike a balance between these two competing interests. The statutory derivative action is a recognition of the weaknesses inherent in the attempt of the common law derivative action to protect the minority shareholder and is an attempt to remedy the weaknesses.'

Mujih, E, 'The New Statutory Derivative Claim: a Delicate Balancing Act Part 1 (2012) 33 Comp. Law. 76 at 78

14.3.1 Grounds for claim

A statutory derivative claim may be brought *only* in respect of a cause of action arising from an actual or proposed act or omission involving negligence, default, breach of duty or breach of trust by a director of the company. The cause of action may be against the director or another person or both (s 260(3)). Note that the exposure of *third parties* to a s 260 claim will depend upon dishonest assistance and knowing receipt as the courts have developed these concepts in the context of breaches of duty by directors (these concepts are usually addressed in trusts courses when examining the liability of strangers to the trust in the event of a breach of duty by one or more trustees and you may find cases you study there relevant here). Claims cannot be brought under s 260 against third parties based on causes of action arising independently from the directors' legal shortcomings (*Iesini Westrip Holdings Ltd* [2010] BCC 420).

14.3.2 Claim procedure

The parties

The claimant in a s 260 derivative claim is the shareholder. Note that because the shareholder is bringing the action to secure relief for the company, the company must be made a defendant to the claim along with the directors and any third parties against whom relief is sought. An application to continue a derivative claim by a *majority* shareholder was rejected in *Cinematic Finance Ltd v Ryder* [2010] EWHC 3387. The court accepted that a derivative action could be brought by a majority shareholder but stated that permission to continue would be given to a majority shareholder only in very exceptional circumstances and it was difficult to envisage what such circumstances might be. In *Stimpson v Southern Private Landlords Association* [2010] BCC 387 (Ch D), the question of the importance of wrongdoer control of the members arose, although the comments in the case on this issue were obiter. In the absence of such control, the fact that it was open to the claimant to requisition an extraordinary general meeting and try to obtain a replacement board that could, if it considered it appropriate, authorise the litigation, was stated to be a powerful and perhaps overwhelming factor against granting permission to continue.

Application for permission to continue claim

Once the claim form has been drafted and either before or after it has been issued, an application must be made to the court for permission to continue the claim (s 261(1)). The shareholder is precluded from taking any further step in the proceedings until the court has given permission for the claim to continue. A two-stage process exists by which the court decides whether or not to permit the claim to continue.

Stage 1: a *prima facie* case

The court must be satisfied that the particulars of claim and the evidence submitted to support it disclose a *prima facie* case for giving permission to continue. If no *prima facie* case is disclosed, the court *must* dismiss the application and make any consequential order it considers appropriate (s 261(2)). If the court does not dismiss the application, the application moves to stage 2. At this stage, the claimant will submit written evidence with his application for permission to continue, supporting his statement of claim, and there is no requirement to involve the defendant.

Confusion has emerged from recent cases as to precisely what a claimant has to establish at this first stage. The burden of proof imposed on a claimant and the range of issues necessarily considered at this stage define the process within which the courts balance protection of the company from the cost and distraction of bogus actions on the one hand, and minority shareholders from unacceptable excesses of majority shareholder rule on the other. If a heavy burden is imposed, many claimants will have to be denied permission to continue at this stage.

In Scotland, the Court of Session in *Wishart v Castlecroft Securities Ltd* [2010] BCC 161 has been described as adopting a "low threshold", stating that, " ... no onus is placed on the applicant to satisfy the court that there is a *prima facie* case; rather the court is to refuse the application if it is satisfied that there is no *prima facie* case". This approach has been contrasted with two English cases in which the approach taken has been that the court has to decide *based on the evidence before it* that there is a prima case both that the company has a good cause of action and that the cause of action arises out of a director's default, breach of duty (etc). (*Iesini Westrip Holdings Ltd* [2010] BCC 420 and *Franbar Holdings Ltd v Patel* [2008] BCC 885 (Ch D)). Presumably, these two cases imply that the claimant must present evidence rather than simply asserting the relevant breach of duty (etc) in the statement of claim. *Stimpson* highlights the question of the extent to which this stage should involve consideration of the factors the court is required to consider at a later stage in determining whether or not it should give permission to continue (see s 263(3) and (4)). The confusion is assisted by the practice of stages 1 and 2 sometimes being combined. Clearly, appellate court guidance is needed. Guidance should separate out (i) which issues are under consideration at stage 1 from (ii) where the burden of proof lies, and how the burden can be satisfied, in relation to each of those issues. If, for example, a breach of duty by a director is clearly established, is this the stage at which the court should look at whether the circumstances for granting permission to continue a claim have been established?

Stage 2

Stage 2 involves a hearing of the application for permission to continue the claim and the defendant and, if it wishes, the company take part. At this stage the court *must* refuse permission to continue if:

- A person acting in accordance with the s 172 duty to promote the success of the company would *not* seek to continue the claim (s 263(2)(a)); or
- The act or omission has been authorised (ahead of time) or ratified (after the event) by the company (s 263(2)(b) and (c).

The court does not have to decide that a hypothetical or nominal director would consider the claim worth pursuing. Rather, permission to continue must be refused if, on the balance of probabilities, such a director would decide *not* to pursue the claim. Only if no director acting in accordance with s 172 would seek to continue the claim will the courts consider themselves bound to refuse permission under s 263(2)(a) (*Airey v Cordell* [2006] EWHC 2728 and *Iesini*). The courts have identified a number of factors that directors would take into account in deciding whether or not to continue to pursue a claim, including, its prospect of success, the enforceability of any judgment obtained, disruption of the litigation to the company's business, costs of proceeding, and the impact on the company's reputation (see *Franbar*).

The second ground for obligatory refusal preserves the difficult issue of which acts and omissions of directors the shareholders can authorise or ratify and which they cannot. This is a controversial area which s 239 of the Companies Act 2006 has gone some way to clarifying. Uncertainty remains, however, because, even in relation to ratification, s 239(7) preserves, 'any other enactment or rule of law imposing additional requirements for valid ratification or any rule of law as to acts that are incapable of being ratified by the company'. *Cook v Deeks* [1916] 1 AC 554 (PC) (see above) is authority for the proposition that ratification will be invalid where it amounts to expropriation of the company's property by the majority shareholder.

In relation to authorisation, as noted in the context of directors' duties, the Companies Act 2006 does not make clear how far an interested shareholder may vote to authorise a transaction for which the Act requires shareholder approval. The principle in *Cook v Deeks* should, arguably, be extended to any case in which the transaction for which authorisation is sought would amount to an expropriation of company property. In such a case, the court would surely be permitted to find that, as a matter of law, the transaction had not been authorised so that the court must refuse permission for a minority shareholder to continue a statutory derivative claim.

If the court is not compelled to refuse permission, it must take into account the following when deciding whether or not to grant permission to continue (s 263(3)):

- whether or not the claimant is acting in good faith in seeking to continue the claim (see *Nurcombe v Nurcombe* [1985] 1 WLR 370 (below));
- the importance that a person acting in accordance with s 172 would attach to continuing the claim;
- whether or not the act or omission could be, and in the circumstances would be likely to be, authorised or ratified by the company;
- whether the company has decided not to pursue the claim;
- whether the act or omission in question is one in respect of which the shareholder could pursue an action *in his own right* (this would most likely be under s 994) rather than on behalf of the company (see *Barrett v Duckett* [1995] 1 BCLC 243);
- any evidence before it of the views of shareholders who have no personal interest in the matter (see *Smith v Croft (No 2)* [1988] Ch 114).

In relation to the first point above, *Nurcombe v Nurcombe* [1985] 1 WLR 370 is an example of the courts being alert to attempts by claimants to use the derivative claim where they have already received a remedy for the wrong done. Such a claimant will be regarded as not acting in good faith in bringing the derivative claim.

CASE EXAMPLE

Nurcombe v Nurcombe [1985] 1 WLR 370

The first defendant (D1) in the derivative action was a director and the major shareholder of the company which was the second defendant (D2). The remaining shares were held by the claimant who was the former wife of D1. In earlier matrimonial proceedings by the claimant for financial provision it had become clear that D1 had diverted the considerable benefit of a contract for the purchase of certain land from the company to a company owned by his second wife. The judge in the matrimonial proceedings took into account that D1 had made a substantial profit out of his dealings in respect of the land and the lump sum awarded to his first wife, the claimant, in the matrimonial proceedings had reflected this. The claimant brought the derivative action, as a minority shareholder, on behalf of the company seeking payment by D1 to the company of the profit on the property transaction which she alleged he had diverted from the company in breach of his fiduciary duty as a director. Held: Dismissing the action, that P had abandoned her right to bring a minority shareholder's action by obtaining, in the matrimonial proceedings, the benefit of a lump sum award based on the inclusion of the profit from the property transaction in the first defendant's assets.

Note that the last but one point in the list above is narrower than the common law principle, established in *Barrett v Duckett* [1995] 1 BCLC 243, that a derivative action would not be permitted to proceed where an alternative adequate remedy was available. The availability of a s 994 petition has been considered in a number of applications for permission to continue. The approach taken to date was reviewed by Justice Newey in *Kleanthous v Paphitis* [2011] EWHC 2287:

JUDGMENT

'78   In *Franbar Holdings Ltd v Patel* [2008] EWHC 1534 (Ch), [2009] 1 BCLC 1, Mr William Trower QC, sitting as a Deputy High Court Judge, gave considerable weight to the fact that the Claimant should be able to achieve all that it could properly want through a section 994 petition and shareholders' action which were already on foot (see paragraphs 53 and 54). In *Iesini v Westrip Holdings Ltd*, Lewison J said (in paragraph 126) that the availability of an alternative remedy under section 994 was one of the factors which would have led him to the conclusion that, had he not adjourned the matter, it would not have been appropriate to allow a derivative claim to proceed.

79   In contrast, the availability of an alternative remedy under section 994 did not appear to the Inner House to be a compelling consideration on the facts of *Wishart v Castlecroft Securities Ltd*, where Lord Reed commented (in paragraph 46) that such proceedings would 'constitute, at best, an indirect means of achieving what could be achieved directly by derivative proceedings'. Similarly, in *Stainer v Lee* Roth J considered a derivative action 'entirely appropriate' and 'the theoretical availability to the applicant of proceedings by way of an unfair prejudice petition … not a reason to refuse permission'; the applicant was 'not seeking to be bought out' (paragraph 52).

80   In the present case, likewise, it was submitted on Mr Kleanthous' behalf that he was not seeking a buy-out of his shares. However, the evidence indicates that Mr Kleanthous is interested in being bought out. Mr Kleanthous himself referred in a witness statement to having said to Mr Paphitis in 2008 that he "hoped [Mr Paphitis] would agree to buy [his] RGL shares at a fair price so that [they] could both move on with [their] separate lives". In a more recent witness statement, Mr Kleanthous said that he had "made no secret about the fact that [he] would be willing to sell [his] shares in RGL at a fair price". Further, there has been reference to a petition being presented under section 994 . In a letter dated 2 June 2010, Mr Kleanthous' solicitors said that they had been "instructed to prepare, in addition to the derivative proceedings, an application under Section 994 of the Companies Act 2006". One is left with the suspicion that Mr Kleanthous has chosen to pursue derivative proceedings alone in the hope that that he will be able to obtain a costs indemnity (with the result that the other shareholders in RGL would be likely to bear the bulk of the costs even if the claims against them failed).

81   In all the circumstances, I agree with Mr Todd that the availability of an alternative remedy in the form of an unfair prejudice petition is a powerful reason to refuse permission for the derivative claim to proceed in this case.'

In *Parry v Bartlett & Another* [2011] EWHC 3146, the judge held that the existence of an alternative remedy under section 994 of the Companies Act for unfair prejudice was only a factor to be taken into account, not an absolute bar to the grant of permission to continue a s 260 claim.

In relation to the final point in the list above, a derivative action was struck-out in *Smith v Croft (No 2)* (1988) because a majority of the independent shareholders' votes would have been cast against allowing the action to proceed and there was no evidence to suggest that they would be cast for other than reasons genuinely thought to be for the company's advantage.

It is noteworthy that in the first two cases in which permission to continue was granted, *Stainer v Lee & Others* [2010] EWHC 1539 and *Kiani v Cooper* [2010] BCC 463, the court merely granted permission to proceed until after disclosure, not permission to proceed to trial. This enables the court to revisit the question of permission at a time when the strength of the case is much clearer.

Permission to continue and discontinuance

If the court gives permission for a derivative claim to continue, the claim continues much like any other action with remedies available that would be available in a case brought by the company against its directors (see Chapter 13). In its report on Shareholder Remedies (No 246), the Law Commission recommended that the consent of the court should be a pre-requisite to any subsequent discontinuance of a derivative action. This recommendation reflected concern that the claimant and the directors could collude, with the claimant being bought-off by the directors which, even at a premium in the eyes of the shareholder, would in many cases cost the directors far less than their liability were the claim to proceed to judgment. Such arrangements would be unlikely to be in the interests of the company. This recommendation has not been adopted. It may be, however, that when judges grant permission to continue, they use the power given to the court in s 261(4)(a), 'to continue the claim on such terms as it think fit', to order that the claim cannot be discontinued without the court's permission.

14.3.3 Costs

A derivative claim is brought by a shareholder for the benefit of the company. The shareholder is an agent acting on behalf of the company (*per* Lord Denning MR in *Wallersteiner*, below and see also *Re Sherborne Park Residents Co Ltd* [1986] 2 BCC 9 9528 considered at section 14.4). For this reason, the court is usually prepared to grant a costs order, typically applied for early on in proceedings, that the claimant shall be indemnified by the company against his liability for costs of both the derivative claim and the application for permission to continue, whether the claim is successful or not.

The authority for such an order, now reflected in the Civil Procedure Rules (CPR 19.9E), is *Wallersteiner v Moir (No 2)* [1975] QB 373. Note that it is only as valuable as the creditworthiness of the company, as it does not provide the shareholder with any form of property interest to secure the sum payable by the company (*Qayoumi v Oakhouse Property Holdings plc* [2003] 1 BCLC 352).

Aware of the danger of imposing a potentially large financial obligation on companies, the courts in both *Stainer v Lee* and *Kiani v Cooper* made costs indemnity orders subject to restrictions. In *Stainer v Lee*, for example, it was capped at £40,000 (with liberty to apply for its extension).

14.4 Personal actions by shareholders

Shareholders may bring legal actions asserting their personal rights as shareholders. The rule in *Foss v Harbottle* is not relevant to these actions. The proper claimant is *not* the company, rather, the proper claimant for a wrong done to a shareholder is the shareholder in his personal capacity. In fact, the company in such cases is usually one, if not the only, defendant. *Wood v Odessa Waterworks Co* [1889] LR 42 Ch D 636 is an example of a shareholder bringing an action on behalf of himself and other shareholders, all in their personal capacity. This is known as a representative action. Representative actions are common when shareholder rights are asserted because there are often a number of shareholders with the same right.

CASE EXAMPLE

Wood v Odessa Waterworks Co [1889] LR 42 Ch D 636

The rights of the shareholders in respect of a division of the profits of the company were governed by provisions in the articles of association. A shareholder, on behalf of himself and all other shareholders, brought action for an injunction to restrain the company from acting on a resolution on the ground that it contravened the articles of association of the company. Held: *Per* Stirling, J, 'What I have to determine is, whether that which is proposed to be done is in accordance with the articles of association as they stand, and, in my judgment, it is not, and therefore the Plaintiff is entitled to an injunction so far as relates to the payment of dividends'.

The precise scope of the personal rights of shareholders is not completely clear. When we examined the rights of shareholders to sue to enforce provisions of the articles of association we saw that there is disagreement as to precisely which rights set out in the articles of association may be enforced as personal rights by shareholders (see Chapter 6). The importance of defining the strict legal rights of shareholders has been eclipsed by the availability of the very popular unfairly prejudicial conduct petition under s 994 of the Companies Act 2006, for which a very wide range of remedies may be granted by the court (see s 996). Section 994 petitions can be brought to protect the 'interests' of one or more shareholders. This concept of 'interests' is broader than 'rights' and therefore s 994 petitions can be successfully brought in fact situations in which no strict legal rights of a shareholder have been infringed. Section 994 petitions are examined in the next section of this chapter.

Confusion often arises where a given fact situation gives rise to both a right of the company to sue its directors and a right of the shareholder to sue the company. Examples are when directors abuse the power to allot shares, or allot shares without first respecting the pre-emption rights of existing shareholders. An improper exercise of powers is a breach of duty by the directors (s 171).

It is a wrong done to the company for which the company can sue the directors for a remedy against the directors. It is also a breach of the articles of association and an individual shareholder can sue the company for acting inconsistently with the articles (through the agency of its directors). *Re Sherborne Park Residents Co Ltd* [1986] 2 BCC 99528 is just such a case. The report is of a hearing of a motion (a preliminary hearing for a specific order, here, an order for costs) in what would today be a s 994 case brought by an individual shareholder.

CASE EXAMPLE

Re Sherborne Park Residents Co Ltd [1986] 2 BCC 99528

A shareholder in a residential leaseholders' management company objected to a planned allotment of shares by the directors and commenced what would now be a s 994 unfairly prejudicial conduct petition. By notice of motion, the shareholder sought an indemnity for costs order against the company arguing that the action was a 'derivative' action because the facts complained of involved a breach of fiduciary duty by the directors. Held: The court declined to make the costs order. Hoffmann J, stated that the allotment was alleged to be an improper and unlawful exercise of the powers granted to the board by the articles of association and that whilst this was a breach of directors' duty owed to the company, the true basis of the action was that the alleged abuse of fiduciary powers was *an infringement of the petitioner's rights as a member* under the articles. A shareholder in such an action might sue as representative of himself and other shareholders who had identical interests but he did not in substance assert a right which belonged to the company alone. In a derivative action, the only true claimant is the company. The availability in derivative claims of costs orders indemnifying a claimant against the costs of the action whether the action is won or lost, is based on the shareholder being in a relationship with the company analogous to agent and principal for the purpose of bringing the action. That was not the case here.

14.4.1 Reflective loss: denial of the personal right to recover

As explained in the introduction to this chapter, when a company suffers a loss which significantly diminishes its assets, shareholders are likely to experience a reduction in the value of their shares. If these losses are caused by a breach of duty owed to the company, the position is clear: the company is the proper claimant and can sue for the breach. The shareholder cannot sue because the duty is not owed to him. Where, however, in addition to the company being owed a duty, the shareholder is also owed a duty by the wrongdoer, the principle that the shareholder has no right to sue to recover purely 'reflective loss' comes into play and is referred to as the 'no reflective loss principle' (*Day v Cook* [2002] 1 BCLC 1).

Where there is a breach of a duty owed to both the company and the shareholder, if the shareholder's loss is reflective loss, the shareholder cannot recover it because the company's claim 'will always trump that of the shareholder' (*per* Arden, LJ in *Day v Cook* [2002] 1 BCLC 1). This is because otherwise double recovery (by the company and the shareholder) will occur, or, if the action were to be allowed on a first come first served basis, a shareholder could recover at the expense of the company. Lord Millett stated the justification for the principle succinctly in *Johnson v Gore Wood & Co* [2001] 2 AC 1 (HL), the leading case on reflective loss.

JUDGMENT

'Justice to the defendant requires the exclusion of one claim or the other; protection of the interests of the company's creditors requires that it is the company which is allowed to recover to the exclusion of the shareholder.'

In *Johnson v Gore Wood* (2001), Lord Bingham summarised the law in three principles:

JUDGMENT

'(1) Where a company suffers loss caused by a breach of duty owed to it, only the company may sue in respect of that loss. No action lies at the suit of a shareholder suing in that capacity and no other to make good a diminution in the value of the shareholder's shareholding where that merely reflects the loss suffered by the company. A claim will not lie by a shareholder to make good a loss which would be made good if the company's assets were replenished through action against the party responsible for the loss, even if the company, acting through its constitutional organs, has declined or failed to make good that loss. So much is clear from *Prudential Assurance Co Ltd v Newman Industries Ltd (No 2)* [1982] Ch 204 ...

(2) Where a company suffers loss but has no cause of action to sue to recover that loss, the shareholder in the company may sue in respect of it (if the shareholder has a cause of action to do so), even though the loss is a diminution in the value of the shareholding. ...

(3) Where a company suffers loss caused by a breach of duty to it, and a shareholder suffers a loss separate and distinct from that suffered by the company caused by breach of a duty independently owed to the shareholder, each may sue to recover the loss caused to it by breach of the duty owed to it but neither may recover loss caused to the other by breach of the duty owed to that other.'

Only one true exception appears to exists to the no reflective loss principle. Where the company is unable to pursue its claim against the defendant because of the defendant's wrongdoing, a shareholder will be permitted to bring an action to recover reflective loss (*Giles v Rhind* [2003] 1 BCLC 1 (CA)).

CASE EXAMPLE

Giles v Rhind [2003] 1 BCLC 1 (CA)

Giles and Rhind were the principal shareholders and directors of Surrey Hills Foods Ltd (SHF). Rhind, having sold his shares and left the company, in breach of an obligation of confidence owed both to the company and to Giles, set up a business in competition with SHF, caused the company's major customer to move its business to his new company and thereby brought about the insolvency of SHF. SHF commenced proceedings against Rhind which it was unable to continue when it went into administrative receivership because it could not afford to provide security for the costs of the defendant as ordered by the court. The action was discontinued on the basis of a consent order by which SHF was precluded from bringing any further action against Rhind. Giles therefore commenced an action against Rhind seeking damages for breach of the obligation of confidence owed personally to him. He claimed, amongst other heads of damage, the diminution in the value of his shares in SHF. Rhind argued that this was reflective loss which was not recoverable based on the no reflective loss principle. Rhind won at first instance. Giles appealed. Held: The appeal was allowed. Giles could continue his action. *Per* Waller LJ, 'Even in relation to that part of the claim for diminution which could be said to be reflective of the company's loss, since, if the company had no cause of action to recover that loss the shareholder could bring a claim, the same should be true of a situation in which the wrongdoer has disabled the company from pursuing that cause of action'.

Although *Giles v Rhind* has been followed (see *Perry v Day* [2005] 2 BCLC 405), the Court of Appeal in *Gardner v Parker* [2004] 2 BCLC 554 has made it clear that the case is authority for a very narrow exception to the no reflective loss principle. Only if the company is unable to sue the wrongdoer 'because of the very wrongdoing of which complaint was being made', will a shareholder not be barred from recovering reflective loss.

KEY FACTS

Proper claimant principle, derivative actions and shareholder personal claims	
Proper claimant principle	
Origins	*Foss v Harbottle* (1843)
Limits: Limited to matters subject to majority rule No application to *personal* shareholder claims	*Edwards v Halliwell* (1950) *Wood v Odessa* (1889)
Exception: Past: common law fraud on the minority Now: statutory derivative claim	*Cook v Deeks* (1916) s 260
Statutory derivative actions	
Based on breach of directors' duties	s 260(3)
Permission of court needed to continue a claim	s 261
Permission must be refused if: no *prima facie* case (stage 1) a director acting in accordance with s 172 would not continue (stage 2) act has been authorised or ratified (stage 2)	s 263(2)(a) s 263(2)(b) s 263(2)(c)
Court required to take following into account in permission decision: Good faith of claimant Importance a person acting in accordance with s 172 would attach to continuing the claim Whether likely to be authorised or ratified Whether the company has decided not to pursue the claim	s 263(3) (a) *Nurcombe v Nurcombe* (1985) (b) (c) (d)

Whether a personal action is available The views of other shareholders with no interest in the matter	(e) *Barrett v Duckett* (1995) (f) *Smith v Croft (No 2)* (1988)
Court usually willing to order a costs indemnity regardless of outcome	*Wallersteiner v Moir (No 2)* (1975) Civil Procedure Rules 19.9E
Personal claims by shareholder	
Range of rights enforceable by individual shareholders unclear	See Chapter 5: enforcement of provisions in the article of association by shareholders (s 33)
Personal actions for breach of individual rights eclipsed by s 994 petitions	See below
Reflective loss: Not recoverable Except where company is prevented from suing by the wrongdoing complained of	*Johnson v Gore Wood* (2001) *Giles v Rhind* (2003)

14.5 Unfairly prejudicial conduct petitions

14.5.1 Introduction

The unfair prejudice petition in s 994 has existed since 1980 when it replaced an 'oppressive behaviour' based remedy introduced in 1948. Between 1948 and 1980 only a couple of cases were reported in which oppressive behaviour had been successfully established. The unfair prejudice petition allows petitions to be made based on a much wider range of fact situations and remedies are awarded in a far higher proportion of cases than under the predecessor section.

Consequently, s 994 petitions are extremely popular. Many petitioners now choose to seek relief pursuant to ss 994–996 who, prior to 1980, would have:

- brought an action asserting a *particular* personal *right*, based on breach of contract, breach of duty or a statutory provision providing him with a cause of action;
- presented a winding-up petition on just and equitable grounds; or
- commenced a common law derivative action to assert the rights of the company and thereby benefit personally indirectly from a remedy in favour of the company.

Lord Hoffmann has played a significant judicial role in the development of this statutory remedy. Three cases in particular stand out:

- *Re a Company (No 00477 of 1986)* [1986] BCLC 376, which makes it clear that in companies with certain characteristics the interests of shareholders protected by s 994 are not limited to their strict legal rights (see below).
- *Re Saul D Harrison and Sons plc* [1995] 1 BCLC 14 (CA), which is an attempt to stem the tide of unfairly prejudicial conduct petitions.
- *O'Neill v Phillips* [1999] 1 WLR 1092 (HL), which is the leading case settling the approach to be taken to determine whether or not conduct of the affairs of the company is or has been unfairly prejudicial to the petitioning shareholder(s) (see below).

The right to petition is set out in s 994(1).

SECTION

'994 (1)

A member of a company may apply to the court by petition for an order under this Part on the ground—

(a) that the company's affairs are being or have been conducted in a manner that is unfairly prejudicial to the interests of members generally or of some part of its members (including at least himself), or

(b) that an actual or proposed act or omission of the company (including an act or omission on its behalf) is or would be so prejudicial.'

14.5.2 Petitioners and respondents

Who may petition

Members of a company, the shareholders for our purposes, are entitled to petition for an order under s 994. This clearly includes registered members, which means those individuals whose names are entered on the company's register of members as the legal owners of shares. By s 994(2) member also includes persons to whom shares in the company have been transferred or transmitted by operation of law. Problems may arise if the board of directors has power to refuse to register a person as owner of shares, as is common in private companies (see Model Articles for private companies limited by shares, Art 26(5)). Note that the beneficiary under a trust of shares is *not* a member: it is the trustee who is the legal owner and registered member. A shareholder can complain of conduct that pre-dates his registration, yet a former shareholder cannot present a s 994 petition even in respect of conduct that occurred whilst he was a member. The case that decided the last point, *Re a Company (No 00330 of 1991)* [1991] BCLC 597, has attracted criticism.

In *Gamlestaden Fastigheter AB v Baltic Partners Ltd* [2007] UKPC 26, a shareholder who petitioned the court pursuant to the Jersey equivalent of s 994 was held to be entitled to pursue his petition and the claim was not stuck out simply because, the company being insolvent and the shareholder also being a creditor of the company, the benefit of any order pursuant to the s 996 equivalent in Jersey would benefit the shareholder only in his capacity as a creditor, and not as a shareholder. The Privy Council advised that it was not necessary to show that the relief had to be of some benefit to the applicant shareholder in his capacity as shareholder. The applicant would have *locus standi* as long as the relief would be of real value to him in facilitating recovery of some part of his investment and it was, in the eyes of the Privy Council, artificial to require that the qualifying loss had to be loss that had reduced the value of the shareholder's equity capital rather than the recoverability of its loan capital.

The Secretary of State can present a petition (s 995) and this is most likely to occur following an investigation into a company pursuant to the Companies Act 1985 (see Chapter 17).

Who may be a respondent?

In theory, any person may be made a respondent to a s 994 petition. A person against whom a remedy is sought must be made a respondent and remedies are usually sought against the controlling shareholders/directors of the company. The company will also be made a respondent, albeit on a nominal basis, even where no remedy is sought against it and any shareholder whose interests may be affected by the remedy sought should also be joined (*Re a Company (No 005287 of 1985)* [1986] BCLC 68). Remedies may also be sought against more remote respondents such as ex-shareholders (liability cannot be avoided by a person transferring his shares) or a third party company controlled by the controlling shareholders.

14.5.3 The behaviour complained of

The company's affairs

The complaint must be about the conduct of the *company's* affairs, not the affairs of a director in his private capacity or a shareholder in his private capacity. A wide interpretation has been given to the affairs of the company. In *Re City Branch Group Ltd* [2005] 1 WLR 3505, for example, the conduct of the affairs of a subsidiary company were regarded as conduct of the company's affairs.

Examples of shareholders acting in their private capacity occurred in *Re Unisoft Group Ltd (No 3)* [1994] 1 BCLC 609 and *Re Leeds United Holdings plc* [1996] 2 BCLC 545. In both cases the petition was dismissed because the behaviour complained of was breach by a shareholder of a shareholders' agreement relating to the rights of the shareholder to transfer shares in the company.

Unfairly prejudicial conduct: general principles

The conduct complained of must be, 'both prejudicial … and also unfairly so' (*Re a Company (No 005685) ex parte Schwartz (No 2)* [1989] BCLC 427). Prejudice must be 'harm in a commercial sense, not in a merely emotional sense' (*Re Unisoft Group Ltd (No 3)* [1994] 1 BCLC 609).

Slade J made it clear in *Re Bovey Hotel Ventures Ltd* (1981) (unreported) (quoted with approval by Nourse J in *RA Noble & Sons (Clothing) Ltd* [1983] BCLC 273 and in subsequent cases), that the court will apply an objective test to determine whether or not conduct has unfairly prejudiced the petitioning shareholder's interests:

JUDGMENT

'The test of unfairness must, I think, be an objective, not a subjective, one. In other words it is not necessary for the petitioner to show that the persons who have had *de facto* control of the company have acted as they did in the conscious knowledge that this was unfair to the petitioner or that they were acting in bad faith; the test, I think, is whether a reasonable bystander observing the consequences of their conduct, would regard it as having unfairly prejudiced the petitioner's interests.'

Trivial or technical infringements of the articles will not be regarded as unfair (*Re Saul D Harrison & Sons plc* (1995)), and if the behaviour complained of can be brought to an end by the petitioning shareholder exercising his votes, the behaviour will not be considered unfair (*Re Baltic Real Estate Ltd (No 2)* [1993] BCLC 503).

14.5.4 The interests of members

The behaviour complained of in the petition must evidence the company's affairs being conducted in a manner that is unfairly prejudicial to the 'interests of members generally or some part of the members' (s 994(1)(a)).

Interests of members as members

The interests protected must be the interests of members *as members* or of shareholders *as shareholders*, although this requirement should not be approached too narrowly. The Privy Council has shown, for example, that where the remedy sought would simply bring relief to a shareholder *as a creditor* of the company rather than as a shareholder, the court may be prepared to treat the shareholders' interests as a creditor as interests for the purposes of the petition (*Gamlestaden Fastigheter AB v Baltic Partner Ltd* [2008] 1 BCLC 468 (PC)). In *Gamlestaden* the petitioner was a shareholder in a joint venture in which the joint venturers had agreed in a joint venture agreement to advance loan capital to the joint venture company as well as to subscribe for shares. Delivering the judgment of the Privy Council Lord Scott stated, 'the investor ought not to be precluded from the grant of relief under [section 994] on the ground that the relief would benefit the investor only as loan creditor and not as member'.

Rights and interests

'Interests' are wider than strict legal rights and to understand the range of behaviour that may be included in s 994 petitions it is helpful to place behaviour in three (albeit overlapping) categories.

First, shareholders have certain personal rights as shareholders, the exact range of which is, as we have seen, unclear. Breaches of a shareholder's personal rights as a shareholder are included in s 994 petitions as evidence of the company's affairs being conducted in a manner that is unfairly prejudicial to the petitioning shareholder.

Example

A company declares a dividend and then refuses to pay the share of the dividend due to one particular shareholder. This would be a breach of the contractual right of a shareholder to his share of a declared dividend. This infringement of the shareholder's legal rights could be included in a s 994 petition.

Second, a company has certain rights, such as the right to insist on its directors acting in accordance with their duties, which, as we have also seen, are not rights that are directly actionable by a shareholder. However, behaviour amounting to a breach of duty owed to the company may be included in a s 994 petition as evidence of the company's affairs being conducted in a manner that is unfairly prejudicial to the petitioning shareholder.

Example

The board of directors terminates a minority shareholder director's directorship in accordance with the power to do so in the articles and excludes him from management of the company. This could be a breach of directors' duties if the directors take these actions because they have fallen out with the minority shareholder, rather than because they believe that to do so is likely to promote the success of the company. Nonetheless, the minority shareholder could include this behaviour in his s 994 petition as evidence of the company's affairs being conducted in a manner unfairly prejudicial to his interests.

In the second example the minority shareholder will be asserting unfair prejudice to his *interests*, rather than any strict legal right.

Finally, although, 'a company is an association of persons for an economic purpose, usually entered into with legal advice and some degree of formality' (*O'Neill v Phillips* (1999) HL *per* Lord Hoffmann) and that, accordingly, in most cases, a breach of rights is required for conduct to be unfair, behaviour may amount to evidence of a company's affairs being conducted in a manner unfairly prejudicial to the interests of the petitioning shareholder even if it neither infringes his strict legal rights nor breaches a right of the company.

The 'rights based approach' is supplemented by an 'interests based approach' and it is necessary to ask: has the majority acted or is it proposing to act in a manner which equity would regard as contrary to good faith? (*Re Guidezone Ltd* [2000] 2 BCLC 321, *per* Parker J), in which case a s 994 petition operates to give relief on an equitable basis. Hoffmann J, as he then was, confirmed this interests-based approach in *Re a Company (No 00477 of 1986)* [1986] BCLC 376.

JUDGMENT

'[T]he court must take into account that the interests of a member are not necessarily limited to his strict legal rights under the company's constitution ... The use of the word "unfairly"... like the use of the words "just and equitable" ... enables the court to have regard to wider equitable considerations.'

Circumstances in which an 'interests based' equitable approach is appropriate

As mentioned in the introduction to our consideration of s 994, many petitions which today would be brought under s 994 were, prior to 1980, brought as petitions for the court to wind up the company on just and equitable grounds. The leading case on just and equitable winding-up is *Ebrahimi v Westbourne Galleries Ltd* [1973] AC 360 (HL) which has been endorsed as authority for how the court approaches the exercise of its equitable jurisdiction under s 994.

CASE EXAMPLE

Ebrahimi v Westbourne Galleries Ltd [1973] AC 360 (HL)

N and E were partners in an unincorporated business. They incorporated a company and transferred the assets of the partnership to it. Initially, they were equal shareholders and were both directors. The company paid the directors remuneration rather than paying dividends. N's son joined the company as a director and shareholder. E was now one of three directors and owned one-third of the company's shares. After a disagreement, E was (1) removed from office under what is now Companies Act 2006, s 168, (2) deprived of his salary and (3) deprived of his role in the management of the company. E presented a petition for the company to be wound up on the ground that it was just and equitable to do so. Held: the company was ordered to be wound up. The company had been formed on the assumption that E would participate in its management and receive a salary. The exercise of the company's strict legal right to remove him from office breached an implied agreement or mutual understanding that E would be a full-time working director. In the circumstances such breach was unjust and inequitable. Lord Wilberforce stated that company law recognises that behind the corporate entity there are individuals with rights, expectations and obligations amongst themselves which are not necessarily submerged in the company structure. He stated that a company's structure is defined by the Act and by the articles by which members agree to be bound and that in most companies and in most contexts, this definition is sufficient and exhaustive, whether the company is large or small. But, he emphasised, 'The winding-up jurisdiction is an equitable jurisdiction. It does not entitle one party to disregard the obligation he assumes by entering a company but *it does, as equity always does, enable the court to subject the exercise of legal rights to equitable considerations*; considerations, that is, of a personal character arising between one individual and another, which may make it unjust, or inequitable, to insist on legal rights, or to exercise them in a particular way.' (emphasis added).

Lord Wilberforce described the typical circumstances in which the court is called upon to provide relief under s 994 based on behaviour that does not amount to an infringement of the petitioning shareholder's strict legal rights and set out what have come to be referred to as the '*Ebrahimi* factors' that are likely to be present before the court will grant such equitable relief. The *Ebrahimi* factors should not be regarded as written in stone. Lord Wilberforce introduced them with a reminder that it would be impossible, and wholly undesirable, to define the circumstances in which equitable considerations may arise. Those circumstances, he stated, typically may include one, or probably more, of the following elements:

▪ An association formed or continued on the basis of a personal relationship, involving mutual confidence – this element will often be found where a pre-existing partnership has been converted into a limited company.

▪ An agreement or understanding that all or some of the shareholders shall participate in the conduct of the business (may be evidenced by the manner in which profits are distributed).

▪ Restriction on the transfer of the members' interests in the company – so that if confidence is lost, or one member is removed from management, he cannot take out his stake and go elsewhere.

In *O'Neill v Phillips* (1999) Lord Hoffmann explained the partnership law parentage of the equitable principles in evidence in successful s 994 petitions.

JUDGMENT

'Company law has developed seamlessly from the law of partnership, which was treated by equity ... as a contract of good faith. One of the traditional roles of equity, as a separate jurisdiction, was to restrain the exercise of strict legal rights in relationships in which it considered that this would be contrary to good faith. These principles have, with appropriate modification, been carried over into company law ... [It follows] that there will be cases in which equitable considerations make it unfair for those conducting the affairs of the company to rely upon their strict legal powers.'

He also stressed that in exercising its discretion the court must strike a balance between the breadth of its discretion and the principle of legal certainty. The way in which the equitable principles operate are, in his view, 'tolerably well settled'.

Key (unsuccessful) cases

Two key cases concerning petitions made under the predecessor section to s 994 demonstrate the approach the courts take to the exercise of its equitable jurisdiction. Both cases demonstrate that where there has been no infringement of rights or behaviour inconsistent with the companies' articles, *more than legitimate expectations* of a petitioning shareholder are needed before the court will provide a remedy.

CASE EXAMPLE

Re Saul D Harrison & Sons plc [1995] 1 BCLC 14 (CA)

The petitioner (P) under what is now s 994, held shares in a company that had been set up by her great-grandfather and was trading at a loss, having substantial assets to draw on. She held a separate class of non-voting shares carrying rights to dividend and to share in the capital on a winding-up. P alleged the company should cease trading and return capital to shareholders rather than continuing to trade at a loss. She argued that she had a legitimate expectation that the company would be wound up once it started to make losses. P also claimed that the majority were only continuing to trade so that they could draw their directors' remuneration. Held: The petitioner was not entitled to relief. There was no unlawful conduct and even if there had been it would have to be found to be unfair. Although lawful acts can also be unfair and there are cases in which the letter of the articles does not fully reflect the understanding upon which the shareholders are associated, this was *not* such a case. P's rights were adequately and exhaustively defined by the articles. Her '"legitimate expectations" amounted to no more than an expectation that the board would manage the company in accordance with their fiduciary obligations and the terms of the articles and the Companies Act'.

CASE EXAMPLE

O'Neill v Phillips [1999] 1 WLR 1092

Phillips (P) owned all of the shares of a company. He transferred 25 per cent of his shares to O'Neill (O), a company employee, and promoted O to the board. P retired from the board and O was appointed Managing Director of the company. The company was initially profitable and although O was only strictly entitled to one quarter of the dividends, P waived a third of his dividend entitlement so that dividends were shared equally between P and O. Preliminary discussions took place with a view to O increasing his stake to 50 per cent but no formal agreement was ever reached. A financial downturn followed. P resumed command of the company and although O remained on the board his status was reduced to that of a branch manager. As O was no longer Managing Director, P decided that O would receive only his salary and one quarter of any dividends. O petitioned under what is now s 994 alleging that there was an 'implied agreement' giving rise to a legitimate expectation that he would receive an equal share of the company's profits and an increase to a 50 per cent shareholding. Held: O's petition for relief would not succeed. Whilst there might be circumstances in which equitable considerations would make it unfair for a controlling shareholder to rely on his strict legal powers, this was not such a case. O had not been excluded from management nor, on the evidence, had P unconditionally promised that O would receive an equal share of profits for all time or an increased shareholding.

Typical lawful conduct that may form the basis of a successful petition

The following conduct may be lawful yet be evidence of the affairs of the company being conducted in a manner unfairly prejudicial to the interests of the petitioning shareholder:

- Removal of the petitioner as a director.
- Denying the petitioner a role in the management of the company (in *Richards v Lundy* [2000] 1 BCLC 376, the petitioner had been unfairly excluded from management as a director and employee where the company was in substance a quasi-partnership).

- Mismanagement of the company's assets (see *Re Elgindata Ltd* [1991] BCLC 959 and *Re Macro (Ipswich) Ltd* [1994] 2 BCLC 354).
- Payment of excessive remuneration to directors (see *Re Cumana Ltd* [1986] BCLC 430 (CA)).
- Non payment of dividends or payment of derisory dividends (in *Re Sam Weller & Sons Ltd* [1990] BCLC 80, the company failed to increase dividends for 37 years despite increasing profits).

Unlawful conduct that has formed the basis of a successful petition

The following unlawful conduct has been successfully included in s 994 petitions as evidence of the affairs of the company being conducted in a manner unfairly prejudicial to the interests of the petitioning shareholder:

- Directors exercising powers for an improper purpose (see *Re Cumana Ltd* (1986), in which a rights issue was timed for when the minority shareholder had no funds).
- Breach of statutory pre-emption rights (now found in s 561) (as in *Re a Company (No 005134 of 1986), ex parte Harries* [1989] BCLC 383).
- Refusal to pay declared dividend (as in *Grace v Biagioli* [2006] 2 BCLC 70).
- Diversion of company business to a majority shareholder in breach of fiduciary duty (as in *Re London School of Electronics* [1986] Ch 211).

CASE EXAMPLE

Simon Rodliffe v Guy Rodliffe, Home and Office Fire Extinguishers Limited
[2012] EWHC 917(Ch)

Home and Office Fire Extinguishers Ltd was established in 1979 to sell and service fire extinguishers and alarms by the parents of two brothers, Guy and Simon, each of whom came to be the only two directors and holders of 50 per cent each of the shares in the company. In 2007–2008 the company was in financial difficulty and Simon was having personal and financial difficulties that were keeping him away from the office. In these circumstances, Guy reduced both his own and Simon's salary. After an argument, Simon attacked Guy with a hammer, for which assault he was prosecuted but acquitted. Simon did not work in the company again. Initially his bail conditions preventing him from visiting the company's offices but in any event, the brothers were unable to work with one another. Guy continued to run the company as sole director. Each brother petitioned the court under s 994 for an order that the other sell his shares to them. The court held that Simon's attack on the other shareholder with a hammer constituted unfairly prejudicial conduct which made it impossible for them to continue their association as directors and shareholders and ordered Simon to sell his shares to Guy at a *pro rata* price.

14.5.5 Remedies and costs

On a s 994 petition the court has power to 'make such order as it thinks fit for giving relief in respect of the matters complained of' (s 996(1)). Section 996(2) then contains a *non-exhaustive* list of orders the court may make. Although the court *may* order the winding-up of the company on a s 994 petition, pursuit of such an order introduces complications and petitioners are discouraged from seeking such an order on a s 994 petition. The relationship between a s 994 petition and a petition to wind up the company on the basis that it is just and equitable for it to be wound up is examined below at section 14.6.3.

JUDGMENT

'In most cases, the usual order to make will be the one requiring the respondents to buy out the petitioning shareholder at a price to be fixed by the court. This is normally the most appropriate order to deal with intra-company disputes involving small private companies.'

CASE EXAMPLE

Grace v Biagioli [2006] 2 BCLC 70 (CA)

Members of a company each took responsibility for developing and managing its business in various countries. The petitioner (P) was responsible for starting up and developing business in France. The other members became unhappy because the French business was not very profitable. Dividends were declared but it was decided to withhold P's dividend and pay an equivalent sum to the other members as management fees. P presented a petition under what is now s 994 seeking a buy-out order. It was argued that buy-out relief was not appropriate as any unfair prejudice could be remedied by ordering payment of the dividends. Held: P was locked into a company where relationships had soured and there were likely to be further disputes in the future. The appropriate remedy was an order that he be bought out at a fair valuation.

Buy-out orders

The most important remedy, listed at s 996(2)(g), is an order 'for the purchase of the shares of the company by other members or by the company itself and, in the case of a purchase by the company itself, the reduction of the company's share capital accordingly'. In *Grace v Biagioli* (2006) a buy-out was described as the usual order to make.

Buy-outs have a number of benefits:

- The possibility of future difficulties between shareholders is removed.
- They allow an otherwise locked-in minority to extract his share of the value of the business: to 'exit'.
- The company and its business is preserved for the benefit of the respondent shareholders.
- The company is free from the claims of the petitioning shareholder.

It is important to understand the effect on a s 994 petition of the respondent having offered or, as a result of the petition being presented, offering to buy out the petitioning shareholder. Essentially, if the respondent makes a reasonable offer to buy the petitioner out of the company, the petitioner will be expected to accept the offer (*O'Neill v Phillips* (1999) *per* Lord Hoffmann).

JUDGMENT

'If the respondent to a petition has plainly made a reasonable offer, then the exclusion as such will not be unfairly prejudicial and he will be entitled to have the petition struck out.'

If the offer is made only after the petition has been made and costs have been incurred by the petitioner, the respondent will also need to make a reasonable offer in relation to costs.

Fair valuation of shares

A reasonable offer to buy out the petitioner, and a court order that the respondent or the company (or, potentially a third party) buy out the petitioning shareholders' shares will be based on a fair valuation of those shares. Both the time at which the shares are to be valued and the basis on which they are to be valued are important aspects of fair value.

Timing of the share valuation

Three potential dates exist for the valuation of the petitioning shareholders' shares: the date of the petition, the date of the trial and the date of the final order in the petition. As a rule of thumb, the appropriate date will be the date of the order in the petition, that is, the date on which the shares are ordered to be purchased. Where, however, the conduct complained of has reduced or depreciated the value of the shares as measured at that date, their value will need to be adjusted to restore the petitioning shareholders' position (*Profinance Trust SA v Gladstone* [2002] 1 BCLC 141).

Basis of the share valuation

Valuation of a private company is a notoriously difficult task as alternative valuation methods exist. Because valuation is not an exact science and potential exists for a low valuation or, contrarily, a high valuation to be presented as objectively arrived at, it is extremely important that the valuation is made by an independent valuer and the court should not seek to circumscribe the valuer's exercise of his expertise (*Martin Boughtwood v Oak Investment Partners XII Ltd Partnership* [2010] EWCA Civ 23 (CA)). Even once the *company* has been valued it is necessary to allocate that value to the share interests held by different shareholders in the company. Assuming, as is common, the company has only one class of shares (and assuming that the company has not been valued on a 'net assets on break up' value but as a 'going concern'), the two bases for the valuation of shareholdings are a *pro rata* valuation and a discounted valuation.

A *pro rata* valuation simply means allocation of an equal value to each share. The value of a shareholders' stake in the company is, on this basis, the value of a share multiplied by the number of shares he owns. In a small company, however, individual shareholders typically own significant shareholdings. It is not uncommon for one shareholder to own a block of shares which confers on him voting control of the company (50 per cent + 1 vote). It is standard practice in valuing a block of shares in a company for the purpose of a sale between a willing buyer and seller to discount the *pro rata* value of a minority holding to reflect the absence of control, hence the term 'discounted value'. A minority shareholding may confer the power to block special resolutions which is referred to as 'negative control' (25%) and a minority shareholding conferring negative control ordinarily would not be discounted to the same extent as a shareholding of less than 25 per cent.

The key question to determine the correct basis of valuation in a s 994 petition is whether or not it is appropriate on the facts to discount the value of the petitioning shareholders' stake below a *pro rata* valuation because it is a minority stake and, as such, the petitioning shareholder was never in a position to exercise much or any control over the company. The rule of thumb (although it will not always be the case) on a petition based on unfair exclusion from management will be for shares to be given a *pro rata* valuation (*Re Bird Precision Bellow Ltd* [1984] 3 All ER 44). In exclusion from management petitions, the very point of the relief is that the petitioner had been in a position to exercise control alongside the other shareholders until the other shareholders began to assert their strict legal rights contrary to the understanding that formed the basis on which the company had been run prior to the unfairly prejudicial conduct of which the petitioner is complaining.

In *O'Neill v Phillips* [1999] 1 WLR 1092, Lord Hoffman set out a five point guide to what constitutes a reasonable offer such that the court will strike out a petition if it is not accepted:

- The offer must be to purchase the petitioner's shares at a fair value: ordinarily at a *pro rata* valuation.
- If the value is not agreed it must be determined by a competent expert.
- The value should be determined by an expert as an expert, not by a more complex procedure.
- Both parties should have access to information about the company which bears upon the value of the shares and both should have the right to make submissions to the expert.
- The respondent should be given a reasonable opportunity to make a costs offer before becoming obliged to pay costs.

Costs

The special costs rules that apply to derivative claims do not apply to s 994 petitions because the rationale for making the company indemnify the claimant shareholder is not present. In s 994 petitions the petitioning shareholder is seeking a remedy for himself, not the company (see *Re Sherborne Park Residents Co Ltd* (1986)). Controllers of a company will not be permitted to use the assets of the company to pay the legal costs of defending a s 994 petition which is essentially brought against them, even though the company has been joined as a respondent (*Re a Company (No 001126 of 1992)* [1993] BCC 325, and *Re Milgate Developments Ltd* [1993] BCLC 291).

14.5.6 Reform and alternative dispute resolution

Section 994 petitions are typically very fact intensive and hence time consuming and expensive proceedings. The costs of proceedings can and has in the past exceeded the value of the remedy in issue. A recent case illustrating the point is *Hawkes v Cuddy* [2007] EWHC 2999 (Ch) (*sub nom Re Neath Rugby Ltd*) in which shares worth no more than £97,000 were argued about for more than four weeks in court at various stages in the proceedings. The Law Commission recognised and addressed the problem in both its Consultation Paper and Report on Shareholder Remedies (see further reading), recommending that courts exercise strong case management of s 994 petitions.

In *Fulham Football Club (1987) Ltd v Richards* [2012] 1 All ER 414 (CA), the Court of Appeal applied *Vocam Europe Ltd, Re* [1998] BCC 396, where an unfair prejudice petition had been stayed where a shareholders' agreement provided for disputes to be arbitrated and overruled *Exeter City AFC Ltd v Football Conference Ltd* [2004] EWHC 831 where no stay had been granted on the ground that shareholders' rights to apply for relief were inalienable, to hold that a s 994 petition will be stayed if it is covered by an arbitration agreement.

14.6 Just and equitable winding-up petitions

14.6.1 Who may apply

Section 124 of the Insolvency Act 1986 provides that a company, its directors, any creditor, the liquidator or a 'contributor' of at least six months standing may petition the court for a winding-up order. One of the grounds on which the court may order a winding-up is that the court, 'is of the opinion that it is just and equitable that the company should be wound up' (s 122(1)(g) of the 1986 Act).

Contributor is defined in s 79 of the Insolvency Act 1986 to mean a person liable to contribute to the assets of the company if it is wound up. A shareholder with partly-paid shares clearly falls within the definition of contributory. Although a shareholder with fully paid up shares would appear not to fall within the definition, such a shareholder has been held to be a contributory provided he has a sufficient interest in the winding-up (*Re Rica Gold Washing Co Ltd* (1879) 11 Ch D 36). Basically, a shareholder with fully paid up shares must prove that there will be a surplus in which he will share to be able to bring a petition.

14.6.2 Foundation of the jurisdiction

The circumstances in which a court will order a winding-up on just and equitable grounds were considered by the House of Lords in the leading case of *Ebrahimi v Westbourne Galleries Ltd* (1973) (see above at section 14.5.4). Having reviewed the authorities Lord Wilberforce described the foundation of the jurisdiction:

JUDGMENT

'The foundation of it all lies in the words "just and equitable" and, if there is any respect in which some of the cases may be open to criticism, it is that the courts may sometimes have been too timorous in giving them full force. The words are a recognition of the fact that a limited company is more than a mere legal entity, with a personality in law of its own: that there is room in company law for recognition of the fact that behind it, or amongst it, there are individuals, with rights, expectations and obligations *inter se* which are not necessarily submerged in the company structure. That structure is defined by the Companies Act and by the articles of association by which shareholders agree to be bound. In most companies and in most contexts, this definition is sufficient and exhaustive, equally so whether the company is large or small. The "just and equitable" provision does not, as the respondents suggest, entitle one party to disregard the obligation he assumes by entering a company, nor the court to dispense him from it. It does, as equity always does, enable the court to subject the exercise of legal rights to equitable considerations; considerations, that is, of a personal character arising between one individual and another, which may make it unjust, or inequitable, to insist on legal rights, or to exercise them in a particular way.'

As we have seen, *Ebrahimi* is now a leading case on the approach to be taken by courts on s 994 petitions. It is important to understand the relationship between s 124 and s 994 petitions.

14.6.3 Relationship with unfair prejudice claims

Ebrahimi was decided when shareholders did not have the right to petition the court for a remedy based on unfairly prejudicial conduct of the company's affairs (s 994). Since 1980, when the unfairly prejudicial conduct petition was introduced, many petitioners who, prior to 1980, would have made a winding-up petition on just and equitable grounds now choose to seek relief pursuant to ss 994–996.

Three questions are of critical importance to a shareholder:

▨ May the court order a winding-up on a s 994 petition?
▨ May the court make an alternative order to a winding-up order on a s 124 petition?
▨ Is a shareholder entitled to a winding-up order pursuant to a s 124 petition if he could obtain an adequate remedy under s 994?

May the court order a winding-up on a s 994 petition?

Although the court technically has power to make a winding-up order pursuant to a s 994 petition, courts will not do so unless asked to make such an order (see *Re Full Cup International Trading Ltd* [1995] BCC 682) and a practice direction ([1990] 1 WLR 490) discouraged s 994 petitioners from asking for such relief:

'Practitioners' attention is drawn to the undesirability of including as a matter of course a prayer for winding-up as an alternative to an order under [section 994]. It should be included only if that is the relief which the petitioner prefers or if it is considered that it may be the only relief to which he is entitled.'

This practice direction is no longer formally in effect but courts continue to discourage the practice of asking for a winding-up order on a s 994 petition (see *Re Copeland & Craddock Ltd* [1997] BCC 294).

Further, the effect of asking for a winding-up order, even in the alternative, is to trigger s 127 of the Insolvency Act 1986, which results in the company being unable to carry on business from the date the petition is presented. Again, as a matter of practice, the court will, unless the petitioner can convince it not to, make an order overriding s 127 so that the company can continue to trade.

The learning point is that s 994 is not intended to be used by a person who is seeking to wind up the company. A shareholder seeking a winding-up order should petition the court under s 124 of the Insolvency Act 1986. The availability of a winding-up order as a remedy under a s 994 petition was considered as part of the Company Law Review and the steering group recommended against including winding-up orders in the remedies available on a s 994 petition.

May the court make an alternative order to a winding-up order on a s 124 petition?

The powers of the court under a s 124 application are set out in s 125 (see below). Again, whilst technically it may make 'any order that it thinks fit', it is not the practice of the court to provide a remedy different from a winding-up on a s 124 petition.

Is a shareholder entitled to a winding-up order pursuant to a s 124 petition if he could obtain an adequate remedy under s 994?

The right of a shareholder to a winding-up order where an alternative remedy is available is dealt with in s 125(2)(b).

SECTION

'125   Powers of court on hearing of petition

(1) On hearing a winding-up petition the court may dismiss it, or adjourn the hearing conditionally or unconditionally, or make an interim order, or any other order that it thinks fit; …

(2) If the petition is presented by members of the company as contributories on the ground that it is just and equitable that the company should be wound up, the court, if it is of opinion—

(a) that the petitioners are entitled to relief either by winding-up the company or by some other means, and

(b) that in the absence of any other remedy it would be just and equitable that the company should be wound up, shall make a winding-up order; but this does not apply if the court is also of the opinion both that some other remedy is available to the petitioners and that they are acting unreasonably in seeking to have the company wound up instead of pursuing that other remedy.'

Essentially, even if a winding-up order would otherwise be available, the court will not order the company wound up if the court is of the opinion that *both*:

- 'some other remedy is available'; *and*
- the shareholder is acting unreasonably in seeking to have the company wound up.

Consequently, even if the shareholder could make an application under s 994 (and in most cases he could), this is *not* sufficient ground for the court to deny a winding-up order (see *Re a Company (No 001363 of 1988) ex parte S-P* [1989] BCLC 579). The key consideration is whether or not the shareholder is acting reasonably in seeking a winding-up order, which involves consideration of all the facts of the case. A typical scenario is that the petitioner has been made or, as a result of presentation of the winding-up petition, is made, an offer to purchase his shares in the company. Courts consider whether or not the shareholder is acting unreasonably in refusing to accept the offer. Where it appears that it would be unreasonable for the petitioner to refuse to be bought out, the court may stay (suspend) the winding-up petition for the details of the purchase to be worked out, in this way protecting the petitioner from the defendant adopting bad faith tactics in the share sale negotiations, as in *Re A Company (002567 of 1982)* [1983] 1 WLR 927.

CASE EXAMPLE

Re a Company (No 002567 of 1982) [1983] 1 WLR 927

T and C were partners in an unincorporated business. They formed a company to run the business and T and C were the directors and shareholders. Later, R joined the company with the result that T, C and R were all salaried directors owning one-third of the company's shares and receiving equal remuneration *qua* directors. No dividends were ever paid. T was removed from office as a director, deprived of his employment and any say in the management of the company's affairs, and the company stopped paying him his remuneration. T petitioned the court under the Insolvency Act 1986 for the winding-up of the company on the just and equitable ground citing a breakdown of mutual trust and confidence. Held: the winding-up petition would be stayed pending finalisation of the purchase of shares subject to which it would be dismissed. This was not because the petition lacked merit but because in the court's view the petitioner was unreasonable in refusing the respondents' (C and R's) offer to purchase his shares at a value reached by machinery which met all his reasonable objections (*obiter*) A case where what is alleged is unfair exclusion from the management of the company's affairs in breach of an express or implied agreement that the member will be allowed to participate in management and be paid remuneration falls within the scope of section [994(1)] even though the member's strict rights *qua* member are not affected. *Per* Vinelott J: 'It seems to me unlikely that the legislature could have intended to exclude from the scope of section [994] a shareholder in the position of Mr Ebrahimi in *Ebrahimi v Westbourne Galleries Ltd* [1973] AC 360'.

KEY FACTS

Unfairly prejudicial conduct and just and equitable winding-up petitions	
Unfairly prejudicial conduct petitions, s 994	
Available to present, not past shareholders	*Re a Company (No 00330 of 1991)* (1991)
Range of respondents and relief unlimited though: Buy-out is usual remedy Application for winding-up discouraged	ss 994 and 996 *Grace v Biagioli* (2006) *Re Copeland & Craddock Ltd* (1997)
Behaviour complained of must be conduct of the affairs of the company which may include affairs of a subsidiary	*Re City Branch Group Ltd* (2005)
Shareholders' 'interests' protected may be: Strict legal rights (eg refusal to pay a declared and due dividend)) Strict company rights (eg breach of directors' duties) Interest of shareholders (particularly in quasi-partnership companies) in legal rights being exercised subject to equitable considerations.	*Grace v Biagioli* (2006) *Re Cumana Ltd* (1986) *Ebrahimi v Westbourne Galleries Ltd* (1973) *Re Saul D Harrison & Sons* (1995) *O'Neill v Phillips* (1999)
Just and equitable winding-up petitions, s 122(1)(g) Insolvency Act 1986	
Available to 'contributors' which includes a fully paid up shareholder provided there will be a surplus.	*Re Rica Gold Washing Co Ltd* (1879)
A general equitable jurisdiction.	*Ebrahimi v Westbourne Galleries Ltd* (1973)
Will *not* be ordered if both: Some other remedy is available to the applicant (such as a remedy under s 994); and The applicant is not acting reasonably in seeking a winding-up order	*Re a Company (No 001363 of 1988)* (1989)

SUMMARY

The proper claimant principle (the rule in *Foss v Harbottle*)

- In any legal proceedings in which a wrong is alleged to have been done to a company, the proper claimant is the company.
- The rule arises from application by the courts of majority rule and the business judgement rule.
- The rule does not apply where:
  - a shareholder is exercising a personal right;
  - the action complained of is action by the company for which more than a simple majority is needed (*Edwards v Halliwell* (1950));
  - a statutory derivative action may be pursued (s 260).

Statutory derivative claims (s 260)

- Grounds for claim: an actual or proposed act or omission involving negligence, default, breach of duty or breach of trust by a director of the company (s 260).
- Claims procedure: the claim is issued followed by an application to the court for permission to continue disclosing a *prima facie* case (s 261(1)).
- Permission to continue must be refused if a person acting in accordance with the s 172 duty to promote the success of the company would not seek to continue the claim (s 263(2)(a)); or there has been authorisation or ratification of the act complained of (s 263(2)(b) and (c)).
- The court must consider a list of factors before exercising its discretion to permit the claim to continue (s 263(3)) (see list at 3.2 above).
- Claimants will ordinarily be entitled to an order of indemnity in relation to costs, regardless of the outcome of the litigation (*Wallersteiner v Moir (No 2)* (1975)) based on the theory that the claimant is in effect bringing the claim as an agent of the company.

Personal actions by a shareholder

- Legal actions asserting the personal rights of a shareholders are personal actions.
- The no reflective loss principle denies a shareholder the right to assert personal rights where his loss simply reflects a loss incurred by the company (*Johnson v Gore Wood & Co* (2001)).
- Where the company is unable to pursue its claim against the defendant because of the defendant's wrongdoing, a shareholder will be entitled to bring a personal action as an exception to the no reflective loss principle (*Giles v Rhind* [2003] 1 BCLC 1 (CA)).

Unfairly prejudicial conduct petitions (s 994)

- A shareholder may petition the court for an order on the ground that *the company's affairs* have been conducted in a manner that is *unfairly prejudicial* to one or more *shareholders' interests*.
- A remedy is usually sought against the controlling shareholders/directors of the company, most commonly for an order to buy out the petitioner's shares in the company.
- The conduct complained of must be both prejudicial and unfairly so (*Re a Company (No 005685) ex parte Schwartz (No 2)* (1989)).
- The test of unfairness is objective, not subjective (*Re Bovey Hotel Ventures Ltd* (1981)).
- Prejudice must be harm in a commercial sense, not in a merely emotional sense (*Re Unisoft Group Ltd (No 3)* (1994)).
- Shareholders' interests protected by s 994 are wider than strict legal rights.
- The interests protected in quasi-partnership cases can be equitable in nature (*Ebrahimi v Westbourne Galleries Ltd* (1973); *O'Neill v Phillips* (1999)).
- The court has power to make such order as it thinks fit for giving relief, the most common order being that the majority shareholder buy the shares of the petitioner (s 996).
- Courts are reluctant to consider or grant a winding-up on a s 994 petition.

Just and equitable winding-up petitions (s 122 Insolvency Act 1986)

- The court may order a winding-up on the petition of (amongst others) a contributor (which a shareholder is likely to be) if it is of the opinion that it is just and equitable to do so (s 122(1)(g) of the 1986 Act).
- It is not the practice of the court to provide a remedy different from a winding-up on a s 124 petition.
- The availability of a s 994 application is not sufficient ground for the court to deny a winding-up order (see *Re a Company (No 001363 of 1988) ex parte S-P* (1989)).

SAMPLE ESSAY QUESTION

> Critically analyse the function of derivative claims and the restrictions imposed on such claims.

Unpack the question

This is the first essential step which you must take time to do properly. You should separate out:

- Explanation of what a derivative claim is
- The role intended to be played/played by derivative claims
- Court control of derivative claims
- Consideration/analysis of whether or not the derivative claim provisions serve the purpose they are intended to serve.

Derivative claims and their function

- Contrast with personal actions by shareholders
- Identify the problem of companies being run for the benefit of majority shareholder directors: the economic agency problem (Chapter 1, section 1.2.4)
- Identify why a special procedure is needed: *Foss v Harbottle*, the principle of majority rule and the proper claimant principle
- Identify the common law development and its difficulty: the need to show fraud on the minority: *Cook v Deeks*
- Explain the replacement of the common law procedure with the statutory claim and procedure: ss 260–263.

The statutory derivative claim

- Explain who can bring a claim: any shareholder: s 260(1)
- Explain the basis for a claim: negligence, default, breach of duty or breach of trust by a director of the company: s 26(3)
- Identify its breadth compared to the common law action and suggestions that this will lead to opening of the floodgates.

Outline court control of claims

Discuss the statutory provisions and cases relevant to:

- The need for permission of the court to continue a claim: s 261(1)
- When a court must refuse permission to continue: no *prima facie* case: s 261(2); where authorisation or ratification has taken place: s 263(2); if a s 172-compliant director would not seek to continue the claim: s 263(2)(a)
- Factors a court must take into account when deciding whether or not to give permission: s 263(3) & (4).

CONCLUDE

Express your reasoned opinion as to whether the statutory derivative action and the procedure surrounding it are satisfactory/work well/serve their purpose.

ACTIVITY

Self-test questions

1. Certain director/shareholders increase the proportion of shares in the company they own by allotting shares to themselves. The proportion of the shares in the company owned by other shareholders is thereby reduced, ie their interest in the company is diluted.
   What legal proceedings can be brought?
2. Directors award themselves excessive remuneration.
   What legal proceedings can be brought?
3. A company with director/shareholders does not pay dividends. It pays remuneration to directors at a level that reduces profits to nil. The majority shareholders (55%) pass a resolution to remove the minority shareholder (45%) from the board (s 168).
   What legal proceedings can be brought?

Further reading

Articles

Boyle, A, 'Unfair Prejudice in the House of Lords' (2000) 21 Comp Law 253.

Hannigan, B, 'Drawing Boundaries Between Derivative Claims and Unfairly Prejudicial Petitions' (2009) 6 JBLaw 606.

Keay, A & Loughrey, J, 'Something Old, Something New, Something Borrowed: An Analysis of the New Derivative Action under the Companies Act 2006' (2008) 124 LQR 469.

Lightman, D, ' Coming of Age? ... the Statutory Derivative Claim Three Years On' [2010] New Law Journal 1750.

von Nessen, P, Goo, S H. & Low, C K, 'The statutory derivative action: now showing near you' [2008] JBL 627.

Mujih, E, 'The New Statutory Derivative Claim: a Delicate Balancing Act Parts 1 & 2 (2012) 33 Comp. Law. 76 and 99.

Payne, J and Prentice, D, 'Section 459 of the Companies Act: The House of Lords View' (1999) 115 LQR 587.

Payne, J, 'Sections 459-461 in Flux: the Future of Shareholder Protection' (2005) 64 Cambridge Law Journal 647.

Reisberg, A, 'European Shareholders' Remedies: the Choice of Objectives and the Social Meaning of Derivative Actions' (2005) 6 European Business Organization Law Review 227.

Reisberg, A, 'Shareholder remedies: in search of consistency of principle in English law' [2005] EBLR 1063.

Sugarman, D, 'Reconceptualising company law: reflections on the Law Commission's Consultation Paper on shareholder remedies', Parts 1 & 2 (1997) 18 Comp Law 226 & 274.

Reports

Modern Company Law for a Competitive Economy, *Company Law Review* (see various documents published as part of the review listed in Chapter 1, Table 1.5).

Shareholder Remedies, Consultation Paper No 42, Law Commission (1996).

Shareholder Remedies, Report No 246 (1997, Cm 3769).

Books

Joffe, V, Drake, D, Richardson, G, & Lightman, D, Minority *Shareholders, Law Practice and Procedure* 4th edn, (Oxford, Oxford University Press, 2011), chapter 1

Hollington, R, *Shareholders' Rights* (5th edn (rev), Sweet & Maxwell, 2007).

Lowry, J, 'Mapping the Boundaries of Unfair Prejudice' in de Lacey, J (ed), *The Reform of United Kingdom Company Law* (Cavendish Publishing, 2002).

Reisberg, A, *Derivative Actions and Corporate Governance* (Oxford University Press, 2008).

15

Restructuring, rescuing troubled companies and takeovers

AIMS AND OBJECTIVES

After reading this chapter you should understand:

▣ When section 110 schemes of reconstruction are available and when they are typically used

▣ When Part 26 schemes of arrangement are available and when they are typically used

▣ The object and effect of a company voluntary arrangement (CVA) and the procedure to put one in place

▣ The availability, object and effect of a small company moratorium

▣ The objectives of administration

▣ How administrators are appointed, the effect of administration and how administration comes to an end

▣ The role and scope of application of the Code on Takeovers and Mergers ('the City Code')

▣ The role and legal status of the Panel on Takeovers and Mergers ('the Panel')

15.1 Introduction

The laws and statutory procedures covered in this chapter are relevant to a number of very different practical situations in which companies or corporate groups find themselves. These situations may be grouped under three headings:

▣ Mergers and acquisitions (sometimes called takeovers) of companies where a change of control occurs.

▣ Restructuring, including demerging, a financially healthy company or corporate group where no change of control occurs.

▣ Corporate rescue activity where a company is in financial difficulty.

These activities frequently involve making changes to the company's shareholdings, to its debt, or both. In this chapter we refer to such changes as 'restructuring' the company or corporate group.

The laws and statutory procedures relating to company restructuring have grown up piecemeal over time with the consequence that the law does not map neatly onto practical situations. Company restructuring statutory procedures can usually be used in a number of very different practical situations; for example, the scheme of arrangement procedure in Part 26 of the Companies Act 2006 can be used to effect such diverse activities as a takeover, a tax-effective return of capital to shareholders, and a compromise with creditors in an effort to stave off insolvency.

Also, a number of legal options may be available to a company in a given situation which must select the procedure best suited to its circumstances and aims. Consider a company in financial difficulty the debt of which needs to be restructured to avoid insolvent liquidation. Depending upon how co-operative its creditors are and how complex the required restructuring of the debt is, the company may simply pursue renegotiation with its creditors or it may use one or a combination of: the company voluntary arrangement procedure in Part I of the Insolvency Act 1986, the Part 26 scheme of arrangement procedure in the Companies Act 2006 and the administration procedure in Part II and Schedule B1 of the Insolvency Act 1986.

Another example is a basically healthy company wishing to sell one of its businesses. Here, although a straightforward business sale agreement may suffice, commercial and tax advantages are often secured by using a section 110 scheme of reconstruction, sometimes called a 'demerger' scheme, or, in complex cases, a Part 26 scheme of arrangement may be used.

The terminology used in relation to restructuring can be confusing and a word of warning is appropriate. Terms are often used in a practical sense, without the need to focus on legal significance, resulting in terms being used that connote a range of different legal activities. 'Merger' and 'takeover' are examples of this. Some of the terms used in statutory provisions relevant to this chapter are also unclear in meaning and scope. For example, whilst the legal meaning of the composite term 'reconstructions and amalgamations' can be established from s 900 of the Companies Act 2006, what constitutes a reconstruction *distinct from* an amalgamation is not legally clear cut.

A by-product of the uneasy fit of the law with practical situations is the absence of a broadly agreed upon structure for presenting the law and statutory procedures covered in this chapter. Bearing in mind the comments above and as this chapter provides an outline only of the relevant law and legal procedures, a structure that begins with the law has been adopted and the material covered in this chapter is organised into four sections as follows: schemes of arrangement and reconstruction, CVAs and small company moratoriums, administration and takeovers.

15.2 Schemes of arrangement and reconstruction

In this section we examine two key statutory procedures by which the structure of a company or a group of companies may be changed, or restructured, schemes of arrangement under Part 26 of the Companies Act 2006 and schemes of reconstruction, also known as demerger schemes, under the simpler Insolvency Act 1986 s 110 procedure. The emphasis is on restructuring of the *shareholdings* of a company or corporate group, rather than simply debt restructuring.

We have already considered in Chapters 7 and 8 processes by which the rights attached to particular shares may be varied and the share capital of a company increased and decreased and, in the final section of this chapter, we consider the legal framework governing changes of control, or 'takeovers'. The statutory processes considered in this section are used where the processes considered in Chapters 7 and 8, or a takeover bid, are not available, the requirements are too cumbersome, the conditions are unlikely to be fulfilled, or there is other good reason to choose one of the statutory schemes. Tax considerations are extremely important in restructuring activity and may lead to a restructuring proposal that can only by achieved using one legal process rather than another.

15.2.1 Section 110 schemes of reconstruction

Availability and usage

The most common use of s 110 of the Insolvency Act 1986, known as a section 110 scheme of reconstruction or a 'demerger scheme', is by a company wishing to separate out one or more of its businesses. The demerger may be a preliminary step in the sale of one or more of its businesses to another company or it may be part of an internal reconstruction of a corporate group designed to deliver commercial and tax advantages. For example, demergers can be used to unlock shareholder value, that is, to overcome the strict rules on maintenance of capital so that shareholders can lawfully receive capital from the company.

Demergers can be achieved by a number of routes. The tax benefits of using a section 110 scheme of reconstruction, coupled with the greater expense and longer timeframe for putting a Part 26 scheme of arrangement in place, make section 110 schemes very attractive. Section 110 cannot, however, be used if a compromise is sought with *creditors*: a Part 26 scheme of arrangement or a voluntary arrangement is required to achieve such a compromise.

A section 110 scheme necessarily entails the winding up of the original, transferor company. Do not be misled by this into thinking that it is therefore a corporate rescue procedure. Section 110 is designed for use where the company is solvent and applies only to a company that is being *voluntarily* wound up.

A typical s 110 demerger is effected by the company transferring its assets to two (or more) newly created companies in return for shares in those companies. The shares in the new companies are distributed to the shareholders of the original, now parent, company in proportion to their shareholdings in the original company and the original company is then wound up. The shareholders may continue to own the two companies or one of them may be sold off.

The section 110 procedure

The procedure to put a section 110 scheme in place is to hold a general meeting at which the following special resolutions are proposed (although private companies can use the written resolution procedure):

- to wind up the company (a members' voluntary winding up);
- to appoint a liquidator;
- to approve a section 110 scheme of reconstruction;
- to authorise the liquidator to enter into and carry out the section 110 scheme of reconstruction.

Following the passing of the resolutions, and subject to the rights of dissenting shareholders, the scheme is binding on all members of the company (s 110(5)) and the merger can be effected in accordance with the reconstruction agreement.

Dissenting shareholder protection

If any shareholder does not vote in favour of the section 110 scheme, s 111 gives him the right to require the liquidator to buy out his shares. The liquidator should therefore also be authorised by resolution at the general meeting to buy out shareholders pursuant to s 111 and the manner by which the liquidator may raise money to do so must be stated in the authorising resolution. In addition to providing for a dissenting shareholder to insist on being bought out, section 111 provides for a shareholder to stop a scheme going forward by giving notice to the liquidator to abstain from carrying the resolution into effect. A shareholder cannot be deprived of the rights afforded by s 111 by a provision in the company's articles of association (*Payne v The Cork Company Ltd* [1900] 1 Ch 308).

Creditor protection

A creditor of the company who is unhappy with a scheme may have negotiated contractual provisions in its loan agreements that are triggered by such a reconstruction. In the absence of such contractual or 'self-help' remedies, the only route available to a creditor to stop a section 110 scheme from progressing is to petition the court for a compulsory winding up order. To secure a winding up order a creditor must demonstrate either that it is just and equitable to wind up the company or that the company is unable to pay its debts (as that phrase is defined in s 123 of the Insolvency Act 1986). Even if one of these grounds can be established, the decision to order a winding up or not is in the discretion of the court (s 122). If a court orders the company to be wound up within a year of the special resolution authorising a section 110 scheme, the special resolution is not valid unless sanctioned (approved) by the court (s 110(6)).

Steps can be taken to significantly reduce the risk of a special resolution authorising a section 110 scheme of reconstruction being (i) stopped by a dissenting shareholder or (ii) rendered invalid by a court-ordered winding up within a year of its passage. One commonly adopted step is to incorporate a new 'holding' company ('holdco') to own the company (or parent company of the group) to be reconstructed. Holdco issues its own shares to the shareholders of the company in return for their shares in the company. It is Holdco that then enters into voluntary winding up and effects a section 110 scheme. Holdco has no creditors which virtually removes the risk of a court ordered winding up. The section 110 special resolution can be passed more than seven days before a winding up resolution so that the shareholder dissent period has expired before the winding up commences.

15.2.2 Part 26 schemes of arrangement

Availability and usage

scheme of arrangement procedure

the statutory procedure set out in Part 26 of the Companies Act 2006 which facilitates changes being made to the rights of creditors or shareholders without securing the unanimous approval of those affected by the changes

The statutory procedure set out in Part 26 of the Companies Act 2006, called the 'scheme of arrangement' procedure, exists to facilitate changes being made to the rights of creditors, shareholders or both without securing the unanimous approval of those affected by the changes. Section 895 states that Part 26 applies where a compromise or arrangement is proposed between a company and its creditors, or any class of them, and its members, or any class or them. Accordingly, a Part 26 scheme of arrangement can be used:

- to restructure debt, with or without changes to shareholdings; or
- to restructure the rights of shareholders, with or without changes to the rights of creditors.

If a Part 26 scheme of arrangement is to be used to effect a compromise by the company and its creditors and/or its shareholders of any rights and liabilities between them, there must be an accommodation by each side. A unilateral release of rights by one group, for example, is not a compromise and will not amount to an arrangement therefore cannot be achieved by a Part 26 scheme of arrangement (*Re Savoy Hotel Ltd* [1981] 3 All ER 346; *Re NFU Development Trust Ltd* [1973] 1 All ER 135). Where such a release is part of a wider arrangement, however, such as the release of claims against one company in return for the substitution of claims against a new company, the procedure can be used (*In the matter of Bluebrook Ltd* [2009] EWHC 2114 (Ch)).

An arrangement involving a change in who the shareholders are, but no change in the rights of those shareholders or any creditors (such as a takeover), whilst not a compromise, can be an arrangement for Part 26 purposes (*Re T & N Ltd (No 3)* [2007] 1 BCLC 563).

The procedure for a Part 26 scheme of arrangement to be put in place is cumbersome and consequently expensive and slow resulting in their use being confined to complex restructurings or situations where no other procedure is available. That said, Part 26 schemes of arrangement are regularly used in all three of the non-winding up situations identified in the introduction to this Part:

- Mergers and acquisitions (sometimes called takeovers) of companies where a change of control occurs.
- Restructuring, including demerging, a financially healthy company or corporate group.
- Corporate rescue activity where a company is in financial difficulty.

Taking each of these in turn, first, Part 26 schemes are regularly used to effect takeovers, including takeovers of companies with shares listed on a stock exchange such as the London Stock Exchange. In fact, they have become the most favoured method by which to structure a takeover of a company with listed shares. Where a private sale or acquisition is negotiated, a Part 26 scheme may be used to effect a reconstruction to merge or demerge companies and businesses and bring about other changes to improve the commercial benefits of the sale or acquisition, including effectively managing the tax implications.

Second, examples of when a Part 26 scheme of arrangement might be used to restructure a financially healthy company are:

- to return capital to shareholders;
- to divide or demerge a company (typically a family owned company) when a founder member or other large shareholder dies or retires;
- in anticipation of a disposal, that is, all or a part of the company or group being taken over or sold to a third party;
- in anticipation of an acquisition of a company or business by the company or group.

Turning finally to use of Part 26 schemes of arrangement by companies in financial difficulty, Part 26 is not restricted to compromises with creditors *before* a company becomes subject to a formal rescue or winding up procedure. Administrators can also use the Part 26 scheme of arrangement procedure within the context of an administration as can liquidators in the course of a winding up, although use of Part 26 by the liquidator of a company in *involuntary* liquidation is rare.

Notwithstanding its complexity, a Part 26 scheme may be the only option available in the circumstances to achieve the desired goal. A good illustration is use of a Part 26 scheme of arrangement to squeeze shareholders out of a company where only 75 per cent of the shareholders approve of a takeover of the company. This is less than the 90 per cent support that would be required where a takeover bid to be made, making a takeover by way of a Part 26 scheme of arrangement achievable where a takeover bid would fail for lack of 90 per cent support. This is one (though usually not the only) reason to structure a company takeover as a Part 26 scheme of arrangement.

The Part 26 procedure

The Part 26 procedure involves two applications to court, one before and one after the summoning of separate meetings of those classes of creditors and shareholders who would be affected were the proposed scheme of arrangement to be implemented.

The first stage in the procedure is an application to the court, usually by the company or the administrator, for an order that meetings be summoned of every affected class of shareholders and creditors for the purpose of securing approval of the proposed scheme (s 896(1)). The fairness of the scheme is not considered at this stage (*Re Hawk Insurance Company Ltd* [1922] 2 Ch 723). The court may, however, decide not to order the meetings, if, for example, it considers there is such a level of opposition to the scheme that the scheme would not be approved by the shareholders or creditors as the case may be (*Re Savoy Hotel Limited* [1981] Ch 351).

The court-ordered meetings must then be summoned. The scheme of arrangement must be approved by a majority in number, representing 75 per cent in value of the class of creditors or shareholders, as the case may be, voting, either in person or by proxy, at the duly summoned meeting (s 899(1)). Only if approved by this majority at each of the court-ordered meetings can the court sanction, ie approve, the scheme.

Identification of the different classes of shareholders and creditors, that is, recognising when a sub-group of shareholders or creditors needs to be regarded as unique and therefore a separate class and accorded a separate meeting is often an area of difficulty in relation to Part 26 schemes. The case law in which this issue is raised is extensive. If a sub-group feels it ought to have a separate meeting, and convinces the court of this, the court will not sanction the scheme without the requisite majority approval by that sub-group at a separate meeting.

The test to determine whether a sub-group is a separate class or not for the purposes of what is now Part 26 was stated by Bowen LJ in *Sovereign Life Assurance Co v Dodd* [1892] 2 QB 573:

JUDGMENT

'What is the proper construction of [the] statute? It makes the majority of the creditors or of a class of creditors bind the minority; it exercises a most formidable compulsion upon dissentient, or would-be dissentient, creditors; and it therefore requires to be construed with care, so as not to place in the hands of some of the creditors the means and opportunity of forcing dissentients to do that which it is unreasonable to require them to do, or of making a mere jest of the interests of the minority.

… The word "class" is vague, and to find out what is meant by it we must look at the scope of the section, which is a section enabling the Court to order a meeting of a class of creditors to be called. It seems plain that we must give such a meaning to the term "class" as will prevent the section being so worked as to result in confiscation and injustice, and that it must be confined to those persons whose rights are not so dissimilar as to make it impossible for them to consult together with a view to their common interest.'

The third stage in the Part 26 procedure is the second application to the court, asking the court to sanction the approved scheme of arrangement. The court is not obliged to sanction the scheme. As explained by Astbury J in *Re Anglo-Continental Supply Co Ltd* [1922] 2 Ch 723, it is the role of the court to exercise its discretion.

JUDGMENT

'In exercising its power of sanction … the Court will see: First, that the provisions of the statute have been complied with. Secondly, that the class was fairly represented by those who attended the meeting and that the statutory majority are acting bona fide and are not coercing the minority in order to promote interests adverse to those of the class whom they purport to represent, and, Thirdly, that the arrangement is such as a man of business would reasonably approve …'

If a Part 26 procedural requirement has not been satisfied, the court will not sanction the scheme. Also, if a reduction in capital is a feature of the scheme, the further legal procedures governing capital reduction must be complied with (ss 641, 645–653) and a court will not sanction a scheme where they have not been complied with. Note, however, that if the court has, by oversight, sanctioned a scheme that involves an unlawful capital reduction, the scheme will not be invalidated on this ground (*British & Commonwealth Holdings Ltd v Barclays Bank* [1996] 1 WLR 1).

The test to be applied to determine the reasonableness of the approval was stated by Maugham J in *Re Dorman Long & Co Ltd* [1934] 1 Ch 635:

JUDGMENT

'[The court must be satisfied that] the proposal is such that an intelligent and honest man, a member of the class concerned, acting in respect of his interests might reasonably approve [the scheme].'

The role of the court is not to substitute its judgment for that of the requisite majority and courts have endorsed the words in Buckley on the Companies Acts, that 'the court will be slow to differ from the meeting'. The key concern of the court is to be satisfied that the shareholders and creditors have acted in good faith and that the majority has voted in a class meeting to promote their interests as members of that class, rather than to promote other interests, such as to promote their interests as members of a different class of shareholders, or, possibly, their interests as creditors (*Carruth v ICI* [1937] AC 707).

A court order sanctioning the scheme has no effect until a copy has been delivered to the registrar of companies (s 899(4)). When the order takes effect it is binding on all creditors, shareholders and the company (or, as appropriate, the administrator, liquidator and all contributories of the company) (s 899(3)).

Section 900 reconstructions and amalgamations

Section 900 extends the powers of the court on a Part 26 application by empowering the court to order a broad range of matters, either by including them in the order approving the scheme of arrangement or in a separate order. The broader powers are available and may be exercised by the court only when a Part 26 scheme of arrangement:

- includes or is connected with a scheme of reconstruction of any company or companies or the amalgamation of any two or more companies; *and*
- involves the transfer of the whole or any part of the undertaking or property of a company concerned in the scheme to another company.

Examples of matters the court may order under s 900 include:

- the transfer of the business or undertaking (including liabilities) of one company to another;
- the allotting of shares or debentures of one company to another person;
- that legal claims against a company be continued against the company to whom the business is being transferred;
- the dissolution of a company without a winding up.

Part 27 and the Cross Border Merger Regulations

Where an application under Part 26 involves a 'merger or division', as that term is defined for the purpose, additional requirements are imposed before a scheme of arrangement can be sanctioned. If the merger or division involves a public company rather than a private company, the requirements are set out in Part 27 and, where the 'merger or division' involves either public or private companies in more than one member state, the additional requirements are set out in the Companies (Cross Border Merger) Regulations 2007 (SI 2007/2974). These provisions are of limited practical relevance in the UK where virtually all mergers and divisions of companies are structured such that they do not fall within the scope of application of the EU-inspired rules.

15.3 Company voluntary arrangements (CVA) and small company moratoria

This section is relevant to companies in financial difficulties. When a company experiences financial difficulty it may struggle to 'service its debt', that is, make interest payments, capital repayments, and/or meet certain covenants, or conditions, specified in its loan agreements. The situation may deteriorate rapidly into one in which there is no reasonable prospect that the company can avoid going into insolvent liquidation, or in which an individual creditor considers it has no option but to seek a winding up order.

It is important that directors and officers of companies understand the options available to facilitate a 'corporate rescue', ie the procedures that can be utilised to allow a breathing space to take stock of the situation and to restructure the company's debt (and, sometimes, the shareholder arrangements) to give the company or group the best chance to trade its way back to financial good health.

The law and procedures outlined in this section (CVAs and the small company moratorium) and the following section (administration) are designed to facilitate restructuring of the rights of creditors and, sometimes, shareholders of a company in financial difficulties. They are governed by the Insolvency Act 1986 and the Insolvency Rules 1986 (both as extensively amended). The general approach to corporate insolvency has changed since the 1986 Act was first enacted, resulting in the law being changed both to facilitate corporate rescue and to make the law operate more fairly in relation to unsecured creditors. These changes were made principally by the Insolvency Act 2000 and the Enterprise Act 2002.

The procedure for putting a CVA in place changes if the company is a small company and the directors propose a moratorium. Unfortunately, the small company moratorium procedure, considered at section 15.3.2, is cumbersome and is not available to a company in administration or liquidation. Consequently, it is not very popular.

15.3.1 Company voluntary arrangements

Part 1 of the Insolvency Act 1986 contains a procedure by which a company may put in place a composition in satisfaction of its debts, or a scheme of arrangement of its affairs, that binds all affected company creditors even though not all of them agree to its terms. The proposal, approval and implementation of such a composition or scheme, called a company voluntary arrangement (CVA), must comply with ss 1–7. A CVA proposal may be made to the company and its creditors either by its directors (s 1(1)) or by the administrator or liquidator of the company (s 1(3)).

A CVA proposal must provide for a nominee, who must be a qualified insolvency practitioner and is called a supervisor, to supervise its implementation (s 1(2)). If the CVA is proposed by the directors, they must give the supervisor (i) notice of the CVA proposal setting out its terms and (ii) a statement of affairs of the company (which will give details of its creditors, debts, other liabilities and assets) (s 2(3)). Within 28 days of such notice the supervisor must submit a report to the court (s2(2)) stating:

- whether, in his opinion, the proposed CVA 'has a reasonable prospect of being approved and implemented';
- whether, in his opinion, meetings of the company and its creditors should be summoned to consider the proposal; and
- proposed dates, times and places for such meetings.

Assuming the supervisor's report is positive, and unless the court directs otherwise, the meetings are then summoned by the supervisor to consider the proposal. Every creditor of the company of whose claims and address the supervisor is aware must be invited to the creditors' meeting (s 3(3)) and all meetings must be conducted in accordance with the Insolvency Rules 1986. At the creditors' meeting, the proposal must be approved by a majority of three-quarters or more in value of creditors present (in person or by proxy). The outcome of each meeting must be reported to the court by the chairman of the meeting and notices of the result given in accordance with the Insolvency Rules 1986.

The shareholders and creditors may decide to approve the proposed CVA with or without amendments. The CVA takes effect if the proposal is approved at both the shareholders' meeting and the creditors' meeting. If it is approved only at the meeting of the creditors, or there is a difference in what is approved by the shareholders and what is approved by the creditors, the CVA takes effect as approved by the creditors subject to the right of a member, within 28 days, to make an application to court whereupon the court may make such order as it thinks fit (s 4A).

Any shareholder or creditor who believes that the CVA unfairly prejudices the interests of a creditor or shareholder or that there has been some material irregularity at or in relation to one or more meetings, may, within 28 days, apply to the court for an order revising or revoking the CVA or directing a further meeting or meetings (s 6).

The CVA binds all creditors of the company as if they were parties to it (s 5), and creditors cannot commence legal proceedings to enforce a debt owing to them unless the company fails to perform the CVA. During the implementation of the CVA, either the supervisor or a person dissatisfied with his actions may apply to court and the court may make such order as it thinks fit (s 7).

company voluntary arrangement (CVA)

a composition in satisfaction of a company's debts, or a scheme of arrangement of its affairs, that binds all affected company creditors even though not all of them agree to its terms, entered into in accordance with the procedure in Part 1 of the Insolvency Act 1986

Example

By CVA, a company agrees to pay £100,000 per year for each of three years to the supervisor for distribution to creditors. If the company fails to pay the agreed sum to the supervisor or the CVA has in some other way not been implemented in accordance with its terms, the CVA is deemed to have come to an end (s 7B). On the CVA coming to an end, the company becomes liable to the creditor for any sum that had been payable under the CVA but was not in fact paid.

15.3.2 The small company moratorium

A procedure allowing small companies to obtain a stay or moratorium in the enforcement of its debts to give it time to put a CVA in place was introduced into the Insolvency Act 1986 by the Insolvency Act 2000. The procedure, set out in detail in Schedule A1 to the 1986 Act, is only available to the directors of a company. It is not relevant to an administrator or liquidator (they do not need it).

The procedure is available only to directors of *small* companies defined to be those companies satisfying two out of three of the following conditions (from s 382(3) Companies Act 2006 (as amended)):

Turnover	Not more than £6.5 million
Balance sheet total	Not more than £3.26 million
Employees	Not more than 50 employees

The procedure cannot be used if it has been used in the previous 12 months.

The directors send a document setting out the terms of the proposed CVA and a statement of the company's affairs to the nominee of the proposed CVA and the moratorium comes into force when the directors file the following documents with the court:

- Document setting out the terms of the proposed CVA;
- Statement of the company's affairs;
- Statement that the company is eligible for a moratorium;
- Statement from the nominee that he has given his consent to act;
- Statement from the nominee that in his opinion:
  - the proposed CVA 'has a reasonable prospect of being approved and implemented';
  - the company is likely to have sufficient funds available to it during the proposed moratorium to enable it to carry on its business; and
  - meetings of the company and its creditors should be summoned to consider the CVA proposal.

When the moratorium comes into effect, the directors must notify the nominee who is required to advertise the moratorium and notify the registrar, the company and any creditor who has petitioned for the winding up of the company (Schedule A1, paragraphs 9 and 10).

During the moratorium, no legal proceedings to enforce debts against the company may be commenced, no winding up petition may be presented and no winding up resolution may be passed. No administrator or administrative receiver may be appointed, no security may be enforced against the company's property and no meetings may be held without the consent of the nominee.

A moratorium initially lasts for no more than 28 days. An extension of up to a further two months may be approved by meetings of the shareholders and creditors during that initial period.

A moratorium ends on the day on which the meeting of shareholders or creditors (whichever is later) is held at which the proposed CVA is approved. If meetings of the shareholders and creditors have not been summoned, the moratorium will end on the expiry of the initial period. The nominee must advertise the coming to an end of a moratorium and notify the court, the registrar, the company and any petitioning creditor.

administrator

an insolvency practitioner appointed by the court under an administration order or by the company, its directors, or the holder of a qualifying floating charge, the principal objective of whom is to rescue the company as a going concern

administrative receiver

a receiver and manager appointed by the holder of a pre-15 September 2003 floating charge, who takes control of the whole or substantially the whole of the business and property of the company. Now largely replaced by administrators as part of the move to a corporate rescue culture

qualifying floating charge

a floating charge entered into after 15 September 2003 which comprises a charge over the whole or substantially all of the company's property the holder of which has under the Enterprise Act 2002 the right to appoint an administrator out of court

15.4 Administration

The rules governing administration and the powers of an administrator are found in Schedules B1 and 1 of the Insolvency Act 1986. Changes made by the Enterprise Act 2002 focused administration on corporate rescue: the principal objective of an administrator is to rescue the company as a going concern (Schedule B1, paragraph 3). Administration has taken the place of administrative receivership in most cases. A provision in a floating charge entered into on or after 15 September 2003 (the date on which the relevant provisions of the Enterprise Act 2002 came into effect), purporting to give the chargeholder the right to appoint an administrative receiver, will be effective only in exceptional circumstances. Moreover, even where a creditor has the right under a pre-15 September 2003 floating charge to appoint an administrative receiver, an administrator is often appointed instead. Ten years on, however, it remains unclear how far *corporate rescue* has been enhanced by the 2002 Act changes. Unless stated otherwise, references to paragraphs in this section are to those in Schedule B1.

15.4.1 Purpose of administration

Paragraph 3 of Schedule B1 of the Insolvency Act 1986 sets out three objectives of administration in order of priority. The administrator is required to perform his functions to achieve the first objective unless he thinks that this is not reasonably practicable to achieve. Only then may he pursue the second objective and only if he thinks that too is not reasonably practicable to achieve is he required to work towards the third objective. The three objectives are to:

- rescue the company as a going concern;
- achieve a better result for the company's creditors as a whole than would be likely if the company were wound up (without first being in administration);
- make a distribution to one or more secured or preferential creditors.

The administrator is also required to perform his functions as quickly and efficiently as reasonably possible.

15.4.2 Commencement of administration

An administrator may be appointed by order of the court or, quickly, straightforwardly and without a court application or hearing, by the company, the company's directors, or the holder of a qualifying floating charge. Considering out of court appointments first, neither the company nor the directors may appoint an administrator if the company is in liquidation or a winding up petition is pending, an administrative receiver is in office or an administration application remains to be disposed of by the court. To prevent administration being used whenever a company hits financially rough waters, this route into administration is also unavailable if the company has had the benefit of a moratorium (or interim moratorium) within the previous 12 months.

A floating charge 'qualifies' for the purposes of appointing an administrator if it:

- states that paragraph 14 of Schedule B1 applies to the floating charge;
- purports to empower the holder to appoint an administrator;
- purports to empower the holder to appoint an administrative receiver.

The floating charge must relate to the whole or substantially the whole of the company's property, or, it, together with other security held by the chargeholder, must meet this requirement. At least two business days' notice of intention to make an appointment must be given to the holder of any prior floating charge (or their written consent obtained) and no appointment may be made if an administrative receiver or liquidator is already in office.

The administration commences when the holder of the qualifying charge has filed a notice of appointment in prescribed form with the court and as soon as it is practicable to do so, the administrator must be given notice that the notice has been filed. A pending winding up petition is suspended upon the appointment of an administrator, for the duration of the administration. Note that if the only reason why a floating chargeholder cannot appoint an administrator is because the company is in liquidation, the chargeholder may make an administration application to the court.

Turning to appointment by order of the court, an order of the court appointing a person to be an administrator may be made only if the court is satisfied that:

- the company is or is likely to become unable to pay its debts; and
- the administration order is reasonably likely to achieve the purpose of administration.

The first condition need not be satisfied if the applicant could appoint an administrator because he is the holder of a qualifying floating charge.

A court-ordered administration takes effect at the time appointed by the order or, if the order is silent, when the order is made, and on the making of an administration order:

- a pending winding up petition will be dismissed;
- if an administrative receiver has been appointed he will vacate office; and
- the administrator may require a receiver of part of the company's property to vacate office.

Paragraph 44 provides for an interim moratorium in relation to insolvency and other legal process (the meaning of which is discussed below) to operate between the making of an administration application to the court and the administration order taking effect (or the court refusing to grant an administration order). An interim moratorium also operates when an administrator is appointed out of court, between the notice of intention to appoint being filed with the court and the appointment taking effect.

15.4.3 Effect of administration

Whilst a company is in administration, every business document and all the company's websites must state the name of the administrator and that the affairs, business and property of the company are being managed by him. Business document, for these purposes, means a hard copy or electronic invoice, order for goods or services, business letter and order form.

Effect on insolvency proceedings and other legal process

When a company is in administration a moratorium on insolvency proceedings and other legal process operates. The company cannot be put into liquidation (except pursuant to a public interest petition to do so) and, without the consent of the administrator or permission of the court:

- no step may be taken to enforce any security over the company's assets;
- no administrative receiver may be appointed;
- no property may be repossessed under a hire purchase agreement;
- no landlord may exercise the right of forfeiture by re-entry;
- no legal process may be commenced or continued against the company whether civil or criminal;
- no step may be taken to enforce any legal judgment against the company.

The precise scope of legal process for the purposes of the moratorium has been litigated a number of times and the court has adopted a purposive approach, interpreting the term very broadly. The moratorium applies to all potential claimants, not just creditors (see, for example, *Biosource Technologies Inc v Axis Genetics plc* [2000] 1 BCLC 286). Quasi-judicial proceedings are included, such as arbitrations (*Bristol Airport plc v Powdrill* [1990] BCLC 585), and criminal proceedings are also included (*Re Rhondda Waster Disposal Ltd* [2000] BCC 653). Note also that cases such as *Re Lomax Leisure Ltd* [1999] 2 BCLC 126 holding that the right of forfeiture of a landlord did not amount to enforcement of security therefore the exercise of the right of forfeiture was not prohibited by those words

administration order

a court order which gives power to manage the company's business to an administrator are no longer important because express language has been introduced into paragraph 43 stating that no landlord may exercise the right of forfeiture.

The basis on which the court should exercise its discretion to permit what is otherwise not allowed, has also come before the courts. The court must have regard to all the circumstances and seek to balance all the 'legitimate' interests, including in an appropriate case, the public interest.

Effect on directors

The appointment of an administrator has no automatic effect on the holding of office by the directors who remain subject to all the duties and obligations of directors but an administrator may remove and appoint directors (paragraph 61). By paragraph 64, however, a company or an officer of a company in administration may not, without the consent of the administrator, exercise a power which could be exercised so as to interfere with the exercise of the administrator's powers: in effect, the powers of the directors of a company are suspended upon the appointment of the administrator.

Effect on employees

Administration does not bring employment contracts with the company automatically to an end. The administrator will review the employee contracts and decide whether or not to terminate them and make employees redundant. If an administrator adopts a contract of employment, the wages or salary of the employee from the point of adoption forward are afforded priority, sometimes called 'super-priority' over the wages and expenses of the administrator as well as the claims of floating charge holders. This super-priority extends to liabilities under all contracts entered into by the administrator. The fact that employees have not been made redundant in the first 14 days of an administration cannot be argued to constitute adoption or evidence relevant to adoption for these purposes (paragraph 99).

Effect on contracts

Administration does not bring contracts with the company automatically to an end. Without more, they remain in place but cannot be enforced without the consent of the administrator or the permission of the court. Many commercial contracts automatically terminate or provide the other party with the right to terminate them in the event of administration (and other insolvency events) so many contractors will seek to terminate or renegotiate the terms of contracts, introducing tighter payment provisions such as cash on delivery or supplying with a retention of title clause (if not doing so already). Liabilities under any contract the administrator enters into will attract the super-priority referred to in the previous paragraph.

Effect on property

Whilst the property of the company remains vested in the company, the administrator has the power to manage the property, including the powers set out in schedule 1 to 'take possession of, collect and get in the property of the company …' and sell or otherwise dispose of it. An administrator may dispose of and take actions in relation to property subject to a floating charge as if it were not subject to the charge (paragraph 70).

The role and powers of administrators

An administrator must be an authorised insolvency practitioner and is an officer of the court. He has power to do 'anything necessary or expedient for the management of the affairs, business and property of the company' (paragraph 59) and Schedule 1 to the 1986 Act lists 23 broad-ranging powers of administrators. He acts as an agent of the company (paragraph 69). The administrator must perform his functions in the interests of the company's creditors as a whole with the objective of rescuing the company as a going concern. Only if he thinks that this is not reasonably practicable to achieve should he seek 'to achieve a better result for the company's creditors as a whole than would be likely if the company were wound up' and, failing the reasonable practicability of that, aim to realise property in order to make a distribution to one or more secured or preferential creditors (paragraph 3).

15.4.4 Ending the administration

An administrator is required to perform his functions as quickly and efficiently as is reasonably practicable (paragraph 4) and, in this spirit, the appointment of an administrator ceases to have effect automatically one year from taking effect. The appointment may be extended by order of the court or, for no more than six months and once only, with the consent of the creditors. In addition to automatic termination, administration can come to an end in a number of circumstances:

- A creditor may apply to court to end the administration.
- The administrator may apply to court to end the administration.
- The objective of the administration may be achieved.
- The company may enter public interest winding up pursuant to s 124A.
- The administration may be converted to a creditors' voluntary winding up.
- The company may be dissolved.

'Pre-pack administrations' are a phenomenon by which the business of a company in financial difficulty is prepared for sale to a new company *before* the appointment of an administrator with the intention that the sale will be made by the administrator immediately after the company goes into administration. This can keep adverse publicity to a minimum. Creditors can feel that they have no real choice but to accept the pre-negotiated package. More than this, although a business may be pre-packed and sold to a new company that is independent of either the directors or the secured creditors of the old company, it is not uncommon for, and conflict of interests can arise where, the business is pre-packed and sold to one or more of the directors or a floating charge holder of the company.

KEY FACTS

Company voluntary arrangements (CVAs)
The CVA is a composition in satisfaction of a company's debts, or a scheme of arrangement of its affairs, that binds all affected company creditors even though not all of them agree to its terms.
A CVA must be approved by the shareholders and also by a majority in excess of three-quarters in value of creditors present (in person or by proxy) at a meeting called for the purpose of approving the CVA.
Failure by the company to make a payment due under a CVA brings it to an end.

Small company moratorium
The small company moratorium is designed to protect small companies from legal actions whilst steps are taken to put a CVA in place.
The small company moratorium is not a popular procedure.

Administration
Administration is designed primarily to rescue the company as a going concern (Schedule B1 Paragraph 3). Administrators can be appointed out of court by directors or a qualifying floating charge holder or by the court.
A pending winding up petition is suspended or dismissed on appointment of an administrator.
An administrator is required to perform his functions as quickly as possible in the interests of the company's creditors as a whole with the objective of rescuing the company as a going concern.
Administrations automatically end one year after taking effect unless they are extended by the court or, with the consent of creditors, for a further maximum of six months.
Many administrations end by the company's business being sold as a 'pre-pack' or the company going into creditors' voluntary liquidation.

354

takeover

the process whereby one company acquires a controlling in-terest in another company

City Code on Takeovers and Mergers

a set of principles and rules, now placed on a statutory footing, designed princi-pally to ensure that shareholders are treated fairly and providing an orderly frame-work within which takeovers are conducted to promote the integrity of the financial markets

15.5 Takeovers

The focus of this section is the Takeover Code ('the Code'), now in its 10th edition (September 2011). The Code was first introduced in 1968 in response to the emergence of hostile takeover bids for companies with shares listed on stock exchanges in the US and the UK.

According to economic theory, hostile takeovers occur because the target company, whilst not necessarily in financial difficulty, is economically underperforming due to poor management. From this perspective, hostile takeovers are efficiency-enhancing transactions in the market for corporate control. An alternative view is that hostile takeovers undermine the ability of boards of directors to take a long-term approach to building the businesses they run. Instead, it is argued, boards must constantly ensure that their share price increases in the short term and that dividend levels are maintained to insulate the company from an opportunistic hostile takeover. The absence of consensus on the benefits and shortcomings of hostile takeovers contributed to the difficulty experienced reaching pan-European agreement on the EU Takeover Directive.

Of all the EU member states, the UK has the longest-lived experience of hostile takeovers. Consequently, the EU Takeover Directive (2004/25/EC) was strongly influenced by the Code. EU-wide consensus on how takeovers should be regulated was difficult to reach, however. It took 15 years to achieve, with the result that a number of the provisions of the Takeover Directive are the product of political compromise. The Takeover Directive establishes a minimum (rather than a maximum) regime of protection for shareholders of companies with shares listed on a regulated market (essentially a main stock exchange in the EU), when a third party seeks to acquire control of the company. Moreover, Article 12 permits member states to opt-out of certain provisions of the Takeover Directive namely, the Article 9 prohibition on target company board action to frustrate a takeover and the Article 11 restrictions on arrangements designed to deny control to a successful bidder.

Before the Takeover Directive was adopted and subsequently implemented in the UK by what is now Part 28 of the Companies Act 2006, the UK system of takeover regulation was a system of 'self-regulation' by the Panel on Takeovers and Mergers ('the Panel') based on the Code. The regime was widely believed to work well. The 'minimum protection' nature of the EU Takeover Directive entitles individual member states to maintain higher levels of protection for shareholders than those provided for in the Takeover Directive. Consequently, the UK has been able to preserve the pre-Directive regime largely intact.

The current UK law regulating takeovers, which places the Code and Panel on a statutory footing, is applicable in a broader range of circumstances than the EU Directive requires and is more comprehensive in its provisions. Moreover, fears that replacement of the self-regulation of takeovers with a statutory regime mandated by the EU Directive would see swift and flexible decision-making replaced by cumbersome process and timetables delayed by legal appeals have so far proved unfounded.

This section considers the operation of the Code in the typical situation to which it was designed to apply, ie a purchaser seeking to obtain ownership of sufficient voting shares of a company, the shares of which are listed on the London Stock Exchange, to exercise control of the company, against the wishes of the target company's board of directors. Before turning to this, it is helpful to place takeovers governed by the Code in the broad context of changes of corporate control. This is particularly important given the limited numbers of such takeovers. In the year ending 31 March 2011, this was 92 (94 bids, two of which lapsed), 16 of which began the offer process as hostile but only five of which remained hostile throughout the takeover process.

15.5.1 Takeovers, mergers, acquisitions and disposals

The legal procedures considered in the previous sections of this chapter are often used to change the ownership of the shares of one or more companies. In most instances, however, those restructurings are internal: The ultimate control of the company or corporate group remains unchanged. In contrast, the Code regulates only real, rather than technical changes of control of companies, and is not engaged in most changes of control of companies.

Most companies do not have shares held by a large number of shareholders and their shares are not listed on a stock exchange. Acquisitions and disposals of such companies typically take place following an approach being made by or to a purchaser who is interested in buying the company and negotiation of the terms of a *share purchase agreement*. The share purchase agreement is negotiated between the purchaser and either (i) the board of the parent company (the seller) of the company to be acquired (the target company), or (ii) where the target is owned by individuals, the shareholders of the target company. Even though a change of control of the company occurs, the term 'takeover' is not typically used to describe these transactions. Nor is the term 'merger' typically used, even where the purchaser is a company and the target, upon becoming owned by the purchaser company, is, in one sense, 'merged' into it (or, at least, becomes a subsidiary in the purchaser corporate group). The language typically used to describe such transactions is 'sale', 'disposal', 'purchase' or 'acquisition'. Note that companies with shares traded on a stock exchange frequently agree to sell substantial parts of their business, or one or more of the different businesses they operate, by private sale agreement. Typically, the parent company negotiates and sells the shares of one or more of the subsidiaries through which the businesses to be disposed of are operated.

For a number of commercial reasons, including the tax implications, a disposal or acquisition may be structured as a sale of the underlying business of the target company to the purchaser. A *business sale agreement*, rather than a share purchase agreement, is then entered into between the buyer company and the seller company. Business sale agreements are legally more complex than share sale agreements because each of the assets and liabilities of the target business to be acquired needs to be assigned to the purchaser. Again, these transactions are not usually described as 'takeovers'. Whilst the term 'merger' is sometimes used, the typical language used is 'sale', 'disposal', 'purchase' or 'acquisition'.

The term 'takeover' is typically used to describe acquisition of *sufficient* shares in a *widely held company*, which shares are usually listed on a stock exchange, to exercise control of the company. The terms 'takeover offer' or 'takeover bid' usually refer to an offer to shareholders of a widely held company to acquire their shares. Use of the term 'takeover' is not confined to a 'hostile' takeover situation. It is used even if the offer to purchase is welcomed by the board of the target company and recommended by the board to the shareholders.

15.5.2 Scope of application of the Code

The Code is essentially a shareholder protection measure. Consequently, it applies to changes of control resulting from the purchase of shares, not to direct purchases of underlying businesses.

Contrary to popular belief, the Code is not confined to the takeover of companies with shares listed on the London Stock Exchange. It applies where there is an offer to acquire, or an attempt to gain a controlling interest (defined as an interest in shares carrying 30 per cent or more of the voting rights), in:

Alternative Investment Market (AIM)

the market for smaller companies operated by the London Stock Exchange. AIM is not a regulated market and companies on AIM are not listed on the Official List nor are they subject to the Listing Rules

- a company with shares traded on a regulated market in the UK (primarily companies with shares listed on the London Stock Exchange);
- any other UK public company with its central management and control in the UK.

The takeover of a plc with shares listed on the Alternative Investment Market (AIM), for example, will be subject to the Code *if its central management and control is in the UK*.

A takeover offer may be recommended to the shareholders by the target company's board (a recommended bid) or not (a hostile bid). The takeover process unfolds very differently depending upon which of these it is. If the takeover is welcomed by the board of directors of the target company, this opens up the potential to structure the acquisition in the most commercially sensible and tax efficient manner.

offeree company

a company in respect of which an offer has been, or potentially may be, made to which the City Code on Takeovers and Mergers applies. Also known as the target or target company

Part 26 schemes of arrangement, considered in section 15.2.2, are used to effect about half of all takeovers subject to the Code. Recognising this development, the Panel has drafted special rules for this type of takeover (see Appendix 7 to the Code).

Part 26 schemes of arrangements are a popular choice to effect recommended takeovers due to their flexibility and the tax benefits that can be secured. In particular, a purchase is able to obtain 100 per cent ownership of a company even if only 75 per cent of shareholders wish to sell their shares.

15.5.3 The nature, purpose and general principles of the Code

The nature and purpose of the Code is stated clearly in its introduction, which was amended in the last revision in September 2011, to state clearly the neutral stance of the Code which is not intended neither to facilitate nor impede takeovers. Note that in the General Principles, the target company is referred to as the 'offeree company', shares are referred to as 'securities' and shareholders are referred to as 'holders of securities'.

QUOTATION

offeror company

a person (whether a company or an individual) who makes or is considering making an offer to which the City Code on Takeovers and Mergers applies. Also known as a bidder

'The Code is designed principally to ensure that shareholders in an offeree company are treated fairly and are not denied an opportunity to decide on the merits of a takeover and that shareholders of the offeree company of the same class are afforded equivalent treatment by an offeror. The Code also provides an orderly framework within which takeovers are conducted. In addition, it is designed to promote, in conjunction with other regulatory regimes, the integrity of the financial markets.

The Code is not concerned with the financial or commercial advantages or disadvantages of a takeover. These are matters for the offeree company and its shareholders. In addition, it is not the purpose of the Code either to facilitate or to impede takeovers. Nor is the Code concerned with those issues, such as competition policy, which are the responsibility of government and other bodies.'

The Takeover Code, 10th edition, September 2011, The Takeover Panel

The Code rules are underpinned by six General Principles which also form part of the Code. They are the same as the general principles set out in Article 3 of the EU Takeover Directive and it is helpful to set them out in full. Note that in the General Principles, the target company is referred to as the 'offeree company', shares are referred to as 'securities' and shareholders are referred to as 'holders of securities'.

QUOTATION

'All holders of the securities of an offeree company of the same class must be afforded equivalent treatment; moreover, if a person acquires control of a company, the other holders of securities must be protected.

1 The holders of the securities of an offeree company must have sufficient time and information to enable them to reach a properly informed decision on the bid; where it advises the holders of securities, the board of the offeree company must give its views on the effects of implementation of the bid on employment, conditions of employment and the locations of the company's places of business.

2 The board of an offeree company must act in the interests of the company as a whole and must not deny the holders of securities the opportunity to decide on the merits of the bid.

3 False markets must not be created in the securities of the offeree company, of the offeror company or of any other company concerned by the bid in such a way that the rise or fall of the prices of the securities becomes artificial and the normal functioning of the markets is distorted.

4 An offeror must announce a bid only after ensuring that he/she can fulfil in full any cash consideration, if such is offered, and after taking all reasonable measures to secure the implementation of any other type of consideration.

5 An offeree company must not be hindered in the conduct of its affairs for longer than is reasonable by a bid for its securities.'

The Takeover Code, 10th edition, September 2011, The Takeover Panel

The rules are interpreted and applied by the Panel in the spirit of these principles.

15.5.4 Outline of the basic takeover bid process

The following paragraphs describe the timetable and steps in a simple takeover that proceeds in accordance with the Code. Before deciding to acquire control of another company (the target), the purchaser (the offeror), conducts due diligence based on publicly available information (unless the target company board co-operates) and makes confidential enquiries. Where this causes rumours of a takeover in the market or untoward movements in the target company's share price, the offeror is required to make an announcement that it does not intend to make an offer or a 'firm intention announcement'.

Rule 1 of the Code requires the offeror to communicate to the target company's board its firm intention to make an offer, immediately following which, a firm intention announcement to the market must be made (Rule 2.2) which, subject to permitted conditions specified, binds the offeror to make the described offer. If the offer is recommended, the firm intention announcement will be a joint announcement of the offeror and the target company and will include the target company board's recommendation of the offer. In any event, after the firm intention announcement, the target company must send copies 'promptly' to all shareholders.

A firm intention announcement initiates the offer period and an offer document containing the contractual offer to purchase the shares in the company must be posted on the target company's website and sent to all shareholders within 28 days of the announcement. The offer must remain open for at least 21 days and the expiry of the initial offer period is called the 'first closing day'. In a hostile takeover, the target company board has 14 days from publication of the offer document to send out its first defence document to shareholders.

Most offers are conditioned on the offer being accepted by holders of a specified proportion of the shares in the target company for which the offer is made. This is called the acceptance condition. This proportion is usually 90 per cent because if 90 per cent of the shares for which an offer is made and 90 per cent of their voting rights are acquired, an offeror can compel holders of the remaining 10 per cent to sell their shares (s 979). The acceptance level achieved must be announced on the business day following the first closing day. If the acceptance condition has not been satisfied by the first closing day, an extension of the offer can be made for up to 60 days from publication of the offer document. If the acceptance condition has not been satisfied by day 60, the offer will lapse unless the offeror decides to proceed based on the actual acceptance level. An offeror is not permitted to proceed unless he has secured over 50 per cent of the voting rights in the target. If the offer lapses, the takeover fails and the offeror cannot make another offer for at least a further 12 months.

If the acceptance condition is satisfied on day 60 (or the condition is, where permitted, waived), the offer must remain open for a further 14 days, until day 74, and may remain open for longer. If the offeror has secured acceptances from shareholders holding 90 per cent or more of the voting rights attached to the shares for which the offer was made and 90 per cent or more of the value of those shares, he will probably wish to exercise his right to acquire the outstanding shares (squeeze out rights). A notice to compulsorily acquire the outstanding shares must be served by the offeror within three months of the offer closing. Alternatively, although the offeror may be comfortable with a small cohort of minority shareholders, minority shareholders in a company in which the offeror

squeeze out

the right of the offeror, under the Companies Act 2006, s 979 to acquire outstanding shares on a compulsory basis where it has acquired (or unconditionally contracted to acquire) not less than 90 per cent (i) in value of, and (ii) of the voting rights carried by, the shares to which the takeover offer relates owns and controls 90 per cent or more of the shares and voting rights can individually insist on being bought out by the offeror on the terms of the takeover offer (see Minority Shareholder Treatment, below).

An offer must state that it will lapse if the takeover either is referred to the Competition Commission or the EU Commission decides to initiate a Phase II merger investigation. It may also be subject to additional conditions above and beyond an acceptance condition. If the offeror has shares listed on the London Stock Exchange, for example, the takeover is likely to be a class 1 transaction for the purposes of the Listing Rules and the offer will be made conditional upon approval of the takeover by the offeror shareholders. These conditions must be satisfied within 21 days of the offer being declared unconditional as to acceptances, ie based on a maximum offer period (60 day), by the 81st day after publication of the offer document.

Consideration for their shares must be posted to target shareholders not more than 14 days following the offer becoming wholly unconditional: on the timetable traced above, no later than 95 days after the publication of the offer document.

This is a very simple illustration of the basic timetable of an offer. Takeovers are rarely so straightforward. The terms of an offer are often revised, for example. The Code rules are detailed, discretions can be exercised by the Panel and delays and difficulties invariably arise. Also, a range of laws in addition to the Code come into play in takeovers.

15.5.5 Minority shareholder treatment

An important aspect of the shareholder protection delivered by the Code is the protection of minority shareholders. Minority shareholders are protected in particular by the mandatory offer requirement in Rule 9. Also, s 983 of the Companies Act 2006 supplements the Code and implements Article 16 of the EU Takeover Directive by providing each minority shareholder with sell-out rights.

Mandatory offers on acquisition of a controlling stake

Rule 9 requires a person who acquires shares carrying 30 per cent or more of the voting rights in a company to make a cash offer to all other shareholders at no less than the highest price paid for the shares already acquired. The reason for this is that in practice control of a company can be exercised by a person owning 30 per cent of its shares. The acquisition of that control is very valuable and the purchaser, therefore, will be prepared to pay a price premium for the shares delivering that control. The mandatory bid requirement supports the purpose of the Code to ensure that shareholders of the same class are afforded equivalent treatment by an offeror. The effect of the mandatory offer requirement is to ensure that the price premium for control is shared amongst all the shareholders. Control for the purposes of triggering a mandatory offer is not defined in the EU Takeover Directive but is left to be defined by member states.

Sell-out rights

If, when the offer period closes, the offeror, already owns or has the right to acquire shares in the company amounting to 90 per cent or more of the value of the voting shares and carrying 90 per cent or more of the voting rights of the company, s 983 of the Companies Act 2006 gives each shareholder the right to require the offeror to buy him out at the same price and otherwise subject to the same terms as the takeover offer.

Note that the 90 per cent threshold trigger for minority sell-out rights is different from the 90 per cent threshold trigger for the s 979 right of the offeror to buy out minority shareholders. The minority shareholder's right to compel acquisition of his shares is triggered based on the entire ownership rights of the offeror in the company. Essentially, the offeror must have 90 per cent of the voting shares and 90 per cent of the voting rights in the company, whether he owned those shares before the takeover offer of as a result of it. In contrast, the buy-out right of the offeror is triggered based on the success of the takeover offer – the offeror must secure acceptance from the holders of 90 per cent or more of the shares to which the offer relates. Where the purchaser is seeking 100 per cent control of the target, this test operates as a disincentive to stakebuilding prior to making a takeover offer.

15.5.6 Key additional legal rules and problem areas in takeovers

Legal requirements above and beyond compliance with the Code apply to takeovers. Precisely which legal rules apply will depend upon all the circumstances, including the legal character of the parties involved. Two sets of supplementary legal rules that almost invariably apply are the Financial Services Authority (FSA) Listing Rules, Disclosure and Transparency Rules and Prospectus Rules and competition law.

FSA Listing Rules, Disclosure and Transparency Rules and Prospectus Rules

In many takeovers, one or more of the companies involved are subject to and will need to comply with the relevant provisions of the FSA Listing Rules, Disclosure and Transparency Rules and Prospectus Rules. Where the offeror company has a primary listing of its equity shares on the London Stock Exchange, for example, it will need to comply with Rule 7 of the Listing Rules which requires shareholder approval of a class 1 transaction, which a takeover usually will be. The disclosure provisions of the Code are materially supplemented in most takeovers by the disclosure requirements of the aforementioned FSA rules.

Competition law

Both domestic and EU level competition laws apply in the UK and one or the other if not both are often engaged in a takeover situation. Beyond this, takeovers involving foreign companies and/or having international effects outside the EU, may trigger the competition laws of other countries, not uncommonly the US.

Competition laws and procedures relevant to the takeover transaction itself need to be considered, such as the need for pre-notification to the EU Commission under the EU Merger Regulation (139/2004/EC), or, where the takeover does not have a 'community dimension' bringing it within the scope of the EU Merger Regulation, the benefit to be secured from notification to the Office of Fair Trading to mitigate the uncertainty of a referral to the Competition Commission under the Enterprise Act 2002.

15.5.7 Action by the target company board

Article 9(2)–(3) of the EU Takeover Directive requires the board to secure shareholder approval of any action or provision to frustrate a takeover. To secure political consensus, member states are permitted to opt out of these provisions of the directive and board defence tactics are permitted in some member states. The UK has not opted out of Article 9(2) or (3). Once a hostile bid has been made, directors of the offeree company are in a conflict of interest position. They are likely to lose their positions as directors and their jobs as executive employees of the company if the bid succeeds. It is difficult to reconcile their own self-interests with those of the company. Yet it is wrong to assume that directors who oppose a bid are motivated by self-interest. They may genuinely believe that the takeover is not in the interests of the company, as was the case in the 2010 takeover of Cadbury by Kraft.

The 'enlightened' aspect of shareholder value enshrined in the s 172 duty of a director requiring directors to have regard to the matters listed in that section, which include, amongst others, the likely consequences of any decision in the long-term and the interests of the company's employees, appears to vanish in a takeover situation. The divergence of the immediate interests of shareholders (to secure the highest offer for their shares as possible) and other stakeholders in the company is reinforced where the shares in the target are held by hedgefunds and other short-term funds. It was reported in the press that close to 25 per cent of the shares in Cadbury were purchased by such funds during the 19-week takeover battle.

The third General Principle of the Code (set out above) and rule 21 require directors to play a neutral role. Essentially, once the directors have notice of a firm intention to make an offer they are unable to take any action to frustrate the takeover offer or deny shareholders the opportunity to decide on its merits. In particular, rule 21 prohibits the board, unless shareholder approval is obtained, from issuing any shares, granting any options in relation to shares or issuing convertible bonds or subscription rights, selling or acquiring or agreeing to sell or dispose of assets of a material amount; or entering into contracts otherwise than in the ordinary course of business.

Defensive tactics may not be in response to a bid but steps may be taken to discourage takeovers long before a takeover situation arises. An example is a poison pill device. The right to enforce an agreement amounting to a poison pill was considered by the House of Lords in *Criterion Properties plc v Stratford UK Properties LLC* [2006] 1 BCLC 729 (HL). Criterion was contractually obliged to buy out a shareholder at an inflated price upon the occurrence of a range of events, including a change of control of the company. The case provides no binding authority on the ability of the board of a company to legally commit a company to a poison pill arrangement. The House identified the question as a matter of considerable public importance but, as disposal of the case did not require it to do so, it did not rule on the issue. It is widely understood that poison pills expose directors to actions for breach of duty.

15.5.8 The Panel on Takeovers and Mergers (the Panel)

The Panel on Takeovers and Mergers ('the Panel') issues and makes rulings on the interpretation, application and effect of the Code. It can require a person to provide it with documents and information and also issues directions to restrain breaches and otherwise secure compliance with the Code and imposes sanctions on those who breach the Code or fail to comply with directions issued by the Panel. Finally, the Panel may order those in breach of the Code to pay such compensation as it thinks just and reasonable. The Panel also co-operates and shares information with bodies performing similar functions in other EU member states and the FSA.

The Panel's functions are put on a statutory footing by Part 28 of the Companies Act 2006 in which the Code is referred to as 'the rules'. The Panel's statutory footing extends to all of its work in relation to takeovers, not just those takeovers the UK is required by the EU Takeover Directive to regulate.

The Panel is authorised to make rules in relation to 'transactions ... that have or may have, directly or indirectly, an effect on the ownership or control of companies' (s 943(2) (a)(iii)). The Panel's rulings on the interpretation, application or effect of the rules are given binding legal effect by s 945(2), and Panel directions to restrain breaches and secure compliance with the rules are given legal effect by s 946. Any rule conferring power on the Panel to impose sanctions for breach of the Code or failure to comply with Panel directions given to secure compliance with the Code is given legal effect by s 952 and any rule conferring the power to order a person to pay compensation is given legal effect by s 954.

Where there has been a breach of a requirement set out in the rules, including a disclosure requirement, the Panel is statutorily empowered to make an application to the court in relation to which the court may make any order it thinks fit to secure compliance (s 955).

The Panel is required to have a rule-making committee (s 943). In practice this committee is called the Code Committee. The rules must also provide for a Panel decision to be subject to review by a Hearings Committee (s 951). A right of appeal against a decision of the Hearing Committee to an independent tribunal, the 'Takeover Appeal Board' must also be set out in the rules (s 951(3)). The Chairman and Deputy Chairman of the Takeover Appeal Board are ordinarily persons who have held high judicial office and as at May 2010 were Lord Steyn (ex-member of the judicial House of Lords) and Sir Martin Nourse (one-time Lord Justice). They appoint the remaining members of the Board and are themselves appointed by the Master of the Rolls.

Litigation has not been common in relation to takeovers in the UK. This record may indicate that the Panel has been doing a good job, a widely accepted view which is part of the explanation. Limited judicial review of Panel decisions is largely the result of the history and origins of the Code coupled with judicial endorsement of an explicit policy to deter tactical litigation to delay and frustrate takeovers which has made judicial review available only in extremely narrow circumstances and only after the fact.

Established in 1968, the Code and the Panel operated as a private institution for over 20 years before the public nature of its functions was judicially acknowledged and performance of those functions confirmed to be subject to judicial review. In *R v Panel on Takeovers and Mergers, ex parte Datafin plc* [1987] 1 All ER 564 (CA)), Sir John Donaldson praised the Panel as a 'truly remarkable body'. He stated that, whilst its decisions were subject to judicial review, people were entitled to assume the validity of the Panel's rules and decisions unless and until they were quashed by the court. This part of his judgment has been superseded by Part 28 of the Companies Act 2006 which, as set out above, now confers legal validity on the Panel's rules, rulings, directions and sanctions and provides a two-stage internal appeal process before judicial review could be contemplated.

It was with the following words that the then Master of the Rolls confirmed that the courts could not be used to delay takeovers:

JUDGMENT

'I should expect the relationship between the Panel and the court to be historic rather than contemporaneous. I should expect the court to allow contemporary decisions to take their course, considering the complaint and intervening, if at all, later and in retrospect by declaratory orders which would enable the Panel not to repeat any error and would relieve individuals of the disciplinary consequences of any erroneous finding of breach of the rules. This would provide a workable and valuable partnership between the courts and the Panel in the public interest …'

SUMMARY

Section 110 schemes of reconstruction

- Commonly used by a company seeking to demerge one or more of its businesses typically to unlock shareholder value or as a preliminary step in a sale of one or more of its businesses.
- Can only be used if the company is to be voluntarily wound up.
- Cannot be used if a compromise is sought with creditors.
- Dissident shareholders are protected when a section 110 scheme of reconstruction is proposed by having the right to request that they be bought out or to stop the scheme being implemented (s 111).
- Creditors that do not have pre-negotiated protections when a section 110 scheme of reconstruction is proposed may petition the court for a winding up under s 123.

Part 26 schemes of arrangement

- May be used in mergers and acquisitions of companies, in the restructuring of financially healthy companies or as part of a corporate rescue package.
- The three basic stages in a Part 26 procedure are an application to court for an order that meetings be summoned, the holding of court-ordered meetings at each of which the proposed scheme is approved by the requisite majority and a further application to the court to sanction the approved scheme.

Company voluntary arrangements (CVAs)

■ The CVA is a composition in satisfaction of a company's debts, or a scheme of arrangement of its affairs, that binds all affected company creditors even though not all of them agree to its terms.

■ A CVA must be approved by the shareholders and also by a majority in excess of three-quarters in value of creditors at a meeting called for the purpose of approving the CVA.

■ Failure by the company to make a payment due under a CVA brings it to an end.

Small company moratorium

■ The small company moratorium is designed to protect small companies from legal actions whilst steps are taken to put a CVA in place. It is not a popular procedure.

Administration

■ Administration is designed primarily to rescue the company as a going concern.

■ Many administrations end by the company's business being sold as a 'pre-pack' or the company going into creditors' voluntary liquidation.

Takeovers

■ The Takeover Directive lays down a minimum level of protection allowing the higher level of protection in the Code to operate.

■ The Code applies where there is an offer to acquire, or an attempt to gain a controlling interest (an interest in shares carrying 30 per cent or more of the voting rights) in any LSE traded company or in any UK public company *with its central management and control in the UK.*

■ A takeover bid for a UK company with shares traded on AIM will be governed by the Code if its central management and control is in the UK.

■ A hostile takeover bid is a bid which is not recommended by the board of directors of the target company.

■ Where a takeover bid is recommended, the share acquisition can be structured as efficiently. Part 26 also allows a takeover to succeed with less than 90 per cent acceptance by shareholders.

■ Six general principles underpin the Code and are also set out in the EU Takeover Directive.

■ A person who obtains 30 per cent or more of the voting rights in a company is believed to have effective control so that a cash offer to all other shareholders at the highest price paid for the already acquired shares is required to share the control premium and advance the first principle of equality of treatment of shareholders.

■ Section 979 gives to the offeror the right to buy out minority shareholders (buy-out rights) and s 983 gives to minority shareholder the right to insist that they be bought out by the offeror (sell-out rights).

The Takeover Panel

■ The key function of the Panel on Takeovers and Mergers ('the Panel') is to issue and make rulings on the interpretation, application and effect of the Code.

■ The Panel was placed on a statutory footing by what is now Part 28 of the Companies Act 2006.

■ Panel decisions are subject to internal review by the Hearing Committee and, from there, independent review by the Takeover Appeal Board.

Discuss the role of the Takeover Code in corporate acquisitions.

Unpack the question

This is the first essential step which you must take time to do properly. You should separate out:

- Explanation of what the Takeover Code is
- Explanation of the meaning of "corporate acquisitions"
- Scope of application of the Takeover Code
- The reasons for the Takeover Code/ its principal aims.

Corporate acquisitions

Put the Takeover Code perspective by outlining the range of types of acquisitions of companies and the typical numbers of takeovers that are governed by the Takeover Code.

The scope of application of the Takeover Code

- Identify the Takeover Code as applying to real changes of control, not restructuring of groups
- Identify the Takeover Code as applying to the purchase of shares, not to direct purchases of underlying businesses. Dispell the misconception that the Takeover Code applies only to takeovers of companies with shares listed on the London Stock Exchange
- Outline the scope of application: offers to acquire, 30% or more of a company with shares traded on a regulated market in the UK (primarily companies with shares listed on the London Stock Exchange); *and* any other UK public company with its central management and control in the UK.

The Takeover Code

- Identify the Takeover Code as first introduced in 1968 as a self-regulatory body enforced by the Takeover Panel in response to the emergence of hostile takeover bids.
- Explain that the UK implementation of the EU Take-over Directive has placed the Takeover Code and the Panel on a statutory footing: s 943.

> **The role of the Takeover Code**
> - Discuss the overall aim of the Takeover Code and the six General Principles underlying the Code and the EU Takeover Directive it implements
> - Overarching: fair treatment of target shareholders and an orderly framework for the conduct of takeovers
> - The General Principles:
>   - Equal treatment
>   - Sufficient time and information
>   - Board neutrality
>   - No false markets
>   - Protection from unsubstantiated bids
>   - No protracted unsettling of the market;
> - Provide examples of code provisions illustrating these principles.

CONCLUDE

Further reading

Useful websites
The Insolvency Service website:
http://www.bis.gov.uk/insolvency
The website of the Panel on Takeovers and Mergers:
http://www.thetakeoverpanel.org.uk/

Articles
Armour, J, Jacobs, J, and Milhaupt, C, 'The Evolution of Hostile Takeover Regimes in Developed and Emerging Markets: an Analytical Framework' (2011) 52 Harvard international Law Journal 221.
Hunter, M, 'The Nature and Functions of a Rescue Culture' [1999] JBL 491.
Xie, B, 'Regulating pre-packaged administration – a complete agenda' [2011] JBL 513.

Reports
Insolvency Law and Practice, 'Report of the Insolvency Law Review Committee' (Cmnd. 8558, 1982) (The 'Cork Report').
DTI, 'Productivity and Enterprise – Insolvency: A second Chance' (Cm. 5234, 2001).
DTI/Treasury, 'Report by the Review Group on the Review of Company Rescue and Business Reconstruction Mechanisms' (2000).

Books
Goode, R, *Principles of Corporate Insolvency Law*, Student (ed) (4th Revised Edition, Sweet & Maxwell, 2011).

16

Winding up and dissolution of a company

AIMS AND OBJECTIVES

After reading this chapter you should be able to:

- Identify the different types of winding up
- Decide whether a document creates a fixed or floating charge
- Determine the order of priority of charges against the same property
- Decide whether or not a charge needs to be registered and if so where
- Advise on the steps a liquidator may take to avoid certain pre-winding up transactions
- Advise on the steps a liquidator may take to swell the asset pot available for distribution
- Advise on the statutory order of distribution of the assets of a company on a winding up
- Appreciate the routes available to dissolution of a company

16.1 Introduction

liquidation

the winding up of a company

Before a company ceases to exists, its affairs should be wound up. 'Winding up' and 'liquidation' mean the same thing. Essentially, in a winding up, any assets the company has are sold to turn them into cash which is distributed to meet the company's liabilities. The name of the company is then removed by the registrar from the register of companies and at that point the company ceases to exist. Most companies cease to exist without being formally wound up. If a company ceases to trade, has no assets, and stops making the required annual returns to the registrar, for example, the registrar may remove its name from the register of companies (see the final section of this chapter).

When a *solvent* company is wound up, all creditors are paid in full and the surplus is shared between the shareholders in accordance with their class rights. As noted in Chapter 7, the shareholders may decide to wind up a company and share out its residual wealth by passing a special resolution.

The situation is very different if a company is *insolvent*. The board of a company finding itself in financial trouble, struggling to pay its debts, including interest payments on its loans, will try to renegotiate the terms of loans and other credit arrangements to reach a voluntary compromise or settlement or composition (a range of terms are used) with its creditors to give the company a breathing space to trade itself back into financial good health.

In addition to informal efforts, three statutory legal processes are available to a company in financial difficulties to try to avoid the need to liquidate and dissolve the company: formal company voluntary arrangements, small company moratoria and administration. All three were considered in Chapter 15.

If efforts to renegotiate legal agreements with its creditors are unsuccessful, and the mechanisms in Chapter 15 are unsuccessful, a company is likely to enter liquidation or, put another way, be wound up. In this chapter we focus on companies entering into *insolvent* winding up. We briefly consider the different types of winding up followed by an examination of the most common forms of loan security: fixed and floating charges. An understanding of the basic types of loan security is important to understand the order in which the liquidator shares out the assets of a company amongst its creditors. We then look at the assets available for distribution in a winding up, the steps liquidators may take to avoid certain pre-winding up transactions and swell the asset pot available for distribution, and the statutory order of distribution of assets. Finally, we identify nine routes to dissolution of a company.

Unless indicated otherwise, statutory references in this chapter are to sections of the Insolvency Act 1986.

16.2 Types of winding up

A company may be wound up whether it is solvent or insolvent. Two types of winding up exist: voluntary winding up and compulsory winding up.

16.2.1 Voluntary winding up

voluntary winding up
the winding up of a company commenced by a special resolution of its members

A voluntary winding up is commenced by the passing of a special resolution by the shareholders (Insolvency Act 1986, s 84(1)(b)). A voluntary winding up will be:

- a members' voluntary winding up, if a statutory declaration of solvency (that they are of the opinion that the company will be able to pay its debts in full within a specified time of no more than 12 months) has been made by the directors in accordance with s 89; or

- a creditors' voluntary winding up, if no such statutory declaration has been made (s 90), or, if a declaration of solvency has been made but, subsequently, the liquidator disagrees with the declaration and is of the opinion that the company will be unable to pay its debts in full within the specified period (s 96).

statutory declaration of solvency
a statement made by the board for the purposes of s 89 of the Insolvency Act 1986 which confirms that the company is solvent and will be able to meet all liabilities which arise within 12 months from the commencement of a voluntary winding up

16.2.2 Compulsory winding up

A compulsory winding up is commenced by presentation of a petition to the court followed by an order of the court (Insolvency Act 1986, ss 122 and 124). The winding up is deemed to have commenced at the time of presentation of the petition, ie earlier than the date of the order (s 129(2)) The principal grounds on which a company may be wound up by the court are:

- the company is unable to pay its debts (s 122(1)(f));
- the court is of the opinion that it is just and equitable that the company should be wound up (s 122(1)(g) (see Chapter 14)).

compulsory liquidation or compulsory winding up
the winding up of a company by order of the court

Creditors typically present a petition seeking a winding up on the first ground whereas minority shareholders typically seek a winding up on the second ground (see section 14.6.1).

16.2.3 Insolvent winding up

The focus of this chapter is *insolvent* winding up, which can be either voluntary or compulsory. A company is insolvent when it is unable to pay its debts. In these circumstances either the company itself passes a special resolution to commence a creditors' voluntary winding up or a winding up petition is presented to the court, most commonly by a creditor who is owed £750 or more and has served an unpaid statutory demand on the company (s 123(1)(a)), or a creditor who has secured a judgment for any sum owed to him and execution of that judgment has failed (s 123(1)(b)).

16.2.4 Sources of insolvency law

The main statute governing winding ups is the Insolvency Act 1986, as amended, most significantly for our purposes, by the Enterprise Act 2002. The main regulations are the Insolvency Rules 1986. The Companies Act 2006 also contains provisions important to winding up and a host of other Acts and statutory instruments are relevant, making the structure of the law unsatisfactory.

QUOTATION

'It has to be said that the structure of English insolvency legislation does not display a particularly rational structure or scheme of arrangement … Overall the Insolvency Act and the Insolvency Rules have become a legislative morass through which even the experienced practitioner cannot pick his way without difficulty.'

Goode, R, *Principles of Corporate Insolvency Law*,
Student (ed) (Sweet & Maxwell, 2005)

In an effort to address this state of affairs, the Insolvency Service (an executive agency of the Department for Business, Innovation and Skills, or BIS), has been working for a number of years on the Modernisation of Insolvency Rules Project, to 'reduce the regulatory and administrative burdens that exist for users of insolvency legislation'. The final phase of the modernisation is 'to produce a new set of Insolvency Rules to restructure and entirely replace the 1986 Rules, which have been amended more than 20 times since they came into force'. Progress can be tracked on the Insolvency Service website referenced under further reading at the end of this chapter.

16.2.5 Effects of a winding up order or appointment of a liquidator

winding up order

a court order to liquidate a company

Once a winding up order has been made (in a compulsory winding up), or a liquidator has been put in place (in a creditors' voluntary winding up), the powers of the board of directors cease. No person may commence or continue any legal actions against the company without the leave of the court and control of the assets of the company passes to the liquidator.

official receiver

a civil servant in The Insolvency Service (an executive agency of BIS) and an officer of the court. The first liquidator of any company subject to compulsory winding up

In a compulsory winding up, the initial liquidator is the official receiver. The liquidator exercises statutory powers as an agent for the company (*Knowles v Scott* [1891] 1 Ch 717). His role is returned to in section 16.4 below after we have examined loan security and, in particular, fixed and floating charges.

16.3 Secured creditors

When a company enters insolvent winding up the liquidator is required to draw up a list of creditors of the company whose claims that the company owes them money have come up to proof. Creditors fall into categories: secured creditors, preferential creditors, unsecured creditors and deferred creditors. Secured creditors are those who, in addition to having a *contractual right* to sue the company for the return of any money owed to them, have taken a *property interest* in one or more items of the company's property as security for the credit they have made available to the company.

The existence of a property right ordinarily permits the holder of that right to take possession of the asset in certain circumstances and thereby remove it from the pot of assets available to the liquidator to liquidate and distribute rateably amongst those creditors who have only contractual rights against the company (unsecured creditors). In this way, the property interest, the security, reduces the risk to the secured creditor of not getting its money back. By reducing risk, security facilitates the lending of money (see *Re Brightlife Ltd* [1987] Ch 200, below at section 16.3.3). As we shall see, not all property right holders have the right to take possession of the charged property. Floating charge holders, for example, do not have the right to take possession, although their rights are greater than those of unsecured creditors.

16.3.1 Classification of loan security

Loan securities can be classified according to a number of criteria. Three classification criteria are commented on in this section.

Mortgages and charges

Although a distinction is often made in property law between a mortgage and a charge, this distinction is not usually important in company law. The term 'charge' is regularly used to describe a loan security whether the security established is a charge or a mortgage. Similarly, for the purposes of registration of charges, for example, s 861(5) states that *charge includes mortgage*. For the purposes of the insolvency process, s 248 of the Insolvency Act 1986 defines secured creditor as a creditor who holds security, which it defines to include *both charges and mortgages*. No attempt is made in this chapter to distinguish security operating by way of mortgage from security operating by way of charge.

Legal and equitable property interests

Loan security may provide the lender with an equitable or legal property right in the charged property. The distinction is important because an equitable property right cannot be asserted against a *bona fide* purchaser of the property for value who does not have notice of the equitable property right. This is important where more than one property right has been granted in relation to the same item of property. In deciding which property interest takes priority, that is, the order in which secured lenders will be entitled to the proceeds of sale of the property, legal rights almost always take priority over equitable rights. The order of priority will, however, be affected by whether or not the charge has been properly registered with the registrar in accordance with the Companies Act 2006. Priority and registration are dealt with at section 16.3.6 below.

charge

a legal or equitable property interest in some or all of the assets of the company created to secure a loan to the company or to secure some other right against the company

Fixed and floating charges

When we study winding up we need to understand not only the rights of secured creditors *vis-à-vis* other creditors but also the rights of different types of secured creditors. In this context it is critically important to classify charges into fixed and floating charges, an important distinction for at least three key reasons.

First, when a company is being wound up there is, in effect, a statutory partial overriding of the property rights of a *floating* chargeholder. Insolvency legislation provides for liquidation expenses, preferential debts and a statutory 'prescribed part' amount to be deducted from the proceeds of sale of property subject to a floating charge before the proceeds are available to pay the debt owed to the floating chargeholder. No similar over-riding occurs in relation to fixed chargeholders. This is part of the reason why it is said that fixed charges are outside the statutory order of distribution provided for in Chapter VIII of the Insolvency Act 1986.

Second, all floating charges created by companies are registrable whereas not all fixed charges are registrable (fixed charges over shares or non-book debts, for example, are not registrable). Because a registrable but ununregistered charge is void against a liquidator, it is sometimes very important to know whether or not a charge is a fixed or floating charge to determine its registrability. Third, a floating charge is vulnerable to avoidance pursuant to the Insolvency Act 1986, s 245, whereas a fixed charge is not (see avoidance of transactions at section 16.4.2 below).

For these three key reasons, amongst others, it is essential to know how to decide whether a particular security interest is a fixed or floating charge. Also for these reasons, banks go out of their way to characterise charges as fixed charges, seeking to establish the much stronger rights of a fixed chargeholder in the event of a winding up, when in reality the charge in question is operated as a floating charge. The distinction between fixed and floating charges was introduced in Chapter 6 where we considered debt financing and you may find it useful to reread the secured funding part of that chapter (section 6.4.6) before reading on.

16.3.2 Fixed charges

A fixed charge, also sometimes called a specific charge, is a property interest in specific property preventing the owner of the property from selling the property or otherwise dealing with it without first either:

- paying back the sum secured against it; or
- securing the consent of the chargeholder.

receiver

a person appointed under a debenture or other instrument secured over the assets of a company to manage and realise the secured assets for the benefit of the charge holder

A fixed charge is created by a deed or other charge document, usually at the same time the loan is made or a credit facility (such as an overdraft facility) is put in place. The rights of the fixed chargeholder will be determined by the language of the charge document which stipulates what the chargeholder may do in relation to the charged property and in which eventualities. Typically, the fixed chargeholder has the right to take possession of the charged property, sell it, and recover from the proceeds of sale the secured sum and costs reasonably incurred. Any surplus proceeds are returned to the company. Additionally, or alternatively, the charge will empower the chargeholder to appoint a receiver to take possession of the property on its behalf. The chargeholder is empowered to take these steps only if and when certain events occur, such as the company defaulting on payment of one or more repayments, or the company entering into liquidation. Figures 6.1 and 6.2 in Chapter 6 illustrate how fixed charges work.

No simple legal definition of a fixed charge exists. It is a non-possessory security that is not a floating charge. Non-possessory means that the person who benefits from the charge does not have possession of the charged property. Possession remains with the company. This is the reason why it is important to have a public register of charges so that third parties, by consulting the register, are able to discover whether or not a piece of property owned and in the possession of the company is subject to any of the registrable charges. Note, however, that whilst all floating charges are registrable, not all fixed charges are registrable. Fixed charges on shares and non-book debts, for example, are not registrable.

The essence of a fixed charge is that control over dealing with the charged property rests with the bank/lender/creditor/chargee/chargeholder. In contrast, property subject to a floating charge may be dealt with (usually sold) by the company in the ordinary course of business without seeking the consent of the chargee.

The meaning of fixed charge has been explored in several significant cases in the past 20 years in which liquidators and the Inland Revenue (now HM Revenue & Customs) have sought to challenge charges described on their face as fixed charges, arguing that they are, in reality, floating charges. In *Re Spectrum Plus Ltd* [2005] 2 AC 680 (HL), Lord Scott emphasised that it is the substance of the rights created and not the form that determines the nature of the charge.

JUDGMENT

'[T]he label of "fixed" or "specific" (which I take to be synonymous in this context) cannot be decisive if the rights created by the debenture, properly construed, are inconsistent with that label.'

Before the relevant sections of the Enterprise Act 2002 came into effect, unpaid taxes of a company that went into winding up were payable as preferential debts. This is no longer the case, but it was the case when the facts of the four major cases exploring the line between fixed and floating charges arose. Accordingly, the taxing authorities were keen to establish that the form of security scrutinised in the cases were floating charges thereby requiring the liquidator to pay the unpaid taxes out of the proceeds of sale of the charged assets before applying any of those proceeds to pay back the chargeholder.

The four leading cases in which a charge named on its face as a fixed charge was examined to determine what rights the parties intended to create and whether or not, as a matter of law, those rights constituted a fixed or a floating charge are:

- *Siebe Gorman & Co Ltd v Barclays Bank Ltd* [1979] 2 Lloyds Rep 142 (overruled in *Re Spectrum*).
- *Re New Bullas Trading Ltd* [1994] 1 BCLC 485 (PC) (overruled in *Agnew*).
- *Agnew v Commissioner of Inland Revenue (Re Brumark Investments Ltd)* [2001] 2 AC 710 (PC) (approved in *Re Spectrum*).
- *Re Spectrum Plus Ltd* [2005] 2 AC 680 (HL).

The leading authority, *Re Spectrum*, a test case on a widely used standard form of debenture, is discussed at section 16.3.4 below when we examine charges over book debts.

16.3.3 Floating charges

Justice Hoffmann (as he then was) explained the role played by floating charges in *Re Brightlife Ltd* [1987] Ch 200. He highlighted the tension between the rights of floating chargeholders and unsecured creditors, stating that responsibility for balancing these competing interests lies with the legislature, not the courts.

JUDGMENT

'The floating charge was invented by Victorian lawyers to enable manufacturing and trading companies to raise loan capital on debentures. It could offer the security of a charge over the whole of the company's undertaking without inhibiting its ability to trade. But the mirror image of these advantages was the potential prejudice to the general body of creditors, who might know nothing of the floating charge but find that all the company's assets, including the very goods which they had just delivered on credit, had been swept up by the debenture holder. The public interest requires a balancing of the advantages to the economy of facilitating the borrowing of money against the possibility of injustice to unsecured creditors. These arguments for and against the floating charge are matters for Parliament rather than the courts and have been the subject of public debate in and out of Parliament for more than a century.

Parliament has responded, first, by restricting the right of the holder of a floating charge and secondly, by requiring public notice of the existence and enforcement of the charge.'

In *Re Yorkshire Woolcombers Association Ltd* (1903), Romer LJ described three key characteristics of a floating charge. A floating charge, he stated, is:

- a charge upon all of a certain class of assets present and future;
- which class is, in the ordinary course of the company's business, changing from time to time;
- in relation to which charged assets, until steps are taken to enforce the charge, the company can carry on business in the ordinary way including removing a charged asset from the security.

In *Agnew v Commissioner of Inland Revenue (Re Brumark Investments Ltd)* [2001] 2 AC 710 (PC) Lord Millett stressed it is the third of these characteristics that is the essential feature of a floating charge and which distinguishes a floating charge from a fixed charge. A fixed charge may have one or both of the first characteristics listed above but may *not* have the third.

Figures 16.1 and 16.2 illustrate how a floating charge may be put in place against a single class of assets or a number of different classes of assets. It is common for floating charges to be put in place against 'all the assets and business of the company'. This is referred to as a general floating charge. The great attraction and benefit of a floating charge is that the company can continue to use the charged assets of the company, buying and selling them in the ordinary course of business, without recourse to the chargeholder, until, that is, the charge crystallises. Until crystallisation, the property interest of the chargee simply floats above the assets, hence the name 'floating charge'.

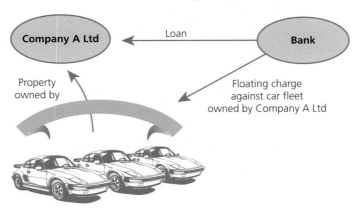

Figure 16.1 Floating charge against single class of assets

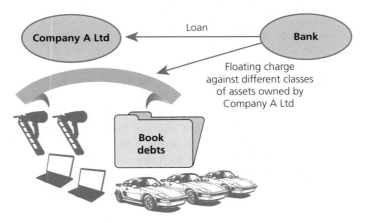

Figure 16.2 Floating charge against different classes of assets

crystallisation

on crystallisation, a floating charge becomes a fixed charge

Crystallisation of a floating charge

The effect of crystallisation

On crystallisation, a floating charge becomes a fixed charge. The right of the company to deal with the charged assets in the ordinary course of business ceases and the rights of the chargeholder/bank are essentially those stated for a fixed chargeholder above, except that if the company is being wound up those rights are subject to the Insolvency Act provisions overriding them.

Also, do not think that because a floating charge becomes a fixed charge at the point of crystallisation it is thereby taken outside the statutory insolvency law provisions applicable to floating charges. Although it is possible to provide in a floating charge that it will crystallise in circumstances that occur *before* the commencement of a winding up, Parliament has acted to neutralise the effect of such provisions by providing in the Insolvency Act 1986 that for the purposes of a winding up, 'floating charge' is defined as, 'a charge which, *as created*, was a floating charge' (s 251) (emphasis added). Consequently, provided the charge started its life as a floating charge, it is treated as a floating charge in a winding up.

When does crystallisation occur?

Crystallisation of a floating charge occurs on/when:

- appointment of a receiver;
- the company goes into liquidation;
- the company ceases to carry on business/sells its business;
- a notice of conversion being given (if the charge document gives the chargeholder/bank the right to convert the charge from floating to fixed on giving notice);
- an event occurs which, under the terms of the charge document, causes 'automatic crystallisation'.

The freedom of the parties to stipulate the crystallisation events was supported by Hoffmann J in *Re Brightlife Ltd* [1987] Ch 200 subject to statutory provisions that cannot be contracted out of.

16.3.4 Charges over book debts

What is a book debt?

book debt
a debt arising in the course of a business that would or could in the ordinary course of business be entered in well-kept books of account of the business

Sums receivable, either immediately or at some date in the future, by a company operating a business ('receivables') are important assets of a company. When they are used to raise capital for the company it is called 'receivable financing'. Book debts are a very important type of receivable. They can be either sold (assigned) to raise capital for the company (the sale price), or charged as security for a loan made to the company. A charge over book debts is registrable with the registrar pursuant to s 860 of the Companies Act 2006, whether it is a fixed or floating charge, yet there is no definition of book debt in the Companies Act 2006.

Consequently, the definition of book debt has been litigated, for example, in the context of one party seeking to establish that a charge over a debt is not registrable because the debt is not a book debt. A fixed charge on a non-book debt does not fall within the list in s 860 of charges that need to be registered and, accordingly, is not registrable. In contrast, a floating charge on *any* property of the company, including book debts, is registrable. In *Independent Automatic Sales Ltd v Knowles & Foster* [1962] 1 WLR 974, Buckley J considered whether or not the debts in question were book debts. If they were, the charges were registrable, and, as they had not been registered, were void against the liquidator.

JUDGMENT

'*Shipley v Marshall* [(1863) 14 CBNS 566], I think, establishes that, if it can be said of a debt arising in the course of a business and due or growing due to the proprietor of that business that such a debt would or could in the ordinary course of such a business be entered in well-kept books relating to that business, that debt can properly be called a book debt whether it is in fact entered in the books of the business or not.'

Book debts example

Company A Ltd manufactures shoes and sells them to wholesaler customers. The customers to whom it sells shoes in December 2006 are B, C, D, E and F. The customers it sells to in January 2007 are D, E, F, G and H. The terms of supply provide for the price to be paid within 45 days of invoice. The sums owed to Company A Ltd are recorded in its books of account as assets. These assets are called 'book debts' and they are choses in action. When the debtor pays the invoiced sum, the book debt is extinguished and the cash payment is deposited in the bank account of Company A

Ltd. If a debtor/customer does not pay the sum due by the due date the Company can sue the debtor to recover the debt. Company A Ltd's list of book debts is constantly changing. The following table illustrates this:

Book Debts of Company A Ltd	
1 January 2007	**1 February 2007**
B owes £10,000	D owes £15,000
C owes £5,000	E owes £1,000
D owes £1,000	F owes £1,000
E owes £1,000	G owes £6,000
F owes £1,000	H owes £9,000

In January 2007, wholesaler B pays the invoice for the shoes it has bought from Company A Ltd in December 2006 by sending Company A Ltd a cheque for £10,000. The book debt owed by wholesaler B ceases to exist and does not appear in the list of book debts of Company A Ltd on 1 February 2007. Company A Ltd has, in its place, a cheque. Company A Ltd deposits the cheque in its bank account. Company A Ltd uses the money in the bank account in the ordinary course of running the business, to pay bills, employee wages, taxes, etc.

Fixed charges over book debts

Charges over book debts are usually floating charges. It is *theoretically* possible to have a fixed charge over book debts *but* the chargeholder/bank must control the property charged.

CASE EXAMPLE

Re Spectrum Plus Ltd [2005] 2 AC 680 (HL)

A standard form charge used widely by banks to take security over book debts, present and future, of a company, was expressed on its face to be a specific charge, meaning a fixed charge. The Inland Revenue challenged the nature of the charge, seeking to have it declared to be a floating charge so that the proceeds of sale of the book debts in the hands of the liquidator had to be used to pay off preferred debts (which, when the facts of the case arose, included unpaid taxes, although this is no longer the case). The charge provided that the company could not deal with uncollected book debts. It also required the proceeds of the book debts (the sums paid by the book debtors to the company extinguishing the book debt) to be paid into the company's current account with the bank. Provided the overdraft limit on that account was not exceeded, the company could draw sums freely out of the bank account and use the sums for its business purposes. Held: The document created a floating charge not a fixed charge. The account into which the proceeds of the book debts was to be paid was not a 'blocked account', that is, one that the company could not draw on without the consent of the chargee bank and therefore the company was free to deal with the proceeds of the book debts in the ordinary course of its business. This did not give the bank the control over the charged asset that is required to establish a fixed charge.

Following *Re Spectrum Plus Ltd* (2005), the leading case on the defining features of a fixed charge and which involved a charge over book debts, there are three stages to the control needed for a charge over book debts to be a fixed charge:

- the company must not be able to sell or use the book debts as security without the consent of the chargeholder/bank (so no using the charged book debts for receivables financing);

- the sum paid to the company by the book debtors must be paid into an account specified by the chargeholder/bank;
- the proceeds in the bank account must be useable by the company only with the consent of the chargee/bank (it must be a 'blocked account'): essentially, the chargee/bank must control withdrawals from the bank account into which the book debt receipts are paid, both in theory and in practice.

Note that although not strictly needed for the decision in the case, the court in *Re Spectrum* did not consider that a court should confine its concern to the language of the documentation creating the charge but should also consider how the charge was operated in practice. Lord Scott, referring to the words of Lord Millet in *Agnew v Commissioner of Inland Revenue (Re Brumark Investments Ltd)* [2001] 2 AC 710 (PC) said, 'It was not enough to provide in the debenture for an account to be blocked, if it was not in fact operated as a blocked account'. Where, therefore, the language of the document gives the chargee bank control over the bank account but as a matter of fact that control is not exercised, the charge will not be a fixed charge.

16.3.5 Registration of charges

Charges created by a company may need to be registered:

- with the registrar of companies;
- in the company's own register of charges;
- with HM Land Registry (charges on registered land) or at the Land Charges Department (charges on unregistered land).

Registration with the Registrar of Companies (ss 860–877)

Section 860(1) of the Companies Act 2006 provides that prescribed particulars of *certain* fixed and *all* floating charges created by a company, together with the instrument, if any, creating them, must be delivered to the registrar within 21 days after creation (s 870). On registration of a charge, the registrar gives a certificate of registration which is conclusive evidence that the requirements of the Act as to registration have been complied with (s 869(6)). The decision to issue a certificate cannot be judicially reviewed (*R v Registrar of Companies, ex parte Central Bank of India* [1986] QB 1114).

If the prescribed particulars are not delivered within 21 days, the charge is void against the administrator or liquidator of the company and any creditor of the company (subject to an extension of the time for registration being granted on which see below). If a registrable charge is not registered in accordance with the Act, criminal liability attaches to the company and every officer in default (s 860(4)). The civil consequences of non-registration are far more important than the potential criminal liability, and it is to avoid the civil consequences of non-registration that registration is normally undertaken by the chargeholder, a course of action expressly permitted by s 860(2).

Although an unregistered registrable charge is void against the liquidator and any other creditor, the loan itself is not void. The creditor becomes an unsecured creditor. Also, s 874 states that when a charge becomes void for want of registration, the money secured becomes immediately repayable. Even if a second chargeholder knew of the creation of the prior unregistered charge, the prior charge is still void against the second chargeholder (*Re Monolithic Building Co* [1915] Ch 643).

If the omission is accidental, due to inadvertence, is not of a nature to prejudice the creditors or shareholders, or it is otherwise just and equitable for the court to grant relief, the company or any person interested may apply to the court to extend the time to register a charge or to rectify the register (s 873). Relief, usually late registration, will only be granted subject to the standard proviso, known as the 'Joplin' proviso, that registration is without prejudice to the rights of parties acquired during the period between the date by which the charge should have been registered and the date of its actual registration

(*Re Joplin Brewery Co Ltd* [1902] 1 Ch 79). It is settled practice that a court will not make an order under s 873 extending time for registration if the application is made after winding up of the company has commenced.

Registration in the Company's own register

register of charges
the statutory register that has to be maintained by every company containing details of all charges over the company's property or any part of it

Every company is required by the Companies Act 2006 to keep available for inspection:

- a copy of every instrument creating a charge over the company's property that is registrable with the registrar (ss 875 and 877). This is a copy of the original debenture; and
- a register of *all* charges (whether registrable with the registrar or not) (ss 876 and 877).

The Act provides for criminal liability to attach to an officer of the company who knowingly and wilfully authorises or permits the omission of an entry in the company's register (s 876). Refusal to allow inspection of the register or any instrument attracts criminal liability for any officer in default *and* the company (s 877(6)). Failure to comply with the statutory provisions does not, however, adversely affect enforceability of charges.

Registration of charges over land

Registered land charges

In addition to registration with the registrar and in the company's register of charges, a charge over registered land owned by the company must be registered in the Land Registry pursuant to the Land Registration Act 2002.

Unregistered land charges

In addition to registration with the registrar and in the company's register of charges, a charge over unregistered land must also be registered with the Land Charges Department pursuant to the Land Charges Act 1972.

16.3.6 Priority of charges

Provided charges have been properly registered with the registrar pursuant to s 860, the following basic rules apply to determine the priority of charges:

- Fixed charges rank in order of the time at which they are created: the first in time takes priority over all subsequent fixed charges over the same property.
- Fixed charges establish stronger rights than floating charges and a later-in-time fixed charge ranks in priority over an earlier floating charge (*Re Castell & Brown Ltd* [1898] 1 Ch 315). Except that if the subsequent fixed chargeholder had *actual* knowledge, at the time its charge was entered into, that the pre-existing floating charge expressly prohibited the company from creating a subsequent charge with priority, the pre-existing floating charge will take priority over the subsequent fixed charge (*Siebe Gorman & Co Ltd v Barclays Bank Ltd* [1979] 2 Lloyds Rep 142, which remains good law on this point). Such a clause is known as a 'negative pledge'. A negative pledge principally operates as a contractual right between the company and the first chargeholder. Note that registration with the registrar of the pre-existing floating charge is *not enough* to confer knowledge on a subsequent fixed chargeholder to stop the subsequent fixed charge from taking priority. The registration system does not, however, require the existence of a negative pledge to be registered. Even if the existence of the negative pledge clause is clear from the public register, the subsequent fixed chargeholder will *not* be saddled with constructive notice of the negative pledge. If the subsequent fixed chargeholder has actual knowledge, because it has actually read the information on the public register, *Siebe Gorman* is authority for the proposition that the pre-existing floating charge will take priority over the subsequent fixed charge.

- Floating charges rank in order of time of creation: the first in time takes priority over all subsequent floating charges over the same property (*Re Benjamin Cope & Sons Ltd* [1914] 1 Ch 800).
- A floating charge over specific assets *may* rank in priority to an earlier floating charge expressed to be a charge over all the assets and undertaking of the company ('a general floating charge') *if* power is reserved to the company in the earlier charge to create a later charge having priority (*Re Automatic Bottle Makers Ltd* [1926] Ch 412).

Figures 16.3 to 16.5 illustrate the operation of these rules.

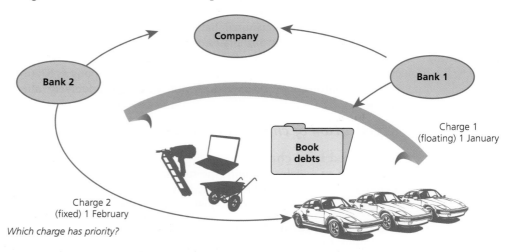

Figure 16.3 Priority of charges: fixed and floating charges

Answer: Bank 2 has prior claim to the proceeds of sale of the premises, *Re Castell & Brown Ltd* [1898] 1 Ch 315.

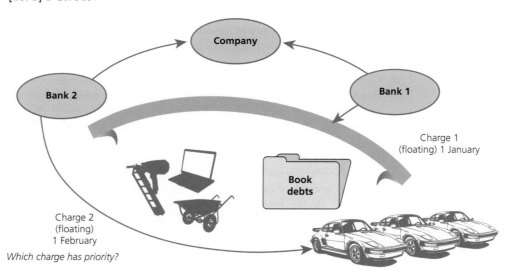

Figure 16.4 Priority of charges: two floating charges

Answer: Floating charge 1 has priority unless the document creating it contains a clause permitting the creation of subsequent charges with priority (*Re Automatic Bottle Makers Ltd* [1926] Ch 412).

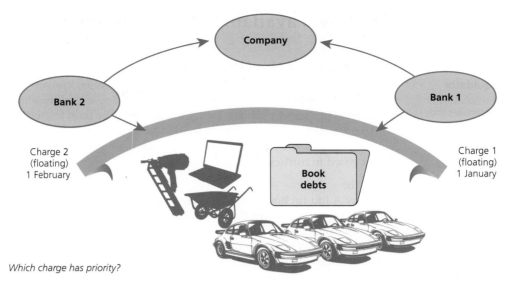

Which charge has priority?

Figure 16.5 Priority of charges: two general floating charges

Answer: Bank 1 has prior claim to the proceeds of sale of the assets, *Re Benjamin Cope & Sons Ltd* [1914] 1 Ch 800.

16.3.7 Fixed and floating charges compared and contrasted

The key differences between a fixed and floating charge are:

- Whilst the floating charge remains floating (before crystallisation), the company/chargor remains free to deal with the charged property in the ordinary course of business.
- Various statutory rules relating to validity and priority are worded to apply to one form of security (eg floating charges) but not the other, including:
  - registration requirements are different: all floating charges are registrable but not all fixed charges are registrable;
  - floating charge property proceeds are available to pay the expenses of winding up, preferential debts and a statutory 'prescribed' part is set aside for unsecured creditors out of them;
  - the liquidator may treat certain floating charges as invalid pursuant to s 245 of the Insolvency Act 1986.
- Priority of charges against the same property: the floating nature of the floating charge until it crystallises, results in it being treated differently from a fixed charge in determining priority of charges.

Note that it is common for banks to take both a fixed charge and a floating charge in the same document thereby seeking to combine the *priority* advantages of the fixed charge with the *flexibility* of the floating charge. It is instructive to look at the language actually used in such documents. In *Re Spectrum* (above), for example, the charge was expressed in the following language:

'A specific charge [of] all book debts and other debts ... now and from time to time due or owing to [Spectrum]' (para 2(v)) and 'A floating security [of] its undertaking and all its property assets and rights whatsoever and wheresoever present and/or future including those for the time being charged by way of specific charge pursuant to the foregoing paragraphs if and to the extent that such charges as aforesaid shall fail as specific charges but without prejudice to any such specific charges as shall continue to be effective' (para 2(vii)).

16.4 Assets available for distribution

16.4.1 Role of the liquidator

liquidator

the person who undertakes the liquidation of a company and who must be a qualified insolvency practitioner

pari passu

the principle of treatment on an equal footing, applied on the winding up of companies so that all unsecured creditors share the assets available to unsecured creditors in proportion to the sum each is owed

The liquidator's role is to collect or 'get in' the assets, convert them into cash and distribute the proceeds in satisfaction of the company's liabilities *'pari passu'*. *Pari passu* means that the money available for distribution will be paid to creditors in proportion to the size of their valid (known as 'admitted') claims against the company. This principle cannot be excluded by contract but it does have a number of exceptions, for which see Goode, listed in further reading.

Example

Company A Ltd (in liquidation) has admitted unsecured creditor claims of £2,000 made up of £500 owed to each of B, C, D and E. The liquidator gets in all the company's assets and realises only £1,000. Ignoring expenses and in the absence of preferential and secured creditors, the £1,000 will be distributed *pari passu*, or 'rateably' amongst the unsecured creditors by paying £250 to each of B, C, D and E. This is referred to as '50 pence in the pound'. The amount received per pound is arrived at by dividing the sum available to distribute by the total sum owing, $1,000/2,000 = 0.5$ or 50 pence per pound. If B, C, D and E had been owed £1,000 each, they still would have received £250 each but this would be 25 pence in the pound arrived at by dividing the £1,000 available for distribution by the £4,000 owed.

Example

Company F Ltd (in liquidation) has admitted unsecured creditor claims of £2,000 made up of £1,000 owed to G, £500 owed to H and 250 owed to each of I and J. The liquidator gets in all the company's assets and realises only £1,000. Ignoring expenses and in the absence of preferential and secured creditors, that £1,000 will be distributed *'pari passu'*, or 'rateably' amongst the unsecured creditors as follows:

Creditor	Is owed £	Receives £
G	1,000	500
H	500	250
I	250	125
J	250	125
Total	2,000	1,000

This is referred to as a payment of '50 pence in the pound'.

Pari passu is not applied to the combined claims of secured and unsecured creditors because secured creditors have property rights, or 'rights *in rem*' in relation to property in the possession of the company. The existence of creditor property rights in the company's property means that the liquidator must take the property to which those rights attach out of the company's general asset pot and put it into a separate pot to be distributed between holders of property rights in those assets: the secured creditors. The statutory order of distribution of assets that must be applied by a liquidator in an insolvent winding up is considered in the following section of this chapter.

Collecting in the assets includes:

- bringing any actions vested in the company, such as actions for breach of contract against a third party;
- disclaiming onerous contracts and property (Insolvency Act 1986 ss 178–182);
- avoiding specific types of transactions that can be avoided pursuant to the Insolvency Act 1986 (ss 238, 239, 244, 245, 423 and Companies Act 2006 s 874);
- making applications to recover contributions from officers and others pursuant to the Insolvency Act 1986.

16.4.2 Avoidance of transactions

Fair dealing provisions in the Insolvency Act 1986 permit a liquidator (or administrator) to reverse certain transactions regarded by the law to be detrimental to creditors and the collective nature of the winding up process because they undermine the *pari passu* principle. The power of the court to make orders in relation to some of these arrangements is very wide, going beyond the power to set aside a transaction. In relation to extortionate credit transactions, for example, the court has the option to order that the transaction remain in place but with varied terms.

The transactions examined in this part of the chapter are 'pre-liquidation' transactions entered into within what Goode refers to as the 'twilight period' before the winding up commences. The Insolvency Act 1986 classifies these transactions into four types:

- transactions at an undervalue (s 238);
- preferences (s 239);
- invalid floating charges (s 245);
- extortionate credit transactions (s 244).

The statutory provisions protect creditors by legally overriding attempts, in the run-up to a winding up, by directors and major shareholders of a company, to put particular persons (individuals or companies) in a more advantageous position than that in which they would otherwise find themselves. The person intended to benefit from the arrangement in question may be a director or major shareholder of the company or, as is often the case, a person who is related or linked in some way to a director or major shareholder. In relation to three of the four types of arrangements, the statute uses the 'connected person' concept to make it easier to successfully challenge an arrangement benefiting a person connected with the company.

Each type of transaction is dealt with below, followed by an examination of the concept of a 'connected person'.

Transactions at an undervalue (s 238)

The liquidator (or administrator) may apply to the court for an order and the court may make 'such order as it thinks fit for restoring the position to what it would have been if the company had not entered into' a transaction with any person at an undervalue. Transaction at an undervalue is defined in s 238(4).

SECTION

'A company enters into a transaction with a person at an undervalue if –
(a) the company makes a gift to that person or otherwise enters into a transaction with a person on terms that provide for the company to receive no consideration, or
(b) the company enters into a transaction with that person for a consideration the value of which, in money or money's worth, is significantly less than the value, in money or money's worth, of the consideration provided by the company.'

In the only House of Lords decision, *Philips v Brewin Dolphin Bell Lawrie Ltd* [2001] 1 WLR 143, Lord Scott regarded as useful the following breakdown of the statutory requirement provided by Millet J when analysing the requirements of s 238(4)(b) in *re MC Bacon Ltd* [1990] BCLC 324 at 340.

JUDGMENT

'To come within that paragraph the transaction must be:
(i) entered into by the company;
(ii) for a consideration;
(iii) the value of which measured in money or money's worth;
(iv) is significantly less than the value;
(v) also measured in money or money's worth;
(vi) of the consideration provided by the company.'

A classic example of a transaction at an undervalue as defined in s 238(4) would be the sale by a company of an executive BMW company car with a second hand market value of £40,000, to a director or, indeed, to any person, for, let us say, £10,000. Gifts are also regarded as transactions at an undervalue so that if the BMW car were given to somebody, the gift would also be vulnerable to challenge under s 238. Before the 1986 Act, transactions at an undervalue were regulated as 'fraudulent conveyances' but the new terminology makes it clear that it is not necessary to prove fraud.

How much, you may ask, would have to be paid for the BMW car in our example for the sum paid to fall outside the language 'significantly less than the value' of the car and the transaction not to be open to challenge as a transaction at an undervalue? No clear rule of thumb is stated in the sparse case law on s 238. Whilst the specific issue of what proportionate shortfall in value amounts to a significant undervalue was not discussed in *Philips v Brewin Dolphin Bell Lawrie Ltd* [2001] 1 WLR 143, the transaction in that case was held to be at an undervalue where the consideration receivable by the company was approximately 60 per cent of the value of the consideration given by the company.

Lord Scott of Foscote focused on the importance of valuing consideration at a realistic appraisal of actual value rather than a speculative estimate of value. This was important because part of the consideration given to the company in the case was the value of another agreement, which had to be ascertained. The 'collateral' contract was described as being 'a precarious thing' at the time the transaction was entered into, and its value 'speculative'. Where the consideration offered is speculative and precarious, the House of Lords held that it is for the party seeking to rely on the value to prove it.

Even if a transaction is at an undervalue, the liquidator must establish two further conditions to successfully challenge a transaction under s 238:

- The transaction must have been entered into at a relevant time which means within the two years ending with the commencement of the insolvency (which in most cases means the presentation of the winding up petition to the court); and
- At the time the transaction was entered into the company must have been unable to pay its debts as they fell due or to have become unable to do so as a result of the transaction.

Finally, even if the liquidator can establish these two conditions, no order will be made if the court is satisfied that s 238(5) applies and the company entered into the transaction:

- in good faith,
- for the purpose of carrying on its business, and
- reasonable grounds existed for believing that the transaction would benefit the company.

At this point, however, it is for the party seeking to rely on s 238(5) to resist the making of an order, to prove that the requirements of s 238(5) are satisfied.

If the transaction is entered into with a connected person (a concept examined in detail below), the requirement that at the time the transaction was entered into the company must have been unable to pay its debts as they fell due, or to have become unable to do so as a result of the transaction, is assumed to have been satisfied and the burden of proof, to show that at the time of the transaction the company was solvent, lies with the party resisting the order.

It is noteworthy that a transaction at an undervalue can sometimes be challenged under s 423 of the Insolvency Act as a transaction defrauding creditors.

Preferences (s 239)

The conditions for a liquidator's successful application under s 239 are as follows:

Factual preference

The company must have given a factual preference. This has two dimensions:

Person dimension: the preference must have been given to a creditor, surety or guarantor of the company;

Effect dimension: the preference must have put that person in a better position in the event of insolvent liquidation.

An example of a factual preference is the granting of a charge to an unsecured creditor, whether that charge is fixed or floating, *for no consideration*. Another example is the premature repayment of an unsecured loan (*Re Exchange Travel Ltd (No 3)* [1996] 2 BCLC 524 and *Wills v Corfe Joinery Ltd* [1998] 2 BCLC 75). Unsurprisingly, the debt is often due to a director. Where payments to the company were redirected to its bank, this was held by Lewison J, in *Re Hawkes Hill Publishing Co Ltd* [2007] BCC 937 not to be a factual preference where the bank had a floating charge over all the assets and business of the company because the bank would have recovered the money pursuant to its security.

Relevant time

The preference must have been granted at a relevant time. Relevant time has two dimensions:

Temporal dimension: the preference must have been given within two years for a connected person, six months for others, of the commencement of insolvency;

Financial dimension: the company must have been insolvent at the time of the grant or have become insolvent as a result of the grant.

Insolvency commences on the presenting of a petition in the case of a compulsory winding up and on the passing of the winding up resolution in a voluntary winding up.

Desire

In granting the preference, the company must have been influenced by a desire to put the preferred person in a better position in the event of the company going into insolvent liquidation. Two key points to remember are:

- Desire is presumed to have existed if the preference has been granted to a connected person. It can, however, be rebutted (*Re Fairway Magazines Ltd* [1993] BCLC 643).
- We do not desire every necessary consequence of our actions (*Re MC Bacon Ltd* [1990] BCLC 324, especially *per* Millet J (as he then was)).

JUDGMENT

'A man is taken to intend the necessary consequences of his actions, so that an intention to grant a security to a creditor necessarily involves an intention to prefer that creditor ... A man is not to be taken as *desiring* all the necessary consequences of his actions. Some consequences may be of advantage to him and be desired by him; others may not affect him and be matters of indifference to him; while still others may be positively disadvantageous to him and not be desired by him, but regarded by him as the unavoidable price of obtaining the desired advantages ... *a transaction will not be set aside ... unless the company positively wished to improve the creditor's position in ... liquidation.*' (emphasis added)

CASE EXAMPLE

Re MC Bacon Ltd [1990] BCLC 324

A company with an unsecured overdraft facility was trading near to its overdraft limit when it lost a major customer. The company's bank demanded a fixed and floating charge security for existing unsecured liabilities on the overdraft *and* any future advances as a pre-condition to continuing support. The company's directors caused the company to grant security in response to the bank's demands. The liquidator applied to set aside the Bank's security under s 239. Held (Millett J): The company had not been 'influenced by a desire' to prefer the bank. The company/directors desired to do everything necessary to stay in business and turn the company around. Their thinking was, either we give the bank security or they call in the overdraft. The preference was therefore the, 'unavoidable price of obtaining the desired advantages.' The company directors did not positively wish to improve the bank's position.

Consequences

The liquidator may apply for such order as the court thinks fit for restoring the position to the pre-preference position. Unlike a transfer at an undervalue, a voidable preference need not diminish the assets of the company. The reason why the preference is unacceptable is because it undermines the *pari passu* principle. Where the preference is a release from an obligation (such as a guarantee), the court may order that a person is under a new or revived obligation guarantee obligation. Where the preference is the grant of a charge, the court will often set aside the charge and when a creditor has been repaid early, the court will order that the sum be paid back to the company with the creditor left to prove for the debt in the winding up.

Invalid floating charges (s 245)

Section 245 enables a liquidator to avoid a floating charge in certain defined circumstances. No application to the court is required. The circumstances bringing a floating charge within s 245 are as follows:

Floating charge

Section 245 is relevant only if a *floating charge* has been granted. Remember that a charge called a fixed or specific charge on its face may, in reality, be a floating charge and therefore challengeable (see *Re Spectrum Plus* above). A fixed charge (in substance) cannot be challenged pursuant to s 245. A floating charge may *also* be challenged in a s 239 application.

Relevant time

The floating charge must have been granted at a relevant time. Relevant time has two dimensions:

Temporal dimension:	the preference must have been given within two years for a connected person, 12 months for others, of the commencement of insolvency;
Financial dimension:	the company must have been insolvent at the time of the grant or have become insolvent as a result of the grant. Insolvency is not a requirement if the charge is granted to a connected person.

Consequences

A floating charge falling within s 245 is invalid except as to money paid or goods and services supplied to the company *at the same time as, or after the creation of the charge* (s 245(2)). The meaning of this subsection has been explored in cases involving:

- Overdraft facilities: where a floating charge is granted to secure an overdraft facility and money has been paid in and out of the account both before and after the grant (such as *Re Yeovil Glove Co Ltd* [1965] Ch 148).
- 'Structured transactions': where money is paid in the context of transactions deliberately structured to appear as if money has been paid on or after creation of the charge. In these cases the court looks at the substance of the transaction, not simply the form (see, for example *Re GT Whyte & Co Ltd* [1983] BCLC 311).

CASE EXAMPLE

Re Yeovil Glove Co Ltd [1965] Ch 148

The company's bank extended an overdraft facility to it on 1 February 2006. On 1 August 2006, when the company was already overdrawn by £50,000, it granted a floating charge to its bank as security for sums advanced both in the past and to be advanced in the future. After 1 August 2006, the bank made further advances totalling £50,000 to the company and the company paid £70,000 into the account.

The winding up of the company was commenced on 1 December 2006 at which point the balance on the overdraft stood at £30,000 overdrawn (£50,000 + £50,000 less £70,000). The question arose whether that £30,000 represented pre-charge advances, post-charge advances or a combination of the two. Held: The court applied *Clayton's Case* ('first in, first out') to movements on the bank account, so that payments into the account were treated as repaying advances in the order in which those advances had been made, that is, the earliest advances were deemed to be repaid to the bank first. On the simplified facts above, the post-charge repayments (£70,000) were treated as repaying the *first* £70,000 of advances which covered all pre-charge unsecured advances and £20,000 of the post-charge advances. It followed that the £30,000 outstanding to the bank was lent to the company after the creation of the charge and therefore s 245 did *not* make the floating charge void to that extent, it being 'money paid … after the creation of the charge' within s 245(2). Note that the facts have been simplified in the extreme for the purposes of this case summary.

CASE EXAMPLE

Re GT Whyte & Co Ltd [1983] BCLC 311

The company's bank made an unsecured loan to the company. Later, when the company was close to being wound up, the bank demanded repayment in full. The company repaid the loan out of the little cash it had remaining and immediately borrowed the money from the bank again but this time on a secured basis: the company granted the bank a floating charge to secure the sum lent. In form, the money had been paid at the same time as the creation of the charge. Held: The floating charge was set aside. The intention of the company was not relevant to s 245. In substance, the transaction simply involved the substitution of an unsecured loan by a secured loan and as no new money had been paid, the sum was not money paid on or after the creation of the charge.

The effect of the grant of late security on unsecured creditors is illustrated in Figure 16.6.

- Each creditor is owed £20,000. 5 x £20,000 = £100,000
- Company X goes into insolvent liquidation with assets of £50,000
- Each creditor receives £10,000 (50p in the pound): *'pari passu'*

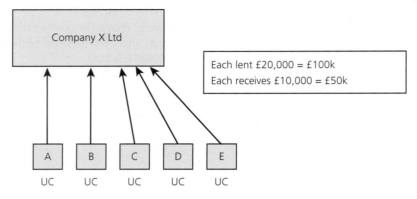

- Three months before the winding up of Company X Ltd commences, a floating charge is granted to E

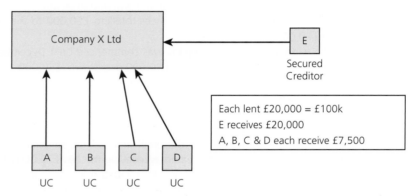

- E now receives £20,000 first
- A, B, C and D now each receive only £7,500 (30/80 x £20,000)
- The liquidator will examine the circumstances of the grant of the floating charge to see if it is void to any extent pursuant to s 245

Figure 16.6 The effect of grant of a late security on unsecured creditors and distribution of the company's assets in a winding up

Extortionate credit transactions (s 244)

In addition to the three avoidance provisions dealt with in detail above, where a company, within three years of the commencement of its winding up, has been a party to a transaction involving the provision of credit to the company, or still is a party to such, the liquidator may apply to the court for an order if the transaction is or was extortionate. The concept of connected persons is not used in this provision. The test to determine whether or not a transaction is or was extortionate is contained in s 244(3).

SECTION

'(3) For the purposes of this section a transaction is extortionate if, having regard to the risk accepted by the person providing the credit –

(a) the terms of it are or were such as to require grossly exorbitant payments to be made (whether unconditionally or in certain contingencies) in respect of the provision of the credit, or

(b) it otherwise grossly contravened ordinary principles of fair dealing and it shall be presumed, unless the contrary is proved, that a transaction with respect to which an application is made, under this section is or, as the case may be, was extortionate.'

Note that the burden of proof is reversed, being placed on the party arguing that the transaction is *not* extortionate. Details of how this section works can be found in insolvency law textbooks.

Connected persons

As we have seen, the rules governing the avoidance of pre-liquidation transactions apply more strictly where the other party to the transaction is connected to the company. Apart from the time limit being extended (from 6 or 12 months to two years), the burden of proof may be reversed (for example in relation to proof of the company's solvency at the time of a transaction at an undervalue), or an otherwise required condition may not need to be proved (for example the insolvency of the company at the time a late floating charge is granted).

This tightening of the provisions in relation to connected persons was introduced in 1986 on the recommendation of the Cork Committee following its review of insolvency laws. Consequently, the concept of being connected to a company for the purposes of the avoidance of pre-liquidation transactions is different from, and must not be confused with, the different concept of being connected to a director for the purposes of directors' breaches of duty (which is dealt with in ss 251–256 of the Companies Act 2006).

Who, then, is a connected person? Section 249 provides that a person is connected with a company if he is:

1 a director of the company;
2 an associate of:
● the company; or
● a director of the company.

Director, in this context, includes a shadow director. Connected persons can be represented diagrammatically as in Figure 16.7.

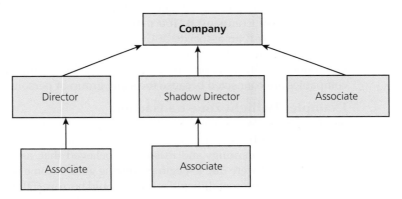

Figure 16.7 Connected persons for the purposes of the fair dealing provisions of the Insolvency Act 1986

Whilst s 249 is short, it raises the question of the meaning of 'associate'. Associate is defined in s 435 and, in contrast to s 249, the definition is detailed and complex. Two key aspects of associate, relative and control, are defined very widely. Unlike the approach taken in other jurisdictions, such as Australia, an attempt is made in s 435 to define these aspects exhaustively.

Relative, defined in s 435(8), includes brothers, sisters, uncles, aunts, nephews, nieces, lineal ancestors and descendants, half blood relationships, adopted and step children, and former spouses. Control, important in deciding both whether or not two companies are associated and whether or not a company is associated with an individual, is essentially 30 per cent voting power over the company (or any company with control over the company), or evidence that the board acts in accordance with instructions (see s 435(10)).

The following table conveys some of the complexity of ascertaining whether or not a person is an associate of a company.

Company A is an associate of its directors and its director's associates who are:	Company A is an associate of Company B if:

1 His:
  ▪ Spouse
  ▪ Relatives (which is very widely defined in s 435(8))
  ▪ Relatives' spouses
  ▪ Spouse's relatives
  ▪ Spouse's relatives' spouses
  ▪ Business partners
  ▪ Business partners' relatives
  ▪ Business partners' spouses
  ▪ (Not business partners' relatives' spouses!)
  ▪ Employees (note, these are employed by him personally, not the employees of the company of which he is a director)
  ▪ Employers (includes any company of which he is a director or secretary)
  ▪ Beneficiaries (and their associates) of certain trust of which he is a trustee
	▪ Both companies are controlled by the same person
	▪ A person has control of Company A and his associates have control of Company B
	▪ A person has control of Company A and he and his associates together have control of Company B
	▪ Both companies are controlled by the same group of persons (for these purposes, any person in a group can be replaced by an associate)

2 And any:
  ▪ Company controlled by him
  ▪ Company controlled by him together with his associates	

As the above suggests, the definition of connected person is far-ranging. That said, consider for example, two directors of Company A, each of whom own 25 per cent of the shares of Company B. You may be surprised to learn that this is not enough to make Company B an associate of Company A. The directors are not associated simply because they are both directors of Company A, and, consequently, the companies are not connected. If, however, the directors, together control Company A, then the two companies are connected because the same group of persons controls both.

Example: Twilight zone transaction

Seven months ago Company A Ltd was struggling to pay its debts as they fell due and the amount by which the company was overdrawn each week was increasing. The directors reviewed future earnings and reasonably believed that, as two major projects they had funded up front were due to begin producing good income returns, they could trade their way out of their present difficulties if they could borrow £50,000 to tide them over for three months. Company A Ltd immediately visited the distress finance department of B Bank plc, a bank with which it had no prior relationship and, the next day, borrowed £50,000 secured by a fixed charge over Company A Ltd's freehold offices and a floating charge over all the assets of the company. All seemed to be going well for six months until the two projects turned abruptly sour. It became clear that they were not going to produce the expected income and the compulsory winding up of Company A Ltd commenced yesterday.

Can the liquidator challenge the fixed or the floating charge under ss 239 or 245? Would it make any difference if B Bank plc was already an unsecured lender to Company A Ltd at the time the charges were granted?

The liquidator cannot challenge either the fixed or the floating charge under s 239 for the following reasons:

▪ The fixed charge is *not* a factual preference because Bank B plc was not an existing creditor, surety or guarantor of Company A Ltd and, in any event, Bank B plc has made a fresh injection of capital which is the only sum secured by the fixed charge.

- The fixed charge is *not* in favour of a connected person, therefore the time at which it must have been created in order to be challengeable under s 239 is within six months before the commencement of the winding up. It was put in place before this period.
- There was *no* desire on the part of Company A Ltd when it created either charge to put the bank in a better position in the event of winding up than it had been before.
- It is also not clear that Company A Ltd was insolvent when the charges were created. Very detailed evidence would need to be examined to determine this point if it were the deciding factor.

The liquidator also cannot challenge the floating charge under s 245 for the following reason:

- Any floating charge within s 245 is void *except as to money paid or goods and service supplied to the company at the same time as, or after the creation of, the charge*. Here, the secured sum, £50,000 was supplied to A Company Ltd at the same time as the creation of the floating charge.
- It is also not clear that Company A Ltd was insolvent when the loan was granted. Very detailed evidence would need to be examined to determine this point if it were the deciding factor.
- Note that the floating charge is *not* in favour of a connected person, therefore the time at which it must have been created in order to be challengeable under s 245 is within 12 months before the commencement of the winding up (twice the relevant period for challenge under s 239). The floating charge was put in place within this period.

If B Bank plc was already an unsecured lender to Company A Ltd at the time the charges were granted, first, in relation to s 239, provided the fixed and floating charges secured only the £50,000, there has been no factual preference and so no successful application could be made. If the fixed and floating charges secured both the £50,000 *and* sums already outstanding to B Bank plc, the charges still could not be successfully challenged under s 239 because they were put in place outside the relevant period for unconnected persons which is six months prior to the commencement of the winding up. Even had they been put in place within the relevant time, it is extremely difficult to establish that a company was influenced by a desire to prefer where its motivation is to finance the company to allow for a trading out of its financial difficulties.

In relation to s 245, the floating charge could be void to the extent that it purported to secure any sum lent to Company A Ltd *before* the time the floating charge was put in place. The floating charge was put in place within 12 months of the commencement of the winding up. The difficult issue on which the validity of the floating charge would turn is whether or not Company A Ltd was insolvent at the time the floating charge was put in place. As indicated above, a liquidator would need to make a very detailed examination of the financial health of Company A Ltd as at the date of creation of the floating charge to determine this point.

16.4.3 Swelling the assets: applications for contributions

The Insolvency Act 1986 provides a liquidator with power to seek orders from the court arising out of a number of types of behaviour, including:

- Misfeasance by officers of the company (s 212);
- Wrongful trading (s 214);
- Fraudulent trading (s 213).

The objective of the liquidator is usually to obtain funds from individual directors (though it can be others) to add to the funds of the company available for distribution to creditors.

Misfeasance by officers of the company (s 212)

Many cases concerning breaches of directors' duties are brought when a company is being wound up. A liquidator may bring legal actions in the name of the company or

wrongful trading

a director continuing to trade when he knew or ought to have concluded that there was no reasonable prospect that the company would avoid going into insolvent liquidation

he may use the procedure provided for in s 212 to bring certain legal actions in his own name on behalf of the company.

Section 212 is extremely broad in scope but it is simply a procedural provision enabling the liquidator to bring an underlying cause of action; it does not create any new causes of action. It permits a liquidator to seek a remedy against an officer of the company, a liquidator or administrative receiver, or any person who took part in its promotion, formation or management, who has misapplied or retained or become accountable for any money or other property of the company or been guilty of any misfeasance or breach of any fiduciary or other duty in relation to the company. Not being a distinct cause of action, the court in *Re Eurocruit Europe Ltd (In Liquidation)* [2007] EWHC 1433 (Ch) held that a claim under s 212 does not have a limitation period distinct from the limitation period applicable to the underlying claim.

Wrongful Trading (s 214)

SECTION

'(1) Subject to subsection (3) below, if in the course of the winding up of a company it appears that subsection (2) of this section applies in relation to a person who is or has been a director of the company, the court, on the application of the liquidator, may declare that that person is to be liable to make such contribution (if any) to the company's assets as the court thinks proper.

(2) This subsection applies in relation to a person if:
  (a) the company has gone into insolvent liquidation,
  (b) at some time before the commencement of the winding up, that person knew or ought to have concluded that there was no reasonable prospect that the company would avoid going into insolvent liquidation, and
  (c) that person was a director of the company at that time ...

(3) The court shall not make a declaration under this section with respect to any person if it is satisfied that ... that person took every step with a view to minimising the potential loss to the company's creditors as ... he ought to have taken.'

The main points to note about s 214 are that only the liquidator may make an application, and the company must be in liquidation and factually insolvent. Only directors can be made liable, although note that it is expressly provided in the section that director included shadow director (s 214(7)).

Basically, if a director knew or ought to have concluded that there was no reasonable prospect that the company would avoid going into insolvent liquidation but continued to incur debts, he risks being ordered to make a contribution to the company's assets in a subsequent liquidation. It is not enough that the directors knew or ought to have known that the company was insolvent. Many businesses trade through financially difficult times when they are unable to pay their debts as they fall due to reach financial health at a future date. In *Re Hawkes Hill Publishing Co Ltd* [2007] BCC 937, Lewison J, unwilling to find that the directors had wrongfully traded, stressed that having the opportunity to trade the company to financial good health where the prospect of such is reasonable is particularly important in the early years of a new business.

JUDGMENT

Of course, it is easy with hindsight to conclude that mistakes were made. An insolvent liquidation will almost always result from one or more mistakes. But picking over the bones of a dead company in a courtroom is not always fair to those who struggled to keep going in the reasonable (but ultimately misplaced) hope that things would get better.

Lewison, J in *Re Hawkes Hill Publishing Co Ltd* [2007] BCC 937

In determining what facts a director ought to have known, the conclusions he ought to have reached and the steps which he ought to have taken, the test applied is the same as that for determining whether or not there has been a breach of the directors' general duty in s 174, the duty to exercise reasonable care, skill and diligence (see Chapter 11). If proper books and records have not been kept which, if kept, would have shown that the company could not have avoided going into insolvent liquidation, it will be held that a director 'ought to have known'.

It is a defence for a director to show that he took every step he ought to have taken with a view to minimising the potential loss to the company's creditors An example of a situation in which the court could not make an order because s 214(3) has been complied with would be where the directors had advised all existing creditors and each potential new creditor of the risks it might be undertaking in advancing credit or further credit.

Fraudulent trading (s 213)

Section 213 is not a commonly used provision because of the need to plead and prove fraud. Far more applications are made under s 214, for wrongful trading.

SECTION

fraudulent trading

for the purposes of s 213 Insolvency Act 1986, the carrying on of the business of the company with intent to defraud creditors of the company or creditors of any other person, or for any fraudulent purpose

's 213

(1) If in the course of the winding up of a company it appears that any business of the company has been carried on with intent to defraud creditors of the company or creditors of any other person, or for any fraudulent purpose, the following has effect.

(2) The court, on the application of the liquidator may declare that any persons who were knowingly parties to the carrying on of the business in the manner above-mentioned are to be liable to make such contributions (if any) to the company's assets as the court thinks proper.'

Points to note in relation to fraudulent trading are that only a liquidator may make an application, liability under the section is not confined to directors; any persons may be required to make a contribution to the company's assets, and actual dishonesty, involving real moral blame, is required (*Re Patrick and Lyon Ltd* [1933] Ch 786). It is not enough to show that the company continued to run up debts when the directors knew it was factually insolvent. There has to be 'intent to defraud creditors' and *Morphitis v Bernasconi and Others* [2003] Ch 552 (CA) establishes that a fraudulent misrepresentation made to a single creditor may not be enough to establish that the business of the company had been carried on with intent to defraud creditors of the company.

16.5 Distribution of the assets

Having got in the assets and realised them, the role of the liquidator is to distribute the assets amongst the creditors and (if any money is left) the shareholders, in accordance with the statutory order of distribution.

16.5.1 Assets subject to fixed charges

Assets subject to fixed charges are outside the statutory order of distribution. The fixed charge holding creditor is entitled to take possession of the charged asset, sell it and take from the proceeds of sale what is owed to him and expenses (the additional amounts the proceeds may be used to meet will usually be stated in the charge or loan document). This is usually achieved by the fixed charge holder appointing a receiver under the terms of the charge. If the asset is insufficient to pay the sum secured, the charge holder will, unless he has a second security, become an unsecured creditor for the outstanding amount of his debt.

It is common for banks to take a fixed charge in relation to specific assets and a floating charge on a broad range of the company's assets in which event, if the specific assets do not provide enough money to pay the sum owed to the bank, the bank becomes a floating charge holding secured creditor for the remainder. If, however, the proceeds of sale exceed the sums due to the fixed charge holder, the surplus amount must be paid to the liquidator.

16.5.2 The statutory order of distribution

The order in which a liquidator is required to distribute the proceeds of sale of the property of an insolvent company is governed by:

- Insolvency Act 1986, principally ss 115, 175, 176A and 386 and Sched 6 (as amended).
- Companies Act 2006, s 1282.
- Insolvency Rules 1986 (SI 1986/1925) (also as amended).
- Insolvency Act 1986 (Prescribed Part) Order 2003 (SI 2003/2097).

The order of payment resulting from these provisions is basically as set out in Table 16.1.

Expenses of liquidation
Preferential debts *pari passu*
Debts secured by floating charges put in place before 15 September 2003 to be paid out of the proceeds of the property subject to the charges
Prescribed part of the proceeds of sale of property subject to floating charges put in place on or after 15 September 2003 to be set aside for unsecured creditors
Debts secured by floating charges put in place on or after 15 September 2003 to be paid out of the proceeds of the property subject to the charges
Ordinary unsecured creditors *pari passu*
Deferred creditors *pari passu*
Shareholders (the 'shareholder last' principle)

Table 16.1 Statutory order of distribution on an insolvent winding up

Significant changes introduced by s 251 of the Enterprise Act 2002 were brought into effect on 15 September 2003 (which explains why this date appears in the list above). Essentially, in relation to floating charges entered into on or after 15 September 2003 only, in return for changes expanding the range of expenses deductible from floating charge property proceeds *and* reducing the range of preferential debts, both of which are good for floating chargeholders, the proceeds that would otherwise be available to floating chargeholders are subject to deduction of a 'prescribed part' to be set aside for the benefit of unsecured creditors (Insolvency Act 1986, s 176A).

Calculation of the prescribed part is governed by the Prescribed Part Order referenced above. The prescribed part is calculated by taking:

- 50 per cent of the first £10,000 net assets of the company; and
- 20 per cent of any net assets of the company exceeding £10,000;
- subject to the prescribed part not exceeding £600,000.

Net assets of the company for these purposes means the sum remaining after payment of liquidation expenses and preferential debts. Interpreting s 176A, it has been held that neither fixed nor floating chargeholders are permitted to participate in the prescribed part in respect of any unsecured part of their debts (*Re Permacell Finesse Limited (in liquidation)* [2008] BCC 208 (floating chargeholder) and *Re Airbase (UK) Limited* [2008] EWHC 124 (Ch) (fixed and floating chargeholder) unless they surrender their entire security and participate in the winding up as an unsecured creditor (*PAL SC Realisations 2007 Ltd v Inflexion Fund 2 Limited Partnership* [2010] EWHC 2850). The fixed and floating chargeholders will be counted as an unsecured creditor for the purposes of sharing any non-prescribed part remaining distributable funds.

Example: Operation of the statutory order of distribution

Company A Ltd borrowed £800,000 from Bank B plc

To secure the repayment Bank B plc took a:

- fixed charge over Company A Ltd's freehold premises; and
- floating charge over all of the company's property.

The charges were created in April 2007 and were properly registered pursuant to s 860 of the Companies Act 2006.

A winding up order was issued against Company A Ltd in May 2008.

Company A Ltd has the following assets:

- Freehold property worth £500,000.
- Stock in trade worth £300,000.

Company A Ltd also owes:

- Unsecured creditors £400,000.
- Preferential creditors £50,000.

The liquidator's costs and expenses are £150,000.

Consider the order in which the liquidator must distribute the proceeds of sale of the company's property to its creditors and in payment of the liquidation costs.

1 Debts secured by fixed charges are paid out of the assets subject to the fixed charge, so B Bank plc received the entire proceeds of sale of the freehold premises, £500,000, leaving the bank with a £300,000 (£800,000 – £500,000) outstanding debt secured by the general floating charge.

2 The statutory order of priority is then applied starting with £300,000:
   - Pay £150,000 costs and expenses of liquidator, leaves £150,000.
   - Pay £50,000 preferential debts, leaves £100,000.
   - Pay any debts secured by a floating charge created before 15 September 2003, which here is 0, leaves £100,000.
   - Where a floating charge is created on or after 15 September 2003: set aside a prescribed part for unsecured creditors, here, out of £100,000:

(50% of £10,000)	+	(20% of £90,000)	=
5K	+	18K	=

   23,000 to be set aside for unsecured creditors.
   - Remaining £77,000 (£100,000 – £23,000) is paid to B Bank plc under the floating charge.
   - B Bank plc has an outstanding unpaid and unsecured debt of £223,000 (£300,000 – £77,000).
   - Prescribed part (£23,000) is paid out to unsecured creditors *pari passu* giving them 5.75 pence in the pound (£23,000/£400,000).
   - B Bank Ltd does *not* participate in the prescribed part.

16.6 Dissolution and restoration

A company, ie the separate corporate personality, continues to exist throughout the winding up process. A company ceases to exist only by the act of removal of the name of the company from the register at Companies House (Insolvency Act 1986, s 201ff). Removal from the register is the point of dissolution of the company. All legal relationships the company has with any person, including its shareholders, are terminated on dissolution. If the company owns any property on dissolution the property passes to the Crown as *bona vacantia* (Companies Act 2006, s 1012).

Dissolution does not solely occur following a winding up. Winding up is an expensive process and is often avoided for that very reason. Removal from the register may take place:

- By the registrar of companies striking the company off the register after an advertisement in the Gazette. The registrar may exercise this administrative power if his inquiries suggest the company has ceased to carry on business (Companies Act 2006, s 1000).

- By the registrar of companies if he has reasonable cause to believe that no liquidator is acting or the affairs of the company have been fully wound up and required returns have not been made for six months (Companies Act 2006, s 1001).
- On application by the company three months after publication of the application to remove in the Gazette (Companies Act 2006, s 1003).
- Automatically, three months after the registrar of companies has been notified a voluntary winding up procedure is complete (Insolvency Act 1986, s 201).
- Automatically, three months after the registrar of companies has been notified a compulsory winding up procedure is complete (Insolvency Act 1986, s 205).
- Automatically, three months after application by the official receiver (who is the liquidator of the company) for early dissolution because it appears to him that (i) the realisable assets of the company are insufficient to cover the expenses of liquidation and (ii) no further investigation into the company is necessary (Companies Act 2006, s 202).
- On completion of administration: three months after notification to the registrar by an administrator that here is nothing to distribute to creditors (Insolvency Act 1986, Sched B1, para 84(6)).
- By order of the court in relation to various circumstances such as reconstructions and amalgamations (Companies Act 2006, s 900(2)(d)).
- Pursuant to an Act of Parliament such as an Act providing for the takeover of one bank by another or a merger of banks.

administrative restoration

a procedure introduced under the Companies Act 2006 whereby the registrar of companies may restore a company to the register without the need for a court order, provided certain criteria are met

In limited circumstances, a company that has been removed from the register may be restored (Companies Act 2006 ss 1024–1042). In addition to administrative restoration to reverse a striking-off by the registrar pursuant to ss 1000 and 1001 (s 1024), a court may, on application within six years of removal, order restoration to enable legal proceedings for damages for death or personal injury to be brought against the company (ss 1029 and 1030). The general effect of an order by the court for restoration to the register is that the company is deemed to have continued in existence as if it had not been removed from the register (s 1032). This step is sometimes necessary to access liability insurance cover of the dissolved company.

KEY FACTS

Winding up: types, main effects, key duties and powers of liquidator	
(References are to the Insolvency Act 1986)	
Types	
Voluntary winding up:	
Members' voluntary winding up	s 84
Creditors' voluntary winding up	ss 84 and 90
Compulsory winding up: main grounds:	
Company unable to pay its debts	s 122(1)(f)
Just and equitable to wind up	s 122(1)(g)
Main effects	
Powers of board cease	
Liquidator exercises statutory powers as agent of company	*Knowles v Scott* [1891] 1 Ch 717
No commencement or continuance of legal action against the company without leave of the court	
Onerous contracts and property may be disclaimed by the company	ss 178–182

Key duties and powers of liquidator	
To 'get in' all assets of the company, convert them to cash and distribute the proceeds	s 143(1)
Powers to avoid certain transactions: Transactions at an undervalue Preferences Invalid floating charges Extortionate credit transactions	s 238 s 239 s 245 s 244
Powers to make applications for contributions from directors and others to the company: Misfeasance of officers Wrongful trading Fraudulent trading	s 212 s 214 s 213
Proceeds to be distributed 'pari passu' subject to, in particular: property rights of secured creditors statutory order of distribution	Distinguish fixed and floating charges ss 115, 175, 176A, 386 and Sched 6 (as amended)

SUMMARY

Types of winding up/liquidation

Voluntary winding up:
- Members' voluntary winding up (s 84).
- Creditors' voluntary winding up (ss 84 and 90).

Compulsory winding up: main grounds:
- Company unable to pay its debts (s 122(1)(f)).
- Just and equitable to wind up (s 122(1)(g)).

Main effects of compulsory liquidation

- The powers of the board of directors cease and the liquidator exercises statutory powers as agent of company (*Knowles v Scott* (1891)).
- No commencement or continuance of legal action against the company without leave of the court.
- Onerous contracts and property may be disclaimed by the company (ss 178–182).

Key duties and powers of the liquidator

- To 'get in' all assets of the company, convert them to cash and distribute the proceeds, (s 143(1)).
- Proceeds to be distributed 'pari passu' subject to, in particular:
  - property rights of third parties including secured creditors (distinguish fixed and floating charges);
  - the statutory order of distribution.

Secured creditors: fixed and floating charges

- Secured creditors have an interest the company's property in addition to contractual rights.
- On crystallisation, a floating charge becomes a fixed charge although a charge that started its life as a floating charge, is treated as a floating charge in a winding up even if it has crystallised (insolvency Act 1986, s 251).
- Charges must be registered in the company's register of charges (s 876 and 877), most need to be registered with the registrar (s 860), and charges over land may need to be registered at the Land Registry or at the Land Charges Department.
- An unregistered charge is void against the liquidator, administrator and other creditors of the company.

Priority of charges

- Fixed charges rank in order of the time at which they are created.
- A later-in-time fixed charge ranks in priority over an earlier floating charge (*Re Castell & Brown Ltd* [1898] 1 Ch 315).
- Floating charges rank in order of time of creation (*Re Benjamin Cope & Sons Ltd* [1914] 1 Ch 800).
- A floating charge over specific assets may rank in priority to an earlier general floating charge if power is reserved to the company in the earlier charge to create a later charge having priority (*Re Automatic Bottle Makers Ltd* [1926] Ch 412).

Four key types of pre-liquidation transactions can be challenged

- Transfers at an undervalue (s 238).
- Preferences (s 239).
- Invalid floating charges (s 245).
- Extortionate credit transactions (244).

Three key provisions impose personal liability

- Misfeasance restorations and contributions (s 212).
- Fraudulent trading contributions (s 213).
- Wrongful trading contributions (s 214).

Dissolution

- A company ceases to exist when its name is removed from the register at Companies House whereupon all relationships terminate.
- In limited circumstances a company may be restored to the register.

ACTIVITY

Applying the law

Assuming that each has been properly registered, put the following charges over the specified assets of Company B Ltd in order of priority:

	Charge	Date created
1	Floating charge over all assets	1 January 2004
2	Floating charge over car fleet	1 January 2005
3	Fixed charge over freehold premises	1 January 2006
4	Floating charge over freehold premises	1 January 2007

Remember that you only need to prioritise charges attaching to the same property.

SAMPLE ESSAY QUESTION

Explain and assess the extent to which a liquidator is empowered to swell the assets of an insolvent company and improve the position of unsecured creditors.

Unpack the question

This is the first essential step which you must take time to do properly. You should separate out:

- Explanation of the concept of a liquidator of an insolvent company and his role
- Explanation of the meaning of swelling the company's assets
- Explanation of unsecured creditors and the priority of secured creditors in the distribution of the assets
- Identifying the specific procedures and powers a liquidator has which could result in enhancing the company's assets/the position of unsecured creditors:
  - Wrongful trading, fraudulent trading, misfeasance applications
  - Twilight transactions.

Liquidators, assets and unsecured creditors

- Explain the concept of the liquidator and his role: to collect the assets of the company and distribute them in accordance with the statutory order of distribution
- Explain that the liquidator may exercise powers to swell the assets as a whole, or to change an asset from an asset subject to a charge to one available to unsecured creditors
- Explain the power to set aside the prescribed part from the charges assets for the benefit of unsecured creditors: Insolvency Act s 176A.

Wrongful trading, fraudulent trading and misfeasance

Outline the availability of a wrongful trading claim:

- Explain the requirements: Insolvency Act s 214
- Focus on the test as whether there is any reasonable prospect of avoiding insolvent liquidation (not simply whether or not the company is insolvent)
- Explain the remedies available: s 214(1): such contribution to the assets of the company as the court thinks proper
- Explain that a remedy is available only against directors past and present.

Outline the availability of a fraudulent trading claim:

- Explain the requirements of fraudulent trading: Insolvency Act s 213

- Analyse what amounts to fraud: *Re Patrick and Lyon Ltd* and intent to defraud creditors: *Morphitis v Bernasconi and Others*
- Explain the remedies available: s 214(1): such contribution to the assets of the company as the court thinks proper. S 213(2).
- Explain that a remedy is available against "any person".

Outline the availability of a claim asserting director misfeasance:

- Explanation that a claim under the Insolvency Act s 212 is simply a procedural route to asserting an otherwise existing claim.
- Explain that a remedy may be available against officers, liquidators, administrators, and person who has taken part in the promotion, formation or management of the company.

Challenging twilight transactions

Explain the concept of the twilight zone: up to two years leading up to the commencement of insolvent liquidation.

Outline the potential to challenge a transaction at undervalue:

- Explain the requirements of the Insolvency Act s 238.

Outline the potential to challenge a transaction or grant as a preference:

- Explain the requirements of the Insolvency Act s 239.

Outline the potential to challenge a floating charge as late and invalid:

- Explain the requirements of the Insolvency Act s 245.

Conclude

Express conclusion that the liquidator has a range of procedures and powers available to expand the assets available for distribution generally and in particular to unsecured creditors.

Further reading

Useful websites

The Insolvency Service
www.insolvency.gov.uk/index.htm

Articles

Keay, A, 'The Avoidance of Pre-Liquidation Transactions' [1998] JBL 515.
Keay 'Wrongful trading and the point of liability' (2006) 19 Insolv. Int. 132.
Oditah, 'Wrongful Trading' [1990] LMCLQ 205.
Savirimuthu, A, 'Morphitis in the Court of Appeal: some reflections' (2005) 26 Comp. Law 245.

Books

Goode, R, *Principles of Corporate Insolvency Law,* Student (ed) (4th Revised Edition, Sweet & Maxwell, 2011).
Sealy, LS and Hooley, RJA, *Commercial Law, Text, Cases and Materials* (4th Edition, Oxford University Press, 2008).

17

Transparency

AIMS AND OBJECTIVES

By the end of this chapter you should be able to:

- Identify the key public disclosures required of registered companies under the Companies Act 2006

- Distinguish core company law public disclosure requirements from securities regulation disclosures required pursuant to the Financial Services and Markets Act 2000

- Understand which basic accounts, reports and statements registered companies are required to prepare

- Discuss the extension of public disclosure into narrative reporting

- Understand the rationale for the audit process and the role of the auditor

- Discuss the legal basis of auditor liability to the company and third parties and the statutory limits on the ability of auditors to limit their liability

- Discuss the powers and procedures available to the government to investigate registered companies and when those powers are in practice exercised

QUOTATION

> 'Sunlight is said to be the best of disinfectants'
>
> Louis Brandeis, 'What Publicity Can Do', *Harper's Weekly* (1913)

17.1 Introduction

Obligatory disclosure of reliable information by registered companies pursuant to the Companies Act 2006 is an important pillar of core company law and the forfeiture of confidentiality it entails is sometimes characterised as the price paid for limited liability by those who chose to run their businesses through companies. Disclosure is sometimes required to existing shareholders only but most information companies are legally required to disclose or make available for inspection is accessible by the general public. For certain disclosures, the Companies Act 2006 distinguishes between small companies, medium sized companies, unquoted companies and quoted companies (see, for example, disclosure of director remuneration, considered at section 9.3.4 and accounts (below)).

Beyond core company law disclosures, additional disclosure obligations apply to companies with securities admitted to trading on a stock exchange. Different levels of disclosure apply depending upon to which particular stock exchange and market a company's securities are admitted to trading. Additional disclosures, beyond those required by the Companies Act 2006, will be required either by law (the Financial Services and Markets Act 2000 and rules promulgated by the Financial Services Authority pursuant to that Act, including the Disclosure and Transparency Rules), by the rules of the market (such as the London Stock Exchange Admission and Disclosure Standards) or, usually, by a combination of both. A company with a Premium Listing of its equity shares on the London Stock Exchange Main Market is subject to the highest level of public disclosure. The various levels of public disclosure imposed by securities regulation are beyond the scope of this book but a brief outline of the scheme of periodic disclosure imposed by the Disclosure and Transparency Rules (DTR) is included in section 17.3, including the obligation to disclose price-sensitive information.

In this chapter we focus on public disclosure mandated by the Companies Act 2006 and we examine the role of auditors as independent professionals who, through the audit process, monitor the integrity of principally financial information disclosed by companies. Finally, because they are an important part of protecting the public interest, we look at the powers of BIS to investigate companies. Rather than having been consolidated into the Companies Act 2006, these powers remain in the Companies Act 1985, as amended.

Gazette

the London, Edinburgh and/ or Belfast Gazette published by The Stationery Office which comes out every business day and in which formal announce- ments concerning companies are made, such as when a winding up order is made or when a wind- ing up resolution is passed

17.2 Public disclosure under the Companies Act 2006

Public disclosure has been an important part of core company law since registration of companies was first made available in 1844. Pursuant to the Companies Act 2006, the public has access to information about companies from various sources:

- Companies House, where information in all documents required to be delivered to the registrar is kept, on 'the register' (s 1080), and may be inspected by the public (s 1085) subject to the limited exceptions to public inspection set out in s 1087 (see, in relation to directors' residential addresses, section 9.3.3).
- A company's registered office (or other notified place) at which it keeps its registers and other documents it is required to make available for public inspection, including its website.
- The Gazette (London, Edinburgh and Belfast editions), in which the registrar is required to place notices of receipt of certain documents, namely those subject to 'Directive disclosure requirements' (see s 1078).

Disclosure in relation to particular activities is covered in this book where that activity is dealt with, such as removal and appointment of directors (see section 9.3.3). Here, we deal with the registers a company is required to keep and make available to the public for inspection and the main *annual* filings: the annual return and the annual accounts and reports.

17.2.1 Company registers available for public inspection

Companies are required to keep the following registers and make them available for inspection by members of the public:

register of members

a statutory register that has to be maintained by all companies containing a definitive list of members of the company

- Register of members (ss 113–121, subject to protections, see below).
- Register of directors (s 162 and see section 9.3.3).
- Register of secretaries (s 275) (if the company has a secretary, see section 9.4).
- Register of charges (s 875 and see section 16.3.5).
- Public companies only: register of interests disclosed to it in the context of a company investigation (ss 808 and 809, see below at 17.5).

If a company keeps a register of debenture holders (which it is not required to do, even if it has issued debentures), it must make it available for inspection subject to similar protections as those applicable to inspection of the register of members (s 743).

A person seeking to inspect the register of members or debenture holders must provide the company with his name, if he is seeking the information in an individual capacity, or the name of the organisation seeking the information, the purpose for which the information is to be used and whether or not it will be disclosed to any other person and, if so, the same information in relation to that or those other persons (ss 116 and 744). A company must comply with a request to inspect or apply to the court for an order that the information is not sought for a proper purpose (ss 117 and 745).

Public companies are also required to keep available for inspection by the public copies of contracts for the purchase of its own shares (s 702).

17.2.2 Annual filings

Annual returns

annual return
a document in prescribed form which every registered company is required to file with the Registrar of Companies on an annual basis pursuant to the Companies Act 2006, s 854, containing basic information about the company

A company must make an annual return on a prescribed form to the registrar (s 854) and pay a nominal fee. The information to be contained in the return is (ss 855, 856, 856A & 856B):

- Registered office address.
- Type of company it is and its principal business activities.
- The names of directors at any time in the preceding year.
- The name of the company secretary at any time in the preceding year.
- Any address different from the registered office at which the register of members or debenture holders are kept.
- A statement of capital.
- A list of shareholders, their shareholdings and changes thereto (a full list is only required every three years and special rules apply to traded companies).
- A statement as to whether any of the company's shares were admitted to trading on a relevant market.

The Secretary of State has power to make regulations changing the information to be contained in annual returns (s 857) and has recently used this power to make the obligation to supply details of shareholders less onerous for companies with traded shares (see s 856B and the Companies Act 2006 (Annual Returns) Regulations 2011 (SI 2011/1487)).

Accounting records and annual accounts and reports

summary financial statement
a shortened form of the annual report and accounts of the company which may be circulated to shareholders instead of the full report. All companies have the choice of issuing summary financial statements

Accounting records

Companies must keep accounting records sufficient to (s 386):

- show and explain the company's transactions;
- disclose the company's financial position with reasonable accuracy;
- enable annual accounts to be drawn up in accordance with the Act.

Reports and Accounts

The directors of companies must prepare annual accounts and reports (ss 394, 415 and 420), and send them to shareholders (s 423) and the registrar (s 441). A small company is exempt from sending its directors' report to the registrar (s 415A and 444). In certain circumstances a summary financial statement can be sent to shareholders in substitution for its full accounts and reports (s 426), although a full copy of the accounts and reports must be sent to any shareholder who wishes to receive one. The contents of summary financial statements for quoted and unquoted companies are prescribed by regulations (ss 427 and 428). The accounts that a company must file under the Companies Act 2006 are in practice often referred to as the statutory accounts.

statutory accounts
the individual or group accounts which are required to be filed with the registrar of companies which may be full accounts or, where permitted, abbreviated accounts

Public companies (which includes all quoted companies) are required to lay accounts and reports before a general meeting (s 437), and quoted companies must additionally make them available on their website (s 430). Quoted companies are also required to propose a resolution at the meeting at which accounts are laid approving the remuneration of its directors (s 439). At the time of writing, this resolution is purely advisory and no remuneration is conditional upon the resolution being passed (s 439(5)), although the government is drawing up reforms which may result in this resolution having a real effect on the remuneration of directors (see also Chapter 9).

A very helpful table summarising the accounts and reports filing requirements for difference categories of companies under the Companies Act 2006 is contained in BIS Guidance for UK Companies on Accounting and Reporting (June 2008) which can be accessed via the BIS Companies Act 2006 website, referenced at the end of Chapter 1. This guidance must be read subject to subsequent changes, in particular, the requirement for a company that is subject to Disclosure and Transparency Rule 7.2 to include in its directors' report or publish separately from that report a 'corporate governance statement' approved by its directors (see ss 419A and 472A) (see below under narrative reporting).

Individual company accounts

The annual accounts and reports are:

- a profit and loss account;
- a balance sheet;
- notes to the accounts (ie to the above two);
- a directors' report;
- a directors' remuneration report (quoted companies only, see section 9.3.4);
- a corporate governance statement (can be a separate statement or contained in the directors' report) (companies subject to DTR 7.2 only);
- an auditors' report (unless the company is exempt from audit, see below).

Group accounts

If a company is a parent company it must prepare group accounts covering all the companies in the corporate group (s 399), unless:

- all its subsidiaries are excluded from consolidation (s 402); or
- it is a member of a larger group (in which case the obligation to prepare group accounts rests with the ultimate parent company (ss 399(2)–401)).

When required, group accounts are prepared in addition to individual company accounts. They consist of a consolidated profit and loss account, balance sheet and notes thereto.

Auditors and the auditing of reports are considered below at 17.4 after considering a relatively new but extremely important aspect of annual reporting. The emphasis in relation to disclosure has been on disclosure of financial information in annual accounts and reports. Recently, however, the information required to be disclosed has been extended beyond financial information to include business information. Reporting of non-financial business information is referred to as 'narrative reporting'. Narrative reporting has proved to be a very controversial issue.

Narrative reporting

At the time of writing, the Government is proposing to put a new framework for narrative reporting in place. It is proposing to replace Directors' Reports with two documents. A high-level Strategic Report will be required for all except small companies, to provide an overview of the company supported by key financial and other information, backed up by an Annual Directors' Statement, required for all companies, (although the obligatory content of this report for small companies is expected simply to mirror the current requirements for directors' reports), providing a framework for detailed narrative disclosures by the company in a more structured way than is currently the case. A company will be able to put both required and voluntary disclosures in its Directors' Statement to provide 'an integrated view of the company as a whole' (see BIS, The Future of Narrative Reporting, The Government Response, March 2012).

The ongoing consultation on narrative reporting began in 2010 with publication of the first of two BIS consultation papers. The concept of narrative reporting was explained in that consultation paper.

QUOTATION

'Narrative reporting

20. The current provisions on narrative reporting reflect European requirements and the extensive debate and consultation on UK company law which led to the Companies Act 2006. The term "narrative reporting" is used to describe the non-financial information that is included in company reports in order to provide a broad and meaningful picture of a company's business, its market position, strategy, performance and future prospects. Narrative reporting – sometimes referred to as the "front half" of the annual report – includes a number of elements, some of which are required by statute or Financial Services Authority (FSA) rules.

These include:

- the Directors' report, including the business review;
- the Chairman's statement and the Chief Executive's review;
- the Directors' Remuneration Report;
- corporate governance disclosures.

21. Some companies also choose to provide separate social and environmental reports. In addition, the FSA's Disclosure & Transparency Rules require some companies to make periodic financial statements, which contain forward looking statements about the company's strategy and objectives. These various elements of narrative reporting should be consistent and clearly presented so that readers can understand the principal factors likely to affect a company's long-term performance, for example:

- by relating long-term performance criteria for directors' remuneration to the company's strategic objectives;
- where appropriate, by linking reporting on social and environmental factors to the principal risks set out in the business review.'

BIS, The Future of Narrative Reporting, A Consultation, August 2010)

Apart from the directors' remuneration report (see Chapter 9 and note that separate proposals for reform of how directors' remuneration is regulated are under development at the time of writing), the most controversial element of narrative reporting provided for in the Companies Act 2006 is the business review. All companies except small companies are required to include a business review within their annual directors' report (s 417). The business review must contain:

- a fair review of the company's business and a description of the principal risks and uncertainties facing the company;
- a balanced and comprehensive analysis of the development and performance of the company's business during the financial year and the position of the business at year end.

Quoted companies are required to include the following additional information in their business reviews:

- the main trends and developments likely to affect the future development, performance and position of the company's business;
- information about environmental matters, company employees and social and community issues and company policies and their effectiveness in relation to these matters;
- information about 'persons with whom the company has contractual or other arrangements which are essential to the business of the company'.

Certain information may be carved out and not reported:

- Disclosure of information about impending developments or matters in the course of negotiations if the disclosure would, in the opinion of the directors, be seriously prejudicial to the interest of the company, s 417(10).
- Disclosure of information about a person if the disclosure would, in the opinion of the directors, be seriously prejudicial to that person and contrary to the public interest, s 417(11).

A recent development in narrative reporting is the requirement in DTR 7.2 for companies with listed securities to prepare a corporate governance statement and include it in its directors' report (DTR 7.2.1) or keep it as a standalone statement (DTR 7.2.9). This requirement is of broader application than the FSA Listing Rules (LR) 9.8 requirement which applies only to companies with Premium Listings on the Main Market of the London Stock Exchange (LSE). The 2006 Act has been amended to accommodate 'separate' corporate governance statements (ss 419A, 446, 447 and 472A) and also to provide for such statements to be audited (ss 497A & 498A) (see the Companies Act 2006 (Accounts, Reports and Audit) Regulations 2009 (SI 2009/1581)).

17.3 Public disclosure under the Financial Services and Markets Act 2000

In addition to Companies Act 2006 disclosure requirements, disclosures are imposed on some companies by rules promulgated by the Financial Services Authority (FSA) pursuant to the Financial Services and Markets Act 2000. Precisely which disclosure rules apply to which companies is complicated but for our purposes, because we are looking at this only at a high level, we will focus on companies with shares traded on the Main Market of the London Stock Exchange, (all of which have shares listed on the official list as this is a pre-condition to securing admission to the Main Market).

The requirements are found primarily in the Disclosure and Transparency Rules (DTR). The basic regime for periodic disclosure and disclosure of inside information provided for in those rules is set out briefly in this section.

For companies with Premium Listings, rather than Standard Listings on the Main Market, a higher level of disclosure is required. Most of these additional disclosures are required by the UK Corporate Governance Code (September 2012) ('the Code'). Compliance with the Code is not mandatory but a company with a Main Market listing is required to include a statement in its annual report and accounts of how it has applied the Main Principles of the Code, whether it has complied with the provisions of the Code, and, if not, the parts with which it has not complied and an explanation why it has chosen not to comply (the 'comply or explain obligation'). The statutory footing for the comply or explain disclosures is Listing Rules 9.8.6 and 9.8.7.

17.3.1 Periodic Disclosure

Annual Financial Report (DTR 4.1.3)

Within four months of the end of the financial year the company must make public an annual financial report including:

- audited financial statements;
- a management report;
- responsibility statements.

Half-yearly financial reports (DTR 4.2.2)

Within two months of the end of the period, a company must make public a half-yearly report including:

- condensed set of financial statements;

- an interim management report;
- responsibility statements.

Interim management statements (DTR 4.3.2)

A company must make public, between week 11 and 20 of each half year period, ie effectively quarterly, an interim management statement providing:

- an explanation of material events and transactions that have taken place during the relevant period and their impact on the financial position of the issuer; and
- a general description of the financial position and performance of the issuer during the relevant period.

17.3.2 Disclosure of inside information

Disclosure of inside information by companies with listed securities is regulated by DTR 2. Basically, a company must disclose price-sensitive information as soon as possible. Price-sensitive information is information which:

- is not generally available;
- relates, directly or indirectly, to the company or the shares; and
- would, if generally available, be likely to have a significant effect on the price of the shares.

Ask: would the information in question be likely to be used by a reasonable investor as part of the basis of his investment decisions and therefore be likely to have a significant effect on the price of the shares? If the answer is yes, it must be disclosed as soon as possible.

KEY FACTS

Main Public Disclosures	
Pursuant to the Companies Act 2006	
Sources of information	Company's registered office Registrar of companies/Companies House The Gazette
Registers	Members (s 113) Directors (s 162) Secretaries (s 275) Charges (s 875) Debenture holders (optional) (s 743) Interests (public company only in context of a company investigation) (s 808)
Annual filings	Annual return (s 854) Accounts (degree of detail dependent on company being small, medium sized, unquoted or quoted) Directors' report Directors' remuneration report (quoted companies only) Auditors' report (unless exempt from audit)
Pursuant to the Financial Services and Markets Act 2000 and Disclosure and Transparency Rules (DTR)	
Periodic disclosure	Annual (DTR 4) Half-yearly (DTR 4) Quarterly (DTR 4)
Disclosure of inside information	Price-sensitive information to be disclosed as soon as possible (DTR 2)

17.4 Audit and auditors

17.4.1 The audit requirement

Section 475 of the Companies Act 2006 sets out a general requirement to have a company's annual accounts audited. An auditor is a person who makes an independent report, the 'auditor's report' to a company's shareholders as to whether, in the auditor's opinion, the company's annual accounts have been properly prepared in accordance with the Companies Act 2006 and the relevant reporting framework. The report must also say whether or not, in the opinion of the auditor, the company's accounts give a true and fair view of the company's state of affairs and the profit or loss of the company (s 495).

In preparing his report the auditor must (s 498) carry out such investigations as will enable him to form an opinion as to whether:

- adequate accounting records have been kept;
- the company's accounts are in agreement with the accounting records.

dormant company

a company which has no significant accounting trans-actions during a financial year

The exemption from audit for dormant and small companies is very important (s 475). More than two thirds of companies that deliver accounts to the registrar take advantage of the audit exemption.

1 Dormant company essentially means a company with no significant accounting transactions, ie no entries in the accounting records (s 480).
2 Small company for the purposes of this exemption (s 477, updated by regulation) essentially means a company with:
   - not more than £6.5m annual turnover; and
   - not more than £3.26m balance sheet.

If the company is to take advantage of the audit exemption, the balance sheet must contain an appropriate statement by the directors: s 475(3). Even if the company would otherwise be entitled to exemption, members representing no less than 10 per cent nominal value of the share capital, or any class of it, may give notice requiring the company to have its accounts audited (s 476).

The auditor is also required to report whether in his opinion:

- the information given in the directors' report is consistent with the annual accounts (s 496);
- where a remuneration report is required, that the auditable part of it has been properly prepared in accordance with the 2006 Act (s 497); and
- where a separate corporate governance statement has been prepared, whether the information given is consistent with the annual accounts (s 497A).

17.4.2 Appointment, functions, duties and removal of auditors

The rules governing the appointment, functions, duties and removal of auditors are set out in Chapters 2, 3 and 4 of Pt 16 of the Companies Act 2006. These rules have been significantly tightened in recent years in an effort to ensure the independence of the auditor from the company.

17.4.3 Auditor liability

Auditor liability to the company

Auditor liability to the company arises both at common law, most likely for negligence based on a lack of reasonable care, skill or diligence, and pursuant to the contract between the auditor and the company which will in almost every case impose a contractual obligation to perform services under the contract with reasonable care, skill and diligence. Provisions in the articles or any contract with the company exempting or limiting the liability of an auditor, or providing an indemnity against any liability of an auditor, in relation to the audit of accounts are void (s 532) subject to two exceptions:

- A company may now agree to limit the liability of its auditors using a 'liability limitation agreement' as that term is used in the Act (ss 534–538) and complying with the Companies (Disclosure of Auditor Remuneration and Liability Limitation Agreements) Regulations 2008 (SI 2008/489).
- A company may indemnify an auditor in relation to the liabilities arising out of successfully defending himself in proceedings, s 533.

The Financial Reporting Council (FRC) has recently published guidance on what is and what is not permitted in relation to auditor liability limitation agreements (Guidance on Auditor Liability Limitation Agreements, June 2008, accessible on the FRC website). Also, auditor liability and the importance of auditors being permitted to limit their liability has been the subject of a recent EC Commission recommendation (Commission Recommendation of 5 June 2008 concerning the limitation of the civil liability of statutory auditors and audit firms, 2008/473/EC) which stresses the increasing trend of litigation and lack of sufficient insurance cover faced by auditors. The aim of the recommendation is to protect European capital markets by ensuring that audit firms remain available to carry out audits on companies listed in the EU.

Auditor criminal liability

An auditor is now exposed to potential criminal liability (s 507) if he:

1 knowingly or recklessly causes an auditor's report on the annual accounts to include a matter that is misleading, false or deceptive in a material particular (s 507(1)); or
2 knowingly or recklessly causes an auditor's report on the annual accounts to omit a statement:
 - that the company's accounts do not agree with the accounting records (s 507(2)(a)); or
 - that necessary information and explanations have not been obtained (s 507(2)(b)); or
 - that directors wrongly took advantage of the exemption from the obligation to prepare group accounts (s 507(2)(c)).

The penalty on conviction is a fine (s 507(4)).

Auditor liability to third parties

Auditor liability to third parties is governed by tort law. Consider an investor who relies on the audited, published accounts of a company to buy the shares of the company only to lose money because the accounts did not present a true and fair view of the finances of the company and the auditor was negligent in not discovering and flagging this. The liability of the auditor in such a case is governed by tort rules on liability for economic loss arising from negligent misstatement, the leading case on which, you will recall, is *Hedley Byrne & Co Ltd v Heller & Partners Ltd* [1964] AC 465 (HL).

Auditor liability for third party economic loss was considered and settled in *Caparo Industries Ltd v Dickman* [1990] 2 AC 605 (HL). Basically, the House of Lords decided that an auditor owes a duty of care to the company, a limited duty of care to shareholders of the company (limited to protection of their shareholder rights) and only owes a duty of care to third parties (and a wider duty to shareholders), where a special relationship exists between the auditor and the third party in question. Reasonable foreseeability of loss by a third party is *not* sufficient to establish a special relationship/auditor liability to a third party.

Subsequent cases have described the need to establish a 'special relationship' pursuant to *Caparo* as the need to show that there has been an assumption of responsibility to the third party by the auditor. In the absence of an *express* assumption of responsibility, the type of parties to whom courts may be willing to find that responsibility has been assumed are believed to be parent companies and directors.

KEY FACTS

Audit and auditor liability	
Audit	
Requirement	s 475
Exemption from audit: Small companies Dormant companies	 s 477 s 480
Auditor liability	
Criminal	s 507
Civil liability: to the company to shareholders to third parties	*Caparo Industries Ltd v Dickman* (1990)
Restrictions on civil liability: Liability limitation agreements Auditor indemnities	 s 534 s 538

17.5 Company investigations

The Secretary of State for Business Innovation and Skills has broad powers to investigate companies pursuant to Pt XIV of the Companies Act 1985 (as amended). This jurisdiction was not included within the remit of the 1998 Company Law Review. Consequently, the governing provisions have not been consolidated into the Companies Act 2006 but remain, and are expected to remain, in the 1985 Act. The powers are in practice exercised by the Insolvency Service (IS), part of the regulatory arm of the Department for Business, Innovation and Skills (BIS). Although the powers are granted in wide terms, the IS will generally only investigate a company where it has reasonable grounds to suspect fraud, serious misconduct, or material irregularity in the conduct of its affairs and approximately 75 per cent of investigations are begun because fraud is suspected.

Most investigations are carried out pursuant to s 477 by requiring companies or 'any person' to produce documents and information. Investigators may be empowered to enter premises and search for documents and information. These investigations are confidential.

Less common but more comprehensive are investigations by inspectors appointed pursuant to ss 431 and 432 to investigate and report to the Secretary of State on the affairs of a company. The appointment of an inspector is a publicly announced event and traditionally their reports had to be published. An amendment introduced in 1989 now permits appointment of inspectors on the basis of non-publication of the report (s 432(2A) inserted by the Companies Act 1989). Investigations may result in a decision not to take further action. Where action is taken it is typically one or more of the following:

- a petition pursuant to s 124A of the Insolvency Act 1986 for the winding up of the company;
- prosecutions being undertaken (often by the serious fraud squad);
- a petition pursuant to the Company Directors Disqualification Act 1986 for disqualification of one or more directors on the grounds of unfitness;
- (less commonly), a petition for relief under s 994 by the Secretary of State based on the company's affairs having been conducted in a manner unfairly prejudicial to its members' interests (see section 14.5).

The findings in published reports may also encourage shareholders, creditors and other parties to bring civil actions. Reports since 1945 can be accessed from the BIS Insolvency Service webpages referenced at the end of this chapter.

SUMMARY

Public disclosure under the Companies Act 2006

- Public disclosure of information is an important part of core company law.
- Companies must maintain key registers (directors, members, company secretaries, and charges) and make them available to the public.
- Annual returns and annual accounts and reports must be filed at Companies House.
- Narrative reporting, providing information about the company over and beyond financial information, is a growing area of law, as at April 2012, is the subject of consultation.

Public disclosure under the Financial Services and Markets Act 2000

- DTR 4 require publication of annual, half-yearly and quarterly reports.
- DTR 2 requires inside information (information likely to be used by a reasonable investor as part of the basis of his investment decision) to be made public as soon as possible.

Audit and auditors

- A company's annual accounts, including its directors' report and (for quoted companies) the directors' remuneration report must be audited (s 475) unless the company is dormant (s 477) or entitled to the small company exemption from audit (s 477).
- The auditor is required to make an independent report, the 'auditor's report' to the company's shareholders on all annual accounts (s 495), that in his opinion the accounts give a full and fair view of the company at the end of its financial year and of the profit and loss for the financial year and have been properly prepared in accordance with the Companies Act 2006 and the relevant reporting framework.

Auditor liability

- Civil liability to the company is principally in contract law, and to third parties may arise under tort law although in *Caparo Industries Ltd v Dickman* (1990) the House of Lords decided that an auditor owes a duty of care to third parties only where a special relationship exists between the auditor and the third party in question.
- Criminal liability is provided for in s 507 based on the standards of knowing or reckless behaviour.

Company investigations

- BIS has broad powers to investigate companies pursuant to Pt XIV of the Companies Act 1985 (as amended), investigations being carried out pursuant to s 477 and ss 431 and 432.
- Reasonable grounds to suspect fraud, serious misconduct, or material irregularity in the conduct of its affairs is generally required for an investigation to be initiated.

ACTIVITY

Self-test questions

1. Which registers are companies required to keep and make available for public inspection?
2. What special rules apply to the register of directors?
3. What information and documents are companies required to send annually to the registrar?

4. Are all companies subject to the same public disclosure regime? Explain any differences that may exist identifying the basis on which companies are classified for public disclosure purposes.
5. Describe in outline the periodic reporting obligations of a company with shares on the official list and identify the legal source of those disclosure rules.
6. What does the term narrative reporting mean and which companies are subject to narrative reporting?
7. What is the function of an auditor and why is his role so important?
8. To whom is a negligent auditor liable and on what legal basis? What, if any, steps may an auditor take to limit his liability?
9. In what circumstances is the Secretary of State entitled to investigate companies under the Companies Act 1985?
10. Compare and contrast the powers of the Secretary of State under s 477 on the one hand and ss 431 and 432 on the other hand.

Further reading

Useful websites

The FSA Listing Rules (LR), Prospectus Rules (PR) and Disclosure Rules and Transparency Rules (DTR) can be accessed on the FSA website:
http://fsahandbook.info/FSA/html/handbook/
The Financial Reporting Council, Guidance on Auditor Liability Limitation Agreements, June 2008, is available at:
www.frc.org.uk/images/uploaded/documents/FRC%20ALLA%20Guidance%20June%20 2008%20final4.pdf
The BIS Insolvency Service website pages on company investigations:
http://www.bis.gov.uk/insolvency/Companies/company-investigation

Articles

Butcher, C, 'Auditors, Parliament and the courts: the development and limitation of auditors' liability' (2008) 24 Professional Negligence 66–77.
Roach, L, 'Auditor liability: the case for limitation: Parts 1 & 2' (2010) 31 Comp Law 136 & 167.

Reports

Department of Trade and Industry, *Company Investigations, Powers for the Twenty-First Century* (2001).

Books

Lidbetter, A, 'Company Investigations by the DTI' in de Lacey, J, (ed) *The Reform of United Kingdom Company Law* (Cavendish Publishing Ltd, 2002).

Appendix

Main changes introduced by the Companies Act 2006		
	Topic	**Companies Act 2006 section numbers**
1.	**Company Formation**	
	New 'UK' Companies rather than English, Scottish, NI companies	s 1183
	Single member companies can be plcs	N/A but see s 7
	Memorandum to be a prescribed form, static document	s 8
	Objects clauses to be unnecessary for new companies	s 31
	Existing company objects clauses to be treated as provisions of articles	s 28
	Consequence is that the '*ultra vires*' doctrine is no longer relevant to non-charitable companies	
	Default articles of association	The Companies (Model Articles) Regulations 2008 (SI 2008/3229)
	Table A (for both Ltds and plcs) replaced by Model Articles for Private Company Limited by Shares and Model Articles for Public Companies	
	Entrenchment of provisions in articles on incorporation or by unanimous agreement of shareholders	s 22
	No need for authorised share capital	N/A but see s 545
	Shares still must have nominal value with right to have shares denominated in any currency and different classes in different currencies placed on a statutory footing	s 542
	Statement of capital and initial shareholdings required	s 10
	Plc authorised minimum nominal value of allotted shares (£50K or prescribed Euro equivalent)	s 763(1)
	may be denominated in Euros	s 765(1)
	Euro equivalent of €75K may be altered by regulations	
	Company Names	ss 53–88
	new regime	
2.	**Company Administration**	
	Company Secretaries	s 270
	Private companies no longer need one; functions can be performed by a director	s 270(3)(b)(ii)
	Power of directors to appoint an authorised person	
	Register of Directors	ss 162–167
	To contain a service address which may be the company's registered office	s 240
	To indicate country of residence of each director	
	Residential addresses to be kept in a separate register not available for inspection	
	Residential address must still be supplied to Companies House but is protected information withheld from public inspection	

Topic	Companies Act 2006 section numbers
Register of members	ss 113–121
Inspection process reformed to protect members from harassment etc	s 116
Annual Returns not to include shareholder addresses except for plc traded on EU regulated markets for shareholders who have held 5% or more of any class	Companies Act 2006 (Annual Return & Service Addresses) Regulations 2008 (SI 2008/3000)
3. **Decisions of Shareholders**	
Private company written resolutions	ss 288–300
Written resolution is now the normal mode of decision-making for private company shareholders	N/A
Only reason for a private company to have a shareholder meeting:	
Remove a director under s 168	
Remove an auditor under s 510	
No AGMs required for private companies	
4. **Communications with Shareholders & Proxies**	
Electronic communications	ss 308, 309, 333, 1143–1148, Scheds 4 and 5
Provisions of 2006 Act apply to all companies	
Not compulsory	
Existing arrangements to communicate electronically can continue with no changes	See: DTR 6
To extend/begin electronic communications by the company to the shareholder by emails and/or website	
Check articles to confirm permitted	
Shareholder approval is needed except for deemed consent to website communication	
Shareholders can communicate with company by email if company has given an address in a meeting notice or proxy paperwork	
Companies subject to DTR	
Rights of proxies	s 324
Enhanced rights for proxies	
Right to appoint more than one to attend, speak and vote	
Articles can give greater rights	

	Topic	Companies Act 2006 section numbers
	Indirect shareholder rights	ss 145–153
	If articles permit, a shareholder may nominate any other person as entitled to enjoy all or any specified rights of the shareholder in relation to the company	s 145
	Shareholders of a company with shares on a regulated market may nominate that person to enjoy information rights, i.e., to receive accounts and reports, and any copies of other communication sent by the company to its shareholders	s 146
5.	**Accounts and Reporting**	
	Companies subject to DTR Periodic financial reporting rules changed for financial periods commencing on or after 20 January 2007	DTR 4
	Business Review (required for all companies other than those subject to the small companies' regime and forms part of the directors' report) for quoted companies to contain forward looking information, environmental, employee, social and community matters and contractual arrangement information	s 417
	X ref directors' liability re directors' report, below	s 463
	X ref directors' specific statutory duty to be satisfied the accounts give a true and fair view	s 393
	Timing for filing accounts with Companies House reduced by 1 month for both Ltds (9 months) and plcs (6 months)	s 442
6.	**Auditors**	
	Individual 'senior statutory auditor' to sign auditors' report	s 503
	New criminal offences (2) for auditors in relation to auditors' report.	s 507
	New exception to voidness of provisions protecting auditors from liability: company can enter into a liability limitation agreement, to limit liability of auditor for negligence, default, breach of duty or trust so far as is fair and reasonable	s 534
7.	**Directors and Directors' Duties**	
	No need to retire at 70 from plc board	ss 293 and 294
	Need at least 1 natural director No directors under the age of 16	ss 155–159
	Tax free payments to directors— prohibition repealed	(s 311, 1985 Act)
	New: liability of directors to the company for statutory narrative reporting: directors' report/remuneration reports/material from them used in summary financial statements	s 463
	True and fair view Duty of directors to prepare accounts for each financial year (s 394) reinforced by new statutory specific duty 'not to approve accounts unless they are satisfied that they give a true and fair view of the assets, liabilities, financial position and profit and loss … of the company'	s 393

	Topic	Companies Act 2006 section numbers
	Companies with securities on regulated market Liability of directors to the company for periodic financial reports Liability of the company to third parties	s 1270, inserting s 90A FSMA 2000
	General Duties of directors replace common law/equitable duties (delayed implementation of conflict of interest provisions (which changed the law) to allow for review of articles and any required amendments to be made)	ss 170–174 and supporting
	Statutory conflict of interest duties to amend and replace equitable duties and old disclosure rules	ss 175–177 and ss 182–187
	Substantial property transactions, loans, guarantees of loans, quasi loans and credit transactions between company and directors largely re-enacted	ss 190–225
	Directors' service agreements exceeding or which may exceed 2 years to be approved by shareholders (was 5 years)	s 188
	Payments to directors for loss of office	ss 215–222
	Derivative actions placed on statutory footing	s 260–264
8.	**Share Capital**	
	X ref Company Formation above re authorised share capital and sterling or Euro denomination of plc authorised minimum	ss 545, 761, 763
	Private company with one class of shares: authority of directors to allot shares is automatic. No need for articles or resolution to provide for such	s 550
	All other allotments to be authorised by articles or general resolution with maximum amount that may be allotted and 5 year limit on power	s 551
	Transferability of shares	s 544
9.	**Capital Maintenance**	
	Reduction of share capital Private company right to reduce capital by special resolution supported by a solvency statement (as an additional alternative to a special resolution confirmed by the court)	ss 641–643, 652
	Financial Assistance Removal of statutory prohibition on private companies providing financial assistance for purchase of own shares (but note remaining common law capital maintenance) Changes (minor) to statutory prohibition on plcs providing financial assistance for purchase of own shares	N/A (see ss 151–158, 1985 Act) ss 677–683
	Minor changes to rules governing acquisition of own shares including redeemable shares	ss 658–737
	Application of share premium account Purposes for which it can be used are reduced (counter to theme of 2006 Act)	s 610
10.	**Distributions**	
	Main changes relate to treatment of distributions in kind	ss 845, 846
11.	**Takeovers Directive**	
	Regulations implementing the directive consolidated in the Act	Part 28 (ss 902–991)

Glossary of terms

Note that an index of expressions defined in the Companies Act 2006 appears in schedule 8 of the Act.

administration order
a court order which gives power to manage the company's business to an administrator

administrative receiver
a receiver and manager appointed by the holder of a pre-15 September 2003 floating charge, who takes control of the whole or substantially the whole of the business and property of the company. Now largely replaced by administrators as part of the move to a corporate rescue culture

administrative restoration
a procedure introduced under the Companies Act 2006 whereby the registrar of companies may restore a company to the register without the need for a court order, provided certain criteria are met

agent
a person with authority to alter the legal position of another person which other person is known as the principal

administrator
an insolvency practitioner appointed by the court under an administration order or by the company, its directors, or the holder of a qualifying floating charge, the principal objective of whom is to rescue the company as a going concern

allotment
shares in a company are taken to be allotted when a person acquires the unconditional right to be included in the company's register of members in respect of the shares

AIM
see **Alternative Investment Market**

Alternative Investment Market (AIM)
the market for smaller companies operated by the London Stock Exchange. AIM is not a regulated market and companies on AIM are not listed on the Official List nor are they subject to the Listing Rules

annual general meeting (AGM)
a general meeting of the members of a company which public companies must hold each calendar year within six months of the financial year end

annual return
a document in prescribed form which every registered company is required to file with the Registrar of Companies on an annual basis pursuant to the Companies Act 2006, s 854, containing basic information about the company

articles of association
the regulations governing a company's internal management including the rights of shareholders, the conduct of meetings and the appointment, removal and powers of directors. Separate Model Articles for public and private limited companies operate as the articles of a company to the extent that they have not been excluded or modified

BIS
the Department for Business, Innovation and Skills (formerly BERR and before that the DTI) is the government department responsible for company law (amongst other things)

bonus issue
fully paid shares of the same class issued free of charge to existing shareholders in proportion to their existing shareholding also referred to as a capitalisation issue

book debt
a debt arising in the course of a business that would or could in the ordinary course of business be entered in well-kept books of account of the business

called-up capital
the sum of the amounts paid for shares when issued, sums subsequently called-up (even if the called amounts have not been paid), and sums due on a specified date without further call

certificated
a paper-based system of holding shares, represented by share certificates

certificate of incorporation
the document issued by the registrar of companies on the registration of a company under the Companies Act 2006 or a predecessor statute

charge
a legal or equitable property interest in some or all of the assets of the company created to secure a loan to the company or to secure some other right against the company

charitable incorporated organisation
a corporate vehicle for charities registered with the Charity Commission rather than with the registrar of companies

City Code on Takeovers and Mergers
a set of principles and rules, now placed on a statutory footing, designed principally to ensure that shareholders are treated fairly and providing an orderly framework within which takeovers are conducted to promote the integrity of the financial markets

common seal
a device used for making an impressed mark (the seal of the company) on a document to authenticate it

community interest company (CIC)
A corporate entity to encourage the provision of products and services to benefit community, social and environmental needs. Companies wishing to qualify for CIC status are required to satisfy the community interest test

Companies House
an executive agency of BIS by which the registrar of companies performs the functions of the registrar including the incorporation and dissolution of registered companies, the examination and storage of information delivered under the Companies Act, and, where required, the making public of that information

company limited by guarantee
a company the articles of which contains an undertaking by members to contribute a specified amount on a winding up towards the payment of its debts and the expenses of winding up

company secretary
the chief administrative officer of the company which all public companies must have and of whose qualifications, knowledge and experience to discharge the role, the directors of a public company must take reasonable steps to satisfy themselves

company voluntary arrangement (CVA)
a composition in satisfaction of a company's debts, or a scheme of arrangement of its affairs, that binds all affected company creditors even though not all of them agree to its terms, entered into in accordance with the procedure in Part 1 of the Insolvency Act 1986

compulsory liquidation or compulsory winding up
the winding up of a company by order of the court

core company law
the law governing the creation and operation of registered companies

corporate governance
the system by which companies are directed and controlled

creditor
a person to whom a debt is owed

CREST
an electronic holding and settlement system in which legal title to a dematerialised share is recorded and by which share transfers are made. Shares held and transferred in this way are called 'dematerialised'

crystallisation
on crystallisation, a floating charge becomes a fixed charge

cumulative dividend
if any dividend due is not paid, it accrues to the shareholder and is payable with the next dividend due at the next payment date. Usually associated with preference shares

debenture
a document which either creates a debt or acknowledges it. Usually, though by no means always, a debenture is secured.

deed
a formal document conforming with the requirements of a deed set out in the Law of Property (Miscellaneous Provisions) Act 1989 and, in the case of a registered company, executed as a deed in accordance with the Companies Act 2006, s 44

de facto **director**
a person who has not been properly appointed but who has assumed the role of a director

de jure **director**
a person who has not only been properly appointed but who has satisfied the legal formalities that have to be observed by directors

derivative claim
a claim brought by a member under the Companies Act 2006, ss 260–269 against a director for an actual or proposed act or omission involving negligence, breach of duty or breach of trust by a director of a company. The claim is brought by the member for and on behalf of the company itself

director
any person occupying the position of a director by whatever name he is called

disqualification undertaking
an out of court procedure whereby a director accepts a binding undertaking not to act as a director for a defined disqualification period without the consent of the court, in lieu of being disqualified under the Company Directors Disqualification Act 1986 (as amended)

distributable profits

profits available for the purpose of paying a dividend as defined in s 830 of the Companies Act 2006

dividend

a payment made to members out of a company's distributable profits, in proportion to their shareholding

dormant company

a company which has no significant accounting transactions during a financial year

enlightened shareholder value

the doctrine enshrined in the Companies Act 2006, s 172, whereby although directors must act in the way they consider, in good faith, would be most likely to promote the success of the company *for the benefit of its members as a whole,* in performing this duty they must have regard to the interests of other stakeholders and the long term consequences of any decision

European Economic Interest Group (EEIG)

a legal entity separate from its members at least two members of which must be from different member states and all members of which must carry on business within the European Union (EU) and have their principal administration within the EU

equity share capital

the issued share capital of a company excluding any part which, neither as respects dividends nor as respects capital, carries any right to participate beyond a specified amount in a distribution

fixed charge

a property interest in specified property preventing the owner of the property from selling or otherwise dealing with it without first either paying back the sum secured against it or obtaining the consent of the chargeholder. Also called a specific charge

floating charge

a security by way of charge over one or more specified classes of assets, present and future, prior to enforcement of which charge, the company is free to carry on business in the ordinary way in relation to those assets, including removing any assets from the security

fraudulent trading

for the purposes of s 213 Insolvency Act 1986, the carrying on of the business of the company with intent to defraud creditors of the company or creditors of any other person, or for any fraudulent purpose

Gazette

the London, Edinburgh and/or Belfast Gazette published by The Stationery Office which comes out every business day and in which formal announcements concerning companies are made, such as when a winding up order is made or when a winding up resolution is passed

general meeting

a meeting of the members of a company

incorporation

the process by which a legal entity, separate from its owners and managers, is formed

insolvent

a company is insolvent and an application to wind it up can be made if it is unable to pay its debts

judgment creditor

a creditor who has sued the company owing him money and obtained judgment from the court in his favour against the company

limited company

a company the liability of whose members to contribute to the company to enable it to pay its debts is limited by shares or guarantee

limited liability partnership

a body corporate, the liability of whose members is limited, formed by registration under the Limited Liability Partnerships Act 2000 which has the organisational flexibility of a partnership and is taxed as a partnership

limited partnership

a partnership having one or more but not all limited partners, ie sleeping partners whose liability in the event of the partnership's insolvency is limited to the amount that such partner has agreed to contribute

liquidation

the winding up of a company

liquidator

the person who undertakes the liquidation of a company and who must be a qualified insolvency practitioner

member

a person becomes a member of a company when his name is entered in the register of members. For companies with a share capital the term is synonymous with shareholder

memorandum of association

the document which under predecessor companies acts set out the basic details of a company: name, place of incorporation, objects, liability of the members and authorised share capital but under the Companies Act 2006 is a shorter document containing the names of the initial subscribers for shares and their agreement to form a company

model articles

the default articles which, by operation of the Companies Act 2006, s 20, form part or all of the articles of a registered company on its formation to the extent that the incorporators do not register bespoke articles

nominal value

the value attached to a share when it is issued. The nominal value of a share need not bear any correlation to the market value of that share

non-executive director (NED)

a director who is not an employee of the company and who has no executive responsibilities

objects clause

the clause in an old style memorandum of association which sets out the business(es) the company proposes to carry on. Under the Companies Act 2006, the objects clause of pre-2006 Act companies has become a provision of the articles of association. A company incorporated under the 2006 Act may but need not have an objects clause in its articles

Official Receiver

a civil servant in The Insolvency Service (an executive agency of BIS) and an officer of the court. The first liquidator of any company subject to compulsory winding up

offeree company

a company in respect of which an offer has been, or potentially may be, made to which the City Code on Takeovers and Mergers applies. Also known as the target or target company

offeror company

a person (whether a company or an individual) who makes or is considering making an offer to which the City Code on Takeovers and Mergers applies. Also known as a bidder

Official List

the list maintained by the FSA as UK Listing Authority pursuant to FSMA 2000 s 74(1) being a list of securities issued by companies for the purpose of being traded on a UK regulated market (the most important of which markets for equity shares is the Main Market of the London Stock Exchange)

ordinary resolution

a resolution of the members of a company passed by a simple majority of 50% plus one vote of those eligible to vote

ordinary shares

defined for the purposes of pre-emption rights as shares other than shares that as respects dividends and capital carry a right to participate only up to a specified amount in a distribution but the term is used more generally including to describe the shares of a company with only one class of shares

ostensible authority

the authority that one can assume a person purporting to be an agent has based on a representation made by a person authorised by the company. Also known as apparent authority

parent company

a company is the parent company of another company if it holds the majority voting rights in that company, is a member and can appoint or remove all the directors, or is a member and controls a majority of the voting rights either alone or pursuant to an agreement with other members of the company

partnership

the relation which subsists between persons carrying on a business in common with a view of profit

pari passu

the principle of treatment on an equal footing, applied on the winding up of companies so that all unsecured creditors share the assets available to unsecured creditors in proportion to the sum each is owed

passing off

a common law tort actionable by a claimant who is the owner of goodwill (sometimes referred to as an unregistered trade mark or reputation attached to a good or service) when another person has made a misrepresentation which leads or is likely to lead to its product or service being associated with the claimant thereby deceiving the public and resulting in damage to the goodwill of the claimant

phoenix company

a new company formed with a name the same as or similar to that of a company that has gone into insolvent liquidation having the same director(s) as the failed company and running essentially the same business that had been run by the failed company the assets of which have been transferred to the second company

poison pill

a device or strategy to frustrate a takeover of the company which is sometimes put in place long before a takeover situation arises

poll

a vote in writing at a general meeting where shareholders or their proxies vote in proportion to their voting shareholdings

pre-emption rights
: the rights of existing equity shareholders to be offered new equity shares first in proportion to their existing equity shareholdings

preference shares
: shares giving the holder preferential rights, usually in respect of dividends and/or return of capital on a winding up

preferential creditors
: creditors entitled to receive payment on a winding up in advance of the floating charge holders and unsecured creditors

premium
: the amount paid for a share over and above the nominal value when it is allotted by the company

price-sensitive information
: information which would, if made public, be likely to have a significant effect on the price of particular securities

private company
: a registered company that is not a public company

pro rata
: rateably or in proportion

promoter
: a person who decides to form a company and takes, or on whose behalf others take all or some of the necessary steps to form it

public limited company
: a company registered as a public company the name of which ends with the letters plc (or the words represented by those letters in full)

prospectus
: a document containing information about the company and its shares which enables prospective investors to decide whether or not to invest and/or is supplied to the financial regulator to obtain admission of shares to the Official List

proxy
: a person appointed by a member entitled to vote at a general meeting to attend the meeting and vote in his place. The proxy can speak at the meeting and vote on a show of hands and on a poll. The proxy need not be a member of the company

qualifying floating charge holder
: a floating charge entered into after 15 September 2003 which comprises a charge over the whole or substantially all of the company's property the holder of which has under the Enterprise Act 2002 the right to appoint an administrator out of court

quantum meruit
: the sum due to a person who has performed services for which no remuneration or means of calculating remuneration has been agreed but for which it was implied that payment would be made

quorum
: the minimum number of people necessary for the transaction of business at a general meeting or board meeting

receiver
: a person appointed under a debenture or other instrument secured over the assets of a company to manage and realise the secured assets for the benefit of the charge holder

redeemable shares
: fully paid-up shares that either will be redeemed (bought back by the company), or may be redeemed at the option of the company or the shareholder, on such date or dates and subject to such terms as are stated in the articles or company resolution

registered office
: the address of the office of a company to which formal notices and legal documents should be addressed and sent

register of charges
: the statutory register that has to be maintained by every company containing details of all charges over the company's property or any part of it

registrar of companies
: the registrar of companies for England and Wales, Scotland or Northern Ireland, as the case may require, to whom documents are sent to form a company and to whom the necessary returns are made during the lifetime of a company

register of members
: a statutory register that has to be maintained by all companies containing a definitive list of members of the company

resolution
: the formal way in which a decision of the shareholders or the directors is proposed and passed

rights issue
: the offer by a listed company of new shares to existing equity shareholders on a *pro rata* basis on a renounceable basis which entails issuing renounceable letters of allotment. The new shares are offered at a discount to the market price and the rights can be assigned for consideration

scheme of arrangement procedure
: the statutory procedure set out in Part 26 of the Companies Act 2006 which facilitates changes being made to the rights of creditors or shareholders without securing the unanimous approval of those affected by the changes

secured creditor
> a creditor who has a property interest in all or part of the property of the company to secure the debt

shadow director
> any person in accordance with whose directions or instructions the directors are accustomed to act, except where that person gives advice in a professional capacity (eg a solicitor or accountant)

share capital
> the shares of a company that have been issued, including those taken on the formation of the company by those who subscribed to the memorandum of association

share certificate
> the documentary evidence issued by a company and held by a shareholder to indicate the ownership of shares

share premium
> *see* premium

share premium account
> an account into which all payments made for shares over and above their nominal value are credited

Societas Europaea (SE)
> a corporate vehicle designed for corporate groups which operate in more than one European Union member state

Societas Privata Europaea (SPE)
> a form of European Private Company (SPE) proposed by the European Commission to assist both large corporate groups wishing to reduce the costs of administering their groups of subsidiaries in Europe and SMEs seeking to operate in more than one member state

sole trader
> an individual who is in business on his own account, ie he is not in partnership nor does he trade through a corporate body

special notice
> the notice required from the proposing shareholders to the company, of ordinary resolutions to remove a director or remove, appoint or re-appoint an auditor

special resolution
> a resolution of the members of a company used for significant decisions requiring a 75 per cent majority of the votes of those eligible to vote which must be described as a special resolution and the text of which must be set out in any notice

squeeze out
> the right of the offeror, under the Companies Act 2006, s 979 to acquire outstanding shares on a compulsory basis where it has acquired (or unconditionally

contracted to acquire) not less than 90 per cent (i) in value of, and (ii) of the voting rights carried by, the shares to which the takeover offer relates

stakeholders
> groups with an interest in the company, such as shareholders, creditors, employees, customers, suppliers and the local communities in which the company operates

statutory accounts
> the individual or group accounts which are required to be filed with the registrar of companies which may be full accounts or, where permitted, abbreviated accounts

statutory declaration of solvency
> a statement made by the board for the purposes of s 89 of the Insolvency Act 1986 which confirms that the company is solvent and will be able to meet all liabilities which arise within 12 months from the commencement of a voluntary winding up

stock transfer form
> the form completed by the transferor of certificated shares to transfer the shares to the transferee

subsidiary company
> a company is a subsidiary of another company, known as its holding or parent company, if that other company holds the majority of its voting rights, is a member and can appoint or remove all of its directors, or is a member and controls a majority of its voting rights either alone or pursuant to an agreement with other members

summary financial statement
> a shortened form of the annual report and accounts of the company which may be circulated to shareholders instead of the full report. All companies have the choice of issuing summary financial statements

takeover
> the process whereby one company acquires a controlling interest in another company

trading certificate
> the certificate issued by the registrar of companies a public company is required to obtain before it can lawfully trade or borrow

UK Corporate Governance Code
> the code on corporate governance published by the FRC, most recently updated and renamed in September 2012 previously called the Combined Code on Corporate Governance

UK Listing Authority (UKLA)

The FSA when it acts as the competent authority under Part IV of FSMA 2000, ie the UK's securities regulator

ultra vires

the expression used to refer to a transaction entered into by a company that is beyond its legal capacity (historically, outside the scope of its objects clause). In this strict sense, *ultra vires* has been abolished in relation to non-charitable registered companies. Sometimes used to refer to a transaction beyond the powers of the directors, which use is best avoided

unincorporated association

an organisation typically formed or run to advance social, environmental or cultural objectives for the benefit of its members, the local community or the public generally, including sports or other social clubs and cooperatives, often charities, not being incorporated or a sole trader or a partnership

unlimited company

a company, the liability of whose members to contribute to the company on a winding up, to enable it to pay its debts, is not limited, by shares, guarantee or otherwise

voluntary winding up

the winding up of a company commenced by a special resolution of its members

winding up

the liquidation of a company

winding up order

a court order to liquidate a company

written resolution

a resolution of the members of a private company proposed and passed in writing in accordance with the Companies Act 2006

wrongful trading

a director continuing to trade when he knew or ought to have concluded that there was no reasonable prospect that the company would avoid going into insolvent liquidation

Index